FAMILY HOME EVENING

R E S O U R C E   B O O K

Published by
The Church of Jesus Christ of Latter-day Saints
Salt Lake City, Utah 1983

Credits

Page 16: Flight into Egypt, *by Christian Dalsgaard. Globe Photos, Inc.*

Page 42: Saulus outside Damascus, *by H. Siegumfeldt. Globe Photos, Inc.*

Pages 58, 150: The Last Supper, *by Carl Bloch. Original at the Chapel of Frederiksborg Castle, Denmark. Used by permission of the Frederiksborgmuseum.*

Page 61: Christ Bearing the Cross, *by Fra Sebastiano Del Piombo. Globe Photos, Inc.*

Pages 62, 152: The Burial of Christ, *by Carl Bloch. Original at the Chapel of Frederiksborg Castle, Denmark. Used by permission of the Frederiksborgmuseum.*

Page 101: Sermon on the Mount, *by Carl Bloch. Original at the Chapel of Frederiksborg Castle, Denmark. Used by permission of the Frederiksborgmuseum.*

Page 151: The Crucifixion, *by Carl Bloch. Original at the Chapel of Frederiksborg Castle, Denmark. Used by permission of the Frederiksborgmuseum.*

Page 158: The Birth of Christ, *by Carl Bloch. Original at the Chapel of Frederiksborg Castle, Denmark. Used by permission of the Frederiksborgmuseum.*

English approval: 6/97

CONTENTS

A PROCLAMATION TO THE WORLD

THE FIRST PRESIDENCY AND COUNCIL OF THE TWELVE APOSTLES OF THE CHURCH OF JESUS CHRIST OF LATTER-DAY SAINTS

WE, THE FIRST PRESIDENCY and the Council of the Twelve Apostles of The Church of Jesus Christ of Latter-day Saints, solemnly proclaim that marriage between a man and a woman is ordained of God and that the family is central to the Creator's plan for the eternal destiny of His children.

ALL HUMAN BEINGS—male and female—are created in the image of God. Each is a beloved spirit son or daughter of heavenly parents, and, as such, each has a divine nature and destiny. Gender is an essential characteristic of individual premortal, mortal, and eternal identity and purpose.

IN THE PREMORTAL REALM, spirit sons and daughters knew and worshiped God as their Eternal Father and accepted His plan by which His children could obtain a physical body and gain earthly experience to progress toward perfection and ultimately realize his or her divine destiny as an heir of eternal life. The divine plan of happiness enables family relationships to be perpetuated beyond the grave. Sacred ordinances and covenants available in holy temples make it possible for individuals to return to the presence of God and for families to be united eternally.

THE FIRST COMMANDMENT that God gave to Adam and Eve pertained to their potential for parenthood as husband and wife. We declare that God's commandment for His children to multiply and replenish the earth remains in force. We further declare that God has commanded that the sacred powers of procreation are to be employed only between man and woman, lawfully wedded as husband and wife.

WE DECLARE the means by which mortal life is created to be divinely appointed. We affirm the sanctity of life and of its importance in God's eternal plan.

HUSBAND AND WIFE have a solemn responsibility to love and care for each other and for their children. "Children are an heritage of the Lord" (Psalms 127:3). Parents have a sacred duty to rear their children in love and righteousness, to provide for their physical and spiritual needs, to teach them to love and serve one another, to observe the commandments of God and to be law-abiding citizens wherever they live. Husbands and wives—mothers and fathers—will be held accountable before God for the discharge of these obligations.

THE FAMILY is ordained of God. Marriage between man and woman is essential to His eternal plan. Children are entitled to birth within the bonds of matrimony, and to be reared by a father and a mother who honor marital vows with complete fidelity. Happiness in family life is most likely to be achieved when founded upon the teachings of the Lord Jesus Christ. Successful marriages and families are established and maintained on principles of faith, prayer, repentance, forgiveness, respect, love, compassion, work, and wholesome recreational activities. By divine design, fathers are to preside over their families in love and righteousness and are responsible to provide the necessities of life and protection for their families. Mothers are primarily responsible for the nurture of their children. In these sacred responsibilities, fathers and mothers are obligated to help one another as equal partners. Disability, death, or other circumstances may necessitate individual adaptation. Extended families should lend support when needed.

WE WARN that individuals who violate covenants of chastity, who abuse spouse or offspring, or who fail to fulfill family responsibilities will one day stand accountable before God. Further, we warn that the disintegration of the family will bring upon individuals, communities, and nations the calamities foretold by ancient and modern prophets.

WE CALL UPON responsible citizens and officers of government everywhere to promote those measures designed to maintain and strengthen the family as the fundamental unit of society.

This proclamation was read by President Gordon B. Hinckley as part of his message at the General Relief Society Meeting held September 23, 1995, in Salt Lake City, Utah.

INTRODUCTION

The *Family Home Evening Resource Book* has two major goals: to build family unity and to teach gospel principles. Although much of the material in this book is for parents with children, care has been taken to provide material for most age groups and family situations. Everyone can benefit from studying the gospel and applying its principles in his life.

Our Heavenly Father has given us commandments that will bring us blessings through obedience. He has granted us our agency to choose good over evil. He has provided for us a Savior, his Son Jesus Christ, to show us the way and atone for our sins. The family home evening lessons and activities in this book will help you develop an appreciation of these blessings and a desire to live for them.

THE RESPONSIBLITY OF PARENTS

In the home, parents and children learn together to apply the gospel's teachings to their lives. You teach your children all day, every day, whether you realize it or not. They pick up your habits, your prejudices, and your values from what you do as well as from what you say. The Lord has called you to be a parent, and he knows you can do it. You are part of his plan for his children.

Don't expect perfection from your children or from yourself all at once. Strive with your children to improve your lives little by little, step by step, line upon line each day. This book has been assembled to help you in your awesome responsibility as a parent.

HOW TO USE THIS BOOK

Unlike former family home evening manuals, this book gives ideas and activities that can be used without repetition by your family for many years. Use this book to create your own lessons most of the time, meeting your own family's needs. Each section of this book can help you if you will use it for its intended purpose.

Family Home Evening Lessons

The book contains thirty-seven regular family home evening lessons on basic subjects that most families will want to discuss. Most of the lessons contain adaptations for younger children (particularly nonreaders) and for teenagers and adults. Each of these groups need special approaches for the lessons to be effective and stimulating.

Questions you are to ask your family are preceded by black dots throughout the lessons and the book. This will make it easier for you to identify the questions quickly as you prepare and give the lessons.

At the end of most of the lessons are suggestions for additional family home evenings that you can develop on the same subject. Often your family may want to continue talking about a topic, or you may want to return to the same topic months later or another year. These extra suggestions can help you give the discussions a new slant whenever you return to that principle over the years. The lessons contain enough material for many years of family home evenings.

The last group of lessons, called "Special Occasions," will help you plan family home evenings for special events and holidays. These may include home evenings honoring someone in your family who may be getting baptized, receiving a patriarchal blessing, or going on a mission. Scan these as you begin to use this book so that you can use them at the appropriate times.

Making Home Evenings Successful

In former manuals, ideas were provided for parents to help them make their family home evenings more successful. This book provides the same kind of help under the section entitled "Making Home Evenings Successful." You may want to read these suggestions on planning and presenting home evenings first.

Over the years there will be many occasions when you will need to solve a special problem or help your children understand a particular principle. The last suggestion, "Creating Your Own Lessons," can help you develop your own lessons to fill such needs. It gives advice on how to choose a topic and organize a good lesson.

Lesson Ideas

The section "Lesson Ideas" contains thirty-seven topics not covered in the regular lessons. Arranged alphabetically, each topic presents brief outlines of several family home evening lessons to stimulate your thinking. Each topic section also includes additional references to related scriptures, chapters in the *Gospel Principles* manual [PBIC0245], and hymns and songs. These ideas provide you with suggestions to create your own lessons that meet the needs and interests of your family.

Building a Strong Family

You will want to study the section entitled "Building a Strong Family" carefully. It can help you better understand your children and improve communications with them. This is a concern of most dedicated parents. It provides many real-life examples of how to effectively resolve some difficult family situations or problems when they arise.

Family Activities

Your family members need to enjoy each others' companionship. The unity and love your family needs can grow as you work, play, and create together. The "Family Activities" section contains hundreds of ideas for fun times with your family.

PREPARING YOUR LESSONS

When preparing and holding your family home evenings, consider the following:

1. Pray. Pray about the needs of your family as you consider topics for home evenings, and pray as you prepare. Although it is not in the lesson outlines, begin and end each family home evening or activity with prayer. Setting the best spirit possible for each experience you have together is vital to your success. You need the help of our Heavenly Father, and he wants to be with you. Remember, your children are his children.

2. Be flexible. Whatever you do as you use this book, be flexible and adjust it to your family. You may want to expand a discussion that is designed for one week into a two-week discussion. Pick the topics you want to discuss in the order that best fits your own family's needs. How much of the material in the book you use is your choice. Substituting stories and examples of your own may be better than using the ones from the book.

3. Save your visual aids. You will be using this family resource book for several years. Preserve any pictures or other items that you make for the lessons. Get a large envelope, and keep everything that you want to save in it. Save sets of pictures, wordstrips, and similar visual aids in smaller envelopes that will fit into the larger one you have prepared.

   This book has been designed so that you will not need to cut out any of the pictures or diagrams included in it. But if you choose to do so, be sure to save these as well so that your book will continue to be of use to you in the years ahead.

4. Relax and enjoy it. The most important thing your children will remember is the spirit they feel in your family home evenings and activities. Be sure that the atmosphere is one of love, understanding, and enjoyment. It is more important to have a good time with one another than to get through a lesson. Don't be afraid to relax and enjoy your times together.

LESSONS

Sample
home evening lessons,
including lessons
for special occasions
and holidays

C O N T E N T S

BUILDING OUR FAMILY THROUGH HOME EVENINGS

Family life is the best method for achieving happiness in this world, and it is a clear pattern . . . [of] what is to be in the next world.
[*Spencer W. Kimball, "Privileges and Responsibilities of Sisters," Ensign, Nov. 1978, p. 103*]

PURPOSE

Help family members desire to be an eternal family, and help them to decide how they can use family home evenings to achieve that goal.

FOR THE PARENT

As Latter-day Saints, we frequently hear the phrases "eternal life" and "eternal family." They remind us that our families are our greatest source of happiness and joy. Only as family units can we receive the highest rewards of exaltation. This truth places a heavy responsibility on every family member.

As your family members learn to love and appreciate the special nature of your family, their commitment to be a successful, eternal family will grow. Family home evenings will take on greater importance and will promote spiritual growth among family members.

Evaluate your family home evenings, and work to improve them. The Lord has given us the family home evening program to help us hold our families together through the perilous times in which we live. Live the principles that you teach, and help your children to live them also. As you do, your family will grow closer and happier.

How you present this lesson will help you set the mood of future family home evenings. Prayerfully prepare to teach the lesson, and seek the guidance of the Holy Ghost. Be honest and sincere as you present it to your family. Let your children feel your great love for them and for the gospel. Do this and you will enjoy many successful and sacred experiences with your family.

PREPARATION

1. Bring a potted plant, a pet, and a baby, or pictures of each item.
2. Make a "Family Home Evening Question and Suggestion Box."
3. Bring or draw a picture of your family.

SUGGESTED HYMN AND SONG

"There Is Beauty All Around" (*Hymns*, no. 169).
"Families Can Be Together Forever," which accompanies this lesson.

SUGGESTED LESSON

We Belong in Families

Begin by reading or explaining the following:

Families

Before we were born, we lived in a family. There we were loved and taught. As we grew in knowledge and understanding, we wanted to become like our Heavenly Father. We wanted to share in his joys. We wanted a family of our own. Our Heavenly Father also wanted us to be able to have families of our own. He sent us to earth to get our bodies, to test us, and to train us to be parents eternally. This is what godhood means. (See chapter 2, "Our Heavenly Family," *Gospel Principles* [PBIC0245], pp. 9–12.)

After we come to earth we can begin to develop our own eternal families. If we succeed with our families in this life, we may return with them to our Heavenly Father. Then we will establish our own heavenly homes and be able to continue to have families. This is our Heavenly Father's plan for us and the highest reward we can receive. He has made it possible for us to return to him, to be with our earthly family, and to become gods and goddesses, having families forever.

Show your family the plant. Talk about the Creation and how Heavenly Father provided all of the things necessary for plants to grow. Discuss with your family some of the plant's needs and how they are met.

Next show the pet or baby animal. Discuss how Heavenly Father planned for its needs to be taken care of. Talk about its needs for food, water, and protection.

Now show the baby. Have your family discuss the baby's needs, such as love, security, guidance, education, social training, and spiritual growth, and how Heavenly Father planned to meet them. Explain that because of the special needs of his children, Heavenly Father planned for us to have families. He patterned our families after his own. He knew that a father and a mother who loved each other and sacrificed to bring children into the world would love them more than anyone else and would try to provide for all of their needs.

Heavenly Father Wants Our Family to Be Happy

Look at the baby again.

• To what kind of family would Heavenly Father want the baby to come?

• What kind of father would he want the baby to have? (One who is loving and who leads his family as our Heavenly Father leads his.)

• What would Heavenly Father want its mother to be like? (Loving and unselfish.)

• How would he want the baby's brothers and sisters to act?

• Are there any perfect families on the earth for babies to come to?

Point out that Heavenly Father knew that no family would be perfect. We are all working and learning together. Still, he wants us to work to become perfect in time. He knows that the closer we come to perfection, the more happiness we will find. This is one reason he has given us the family home evening program. If we make family home evenings effective in our homes, then we will find our families becoming better and happier.

Our Family Is Unique

Explain that all families are different. Let family members name some of the things that make them different from other families, such as size, age, background, talent, tradition, or personality.

Discuss some of the things that you like best about your family, then discuss the things you would like to improve. Talk about your family members' special gifts and talents. Discuss the goals that you have as a family. Then point out that because you are a family, you can all work together, each person using his gifts and talents, to reach your goals.

Family Home Evenings Can Meet Our Needs

Explain that your family home evenings can and should meet your family's needs. Only you know all your gifts, strengths, weaknesses, personalities, and needs and how to use them to help each other.

Pass the home evening resource book around, and let the family members look through it. Discuss how it is designed to help you meet your own needs and create your own family home evenings. Emphasize how you want your family home evenings to be successful in every way.

• How do you feel about our family home evenings?

• Are they really helping us grow toward perfection?

• Are they helping us feel closer to each other?

• How could we improve them?

Now talk together about some of the things you would like to see family home evenings do for your family. Make sure that the discussion is positive. Look through the book again,

and see how it can help you with your goals. Plan together how you would like to use it.

Show the "Family Home Evening Question and Suggestion Box." Tell your family that you will leave it where they can put a question or suggestion in it whenever they get an idea. Tell them that they can suggest lessons they would like to hear, questions they want answered, and suggestions for improving family home evenings.

Let's Make It Work

Express your feelings about the home evening program that Heavenly Father has given your family so that you can work toward exaltation together. Share your enthusiasm for what you want to do together in family home evenings. Bear your testimony of the gospel and the love that Heavenly Father has shown you.

Now show the family picture that you have selected or drawn. Tell your family that to you they are the most important family on the earth. Be specific about what you feel is best about your family. Let them know how much you love them and believe in them. Express your faith that your family can return to the presence of your Heavenly Father together.

Invite each family member to share his feelings about your family, the gospel, and the family home evening program.

Challenge family members to help the family succeed by doing all that they can to make family home evenings a good experience.

ADAPTING FOR YOUNGER CHILDREN

Begin with the object lesson involving the plant, pet, and baby presented under the heading "We Belong in Families." Briefly discuss the section "Heavenly Father Wants Our Family to Be Happy."

Explain that you want your family to be happier and that your family home evenings can help you become a better family.

Let your children look through the new book. Help them feel excited about the pictures, games, and activities that are in it and about how much

fun your family home evenings are going to be. You may want to choose to do one of the activities in the "Family Activity" section of the book as an example of fun activities you can have during family home evening.

Finish by showing your family picture and expressing your feelings and testimony as described under the lesson heading "Let's Make It Work."

ADAPTING FOR TEENAGERS AND ADULTS

Begin the lesson by explaining and discussing the material under the heading "Families."

Use the discussion in the section of the lesson entitled "Heavenly Father Wants Our Family to Be Happy." Talk about your own family and what goals you have. Discuss with your family what they would like to see family home evenings do for them.

Talk about how you can use the new book as explained under the lesson heading "Family Home Evenings Can Meet Our Needs."

Look through and discuss the book and the new ideas it offers. Investigate the different sections. Read through the introduction and the message from the First Presidency.

Use the "Family Home Evening Question and Suggestion Box" so that family members may write down ideas when they think of them.

End by showing your family picture and expressing your feelings as done in the section of the lesson entitled "Let's Make It Work."

SUGGESTIONS FOR FUTURE HOME EVENINGS

Appreciating Family Members

Have a family home evening honoring different family members. Take as many evenings as you need to do this.

Emphasize what each person has contributed to the family. Choose special incidents in the life of the family member that set good examples or teach gospel principles (for example, a brother's determination to learn to ride a bike despite many bumps and bruises demonstrates sticking to a project and never giving up, or a sister who shared her time with the baby

exemplifies service and love). (See Mosiah 4:15.)

Use pictures of family members at different ages and other mementos to illustrate their contributions to making your family special.

Knowing Your Family Heritage

If family or personal histories, journals, diaries, or letters of family ancestors are available, build a family home evening around finding and appreciating your family heritage.

Relate your family's history, staying with the direct line. Illustrate the history with stories about particular ancestors.

If these materials are unavailable, spend an evening planning and beginning a project to compile your family's history. Begin with your own family history, starting with brief biographies of yourselves up to your marriage, then going into more details about such topics as where you lived, the occupations of family members, and the coming of the children.

The Family Can Be Eternal

Build a lesson on the material in chapter 36, "The Family Can Be Eternal," of *Gospel Principles*, pages 221–25.

Becoming Eternal Friends

Hold a special family program. Hold it on a special date, such as on your wedding anniversary, or on any convenient night. Plan a special meal, setting, and program. Family members may wish to exchange homemade gifts or original verses expressing their feelings. You may wish to prepare a display of family pictures and mementos of family events or achievements.

Plan activities, but make sure that the purpose of the night is understood—to pay honor to the family and to express loyalty and love to each other as members of the family.

Keep in mind the following counsel from Elder Marvin J. Ashton:

"One of the great purposes of family evenings and home teaching is to have family members realize that a brother can be a friend, and that a sister can be a friend, and that a father and a mother can be more than parents, they can be friends.

"I would hope and pray that we may catch the wisdom and the inspiration of building a home so that our members in that sacred unit can look upon a father and say, 'He is my best friend,' or 'My mother is more than a mother, she is my friend.' When we realize that parents and family members can be more than blood relations and are in very deed friends, then we will have a glimpse of how our Heavenly Father wants us to live, not only as brothers and sisters but as very close friends." (In Conference Report, Oct. 1969, pp. 28–29.)

Appreciating the Important Things

Begin a family home evening time by reading the following letter from a prisoner of war to his family:

"Dearest Marjorie, Cameron, Heather, Warren, Holly, Heidi. Above all I seek for eternal life with all of you. These are important: temple marriage, mission, college. Press on. Set goals, write history, take pictures twice a year." (George Durrant, "A Gift from Heaven," *Ensign*, Mar. 1971, p. 5.)

Explain that because he was a prisoner of war, the author of the letter could write only a few words, so he had to choose carefully what he wanted to say to his family.

Have family members imagine that they are away from home under trying circumstances or in some way unable to be united with their loved ones. Have them write a brief letter to their family saying what is most important to them.

Allow time to share the letters, and let each person explain what he wrote and why if he wishes to do so.

Building Family Identity

Let the family members design a flag or banner for the family. Discuss what is unique about your family (see "Our Family Is Unique" in the regular lesson). Decide what aspects of your family are worth symbolizing in the flag. Then design and make the flag.

Family members may wish to set up some guidelines about when and where the family flag will be flown.

Be sure your family understands that a family flag does not take the place of your country's flag nor your allegiance to it.

THE COMMANDMENTS– GIFTS FROM A LOVING FATHER

He that keepeth the law, happy is he.
[*Proverbs* 29:18]

PURPOSE

Help family members appreciate that the commandments are blessings given by a loving father to bring us joy.

FOR THE PARENT

One of the saddest experiences of life is when we must watch someone we love break the commandments and follow ways that lead to unhappiness. As parents, we can help to protect our children from following such a course by teaching them early that the commandments are one of the greatest gifts our Father in Heaven provided for us during our stay in mortality. They are guidelines to happy living. They protect us from all the serious pitfalls of life. They are the pathway to peace and joy.

We must not only teach our children these truths but we must live so that our children can see the joys that we derive from keeping the commandments. The commandments were not meant to be a burden to us, but a wonderful blessing. They are gifts from our Heavenly Father, who loves us and wants us to share in his joys. Keeping them will increase our love and appreciation for him (see Deuteronomy 6:1–25, John 15:14).

PREPARATION

1. Prepare a chart with the phrase "Commandments I Am Thankful For" written across the top. You will add to it during the lesson.

2. Have a marker ready to write on the chart.

SUGGESTED HYMN AND SONG

"How Gentle God's Commands" (*Hymns*, no. 67).
"My Heavenly Father Wants Me to Be Happy" (*Sing with Me*, B–60).

SUGGESTED LESSON

Loving Parents Give Rules for Their Children

Share with your children how you felt while you were awaiting each of their births. Talk about your hopes and fears for them. Tell them how you loved them when you first held them

WICKEDNESS NEVER WAS HAPPINESS

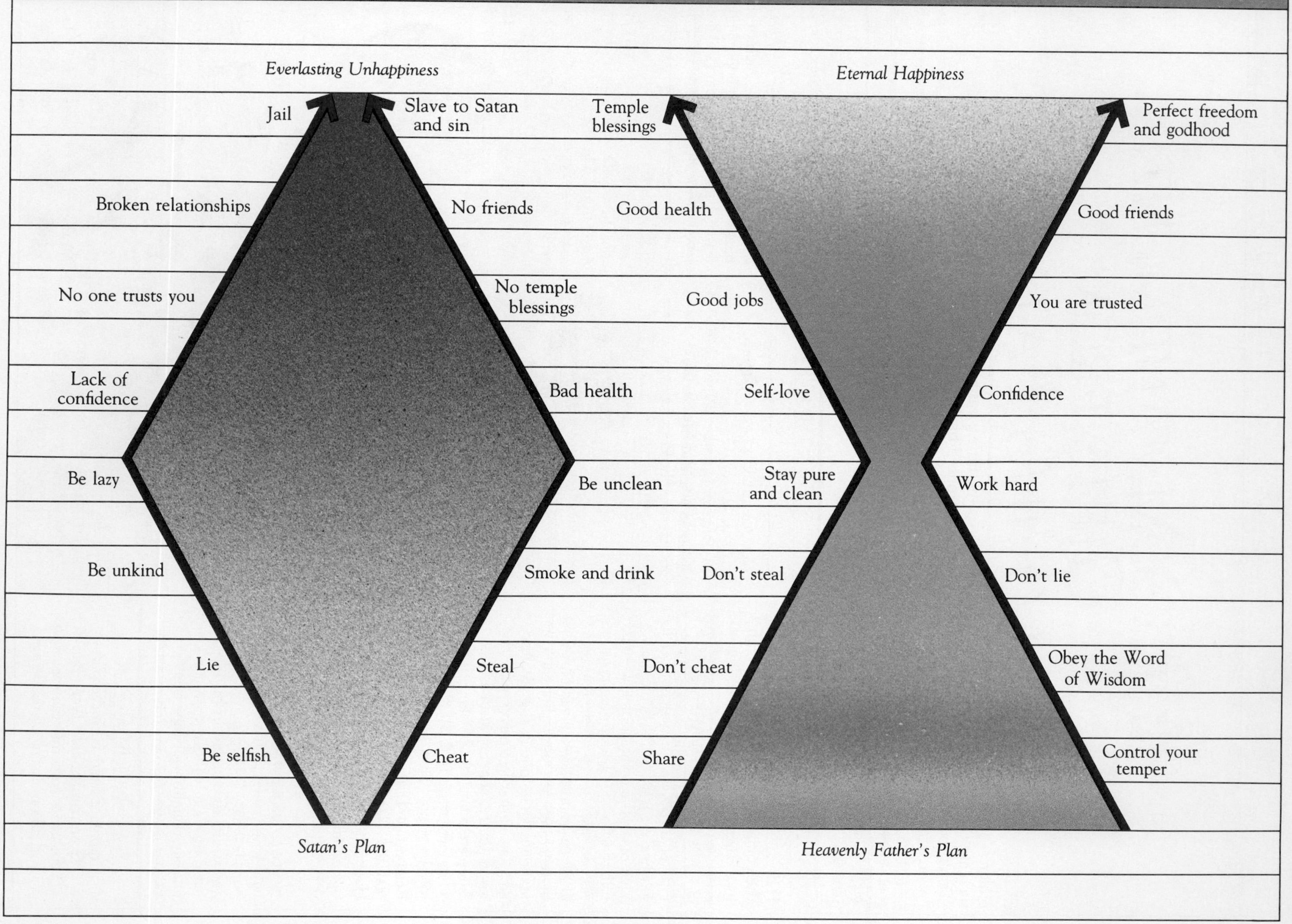

Eternal Happiness

Perfect freedom
and godhood

Good friends

You are trusted

Confidence

Work hard

Don't lie

Obey the Word
of Wisdom

Control your
temper

Heavenly Father's Plan

Temple
blessings

Good health

Good jobs

Self-love

Stay pure
and clean

Don't steal

Don't cheat

Share

Everlasting Unhappiness

Slave to Satan
and sin

No friends

No temple
blessings

Bad health

Be unclean

Smoke and drink

Steal

Cheat

Jail

Broken relationships

No one trusts you

Lack of
confidence

Be lazy

Be unkind

Lie

Be selfish

Satan's Plan

in your arms and how, more than anything else in the world, you wanted them to be safe and happy. Relate how at first you could personally care for them and protect them, but as they grew older they began to do things for themselves.

Have your children help you list some rules you might have made to protect your baby as he began to grow and explore his world.

Explain that the first rules parents give children are for their physical safety, such as "Don't go in the street" or "Don't touch the hot stove." But as children get older, parents also want to protect them from ways of behaving that will bring them unhappiness. They then make rules to teach them good behavior. List a few of these rules, such as "Be kind to everyone," "Share with others," and "Be willing to help others."

Our Heavenly Father is also our parent. He loves us even more than our earthly parents. He is also much wiser than any earthly parent. He knows what will bring happiness and unhappiness, and he guides us to happiness. He planned it that way because he loves us.

"Wickedness Never Was Happiness"

Explain that sometimes people feel that the commandments are hard to keep and restrict us from doing what we want to do. It sometimes looks as though the ones who break the commandments find pleasure or worldly success. Keeping the commandments may seem difficult at first.

Read Alma 41:10 together. Then display the "Wickedness Never Was Happiness" chart included in the lesson. Look at Satan's plan. Discuss how Satan makes it look like more fun to break the commandments. That is how he tempts us. When a person follows his plan, at first it seems to give him more freedom. But as he continues to make wrong choices, the consequences begin to bind him, and soon he finds that he is a prisoner to Satan. He may have "fun" at first; but, unless he repents, the price he pays is everlasting unhappiness.

See if your family can match up some of the specific broken commandments on the chart with their consequences, such as "Smoke and drink" brings

"Bad health," and "Lie" results in "No one trusts you."

Now look at Heavenly Father's plan. Explain that a person who chooses to keep the commandments may at first feel restricted. Sometimes it seems that there are many things he can't do. But as he trusts in Heavenly Father's love and continues to make right choices, his life begins to open up to greater freedoms, and he receives joys and blessings he never dreamed of. He will then rejoice that he gave up the little pleasures that would have robbed him of real and lasting joy. He will know of Heavenly Father's love because he will get good and happy results from what he does in his life. (See 1 Nephi 3:7, 22:31.)

Choose a few of the commandments, and discuss why they might be hard to keep at first. Then match them to their blessings on the chart. Try to think of other examples of commandments that bring blessings to your lives, and let your children write them on the chart if they would like to. Happiness in our everyday life comes from keeping the commandments of our loving Heavenly Father. Each commandment shows his love for us and his wisdom in guiding us.

Give a personal example of a time when keeping a commandment brought you a special blessing or happiness. Share your feelings about keeping that commandment. If you cannot think of one, tell the story of Nephi as he returned to Jerusalem to get the plates of Laban (see 1 Nephi 3–5).

• What was Nephi commanded to do?

• Why did Nephi find it hard to keep the commandment to obtain the plates?

• What would have happened if he had given up?

• How many people found happiness because of Nephi's decision to keep the commandment given him?

Relate the following about the Nephites after they were visited by the Savior:

A Happier People

When Jesus visted America after he was resurrected, the people who saw him accepted him with all their hearts. They not only repented, but

they told all the people who hadn't seen Jesus personally about his visit and the things he taught and the great works he performed. In just a few years all the people in the land were converted.

They were so careful in keeping all of the comandments that the Book of Mormon tells us "there were no contentions and disputations among them, and every man did deal justly one with another" (4 Nephi 1:2; see also 4 Nephi 1:17). As they followed the Lord's plan for living, many of their problems began to go away, "Surely there could not be a happier people among all the people who had been created by the hand of God" (4 Nephi 1:16).

• Why were these people so happy?

• Why would keeping the Lord's commandments make them happy?

• How can obeying the commandments help make our family happy?

Let's Be Thankful

Challenge family members to think of commandments that have brought them happiness because they have kept them.

Show your family the chart you are going to develop entitled "Commandments I Am Thankful For." Tell them that you would like to list commandments that you have found by personal experience to be blessings. Write down one or two that you have good feelings about, and tell your children why you have come to appreciate them. Invite them to share their experiences with you and add their favorite commandments to the list. Be sure to bring out that keeping the commandments gives us the healing and comforting influence of the Spirit.

Display the chart all week, and add to it as any family member thinks of more commandments. This would be a good topic of conversation as you eat your meals together. Also remember in your family prayers to thank Heavenly Father for the blessing of his commandments.

ADAPTING FOR YOUNGER CHILDREN

Start with the following story:

Mother Bear Protects Her Cubs

In the spring when Mother Bear came

out of her cave, she brought her two new baby cubs with her. She began from the very first day to teach them how to be safe. She taught them to climb up high in a tree whenever there was danger. It was a rule that they had to obey. They couldn't come down until Mother Bear let them know it was safe. If they did, she would chase them back up again. They learned the rule very well.

One day, while they were wandering through the forest, they came upon a hungry cougar that thought a baby bear would be good to eat. Mother Bear gave a warning, and both cubs scrambled up the nearest tree. Then Mother Bear fought the cougar and chased him away. The baby cubs were glad their mother had made rules to keep them safe.

Explain that most animal mothers want to protect their babies. Human parents love their children and want to protect them even more. Your young children will love to hear about how you felt about them when they were born. Share with them the rules you made to keep them safe.

Tell them that our Father in Heaven is our parent, too. He loves us the most of all. He also gave us rules. His rules keep us safe and happy. We call his rules "commandments." He promises us that if we will obey his commandments we will be able to live happy lives and return to live with him.

A Treasure Hunt

Next let your young children go on a treasure hunt. Make pictures for the clues or rules of where they are to look. Give them the first clue, perhaps a picture of their bed, and let them go there where you have the next clue hidden. That clue will have a picture of the next place to look. Continue until they find the treasure at the last place. The treasure should be some small treat.

Before they start, explain that you are going to let them practice following a rule to find a treasure. The rule is to follow the pictures.

After they have found the treasure, tell them that Heavenly Father's treasure for us is happiness. His commandments are the clues or rules we must

follow to gain his treasure of happiness.

Let each child make a picture for the "Commandments I Am Thankful For" chart. Give suggestions such as—

1. Tithing (they can draw pennies or themselves giving tithing to the bishop).

2. Sharing (they can draw toys they share with brothers and sisters).

3. Going to church (they can draw

the meetinghouse with your family in front of it).

Help them to remember to say thank you to Heavenly Father for the commandments in their prayers.

ADAPTING FOR TEENAGERS AND ADULTS

Start with the story and a discussion of the ideas under "A Happier People."

Explain that you make rules as an earthly parent for them because you love them and want to help them become their best selves. You want to save them from unhappiness and heartache. Admit that you may make mistakes but that they have a wise and loving parent who loves them even more than you do and who knows exactly what will bring them happiness and unhappiness. Heavenly Father has given us guidelines in the form of commandments to show us the way to live so that we may share in his happiness.

Discuss the "Wickedness Never Was Happiness" chart presented in the lesson. Then relate personal experiences you have had that have helped you know that the commandments were given for our happiness. Invite your family to share their experiences of when they have found happiness through keeping one of Heavenly Father's commandments.

Conclude by explaining that as we gain testimonies of some of the commandments, we also gain a trust in our Heavenly Father that helps us keep the others while we are learning about them.

Bear your testimony that Heavenly Father does love us and that the commandments are the only way to lasting happiness. Express your gratitude for the commandments, and encourage your family to express their gratitude for them in prayer during the coming week.

SUGGESTIONS FOR FUTURE HOME EVENINGS

The Commandments Protect Us and Free Us

Have family members discuss what it means to be free. Then ask the family to imagine a busy intersection and what it might be like if there were no traffic laws and signals.

- What might happen to an individual driver or pedestrian? (At best, he would lose time in traffic tie-ups. At worst, he might be hurt or killed in a traffic accident.)
- Why do these traffic laws exist: to hinder us and hold us back or to help the traffic flow more smoothly and more freely?

Compare the need for such laws with our earthly lives.

Read John 8:31–32. Ask how the truth makes us free and what it frees us from. Explain that every action has a consequence—we choose the consequences by choosing the actions.

Have family members each select a commandment and describe the consequences first of breaking the commandment then of keeping it. Ask them to decide in which case we are really free. Then read John 8:33–36.

Younger family members may enjoy drawing a house with a picture of themselves inside. Each part of the house can be labeled with a different commandment, such as the foundation, loving God; one wall, keeping chaste; another wall, being honest; the roof, honoring parents; and the door, not coveting. Explain that all together, the commandments protect and shelter us from the world.

Obedience Brings Great Blessings

Have a family member tell the story of Adam's sacrifice (Moses 5:4–9) or Naaman the leper (2 Kings 5:1–14). Point out that the blessings came *after* obedience to the commandment.

Then read Doctrine and Covenants 130:20–21. Have family members suggest some laws and the blessings that follow from obeying them. Younger family members may wish to write the commandment and draw a picture showing the blessings that come from obeying it.

Older family members may wish to discuss the importance of obedience and what obedience means to a celestial being. Such a discussion might help them understand how the practice of obedience can lead to the habit of doing things simply because they are the right things to do without having to choose and push oneself to be obedient.

Delight in the Law of the Lord

Read Psalm 1. Ask family members what it means to delight in something. Have them list a few things they find especially enjoyable.

Then ask them what they would be willing to do or to give up in order to continue to enjoy those things. Sug-

gest that it is their delight or enjoyment that prompts them to make the sacrifice or to put forth the effort.

Ask why the man in the psalm who delights in the law of the Lord is blessed. You may wish to refer to Matthew 6:19–21 during this discussion. Have family members suggest ways in which they can learn to delight in the law of the Lord, such as obeying the commandments, experiencing the blessings, praying for the witness of the Spirit, studying the scriptures, applying gospel principles in their lives, serving the Lord by serving others, and learning about eternal life and the promises that go with the covenants.

The Purpose of the Commandments

God gives commandments to men to bring about their full happiness. Have someone read Moses 1:39.

Discuss how keeping the commandments prepares us for eternal life.

- What is meant by the term "eternal life"? (To become like our Heavenly Father and to live as he lives.)

Read Revelation 21:7 and Doctrine and Covenants 84:38. Ask family members to imagine how they would feel if God were subject to some of the imperfections of men.

Have family members explore the idea that the greatest blessings also carry the greatest responsibilities. Emphasize that by obedience to the commandments man can overcome his faults and become like God.

Encourage each family member to pick out one commandment and practice living it until he has become perfect at it.

You may also wish to refer to Doctrine and Covenants 88:21–24, 35, and 130:20–21 when giving this lesson.

Know the Lord's Laws

You may wish to build a family home evening around the study of the Ten Commandments (Exodus 20:3–17) showing how our laws are based on the Lord's code of behavior. You may find it necessary or useful to devote separate home evenings to discuss different commandments. In the manual, you will find lesson suggestions under specific topics in the section "Lesson Ideas" or in the index.

THE GOSPEL IN OUR DAILY LIVES

Be ye doers of the word, and not hearers only, deceiving your own selves.
[James 1:22]

PURPOSE

Teach your family that the full blessings of the gospel come only through actively living the gospel.

FOR THE PARENT

Sometimes a member of the Church may wonder, "I belong to the Church. I know the gospel is true and try to teach my children about it. So what is wrong? Why am I unhappy?" We all need to realize that the blessings of the gospel do not come from just knowing about it or belonging to the Church. Blessings come from actually living gospel principles in our everyday lives.

The home is the most effective place to teach children how to use these principles and reap the blessings of the gospel. When you, as parents, work to change and grow with your family, your children will see that living the gospel is an important part of life. They will see that people can change and become better. This will help them commit themselves to put the gospel to work in their own lives. Your commitment to apply the gospel in your life will be the strongest influence for helping your children to do the same. Then the gospel can bring into their lives those blessings that Heavenly Father is waiting to give them. (See Deuteronomy 26:16, Joshua 24:15.)

PREPARATION

1. Center this family home evening on a special, favorite meal. Seat family members around the table, and begin your lesson. Do not have the prayer or let them begin to eat until the appropriate time in the lesson.

2. Make a chart. Divide the cart into halves. On the top of the left half, write "Physical Needs," on the right side write "Spiritual Needs." Have a marker ready to write on the chart.

3. Make wordstrips with different gospel principles written on them, and put one or more under each family member's plate. Some examples are "kindness," "honesty," "prayer," "reverence," "obedience," and "self-control."

4. Make the following wordstrips: "irreverence," "selfishness," "unkindness," "laziness," "dishonesty," "disobedience," "anger," and "lack of prayer." Have a plate ready on which to collect them.

SUGGESTED HYMN AND SONG

"Let Us All Press On" (*Hymns*, no. 98).
"I Want to Live the Gospel" (*Sing with Me*, B–65).

SUGGESTED LESSON

Physical Food and Spiritual Food

Begin your lesson by having family members sit down to a special dinner that you have prepared. Do not let them begin to eat. Instead, have them look at the food and discuss why they especially like each item and why the food is good for them.

Discuss the importance of a balanced diet and how our bodies need many different things to stay healthy.

On the left side of the chart list some of the ingredients of a good, balanced diet.

Point out that the gospel contains the ingredients for a good, balanced diet for our spirits. On the right side of the chart add some of these spiritual ingredients.

Your chart may look something like the following:

Physical Needs	Spiritual Needs
Grains	Feeling the Spirit
Fruits	Being loved
Vegetables	Contributing
Milk products	Belonging
Meat	Having self-confidence
Protein	Forgiving
Minerals	Feeling secure
Vitamins	Serving
	Sacrificing
	Being forgiven
	Receiving inspiration
	Developing our talents

Now tell them that since they have discussed their dinner and how they feel about it, they can all leave the table.

• Do you think this is a good idea?

• Are you still hungry?

• Why didn't the food do you any good?

Emphasize that we must eat the good food if our bodies are to benefit from it. Point out to your family that just as food feeds our bodies, the gospel feeds our spirits. It is spiritual food.

• Can we benefit by knowing about

the gospel, being around it, understanding it, discussing it, or even feeling that it's true if that is all we do?

- What do we need to do before the gospel can really help us? (We must live it for it to do us good just as we must eat the food for it to do us good.)

Now have your prayer, and begin to eat while you finish your discussion.

We Need the Blessings of the Gospel

Have the family members take out the wordstrips from under their plates. Talk about why you need to live the principles written on them if you want to satisfy the spiritual needs you just listed. For example, for the wordstrip "kindness," you might ask:

- How does kindness help us?
- What would happen to our lives without kindness?
- How does being kind help us to stay spiritually healthy and happy?

After you discuss each wordstrip, explain that living all the principles of the gospel is like eating a balanced diet. By doing all of the things that our Heavenly Father has asked us to do we will stay spiritually happy and healthy.

What Can We Do?

Tell the following story. Hold up the wordstrips indicated in parentheses in the story. Place them one by one on the plate that you have provided.

David

David belonged to the Church, and he said he believed it was true. He went to church every Sunday; but he thought that most of the time it was boring, so he didn't pay much attention. He thought it was more fun to talk and joke with his friends. (Hold up the wordstrip "irreverence.")

He liked family home evenings because his father told such good stories and his mother made such good treats (hold up "selfishness"), but even during the lessons he enjoyed teasing his sisters ("unkindness").

During the week, David's life was filled with problems. He played instead of doing his homework ("laziness"), and then copied his friend's work ("dishonesty"). He didn't obey his parents ("disobedience") and

wondered why they picked on him when he got into trouble. He had a terrible temper ("anger"), and figured that other people deserved to be treated unkindly because he didn't have many friends. He forgot about his prayers most nights ("lack of prayer"). He just didn't think he had time.

One day in Primary, David heard his Primary teacher say, "The gospel brings us so much happiness."

David thought, "The gospel doesn't bring me happiness."

- Why didn't David find happiness in the gospel?

Show the plateful of negative wordstrips.

- Would such a meal be good for our spirits?
- Why not?

Discuss some of the things that David needed to do to bring the blessings of the gospel into his life. You may want to use the other set of wordstrips.

Let family members talk about some of the things that cause unhappiness in their lives. See if they can think of ways that living the gospel could improve their lives. Praise them for the good choices they do make, pointing out the blessings that come from making such right choices. Help them realize how many more blessings they could receive by living the gospel more fully.

Each Person Must Do It for Himself

- What could David's parents do to help David live the gospel?

Explain that although they could teach him and pray for him and try to remind him, only David can make the decision that he is going to make the gospel work in his life. He is the only one who can live for the blessings that Heavenly Father is waiting to give him.

Tell your family that you will be teaching the gospel to them in your family home evenings and sharing some of the experiences from your life. Explain that the only way that family home evenings can help you is if each person applies the things he learns to his life.

Explain that applying the gospel means living it every day and learning

to do the things that Heavenly Father has commanded us to do.

You Can Do It

After the dinner is over, challenge family members to put the gospel into practice in their lives more and more each day. Share with them your commitment to change and to grow. Discuss with them some of the things that might make it hard to begin to change the patterns of their lives, such as pride, habit, fear of what others may think, or lack of faith that such a change will really bring happiness. Admit that you know that it will take effort every day to grow and change, but remind the members of your family of the great blessings that will come to them as they make that effort.

Discuss some of the lessons you will be having in family home evening. Point out specific blessings that can come to you as a family as you make an effort to live what you learn. Close by challenging each family member to commit himself to live the principles he learns each week (see Matthew 6:33, 7:24; 1 Nephi 3:7).

ADAPTING FOR YOUNGER CHILDREN

Begin by asking the following questions. Have the children raise their hands for the answer that shows what Heavenly Father wants them to do.

1. When mother is busy fixing dinner you should—
   a. Go play with your friends.
   b. Help her.
2. When your little sister is crying you should—
   a. Call her a crybaby.
   b. Give her a hug and find a toy to share with her.
3. When your father asks you to do something you should—
   a. Do it quickly.
   b. Pretend you didn't hear him.
4. When your brother breaks one of your crayons you should—
   a. Forgive him.
   b. Punch him and go tell your mother.
5. When you have a problem that worries you, you should—
   a. Cry about it.

b. Discuss it with your parents and pray to Heavenly Father about it.

Make up other questions that fit the needs of your children.

After the questions, tell your children how proud you are that they know what Heavenly Father wants them to do. Then explain to them that there is something even more important than *knowing* what Heavenly Father wants them to do. See if they can guess what it is as they listen to the following story:

Sammy Shares

Sammy had a wonderful lesson in Primary. He learned about sharing. His teacher told him that Heavenly Father was happy when people shared. She said that if the children shared, they would be happy, too. Sammy went home and told his mother and father. They were proud that Sammy knew about sharing.

Later that day, Sammy was playing with his clay. His little sister, Jane, saw him and wanted to play with the clay, too. Sammy didn't want to give Jane any of his clay. Sammy's mother reminded Sammy about sharing. Then Sammy remembered that Heavenly Father wanted him to share. He wanted to do what Heavenly Father wanted, so he gave some clay to Jane. Mother and father were happy. Jane smiled happily as she pounded the clay. Sharing did make Sammy happy. Sharing was much better than just knowing about sharing.

Remind your children of the times when they have made the right choices and tell them how wonderful they were. Also remind them of some of the things that they have learned in family home evening and how they tried to live them. Let them tell you how they felt when they really did the things that they learned about.

Praise them for all of their efforts, and tell them that you all want to work very hard to do the things you learn about that Heavenly Father wants you to do. Remind them throughout the week to do what they *know* is right.

ADAPTING FOR TEENAGERS AND ADULTS

Begin by having the dinner as suggested in the regular lesson. Use the discussion under the heading "We Need the Blessings of the Gospel."

- What is likely to happen to a person's faith who belongs to the Church and understands the truth but makes no real effort to live the gospel?

Discuss James 1:22.

- What does "deceiving your own selves" mean? (Thinking we can know but not do.)

Also read and talk about Matthew 5:48.

- Does Heavenly Father expect perfection immediately?

Explain that the more principles of the gospel we can live in our lives, the more spiritual blessings we will receive. Read and discuss Doctrine and Covenants 82:10. We do not have to be perfect before the Lord will give us blessings; he is eager and waiting to bless our lives (see D&C 10:65–66).

He wants us to be happy.

You may want to use the section "Each Person Must Do It For Himself."

• In what ways is it possible for one person to help another live the gospel?

• Can a person be helped if he is unwilling to receive help?

Conclude your lesson with section entitled "You Can Do It."

SUGGESTIONS FOR FUTURE HOME EVENINGS

Increasing in Ability to Live the Gospel

Have two family members stand side by side. Then have them take three normal steps forward. Ask them what they think President Kimball meant when he said we should "lengthen our stride." (Take bigger steps in our journey toward perfection.)

Have family members suggest some gospel principles in which they need to improve, such as honesty, kindness, self-control, tithing, unselfishness, missionary work, and service. Ask how they can take bigger steps in learning to live these principles. Have family members suggest and write down ideas for taking bigger steps in each of the areas. Have family members choose one or two of the ideas to work on during the coming week, and get their commitment to try to improve in those areas.

You may wish to read to them or give them a copy of the following statement by Elder Heber J. Grant, "That which we persist in doing becomes easier for us to do; not that the nature of the thing itself is changed, but that our power to do is increased" (in Conference Report, Apr. 1901, p. 63). Suggest that the more they practice any gospel principle, the easier it will be to live it.

Living the Gospel Begins with Our Thoughts

Begin by telling the family about Larry and Jerry:

Larry spent much of his time daydreaming. He loved to think about what it would be like to be rich. He planned what he would buy if he had lots of money, and he imagined living in luxury.

Jerry spent much of his time thinking, too. He liked to think about what was really important in life. He thought about people and what truly brought them happiness. He thought about the gospel and why Heavenly Father gave us the commandments.

Later, both Larry and Jerry were given an opportunity to make a great deal of money very easily. To do it, however, they would need to "stretch the truth" to convince others to invest money also.

• Who was more likely to give in to the temptation, Larry or Jerry? (Larry.)

Ask them to explain why they think one was weaker than the other.

Have someone read Matthew 6:19–21. Then ask family members to suggest other "treasures" their hearts might be set upon. As each is suggested, quote Proverbs 23:7, "For as he thinketh in his heart, so is he." Then ask whether the suggested "treasure" or thought will bring a man closer to God or pull him farther away from him.

Explain how the things we think about often end up controlling our actions. Read aloud Luke 6:45. Discuss how a person can control and direct his thoughts (for example, by seeking the right surroundings, reading scripture and good books, praying, or singing hymns).

End by reading Doctrine and Covenants 121:45. Discuss the great blessings that come from virtuous thoughts.

Learning to Show Faith by Our Works

Spend an evening discussing James 2:14–26. Talk about each verse and what it means. Then have each person rate his own faith by privately responding to the following questions, answered by *always*, *sometimes*, or *never*:

1. Do I forgive quickly?

2. Do I gladly help my neighbors?

3. Am I honest?

4. Do I stand up for the right even when my friends mock me?

5. Do I willingly accept Church callings?

6. Do I give of my time to each family member?

7. Do I pray sincerely every day?

8. Am I kind to strangers, friends, and family members?

9. Do I refrain from judging other people as being either better or worse than me?

10. Do I avoid even the appearance of evil?

Family members may score themselves by giving ten points for every time they answered *always*, five for every time they answered *sometimes*, and none for every time they answered *never*. (They need not tell others their score.)

Have each family member choose one of these areas in which to strengthen his faith by improving his works. Suggest that he work on these principles one by one until his score is one hundred.

Using the Gospel to Take Care of Our Needs

Have the family list different kinds of problems people have, such as fights with brothers and sisters, money problems, sickness, not having any friends, poor grades in school, failure in business, or the death of a loved one.

Discuss how the gospel helps us with our problems. Go over each of the problems on the list and discuss how living the gospel could help a person with that problem. Point out that living the commandments can solve some kinds of problems (for example, if we are honest in our dealings, we will never have to be ashamed of being caught in a dishonest act).

Explain that living the commandments, however, does not guarantee that we will never have other kinds of problems. Knowing who we are, why we are on earth, and where we are going can help us endure and cope with these other problems. Express your appreciation for the sacrifice that the Savior made, which conquered the lasting effects of the most damaging of problems, sin and death.

Use the story of Elisha in 2 Kings 6:8–17 to illustrate how the Lord can be with us. He will give us whatever support we need to live our lives successfully if only we will look to him and the gospel for aid to meet our own personal challenges.

STUDYING THE SCRIPTURES TOGETHER

My soul delighteth in the scriptures, and my heart pondereth them, and writeth them for the learning and the profit of my children.
[2 Nephi 4:15]

PURPOSE

Encourage family members to study the scriptures together regularly.

FOR THE PARENT

All Church members have been counseled by our leaders to study the scriptures. Though we know how important this counsel is, it is not always easy to follow. The scriptures are not always easy reading. They sometimes seem difficult to understand.

The scriptures are, however, the word of God to his children through the ages. They show his great love and assure us that he cares for us today as he has always cared for his children. The Lord said, "Learn of me, and listen to my words; walk in the meekness of my Spirit, and you shall have peace in me" (D&C 19:23). This peace can dispel worry and fear in a confused and troubled world.

The scriptures contain sound advice, beautiful poetry, and history. If we read the scriptures regularly, praying and desiring to understand, they will be a great blessing to us and to our families. (See 2 Nephi 4:15, Mosiah 1:7, D&C 33:16.)

PREPARATION

1. Have a copy of the standard works for each family member if possible.
2. Make the following three wordstrips or simple posters: "God loves his children," "We can learn to know Jesus," and "We can get help."

3. Use the pictures of families from the scriptures included with the lesson.

SUGGESTED HYMN AND SONG

"An Angel from on High" (*Hymns*, no. 224).

"Tell Me the Stories of Jesus" (*Sing with Me*, B–46).

SUGGESTED LESSON

The Scriptures Are the Word of God

If you have enough copies of the standard works, give one book to each member of your family. If you don't have enough for each person, let them share those books that you do have.

- What are these books called? (The standard works, scriptures.)
- Why are they important to us? (They contain the truth. They contain the word of God.)

Explain that Heavenly Father gave us these books for special reasons. Have your family read 1 Nephi 19:22–24. Nephi lists three reasons for having scriptures. Display the wordstrips or posters as you identify these three reasons:

1. God loves his children—"that they might know concerning the doings of the Lord in other lands, among people of old" (vs. 22).
2. We can learn to know Jesus—"that I might more fully persuade them to believe in the Lord their Redeemer I did read unto them" (vs. 23).
3. We can get help—"for I did liken all scriptures unto us, that it might be for our profit and learning" (vs. 23).

The Scriptures Show That Heavenly Father Loves His Children

Refer to the first wordstrip or poster, "God loves his children." Show the four pictures of families from the scriptures that Heavenly Father has helped. Discuss who the people are, what happened to them, and which book contains their story:

1. Joseph, Mary, and the baby Jesus left for Egypt (Matthew 2:13–15).
2. Moses and the children of Israel journeyed to the promised land (Exodus 3:7–8).
3. Lehi and his family traveled to America (1 Nephi 18:8, 23).
4. The Mormon pioneers moved west (D&C 136:1–10).

Remind your family that the scriptures tell us that Heavenly Father loves his children and wants to help them. We can be sure that he cares for us today and will bless us as he has blessed his children in the past.

The Scriptures Tell Us about Jesus

Show the second wordstrip or poster, "We can learn to know Jesus." Ask each family member to tell his favorite story about Jesus. After each person has responded, point out which book of scripture contains that story.

Look up some of the stories you have shared, and let your children see exactly where they are found. Let them read a few verses so that they can become familiar with the language of the scriptures.

Ask the following questions, and if your family members think the answer is in the book they are holding, tell them to stand up:

- What book tells about Jesus' birth and life on earth? (The Bible.)
- What book tells about his visit to

the American continent? (The Book of Mormon.)

- What book has instructions that Jesus gave to Joseph Smith? (The Doctrine and Covenants.)
- What book tells about when Heavenly Father and Jesus appeared to Joseph Smith in the Sacred Grove? (The Pearl of Great Price.)

Be sure your family understands that all of the standard works tell us something about Jesus. The more we read about Heavenly Father and Jesus, the better we will know them.

The Scriptures Can Help Us

Show the third wordstrip or poster, "We can get help." Explain that Heavenly Father gave us the scriptures so that by reading about the lives of other people, their problems, and how they solved them, we can learn to handle our own problems better.

Read the following problems. After each one is read, have a family member look up and read the listed scriptures that would help in handling that problem. (Help smaller children.)

1. You are worried or fearful about something (Isaiah 41:10, D&C 112:10).

2. You are sad because you have done something you shouldn't have (Isaiah 1:18, Moroni 6:8, D&C 58:42).

3. You feel bad because someone has been unkind to you (Proverbs 15:1–2, Matthew 6:14–15, Luke 6:27–30).

We Can Study the Scriptures Together

Explain that the scriptures can help us and be a blessing to us only if we will read them regularly and think and pray about them. Every family home evening lesson begins with a scripture. Encourage family members always to have the standard works with them at family home evenings so that they can look up scriptures during the lessons.

Help your children read directly from the scriptures. Help them to understand what is said so that the scriptures will become familiar to them. Point out that every Latter-day Saint home should have these books and use them.

If you are not now reading the scrip-

tures regularly as a family, discuss how to begin. Decide on a time, a place, and the book you would like to read first. Some families have found early morning, before or after breakfast, to be the best time for scripture reading. Others choose to do it at dinner time or before family prayers at night. Discuss all these possibilities with your family, and decide what is best for you.

Emphasize that reading the scriptures only ten minutes or one chapter a day can greatly increase the spirituality of your home.

If you are already reading together, have one or two family members share what reading the scriptures regularly means to them.

ADAPTING FOR YOUNGER CHILDREN

Hold each of the four standard works, one at a time, in a way that shows your appreciation and reverence for it as you tell the children its name. Explain that they are very special books because they contain the words of our Heavenly Father. They contain true stories and tell us about Jesus and how we can be happy. They tell us how much our Heavenly Father loves us and that he will always help us.

Sing "Tell Me the Stories of Jesus" with your children. Then tell them the story of Jesus blessing the Nephite children (see 3 Nephi 17:18–25). Show them where this story is located in the Book of Mormon.

Next tell them your favorite Old Testament story, and show them where it is found in the Bible.

To study the scriptures with your younger children, read or tell bedtime stories from the scriptures, or read from *Old Testament Stories* (stock number PBIC0336), *New Testament Stories* (PBIC0347), *Book of Mormon Stories* (PBIC0325), *Doctrine and Covenants and Church History Stories* (PBIC037A), or *Scripture Stories* (PBIC0358). (Prerecorded sound tapes are also available. Check the current distribution center catalog in your meetinghouse library.)

Remember to tell your children which book the story comes from each time you read or tell a story so that they will become familiar with the standard works.

ADAPTING FOR TEENAGERS AND ADULTS

Have each family member tell his favorite scriptural passage, story, or parable. Stimulate their thinking by first telling one of yours. After everyone has had an opportunity to respond, ask why they chose that particular verse or story. Responses should show different ways the scriptures can teach and help us.

Have someone read 1 Nephi 19:22–24. Identify the three basic reasons why Nephi exhorted his people to read and ponder the scriptures. Use the regular lesson to discuss these three reasons, adapting it to the interests of your family.

If you do not have a regular program for scripture study in your family, use the following personal experience related in the April 1975 general conference by Bishop H. Burke Peterson to help your family begin one:

"May I relate a personal experience from the Peterson family. Several years ago after wrestling with the problem for some time, my wife and I, sensing the urgency of our parental charge, devised a new battle plan. You see, up to that point, Satan had been winning the battle of 'Should we or should we not read the scriptures together in the Peterson home?' We had tried off and on for years with no sustained success. Our big problem was that someone or something always interrupted our schedule. With a 17-year spread in our children's ages, we felt we had a special challenge.

"As we studied and prayed over it, we concluded that the best time for our family of girls to read would be when no one else wanted our time. Since the older girls had to be in seminary by 7:00 A.M., our controllable time had to be early. We decided on 6:15 in the morning. We knew it would be a challenge to get teenage support. The idea was good, but its implementation was most difficult and it still is. Our family is still struggling.

"Our great new plan had its birth one hot August day in Phoenix, Arizona. My wife suggested we give them a whole month to think about it and prepare for it. We went about their mental preparation in a very positive way. The plan was to start the first day of school in early September. To their protests that it was impossible to have their heads all filled with rollers in time, or that it was not likely they would feel happy so early in the morning, or that they might be late to seminary, or not have time to eat breakfast either, we replied very cheerfully that we knew they were clever enough to cope with any minor problems that might arise.

"At its announcement, we also told the girls we had been praying for guidance in this family problem. This made it easier, because they had been schooled in prayer and had been taught not to question its results.

"The historic first morning finally came. My wife and I got up a little early so we would be sure to be wide awake and happy. Our initial approach must meet with success. We entered each bedroom singing and happy at the thought of the prospects before us. Purposely we went to one special bedroom first. Here slept a daughter who would be able to get up early but who couldn't wake up before noon. We sat her up in bed and then went to the others and started them all into the family room. Some stumbled, some fell, some had to be carried in, some slept through that first morning—and I might say through subsequent mornings too.

"Little by little, we have learned over the years what reading the scriptures 15 minutes each morning can do for our family. You should know that we don't try to discuss and understand each point we read. We try to pick out only a couple of thoughts each morning to digest. You should also know we still have to struggle with the plan's performance, even though we now have only two children at our home.

"Can you imagine how a parent would feel to ask a little girl, 'What did King Benjamin mean when he said, "When ye are in the service of your fellow beings ye are only in the service of your God"?' (Mosiah 2:17.) And she would respond, 'I suppose he means that I shouldn't be selfish and should do little things for my sisters because it makes Heavenly Father happy—and Daddy, I want him to be happy with me, so I'm going to try harder.' Innu-

merable are the blessings that will accrue to the family that persists in this noble effort of reading the scriptures together daily." (In Conference Report, Apr. 1975, pp. 79–80; or *Ensign,* May 1975, p. 54.)

Encourage your family to set up a program of scripture reading as discussed in the final section of the regular lesson.

SUGGESTIONS FOR FUTURE HOME EVENINGS

Getting to Know the Scriptures

Have a separate lesson on each of the standard works (you may wish to treat the Old and New Testaments as separate books). In each lesson, discuss where the works came from, what they contain, and some of their important messages. (See chapter 10, "Scriptures," in *Gospel Principles* [PBIC0245], pp. 49–52.)

Where Is It?

Have a family home evening on locating scriptures. Write the names of the books (Omni, Helaman, Haggai, etc.) on flash cards. As each card is shown, family members tell in which standard work that book is found.

For older members, use individual scripture stories, names of prophets, or familiar passages. The names of books can also be mixed up and then arranged in the order in which they are found in the standard works.

A Scripture Game Night

Have an evening of games. You can include games such as the following:

1. Question and answer games. Ask questions such as "What prophet called down fire from heaven?" or "What book comes after Zechariah?" Then let family members find the answer in the standard works (Elijah, in 1 Kings 18, 2 Kings 1; and Malachi).

2. Scripture chase. Use a word or phrase, such as "Love is necessary to do God's work." Then have family members race to find the appropriate scripture (D&C 4:5).

3. Matching games. Play matching games, matching such things as scriptural characters with events or people with places.

Adjust game difficulty to fit your family's age and knowledge.

You may wish to award points or prizes to make the games more interesting. If so, be careful that each family member has a chance to share in the prizes.

How to Study the Scriptures

Have a lesson on ways to study scriptures. Discuss how to outline, read for understanding, or mark passages. Use references and the Topical Guide in the Latter-day Saint edition of the King James Version of the Bible, and relate the scriptures to our own day (see 1 Nephi 19:23).

Adapt the lesson to fit the age level of your family (this would not work well for very young children). Older children and adults may wish to practice these skills and compare results.

The Scriptures in Our Lives

Read aloud Joseph Smith—History 1:1–14. Show how the scriptures helped Joseph Smith find the answer to his problem. Then ask family members to suggest passages of scripture that have made a difference in their lives or the lives of people they know. Discuss how the scriptures can help us solve our daily problems. Point out that the scriptures are personal messages to us from our Heavenly Father.

The Need for Personal Scripture Study

Discuss the importance of a personal program of scripture study. Take time to have each family member set up a practical scripture study schedule of his own if he does not have one. Family members may select their own part of the standard works to study. Have them schedule their reading on a calendar as a visible reminder.

Have family members keep track of their reading, and promise the whole family a treat if they meet some agreed percentage of their goals.

End with a twenty-minute quiet period during which the members of your family can begin their scripture study program.

Young children may not be capable of scripture reading on their own, but they do enjoy hearing the scriptures read aloud. A regular program of reading scriptures to them will help make later scripture reading a familiar and enjoyable experience.

I Am a Child of God

Have we not all one father?
[*Malachi 2:10*]

PURPOSE

Help family members realize what it means to be children of God.

FOR THE PARENT

From our earthly parents we have inherited our physical characteristics. We have also inherited qualities of nobility, goodness, and eternal worth from our Heavenly Father. Think of the potential of your children. Think of what it could mean to them to really sense their potential. Do you really believe that you are a child of God? Does that knowledge make a difference in your daily life?

PREPARATION

1. Have two items that have obvious similarities and differences, such as a combiniation of two of the following: a small rock, a small ball, an orange, or an apple.

2. Bring a family picture with the parents and all the children, including grandparents if possible, or several pictures of family members, so that everyone is represented.

3. On a sheet of paper, write "Our Heavenly Father."

4. Have a chalkboard or poster to write on and some chalk or a marker.

5. Have a card or poster for each family member.

6. For younger children, bring a picture of each family member as a baby.

SUGGESTED HYMN AND SONG

"O My Father" (*Hymns*, no. 139).

"I Am a Child of God" (*Sing with Me*, B–76).

SUGGESTED LESSON

Who Are You?

Hold a small rock in your hand, and ask your children:

• What is this?

Hold an orange in your other hand.

• What is this?

Ask your family to name as many ways as they can in which these two objects are different. Then ask them to identify how they are similar.

Hold up the family portrait or the separate pictures of family members, and ask:

• Who are these people? Who is this?

• In what ways are the members of our family different from each other? (Facial characteristics, size, age, talents, and any other ways family members might mention.)

• In what ways are members of our family alike? (Color of hair, eyes, freckles, interests, hopes, desires to learn, or whatever your family members identify.)

Point out that we inherited some of these characteristics from our parents.

• In what way is our family different from other families? (Looks, house we live in, goals, number of family members.)

• In what ways are we like the people in other families? (We enjoy playing, smiling, crying, praying.)

Hold up the paper on which you have written "Our Heavenly Father."

• How are we related to our Heavenly Father? (We are his actual children in the spirit.)

We Belong to Two Families

Place the family portrait(s) beside the piece of paper just discussed. Explain to the family that just as they are members of an earthly family, they are also members of a heavenly family.

Point out that one way we are like

Verse	Child's Favorite Part
I am a child of God, And he has sent me here, Has given me an earthly home With parents kind and dear.	Kind parents
I am a child of God, And so my needs are great; Help me to understand his words Before it grows too late.	My needs
I am a child of God, Rich blessings are in store; If I but learn to do his will I'll live with him once more.	Blessings Live with him
Lead me, guide me, walk beside me, Help me find the way. Teach me all that I must do To live with him someday.	Teach me, walk beside me Live with him

Draw the following chart on a chalkboard or poster, and ask your children for words that describe what our Heavenly Father is like. Some examples are below:

Heavenly Father is—	His children can be—
Loving.	
Forgiving.	
Helpful.	
Wise.	
Interested in the future.	

Your family list may not be exactly like the one illustrated.

Under the heading "His children can be," write the same qualities you list in the left column. Ask for examples of these very qualities that have been observed in family members during the past week.

Our Worth and Our Potential

Explain to your children that because they are God's children, they are worth very much.

• What is it about us which Heavenly Father would love so much? (First of all, he loves us because we are his spirit children; we are his family. Secondly, he loves us because of what we are capable of doing and becoming.)

Remind your children that their worth, like their family membership, is unquestionable.

• What if someone were to tell you that you are not a child of God?

After listening to their answers, reinforce the fact that regardless of what others may say, they are still children of Heavenly Father. Point to the list that you made as you ask the following question:

• What if someone were to tell you that you could not develop these qualities?

After they have answered, read and discuss this statement by Lorenzo Snow: "We are the offspring of God, born with the same faculties and powers as He possesses, capable of enlargement through the experience that we are now passing through in our second estate" (*Millennial Star*, 3 Dec. 1894, p. 772). Be sure each

each other and like the members of all other families on the earth is that we are all children of God.

Recite the words to the song "I Am a Child of God" (*Sing with Me*, B–76). After each verse ask a child in the family to tell you what words or ideas in the verse they liked best. (See the facing chart as an example.)

Reviewing the song this way can help your children understand and respond to the words. Listen to their thoughts, and use them later in the lesson.

You might comment, for example, on your own desire to be a kind parent or how one of our needs is to know the truth about God and about blessings that have come by doing his will.

Explain to your children that they will always be members of your family and

that you will always be their father and mother. Nothing can change that. The same is true of God's family. He will always be our Father. We will always be his children. But to return to him we must live his commandments. That's what the chorus in "I Am a Child of God" means when it states,

"Teach me all that I must do
To live with him someday."

What We Inherit from God

Remind your family that just as we are similar to our earthly parents, we are, as children of God, similar to him. As we can grow up to be like our earthly parents, so we can also grow spiritually to be like our Heavenly Father. (See chapter 2, "Our Heavenly Family," *Gospel Principles* [PBIC0245], pp. 9–12.)

person knows what the phrase "second estate" means.

Give some practical examples to apply these ideas. For example, when they feel discouraged, encourage your children to look in a mirror and say such things as, "I am a child of God. I can learn and grow. I can be kind to others. I can succeed."

Have each family member make a small card or poster with the following on it to place by his bed:

I am a child of God, and I can become more_____ .

Explain that each morning before prayer the family member looks at the card and identifies a godly quality he could develop to fill in the missing word, such as loving, forgiving, educated, or accomplished. He should use whatever quality he may feel he needs to develop at the time. Encourage family members to seek the Lord's help in being true to their capacity to become like him. In the evening, they should ponder the chances they had during the day to work on their potential. Challenge each person to examine the experiences he has had each day and share with his Heavenly Father what he, as one of God's children, has learned from them.

ADAPTING FOR
YOUNGER CHILDREN

If possible, display a picture of each family member as a baby. Let the children try to find their own pictures and identify the others. Tell them about the circumstances surrounding their birth. You may wish to describe your feelings as a parent as your prepared for their coming to your home. Describe how you felt when you saw, held, and loved them for the first time. Then ask them to imagine how Heavenly Father must feel to see them growing and learning.

Share how a knowledge that you are a child of God has helped you to choose the right. A specific example of a righteous choice they would understand would be helpful. You could recall how you were tempted to be unkind and then remembered that you were a child of God and so did a kind thing instead. Use some example from your recent experience so that the child will see the point clearly.

Sing "I Am a Child of God" with your children. Then tell them what the words mean to you.

At bedtime, during different nights of the week, spend some time with each child to share with him your knowledge of his worth to you and to God. Give examples of how Heavenly Father and you have confidence in his ability to succeed in life.

ADAPTING FOR
TEENAGERS AND ADULTS

Use the family picture, discussing similarities between family members and their earthly parents. Proceed from there to discuss the concept that all persons are children of God.

• Do people sometimes teach or imply that we are something less than children of God?

Give examples and the implications of such beliefs on how one feels about oneself.

• What difference would it make in how a person acted if he really believed he were a child of God?

Analyze the words of "I Am a Child of God," and let your children tell what it means to them as young adults. Then make the chart on the chalkboard or poster about what Heavenly Father is and how we can become like him as suggested in the section "What We Inherit from God."

As you discuss the idea of worth and potential, have your family members analyze Doctrine and Covenants 18:10 and Moses 1:39 together so that they will get a feeling of how important we are to our Heavenly Father as his children.

Making the personal poster for each family member to take to his room for consideration in daily prayer could be the most important part of this lesson for teenagers and adults. Explore in depth the development that could come from such an activity.

SUGGESTIONS FOR FUTURE
HOME EVENINGS

Heavenly Father Loves Us without Reservations

Explain that God is the perfect parent. He loves each of us unconditionally. No matter what we do, he

loves us. He can bless us when we obey his commandments, and he must deny us blessings when we do not. But he always loves us and wants us to grow to our full potential (see Moses 1:39).

Discuss with your family what that unconditional love means to them. Have the family read the parable of the prodigal son (Luke 15:11–32).

Discuss the joy our Heavenly Father feels when we repent and try to return to him. Assure them that as they repent and go to their Heavenly Father in prayer, he will put his love into their hearts (see Moroni 7:48) and they will *know* that he loves them.

Each Person Is Heavenly Father's Child

Seat the family in a circle. Place a bottle on its side in the center, and spin the bottle. When it stops, have all the others in the circle tell one thing that describes the person at whom the bottle points. (For example: "He is a boy." "His name is Terry." "He is ten years old." "He laughs a lot.") If no one else mentions it, add, "He is a child of Heavenly Father." Repeat this until everyone in the circle has been described.

Point out that even though each person's description may be different, he is a true child of God.

Then discuss whether Heavenly Father likes one person better than another for any reason, such as his disposition, age, or hair color. Read and discuss Acts 10:34–35. Explain that every person is important to Heavenly Father because every person is his child.

Children Love and Respect Their Parents

Explain that we are always God's spirit children and that he loves us. Explain that we can also become his children in a special way. Read Moses 6:65–7:1. Then tell them that God will not stop being our Father, but we can turn away from being his children.

• How? (By not respecting him and obeying his commandments.)

Discuss with your family how obedience makes us children of our Father in Heaven in a special sense.

Read Abraham 3:25, and discuss what it means.

NATURE–EVIDENCE OF HEAVENLY FATHER'S LOVE

Yea, all things which come of the earth, in the season thereof, are made for the benefit and the use of man, . . .

And it pleaseth God that he hath given all these things unto man; for unto this end were they made to be used, with judgment, not to excess.
[D&C 59:18, 20]

PURPOSE

Help your family become aware of and appreciate how our Heavenly Father blesses us through the things around us.

FOR THE PARENT

Everything about us in this world shows that God loves us. Miracles abound on every side if we will just look. It is important that you and your children sense the great love our Father in Heaven has for each of us. We are his children, and our happiness and success are his greatest concern. He has said, "This is my work and my glory—to bring to pass the immortality and eternal life of man" (Moses 1:39).

Think how this appreciation could provide your children with a sense of real security, a feeling of personal confidence, the assurance that someone understands and cares. All of us would like to have these feelings.

Everything in our environment evidences in all its wonder, both in the way it functions so efficiently and in the way it enriches our lives with its beauty, that God organized the

universe for his children (see Alma 30:44). The body is a marvel of engineering. Families, the Church, societies, and even governments were inspired for our growth and security. God revealed the plan of salvation with agency, responsibility, and repentance for our exaltation. He sent his Son to show us the way and atone for our sins.

All good things come from him because of his great love for us. Our sensitivity to his grace and appreciation of his love can grow each day as we observe what he has done for us. (See D&C 59:18–21.)

PREPARATION

1. Have magazines, newspapers, glue,

I will give you
rain in due season,
and the land shall
yield her increase,
and the trees of
the field shall
yield their fruit.

Leviticus 26:4

and anything else you need to do the lesson activities you have chosen for family participation.

2. Have a sheet of paper and a pencil with which to make a list for each family member.

SUGGESTED HYMN AND SONG

"Praise God from Whom All Blessings Flow" (*Hymns*, no. 214).

"My Heavenly Father Loves Me" (*Sing with Me*, B–59).

SUGGESTED LESSON

Appreciating God's Creations

Give each family member a sheet of paper and a pencil. Challenge each person to list everything he thinks shows us that God loves us. If the family members hesitate, suggest such things as water, food, flowers, sunsets, lakes, birds, animals, a body, the scriptures, the Church, parents, and the Savior. Or use pictures from magazines or newpapers to stimulate their thinking. Accept each response so that your children will be encouraged to share how they feel.

You may have family members who know about the water cycle, the respiratory system of the body, or the balance of life in nature. If so, let them explain them. Emphasize the things your family already appreciates, and give your children a chance to express what they know.

Expanding Our Appreciation

Have one of your family members read Moses 6:63.

- What things bear record of God? (Everything.)

- Are those things that bear record of God spiritual or temporal (physical)? (Both.)

Explain that during the week all of you look each day for different things around you that show the love of Heavenly Father. At dinner have each family member tell what he noticed that day. Also thank Heavenly Father in family prayers during the week for what he has done for you as you become more aware each day of new things you discover.

Your family may enjoy making a

scrapbook or collage of pictures from magazines, newspapers, your own drawings, or from any other source. Have the family members choose things they think show that God loves them and that he has made this world and everything in it for us, his children.

ADAPTING FOR YOUNGER CHILDREN

The song suggested for this lesson, "My Heavenly Father Loves Me," is particularly appropriate to help younger children feel something about the beauty of the world Heavenly Father has given us.

Tell the children how wonderful it is that our Heavenly Father has given us all that we need to make life here possible and beautiful. Discuss some of the things he has given us to make life possible, such as the following:

Air

- How did the Lord keep the air from floating away from the earth? (Gravity.)

- What is in the air that our bodies use? (Oxygen.)

- What do our lungs return to the air as waste? (Carbon dioxide.)

- With all the people and animals on earth using oxygen and breathing out carbon dioxide, why don't they use up all the oxygen? (One reason is that the plants the Lord put on earth use carbon dioxide and give off oxygen.)

Emphasize how carefully the Lord planned to make the air just right for us.

Water

- Can you chew water?

Demonstrate: Give each person a small piece of ice, and have him put it in his mouth and chew it.

- Can you breathe water?

Demonstrate: Put a small amount of water in a pan on the stove, and let it boil until the pan is empty.

- Where did the water go?

- Where does the water go when we hang out wet clothes to dry? (It evaporates into the air.)

Explain that almost all air has some

water in it. It is called water vapor, which is a gas. We cannot see it in the air but we breathe it.

Summarize by explaining that water has three forms: gas, liquid, and solid. Emphasize how marvelous it is that God has provided us with the wonders of water.

Food

Tell or read the following story:

Food for Pat and Patty

Pat and Patty were twins. They lived on a big farm fifteen miles from town.

One winter they were snowbound for two months. It was impossible to get to town.

"Mother, we'll starve!" exclaimed Pat.

"No, we'll just use the food the Lord has provided," mother answered.

"What food?" asked Patty.

"We have some seeds," said mother.

"Seeds?" questioned Pat and Patty.

"Yes, seeds. We have some wheat we can grind into cereal and flour. We have lots of dried beans to cook. We have corn we dried and peas we canned. And then we have roots."

"Roots?" asked Pat and Patty.

"Yes," answered mother. "We stored beets, carrots, and potatoes. Besides we have some leaves."

"Leaves?"

"Yes, vegetable leaves—spinach we canned and cabbage we stored in the sand. And we have fruit."

"I know," said Patty, "apples. We also canned peaches."

"And we have meat," said Pat, "from our pigs, cows, sheep, and chickens."

Emphasize how carefully the Lord supplied us with the food we need.

Seeing Nature

Take a nature walk with your children. Stroll around your neighborhood, and point out how beautiful the things are that you see around you every day. There may be some special places near your home, such as a wood, the seashore, the mountains, or a desert. Take advantage of these places to inspire a love of nature in your children.

Have the children make a nature collage. Each day they could glue a scenic picture, a dried leaf or flower, or a seashell to a poster or a piece of cardboard or wood. Let your children choose the pictures or things they want.

End the lesson with the song "Thanks to Our Father" (*Sing with Me*, A–3). The words express thanks for everything our Father in Heaven has given us.

ADAPTING FOR TEENAGERS AND ADULTS

You can adapt the material in the regular lesson for all ages, depending how deeply you explore the glory of God's creations.

Add topics such as the following:

1. The balance of nature. Discuss the relationships between insects, fish, birds, mammals, and vegetation. Emphasize how the balance of nature benefits man.

2. The body's systems. Discuss how the body's systems, such as the digestive, respiratory, blood, and nervous systems, work together. Also discuss the body's ability to heal itself.

3. The history of knowledge. Discuss how God has helped man discover knowledge and develop technology in this dispensation, including developments in light, radio, television, satellites, air travel, space travel, computers, and medicine.

4. The workings of God among his people. Discuss how carefully God has planned for all his people in all dispensations and among all cultures.

To increase their appreciation of nature and of the scriptures, have older children match special verses with beautiful pictures. Pick some of your favorite verses and match them with pictures you have or drawings that family members make themselves. Appropriate pictures could come from magazines, art calendars, or original photographs. See the example included in the lesson.

The following verses could be used:

1. "Thine, O Lord, is the greatness, and the power, and the glory, and

the victory, and the majesty: for all that is in the heaven and in the earth is thine" (1 Chronicles 29:11).

2. "To every thing there is a season, and a time to every purpose under the heaven" (Ecclesiastes 3:1).

3. "He hath made every thing beautiful in his time" (Ecclesiastes 3:11).

You may also consider Psalms 65:9–13, 96:11–12, 106:1; Isaiah 32:18; Romans 11:36; Doctrine and Covenants 59:16–21; Moses 3:9; and Abraham 5:9.

Teenagers love to have posters in their rooms. Make some using these scriptures and pictures of your choice.

SUGGESTIONS FOR FUTURE HOME EVENINGS

We Can Appreciate Our Heavenly Father's Love

Visit a zoo, aviary, park, botanical garden, planetarium, or natural history museum; or have a family outing in the country, mountains, or seashore. During or after the outing, discuss how the beauties of nature were prepared by God for our good.

Staring at the Stars

On a night when the sky is clear, go outside as a family and look up into the sky. Ask questions such as the following:

• Why can we see only part of the moon?

• What are the names of the stars?

• Can you point out and name some of the constellations?

• Can you identify any of the planets?

Discuss who created the heavens. Share the story of Korihor the unbeliever who asked Alma for a sign that there is a God (see Alma 30:43).

Alma answered him, "All things denote there is a God; yea, even the earth, and all things that are upon the face of it, yea, and its motion, yea, and also all the planets which move in their regular form do witness that there is a Supreme Creator" (Alma 30:44).

• What do you think of this evidence that there is a God who created the heavens and the earth?

Tools of Appreciation

Discuss what tools we have to appreciate nature (eyes, ears, nose, hands, mouth, and mind).

• How can we use these tools to deepen our appreciation for and understanding of the natural world?

Go on a nature hike using all the tools God has given you. Listen for sounds. Feel smooth flower petals and rough tree bark. Smell the damp earth and a flower. Notice patterns on leaves, flowers, and rocks. Notice differences and similarities. You may wish to use a magnifying glass to look at spider webs, leaves, or tiny insects.

Hold a testimony meeting at the end of the hike, and give family members an opportunity to express their feelings about the abundance and variety of life and the glory of the world.

How Do I Know He Loves Me?

Ask family members to take fifteen minutes to list scriptural evidences of Heavenly Father's love for them, or prepare a list of scriptures (see "God, Love of," in the Topical Guide of the Latter-day Saint edition of the King James Version of the Bible).

Have family members read and explain how each scripture shows us God's love. Young children may wish to tell of other ways they can know that Heavenly Father loves them.

Where Love Is Given, It Should Be Returned

Spend an evening of expressing love for our Heavenly Father. Have family members read Psalms (for example 23, 24, 27, 150). Let them tell how they feel about God and the blessings he has given them. You may also sing hymns of thanksgiving and love.

Creating Our Own Praise for God

Family members may enjoy creating songs, poems, or pictures to express their love for our Heavenly Father. For example, they may enjoy creating psalms of their own like those mentioned above or those found in 2 Nephi 4:16–35, Mosiah 4:9, and Luke 1:46–55. Encourage everyone to participate. Avoid negative criticism. Accept each expression even if the poem does not rhyme, have rhythm, or display an expressive choice of words.

HEAVENLY FATHER ANSWERS OUR PRAYERS

Draw near unto me and I will draw near unto you; seek me diligently and ye shall find me; ask, and ye shall receive; knock, and it shall be opened unto you.
[D&C 88:63]

PURPOSE

Help family members develop a sincere desire to pray, and help them know that they will always receive an answer because Heavenly Father loves them.

FOR THE PARENT

One of the greatest things that you can teach your children is to talk to their Heavenly Father, to help them know that they can always turn to him in prayer and that he will listen to them and answer their prayers.

Consider if the members of your family feel comfortable in going to their Heavenly Father in prayer with their thoughts, their problems, and their needs. If your children have learned to pray, you need not fear for them as they grow older and you are not always there to guide and help them. You will have the assurance that no matter how difficult the decision or how many the trials they may have to face, they can always have the help and comfort of a loving and wise Heavenly Father (see 2 Chronicles 7:14, Matthew 7:7–8).

PREPARATION

1. Prepare for this lesson by reading in the scriptures as much about prayer as you can (for example,

Alma 13:28, 3 Nephi 14:7–8). Reflect on your own experiences with prayer. Also read chapter 8, "Praying to Our Heavenly Father," in *Gospel Principles*, pages 37–40.

2. Ask each family member to be ready to share an experience when his prayers were answered.

SUGGESTED HYMN AND SONG

"Sweet Hour of Prayer" (*Hymns*, no. 166).

"I Thank Thee Dear Father" (*Sing with Me*, A–8).

SUGGESTED LESSON

Heavenly Father Listens to Our Prayers

Begin by reading the following statement by Bishop H. Burke Peterson:

"I want you to know that I know that whenever one of Heavenly Father's children kneels and talks to him, he listens. I know this as well as I know anything in this world—that Heavenly Father listens to every prayer from his children. I know our prayers ascend to heaven. No matter what we may have done wrong, he listens to us.

"I also believe he answers us. I don't believe he ignores his children when they talk to him." ("Prayer—Try Again," *Ensign*, June 1981, p. 73.)

- Do you think Heavenly Father listens to everyone's prayers?

- Why would he listen even to someone who has made mistakes? (Because he loves everyone. We are all his children, and he wants to help us.)

- Do you think that Heavenly Father listens to your prayers?

Tell the following story to your family, and ask them to listen and think how the story can be compared to prayer:

It was Saturday morning, and father was home. He had brought some work from the office to complete and went into the study to be alone.

Soon his little daughter came into the room crying. Someone had broken her new doll. Her father told her not to worry: he would fix her doll. She thanked her father and ran happily back to play.

- Did the father listen to his daughter when she needed his help?

Next his son came in. He asked his father for money to buy a new model boat to take sailing with his friends. His father took time to explain that the boy had already received his weekly allowance two days ago with the understanding that it was to take care of such things.

- Did the father stop to listen to his son when he needed his help?

- Was his answer yes or no this time? Why?

His teenage daughter came in next. She wanted a new dress for the com-

ing dance. Her father told her that she would have to wait. He told her that if she saved as much as she could herself, he would help her buy the new dress.

- Did the father listen to his teenage daughter?

- How did the father answer this time? (Wait, or yes, but not at this time.)

His teenage son interrupted the father next. The son was doing his homework and needed help with a problem. His father gave him some suggestions, but did not work the problem for him. A few minutes later, his son returned to say, "Thank you for the idea you gave me. It worked!"

- Did the father help his teenage son? How?

Finally, the youngest child came in. His father looked down at the boy and asked kindly, "What do you want, son?"

"I don't want anything," the little boy answered as he reached his arms around his father's neck and kissed him. "I just wanted to be with you."

- Why do you think the children went to their father for assistance?

- What evidence is there that shows us that the father loved his children?

- How can this story be compared with prayer?

Our Prayers Are Always Answered

Point out that all fathers are not always available as the father in the story was, but our Heavenly Father always listens. Explain to your family that they can always pray to Heavenly Father, no matter when or for what reason. He will answer them.

Have someone in your family read aloud Matthew 7:11.

- What do you think this scripture means?

Now have the members of your family share their examples of when their prayers were answered.

Explain to your family that because Heavenly Father loves them he will always answer their prayers in the way that is best for them. Sometimes the answer will be yes; sometimes, no; sometimes, wait; and sometimes he will let us work it out ourselves. Explain that Heavenly Father knows what is best for us, and he will give us "good things" or the things that will help us the most, because he loves us.

We Do Not Always Recognize Answers to Prayers

- Have you ever felt that your prayers were not answered?

Explain to your family that sometimes we do not realize that Heavenly Father has answered our prayers, but later we see that he has given us an answer. Tell the following story to illustrate:

Brother Robinson had just moved his small family into their new cabin home near the forest where he worked. He was grateful for his daughter and his beautiful wife, who would soon have their second child.

The family knelt in prayer together one night around the dinner table. They thanked Heavenly Father for their blessings and asked for his protection.

As the family sat at the table together, they could hear the frightening sounds of the wind as it whistled through the trees in the nearby forest. Suddenly the wind uprooted a giant tree. Five different trees fell, one knocking down the other. One tree crashed through the roof of their small cabin, breaking the boards over their heads. One of the boards fell on Brother Robinson and cut his head.

Fortunately, no one was seriously injured, but Brother Robinson's family had to leave their home and return to live with relatives in the city for the winter. Brother Robinson had to leave them and return to the logging camp to continue working.

• Do you think the family's prayer was answered?

Brother Robinson recalled his feelings at the time, "My home was in shambles, and I was separated from my family. I felt as if the Lord had not heard our prayers, and I wondered how he could have allowed this to happen to us."

Brother Robinson continued, "Later I realized how wrong I was in thinking that the Lord had not heard our prayers, for the snowstorms were so terrible that year that many families were snowed in all winter. We would have been left to ourselves with no help or supplies and no doctor to deliver the baby. I could have lost my wife or our new baby girl—or both! I realized then that the Lord had heard and answered our prayer for our protection."

Explain that sometimes, like Brother Robinson, we do not recognize answers to our prayers because we do not see everything as clearly as our Heavenly Father does.

• Have you ever prayed for something and not recognized the answer to your prayer until later?

Let the family members give examples.

Remind your family that Heavenly Father answers all their prayers and they can always trust him to know what is best for them (see D&C 88:64, 112:10). As an example, tell the story of Daniel in Daniel 6:1–23.

What Difference Does It Make?

• What difference does it make to you if you know that Heavenly Father really listens to you when you pray?

Tell your family that if they know that Heavenly Father is listening to them and cares about them, then it should make a difference in how they pray, in what they ask for, and how they feel about the answers they receive (see 2 Nephi 32:9, Alma 34:26, D&C 46:30).

Express to your family the assurance you feel knowing that they can feel close to Heavenly Father and turn to him in sincere prayer whenever they need his help.

Challenge your family members to pray with more sincerity, trusting that Heavenly Father will answer their prayers.

ADAPTING FOR
YOUNGER CHILDREN

Explain that when we pray we are talking to Heavenly Father. He loves us and knows what is best for us. We can trust him and the answers we get from him. Tell the following stories:

An Answer to Prayer

A four-year-old boy had moved with his family to a new city. They had brought along his dog. The little boy was glad to have him to play with. One day the boy could not find the dog.

The whole family looked everywhere for him, from the area around their house to the dog pound. They wondered if the dog was trying to go back to their old home.

Three days later, the family rode in their car together to see some of the new city they lived in. As they drove down a highway, they saw a little dog running along the road. It was their own dog.

After they got the dog into the car, the little boy said, "I knew we would find him. When he didn't come back, I went into my bedroom and asked Heavenly Father to bring him back, and he did." (See "An Answer to Prayer," *Church News*, 2 Aug. 1980, p. 16.)

• How was the boy's prayer answered?

Be sure your children understand that Heavenly Father does not always bring back lost animals or toys but that many times he helps us in situations such as this.

Amy Learns about Prayer

Amy's new baby brother was coming home from the hospital today. She was very excited. When he was born he had been very sick and had to stay in the hospital. Her father said they should pray to Heavenly Father and ask him to help baby Joshua to get better.

Amy did pray. She knew that her father and mother were praying, as well as her grandparents. But Joshua didn't get better.

Amy asked her father why Heavenly Father didn't listen to their prayers. Her father had told her that Heavenly Father does listen every time we pray, but he knows what is best for us and we have to trust him. Sometimes he answers yes and sometimes no.

Heavenly Father heard their prayers, and soon Joshua was better and was able to come home.

• How did Heavenly Father answer Amy's prayer?

• Was Amy's prayer answered right away?

Explain to your children that Heavenly Father answers all of our prayers. Sometimes we have to wait. Sometimes we ask our parents for things that we shouldn't have, and they tell us no. They know what is best for us. Sometimes what we ask our Heavenly Father is not good for us, and he tells us no. We have to trust him.

Tell the story about Brother Robinson. Share an experience from your own family when your prayers were not answered in the way you expected them to be.

Explain that we must have faith when we pray and want Heavenly Father to answer our prayers in the way that he knows is best for us.

ADAPTING FOR TEENAGERS AND ADULTS

Ask your family how they feel about Bishop Peterson's statement in the section "Heavenly Father Listens to Our Prayers." Ask the questions noted there.

Use the sections "Our Prayers Are Always Answered" and "We Do Not Always Recognize Answers to Prayers." The story of Brother Robinson could be read and discussed. The following story could also be used for teenagers:

Roberto

Roberto joined the Church while he was still in high school. Though several years had passed since he had joined the Church, his parents still were not members.

Each day Roberto prayed that his parents would join the Church. He was grateful for the gospel. It had made a difference in his life. Surely, he thought, his parents could see the difference in the way he acted now. Surely they would want to know why the Church had changed him so. But Roberto's parents refused to listen to him. They even became angry with him when he tried to talk to them about the Church.

Roberto continued praying for his family. He asked that the Lord would soften their hearts and that one day they would want to join the Church.

Members of Roberto's branch started visiting his family. Some of the sisters made friends with Roberto's mother and sister and invited them to Relief Society. Soon Roberto's mother and sister attended some of the Relief Society homemaking meetings and enjoyed doing the things they learned there. Once his whole family attended a branch activity.

Later the missionaries came to visit Roberto's family, but Roberto's family sent them away.

Roberto felt as if his heart would break. He loved his family; he knew they were good people. He continued setting an example himself, and praying for them. But Roberto's family still refused to join the Church.

- Did Heavenly Father listen to Roberto's prayers?
- How were Roberto's prayers answered?

Explain that sometimes the answer is no or wait. We also need to realize that others have their agency. Though we can pray for them, they may not choose to do the things we are praying for them to do.

Explain that we need to remember to do our part in getting an answer to our prayers, too. Point out that Roberto tried to do his best to help his family by setting a good example.

- How did Roberto's prayers help his family? (Others were touched to help his family learn about the gospel too.)
- Have you ever received no in answer to your prayers and later understood why?
- Why does Heavenly Father sometimes answer no?

Conclude your lesson by discussing the section "What Difference Does It Make?"

SUGGESTIONS FOR FUTURE HOME EVENINGS

How to Pray

In Matthew 6:5–15, the Savior gave some directions and a model for prayer. Ask family members to suggest different ways people pray. Discuss how these ways fit with what the Savior taught. Discuss what language to use while praying, saying silent prayers, using memorized prayers or repetitious wordings, what we should and should not ask for in our prayers, and relying on the Spirit as we pray.

When to Pray

Have family members find scriptures that explain when to pray (see "Prayer, Pray," in the Topical Guide of the Latter-day Saint edition of the King James Version of the Bible).

They may also wish to relate stories from Church history or from their own experience about times when prayer was needed and helped someone.

Develop the idea that personal prayer ought to be a part of daily life, not just a bedtime routine.

We Have the Right to Pray to Our Heavenly Father

Ask family members who they have the *right* to go to for help if they need something for school, need new clothes, want permission to use the car, want to invite friends into the home, or want something to eat.

- Why do you have this right?

Explain that in addition to their earthly parents, family members also have a Heavenly Father who loves them. They have a right to go to him for help as well.

Have some of them play the role of a parent responding to a child's request.

Read 3 Nephi 14:7–11 or Luke 11:9–13.

Prayer Requires Action

- What should you do before and after you pray?

You may wish to read James 2:14–20 or the following statement by President David O. McKay: "Sincere praying implies that when we ask for any virtue or blessing we should work for the blessing and cultivate the virtue" ("Essential Virtues in Effective Prayer," *Instructor*, Nov. 1953, p. 321).

You may also wish to suggest some common things family members might ask for in their prayers. Then have them reply by suggesting what they might do to help bring about the blessing asked for.

Fasting and Prayer

Read aloud Alma 5:46. Explain that Alma is speaking to the people of Zarahemla and explaining how he gained a testimony.

- Why did Alma fast with his prayers?

Ask family members to tell about any other occasions in the scriptures when prayer was accompanied by fasting. Discuss what fasting adds to prayer and why it is sometimes necessary. (See Mark 9:29, D&C 59:13; see also chapter 25, "Fasting," *Gospel Principles*, pp. 157-60.)

WE CAN CHOOSE

Ye are free; ye are permitted to act for yourselves.
[Helaman 14:30]

PURPOSE

Help family members understand that they have the agency to make righteous choices.

FOR THE PARENT

Our Heavenly Father has given each person the agency or power to choose for himself. He has sent us to earth to learn how to choose wisely.

Unfortunately, many people feel that they cannot make choices, that circumstances or events outside themselves control them. "I can't help it," a person may say. "That's just how I am."

Most of us do not fully understand the freedom that knowledge of our agency brings. The knowledge that we can choose our responses frees us. It allows us to leave old teachings and habits, to repent, and to truly follow the Savior. (See chapter 4, "Freedom to Choose," *Gospel Principles* [PBIC0245], pp. 18–21.)

PREPARATION

1. Have a piece of paper and a pencil for each family member.
2. If you have young children, bring a bowl of different colored jelly beans, small candies, or treats. Have more than one of each color and enough colors so that each family member can choose one from several.

SUGGESTED HYMN
AND SONG

"Choose the Right" (*Hymns*, no. 110).

"Dare to Do Right" (*Sing with Me*, B–81).

SUGGESTED LESSON

Pass out a piece of paper and pencil to each family member. Give your family several minutes to list every choice they can think of that they have made that day. You may need to give an example to get them started (for example, what clothes to wear or who to play with). Have each person read his list aloud and then put it aside until later in the lesson.

Our Agency Is Part of Us

The Lord explained to Moses the basic conflict between Heavenly Father's plan and Satan's opposition. Depending on the ages of your children, read or explain in your own words Moses 4:1–4.

Lead a discussion by asking questions like these:

- What did Jesus say about Heavenly Father's plan? ("Thy will be done.")
- What did Satan want to destroy? (Our agency.)
- What is agency? (The ability to act or choose.)
- What did Satan say about Heavenly Father's plan? (He said that if he were sent, not one soul would be lost.)
- Was Satan telling the truth?

Explain that Satan's plan could not work; it could never help us return to Heavenly Father. To live with Heavenly Father, we must become like him, which means more than just not making mistakes. It means learning to make wise choices.

Have the family look at their lists, and ask them to imagine what it would be like if they were not allowed to make any of those choices. For ex-

ample, what if they could not choose what clothes to wear, what time to get up, or how to spend any of their time during the day? Would they be stronger or weaker? What if all choices were made for them or there were no choices at all—just one possibility? Would they be stronger or weaker? Point out that, even though they might never make a mistake, they would be dependent and weak. As we make wise choices, we increase our ability to make greater choices and grow. (See 2 Nephi 28:30; D&C 50:24, 93:28.)

The Choice Is Ours

Have someone read or tell Viktor Frankl's story. Use the story to help your family recognize choices that they sometimes overlook.

A Prisoner's Choices

During World War II, Viktor Frankl was kept in a Nazi concentration camp for three years. During that time, he could make few of the choices we take for granted. He could not choose how to wear his hair; his head was shaved. He could not choose what clothes to wear; he was given a prison uniform. He could not read or write or talk freely. Someone told him when to get up and exactly what to do every minute of the day. He was treated cruelly, and if he did not work hard enough, he was in danger of being killed.

- What choices could Viktor Frankl make?

He later wrote this about his experiences:

"We who lived in concentration camps can remember the men who walked through the huts comforting others, giving away their last piece of bread. . . . They offer sufficient proof that everything can be taken away from a man but one thing: the last of the human freedoms—to choose one's attitude in any given set of circumstances, to choose one's own way.

"And there were always choices to make. Every day, every hour offered the opportunity to make a decision." (*Man's Search for Meaning*, trans. Ilse Lasch, rev. ed. [New York: Simon and Schuster, 1962], p. 65.)

Viktor Frankl found out that no one could force him to be bitter and angry, no matter how much they hurt him. He could still enjoy the beauties of nature; he could love and show kindness to other people.

Point out that everyone uses agency each day, even if he is not aware of his choices. For example, everyone must choose his attitudes each day as Viktor Frankl did. These are often very private choices that others do not notice. But it is easier to make these choices correctly when we realize that we are free to choose. No one can ever *make* us angry or dishonest.

Show the four pictures that accompany the lesson to the members of your family. Let each family member describe one of the pictures and tell what choice the picture represents.

Point out that Heavenly Father is anxious to help us make wise choices. He especially wants to help us when we feel we cannot choose without help. He has given us prayer and the Holy Ghost to guide us when we choose.

Ask the family to reconsider their lists. Have them add choices they may not have thought of at first. Then ask everyone to keep their lists during the next week and add to them every night. Challenge them not only to become aware of their daily choices, but to learn to make them wisely.

ADAPTING FOR YOUNGER CHILDREN

Show the bowl of jelly beans or whatever treat you have brought. Let each child choose and eat one. Tell them that they have many choices each day and that some are much more important than the one they have just made.

Ask them to listen as you read a story about a boy named Brent, who made many choices. Ask them to hold their thumbs up when they think Brent chose right, down when they think he chose wrong, and toward themselves when they are not sure. After each sentence, stop to note where your children point their thumbs.

Brent's Day

Brent stayed in bed after mother called him twice. When he did get up, he dressed himself except for tying his shoes.

At breakfast he took a piece of bacon from his sister's plate while she was

not looking. After breakfast he let Sally, his sister, play with his new truck because he felt sorry that he had taken the bacon.

He came in promptly when mother called him for lunch, even though he was having fun.

When mother told him to take a nap, he and Sally whispered and giggled and did not go to sleep.

Later, he shared half his cookie with Billy Jones.

He did not cross the street when the other kids did because his father had told him not to.

He picked one of Mrs. Brown's red tulips because it was so pretty. He gave the tulip to mother. He obeyed his mother and went and told Mrs. Brown he was sorry to have picked her tulip and asked if she wanted him to pay for it. He didn't talk back to Mrs. Brown when she scolded him for picking one of the tulips she liked so much. He felt bad and told her he would never do it again.

He brought the paper to his father when he came home. He helped mother set the table by putting the napkins on. He fed his dog.

During dinner, he tried to feed his spinach to the dog after father had told him to eat it.

When it was time to go to bed, he undressed himself and hung up his clothes. He prayed to his Heavenly Father. Then he went to sleep without whispering and giggling with Sally.

Discuss the story of Brent and the many choices he made. Sometimes he made the right choice, sometimes he didn't, but he kept trying.

Ask the children to think of some choices they make every day. Use the pictures with this lesson to give them ideas.

Explain that some choices will be more important than others but that all choices have a consequence. One consequence might be how they feel. For example, if they choose to be kind to their brothers and sisters, they will feel happy. Other consequences might be what happens. For example, if they choose not to tie their shoes they may trip and fall or their shoes may come off.

Mention one good choice each child has made during the past week. Encourage them to think about the choices they make during the coming week.

During the week, give your children little opportunities that will help them learn to make choices. For example, let them help decide what to have for dinner, what tablecloth to use on the table, or what they are going to wear that day. When they learn to make simple choices, they can start to learn how to make more important choices.

At mealtime during the week talk about the choices the children have made that day.

ADAPTING FOR TEENAGERS AND ADULTS

Have everyone write down the name of someone they admire and would want to be like. Make a list of the qualities these people have, such as self-discipline, cheerfulness, or patience, and discuss them.

Ask the family to think about their own behavior during the day.

- What things prevented you from being the kind of person you would like to be? (Have everyone write these down. Then make a list together.)

Explain that rather than blaming our circumstances or someone else, we must realize that we each have control over what we do. We have our agency. No one can make us do something if we are not willing to be influenced by them.

Tell and discuss the story of Viktor Frankl.

- Do you ever feel that you are a prisoner of your circumstances, your moods, your upbringing, or your habits?
- How does the way other people treat you determine how you treat others?

Choose several items from the second list, and explore together how you could control the events and attitudes that seem to control us.

Ask everyone to recall a time when he has reacted positively in a negative situation, or have family members think of people they know or have read about who have done this.

You may want to use the section "Our Agency Is Part of Us" to start a discussion of Heavenly Father's plan and Satan's opposition. Our Heavenly Father's plan shows his great love for us. He was willing to let us make mistakes, though they grieve him, in order to allow us to grow.

Ask each person to choose one quality from his first list to work on during the week. Encourage him to choose one he has some trouble with and to notice during the week how he can use his agency to develop it.

SUGGESTIONS FOR FUTURE HOME EVENINGS

Making Choices Ahead of Time

Read and discuss the following statement by President Spencer W. Kimball:

"Indecision and discouragement are climates in which the Adversary loves to function, for he can inflict so many casualties among mankind in those settings. . . . If you have not done so yet, decide to decide!" (In Conference Report, Apr. 1976, p. 70; or *Ensign*, May 1976, p. 46.)

Give each family member a situation in which an important gospel choice has to be made. Adapt the situations to the needs of your family. Have them decide what they would do in each situation. You may wish to have them act out the situation and the way they would handle it. Following are some suggestions:

1. Your friend asks you to smoke a cigarette with him.
2. You find some money that you know someone has lost.
3. Mother has asked you to play with your little sister when you would rather read.
4. You don't have enough money to buy something you want very much and also pay your full tithing.

Afterward, point out that if they make the right choice now, it will be easier for them to make the right decision if that situation comes up in their lives. Suggest that they pick out some important situations, such as temple marriage, not smoking, and remaining chaste, that they will face some day and decide *now* what their decision will be.

Jesus Chose to Follow His Father

Ask your family if they think that following God's commandments means giving up our agency. Read John 6:38 and 12:49. Discuss how Jesus used his agency. Be sure to point out that he always did what his Father in Heaven commanded.

Choices, Decisions, and Consequences

First show how every law our Heavenly Father has given us has a consequence (see D&C 130:20–21). You may wish to have family members read scriptures that show the consequences of living or not living the commandments. For example—

1. If we are pure in heart, we will see God (Matthew 5:8).

2. If we earnestly pray for love and follow the Savior's example, we will be filled with love (Moroni 7:48).

3. We will be judged the way we judge others (Matthew 7:2).

4. If we don't repent, we must suffer even as the Savior suffered at Gethsemane (D&C 19:16–17).

Let your family contrast the blessed and happy state of those who follow Jesus and obey the commandments (see D&C 76:55–60, 4 Nephi 1:15–18) with the miserable slavery of those who follow Satan (see 2 Nephi 2:27–29, Alma 36:12–16).

Create a chart showing the consequences of obeying or disobeying our Heavenly Father's laws. The chart might look like this:

Result of Good Choices	Result of Bad Choices
The Holy Ghost stays with us.	The Holy Ghost leaves us.
We gain faith.	We lose faith.
We gain spiritual blessings.	We do not get spiritual blessings.
We find happiness.	We find misery.

Conclude that our Heavenly Father planned for us to have a choice. Help family members to understand that we can choose eternal life.

Does Heavenly Father Always Tell Us What to Do?

Read Doctrine and Covenants 58:26–28. Have family members discuss what is a good balance between being told what to do and doing good without being commanded. Ask them to name some things that they might do on their own with which Heavenly Father would be pleased. Then let family members share some experiences about how choosing to do something good without being told has helped them grow.

Appreciating Our Agency

Have the family sit in a semicircle with yourself at the center. Explain that during this home evening they will participate in an experiment and that they must do exactly as you tell them and nothing else. Have someone give the opening prayer before starting the experiment.

To begin, tell the family that they cannot speak unless they are spoken to or move unless they are told to. Then for the opening hymn, scripture reading, and other remaining opening activities, tell them exactly what to do and how to do it, including what words to say. (Be sure you do not tell them to do or say anything contrary to gospel principles.)

When your family becomes restless and uncomfortable, end the experiment. Ask them to discuss their feelings and reactions. Help them to see that our agency is a priceless gift given to us by God and that it is necessary for us so that we can learn from our own experience.

End the lesson with a free choice of the closing hymn and prayer.

Our Choices Influence Others

Begin by asking the family questions such as the following:

• What might happen if a missionary chooses not to give in, but fervently bears his testimony when an angry investigator tells him to leave?

• What might happen if a courageous young basketball player decides to tell his nonmember teammates about the Word of Wisdom?

Let the family members suggest what might happen. Then tell what did happen:

In the first case, the investigator called the missionaries the next day and invited them back because he could not forget the conviction of the missionary's testimony. Later, the investigator and his family joined the Church. (See "3 R's of Free Agency: Right, Responsibility, Results," *New Era,* Apr. 1973, p. 5.)

In the second case, a sixteen-year-old boy lived the Word of Wisdom in spite of his friends on the basketball team, who used tobacco. Because of his example, he gained the admiration and respect of his teammates; and before the year was over, none of them used tobacco. (See "Our Individual Responsibility," *Improvement Era,* Dec. 1968, p. 92.)

Have family members relate other examples they know of in which right choices affected the lives of others.

Our Daily Choices Determine Our Future

Make a chart with the phrase "Toward Heavenly Father" written across the top and "Toward Satan" written across the bottom. Make up and tell a short story (use events that are familiar to your family) about the moral decisions and choices a person might face during one day—the important daily choices and decisions in our lives, such as whether or not to cheat, lie, gossip, or be dishonest in any way. For each decision or choice the person in the story makes, let family members vote on whether it was a good choice or a bad one, and mark a dash on the chart, moving from left to right. If the choice is a good one, slant the dash upward; if it is a bad one, slant the dash downward. Add dashes so that they follow one another. Your completed chart might look like this:

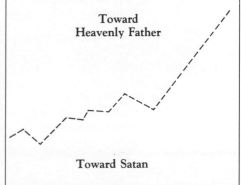

Toward Heavenly Father

Toward Satan

At the end of the story, use the chart to show how a person's choices can move him closer to or away from his Heavenly Father during a day.

HEAVENLY FATHER PROVIDED US A SAVIOR

For God so loved the world, that he gave his only begotten Son, that whosoever believeth in him should not perish, but have everlasting life.
[John 3:16]

PURPOSE

Help the family appreciate the love of our Heavenly Father for us in sending his Beloved Son to the world to redeem us from sin and death.

FOR THE PARENT

Our Heavenly Father loves each one of us because we are actually his children, not merely one of his creations. Because of his love, he sent us to earth to grow and progress. But on earth he knew there would be many dangers. By sinning we would cut ourselves off from our heavenly home and by dying we would be separated from our physical bodies. Heavenly Father, in his great love, sent his Only Begotten Son, Jesus Christ, to rescue us from sin and death and to make it possible for us to return to him (see Abraham 3:27).

Imagine how hard it must have been for Heavenly Father to see Jesus suffer so terribly. But he allowed it because of his love for us and his desire for us to progress. Help each member of your family come to appreciate the love Heavenly Father has for us.

PREPARATION

1. Prepare the following wordstrips: "Map," "Means of transportation," "Money," "Stamps," "Clothing,"

and "Books." Distribute the word-strips among members of the family before you start family home evening.

2. Bring a chalkboard and chalk or a large piece of paper and a marker.

3. Be prepared to show the picture of Jesus and the children from lesson 36, "He Is Risen!"

4. Provide a paper and crayon for each child.

SUGGESTED HYMN
AND SONG

"God Loved Us, So He Sent His Son" (*Hymns*, no. 178).
"I Thank Thee, Dear Father" (*Sing with Me*, A–8).

SUGGESTED LESSON

Heavenly Father Loves His Children

Ask the family members to pretend that you are going to send them away to school. Tell them that you love them and will miss them but that this additional schooling will be for their good and will help them progress. Explain that you will provide what they need to take them there, keep them while at school, and bring them back when school is over.

Have the family members display, one at a time, the wordstrips representing the items you will give them. As each wordstrip is shown, discuss with them what would happen if they did not take care of that item and use it properly. Contrast this with what would happen if they did use wisely what you have provided.

• In which case could you probably complete school successfully and return home?

Tell them that a long time ago, before any of us can remember, we were in a similar situation. We lived in heaven with our Heavenly Father.

• What happened there that was similar to what we have pretended?

Let your family discuss the council in heaven as they answer this question (see chapter 2, "Our Heavenly Family," *Gospel Principles* [PBIC0245], pp. 9–12).

Help your family imagine the great love Heavenly Father had for his family as he gathered them together and presented his plan. He planned to send us to earth where we could inherit a body, learn, grow, and return to him.

Describe your love, as parents, for your children. They are your actual physical offspring. Talk about how you cared for their every need while they were small, taught them to walk and talk, and how you now try to provide for them in every way. Express sincerely your feelings that the greatest reward you could receive in life is to have them become valiant members of the Church and that the greatest reward you could ask for after this life is to be together with them as a family.

Compare this to how Heavenly Father feels about us. We are his actual spiritual children, and he loves us as our heavenly parent.

Read Moses 1:39 to show that Heavenly Father's main goal or objective is to help us return to him.

Emphasize that when Heavenly Father sent us here, he wanted to give us all the help he could so that we could be successful in our earthly journey.

Read the following parts of Abraham 3:23–25, and have your family listen for what Heavenly Father planned to give us to help us make the most of our schooling and return to him:

"And God saw these souls that they were good. . . .

"And there stood one among them that was like unto God, and he said unto those who were with him: We will go down, for there is space there, and we will take of these materials, and we will make an earth whereon these may dwell;

"And we will prove them herewith, to see if they will do all things whatsoever the Lord their God shall command them."

As your family members discover what Heavenly Father has given us, list them on the chalkboard or poster; for example, an earth to live on, experiences to prove us, and commandments to guide us. Discuss, one at a time, what will happen if we do not use these gifts properly, and contrast those results with what will happen if we use them wisely.

We Need a Savior

Tell your family that Heavenly Father knew there was one more thing we needed in order to return to him. It is the most important one of all.

• What was it? (A Savior [see chapter 3, "Jesus Christ, Our Chosen Leader and Savior," *Gospel Principles*, pp. 15–17].)

Read Abraham 3:27.

• Who volunteered and was chosen to be our Savior? (Jesus.)

Add "Savior" to your list.

• Why do we need a savior?

Allow your family to discuss this question, then explain our universal need for a savior. Without a savior we could not return home to our Heavenly Father. When Heavenly Father sent us here, he gave us commandments. When we break a commandment, we need someone to help us. Through the Atonement, Jesus made it possible for us to repent and return to our Heavenly Father.

Jesus Makes It Possible for Us to Return to Heavenly Father

Discuss with your family what Jesus did for us. Using your family's suggestions, make a chart similar to the following on a chalkboard or poster:

What Jesus Did for Us	
He atoned for Adam's sin	so little children can be saved.
He gave us the gospel	so we can live with him.
He showed us how to live	so we can be happy.
He suffered for our sins	so we can be forgiven.
He died and was resurrected	so we can be resurrected.

• Which of these is a free gift to us, one we receive no matter what we do? (The Resurrection.)

• Which of these must we do something about before we can have the gift? (His paying for our sins. We must repent in order to be forgiven and live a happy life.)

Emphasize that the gift of eternal life, the privilege of returning to the celestial kingdom and living with Heavenly

Father and our families, is a gift we have to work for by repenting and living the gospel. Jesus, in the Garden of Gethsemane, suffered for the sins of the world. If we truly repent, Jesus will take away our sins so that we can return to our Heavenly Father. (See 2 Nephi 9:6–26.)

- How do you think Heavenly Father felt when his beloved Son, Jesus Christ, had to suffer and die for all of us? (Both glad and sad.)

- Why? (Because he was glad that Jesus was willing to do it, but sad that Jesus had to suffer.)

To help your family appreciate Heavenly Father's love, decide on some topics to discuss further at the dinner table each day during the coming week, such as Jesus' example, the reality of the Resurrection, and the chance to learn good from evil. After each daily discussion, suggest that your family members remember to thank Heavenly Father in their prayers for that particular blessing.

ADAPTING FOR YOUNGER CHILDREN

Relate briefly and simply the story of the council in heaven. Emphasize the love that Heavenly Father has shown for each of us in his plan to send us to earth to receive a body.

Help your children understand that because of Heavenly Father's love for us, he sent our older brother, Jesus, to help us. To help them understand what Jesus did for us, tell the following story:

Michael's Danger

Michael went to the park with his family. While they were at the picnic table, he ran over to the tall slide and climbed up it. He liked to climb stairs. He had just learned how to climb. But when Michael reached the top of the slide and looked down he became very frightened. He was so high up.

Michael started to cry. He didn't know what to do. He was too scared to climb back down, but he was also too scared to go down the steep slide. Mandy, the child behind Michael on the slide, said she would help Michael back down the stairs. But Michael was too afraid to let Mandy help him.

From the picnic table, Michael's father saw Michael on the slide. He knew Michael was scared. So he sent Stephen, the older brother, to rescue Michael. Michael saw Stephen coming. Soon Stephen was standing at the bottom of the long slide. Stephen talked softly to Michael and quickly talked Michael into sliding down into his strong arms. Michael ran happily back with Stephen to the picnic table. He was glad to be safe with his father, mother, brothers, and sisters again.

Going up the tall slide for Michael is much like our leaving Heavenly Father and coming to the earth. It is new, exciting, and different. But there are dangers. Without help we would not be able to get back to safety. Not just anybody can help. The person must be able to help and must also be someone we know and trust.

Jesus is our Savior and helps us when we are in this earth life. Only he can rescue us. Our Heavenly Father loves us so much that he sent his Son, Jesus Christ, to earth to make it possible for us to come back to our heavenly home.

Show your children the picture of Jesus and the children (see lesson 36, "He Is Risen!"). Talk with them about some of the things Jesus may be asking these children to do that will help them return to Heavenly Father, such as be kind to each other, obey your parents, and share your toys.

Let them draw a picture of one thing Jesus wants them to do that they will try to do this week. Post the pictures where they can remind the children during the week.

ADAPTING FOR TEENAGERS AND ADULTS

Use the discussion, including Moses 1:39 and Abraham 3:23–25, under the heading "Heavenly Father Loves His Children."

Present the information under "We Need a Savior," and use the chart and questions under "Jesus Makes It Possible for Us to Return to Heavenly Father."

Have your family sing the first verse of "How Great the Wisdom and the Love" (Hymns, no. 68), or have someone read the words aloud (you may want to do both). Ask them to

listen carefully to the words, then discuss the meaning of each line. For example:

"How great the wisdom and the love."

- Why was it wisdom as well as love?

"That filled the courts on high."

- What does this refer to? (The council in heaven.)

"And sent the Savior from above."

Heavenly Father sent his Son.

"To suffer, bleed, and die!"

- What was accomplished by his suffering, bleeding, and dying?

You may want to discuss related topics throughout the week at dinner time as recommended in the regular lesson.

SUGGESTIONS FOR FUTURE HOME EVENINGS

The Salvation of Little Children

The Atonement made possible the salvation of little children in the celestial kingdom.

Have your family think of all the scriptures they can that have to do with children and their special place in heaven (for example, Matthew 18:3; Mosiah 3:16; Moroni 8:10–23; D&C 29:46–47, 137:10; and Moses 6:54).

If you have the the Latter-day Saint edition of the King James Version of the Bible, look up "Salvation of Little Children" in the Topical Guide for more scriptures.

Ask a question about the salvation of those who are retarded mentally and do not become accountable before the Lord. Be sure to bring out that their salvation is also assured as that of little children.

End the family home evening by expressing your appreciation and joy that so many of our Heavenly Father's children have salvation in the celestial kingdom because of Jesus Christ. Since the beginning of the world, there must have been billions who died before accountability.

- What does this mean to you about Heavenly Father's love?

Understanding the Atonement

Using chapter 12, "The Atonement," in Gospel Principles, pages 65 through 72, develop a lesson on the Atonement.

JESUS MADE REPENTANCE POSSIBLE

Behold, he who has repented of his sins, the same is forgiven, and I, the Lord, remember them no more.
[D&C 58:42]

PURPOSE

Help your family appreciate the gift of repentance, which gives us an opportunity to overcome our weaknesses and grow from experience.

FOR THE PARENT

Can you imagine how you would feel if you could never be forgiven for any wrongs you committed? Think of the great burden you would have to carry, always remembering all the mistakes you have made in life, never being able to be free of them and really grow, never realizing the possibility of becoming like your Heavenly Father or being able to return and live with him again.

How grateful we should be to our Savior, Jesus Christ, who loved us so much that he suffered and died for us so that we could repent. Because of his atonement, we can be forgiven of our sins if we truly repent, and we can go on—unburdened, wiser, and stronger—to achieve our full potential.

PREPARATION

1. Obtain a baby picture of each member of the family, including parents. Do not identify the pictures.

2. Refer to the pictures of Jesus in Gethsemane and Jesus on the cross from lesson 14, "Partaking of the Sacrament."

3. Provide a piece of paper and a pencil for each family member.

SUGGESTED HYMN AND SONG

"I Stand All Amazed" (*Hymns*, no. 80).

"I Want to Live the Gospel" (*Sing with Me*, B–65).

SUGGESTED LESSON

When You Were a Baby

Display the baby photographs of each family member. Children, especially younger ones, will enjoy guessing who the different family members are in the pictures.

Discuss with your family what your youngest child was like as a baby. Explain that he was very special. He was pure and innocent of wrong doing because he had just come from Heavenly Father and his heavenly home. Point to each of the other pictures. Explain that all of you were pure when you left Heavenly Father's presence, that you didn't have any sins.

We All Make Mistakes and Sin

Show a baby picture again, and explain that Heavenly Father knew that we would not always stay as pure as we were when we were babies. Explain that he knew that we would all grow up and that while we were learning to do right we would make some mistakes and sin. Of course it would be better if we never did sin and could remain innocent like a little baby, but all of us are tempted and all of us sin.

Explain that Heavenly Father knew that the burden of our sins would keep us from growing spiritually and from reaching our greatest potential here on earth.

Explain that we also would not be able to return to live with our Heavenly Father if our sins could not be taken away or removed, for no unclean thing or sinful person can live with him.

- Why could a sinful person not live with Heavenly Father again?

Have a member of your family read 1 Nephi 15:33–35 aloud. Point out that our sins keep us burdened down and make it impossible to return to Heavenly Father's presence one day (see 2 Nephi 9:23).

Jesus Paid for Our Sins

Show the pictures of Jesus in Gethsemane and Jesus on the cross (both in lesson 14, "Partaking of the Sacrament"). Explain that Heavenly Father sent Jesus to help us overcome sin. Jesus suffered and died to pay for our sins. He was the only one who could pay for our sins. We could not be forgiven by our own efforts alone.

Because of Jesus' sacrifice and atonement, we can repent and become pure again. We can be free to progress and be clean to live with our Father in Heaven again one day. Read Doctrine and Covenants 58:42 aloud.

We Can Repent and Grow

Have a family member read aloud Doctrine and Covenants 19:16, "I, God, have suffered these things for all, that they might not suffer if they would repent."

Explain that if Jesus had not atoned for our mistakes we could not be forgiven and would have to continue to suffer for them. However, because he suffered for us, we can be forgiven if we repent. To help illustrate this process, have someone read or tell the following story by President David O. McKay:

"One day, a group of small boys were swimming. Perhaps it would be more accurate to say, they were learning to swim; for none could take more than a few strokes. Just below them a short distance down the stream was a treacherous hole much beyond their depth. Into this, either through bravado or accident, one daring youngster either plunged or fell. He became helpless to save himself; and for a moment his companions were powerless to aid him. Fortunately, one with presence of mind and quick action, jerked a long stick from a willow fence and held one end of it toward the drowning lad. The latter grasped it, held on tightly, and was saved.

"All the boys declared that the venturesome lad owed his life to the boy who furnished the means of rescue." ("The Gospel of Work," *Instructor*, Jan. 1955, p. 1.)

Explain to your family that Jesus is like the rescuer and his atonement is like the stick. Jesus offers us the Atonement as the way to receive forgiveness. When we repent, we reach out to accept the Atonement just as the drowning boy reached out to grasp the stick. If we accept the Atonement by repenting, we will be forgiven and not have to continue suffering for our sins. We can learn from our mistakes and continue to progress. We will be stronger and wiser if we have overcome our faults and have learned from our experiences.

Repentance Quiz

To help your family understand more about the gift of repentance, pass out papers and pencils, and take the following true-false quiz as a family. You may want to divide your family into two teams. Small children could work with older children in answering the questions. Choose ahead of time whether you will discuss the answers after each question or after you finish the entire quiz.

1. The suffering and death of Jesus nearly two thousand years ago does not affect our lives today. (False. If Jesus had not atoned for our sins, we could not repent and grow. We could never return to live with our Heavenly Father again. Every person that has ever lived or will live upon the earth is affected by Jesus' sacrifice.)

2. When we make a mistake or sin, Jesus stops loving us. (False. Jesus never stops loving us. It is because of his love that we have the gift of repentance.)

3. Because Jesus suffered and died for our sins, they are automatically forgiven. (False. Jesus can forgive only those who are sorry for their sins and who repent of them.)

4. When we repent of a sin, we are completely forgiven and we do not need to worry about it any more. (True. When we have repented of a sin the Lord not only forgives us, but our sin is also forgotten [see Isaiah 1:16–18, D&C 58:42].)

5. When we repent of our sins, we can learn through correcting our mistakes and continue to grow and progress spiritually. (True. When we repent of our sins, we are free to go on and not be held back because of them. Our weaknesses can even become our strengths. [See Ether 12:27.])

Be Grateful for the Gift of Repentance

Share your testimony of Jesus as your savior, and express your gratitude for his love and sacrifice that made repentance possible. You may wish to relate an experience about how repentance has blessed your life and helped you grow. Older children may also wish to bear their testimonies about how much repentance means to them.

Conclude your home evening by singing "I Stand All Amazed," or read the words of the song aloud together.

ADAPTING FOR YOUNGER CHILDREN

Begin with the baby pictures, and let the children guess whose pictures they are. Explain simply how we all make mistakes as we grow up. Tell them that Jesus made it possible for us to repent. Explain that *repent* means to change from doing something wrong to doing the right thing. We can receive forgiveness if we make mistakes after we are sorry and do not do them anymore. Explain that *forgiveness* means that the Lord will not remember our mistakes any more.

Tell the following story:

Julie Repents

Julie went to play with her friend Lisa. Lisa had some new clothes for her doll, and they spent the afternoon trying them all on the doll. It was fun to see the doll in so many different clothes. When Julie put on her coat to go home, she slipped one of Lisa's new doll dresses into her pocket. She didn't think Lisa would miss it because she had so many other clothes for her doll.

Julie put the dress on her doll when she got home, but it didn't seem as much fun to play with the dress this time. She knew that the dress belonged to her friend, and she was sorry she had taken it. At dinner Julie didn't feel like eating. She was worried about the dress and didn't feel good inside. All she could think about was that she had taken the dress. She knew it was wrong.

After dinner she told her mother what she had done and asked her to go with her to Lisa's house to take the dress back. Julie gave the doll dress to Lisa and told her that she was sorry she had taken it. Lisa quickly forgave Julie and told her everything was all right. Then Julie told her mother that she would never again take anything that belonged to someone else. Julie skipped all the way home. She felt good now; she was happy.

Explain to your children that Julie did something wrong, but she was sorry and changed. She did the right thing by taking the dress back. This is what it means to repent. Before Julie took the dress back, she was worried and felt badly, but after she was happy and felt good. Remind the children that when they make a mistake they can feel sorry and change just like Julie did.

ADAPTING FOR TEENAGERS AND ADULTS

Use the baby pictures, and review the

section "Suggestions for Future Home Evenings" in lesson 9, "Heavenly Father Provided Us a Savior."

Explain that the price we must pay to accept Jesus' atonement is repentance, which may include deep sorrow and painful remorse. President Spencer W. Kimball wrote:

"However he tries, a man cannot escape the consequences of sin. They follow as the night follows the day. Sometimes the penalties are delayed in coming, but they are as sure as life itself. Remorse and agony come. . . . Remorse may be pushed aside with bravado and brainwashing, but it will return to prick and pinch. It may be drowned in alcohol or temporarily shocked into numbness in the increasing sins which follow, but the conscience will eventually awaken, and remorse and sorrow will be followed by pain and suffering. . . . And the longer repentance is pushed into the background the more exquisite will be the punishment when it finally comes to the fore.

"The words of Alma give us what is perhaps the best scriptural account of the exquisite suffering of the sinner.

" 'But I was racked with eternal torment, for my soul was harrowed up to the greatest degree and racked with all my sins.

" 'Yea, I did remember all my sins and iniquities, for which I was tormented with the pains of hell; yea, I saw that I had rebelled against my God, and that I had not kept his holy commandments.

" ' . . . the very thought of coming into the presence of my God did rack my soul with inexpressible horror.

" 'Oh, thought I, that I could be banished and become extinct both soul and body, that I might not be brought to stand in the presence of my God, to be judged of my deeds.' [Alma 36:12–15.]

"If men would only let their sins trouble them early when the sins are small and few, how much anguish would be saved them!" (*The Miracle of Forgiveness* [Salt Lake City: Bookcraft, 1969], pp. 141–42.)

Discuss the section in the lesson entitled "We Can Repent and Grow." You could also take the "Repentance Quiz."

Discuss in depth Ether 12:27, such as follows:

When we try to follow the Savior and become more like him, we come unto him. —— **And if men come unto me**

As we study the scriptures and pattern our lives after the Savior, we recognize what in our lives needs improvement. —— **I will show unto them their ªweakness.**

God has allowed us to have the capacity to make mistakes here on earth. —— **I ᵇgive unto men weakness**

Our Heavenly Father allowed this condition that we might be humble and desire to turn to him for our strength and realize that we need him in all we do. —— **that they may be humble;**

The gift of the Atonement has paid for our sins (see Romans 3:24, 4:7). —— **and my ᶜgrace is sufficient**

It is necessary to be humble first in order to be teachable and want to change and improve. —— **for all men that ᵈhumble themselves before me; for if they humble themselves before me,**

Jesus made it possible for us to repent and progress. Without faith in his atoning sacrifice, we cannot reach out and accept the gift of the Atonement. —— **and have faith in me,**

Even those things we consider to be our greatest faults can become our strengths if we turn to Jesus for forgiveness and strength. —— **then will I make ᵉweak things become strong unto them.**

Point out that God does not want us to worry about our sins once we have overcome them and repented.

Together read, discuss, and memorize Doctrine and Covenants 58:42. You may also want to discuss Isaiah 1:18.

Conclude the lesson by bearing your testimonies of the Savior and sharing your experiences of the blessing of repentance.

SUGGESTIONS FOR FUTURE HOME EVENINGS

Understanding the Steps of Repentance

There is good material on repentance in chapter 19, "Repentance," of *Gospel Principles* [PBIC0245], pages 117 through 123. Discuss the definition, the steps, and the need for repentance using that information.

Learning to Forgive Oneself

Many people take all the steps of repentance except the last one, forgiving themselves. Tell the story of how Saul of Tarsus, persecutor of the Saints after Jesus' death, became Paul the Apostle. He became a devoted and successful missionary. (See Acts 9:3–19.)

- If Paul had not been able to forgive himself for his serious sins after he repented and became converted, how effective a missionary would he have been?

- If we do not forgive ourselves after we have repented, how effective can we be in whatever we do?

Developing the Spirit of Repentance

Have a home evening for older children, teenagers, and adults on the spirit of repentance. Emphasize that although the steps we often discuss are important, the attitude of repentance is also very important.

- Why is this so?

- Can one truly repent without a desire to do so?

Explain that repentance is a direction in life, a habit of constant improvement, a spirit of being teachable and willing to grow each day from honestly looking at ourselves and striving to overcome (see 2 Nephi 2:21).

Forgiving Others

Begin by asking your family:

- What one thing did the Savior repeat with emphasis after he gave his famous prayer we call the Lord's Prayer. (The admonition for us to forgive others [see Matthew 6:12–15].)

The Savior further emphasized this important principle when he talked to Peter about how many times we should forgive each other (see Matthew 18:21–22). Then Jesus told one of his parables about two men who owed money. Read the parable in Matthew 18:23–35, and discuss the importance of forgiving others.

In our day this same principle has been highlighted by the Lord in many sections of the Doctrine and Covenants. Read together Doctrine and Covenants 64:8–10, and discuss what the verses mean to you.

Have a Scripture Night

Spend a home evening to locating, reading and discussing your favorite passages of scripture about repentance and the atonement of Christ, which made the forgiveness of sin possible for all of us. If you need help in locating appropriate passages, look under "Repent, Repentance" in the Topical Guide of the Latter-day Saint edition of the King James Version of the Bible.

You may wish to have a scripture chase game, in which you state a topic or phrase from a scripture and let family members race to find it in their copies of the scriptures. The person who finds it first wins and reads the complete passage out loud.

You may also wish to combine these suggestions with the following activity.

Singing the Hymns of Atonement

Have a spiritual evening of hymns about the atonement of Jesus Christ. Let family members take turns naming their favorite hymn to sing, such as "Behold the Great Redeemer Die" (*Hymns,* no. 230), "God Loved Us, So He Sent His Son" (*Hymns,* no. 178), or "How Great the Wisdom and the Love" (*Hymns,* no. 68). Family members may wish to tell why this hymn is important to them or what it means to them. A brief discussion before the hymn will make the singing more meaningful.

MY FAITH IN CHRIST CAN GROW

We believe that the first principles and ordinances of the Gospel are: first, Faith in the Lord Jesus Christ.
[*Articles of Faith 1:4*]

PURPOSE

Help your family increase their faith in Jesus Christ.

FOR THE PARENT

Children have a natural faith in anything their parents tell them. If they learn about Jesus at an early age, they will have a simple faith that he lives and that he loves them. This will help to bring his Spirit into their lives. That is why you are commanded by the Lord to teach your children faith in Jesus Christ while they are young.

Their childlike faith grows as you provide opportunities for them to pray, to learn about the Savior, and to apply their faith to their lives.

If you want your family to have faith in Jesus, they must see you praying, studying the gospel, and following the teachings of the Savior. Example is much more important than anything you can tell them. The words you say will have more meaning when your children see your example.

By sharing faith-building experiences with your family members, you will help them grow in faith until they become strong enough to successfully face the temptations and trials in their own lives.

PREPARATION

1. Bring a chalkboard and chalk or poster and marker.

2. Bring a seed and, if possible, a picture of the plant it becomes.

3. Prepare the chart "Our Faith in Jesus Christ Can Grow" as illustrated under the heading "How to Help Our Faith Grow."

4. Prepare a slip of paper for each family member with the phrase "I will increase my faith in Jesus this week by—" written on it.

SUGGESTED HYMN AND SONG

"Come, Follow Me" (*Hymns*, no. 14).
"The Light Divine" (*Sing with Me*, B–26).

Explain that this is faith.

- What do you think the mists of darkness represented? (Temptations that make it hard to keep our minds and hearts on the goal of eternal life.)
- What mists of darkness do we have in life today?

Explain that all people have times in their lives when mists of darkness surround them. Problems arise that seem unsolvable. Hardships come that seem unnecessary and unfair. Suffering, failure, family problems, war, false teachings, and confusion about why things are happening sometimes combine to make us lose sight of where we are going. When this happens, some people give up and lose their way, but others are able to keep going and even keep a cheerful attitude and help others. Faith makes the difference. At this time you may want to share examples from your own life or from the lives of others who have conquered trials through faith.

We Can Develop Faith in Jesus Christ

Tell your family that one of the best ways to prepare yourself to face life successfully is to develop faith in Jesus Christ. Have someone quote or read the fourth article of faith. Faith in Jesus is the *first* principle of the gospel. (See chapter 18, "Faith in Jesus Christ," *Gospel Principles* [PBIC0245], pp. 110–16.)

- What is faith? (A belief in something that can't be seen or proved by scientific methods. A trust that is so strong it causes us to act on it.)
- Why is faith in Jesus Christ so important?

To answer this question, read John 14:6.

- What does *way* mean?
- What did Jesus mean when he said that he is the way?

Discuss how Jesus leads the way back to our Heavenly Father. We belong to his church and follow his example. We have faith in his great sacrifice, which will enable us to return to our heavenly home if we prepare ourselves.

- Why can we have faith that Jesus is the way back to Heavenly Father?

SUGGESTED LESSON

Faith in Christ Brings Us Strength

Begin by telling your family about Lehi's dream (1 Nephi 8, 11–12, 15:21–36):

Lehi was a prophet who lived long ago. His dream was about the way to eternal life. In his dream, Lehi saw a beautiful tree. The tree stood for the love our Heavenly Father has for us. It's fruit was eternal life. There was a straight and narrow path leading to the tree. Along the path was a rod of iron. The rod of iron represented the word of God, or his commandments. A river ran beside the path, and it was full of filthy water. The river rep-resented the wickedness and sin in the world that people can fall into. As Lehi watched people moving along the path, there arose mists of darkness that made it hard for them to see where they were going. Many of the people clung to the rod of iron to stay on the path. Others wandered in the mists of darkness and were lost. Those who held to the rod reached the tree.

- What made some of the people able to hold on and move forward through the mists of darkness instead of becoming confused, letting go, and losing their way? (They believed that the rod would lead them safely through the darkness to the tree. They trusted it.)

(Because Heavenly Father sent him to show us the way, because Jesus does and says only what Heavenly Father wants him to, and because of our own testimonies.)

To Have Faith in Jesus, We Must Know Him

• Why are we sometimes afraid of strangers? Because we don't know them and don't know if we can trust them.)

Discuss why it is hard to have faith in someone whom we do not know. Explain that faith comes from knowing and trusting someone. To have faith in Jesus, we have to know him. Use your chalkboard or poster to write down some of the things that your family knows about Jesus, such as—

1. He is the Son of God.
2. He lives.
3. He loves us.
4. He loves everyone.
5. He died for us.
6. He is our Savior.
7. He is patient.
8. He is forgiving.
9. He has power over the elements of the earth.
10. He knows what is best for us.
11. He wants us to be happy.
12. His teachings come from Heavenly Father and will lead us back to him.
13. He and Heavenly Father appeared to Joseph Smith.

Faith Grows

Tell your family that you know they already have faith in Jesus because of some of the things they think, say, and do. Name some of the ways they show their faith. For example, they were baptized into his church. They hold family home evening. They go to church. They pray to their Heavenly Father the way Jesus taught them to.

Read Matthew 17:20.

• Why did Jesus compare faith to a seed?

Show the seed that you brought, and explain that although it is small it has the ability to grow into a big plant. Hold up the picture of the plant. Tell the family that the mustard seed was

chosen by Jesus to teach faith because it is a small seed that grows into a tree.

Faith usually begins as a small thing. Sometimes it begins with only the desire to believe. Like the seed, it has within it the ability to grow in strength and power. To grow, it needs to be planted and taken care of. (See Alma 32:28–43.)

The seed of faith is planted in our hearts. As we take care of it and it begins to grow, our faith fills our lives with blessings, and we find miracles happening in our lives. These may not be miracles like the moving of a mountain, but we will notice changes taking place in ourselves and those around us that we thought would never happen. We will feel the blessings of Heavenly Father in our lives and have reason to rejoice. We will have the confidence and strength to hold on to the iron rod until we reach eternal life.

How to Help Our Faith Grow

• What can we do to help our faith in Jesus Christ grow?

After your family has responded to this question, hold up the chart you have made "Our Faith in Jesus Christ Can Grow," using the sample below:

Our Faith in Jesus Christ Can Grow

1. *Pray* to Heavenly Father, and ask him to help your faith in Christ grow.
2. *Learn* all you can about the Savior.
3. *Follow* Jesus' example and his teachings.

Discuss each step as you read it, using the following ideas:

1. Prayer is important in making our faith grow because the feeling of sureness or testimony of Jesus Christ can come only from Heavenly Father. It comes by revelation through the Holy Ghost. We need help from our Heavenly Father to know Jesus and to understand and have faith in the things we learn about him.

2. We must continue to learn all we can about our Savior. We have the scriptures to teach us about his life and teachings. We have our

Church classes and sacrament meetings. We also have seminary, family home evening, and the Church magazines to teach us about him and what he wants us to do.

3. The best way we can develop faith in Jesus is to live his teachings. This is how we learn that they bring good results and joy to us. In fact, faith is believing and trusting him enough to do what he wants us to do even when it is difficult. By using our faith in this way, it will grow. We will also find that we know and understand the Savior better.

Tell the following story or a similar one from your own experience:

Margie Follows the Teachings of Jesus

Margie stopped at the teacher's desk on her way out of the classroom for lunch. She looked at the prisms he had displayed and couldn't resist picking one up and making a rainbow in the light. She watched the rainbow dance up and down the wall. She shook the prism to make the rainbow dance faster. As she shook it, the prism slipped from her hand. She tried hard to catch it but instead knocked two more prisms off the teacher's desk. She looked in horror at the broken glass at her feet. Then she looked around and saw that she was alone and that no one had seen the accident. She ran from the room.

During lunch, Margie did not feel hungry. She did not feel like playing with her friends. She felt too miserable. She knew that she had done something wrong. She knew that Jesus would want her to admit her mistake, but she didn't know if she could stand the humiliation. She had never been in trouble at school before. She was frightened and upset.

Finally Margie decided she would tell her teacher as soon as lunch was over. She was so nervous about it that she lagged behind until she was the last one to return to class.

There she found her teacher angrily demanding, "Which one of you broke these prisms?"

The class was silent. Margie almost failed in her resolve.

"I did it," Margie said at last. "It was an accident. I'm so sorry."

The teacher looked surprised. Then he quietly asked her to help him clean up the glass. To Margie's surprise, her heart felt happy as she worked. All of the bad feelings that had been with her during the lunch period were gone, and in their place was a feeling of peace. Margie knew that she had made a mistake, but she also knew that she had handled it in the right way. She had done what Jesus wanted her to do.

• How do you think this experience helped Margie's faith in Jesus to grow?

• Do you think that next time it will be easier for her to follow Jesus' teachings?

• Why?

Faith in Jesus grows from this kind of experience. Invite family members to share similar experiences they have had.

We Can Make Our Own Faith Grow

Conclude by talking about how your faith in Jesus Christ will grow only as you work to make it grow. By praying, studying about the Savior, and living his teachings, you will know for yourselves that you can trust in him. You will know that following him will bring happiness and peace. Then when you encounter difficulties, you will have the faith to keep his commandments, knowing in a very personal way that he will never let you down.

• What do we need to do to build our faith?

Pass out the papers you have prepared, and ask family members to think of at least one thing they can do to help their faith in Jesus Christ grow. Help them choose something they can do right away so they can have a successful experience. Tell them to pay special attention to how they feel as they do the assignment they set for themselves.

Bear your testimony, and express your love for your family. Let them know that you want them to have all the blessings that come to the faithful. Challenge all the family, including yourself, that when temptation comes they will be strong.

ADAPTING FOR YOUNGER CHILDREN

Tell your children that you are going to talk about having faith in Jesus. *Faith* means believing that Jesus lives and loves us and that he will bless us if we do what is right. If we trust him and follow his teachings, we will be happy. Our faith in Jesus can grow by learning about him.

Share some stories about Jesus and what kind of person he is with your children. Choose your favorite stories, and retell their favorites. After each story, tell them what it teaches you about Jesus and why it helps you to have faith in him. Your children may not yet understand what faith is, but they will benefit from hearing the stories about Jesus, and their faith will grow.

The following is an example of a story you might tell your children:

Jesus Blesses the Children

One day Jesus was teaching people. Some of the people wanted Jesus to bless their little children, and they started to take their children to where Jesus was sitting. Jesus' disciples, who were the men who helped Jesus, tried to keep the people from bringing the little children to Jesus.

Jesus saw this and told the disciples to let the children come to him. He said, "Suffer the little children to come unto me, and forbid them not: for of such is the kingdom of God" (Mark 10:14).

The children came and climbed on Jesus' lap, and he blessed them and showed them how much he loved them. (See Mark 10:14–16.)

• How do you think Jesus felt about little children?

Tell your children that during the week you are going to work together to develop more faith in Jesus by learning more about him. Then share stories of Jesus with the children throughout the week at mealtimes or at bedtimes (for example, the story of Jesus blessing the Nephite children in 3 Nephi 17:17–25).

ADAPTING FOR TEENAGERS AND ADULTS

Start with the example of the iron rod as in the regular lesson. You may want to read all or part of it from the scriptures.

Ask your family members to share examples of people they know who have shown great faith.

Have someone quote the fourth article of faith.

• Why is faith in Jesus Christ the first principle of the gospel?

Read John 14:6, and discuss what it means that Jesus is the "way."

• How could you develop more faith in Jesus Christ?

Read and discuss the ideas under the section "Faith Grows." Also discuss the chart.

You may want to tell the following experience of Elder Paul H. Dunn or one from your own life:

Living the Teachings of Jesus

"Some time ago I had a challenge as a father when one of my daughters, during her junior high school days, came to me with a social problem which was very disturbing. My daughter at the time was involved with a social group consisting of seven girls (four members of the Church and three nonmembers). The four had a silent pact, as it were, to try to convert the other three. As they were lunching together, which they frequently did, one of the young Latter-day Saint girls commenced to tell an off-color story. It was in poor taste and totally out of order.

"My daughter came home that night and recounted the situation; in fact, she was even bold enough to tell me the story. It was a problem! 'Now,' she said, 'Dad, don't tell me what's right and what's wrong. . . . But,' she said, 'what do you *do* when you find yourself in this kind of a situation? How do you handle it?'

" . . . She was saying, in effect, 'Will you give an answer and, at the same time, keep me popular.' . . .

" . . . I turned, after some discussion, to the cleansing of the temple experience recorded in Matthew, Mark and Luke. . . . As I read the . . . story, I asked her, 'What do you get out of this story?'

"She said, 'Well, the Savior was upset.'

46

"I said, 'May I just suggest one thought. He was saying to his peer group that there comes a time in every person's life when he has to stand up and be counted, and while it may not be the popular thing to do, there are times when you have to do what's right even though it isn't easy. You may have to stand alone a few times.'

"I said, 'You think about that. Then you and I'll have another talk.' . . .

" 'Dad,' she said, 'you missed the *point.* You *can't* do that and be popular.' "

Stop telling the story, and ask:

• What would you do if you were the daughter?

Explain that the next evening she had another talk with her father and explained what she had done:

"She said, 'Dad, it is an interesting thing. I took the cleansing of the temple story today to task and tried it out.'

"I said, 'Oh, did you clean out the junior high?'

" 'No,' she said, 'I called M—— (who was the girl that had told the off-color story, her L.D.S. friend) and said, "Can you walk home with me?" "Yes." So we walked home. I brought her into the bedroom and sat her down and I said, "M——, I just want you to know that our friendship means a great deal to me. Yesterday . . . when you told that story it reduced all of us in the eyes of our non-Latter-day Saint friends. . . . While . . . you thought this was a clever way to be noticed, I wonder if the next time you feel that you have to do this would you warn me in advance so that I can be excused?"

"M—— broke down and put her arms around this daughter and said, 'Will you forgive me?'

"She said, 'Dad, we cried for half an hour.' Then the climax: 'You know what, Dad?'

"I said, 'No, what?'

"She said, 'The New Testament really *works,* doesn't it?'

" 'Yes, the New Testament really works.' " (*Happiness Is . . . ,* Brigham Young University Speeches of the Year [Provo, 18 Apr. 1967], pp. 6–9.)

• Do you think that this experience helped Elder Dunn's daughter understand Jesus' teachings?

• Do you think that next time it will be easier for her to follow Jesus' teachings?

Faith in Jesus grows after this kind of experience. Invite family members to share similar experiences they have had in living the teachings of Jesus.

Pass out the papers for the challenge as described in the family lesson, and have each person set a reasonable goal to increase his faith in Jesus Christ.

SUGGESTIONS FOR FUTURE HOME EVENINGS

Learning Faith in Christ through the Scriptures

There are many examples of faith in the scriptures. Have family members be prepared to relate a favorite scripture passage that demonstrates faith. Have them give the background to the scripture and the details that show the importance of having faith in Jesus Christ. After each story, discuss briefly what faith did for those in the story or what the scripture tells us about faith.

Some scripture stories you might use include—

1. Helaman and the two thousand young warriors (Alma 56:41–47, 57:24–27).
2. The brother of Jared (Ether 3:1–13).
3. Jesus rebuking his Apostles (Matthew 17:14–21).
4. Doubting Thomas (John 20:19–29).
5. Joseph Smith's vision (Joseph Smith—History 1:11–20).
6. The last days of Moroni (Moroni 1, 7:33, 10:32–34).
7. Alma among the Zoramites (Alma 31–32, especially Alma 32:27).

The Differences between Belief, Faith, and Knowledge

Introduce the lesson by asking about the differences between belief, faith, and knowledge. Then have the father (or oldest son in the family) lift each child in turn. Explain that the father is strong enough to hold the child. They know this because they have experienced it. Tell them that their

father loves them and would not hurt them. Ask them if they believe this. Then ask a child to stand with his back to his father, eyes closed, and fall backward while his father catches him. Whatever the child actually does, explain that his willingness to do what he was asked shows faith in the promises made by his father. He knows his father can hold him up. He believes his father would not let him be hurt. He demonstrates his faith by willingly accepting his father's promise and by doing what he is asked to do.

After the children have done the activity, have family members list some of the promises Jesus has made to those who believe and have faith in him (for example, John 4:14, 11:25; D&C 5:16).

Discuss how belief and faith work to bring about the promise. Explain that, like the father in the family, Jesus has made us a promise and that if we will have faith that he lives and will keep his promises, we can have eternal life.

The Power of Faith in Christ

Have an evening of faith-promoting stories from the lives of family members, ancestors, or other Church families, such as pioneers or Church leaders. Such an evening should start with a hymn such as "I Need Thee Every Hour" (*Hymns,* no. 79) or "Father in Heaven, We Do Believe" (*Hymns,* no. 41) and the reading of appropriate scriptures.

Learning to Exercise Faith

Start the evening with a series of physical exercises, such as sit-ups, running in place, or push-ups. While these are going on, talk about how exercise strengthens muscles.

• What else needs exercising? (Our spirits and our faith.)
• What will exercise do for faith? (Make it stronger and healthier.)
• How can we exercise our faith? (By bearing testimonies, sharing the gospel with others, praying, studying the scriptures, and living the commandments.)

Explain that like physical exercise, building faith usually does not happen overnight but requires constant effort. Read and discuss James 1:22 through 2:26.

JESUS IS MY EXAMPLE

I am the light of the world: he that followeth me shall not walk in darkness, but shall have the light of life.
[John 8:12]

PURPOSE

Help family members follow Jesus' example when they make their daily decisions.

FOR THE PARENT

In this lesson you will review some of the attributes possessed by Jesus that you and your family would want to acquire to become more like him and our Heavenly Father. You can teach each other the habit of asking "What would the Lord have me do?" as you make your daily decisions.

PREPARATION

1. Prepare for the activity that will take place in the darkness or with the use of a blindfold.
2. Prepare the chart entitled "What Would the Lord Have Me Do?"

SUGGESTED HYMN AND SONG

"Come, Follow Me" (*Hymns*, no. 14). "Teach Me to Walk in the Light" (*Sing with Me*, B–45).

SUGGESTED LESSON

"I Am the Light of the World"

Turn out all the lights in the house, or use a blindfold if it is still light. Ask one of the family members to perform a difficult task, such as writing a sentence on a piece of paper or finding several household items and

putting them in one place. Then turn on the lights or remove the blindfold, and show how easily the same task can be done in the light.

Have a family member read aloud John 8:12.

- How is Jesus the Light of the World? (He is the one who lights our way.)
- How does he give us light? (He gave us his example and teachings.)
- Why is it easier to make the right decisions with the aid of Jesus' light? (His examples and teachings light the way for us. We can see the paths we should take more clearly.)

Memorize John 8:12 together as a family. Then sing "Teach Me to Walk in the Light."

Jesus Gave Us His Example

- What are some of the things for which Jesus has given us his example, things that apply to our own lives?

Direct your discussion according to the needs of your family. Following are some examples:

1. He showed us the way to be baptized (Matthew 3:13–17).
2. He loved little children (Mark 10:13–16).
3. He helped the sick and the handicapped (Mark 6:53–56, 7:31–35).
4. He was kind (John 4:6–10).
5. He did not get angry with those who offended him (Matthew 27:29–31).
6. He forgave those who were cruel to him (Luke 23:34).
7. He showed us how to pray (Matthew 6:5–13).

8. He taught the importance of truth (John 8:32).
9. He resisted all temptation (Matthew 4:2–10).

In your discussion, show how Jesus always chose to do the will of the Father. He exemplified the principle of love toward others.

Tell the following story, and ask family members to listen for ways Kaye could use Jesus' example:

Kaye's Decision

Ten-year-old Kaye stayed home while her mother went to buy food for the family. Her mother had asked her to clean up her room and to practice her violin.

Kaye quickly cleaned up her room. Then without thinking, she turned on the television. The program that was on interested her very much.

"I am supposed to practice my violin," thought Kaye. "But I don't like to practice. Besides, I want to watch this show."

She was tempted to watch the front yard to see when her mother would arrive home. Then when her mother came, Kaye could quickly turn off the television, take out the violin, and make it look like she was practicing.

- How would the example of Jesus' resisting Satan's temptations help Kaye with her temptation?
- What would the Lord want Kaye to do now?

What Would Jesus Have Me Do?

Bring up some positive examples in your home during the day or the week when stopping to think helped a family member make a better decision. If

48

family members bring up some negative examples, be careful not to accuse or embarrass anyone. Keep the discussion positive.

For decisions between right and wrong, we should ask ourselves, "What would the Lord have me do?"

• How could you be reminded to ask yourselves this important question during the week?

To help family members follow Jesus' example, have them keep a record of their decisions during the coming week. Make a simple chart like the following for each family member. Have them place a happy face on the chart when they choose to do what Jesus would have them do. The parents should do this also. By their example the children can better learn how to follow Jesus.

What Would the Lord Have Me Do?		
Name_____		
Day	Decisions	Followed the Savior
		☺

During the week, compliment each family member on how well he is doing.

ADAPTING FOR YOUNGER CHILDREN

Use the introductory activity from the regular lesson, and sing "Teach Me to Walk in the Light." In your own words, tell how Jesus was always loving, kind, and truthful. Explain to your children in simple terms the idea of asking yourself, "What would the Lord have me do?" Then read the following story about John:

John Was Happy

John was on his way to school. He was hurrying because he wanted to have fun playing before school began. He passed Jenny. She was on her tricycle. But she was not riding. She was just sitting there. Jenny was only three, and John was six.

John said, "Hello Jenny." Then he saw that Jenny was crying. John stopped. "What is the matter, Jenny?" he asked.

"I can't find my house," Jenny cried.

John knew where Jenny's house was, but if he stopped to take her home, he wouldn't get to school in time to play.

• What would you do if you were John?

• What would the Lord want John to do?

John didn't want to stop, but when he saw the tears on Jenny's face, he couldn't leave her there lost. He said, "Don't cry anymore, Jenny. I'll take you home." He helped her turn her tricycle in the right direction and walked beside her. Jenny stopped crying. When she saw her house, she looked happy.

• How do you think John felt?

• How do you think he would have felt if he had left Jenny crying and had gone to school in time to play?

You may wish to display a picture of Jesus on a chart. Below it, down the left side, write the name of each child. Draw a line across the paper separating each name.

When a child does something to make someone happy, let him paste or tape a happy face in his space.

Let the children make the happy faces during the home evening. The outline can be made by tracing around a coin or button.

ADAPTING FOR TEENAGERS AND ADULTS

After holding the activity involving darkness, singing the hymn, and studying the appropriate scriptures, have someone read the following story:

"Inasmuch As Ye Have Done It unto One of the Least of These"

Roger sat at the dinner table, tired but happy. It was Saturday, and he had spent eight hours at the university library studying for three midterm examinations he was scheduled to take on Monday. He had wanted to play tennis and go to the football game, but had studied instead. He was glad he had not done those things, confident that he was prepared for his tests. Roger wanted to maintain his high grade point average because he would be applying for graduate school in the spring. But he still wondered, "Why do professors seem to schedule tests on the same day?"

Roger's roommates had all gone on dates that evening. Roger was preparing his Gospel Doctrine lesson on following the example of Jesus for the next morning. He was glad to be alone with his thoughts.

When the doorbell rang, Roger reacted with a frown. "Who would be coming here on a Saturday night?" he muttered.

Still frowning he let the lesson manual fall shut and pushed his chair from the table. When he opened the door he found an unshaven, scraggly dressed man about forty years old. The man's breath smelled of tobacco and liquor.

"I just drove into town," the man said, "and my car stopped right here in the middle of your street." The man explained how he hadn't eaten all day and that his friend had a son attending the university whom he wanted to find. "Could you spare me a bite to eat, and then help me find out what's wrong with the car? You could probably help me find my friend's son, too, couldn't you?"

Roger tried to think of an excuse. After all, there were several other houses on the street, in which families, not students, lived. They probably had more food. They probably wouldn't have to worry about teaching Sunday School and were not as tired as he was tonight. Besides, he thought, this man might even ask to stay overnight.

On the other hand, Roger did know something about cars. If he used his school directory, he could probably find the person this man was looking for. But what if he couldn't? What would his roommates think if they saw this unkempt man in the apartment? And he still hadn't prepared his Sunday School lesson.

• What do you think you would do if you were Roger?

• What would the Lord have you do? Why?

Read Matthew 25:31–46.

• Who is Jesus talking about when he says, "Ye have done it unto one of the least of these my brethren" (Matthew 25:46)?

• Why are the hardest commandments to keep, such as showing love to *everyone*, the ones that bring us the most personal growth?

Discuss how Roger's decision would make a difference in the lesson he would give on following Jesus' example. Bring out the idea that when we follow Jesus, our faith in him grows, and we find it easier to follow him.

SUGGESTIONS FOR FUTURE HOME EVENINGS

What Is an Example?

These suggestions work best with young children.

Play "Do as I Do." Each member of the family takes a turn as leader. The leader stands in front of the others and performs some action like clapping, touching his nose, winking or saying something. The rest of the group then imitates his actions. Parents or the one conducting the family home evening may want to be leader after the others have had a turn so they can introduce a few examples of reverent behavior for the others to follow, such as folding arms or kneeling as if for prayer.

Discuss the idea of using Jesus as our example.

Developing a More Christlike Life

These suggestions work best with teenagers and adults.

Elder Neal A. Maxwell has given twelve guidelines that will tell us how well we are progressing toward a more Christlike life. You may wish to devote several family home evenings to a discussion of one or more of them. They are—

1. Achieving the right balance between self-contentment and ambition.
2. Following counsel as Moses followed Jethro's counsel (Exodus 18:17–24).
3. Not being too absorbed in one aspect of life, like Martha (Luke 10:41–42).
4. Praying for right things.
5. Having right reasons for our good behavior.
6. Taking gratefully what life brings.
7. Loving our enemies.
8. Being free from envy of those who do better than we.
9. Forgiving *and forgetting*.
10. Using our adversities as tools to grow.
11. Becoming more patient.
12. Becoming more willing to follow the Lord wherever he may lead us. (See "The Christ-Centered Life," *Ensign*, Aug. 1981, pp. 13–17.)

You may wish to simplify these guidelines to make a twelve-item self-evaluation test. Have family members spend fifteen or twenty minutes responding silently to the items to evaluate their own progress. Family members should not be required to reveal their responses.

BAPTISM AND THE NAME OF CHRIST

All those who are true believers in Christ took upon them, gladly, the name of Christ.
[*Alma 46:15*]

PURPOSE

Help family members understand what it means to take upon them the name of Jesus Christ when they are baptized.

FOR THE PARENT

Moroni said that "all those who were true believers in Christ took upon them, gladly, the name of Christ, or Christians . . . because of their belief in Christ" (Alma 46:15).

As we take upon us the name of Christ, we covenant to be obedient to the principles of the gospel. All we do should be based on Christ's example. If we do this gladly, we will find joy in living the gospel. We will feel good about ourselves and have the desire to do what is right. At baptism we covenanted to take upon us the name of Christ. This lesson is to help you and your children realize the importance of this covenant. (See chapter 20, "Baptism," *Gospel Principles* [PBIC0245], pp. 124–30.)

PREPARATION

1. Prepare two pieces of paper for each family member, one with his first name on it and one with his last name on it. Then hide them in the room.

2. Number six slips of paper, one through six, and place them in a hat or bag from which to draw them.

SUGGESTED HYMN AND SONG

"Come, Follow Me" (*Hymns*, no. 14). "The Things I Do" (*More Songs for Children*, p. 18).

SUGGESTED LESSON

Important Names

Tell your family members that there are two pieces of paper hidden in the room that belong to them. Have each family member hunt for the two papers that belong to him. After all have found their names, explain that they had to search until they found the only paper with their first name, but they could take the first paper they found with their last name. Their first names belong to them individually, but their last name belongs to everyone in the family and shows they are a member of the family. Talk about how important your family name is, how proud you are of your name. If you know any historical or special facts about how your family name came to be, use them. Try to develop a feeling of love and pride for your family and family name.

Explain that your family stands for certain things. Ask your children what some of these are. You might get answers such as we believe in the gospel, we are honest, or we try to be friendly. Tell your children that what they do reflects back on your family. Each of us have the responsibility to help make our family name respected.

Point out that just as we were born into our family when we came to earth, we are born into another family when we are baptized. At baptism we become members of Jesus' church or members of his family. We make a covenant with Heavenly Father to take upon us the name of Christ.

I Take Upon Me the Name of Christ

Tell your family that after Jesus was killed, his faithful followers, those who had been baptized, were persecuted. Paul the Apostle came to Antioch in Syria where a group of Church members were to teach people about Christ.

Have someone read Acts 11:26 aloud.

Explain that the enemies of the disciples started calling the followers of Jesus "Christians" after the name of Christ to set them apart. The name was given as an insult, but was accepted gladly by the followers of Jesus. They were glad to be called Christians and were proud of the name.

• How does it make you feel to realize that you have actually taken upon you the name of Christ, that you are a Christian?

• Are you glad to be called a Christian? Why?

Tell your family the following story, which illustrates how one little girl felt about becoming a Christian:

Sarah's Choice

Sarah was eight years old. She was excited to be eight but worried at the same time because she wanted to be baptized. Her mother and father were not active in the Church, and she didn't know what they would say. Sarah had learned from her Primary teachers how important baptism was. She knew that if she was baptized she would be promising Heavenly Father that she would go to church, even if she had to go alone. She would also be promising to live right and obey the commandments.

- Do you think this was a hard decision for Sarah to make?

Sarah prayed about it and decided that it was important that she be baptized. She knew it was what Heavenly Father wanted her to do. Her parents agreed that she could be baptized.

She felt good when she was baptized. She knew Heavenly Father and Jesus were happy. She knew that if she worked hard, the Holy Ghost would help her keep the commandments and be a good influence on her family.

- How do you think Sarah felt when she took upon her the name of Christ and became a member of his family?

Remind your family that when we make the commitment to be baptized and take upon us the name of Christ, we need to live our lives as Heavenly Father and Jesus would want us to.

Suggest to them that if they encounter a situation where they are having a hard time making a decision, they ask themselves, "What would Jesus have me do?"

I Am Glad to Be Called a Christian

Discuss some of the commandments we should be keeping that will help us to act as a Christian or as Jesus would want us to act. Use the pictures in the lesson to help identify these commandments. Explain that each person is going to work on one commandment during the week. Let your family talk about how they could keep the commandments pictured.

Show the family the hat or bag with the six slips of paper in it. Let each person draw out one of the slips. The number on the slip of paper that each person picks identifies one of the six pictures included in the lesson. Each person should work on the commandment represented by that picture.

Encourage each family member to pray about what he is going to do to keep the commandment he picked. Remind the family occasionally during the week that they are trying to live as Christ would have them live.

Conclude by telling the following story by President George Albert Smith:

What Have You Done With My Name?

"A number of years ago I was seriously ill. . . . With my family I went to St. George, Utah, to see if it would improve my health. . . .

"In St. George, . . . I became so weak as to be scarcely able to move. It was a slow and exhausting effort for me even to turn over in bed.

"One day, under these conditions, I lost consciousness of my surroundings and thought I had passed to the Other Side. I found myself standing with my back to a large and beautiful lake, facing a great forest of trees. There was no one in sight. . . . I realized, or seemed to realize, that I had finished my work in mortality and had gone home. . . .

"I began to explore, and soon I found a trail through the woods which seemed to have been used very little, and which was almost obscured by grass. I followed this trail, and after I had walked for some time and had traveled a considerable distance through the forest, I saw a man coming towards me. I became aware that he was a very large man, and I hurried my steps to reach him, because I recognized him as my grandfather. . . . I remember how happy I was to see him coming. I had been given his name and had always been proud of it.

"When Grandfather came within a few feet of me, he stopped. His stopping was an invitation for me to stop. Then . . . he looked at me very earnestly and said:

" 'I would like to know what you have done with my name.'

"Everything I had ever done passed before me as though it were a flying picture on a screen—everything I had done. Quickly this vivid retrospect came down to the very time I was standing there. My whole life had passed before me. I smiled and looked at my grandfather and said:

" 'I have never done anything with your name of which you need be ashamed.'

"He stepped forward and took me in his arms, and as he did so, I became conscious again of my earthly surroundings. My pillow was as wet as though water had been poured on it—

wet with tears of gratitude that I could answer unashamed.

" . . . Honor your fathers and your mothers. Honor the names that you bear, because some day you will have the privilege and the obligation of reporting to them (and to your Father in heaven) what you have done with their name." ("Your Good Name," *Improvement Era*, Mar. 1947, p. 139.)

- Do you think President Smith was glad he had acted like a Christian and kept Heavenly Father's commandments?

Emphasize that because he had so lived, he made his grandfather and Heavenly Father happy.

- Do you live in such a way that others can tell you are part of Christ's family?
- Are you glad to be called by Jesus Christ's name?

Challenge each family member to live as one who has sincerely taken Jesus' name upon him.

ADAPTING FOR YOUNGER CHILDREN

Use the activity in the lesson section "Important Names." Make the first-name slips of different colored paper and the last-name slips of one color, or write each child's name in a different color for the first name and in the same color for all of the last names. Hide the papers, and help your children find their own by telling them the color or colors they are looking for.

After each child has found his name, talk about the names and why you chose them. Point out that they each have a different first name but that they all have the same last name. Talk about your family name and how proud you are of it and of being a family.

Explain that when they become eight years old they will be old enough to be baptized.

- What will happen when you are baptized?

Let the children tell you what they know. Make sure they realize that Heavenly Father wants each of us to be baptized. Tell them we need to do the right things to be ready for baptism and that we promise Heavenly Father and Jesus to keep the commandments after baptism. This means that we act in the way Jesus would have us act. When we do this we are showing we love Jesus.

Show your children the pictures of the commandments. Let them discuss the ones they can identify, and explain the rest. Talk about how they can keep each one.

You might want to tell them about the day you were baptized, or let an older child describe his baptism.

End by singing the song "Baptism Day" (*More Songs for Children*, p. 10).

ADAPTING FOR TEENAGERS AND ADULTS

Begin with the section "Important Names" from the lesson. Also use the information about Paul and the disciples in Antioch from the section "I Take Upon Me the Name of Christ."

Explain that the followers of Alma in the Book of Mormon were also called Christians (see Alma 46:15).

• What do you think the word *Christian* meant to Paul and the disciples of his time? To Alma and his followers?

• What does the word *Christian* mean to you?

Let your family discuss what being a Christian means today. Emphasize that because The Church of Jesus Christ of Latter-day Saints is the true church of Christ, we have a great responsibility to live as Christians.

King Benjamin told his people to repent and enter into a covenant with Christ. Read Mosiah 5:7–15.

• What does it mean to be "spiritually begotten" of Christ (Mosiah 5:7)?

Read Galatians 3:26–29.

• How do we become children of God through faith?

• What does it mean to "put on Christ" (Galatians 3:27)?

Discuss specific ways in which you as a family could become better Christians. Have each family member choose one area in which he would like to improve. Ask if there are any times when it is difficult to take Christ's name upon us. If so, then these are the areas we need to work on. You may want to use the pictures as discussed in the section "I Am Glad to Be Called a Christian."

Conclude by reading the story of President George Albert Smith. Tell your family that some day we will stand before Christ and account for the covenant we have made to take upon us his name. Encourage them to think and pray how they can become better Christians so that they will be able to tell Christ that they have done nothing of which to be ashamed.

SUGGESTIONS FOR FUTURE
HOME EVENINGS

When Someone Is Going to Be Baptized

If someone in your family is preparing to be baptized in the near future, use lesson 29, "Preparing for Baptism."

Knowing What Baptism Is by Watching One

Plan with your family to attend a bap-tism. Before going to the baptism service, discuss with family members what is going to take place. Encourage them to listen to any talks given and to the prayers, including the baptismal prayer.

After returning home, let each family member express his feelings and impressions of the baptism. This will be an excellent opportunity to explore what they know about baptism and its meaning and purpose.

Inviting a Nonmember to a Baptism

You may want to invite a nonmember friend or family to attend a baptism with you. After the service, have a home evening together to discuss what you saw and what it meant to each of you. This would give the nonmembers a chance to ask questions in a more relaxed setting where everyone can make observations and comments.

The Sacrament and Baptism

Discuss the sacrament and its connection with the covenants we make when we are baptized. Remind your family that at baptism our sins are washed away. But we are not perfect and will make mistakes again. Stress that we must try as hard as we can to keep all the commandments but that Heavenly Father has provided a way for us to overcome our mistakes. If we truly repent, he will forgive us, and we can renew our covenants with him when we partake of the sacrament. One of the covenants is to take upon ourselves the name of Christ.

Express your gratitude to Heavenly Father for providing this way for us to overcome our sins. You may wish to refer to lesson 14, "Partaking of the Sacrament," for other ideas and helps.

Baptism and What It Means

Make one or more family home evening lessons from the material in chapter 20, "Baptism," in *Gospel Principles*, pages 124 through 130. This chapter discusses (1) why we must be baptized, (2) how we should be baptized, (3) who should be baptized, (4) the baptismal covenants, and (5) how baptism gives us a new start.

The Covenants of Baptism

Begin by asking the following question:

• What is a covenant? (An agreement or promise between two or more people.)

Discuss how being baptized establishes a covenant between Heavenly Father and the person baptized.

• What are the promises that we make at baptism?

Read Mosiah 18:1–17. Discuss in detail the covenants the followers of Alma made when they were baptized and the covenants Heavenly Father made (Mosiah 18:8–13). Help your family to realize that these are the same covenants we make and Heavenly Father makes when we are baptized. Read verse 11, and ask your family why they think these people clapped their hands for joy.

Let the members of the family who have already been baptized express the happiness and joy that come to them as they try to keep their baptismal covenants. Suggest that next time they partake of the sacrament, they think about these covenants and how well they are keeping them. Suggest that remembering and trying to keep the covenants helps us to renew them when we partake of the sacrament.

The Straight and Narrow Path

On a poster or a large piece of paper, draw a path moving upward. Near the middle of the path draw a door or gate across the path. Label the path "Way to Eternal Life."

Have family members read 2 Nephi 31:13–18 and suggest labels for the parts of the pathway before the gate (for example, repentance and faith) and the gate itself (baptism and the gift of the Holy Ghost).

Ask the family what labels they might put on the pathway after the gate. After they have discussed the possibilities, have someone read 2 Nephi 31:19–20, and complete the labeling.

• What is meant by "feasting upon the word of Christ"? (Reading and studying the scriptures.)

• What does the phrase "endure to the end" mean? (Keeping Heavenly Father's commandments throughout the rest of our lives.)

Explain that baptism is not an end but a beginning. Conclude by reading 3 Nephi 31:21. Bear your testimony about the truthfulness of Nephi's words.

PARTAKING OF THE SACRAMENT

He took bread, and gave thanks, and brake it, and gave unto them, saying, This is my body which is given for you: this do in remembrance of me.

Likewise also the cup, . . . saying, This cup is the new testament in my blood, which is shed for you.
[*Luke 22:19–20*]

PURPOSE

Help family members more fully appreciate the sacrament as an aid in remembering and keeping the commandments of the Savior.

FOR THE PARENT

Nothing seems more basic in our worship of the Lord than learning to partake of the sacrament meaningfully. We teach our children to partake before they learn to speak. We also need to teach them what the sacrament means to them personally. As you and your family evaluate your experiences in partaking of the sacrament, consider the following:

1. Do I think about the words of the sacrament hymn?
2. Do I listen to the sacrament prayers?
3. Do I remember that Jesus suffered and died for me?
4. Do I feel sorry for mistakes I have made?
5. Do I promise to do better?
6. In what way can I improve?

The manner in which the sacrament is administered is prescribed by scripture, but the way in which we receive it should not simply be habitual or mechanical, but an individual, heartfelt act of renewal and recommitment to serve the Lord. Encourage each member of your family to rediscover a rev-

erence for the sacrament and what it can mean in his life. (See chapter 23, "The Sacrament," *Gospel Principles* [PBIC0245], pp. 144–49.)

PREPARATION

Make family assignments for presenting the pictures and information in the lesson.

SUGGESTED HYMNS AND SONG

"Jesus, the Very Thought of Thee" (*Hymns*, no. 148).

"I Stand All Amazed" (*Hymns*, no. 80).

"To Think about Jesus" (*Sing with Me*, B–55).

SUGGESTED LESSON

Who Is Jesus Christ?

Without explanation, show a picture of Jesus, and allow your family to identify him by asking such questions as—

• Who does this picture represent?
• Where did you learn about him?
• Why is Jesus, who lived two thousand years ago, so important that we are taught about him today?
• Why is his death so significant?
• Why is Christ important to our family?
• What did Jesus say of himself? (Have someone read John 8:12 aloud.)
• What did our Heavenly Father say about his Son, Jesus Christ? (Have someone read John 3:16.)

Jesus Asked That We Always Remember Him

Explain that during his three-year

ministry on earth, Jesus clearly marked the path we should follow. He taught by example and word how people should behave and what attitudes they should develop. His was a life of love and service to others. He taught that the two great commandments were to love the Lord above all else and to love our neighbors as ourselves.

• Who are our neighbors? (Our brothers, sisters, parents, relatives, friends, and enemies.)

Show the picture of the Last Supper, accompanying the lesson, and discuss with the family the last few hours of our Savior's life.

• Who are the men in the picture?
• Why are they gathered together?

Briefly tell the story of the Last Supper:

The Last Supper

On the day of the feast of the Passover, Jesus sent two of his Apostles into Jerusalem to arrange for the feast. They prepared a room where they could be together.

This was the last time Jesus would meet with his beloved Apostles before his death. He served them in love. He knelt before them and washed and dried the feet of each of his disciples. He even washed the feet of Judas, whom he knew would turn against him.

During the evening, he told his Apostles that one of them would betray him. When Judas had left the gathering, as if on an errand for the Savior, Jesus tried to strengthen the others by giving them what he called "a new commandment." He commanded, "Love one another; as I have loved you" (John 13:34). He explained, "By this shall all men know that ye are my disciples, if ye have

love one to another" (John 13:35). He comforted them by saying that he would send the Holy Ghost to be with them, to strengthen and guide them.

Jesus tried to tell them that he would soon leave them, but they did not understand. Desiring that they remember him and keep his commandments, he introduced the sacrament. He broke bread and blessed it and passed it among his disciples saying, "Take, eat; this is my body" (Matthew 26:26).

Next he took a cup of wine, blessed it, and gave it to his Apostles to drink. He said:

"Drink ye all of it;

"For this is my blood of the new testament, which is shed for many for the remission of sins." (Matthew 26:27–28; see also the Joseph Smith Translation in the footnotes of the the Latter-day Saint edition of the King James Version of the Bible.)

- Do you suppose they thought, "We will remember"?

Matthew, one of the Apostles present on that sacred occasion, wrote that after the supper and the sacrament, Jesus and his Apostles sang a hymn. Then they went to the Garden of Gethsemane.

Jesus' Suffering, Trial, and Death

Have the assigned family members show and explain the pictures in the following order:

1. Jesus in Gethsemane
2. Jesus on the way to Calvary
3. The Crucifixion
4. Jesus buried in the tomb
5. The Resurrection

As family members show and discuss the pictures, remind them that each scene suggests that Jesus loved them and was willing to endure great pain and death so that they could live in Heavenly Father's presence.

- How do you think the Apostles felt about the last evening they spent with the Savior after his death and resurrection?

- What difference do you think it made to the Apostles in the way they viewed their promise to remember him after they had watched his arrest, his trial, his cru-

cifixion, his death, and finally his resurrection?

- Did the Apostles have opportunity to partake of the sacrament again?

Have the family read Acts 2:42, 20:7, and 1 Corinthians 11:23–30.

A Knowledge of Christ's Love Brings a Change in Attitude

Explain that just as the Savior wanted his Apostles to partake of the sacrament to remember him, so he wants us to remember his love, his teachings, his sacrifice for us.

- How does the knowledge that the Savior gave his life for you make a difference in the way you feel about the sacrament?

- How can this knowledge help you control your thoughts and renew your commitment to remember the Lord?

We Will Remember and Renew Our Covenants

Suggest to the family that before their next sacrament meeting they review

their actions since the last time they partook of the sacrament. Challenge them to think seriously about how they can remember Jesus while they partake of the sacrament at the next sacrament meeting. After the sacrament meeting, discuss your feelings and thoughts and determine if this reminder helped.

Close your home evening by singing or reading the words to "I Stand All Amazed" (Hymns, no. 80).

ADAPTING FOR YOUNGER CHILDREN

As you display the picture of the Last Supper, ask the children which man is Jesus. They will probably know. They also may know that the other men are Jesus' Apostles. Ask them to tell what the men are doing.

Explain that Jesus knew he was going to die and that he wanted his friends to remember him and do the things he had taught them, so he gave them the sacrament.

Help the children understand that this ordinance has meaning, otherwise they might think of it simply as a treat during church. Explain that the sacrament is given to help us remember Jesus' love for us and to help us do the things he wants us to do.

To apply this lesson and impress it on their minds, display a picture of Jesus by the place where you eat your meals. Then, Sunday morning during breakfast, suggest that the family talk about Jesus. Each child could tell one thing about Jesus, something the Savior did while he was here on earth. Then have each child tell something Jesus wants us to do. Remind the children that they will be taking the sacrament in sacrament meeting.

• What can you think about during the sacrament? (They may suggest thinking about their favorite story of Jesus or about something they can do to make someone happy.)

As you travel to your meeting, you could ask the children to sing a song about Jesus to help you remember what you should be thinking about during the sacrament.

Perhaps each child could paste a small picture of Jesus on a piece of construction paper. Help him write, "I will think of Jesus" on it. Let the children take them to church to look at while the sacrament is passed.

As you return home after the meeting, ask each child to tell what he thought about during the sacrament. Begin by telling what you were thinking. Praise the efforts of the children. Do not chide them if they occasionally forget. Encourage them to keep trying.

ADAPTING FOR TEENAGERS AND ADULTS

Instead of just telling the story of the Last Supper, read the scriptures. Compare the four gospels, emphasizing what each one adds to the account (see Matthew 26:26–29, Mark 14:22–25, Luke 22:17–20, John 6:50–65).

If you have the the Latter-day Saint edition of the King James Version of the Bible, read the footnotes that give the Joseph Smith Translation of the passages. They add special insights that you may want to discuss.

Review with your family the pictures and discussion at the end of the lesson.

Also discuss with family members the special meanings associated with the two parts of the sacrament. The bread is in remembrance of his body, which broke the bands of death so that each of us might also be resurrected. The water is in remembrance of his blood with which he bought for us redemption from our sins if we repent.

Discuss with family members how they can better remember during the passing of the sacrament by reviewing in their minds the sacrifice of the Savior, by giving silent prayers of thanksgiving, and recommitting to keep his commandments.

Teenagers and adults will want to do something to improve their appreciation of the sacrament. The application in the regular lesson could be helpful. (See the section "We Will Remember and Renew Our Covenants" in the lesson.)

SUGGESTIONS FOR FUTURE HOME EVENINGS

To Remember the Savior, We Must Know About Him

The sacrament is partaken in remembrance of the Savior. Spend an evening learning about the Savior.

For young children, tell selected stories taken from his life, such as 3 Nephi 17:5–25 and Matthew 19:13–15.

Encourage older children and adults to read and discuss the gospels or chapter 11, "The Life of Christ," in *Gospel Principles*, pages 53 through 63. Explain that this will help them partake of the sacrament more meaningfully.

How Do We Remember the Savior?

Ask family members to suggest ways they can remember the Savior in their daily lives. Discuss how they can show that they remember the Savior through their daily behavior, the choices they make, the language they use, and how they treat each other and their friends.

Make a chart with the names of family members down the left side and "I Remembered" written across the top. During the coming week, each time that a family member reports an ex-

ample of remembering the Savior, he places a star or other marker after his name.

The Sacrament Is a Renewing of Promises

Have someone read or recite the sacramental prayers (D&C 20:77–79). Discuss the promises we make when we take the sacrament.

For young children, write these promises on wordstrips to display under a picture of the Savior as each promise is discussed (for example, "Take his name upon us," "Keep his commandments," or "Always remember him").

Discuss also the promise God makes to us if we are worthy. Explain that he will give us his Spirit.

Relate these prayers and promises to the covenants made at baptism.

You may want to arrange to have this lesson follow one on baptism.

God Knows Our Hearts

Help your family to think seriously about taking the sacrament worthily. Have someone read Mormon 9:29, followed by 1 Corinthians 11:28–30. Discuss what these scriptures mean.

Have each family member suggest activities and ways he can prepare himself for taking the sacrament worthily. Encourage family members to set up a plan and follow it.

Taking the Sacrament Is an Act of Worship

Hymns are an important part of the sacrament service. Have the family sing some of the sacrament hymns found in *Hymns: The Church of Jesus Christ of Latter-day Saints*. Family members will profit from this by learning the words and learning to appreciate both the songs and the inspiration of the Savior's life and mission. Following are some suggested hymns:

1. "Behold the Great Redeemer Die" (*Hymns*, no. 230).
2. "God Loved Us, So He Sent His Son" (*Hymns*, no. 178).
3. "How Great the Wisdom and the Love" (*Hymns*, no. 68).
4. "Jesus of Nazareth, Savior and King" (*Hymns*, no. 86).
5. "We'll Sing All Hail to Jesus' Name" (*Hymns*, no. 217).

PICTURES AND
DISCUSSION

Jesus and His Disciples Sang a Hymn

Matthew, one of the Twelve Apostles who was present during the Last Supper (see the picture on page 58), writes that after the supper and sacrament, Jesus and his Apostles sang a hymn (see Matthew 26:30).

• Why did Jesus and the disciples sing a hymn?

A hymn may also be a psalm. There are one hundred fifty psalms in the Old Testament. Possibly Jesus and his disciples sang an Old Testament psalm as an indication to God that they praised his name, desired to do his will, and sought guidance to fulfill the mission before them.

Jesus Prayed in Gethsemane

Matthew provided a vivid account of what happened in the Garden of Gethsemane. Read Matthew 26:36–44.

Jesus asked Peter, "What, could ye not watch with me one hour?" (Matthew 26:40).

• Could this question also apply to persons whose minds are not on the sacrament while it is being passed?

Jesus on the Way to Calvary

Jesus was betrayed, taken by soldiers, and subjected to several trials. He was beaten and spit upon. A crown of thorns was placed upon his head. The Gospel of John states, "And he bearing his cross went forth into a place called the place of a skull, which is called in the Hebrew Golgotha" (John 19:17).

• Why did Jesus submit to the trials, the beatings, and the crucifixion? (Jesus had committed himself to fulfill a mission. His submission was an act of love for the Father and for us.)

• Could Jesus have spared himself from the sufferings and death imposed by his persecutors? (Yes. He said that he could have prayed to the Father and received more than twelve legions of angels to help him [see Matthew 26:52–54]. Also, he made it clear that no man could take his life from him, but rather he was giving his life himself [see John 10:18].)

Jesus Was Crucified

Read the following scripture, and show the bottom picture on page 61:

"And when they were come to the place, which is called Calvary, there they crucified him. . . .

"Then said Jesus, Father, forgive them; for they know not what they do." (Luke 23:33–34.)

- What do we learn about Jesus when we consider this statement, which he made while his persecutors were putting him to death? (We learn that he had love, even for those who were ignorant and wicked.)

- How does this make you feel?

Jesus Was Buried in the Tomb

When Jesus died on the cross that Friday many centuries ago, Joseph of Arimathaea and other disciples prepared his body and laid it in Joseph's sepulcher (see John 19:38–42).

- How do you think Joseph of Arimathaea and the others who loved Jesus felt as they took Jesus down from the cross?

Have the family express themselves freely, revealing how they themselves might have felt.

He Is Risen!

Jesus had power to take his body up again. He was resurrected and rose from the dead the next Sunday morning, the first day of the week. He was the first person to be resurrected, and he made it possible for all of us to someday be resurrected.

Read the following scripture:

"For as in Adam all die, even so in Christ shall all be made alive" (1 Corinthians 15:22).

- Does everyone who comes to this earth have to die? (Yes.)

- Do we have to believe in Adam for this to happen to us? (No.)

- Will all of us be resurrected? (Yes.)

- Do we have to believe in Christ to be resurrected? (No.)

Explain that the Savior freely gave this gift of the resurrection to all the children of our Heavenly Father. Have each family member express how he feels about this great gift.

LEARNING TO RECOGNIZE THE SPIRIT

Yea, ye have heard his voice from time to time; and he hath spoken unto you in a still small voice.
[1 Nephi 17:45]

PURPOSE

Help family members to recognize guidance from the Holy Ghost.

FOR THE PARENT

Think about the gifts of the Spirit. Would you like your family to know truth from error? Do you hope your children will learn to recognize answers to prayers? Would you like them to have a knowledge of spiritual things, to receive help in choosing wisely, to receive warnings of dangerous or harmful situations, and to gain the ability to teach and influence others? All of these great blessings and more come through the Holy Ghost (see 1 Corinthians 12:8–12, D&C 46:11–32).

Most members of the Lord's Church know that they have the right and privilege to the constant companionship and guidance of the Holy Ghost. But many of us still need to learn to make such guidance a part of our daily lives. Sometimes we even fail to recognize experiences that we do have with the Holy Ghost. Motivating your family to seek and listen to the promptings of the Spirit is one of the most important things you can do.

Prayerfully prepare this lesson so that you can receive the guidance of the Spirit as you teach your family. Remember that "the Spirit shall be given unto you by the prayer of faith" (D&C 42:14).

PREPARATION

1. Bring a poster and marker or chalkboard and chalk.

2. Paste a picture of a person on a sheet of paper. Beside the head write, "mind." Beside the chest write, "heart."

3. Prepare slips of paper with one of the following phrases on each: "Feeling pain," "Tasting salt," "Hearing music," "Seeing the color green," and "Smelling shoepolish."

4. Have family members bring their journals.

SUGGESTED HYMN AND SONG

"The Spirit of God Like a Fire" (*Hymns,* no. 213).
"The Still Small Voice" (*Sing with Me,* B–92).

SUGGESTED LESSON

Begin with the following story:

Following the Holy Spirit

"I was once saved from death or serious accident because my father hearkened to the voice of the Spirit. If he had not responded instantly to the whisperings of the still small voice, my life might have ended then or had its course totally changed.

"One of my earliest childhood recollections is of riding a horse through an apple orchard. The horse was tame and well broken, and I felt at home in the saddle.

"But one day something frightened my mount, and he bolted through the orchard. I was swept from the saddle by the overhanging limbs, and one leg slipped down through the stirrup. I desperately hung to an almost broken leather strap that a cowboy uses to tie a lariat to his saddle. My weight should have broken the strap, but somehow it held for the moment. Another lunge or two of the stampeding horse would have broken the strap or wrenched it from my hands and left me to be dragged to injury or death with my foot entangled in the stirrup.

"Suddenly the horse stopped, and I became aware that someone was holding the bridle tightly and attempting to calm the quivering animal. Almost immediately I was snatched up into the arms of my father.

"What had happened? What had brought my father to my rescue in the split second before I slipped beneath the hoofs of my panic-driven horse?

"My father had been sitting in the house reading the newspaper when the Spirit whispered to him, 'Run out into the orchard!'

"Without a moment's hesitation, not waiting to learn why or for what reason, my father ran. Finding himself in the orchard without knowing why he was there, he saw the galloping horse and thought, *I must stop this horse.*

"He did so and found me. And that is how I was saved from serious injury or possible death." (Bruce R. McConkie, "Hearken to the Spirit," *Friend*, Sept. 1972, pp. 10–11.)

We Need the Guidance of the Holy Ghost

- What prompted Elder McConkie's father to run into the orchard?
- Why did he respond to the prompting? (He recognized that the Holy Ghost was communicating with him.)

Tell your children that Heavenly Father knows each of us. He knows our names and our talents and he knows what is in our hearts. He wants each person to live his life successfully and to find true happiness. Explain that because of his great love for us, he has sent a special personage, the Holy Ghost, to be with us and help us (see 1 Nephi 10:17).

After we are baptized we receive the gift of the Holy Ghost to be our constant companion and guide if we live worthily and seek his help (see D&C 35:6, 121:46; Articles of Faith 1:4).

The Holy Ghost is a member of the Godhead (see 1 John 5:7, D&C 20:28). That means he works with our Heavenly Father. He wants us to have the same things that Heavenly Father has. It is his job to bring messages to us from our Father in Heaven. If we listen to the messages, we will get the help we need for our lives when we need it. This is why the Holy Ghost is so important to each one of us. He helps, teaches, and protects us so that we will not have to face the trials and temptations of the world alone.

On the chalkboard or poster list some ways the Holy Ghost helps, teaches, and protects us. Have your family name as many ways as they can. Be sure the following ideas are covered. The Holy Ghost—

1. Warns us of danger or evil (as in Elder McConkie's story).
2. Gives us our testimonies (Alma 5:46).
3. Helps us know and choose the right (D&C 11:12).
4. Helps us understand things (D&C 6:15).
5. Helps us recognize truth (Moroni 10:5).
6. Guides us in important decisions (2 Nephi 32:5).
7. Teaches us (John 14:26).

8. Inspires us (Luke 12:12).
9. Comforts us (Galatians 5:22).
10. Helps us remember things (John 14:26).
11. Helps us understand and communicate with each other (Alma 12:3).

Help your family understand that as they learn to be guided by the Spirit they will begin to perfect themselves.

Learning How the Holy Ghost Speaks to Us

It is through the power of the Holy Ghost that visions, dreams, and prophecies usually come. But most of the time when he speaks with us it is in a quiet, almost unnoticeable way. That is why we often refer to him as the still small voice. (See 1 Kings 19:11–12.)

Show your family the picture you prepared. Explain that the still small voice is not always a voice that we hear with our ears. Instead, it speaks in our minds and in our hearts. When we listen for it we are listening for a thought and searching our hearts for a feeling (see D&C 8:2). The thought and the feeling often come together. The feeling is of peace, right, and sureness. It is a warm, good feeling. (See D&C 9:8–9.) As long as we seek and follow these good thoughts and feelings from the Holy Ghost, we will continue to receive guidance.

Read 1 Nephi 17:45 together. Ask what Nephi meant when he told his brothers that they were past feeling the words of the still small voice. If we ignore the thoughts and feelings that we are given, they become weaker. Finally they cease coming altogether, and we will be left in darkness.

- What else might interfere with the working of the spirit in our lives? (Not keeping the commandments [see Helaman 4:24].)

We Can Recognize the Spirit

Have family members select one of the wordstrips that you have prepared. Let each of them imagine they are describing the sensation to someone who has never experienced it.

Afterward, explain that there are some things we can learn only through our own experiences. This is why we must make an effort to look for the guidance of the Spirit in our own lives. We must each learn to be so familiar with it that when we have an important need we will understand how to get guidance and help. The more experiences we have with the Spirit, the more confident we will feel about recognizing his presence.

Tell the following story:

Kevin Listens to the Spirit

Kevin and Todd were brothers. They were also best friends. But lately something was wrong, and Kevin didn't know what it was. Todd was not at all easy to get along with. He had been very unkind to Kevin. Kevin wondered if he had made Todd angry until he realized that Todd was acting that way with everyone. Kevin tried harder to be kind to Todd, but his efforts were wasted. Todd just didn't seem to want to be Kevin's friend anymore.

One evening, Kevin and Todd argued. Kevin felt both angry and ashamed. He felt that Todd was acting impossible, but he also knew that he wasn't trying very hard himself anymore. He didn't like things this way. He wanted to be friends again.

That night as he prayed, Kevin asked Heavenly Father to help him improve his relationship with Todd again. He promised that he would rebuild his friendship with Todd if only he knew how. He also told Heavenly Father that he was sorry for the wrong things he had done to Todd.

As he climbed into bed, Kevin thought about the problem. He wondered what Heavenly Father would want him to do. Then he thought, "Go tell Todd that you love him." Kevin knew he couldn't do that! Love was shown in his home but not in that way—especially between brothers. He started to push the thought away, but it came again, "Go tell Todd that you love him."

Suddenly Kevin remembered that the Holy Ghost spoke through thoughts. He wondered if the Holy Ghost was speaking to him. Even as he began to wonder, he had a warm feeling and knew that his prayers were being answered.

Knowing that he must obey, he slipped out of bed and tiptoed to Todd's room. His heart pounded and he felt tense. He wondered why it should seem so hard to do such a simple thing.

"Todd," he said.

"What do you want?" asked a gruff voice from the dark.

"Todd, I . . . I want you to know that I love you."

For a minute there was no sound. Kevin thought maybe he had made a mistake. Then Todd quietly replied, "I love you, too."

Kevin felt relieved and happy. He sat down on Todd's bed, and they began to talk. Soon they worked out their problems and felt closer than ever before.

- How did Kevin know that he was being guided by the Spirit?

- Why was Kevin able to get the Spirit? (He cared. He prayed. He thought about his problem. He lived worthy of help.)

Explain that the still small voice came to Kevin as a thought on how to solve his problem. Sometimes it comes as a thought or a feeling that we shouldn't do something we're about to do. We may be looking for something and suddenly think of the place to look. Or we may suddenly understand something that has been unclear to us or know that something is true.

Explain that sometimes, even though we have prayed for help, we don't recognize our thoughts and feelings as coming from the Holy Ghost in answer to our prayer. Discuss how sometimes we might feel confused about what is our imagination and what is the Holy Ghost. We must remember that if the thought is good and tells us to do what is right, then it comes from God (see Moroni 7:13), and we should follow it. Read the first sentence of Ether 4:12 together.

Explain that as long as we do what we really feel is right, we will feel peaceful and happy. As we pray for help and look for it, we will find it easier to recognize the still small voice of the Holy Ghost, and we will become more familiar with it.

Times We Have Been Helped By the Spirit

Let your family share experiences they have had with the Holy Ghost. Relate a personal experience. But remember that spiritual experiences are sacred and should not be talked about unless we feel prompted by the Holy Ghost.

Challenge them to begin to watch for times when the still small voice whispers to them. Encourage them to record spiritual experiences in their journals. Give them a few minutes at the end of the lesson to record any experiences they have had.

Look up Alma 37:37, and read it together. Bring out that we can always be directed in our lives by our Heavenly Father.

- How does this direction come? (Through the Holy Ghost.)

Bear your testimony of the importance of listening to the Spirit. Point out that they might have felt warm, good feelings during this lesson and that those feelings were from the Holy Ghost telling them that the things they were hearing were true.

ADAPTING FOR
YOUNGER CHILDREN

Tell your children that Heavenly Father knows each of them. He loves them and wants them to be happy. He has given us someone who helps us choose what is right and helps us when we have a problem. He is the Holy Ghost. We do not see him or hear his voice, but he can quietly put ideas into our minds and feelings in our hearts. The Holy Ghost is a loving, friendly helper who helps us to choose the right. He can help us in many different ways.

Tell the following stories:

Jamie Is Lost

Jamie was lost. He and his family had gone on a hike. He saw a squirrel and started to chase it. When he couldn't catch it, he tried to find his family, but they were gone. Jamie was afraid. He remembered that his Primary teacher had told his class to pray if they were ever in trouble or afraid. So Jamie said a prayer and asked Heavenly Father to help him find his family. Jamie didn't feel so afraid anymore. He felt as though someone was helping him, so he started to walk down the hill. Soon he heard his father calling his name. He called back, and his father came running. Jamie was glad he had prayed, and he knew Heavenly Father had helped him.

Car Trouble

The Holt family left for their vacation. They were excited about taking a trip. After about an hour, their car began to sound funny. Father stopped the car along the side of the road. He got out to see what was wrong. When he got back in the car it would not start. Everyone was worried. The small children started to cry. Mother said, "Let's say a prayer." Father asked Heavenly Father in the prayer to help them know what was wrong with the car and to help them know everything would be okay. After the prayer everyone in the family felt good. They knew things would be all right. The children stopped crying. Soon another car stopped and some kind people helped father fix the car. Soon the Holts were on their way again.

In each of the stories someone needed help.

- How did they get it? (They prayed.)

- Who helped them? (Heavenly Father sent the Holy Ghost to help them.)

- How did the Holy Ghost help? (He put thoughts in their mind, made them feel better, or helped them not be afraid. He also prompted other people to help.)

Explain that the Holy Ghost can help us in many different ways. If we need help, we can pray to Heavenly Father, and the Holy Ghost will help us.

ADAPTING FOR TEENAGERS AND ADULTS

Some families have had experiences listening to the Holy Ghost and still do not have a clear understanding of how the Spirit works. The following questions may help you discover and meet the individual needs of your family. They will help you evaluate what needs to be taught. If your family members do have a good understanding of how the Spirit works, use

the questions for a discussion. Remind your family to work for the blessings of the Holy Ghost constantly.

Use the questions only to get them thinking of their personal need to learn about the Holy Ghost. Then go on to teach the regular lesson. Be familiar with all of the material in the lesson so that you can give it easily if you observe a need to do so.

1. How often do you have experiences with the Holy Ghost?

2. Do you feel satisfied that these experiences come as often as they should?

3. Do you feel that you receive personal revelation to guide your life?

4. What does having the Holy Ghost as your constant companion mean? (Worthy Church members may rely on the Holy Ghost to help them meet significant problems in life.)

5. Do you feel that the Holy Ghost is your constant companion?

6. Do you feel that having the constant companionship of the Holy Ghost is a realistic goal?

7. Have you ever been through a period of time when you felt that you did have the constant companionship of the Holy Ghost?

8. What can you do to help you be closer to the guidance of the Holy Ghost?

9. How can you tell the difference between the promptings of the Holy Ghost and your own imagination?

10. For what kinds of things do we need the guidance and help of the Holy Ghost?

11. What kinds of things might Heavenly Father expect us to decide and solve for ourselves?

Explain that Heavenly Father has given us the Holy Ghost to help us live our lives successfully. He was not meant to be a reward for when we are perfect. Learning to be guided by the Holy Ghost is, in fact, neccessary to help us reach perfection.

Consider using the story of Elder McConkie, making the list of things the Holy Ghost does for us, showing the picture with the indication of

mind and heart, and telling the story of Kevin. All of these would be interesting to teenagers and adults if used effectively.

Conclude with the discussion and challenge under "Times We Have Been Helped By the Spirit."

SUGGESTIONS FOR FUTURE HOME EVENINGS

Understanding the Holy Ghost

Using the book *Gospel Principles* [PBIC0245], chapter 7, "The Holy Ghost," pages 33 through 35, and chapter 21, "The Gift of the Holy Ghost," pages 131 through 134, discuss the following:

- Who is the Holy Ghost?

- What is his relationship to the Father and the Son?

- Why is the influence of the Holy Ghost necessary in our lives?

- What is the gift of the Holy Ghost?

- How do we obtain this gift?

Family members may wish to find scriptures to help answer these questions. Some scriptures are quoted in *Gospel Principles*.

Using the Gift of the Holy Ghost

Have family members list some important decisions they will be making in their lives, such as taking a job, deciding on further education, deciding whom to marry, or accepting calls to service. Ask family members to suggest ways of reaching wise decisions about the listed items.

Have someone read Doctrine and Covenants 9:8–9 and 6:22–23. Revise where necessary the family's earlier suggestions about how to make decisions to include the counsel the Lord gives in these scriptures.

You may wish to read and discuss the following comments by Elder Boyd K. Packer:

"Put difficult questions in the back of your minds and go about your lives. Ponder and pray quietly and persistently about them.

"The answer may not come as a lightning bolt. It may come as a little inspiration here and a little there, 'line upon line, precept upon precept' (D&C 98:12).

"Some answers will come from reading the scriptures, some from hearing speakers. And, occasionally, when it is important, some will come by very direct and powerful inspiration. The promptings will be clear and unmistakable." (In Conference Report, Oct. 1979, p. 30; or *Ensign*, Nov. 1979, p. 21.)

Recognizing the Promptings of the Spirit

Ask one or more family members in advance to find experiences from the lives of their ancestors or others in which the promptings of the Spirit brought needed guidance or comfort into someone's life. They could seek such experiences out of family histories, the scriptures, or Church books. Have family members relate these experiences about how the Holy Ghost has led others. You may wish to emphasize the great love our Heavenly Father has for us, which leads him to provide us with this great gift.

Distinguishing Between Our Desires and the Promptings of the Spirit

Sometimes our own hopes and desires are so strong that they may seem right and we may mistake them for the promptings of the Spirit. Introduce this idea by telling a story in which someone prays for guidance and then makes a decision in keeping with his own desires, which are obviously not in keeping with the gospel. End the story by asking family members what went wrong. Use this example for a discussion on how we can tell the difference between our own wants and the whisperings of the Spirit.

Have family members suggest some signs of true promptings of the Spirit, besides a burning in the bosom. The suggestions might include—

1. The promptings do not violate any gospel principles, such as the free agency of another.

2. The promptings are in harmony with the teachings of the scripture and of the prophets.

3. The promptings are in harmony with the order of the Church.

4. The promptings bring peace to the soul.

5. The promptings do not raise doubts and questions.

6. The promptings result in lasting happiness when we follow them.

7. The promptings may be contrary to our desires when we have asked for the wrong things.

Remembering How the Holy Ghost Has Helped

Tell the family you are going to give them a short quiz. Then give each family member a blank sheet of paper and let him divide it into four columns. As a heading to each column write, "Number," "Yes," "No," "Not sure." In the number column have each person list the numbers 1 through 13.

As you read the following questions, have each family member indicate whether he has experienced the feeling described by checking either yes, no, or not sure:

1. Have you ever had a strong inward feeling or witness while reading the scriptures that they were of God?

2. Do you believe strongly that Joseph Smith was a prophet of God or that our present prophet is the Lord's prophet.

3. Do you feel that the Spirit has guided you to love your friends or members of your family more by helping you to forgive them or to help them?

4. Have you ever felt that you have been given an answer to a prayer and directed in your mind as to what you should do?

5. Do you believe strongly that you lived before you were mortal and that there is life after death?

6. Have you ever been inspired in a talk or discussion to explain a principle better than you could have on your own?

7. Do you have an assurance that Jesus is the Savior of the world?

8. Do you know that he is indeed the Son of God?

9. Have you felt during a general conference, a sacrament meeting, or other Church gathering that your priesthood leaders were influenced by divine power?

10. Have you ever felt the Spirit while someone was administered to, or have you been spiritually uplifted during the sacrament or the performance of a priesthood ordinance?

11. Have you ever felt God's love for you or experienced a closeness to him at some particular time?

12. During a time of repentance have you felt the witness of the Spirit that you were forgiven?

13. Have you felt a comforting spirit during a time of bereavement, sorrow, or personal difficulty?

Explain that each of these experiences is an example of the promptings of the Holy Ghost. Have family members think about times they have been influenced by the Holy Ghost using these thirteen questions as a guide.

Then ask family members to tell briefly about one of the experiences or to bear their testimony.

Learning to Commune with the Spirit

Commune means to communicate intimately. It includes both talking and listening. Read and discuss the following statement by Elder H. Burke Peterson:

"Listening is an essential part of praying. Answers from the Lord come quietly—ever so quietly. In fact, few hear his anwers audibly with their ears. We must be listening so carefully or we will never recognize them. Most answers from the Lord are felt in our heart as a warm comfortable expression, or they may come as thoughts to our mind. They come to those who are prepared and who are patient." (In Conference Report, Oct. 1973, p. 13; or *Ensign*, Jan. 1974, p. 19.)

• How do you pray?

• Do you ever take time to listen for the Spirit's answers?

Suggest that, as an experiment during the next week, family members set aside a few minutes during or after their morning and evening prayers to listen for the promptings or the influence of the Spirit. Suggest that they ponder the experiences they have. Some may wish to record these experiences in their journals. Suggest that they remember to thank their Heavenly Father in their next prayers for the comforting influence of the Spirit.

GAINING A TESTIMONY THROUGH THE HOLY GHOST

For he that diligently seeketh shall find; and the mysteries of God shall be unfolded to them, by the power of the Holy Ghost.
[1 Nephi 10:19]

PURPOSE

Help family members realize that the Holy Ghost can help them develop a testimony if they sincerely desire it.

FOR THE PARENT

We must receive a testimony of the gospel by revelation through the Holy Ghost. It doesn't just happen. We have to work and live for it. We have to study and practice the gospel principles and pray to our Father in Heaven for that knowledge.

Perhaps more than anything you would like to give your children a testimony of the gospel. But every person must get a testimony for himself, and this is not always easy. Although you cannot give your children a testimony, you can inspire them to desire one. Many young people have a testimony and do not realize it. You can help them realize they have one.

PREPARATION

1. Have family members prepared in advance to take one or two minutes to tell about something they wanted very much and how they worked to get it.
2. Get some fast growing seeds. Prepare containers (planter boxes, flower pots, or plastic or paper cups) in which you can plant these seeds.

SUGGESTED HYMN AND SONG

"I Know That My Redeemer Lives" (*Hymns*, no. 95).
"I Know My Father Lives" (*Sing with Me*, B–39).

SUGGESTED LESSON

We Work Hard for Something We Really Want

Ask each family member to take one or two minutes to tell of something they wanted and what they did to get it. If they can't think of anything, tell the following story:

Christopher's Puppy

Nine-year-old Christopher went shopping with his mother. At the pet store, he saw a puppy that he wanted. He asked his mother to buy it for him. She told him if he really wanted it, he would have to earn his own money to buy it. His mother told Christopher that a puppy required lots of care and attention and Christopher would have to be responsible for doing this.

Christopher wanted the puppy very much, so for the next several weeks he did every job he could find for his parents and neighbors to earn the money. He was very excited when he finally had enough money to buy the puppy.

He enjoyed the puppy and took good care of it. He learned that it took lots of work to keep it healthy and happy.

Tell your family that they are going to learn about something that is much more important than a pet or any

wordly possession. It is something that no one can injure or take without their consent. It is something that will influence our lives forever. It is a testimony.

- Why would you want a testimony? (Bring out that a testimony can give us purpose, peace, and joy in our lives.)

How We Can Gain a Testimony

Help your family define a testimony. Guide them to discover that it is a knowledge of the reality of God, the Eternal Father, and his Son, Jesus Christ. This testimony can come only by revelation through the Holy Ghost.

- Can our parents, brothers, sisters, or friends give us a testimony?
- What can we do to gain our own testimony?

Help your family bring out the following points:

1. The first step in gaining a testimony is to *want* one (see 1 Nephi 2:16).
2. We must *ask* our Heavenly Father to help us gain a testimony (see D&C 42:51).
3. We must want a testimony enough that we are willing to *work* to gain one (see Ether 12:6).
4. We will *enjoy* our testimony as we study and grow and increase in our knowledge of the truth (see John 8:32).
5. We must *care* for our most prized possession, our testimony, by keeping the commandments of our Heavenly Father (see Mosiah 2:41, Alma 32:41).

- When a person strongly desires a testimony, what must he do?

In the discussion include attending church meetings, listening attentively, living the gospel principles taught at church, studying the scriptures to gain a greater knowledge of these truths, and fasting and praying—praying in faith that you will learn the truth by revelation through the power of the Holy Ghost (see Alma 5:45–47).

Gaining a Testimony Is an Ongoing Process

We must not be discouraged if it takes a long time to gain a testimony. Many have this problem, but they are stronger after struggling. The testimony they gain is worth the struggle.

In the Book of Mormon we read about Alma who was a great and righteous leader. He told his people that the gospel (the word of God) is like a seed that needs caring for every day so it will grow (Alma 32:28–43). Our testimony of Heavenly Father is like that seed. We must care for it every day.

Alma continued to say that if a tree is just beginning to grow, we will nourish it with great care so that it will grow more roots and produce fruit. But if we neglect it and do not nourish it, it will not bear fruit.

Encourage the family to nourish the word of the Lord in them, thinking of the fruit that will come—everlasting life.

Have one of the family read Moroni 10:4 aloud.

Then have another member of the family read what President Spencer W. Kimball said of this scripture:

"That is no casual promise. It is a positive one, and every soul in this world may have a revelation. . . . That revelation will be a testimony, a knowledge that Christ lives, that Jesus Christ is the Redeemer of this world. Every soul may have this assurance, and when he gets this testimony, it will have come from God and not from study alone. Study is an important element, of course, but there must be associated with study much prayer and reaching, and then this revelation comes." ("President Kimball Speaks Out on Testimony," *New Era*, Aug. 1981, p. 4.)

Tell your family the following story in your own words:

Rose

Rose lived in a small city in Germany. She was only fourteen years old when she first met some Mormons. As she listened to them, she became interested in many of the doctrines of the Church, but she did not know if the Church was true. Her friends and even her parents began to turn against her because she associated with the Mormons.

When Rose was sixteen years old, some of her Mormon friends told her President David O. McKay was going to come to Hamburg. They were very excited and talked about nothing else. They all started to save their money for their train fare to Hamburg. Some of the members asked Rose to go with them. She was very interested in the Church and felt she just had to see this man that the Mormons told her was a prophet. She had such a strong desire to see the prophet that she felt she would do almost anything to make the trip.

The Saturday arrived that President McKay was to come, and still Rose did not have permission to go. Her father, thinking she could not possibly get any money or a way to go, told Rose, "If you can get the money to go, try it."

Rose hurried to work and told her boss she wanted to go to Hamburg. She told him her train left at 3:00 P.M. and she would get all of her work

done before she left. Rose said, "I prayed hard all that day. A prophet was coming, and I needed to know the truth."

She watched the clock, upset when it was 2:40, and her boss had still not given her permission to leave.

When he thought it was too late for her to make the 3:00 P.M. train, her boss said, "Why don't you see how far you can get to see your prophet?"

Rose ran hard to get to the station. She still had no ticket and no money. When she got to the ticket counter, the clerk selling tickets said, "Go right on in, Rose." Her father was a railroad official, and the ticket agent had seen Rose with her father and recognized her. When Rose came to the platform, the train was ready to pull out. She still had no ticket.

Someone said, "Hi, Rose. Are you going to Hamburg?" Rose turned and there stood one of her father's friends who was the conductor of the train. Rose told him she was going, but she had no pass. He said, "That's okay Rose. I'll take you to Hamburg because I know your father, but you won't have a way back home because no one in Hamburg knows you."

Rose hurriedly got on the train and sat down. She was so exhausted from running so hard that she just trembled and cried. She got to Hamburg and still had to find the convention hall where the prophet was to speak. Again she had to run all the way because she had no money for bus or train fare.

When she arrived at the convention hall, she found a place by a window where she could stand. The building was crowded with people. Suddenly she saw a movement, and the whole congregation stood up as if they were one person. They began singing, "We thank thee, O God, for a prophet." Rose said, "I saw a man with white hair smiling kindly. No voice told me. But a feeling engulfed my whole being; and I *knew* that this man whom I had never met before, never spoken to before, nor even heard speak was a prophet of God. The Holy Ghost made it known to me.

"Little did I realize that this testimony would in time cause me to lose my

family and my friends. But no matter what, I knew this man was a prophet of God, and I could not deny it."

Rose's two years of studying, fasting, and praying were not in vain; her desire to know was fulfilled. She had received this witness from the Holy Ghost.

Our Own Testimony

Explain to your family that our testimony from the Holy Ghost may not come as dramatically as Rose's did, but if we earnestly desire, seek, and pray, we will receive the same witness.

Explain that some of us come to that understanding in a different way. Tell the story of Charles or one like it, and have your family identify how he received his testimony:

Charles

Charles and Ruth were members of the Church, and everyone considered them good, active members. They enjoyed the meetings and frequently commented on the spirit that seemed to prevail in the Church gatherings.

One day after fast and testimony meeting, Charles said, "Why don't I have a testimony like others in our ward seem to have? They are always eager to bear testimony to the truths of the gospel—that the Book of Mormon is true, that Joseph Smith was a prophet, that Jesus is the Christ, that God lives. Why can't I say those things? I guess I just don't have a testimony."

Ruth responded, "You do have a testimony."

"If I do, why don't I get up and say so? Why do I feel that I don't have one?" countered Charles.

The discussion was dropped, and the days and months passed by for Charles and Ruth without much change.

One day their young son, Mark, was involved in a bicycle accident and was rushed to the hospital. When Charles and Ruth arrived at the hospital and saw the condition of their son, Charles quickly said, "Ruth, I'm going to call our home teacher, Brother Reed, and have him come help me administer to Mark."

Soon Brother Reed arrived, and they gave Mark a blessing. In time the

bruises and broken bones healed, and Mark was able to move about normally.

Ruth and Charles often spoke about the accident. Once Ruth asked, "Charles, why did you call Brother Reed to help you bless Mark?"

"Because," replied Charles, "I knew that we held the priesthood and that if we blessed Mark he would be well again."

"I thought you said that you didn't have a testimony. Charles, don't you see that you called Brother Reed because you do have a testimony, or you wouldn't have had that faith."

Charles thought a moment, and then smiling with surprise he said, "I do, don't I? I knew Mark would be all right. I do have a testimony!"

• How did Charles get his testimony? (In a slow, quiet way as he lived the gospel each day.)

• What showed that Charles desired a testimony and that he earned it?

Discuss this with your family. Remind them that in the first story you talked about, Christopher's desire for a puppy was so great that he was willing to work hard to earn money for it. He cared for his puppy daily and enjoyed it. Help them realize that the worth of a testimony is not to be compared in any way to the worth of any worldly possession, but the story pointed out how important desire is in obtaining and nurturing a testimony.

Bear your testimony of how you desired to have a testimony, how you now desire to know the gospel is true, or how you desire that your testimony will grow.

After you are through, have your family plant the seeds. Compare this to the growth of a testimony.

• What must we do to make the seeds grow? (Give them sunlight and water.)

• What must we do to make our testimonies grow? (Study, pray, and live the gospel principles.)

Plant the seeds in several containers. After the seeds begin to sprout, put one container in a dark closet for a few days and see what happens to the plant. Then don't water another container for a day or two and see what happens to it. The seeds will start to shrivel and die. As this happens, explain to the family that this is what will happen to their testimonies if they don't do the right things to keep them growing. Have a time each day when you water your seeds, put them in the sun, and watch them grow. Reinforce the importance of doing something *each day* to help your testimonies grow.

ADAPTING FOR YOUNGER CHILDREN

Although the word *testimony* is a big word, you can explain to small children that it means to know that something is real.

- What does *real* mean? (Something that is not pretend or is not make-believe. Something that is true.)
- Is your shirt (or any other article of clothing) real?
- Is the chair you are sitting on real?
- How do you know they are real? (You can see them and feel them.)
- Is the sun real?
- How do you know it is real? (You can see it in the sky, and you can feel its warm rays when it shines on you. Even if you couldn't see it, you would still know it was real because you can feel the warmth from its rays.)

Show your children the Bible.

- Is this book real?

Tell them the book is. Explain that the Bible tells us about Heavenly Father and his Son, Jesus Christ. We know they are real because the Bible tells us they are, but there is another way we can tell they are real just as there is more than one way we can tell if the sun is real. That way is a testimony or a feeling we get inside us when the Holy Ghost tells us these things are true. It is a good, warm feeling inside us. When we do what is right, we get that good, warm feeling. When we help someone or do what our mother or father wants us to do we get that feeling. That is the Holy Ghost letting us know that Heavenly Father and Jesus Christ are real.

- Can you think of a time when you had that good, warm feeling inside of you?

Direct your children in their answers toward a time when they had a special experience that made them feel good. If they can't think of anything, tell the following story:

Lindsay's New Brother

Five-year-old Lindsay could hardly wait for her father to bring her mother and new baby brother home from the hospital. Even though she enjoyed having grandmother stay with her, she still missed her mother. When she heard the car, she ran out the front door as fast as she could. It seemed it took her father forever to get her mother and the new baby in the house. When her mother was all settled on the couch, her grandmother told Lindsay to sit in the big chair.

"Would you like to hold your new brother?" grandmother asked Lindsay as she placed the baby on her lap. "Lindsay, you know this baby boy was with Heavenly Father just a few short days ago. Heavenly Father sent him to our family to love, guide, and train. You must always be kind and good to him."

As Lindsay held her new brother and looked at him, she had a good, warm feeling inside. She knew Heavenly Father had sent her little brother to their family.

Bear your testimony to your children. Tell them of things that make you know that Heavenly Father and Jesus are real. Encourage your children to tell of things that make them know Heavenly Father is real, and explain to them that this is a testimony.

Each day when you help your children with their prayers, ask them what has happened that day to help them know that Heavenly Father is real. Keep reminding them that the feeling they have that he is real is called a testimony.

ADAPTING FOR TEENAGERS AND ADULTS

You may want to start by telling your family the story of Christopher. Ask them to identify what in the story parallels the steps in gaining a testimony as they listen.

Read and discuss Alma 32:28–43 in depth. Also encourage your family to

participate in a discussion about Moroni 10:4 and President Kimball's statement regarding this scripture.

Tell your family the story of Rose. After you have talked about Rose receiving the witness from the Holy Ghost that David O. McKay was a prophet, continue the story:

Rose (Continued)

For seventeen-year-old Rose to be baptized when her parents gave their consent so reluctantly was very difficult for her. She had been raised in a religious home and had always been taught to honor her father and mother. Now she was going against their desires. Her parents allowed her to live at home after she was baptized, but there was little communication between them.

When Rose turned eighteen, her branch president called her on a local mission. Her parents were very upset and told her that if she went they would no longer consider her their daughter. Rose was torn, but she finally decided to go. She served a mission, never missing a week of writing to her parents, but she never heard from them.

After her mission, she did not return to her hometown but got a job in another city. She met a young man who was a member of the Church, and they were married in the Swiss Temple. She sent word to her parents, still she heard nothing from them. She continued to write faithfully to her parents although they never answered her letters.

Finally, nine years after she was baptized, she heard from her parents. Her father had had a heart attack. He was afraid he was going to die, and he wanted to see his daughter again. Rose says of those years when she was separated from her parents whom she loved dearly, "It was very difficult for me. I never doubted or wondered if I had made the right choice. I had had the witness from the Holy Ghost that the Church was true, and there was no choice to be made. I had to do the things I did because I knew it was true and I knew God knew that I knew it was true!"

President Spencer W. Kimball has

told us, "You have to *fight* for a testimony. You have to *keep* fighting!" ("President Kimball Speaks Out on Testimony," *New Era*, Aug. 1981, p. 6.)

• What does his statement mean to you?

Discuss your own testimonies as suggested in the regular lesson.

SUGGESTIONS FOR FUTURE HOME EVENINGS

The Testimonies of Others

Invite grandparents in for an evening, or make arrangements to go to their home. Let the grandparents tell of their experience in having a witness or guidance from the Holy Ghost in their lives. Let your family ask questions so that the discussion will help them realize how the Holy Ghost may work to help them in their own lives. Relate experiences that you have had with the Holy Ghost.

Be sure to create a reverent atmosphere for this lesson.

Compiling a Family Record of Inspiration

Have each family member record in writing an experience where he received inspiration or promptings from the Holy Ghost. Children can refer to their confirmation. You may need to help them with the ideas and writing.

After reading the experiences during family home evening, bind them in a folder so they can be reread by family members at other times. As family members have further inspirational experiences they may wish to add them to the folder.

Inviting the Holy Ghost to Be with Us

After discussing or explaining how important it is that we have the Holy Ghost with us always, have family members suggest items for a list of things we might do that would restrain the Spirit and a list of those things that would bring us closer to the Spirit and build our testimonies. After completing the lists, find scriptures that complement the things listed (see the example below).

Gaining a Testimony Through Scriptural Examples

Make a list of persons in the scriptures who gained a testimony. Discuss such items as what they did, how old they were, and how the witness came. Some examples might be—

1. Samuel (1 Samuel 3).
2. Moroni (Mormon 1:13–15).
3. Joseph Smith (Joseph Smith—History 1:1–20).
4. Nephi and Sam (1 Nephi 2:16–24).

Then explain that each person must gain a testimony in his own way but that each person is entitled to a testimony if he seeks it sincerely and hoenstly. Parents of young children may want to use the illustrated books of scripture stories published by the Church.

The Difference between Testimony and Conversion

Discuss the following passages from an address by Elder Marion G. Romney:

"Membership in the Church and conversion are not necessarily synonymous. Being converted, as we are here using the term, and having a testimony are not necessarily the same thing either. A testimony comes when the Holy Ghost gives the earnest seeker a witness of the truth. A moving testimony vitalizes faith; that is, it induces repentance and obedience to the commandments. Conversion, on the other hand, is the fruit of, or the reward for, repentance and obedience. (Of course one's testimony continues to increase as he is converted.)

"Conversion is effected by divine forgiveness, which remits sins. The sequence is something like this. An honest seeker hears the message. He asks the Lord in prayer if it is true. The Holy Spirit gives him a witness. This is a testimony. If one's testimony is strong enough, he repents and obeys the commandments. By such obedience he receives divine forgiveness which remits sin. Thus he is converted to a newness of life. His spirit is healed. . . .

"Somebody recently asked how one could know when he is converted. The answer is simple. He may be assured of it when by the power of the Holy Spirit his soul is healed. When this occurs, he will recognize it by the way he feels, for he will feel as the people of Benjamin felt when they received remission of sins. The record says, ' . . . the Spirit of the Lord came upon them, and they were filled with joy, having received a remission of their sins, and having peace of conscience, . . . ' (Mosiah 4:3.) . . .

"Getting people's spirits healed through conversion is the only way they can be healed. I know this is an unpopular doctrine and a slow way to solve the problems of men and nations. . . . Nevertheless, I know and solemnly witness that there is no other means by which the sin-sick souls of men can be healed or for a troubled world to find peace." (In Conference Report, Oct. 1963, pp. 24–26.)

Things That Restrain the Spirit	Things That Invite the Spirit	Scriptures
Speaking unkind or harsh words in anger.	Working through a serious problem, using consideration and kindness in guiding the discussion.	"Wherefore, my beloved brethren, let every man be swift to hear, slow to speak, slow to wrath: "For the wrath of man worketh not the righteousness of God. . . . "If any man among you seems to be religious, and bridleth not his tongue, but deceiveth his own heart, this man's religion is vain." (James 1:19–20, 26.)

LOVE AT HOME

A new commandment I give unto you, That ye love one another; as I have loved you, that ye also love one another.
[John 13:34]

PURPOSE

Help family members show greater love and appreciation for each other.

FOR THE PARENT

Often it seems easier to be kind to people we hardly know than to our own family members, the people we love the most. Sometimes we can be thoughtless and even cruel to our family by our words and actions.

The Savior taught us to love one another as he loves us. He loves us even when we are not doing everything we should. We should learn to love our own family members in this same way.

PREPARATION

1. Write a note to each member of your family, telling each one why he is special to you and that you love him. Put each note where the person can easily find it during the day of the home evening, such as in a lunch pail, on a pillow, or in a pocket.
2. Make a chart similar to the chart entitled "Love one Another," which accompanies this lesson.
3. Have a pencil and paper for each person.

SUGGESTED HYMN AND SONGS

"There Is Beauty All Around" (*Hymns*, no. 169).
"A Happy Family" (*Sing with Me*, D–1).
"Love One Another" (lesson 36, "He Is Risen").

SUGGESTED LESSON

If Jesus Came to Visit Us

Begin the lesson by asking the following questions:

- How would you feel if Jesus came to visit us in our home?
- Would we want to change the way we act toward each other?

Explain that the Savior would be unhappy if family members were not kind and loving to each other. He cares about each one of us and wants us to feel the love that he and Heavenly Father have for us. We cannot feel their love and support in our home when family members do not show love and kindness.

Inviting the Spirit of the Lord into Our House

Find out if the family members discovered the notes that you wrote. Have each family member tell how he felt when he read his note.

- In what way did it affect your day?

Explain that when we express our love for one another, even in little things, both the receiver and the giver feel good inside.

Explain that when we show our love and appreciation for one another at home we also help bring a good spirit into the home. This is the kind of feeling our Heavenly Father and Jesus want us to have in our home. This is why we were commanded to love one another. A happy home is one that is filled with love, one that invites the Spirit of the Lord to be there. (See Galatians 5:13–14, Ephesians 5:25, 1 John 4:7.)

Tell the following story:

A Family Night

It was almost time for family home evening in the Reynolds home.

Jeanette was busy in the kitchen taking the last batch of hot cookies out of the oven. She had worked all afternoon to prepare refreshments. Father called all the children to come into the living room.

Debby, Jeanette's little sister, ran down the stairs and grabbed a handful of cookies on her way through the kitchen. Jeanette angrily caught her blouse sleeve as she dashed past, and the sleeve ripped. Debby hollered, "Look what you did!"

"Well, if you had just asked first," cried Jeanette. "It's not my fault."

Soon the two girls were arguing, and mother had to come into the kitchen to stop them. She became upset herself when she saw Debby's torn blouse.

Finally father got everyone into the living room together. Debby sat down in one corner of the room, and Jeanette in the other. Even after the opening prayer, everyone in the family felt uncomfortable. The warm spirit they usually felt during their family nights was not there.

During the lesson mother brought some photo albums out and handed them to the children. "I thought you might enjoy looking through these old pictures tonight," she said.

Everyone gathered together to see the pictures. The little children were especially excited to see themselves. They laughed and pointed whenever they found themselves in a picture. Mother held up a picture of Debby and Jeanette when they were little. "Remember when you two got into my oil paints?" she asked. The girls had to laugh when they saw themselves in the picture covered with red and blue paint.

Soon all the family was caught up in

reminiscing. Even Jeanette and Debby talked about the fun times they had together on their camping trip.

The spirit had changed. Everyone in the family could feel the spirit of love in their home again. When they knelt together in prayer, they felt the Spirit of the Lord with them.

• What happened to the spirit in the Reynolds home when the children started arguing?

Have someone read Mosiah 4:14.

• How did this affect their family home evening at first?

• Why did the spirit change when everyone started sharing good thoughts and acting kindly to one another again?

• Why is it important that we try to be thoughtful and loving to each other in our home?

Explain to your family that, just as in the Reynold's home, when family members are kind and loving toward one another, the Lord's Spirit can also be in their home. But when they argue or are angry with one another, the Spirit leaves.

A Game About Love

Without revealing the name of the person, have family members tell of an incident in which another family member demonstrated love. Each person could begin by saying, "I'm thinking about someone that did . . . to show his love." Have the other family members guess who the loving family member is. Make sure that everyone has a turn and that each member is used as an example of love so that no one feels left out.

When It Is Hard to Show Love

Explain that it is easy to be polite and kind to friends and people we don't have to live with, but it is not always easy to be kind and loving to those closest to us, our own family members. Sometimes a family member may say or do something that offends another family member, which may result in bad feelings. We can overcome those bad feelings and learn to be more loving toward one another if we really try. (See 1 Corinthians 13:4.)

Use the following story to show how expressing love helps us overcome negative feelings toward each other:

It Works

"I will not iron your shirt. Iron it yourself," Sybil said to her brother Phillip, who was two years younger than she.

"No, you won't iron mine, but you'd jump at a chance to iron a shirt for Tim Cruthers," retorted Phil as he ran outside.

"It worries me, Sybil," mother said, "to see you and Phillip treat each other the way you do."

"Oh, he makes me so mad that I can't stand him!"

"Would you be willing to try an experiment—just you—without his knowing anything about it?"

"Tell me what it is first."

Mother challenged her, "No matter what Phil does or says, you do and say only those things that show your love for him. See what happens. I'll be an interested observer."

"Oh, that would be hard. I'm not sure I could do it. Do you think he'd change? It would be good to have a brother who was a friend. You know, Marianne and her brother have the best relationship with each other. Maybe she can give me some pointers. I'll think about it, mother."

On her way to school next morning, Sybil stopped at Marianne's house so they could walk together as usual. Marianne was carrying a heavy load of posters. As they came out, Phil passed by. Sybil called out to him, "Oh Phil, please carry my books so I can help Marianne with these posters."

"Yes, I will, just like you ironed my shirt."

"I'm sorry about that. I'll iron it tonight."

But Phil showed no signs of having heard her.

Having missed lunch that day to prepare for a test, Sybil was very hungry when she got home. She made herself a sandwich. Just as she was about to take a bite, Phil came in and said, "Hey, Syb, make one of those for me."

She opened her mouth to say, "Yes, just like you carried my books," but instead she said, "Here take this one. I'll make myself another."

Phil looked shocked. He grabbed the sandwich and ran.

A few days later, mother said to Sybil, "I think it's beginning to work, though Phil is still suspicious of your motives."

Sybil shook her head, "I think I feel a little better toward him. But it's even harder than I thought it would be. Once I slipped back into the old way and really let him have it."

"It will take a while for him to feel that you are sincere. But, in the meantime, I must say it is more peaceful around here."

About a week later, Sybil excitedly said to mother, "It works! You know I was doing the dishes alone. It was Margaret's turn, but she had a cold so father sent her to bed. And, would you believe it, Phil came out and said he'd dry them. We had the best talk. I really do love him."

• Why did Sybil and Phil change their attitudes toward each other?

Point out that it only took one of them to show love to change the situation.

• Why is it important that we express our love for one another? (By serving and helping one another, we will help our love for each other to grow.)

How We Can Make Love Grow

Have your family look up and read the following scriptures:

"Beloved, let us love one another: for love is of God" (1 John 4:7).

"Charity is the pure love of Christ, and it endureth forever; and whoso is found possessed of it at the last day, it shall be well with him.

"Wherefore . . . pray unto the Father with all the energy of heart, that ye may be filled with this love." (Moroni 7:47–48.)

Explain to your family that they can turn to Heavenly Father when they need help learning to love one another. If they will pray with all their heart, they will be filled with his love and their ability to love others will grow.

Remind your family that Jesus' love is unconditional. That means he loves us no matter what we do and say. Explain to your family that if they are to truly love one another as Jesus commanded them, they need to love each other in this same way. Have a family member read John 13:34.

• How would we act if we loved each other the way Jesus loves us?

Discuss with your family things they could do to overcome bad feelings or to help the feeling of love grow in your home. Read the examples below, and add those of your own:

1. Sincerely pray for help to get rid of angry, impatient, or hurt feelings.

2. Look through family photo albums, and talk about the things that the children did when they were little or that the family experienced together. Husbands and wives could look through wedding pictures or honeymoon photos.

3. Challenge family members to experiment as Sybil did, showing nothing but love for a week no matter how any other member of the family acts.

Love One Another Chart

Show your family the chart entitled "Love One Another." Explain that each time they see a family member showing love to someone in the family, they are to color in one of the rays around the heart. They are also to write that person's name down on the chart. Each family member could have his name on the chart several times.

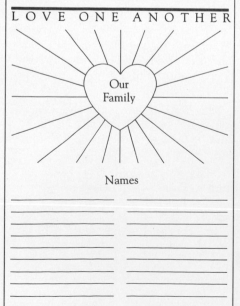

LOVE ONE ANOTHER

Our Family

Names

Put the chart up in a place where all the family members can easily see, read, and color it, such as on the refrigerator or a bulletin board.

Challenge each family member to show love in your home throughout the coming week so that all the rays of the heart will be filled in before your next home evening. Challenge them to feel the spirit of love in your home.

ADAPTING FOR YOUNGER CHILDREN

Tell the children that you are going to pretend that a special visitor is coming to your house. His name is Jesus. Ask them to think how excited they would feel to have Jesus come to visit them.

• What should we do to get ready? (Clean the house. Dress in nice clothes.)

• How will we act when Jesus comes?

The children could act out the things they would do.

Explain to the children that if Jesus were here they would have a good feeling. They would know he loves them.

Tell the children that if Jesus were in your home they would want to try very hard to be good and to show their love for one another.

Explain that each day they can have that good feeling in their home by sharing, by not fighting, and by being kind to one another.

Sing "A Happy Family" (*Sing with Me*, D–1).

• What does the song say we all do in our family? (Love each other.)

• How do you think mother knows you love her? (Help the children name some things they do that show love.)

• How does father know you love him? How does sister? How does brother?

You might use pictures from books and magazines to illustrate some of the things you talk about that show love.

Explain that you always want to have love in your home so that a good spirit can be there.

Little children can also participate in helping with the chart entitled "Love

One Another." Explain that when they see someone who is showing love in the family they can come and tell you. You will write that person's name on the chart for them. You could also help them color in a part of the chart.

Explain to the children that they can also be a good example in showing their love throughout the week.

ADAPTING FOR TEENAGERS AND ADULTS

Use the section "If Jesus Came to Visit Us," and ask the questions there. Both teenagers and adults could benefit by trying the experiment with notes of love and by expressing their feelings toward the family.

Discuss the importance of love in the home.

• What happens to the spirit in our home when we argue?

• Why does that spirit change when we are showing our love for one another?

Both adults and teenagers could participate in the activity in the section "A Game About Love."

Also use the section "When It Is Hard to Show Love."

For teenagers, adapt the story "It Works."

Take time to read and discuss the scriptures in Moroni, John, and 1 John that are noted under the heading "How We Can Make Love Grow."

Have your family list three of their favorite scriptures about love. Let each person read one or explain it. Have each family member tell what his favorite scripture means to him personally even if that scripture was dicussed by another family member.

Observe the good things members of the family do throughout the week in your home, and let them know that you appreciate and love them.

SUGGESTIONS FOR FUTURE HOME EVENINGS

Discovering Qualities of Love

Tell the family that they are going to play a game. Begin the game by saying, "I am thinking of something." Then give the following clues:

1. We cannot see it.

2. We can feel it, but not with our hands.

3. It can be divided up indefinitely.

4. We will never run out of it.

5. It makes us happy.

6. It makes us want to do things for others.

7. It makes us humble.

8. It gives us patience.

9. It makes us want to avoid unrighteous actions.

10. It helps us to be contented with what we have.

After each clue, give family members a chance to guess what it is you are thinking of. Add other clues as you think of them until the family discovers the answer or reaches a time limit.

When they have dicovered that "love" is the answer, have family members take turns explaining how love fits each of the clues that you have given. For example, the clue "It can be divided up indefinitely" means that we can love everyone without decreasing our love for any individual.

Read and discuss Paul's definition of love (charity) from 1 Corinthians 13:4–7, 13.

Suggest that family members choose one of the qualities of love they have discussed and try to apply love throughout a whole day to test whether it is a true quality.

Increasing Family Love

Choose a time a few days before family home evening when you can observe most of the family at home for an hour or two. Without being observed, keep score on the ways that family members show love. This will give you a sample of the level of love in your family.

During home evening, give each person a chance to respond to the following questions:

- What made us unhappy or upset today at home?

- What did you enjoy most today at home?

- How did you contribute to the happiness of someone else?

Share with the family the results of your observations. Challenge the family to increase the level of love in their home. Take another survey during the next week, and ask other family members to do the same. At the end of the week, discuss your findings.

Ways of Expressing Love

Take the family on a walk around your home, your neighborhood, a nearby park, or a woodland or farm. Invite each person to look for ways love is shown. For example, have family members point out an item and tell how love has been expressed, such as "My aunt loves me: she took many hours to knit this sweater," "Our neighbor shows love when he waters his flowers," or "We can learn a lesson in love by watching the mother bird bring food to the baby birds."

Point out that sometimes we express love by saying no. A mother does not let her little child play in the street where it is not safe.

It is important for teenagers to know that parents may express their love by saying no. Read and discuss Revelation 3:19.

- Why does God rebuke his children?

- How can this apply to earthly parents and their children?

Saying I Love You

Divide the family into teams. Within a time limit, see which team can make the longest list of ways to say, "I love you." Reward the winning team members with hugs or treats.

Discuss the lists, and choose the best items from each. Have a family member act as a secretary and copy these items on small cards, one to each card. Mix up the cards, and give each player the same number. Also write "I love you" on enough cards for each family member to have four.

During the coming week, each player tries to see how many cards he can cancel by saying or doing the thing on the card sincerely and at an appropriate time to another family member. The player may want to write on the card when and how that card was used in order to be ready to report at the next family home evening. Anyone who uses up all of his cards can receive special recognition.

Having Fun Expressing Love

Play "Spin the Bottle." Seat family members in a circle with a soda bottle on its side in the middle of the circle. Before each turn, announce what the person whom the bottle points to will do. Then spin the bottle. For example, after the bottle stops spinning, have the person that the bottle points to give someone a hug or a kiss, tell something helpful that someone did for him lately, say what he likes about someone, do something for someone that can be done quickly, or promise to do a small deed for someone during the next day. You can add other things to do that are appropriate for your family.

Learning to Love through Service

Have family members write down on slips of paper things that someone else could do for them that would be helpful and appreciated. Emphasize that these should not be trivial but needed services. Have them sign the slips and place the slips in a box or bowl.

Then read 3 Nephi 14:12 or Matthew 7:12, and have family members tell what they think Jesus is asking of them. Explain that serving and sacrificing for someone else usually increases our love for that person.

Read John 3:16. Point out that by sacrificing and serving, Jesus perfected his love for us. Ask family members to tell of any examples in their own lives or in the lives of others where service resulted in increased love or overcame feelings of envy.

Suggest that each member put this principle to the test. Tell the family that they are not required to but that each person is free to draw as many slips from the bowl as he wishes and perform the service indicated. (If a person draws one of his own, he can return it and draw another.) Have those who participate in the experiment keep track of the results and report back at another family home evening.

Understanding Unconditional Love

These suggestions work best with teenagers and adults.

Read Matthew 5:43–48 or 3 Nephi 12:43–45.

Have family members define what is meant by unconditional love. They may wish to give examples, such as "I will go on loving you even if you do things I don't like," or "I will love you whether you love me or not." Discuss the examples given, and help them to refine and clarify their definition of unconditional love.

Have a scripture search for examples of unconditional love. As you find scriptural examples, draw parallels for your own family—liken the scriptures to yourselves (1 Nephi 19:23)—so that family members can see how the same unconditional love can be applied in their own lives. Emphasize that this doctrine is not vain and idealistic, that we can learn to love our enemies and have compassion and charity for all if we will exercise our faith in Jesus Christ and apply his teachings.

UNITY THROUGH FAMILY PRAYER

Counsel with the Lord in all thy doings.
[*Alma 37:37*]

PURPOSE

Help family members draw closer to each other and to the Lord through family prayer.

FOR THE PARENT

For those who take their real feelings and concerns to the Lord, family prayer can be one of the most unifying and strengthening parts of the day. This lesson is designed to help your family understand the rich blessings available through praying together and to help you discuss how you can reap these blessings more abundantly.

Consider the following story as you prepare for this lesson:

"One father, a quiet, unassuming man, found it hard to express his love for his family. At his wife's prompting they began holding family prayer, and it became an opportunity to voice what was in his heart. To their daughter, who had misinterpreted her father's manner as indifference, the experience was a revelation. His prayers were simple and sometimes clumsily worded, but to hear him say, 'Bless my lovely daughter to do good' thrilled her.

"A timid boy who thought of himself as a 'scaredy cat' felt new pride and self-esteem when his father and mother thanked God for their 'kind, gentle son.' And the boy's self-confidence continued to grow through prayer when even his little brother thanked Heavenly Father for his 'big, strong brother.'

"In preparation for a family outing in our own family, my husband asked the Lord to bless our family to get along and to enjoy each other's company. The preaching we had done had gone unheard, but that reverent prayer brought cooperation.

"Our teenage son was tense and sullen whenever we tried to discuss any problem with him. We decided it was important to plan the discussion when he would be most receptive, and that seemed to be at family prayer time in the mornings. It was then that the house was quiet and we shared a humble, sincere feeling. We found the tenseness eased when prayer preceded our discussions.

"During these quiet moments of family prayer, we are keeping in touch with each other and with our Father in heaven." (Ann H. Banks, "The Extra Blessings of Family Prayer," *Ensign*, Jan. 1976, p. 37.)

PREPARATION

1. Bring a piece of paper and a pencil for each family member.

2. Draw a large version of the bridge shown in the lesson, and cut out the stones of the bridge so that the bridge can be put together like a puzzle. Have a sheet of colored paper and glue ready to put the bridge together at the end of the lesson. See the section "Family Prayer Can Strengthen Us" for instructions on using the bridge.

3. Have a colored pen or crayon.

4. Bring crayons and paper for younger children.

SUGGESTED HYMN AND SONG

"Sweet Hour of Prayer" (*Hymns*, no. 166).
"Family Prayer" (*Sing with Me*, D–6).

SUGGESTED LESSON

How Close Do We Feel to Each Other?

Begin by briefly discussing the following questions and ideas:

• Have you ever felt alone in a big crowd?

Relate an experience you have had—at a ball game, on a subway or bus, or in a large city—when you felt alone among a group of strangers or casual acquaintances. Let one or two family members relate their experiences.

• Why did you feel alone even though there were other people around?

• What makes you feel close to other people?

Conclude that knowing that someone else is interested in our problems, successes, and concerns makes us feel close to them.

Tell about a time when you have been among friends or loved ones and still felt alone. Perhaps you had a problem that you felt no one could help you with or a concern no one seemed to care about. Point out that even among the members of your own family—those who love you most—it is possible to feel alone. Express your desire that this lesson will help them find one important way to draw closer to each other and to Heavenly Father so that none of them will feel that they face life alone. (See D&C 88:62–64.)

Hand out a piece of paper and a pencil to each person. Ask each person to make two columns. In the first column, have them list at least five things they have been concerned or worried about during last week. Give them examples if necessary to get them started, such as taking a test, making friends at school, or starting a new job. In the second column, have them list at least five things that made them happy during the week. Collect the lists, and put them aside for use later in the lesson.

Family Prayer Can Strengthen Us

Place the stones of the bridge that you have drawn and cut apart, except for the keystone (the stone in the center of the bridge), in a pile on the table or floor. Ask everyone to imagine that they are standing on the banks of a deep, fast-flowing river with this pile of stones.

• How could we use these stones to get across the river? (By building a bridge with them.)

Have someone try to put together the picture of a bridge on the table or floor.

• Would this kind of bridge be strong and stable? Could we cross the dangerous river safely?

Point out that there are gaps between the stones and that a bridge like this would collapse.

• What is missing from the bridge that would make it stronger?

Hold up the keystone. Explain that without this one piece, the other pieces of the bridge will not hold together, however strong they are individually. With the keystone, all the pieces can work together and support each other.

Write the phrase "family prayer" on the keystone with a colored pen or crayon. Then on each stone write the name of one of you family members.

• How can praying together in our family be compared to the keystone in a bridge?

Read 3 Nephi 18:21.

• When has family prayer helped us and made our family stronger?

After your family has discussed these questions, have them think about family prayer being a keystone as you, or someone else, tell Brent's story:

The Love of an Older Brother

"One of the greatest joys of my life came when my family was spiritually united in seeking the Lord's aid in my behalf, supporting me through a time of intense struggle. I learned by experience why the Lord placed us in sacred groups called families.

"When I was a junior in high school I contracted a kidney disease. Over the next few years my health gradually declined until my condition became critical. Despite the best medical care, the disease eventually destroyed both of my kidneys. . . .

"I learned a great deal during those three years on a kidney machine. My faith in the Lord grew as I watched his hand guiding my life. I was close to my family, and in spite of the machine I loved life more than ever before. I had never been so free, nor as happy. Yet, I yearned to be free of my mechanical companion.

"This goal, like so many others, became a family project. We often spent family home evenings and family interviews discussing alternatives to dialysis and the justifications for a transplant.

"I recall one memorable week when the family was all together. . . .

"During that week we spent a great deal of time talking about my health. We had all researched the possibility of a transplant, and each member of the family had personally volunteered to be my donor. . . .

"Then one evening a marvelous and unexpected event occurred during family prayers. My father was voice, and when the prayer was completed we all knew what was to transpire. With tears in our eyes we discussed our feelings. Yes, each had felt the same confirmation. We should go ahead with the transplant."

Explain that Brent's brother Craig gave him one of his kidneys. After the operation, Craig was very ill, and Brent's body was trying to reject the new kidney. Then continue with Brent's story:

"The medical reports indicated that I was rejecting the new kidney. It appeared that we had failed. Drastic medical measures were taken, but with little success. As it turned out, the most powerful aid of all was prayer. Etched deeply into my soul is the memory of many nights when family members knelt around my bed and one by one prayed to our Father in Heaven. I listened as my brothers wept, praying that I might live. Then, silently, none of us able to speak, we'd touch hands to say good-night. And they were good nights, for we each experienced the pure love of Christ.

"The kidney rejection was finally overcome; Craig, too, rapidly regained his health and strength. Today, my doctors report that I am one of the healthiest kidney recipients in history. . . .

"I can testify that one of the greatest

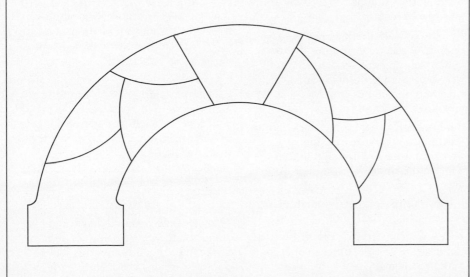

joys of mortality comes when a family is spiritually united in seeking the Lord's aid and comfort." (D. Brent Collette, *Ensign*, Oct. 1981, pp. 42–44.)

• In what way was family prayer like a keystone to Brent and his family?

• Do you think Brent could have faced his long struggle with illness, no matter what the outcome, without the united prayers of his family?

• Why was Brent able to feel such support from his family?

Point out that—

1. The whole family knew about Brent's problem.

2. They loved each other and wanted to help.

3. They prayed together.

4. They did all they could.

Explain that this helped to bring Heavenly Father's blessings.

• Do you feel that other family members know and care about the concerns and joys you wrote down?

Show the lists you collected. Read one or two items from each person's list. Have the family guess who wrote each item you mentioned. Choose items that might not be easy to match with the person who wrote them. You might ask, "During the week, which one of us was concerned about this problem?" or "Who was happy about this during the week?"

A Two-Part Process

Suggest that effective family prayer is a two-part process:

1. We must be aware of each other's feelings and concerns (see 1 Peter 3:8–9).

2. We must talk to Heavenly Father about specific problems that are on our minds (see Alma 34:18–27).

• What if Brent's family had not prayed specifically about his problem during the time of his illness? Do you think they would have known what to do and how they could help?

• What difference did the family's prayers make?

• Why can we get help by praying together as a family that we could get in no other way?

Point out that when we pray together about specific problems, Heavenly Father can show us ways to help each other that we might never have seen. Have someone tell the following story:

Sue Helps

Sue Crandall was concerned about her younger brother, Tim. Every morning they got on a small yellow bus that took them to school a few miles from their home. This was Sue's fourth year, so she was used to riding the bus. She even looked forward to the ride as a time to talk to her friends each morning.

But Tim felt differently. So far, after one week of school, he had cried every morning on the way to the bus stop. Sue's mother had been firm. "You'll get used to it, Tim," she'd say. "Soon you'll have lots of friends on the bus." But Sue could see her mother getting more worried each day as Tim got on the bus sniffling and wiping his red eyes.

Saturday morning, as the Crandall family knelt around the breakfast table, Sue's father said something that made Sue stop and think. Right after he thanked Heavenly Father for his beautiful children, he said, "Bless Tim that he will be able to make friends on the bus this week. And help us find a way to help him."

As the family ate their eggs and toast that morning, Sue thought long and hard. She realized that she had felt sorry for Tim all week, but she hadn't done anything to help. She'd sat with her own friends every morning as her little brother slumped silently on the first row of seats.

By Saturday afternoon, Sue had a plan. She asked her mother if they could pick up her friend Karen and her second-grade brother, Todd, on their way to the bus stop Monday morning.

Sure enough, by the time the children reached the bus stop on Monday, the two boys were so busy talking that Tim hardly noticed his mother drive away.

• How did the prayer Sue's father offered help Tim?

• Can we support each other if we are not aware of each other's concerns and problems?

Suggest that your family could be stronger and feel closer if your prayers together were more specific—if you prayed about the real feelings and concerns of each family member, as well as about group concerns.

Glue the bridge pieces together on a sheet of colored paper. Write the scripture from the beginning of the lesson under the bridge. Post it where your family can see it during the week. Suggest that during the week they make a special effort to pray about family member's concerns. Before each family prayer, you could have a discussion to find out needs and concerns. You might find that mealtime is a good time for this kind of discussion. During the next family home evening, discuss whether this has made your family feel closer.

Be sure to close this family home evening with family prayer.

ADAPTING FOR YOUNGER CHILDREN

Tell the family about a time when each of your children was sick or had a special problem. Tell them how you prayed for that child, how much you love him, and how thankful you were when your prayer was answered. Explain that Heavenly Father has great love for each of us. He always wants us to tell him about our problems and concerns so that he can help us.

Tell the story of Sue and Tim. Talk about how we can help each other better when we pray about our problems.

Pass out a piece of paper to each person. Have everyone draw a picture that will remind him of the lesson, such as a family praying or Sue and Tim on the bus. Have each person tell about his picture.

Close your family home evening with family prayer. In your prayer, express your love for each member of the family, and mention a special concern or need each has.

ADAPTING FOR TEENAGERS AND ADULTS

Most teenagers and adults will understand the feeling of being alone in a crowd. Let them discuss this feeling. Contrast it with the feeling of being with people who love them and are interested in them.

Many people—teenagers especially—are not always willing to tell others what their concerns are. As you introduce the activity of making two lists, you may want to discuss how you can overcome this embarrassment about sharing personal problems through keeping confidences and never violating a trust.

Use the bridge activity.

You may want to discuss in greater depth your own family's experiences with prayer. Recall how your prayers for each other have been answered. Help the family understand that some of the richest and most unifying experiences come when the family together seeks the Lord's help and blessing.

Use the story of Brent, and discuss it.

Accept your family's suggestions as to when, each day, they can spend a few minutes discussing each other's needs and concerns. Encourage them to be aware of these problems when it is their turn to offer family prayer.

SUGGESTIONS FOR FUTURE HOME EVENINGS

Making Prayer More Meaningful

Give each family member a paper on which the letters *f, a, m, i, l, y, p, r, a, y, e, r* are listed down the left-hand margin.

Challenge the family to think of things beginning with these letters that they might do to make family prayer more meaningful. The combined lists will give your family a picture of their responsibilities for effective family prayers. For example, the lists might include *f, feel* humble and sincere; *a, ask* in faith; *m, make* a commitment to live as you pray; *i, invite* the Lord's Spirit to be with you; or *l, love* the Lord, family members, friends, and enemies.

Conclude by discussing other ways you can make family prayers more spiritual and rewarding, such as preparing by reading short scriptural passages or singing a hymn. Plan ways to make family prayer a highlight of the day rather than something family members want to hurry through so they can do other things.

The Essential Steps of Prayer

Teach family members the basic steps in proper prayer, using your own words:

1. Address Heavenly Father in hallowed terms, such as "Our Father in Heaven."

2. Express gratitude for past blessings.

3. Ask for needed blessings, both temporal and spiritual. (Include the needs and problems of others, and seek protection from evil influences.)

4. Close by saying, "In the name of Jesus Christ, amen." Each person adds a sincere "amen" as an indication of agreement and rededication.

Family members might add other ideas. Refer to the Lord's Prayer (Matthew 6:5–13) as you discuss these steps. Ask family members to watch for these steps in prayer at home and in church.

Praying for Others

Family members should be concerned for each other's welfare in their prayers. Review with the family the story of Alma's conversion (Mosiah 27). Discuss the importance and power of his father's faithful prayers in Alma's behalf. Stress that we should never give up on a loved one who needs our encouragement and support.

If a member of your family is facing some challenge, such as inactivity in the Church, a medical problem, an examination at school, going on a mission, going away to college, or facing a new job, help family members put Alma's example into practice.

To remind family members, you can post the following on a family bulletin board: "The effectual fervent prayer of a righteous man availeth much" (James 5:16).

Encouraging Regular Family Prayers

If you do not have regular family prayers, discuss family prayer and what it can do to increase family unity, love, and strength. You may wish to use one of the other suggested family home evenings on prayer to motivate your family to pray together. When they are properly prepared and want to have family prayers, make a plan for

holding family prayer regularly.

If family members' schedules seem to interfere, read and discuss Luke 10:38–42. Discuss what our proper priorities should be. You may wish to appoint one family member to remind the others or to call them to prayer at the proper time. Or you may wish to have them post the scheduled time and place on cards in mirror frames or on bedroom doors as reminders. Plan ways to make your family prayers spiritual experiences.

Appreciating Family Prayer

Share the experience of Elder John H. Groberg during his three-month journey from Salt Lake City to Tonga as a young missionary (see Conference Report, Apr. 1982, pp. 75–79; or *Ensign*, May 1982, pp. 50–52). (If you do not have a copy of this address, check with your meetinghouse library.) Discuss how his family's prayers sustained him in a distant land when he felt frightened and alone. If family members have had experiences when family prayer has strengthened someone, have family members relate them. Explain how family prayer can be more effective through love and unity among family members. Have family members suggest ways that family prayer can increase family unity.

You may wish to conclude with excerpts from Elder Groberg's conference address:

"No matter what other inheritance you leave your family, give them the inheritance of knowing through experience that, forever, you will be praying for them and they for you. . . .

"I testify that time and space are no barriers to these righteous influences, and no matter where we are or what our situation is—even in the depths of discouragement, far from our loved ones—we too can feel and be strengthened by those soul-stirring words, 'and bless John or Jane or whomever on his or her mission,' for indeed life is a mission. We are all here on assignment to learn to love and serve one another; and we can't do this as well as we should unless we have consistent, fervent family prayer." (In Conference Report, Apr. 1982, pp. 78–79; or *Ensign*, May 1982, p. 52.)

THE PRIESTHOOD IN OUR HOME

Behold, I will lead thee by my hand, and I will take thee, to put upon thee my name, even the Priesthood of thy father, and my power shall be over thee.
[*Abraham 1:18*]

PURPOSE

Help family members appreciate the blessings of having the priesthood in the home.

FOR THE PARENT

Our Heavenly Father has great power, which is called the priesthood. By this power the heavens and the earth were created. Through this power, delegated to men, all the children of Heavenly Father can be blessed (see Abraham 2:1).

Every priesthood holder has the right and privilege to use this priesthood to lead and bless his family. Your children should grow up knowing the blessings of the priesthood.

If you do not have the priesthood in your home, you may receive the blessings of the priesthood through relatives, home teachers, and your bishop or branch president. Our loving Heavenly Father gave the priesthood to his children so that he could guide and bless us.

PREPARATION

Bring a poster board or a large piece of paper and some markers or crayons.

SUGGESTED HYMN AND SONG

"Come, Sing to the Lord" (*Hymns*, no. 32). "I Thank Thee, Dear Father" (*Sing with Me*, A–8).

SUGGESTED LESSON

Abraham Received the Priesthood

Turn to Facsimile No. 1 in the book of Abraham.

- What do you see? (Abraham is lying down on an altar. A wicked priest with a knife is trying to kill Abraham.)

- Why did this wicked priest want to kill Abraham? (Because Abraham worshiped Heavenly Father and would not bow down to worship false gods made of stone or wood.)

Read Abraham 1:1–19 with your family; or, if your children are young, tell the story in your own words:

Abraham was a good man who tried to serve Heavenly Father all his life. He wanted one great blessing that he did not have. He wanted to have the priesthood because he knew it would help him to be a better servant of the Lord and would help him bless his family.

Abraham's father could not give him the priesthood as righteous fathers do because he had forgotten Heavenly Father and turned to worshiping idols. Abraham's father even let wicked men take Abraham and tie him to an altar like the one in the picture. There they were going to kill him. But Abraham cried out to Heavenly Father, who heard Abraham and saved his life.

Heavenly Father told Abraham to leave his father's house and go away into another country. He promised Abraham the great blessing that Abraham most wanted, the priesthood of God. He also promised Abraham that through this priesthood all the families of the earth would be blessed. (See Abraham 2:6–13.)

Our Family Is Blessed by the Priesthood

Explain to your family that this priesthood or power of God that Abraham was given is the same priesthood that the fathers or sons in your family have. One of the reasons the Lord has given men the priesthood is so that they can bless their families. Every member of your family who is a member of the Church has had some blessings from the priesthood.

Let each person tell about a blessing he has received through the power of the priesthood. For example—

1. Talk about the blessings the children received as babies. Tell about the event, who attended the meeting, who assisted the father or gave the blessing, how the baby was dressed, and how the name was chosen. Any details you can remember will be fascinating to the child about whom you are talking as well as to other family members. Be sure to include an expression of how you felt on these occasions.

2. A family member who has been baptized and confirmed could tell about that experience and how he felt.

3. A family member could tell about receiving an annointing and blessing when he was ill.

4. Someone in your family could share his feelings about receiving a father's blessing.

5. Share your feelings about going to the temple to be sealed if you have had a temple marriage, being careful not to discuss what goes on in

the temple. You could tell how you are looking forward to this great blessing if you have not yet been through the temple.

You may want to tell the following story:

Tommy's First Day at School

Tommy was getting ready to go to school for the first time. He had been excited about beginning school, but now that the first day had finally come, he was frightened.

Tommy was quiet all morning. His mother had made his favorite breakfast, but Tommy did not smile when he saw it. He picked up the spoon and tried to eat, but could not.

His mother asked, "Do you feel sick, Tommy?"

Tommy answered, "I think so. At least I don't feel like going to school."

Tommy's mother felt his head to see if he had a fever. She looked in his throat, but it was not red. She said, "I can't see anything wrong, Tommy. Show me where it is that you don't feel well."

Tommy said, "I just feel funny inside."

Tommy's father looked at him and said, "I think I know what might be wrong with you, Tommy. This is your first day of school. Maybe you feel funny inside because you will be away from home all day and you don't know what to expect. Are you a little frightened? I know that feeling, too, Tommy. I had the same feeling when I started my new job last week.

"I can do something to help you if you would like. I can give you a special blessing before you go to school today. This blessing can help take away that frightened, funny feeling you have inside."

"I'd like that, dad," said Tommy.

Tommy's father placed his hands on Tommy's head and gave him a special blessing.

That afternoon Tommy came bounding in the door calling, "Mom, mom, I'm home."

"How did you like school, Tommy?" asked his mother.

"Well, it was better than I thought it would be. My teacher is nice," said Tommy.

"Dad said you would feel better after he gave you a special blessing, didn't he? I'm glad your father knew just what to do to help you."

Sharing these experiences should remind each family member what a great blessing the priesthood can be. The Lord has given us the priesthood because we are his children and he loves us. It is our Heavenly Father's way of blessing his children, and he wants us to receive every blessing we are worthy to have.

We Will Remember Our Blessings

Let the children make a poster that says, "The Priesthood Blesses Our Family." Let each family member sign or print his name around the edges of the poster. Then write by each name the priesthood blessings that person has received.

Put up the poster somewhere so that your family will see it each day at dinner time. Discuss the different blessings during dinner each day.

ADAPTING FOR YOUNGER CHILDREN

Tell the picture story "Abraham Received the Priesthood" that accompanies the lesson.

Explain how your family has been blessed by the priesthood. Tell the children about the day they were blessed and given a name by a priesthood holder as suggested in the regular lesson. With younger children, this part of the lesson could be expanded so that you take time telling each child about his birth and your special love for him. Describe other priesthood blessings you may have had, such as a father's blessing or a blessing during illness. Help the children realize that having the priesthood to bless them is like having Heavenly Father close by us all the time.

Tell the story "Tommy's First Day at School," and discuss it.

Let the children help you make and decorate a poster that says, "The Priesthood Blesses Our Family." Put up this poster in your home where it can be seen at dinner time. Each night during the week, tell a bedtime story that illustrates some priesthood blessings.

ABRAHAM RECEIVED THE PRIESTHOOD

Abraham   Abraham's father   House   Families

was a good man who tried to serve Heavenly Father all his life. He wanted one great blessing that he did not have. wanted to have the priesthood. He knew it would help him to a better person and would help him bless his . could not give him the priesthood as righteous fathers had done. had forgotten Heavenly Father and had turned to worshiping idols. Heavenly Father told to leave his father's and go away into another country. He promised the great blessing that most wanted, the priesthood of God. He also promised that through this priesthood all the of the would blessed.

ADAPTING FOR TEENAGERS AND ADULTS

Turn to Facsimile No. 1 in the book of Abraham, and discuss what you see. Then read the explanation printed below it.

• How did Abraham get into this perilous situation?

Read Abraham 1:5–7.

• How was he rescued?

Read Abraham 1:15–18.

• Abraham sought to have the priesthood but could not be ordained by his own father. Why?

The Lord told Joseph Smith who ordained Abraham. Read Doctrine and Covenants 84:14.

When the Lord promised to give Abraham the priesthood, he declared that through this priesthood all the families of the earth would be blessed. Read Abraham 2:11.

Discuss some of the ways that the families of the earth have been blessed by the priesthood. Everyone in the Church has received blessings through the priesthood at some time in his life.

• Can you trace the priesthood lineage in your family?

• Who ordained the priesthood holders in your family?

• Who ordained the men that ordained your family members?

• Can you trace the priesthood lineage of the person who baptized you or set you apart to a position in the Church?

Ask each person to recall and share his feelings about at least one blessing he has received through the priesthood, such as the blessing of babies, baptism, confirmation, father's blessing, blessing during illness, temple endowments, and temple marriage.

Conclude by having the oldest priesthood bearer in the family express his feelings concerning the use of his priesthood to bless those he loves. Introduce this by telling the following story:

Mike Makes a Decision

Mike had graduated from school nearly a year ago, and he would soon be nineteen. All through the past year he had tried to decide whether to go on a mission.

Quite a few of his friends had already gone on their missions, and this is what bothered Mike most. It seemed to him that some of them had gone for the wrong reasons—not because they were committed to serve the Lord, but to please their parents or girl friends. Mike wanted to be sure that if he went, he would go for the right reasons.

One Sunday evening after an inspiring sacrament meeting, Mike asked his father if they could talk privately because he had a problem on his mind that he would like to discuss.

His father said, "Why not right now?" The two of them went into Mike's room and shut the door.

Mike and his father talked for quite a while about all the things that had been bothering Mike. Then his father asked, "Mike, would you like a special blessing to help you?"

"Yes, I would," Mike answered.

Later that night as Mike said his prayers before going to bed, he told the Lord again that he wanted to be sure that he was really committed to serve so that he could feel good about going on a mission. He expressed his love for the Lord and thanked him for his good family and all the other blessings he had received throughout his life. Suddenly he had a warm, good feeling come over him. He knew in his heart how much his Heavenly Father loved him. As he arose from his knees, the words kept going through his head over and over again, "I want to serve the Lord. I want to serve the Lord." Mike knew what to do.

Discuss any future events in your family where a priesthood blessing might be appropriate, such as leaving home for college, mission, work, or marriage; the birth of children; or special assignments or responsibilities. Counsel each family member to remember to call on the priesthood bearers in the home for blessings on these special occasions. Sharing the spiritual experiences of giving and receiving blessings through the priesthood will strengthen and unite your family.

SUGGESTIONS FOR FUTURE HOME EVENINGS

Authority in the Priesthood

Tell the following experience that Elder Hugh B. Brown had before becoming an Apostle and member of the First Presidency:

"I was at one time an army officer. As

such, I became accustomed to having men stand at attention and salute me and call me 'sir,' and frankly, I liked it.

"Often men came and asked for favors—perhaps a furlough or a leave or some thing that they thought I could grant—because they knew that I was an officer of the King [of England] and that I had the right to speak in his name. And so as they came I handed the 'blessings' down to them and I became more haughty and self-important with each event.

"One day a messenger came to my hotel just off Piccadilly Circus. He said, 'You are wanted immediately in the hospital.'

"I thought, 'Well, here is another boy that wants something. I will go down and see what is wanted.'

"I called a taxi and went to the hospital.

"When I arrived the doctors stood at attention and saluted, and that fed my ego. The nurses treated me with great respect and that pleased me even more.

"They directed me to a little room and as I pushed open the door, I saw an emaciated young man lying on a cot. I recognized him as a former Sunday School student of mine in Cardston, Canada.

"When he greeted me, he did not use my rank in his salutation, but simply said, 'Brother Brown, I sent for you to ask if you would use your authority in my behalf.' (I thought, 'Well, this is what I expected. What does he want?')

" 'Brother Brown,' he said, 'you know I have a widowed mother; I am her only son; the doctors say I cannot live; will you give me my life!'

"I thought, 'My goodness, the King of England can't give him his life. To what is he referring?'

"Then he startled me with a request: 'Will you administer to me!'

"At that moment . . . my uniform, with the insignia on it, seemed to melt away, and I stood before that young man in a uniform with insignia indicating authority. I could not have worn that uniform, which was next to my skin, if I had not had some au-

thority given to me. I stood there thinking of that authority, and I was humbled but inspired.

"I went over to his cot and knelt beside him. I put my hands on his head and said, 'In the name of Jesus Christ and by the authority of the holy priesthood, I bless you and promise you that you will get well and return to your mother.' God honored that promise.

"I went into that hospital a proud British officer, and I came out a humble Mormon elder. Ever since then I have earnestly tried to remember that there is a power and authority given to man, not from the king or the president, but from the King of Kings, and if we live properly and do not forget that we have been so endowed, we may exercise that authority in behalf of those who need our ministration." (*Be What You Will to Be*, Brigham Young University Speeches of the Year [Provo, 14 Feb. 1967], pp. 8–9.)

Read the fifth article of faith. Then have someone read Exodus 4:10–16 and 28:1.

• Where did Moses receive his authority to call Aaron to do the Lord's work?

The Lord followed this same procedure when he was himself on the earth. Have someone read John 15:16.

Discuss how priesthood holders are organized into offices to do the work for which they are called (see chapter 14, "Priesthood Organization," *Gospel Principles* [PBIC0245], pp. 79–87.)

Adapt this lesson to the age levels of family members.

Priesthood Ordinances

Prepare your family for special occasions when priesthood ordinances or blessings will be given, such as for baptisms, ordinations, or patriarchal blessings. Use the appropriate lesson from the section "Special Occasions," lessons 27 through 37.

How Priesthood Holders Magnify Their Callings

Use a magnifying lens to demonstrate the meaning of the word *magnify*.

• What is magnified when men honor and use their priesthood? (Their lives and service.)

Have family members suggest ways that callings in the priesthood can be magnified. If there are Aaronic Priesthood holders in the home, ask them to think of their priesthood duties and how they can magnify their callings. Review Doctrine and Covenants 20:38–67.

Discuss how honoring his priesthood all the time will prepare a priesthood holder to bless his family when some emergency or special event takes place (see D&C 121:36).

Honoring the Priesthood

Priesthood leaders have the responsibility to teach, advise, and counsel us as well as to preside over meetings and perform ordinances. We can turn to them for help when we have difficult problems.

Discuss with your family how home teachers, bishops or branch presidents, stake presidents, and General Authorities fulfill these functions.

You may wish to use wordstrips with the priesthood offices printed on them. As you discuss each office, attach the wordstrip to a poster or flannel board. Or you may wish to use a chalkboard. Have family members suggest ways they can honor the priesthood that the officer holds (such as seeking, listening to, and following their leaders' counsel; reading conference addresses; or sustaining priesthood officers).

Recall examples of counsel and advice from priesthood leaders that have blessed you and your family.

Love and the Priesthood

These suggestions work best with teenagers and adults.

Read and discuss Doctrine and Covenants 12:8, 121:41–42, and 1 Corinthians 13 (*charity* in this scripture means "love for our fellowmen").

Have family members who hold the Melchizedek Priesthood describe one or two of their responsibilities for serving other people. Then have them describe how these scriptures apply to the way they carry out those responsibilities.

If there are no priesthood holders in your family, discuss how to apply these scriptures as leaders, teachers, or family members. Be careful not to allow any criticism of priesthood leaders.

A HOUSE OF ORDER

Behold, mine house is a house of order, saith the Lord God, and not a house of confusion.
[D&C 132:8]

PURPOSE

Commit family members to make your home a "house of order" (D&C 132:8).

FOR THE PARENT

All parents hope to raise happy, healthy children who love the Lord and are willing to serve others. This is one of the heaviest responsibilities that God has given men and women. Our Heavenly Father will help us if we will seek and accept his guidance by praying, studying the scriptures, and following the counsel of his chosen leaders.

The Lord said, "Mine house is a house of order . . . and not a house of confusion." If we pattern our homes according to our Heavenly Father's guidance, we will be better parents. An orderly home is a home where parents preside, direct, and teach; where all have responsibilities and are considerate and thoughtful of each other; and where family members are knit together with love. (See D&C 88:119.)

PREPARATION

1. Have several pieces of paper that can be cut into two-inch strips as needed and a marker of some kind to write on them. You will need three or four strips per family member.

2. Have a piece of colored paper for each family member to make a poster.

SUGGESTED HYMN AND SONG

"Today, While the Sun Shines" (*Hymns*, no. 215).
"When We're Helping" (*Sing with Me*, D–5).

SUGGESTED LESSON

Begin with a game called "Come to Order." Explain that the word *order* means, among other things, the way in which things are placed or a condition in which everything is in its right place. Line up your family in different orders, such as the following (be sure that the father or family head is the one giving the directions if possible):

1. Line up according to age, from the oldest to the youngest.

2. Line up according to the size of feet, from the littlest to the biggest.

3. Line up according to height, from the tallest to the shortest.

When everyone is seated again, point out that to play this game, someone had to select the order, and the others had to follow that direction.

Explain to your family that order comes to a home when everyone understands and carries out his responsibilities. The opposite of order is confusion. Confusion comes when people do not know what is expected of them.

We Can Make Our Home a House of Order

Heavenly Father has said that his house is a house of order. Have someone read Doctrine and Covenants 132:8.

Explain that Heavenly Father gives us directions out of his great love. If we will follow those directions, we will be happy and can accomplish all we should. He would like us to follow this same pattern in our homes so that they may be houses of order also.

Through his prophets, the Lord has explained what he expects of parents and children. As always, his directions are given because he loves us and wants us to be happy. The Lord has given responsibilities to both parents and to children. In order to have a loving and happy family, each person must do his part.

Parents Have Responsibilities

Discuss with your family some of the responsibilities Heavenly Father has given parents. Start with the three important ones listed below. As you talk about each one, write each of the headings below on a strip of paper for each parent, and place one of the strips of paper on the floor in front of each parent.

Preside

• What does the word *preside* mean? (To give direction or take charge.)

To point out how important it is to have someone preside in any group, do the following experiment. Ask each family member to think of his favorite game. When you tell them to start, have all the family members tell, at the same time, how to play their games. After a minute, call the group back to order.

• What happened when everyone gave directions for a different game at the same time? (The result was confusion.)

• Could you tell what all the others were saying?

Point out how much easier it would have been to understand everyone's favorite game if someone had taken charge and called on one person at a time to explain his game.

Explain that Heavenly Father has given parents the job of presiding in the home because they love their children. He knows that they will try to give directions and make decisions that will be the best for their children.

While parents are equal partners in the home, it is the father's responsibility to be the patriarch, or head of the house (see Ephesians 5:23–25). If the father is not present, the mother presides no matter how old the sons are or what priesthood they may hold.

Teach the Gospel

Parents have been told by the Lord to teach their children. Have someone read Mosiah 4:14–15 and Doctrine and Covenants 68:25. Point out that having family home evenings helps you carry out this responsibility.

Be an Example

One of the best ways parents can teach their children is by example. In Jacob 2:35, Jacob points out the effect of bad example. Husbands and wives should show love and respect for each other and for their children by their actions as well as by their words.

Explain that parents are human and sometimes fail to set the proper example at all times. Sometimes parents get tired, feel discouraged, or lose their tempers. But they do love their children and are trying to be good parents though they may make some mistakes.

Children Have Responsibilities Too

Our Heavenly Father has also told us what he expects children to do in the home. Children share with their parents the responsibility of making a happy home and a house of order. Discuss the following responsibilties and make a strip with the words written on it for each child. Place a strip of paper on the floor in front of each child.

Obey

Have someone read Ephesians 6:1. Explain that parents and children should counsel together in making family rules and decisions. If children understand why a rule is made, it is easier for them to accept that rule. When the family, under the direction of the parents, has made a rule or decision, all are responsible to obey that rule and abide by that decision.

Honor Parents

Discuss how we honor our parents. Explain that *honor* means to show respect. We honor parents when we follow their teachings and do the things we know they would like us to do.

Read Ephesians 6:2–3.

• How could honoring parents help us to "live long on the earth?"

Point out your concern for your children's health and safety. Relate a personal experience of a time when following a parent's advice saved someone from harm, or use the following story:

Jon and Brad were admiring Jon's older brother's new bike.

"What a beauty," said Brad, "I'd give anything to be able to ride it!"

"Bob is only six like us," Jon said, "and he rides his brother's bike all over. You know, my parents have never really said I couldn't ride the bike."

"Neither have my parents, but I know what they'd say if I asked them. They'd say that I should wait until I'm older and big enough."

"Well, our parents don't need to know if we just take a short ride around the school yard."

As they rode around the school yard, they skidded on some gravel and took a painful fall that left them scraped and bruised.

After the accident, both Jon and Brad understood why their parents would not have let them ride the bike had they asked. Following their parents advice would have saved them trouble and pain.

Contribute

Explain that each family member is personally responsible to help make the family happy and strong. Children should contribute by not just taking from the family but by giving to the family as well.

• How can you contribute to the family? (You may want the family members to answer this question to themselves.)

Ask your children to name other ways they can help make your home a house of order. Write each one on a strip of paper, and place it in front of the children to whom it applies.

Conclude the lesson by telling the children how much you love them and how hard you are trying to be a good parent. Children need to hear often that their parents love them so that they will understand that directions, rules, and order in the home come from that love.

Let each family member make a poster of his responsibilities in the family. Have each child paste the strips of paper he has in front of him onto a piece of colored paper, write his name at the top, and decorate it. The poster could then be put up by the child's bed or wherever it could be seen each day as a reminder.

ADAPTING FOR YOUNGER CHILDREN

Explain to your children that Heavenly Father has given parents children so that the parents can protect the children and teach them what is right. He wants our homes to be happy.

Tell them that each family member has responsibilities. Explain that *responsibility* means that they are in charge of something, such as the responsibility to pick up their toys after they are finished playing with them. Heavenly Father has given both parents and children responsiblities.

Use the sections "Parents Have Responsibilities" and "Children Have Responsibilities Too" from the regular lesson.

ADAPTING FOR TEENAGERS AND ADULTS

You may wish to start with the game "Come to Order," but make the directions more complicated, such as—

1. Line up according to birth dates, from the first of the year to the last.

2. Line up in alphabetical order, using first names.

3. Line up by how much you like a certain food.

After you finish playing the game, have someone read Doctrine and Covenants 132:8. Discuss the various meanings of the word *order,* how they might pertain to this scripture, and what God meant when he called his house "a house of order."

Follow through with the rest of the lesson from the section entitled "We Can Make Our Home a House of Order." As you discuss how honoring parents could in fact prolong your life by keeping you safe from physical injuries, also consider how honoring your parents' teachings could give you spiritual protection (see Exodus 20:12).

• How does the role of parents change as children get older, get married, or move away from home?

• How does the role of children change in those same instances?

Suggest that during the following week all family members evaluate themselves personally as to how well they are fulfilling their responsibilities in your home.

SUGGESTIONS FOR FUTURE HOME EVENINGS

Developing Family Rules

Discuss the basic goals of your family, and list them on a poster or chalkboard. Go over the rules you have established in your home, and show how each rule relates to one of those goals.

If you do not have clearly formulated rules, you may wish to define some. By letting each family member help make the rules, you can build a sense of family loyalty. Family members will want to keep the rules because they will understand why the rules are reasonable and important.

You may also find that some traditional rules are not really relevant to any important goals; and, after discussion, you may wish to eliminate them. You may also end up with more rules than goals since some goals may require more than one rule. Following are some examples:

Family Goals	Family Rules
We want to be a loving family.	We will all try to attend any event in which one of our family members is involved to show our support.
We want to be a healthy family.	We will obey the Word of Wisdom.
We want to be active in the Church.	We will all attend sacrament meeting together. We will accept Church callings when asked.
We want to be alert at school and work.	We will always be home by ten o'clock on school nights.
We want to be morally clean.	We will not date until we are sixteen. We will not do anything that will lead to immorality.
We want to develop our individual talents.	We will practice one hour each day.
We want to be kind.	There will be no quarreling in our house.
We want to be together as a family in eternity.	We will have family home evening every week. We will plan to be married in the temple and keep the commandments.

Family Councils

Plan to hold family councils regularly. You could discuss such subjects as family scheduling, family responsibilities, a family garden, or the family vacation. You may wish to devote a family home evening to discussing and preparing for a family council, setting up the procedures and the agenda, and fixing the schedule. Family councils do not take the place of family home evening lessons each week. You should plan regular lessons or activities as well.

Solving Problems as a Family

As a family, select some family need or problem that you feel would be a good project to fulfill or solve. Plan together how you can work on it as a family. Set a time limit in which you will accomplish the need or solve the problem. For example, you might decide, "We will not have arguments in our home for one full week. We can discuss quietly any conflict that may arise, and settle it peacefully and in friendship."

Plan a reward night when your family will celebrate their success in the project. Even if you do not have full success, reward the efforts of family members, and comment on how much better things were as you all tried to reach the desired goal.

Patriarchal Order in the Home

Teach family members about the principle of the patriarchal order, starting with father Adam. Relate this order to your own family and the extended family. This will give family members a sense of the continuity of Heavenly Father's family here on earth.

FAMILY UNITY

He commanded them that there should be no contention one with another, but that they should look forward with one eye, having one faith and one baptism, having their hearts knit together in unity and in love one towards another.
[Mosiah 18:21]

PURPOSE

Help family members create a greater sense of unity and belonging.

FOR THE PARENT

What did "family unity" mean to the pioneer family who made their way by ox cart across the plains? Or to the hardy people who settled your country? For many of these people, family unity was both a necessity and a natural result of their way of life. Their families lived and worked together. They relied heavily on each other for companionship, safety, and survival.

But in our fast-paced world, many of us change jobs and homes several times in a lifetime. As a result, we have learned to depend less on family. In many of our homes, where television and outside activities compete for our attention, family members may actually feel isolated from one another.

Today, like families in the past, your family has a strong need for unity. Your family came to this earth from a loving home with our Father in Heaven. We lived in a family with Heavenly Father. We live in a family now, and we may live with our family eternally if we are worthy.

PREPARATION

1. Draw five blank lines on a piece of paper on which to spell the word *unity*.

2. Prepare and place the ingredients for a simple cake or other dessert in separate containers. Preheat the oven, and prepare the pans for cooking the dessert.
3. Cut out paper links for a chain, as many links as there are members in your family. Write the name of a different member of the family on each link. Bring staples or tape to finish the chain.
4. Bring pencil and paper for each family member.

SUGGESTED HYMNS AND SONGS

"O My Father" (*Hymns*, no. 139).
"There Is Beauty All Around" (*Hymns*, no. 169).
"We're All Together Again" (*Sing with Me*, D–8).
"Mother and Father" (*Sing with Me*, D–7).

SUGGESTED LESSON

What Makes a Happy Family?

Explain to your family that one element that is absolutely necessary to every happy home is easy to overlook. Hold up the paper with five blank lines on it, and ask the family to think of the word that fills in the blanks and tells what is missing from the family in the following story:

What Is Missing?

The Carter family has six children. Mark, the oldest, has served a mission for the Church. All the other children plan to serve missions too. The Carter children are good students, and they have many friends. Mark attends college, and the youngest child, Susan, is in second grade.

Brother Carter is active in his priesthood quorum. He often does kind things for the people he home teaches. Sister Carter enjoys teaching her Sunday School class. Both parents attend the temple regularly, and the family faithfully attend ward meetings and activities.

The Carters live in a nice neighborhood. Brother Carter has a good job.

- So far, does anything necessary to the happiness of this family seem to be missing?
- Knowing only these facts, would you rate this family as happy or unhappy? (From all appearances, the Carters seem to be a happy family.)

Continue with the story:

One weekend Mark Carter went with his roommate, Blaine, to the Jackson house. On the way back to school, Mark said, "You have a great family. They seem so close and happy. I wish my family could be like that."

Blaine replied, "Yeah, I really love to go home."

"Well," said Mark, "I love my family, too, but I sure hate to go home. The younger kids fight with each other constantly. Mom and dad are gone all the time, too. When they are home, they're always shouting at us because they seem to be in such a hurry.

"What a good time we had eating dinner at your house—everyone talking about what they did during the day. Everybody wanted to share what was going on in their lives with the rest of the family. Afterward, everyone cleaned off the table and did the dishes.

"Mealtime at our house is a completely different story. Mom calls the children to come to the table, but they come dragging in one at a time. We're almost never all at the table when dad blesses the food. He says the blessing when he sits down at the table whether or not anyone else is there. We all eat in a hurry. Then everyone scatters to avoid doing the dishes.

"I sometimes think that if we could have family home evening it would help. But everyone usually has something else he'd rather be doing like watching television, working on homework, talking to friends on the telephone, or preparing a lesson for Church. Yet, mom and dad seem to think we're doing all right as a family."

• What is missing from Mark's family?

• What do you think makes a happy family?

Fill in the blanks with the word *unity.*

Have everyone tell what they think *unity* means. Include ideas like making time for each other, working together, playing together, trying to reach goals together, being willing to listen to and help each other.

• Do you think our family is more like Mark's or Blaine's?

• When have we felt unified, working together and really caring about each other?

Unity Is Essential

Take your family into the kitchen. Show them each of the ingredients for the cake. Point out that these ingredients are good all by themselves, but unless they are mixed together they couldn't be called a cake.

Mix the cake, and pour it into pans.

Let each person help prepare it. Bake it while you finish the lesson.

Explain that each family member has his own strengths, talents, and interests. By himself each person could accomplish many things. But without a feeling of unity, a desire to work together and support each other, all of the separate people who live in your house couldn't be called a real family.

Unity in Heavenly Father's Family

Ask each person to tell what he thinks it felt like to live with Heavenly Father. As you describe two of our Heavenly Father's sons, have the family listen for what one son did to break up the family and what one son did to bring it together:

Our Father in Heaven has a large family of sons and daughters. One of Heavenly Father's sons is very selfish. He chose not to follow his Heavenly Father's plan for the family. He persuaded many of his brothers and sisters to leave the family. He is still trying to gain more followers. He is proud and willing to do anything to get his own way and thinks of his own desires first.

Another son, Heavenly Father's firstborn, loves his Father in Heaven very much and always obeys him. He also loves all of his brothers and sisters. Even though he is his father's first son, he is never proud. He always puts his family first, never his own desires. He was even willing to die so that our heavenly family could always be together.

• Who were these two sons? (Satan and Jesus.)

• What does Satan's bad example show about the result of one person's selfishness and unwillingness to be part of the family? (It can destroy unity.)

• What can we learn from Jesus about what we must do to have unity in our family (see John 5:30)?

Unity in Our Family

Point out that we must be willing to think of others in the family and how our actions affect the whole group. We must be willing to do what is best for all, not just what we want. Mention several small daily acts of unselfishness that you have seen each family member do and how each act

helped bring the family closer together.

Express your gratitude that Jesus has been the kind of brother who would make a very great sacrifice to make it possible for you to return to Heavenly Father's home. Express your desire to help your family return together and to do whatever you can to make that possible. Explain that each person will need to help. Suggest that each person—when he has to choose between something he wants and something that would be good for the family—think, *"We* not *me."*

Begin the paper chain activity by handing each family member the link with his name written on it. Then have the father staple, paste, or tape the two ends of his strip together in a circle first. While he does this, he could tell the children about his courtship: how he felt about their mother, what drew them together, and how they dreamed about their future together. Then the mother could tell about their wedding and early life together as she runs her strip through the circle and fastens the ends, making a two-link chain. The parents could explain that their lives became closely connected when they formed a family.

Have the oldest child connect his link to the chain and continue to the youngest. As each family member adds his link, express your love and need for that person in the family. Add something special about him so that he will realize that he is an important part of the family.

Building More Unity in Our Family

Have each person suggest possible goals for developing greater family unity. For example, you could arrange to be together at mealtimes more often. Share ideas on how you can support each other better even when you are not together. Decide on specific ideas to begin using in your home.

Express your desire to make your home a happy, secure place for each family member. Hang the chain in a place where it can remind everyone how important the family is.

If your family knows the song "Mother and Father," they may enjoy adapting it. Pass out the paper and pencils, and together write a verse about each child in the family. Close your family home evening by singing the verses you have written.

After the closing prayer, enjoy the cake or dessert that you have made together.

ADAPTING FOR YOUNGER CHILDREN

Explain that Heavenly Father planned for us to live together as a family. Each one of us is important to our family. We love each other and should try to help each other.

Make the paper chain. Be sure to express love and a need for each family member as his link is added to the chain. Each child might enjoy making his own family chain.

Tell about a time you did something as a family. Stress that having each member of the family there made it more fun.

Tell the following story:

A Day at the Park

The Whites had been planning their Saturday trip to the park all week long. But when Saturday morning finally came, four-year-old Lisa was sick. Jimmy and Brian said they still wanted to go to the park. Mother said she would stay home with Lisa, so father, Jimmy, and Brian packed their lunches and left for the park.

Jimmy and Brian jumped out of the car as soon as they stopped and ran to the swings. They rolled in the grass and played on the climbing bars and slide all morning. But when they sat down on the grass to eat lunch, Jimmy said, "I wish Lisa and mommy were here. It's not as much fun without everybody."

Brian said, "I miss them, too. And I know how much Lisa likes to play at the park."

Father suggested they go home and eat their lunch. When they got home, Lisa was excited to see them. She was feeling better, so they all ate lunch together in the backyard.

Brian said, "Next time we go to the park, we can all go together."

"And it will be a lot more fun," added Jimmy.

ADAPTING FOR TEENAGERS AND ADULTS

Use the story "What Is Missing?" and the discussions under the headings "Unity in Heavenly Father's Family" and "Unity in Our Family." But you may want to replace either the cake activity or the chain activity with the following one:

Have family members take turns sitting in a chair in the middle of the room. Have the family think about two or three things they could do to support that person. You may need to give an idea or two to get them started. For example, if one member of the family is involved in a school activity, you might suggest that the family could be sure to attend the event together.

After each person has had a turn, challenge everyone to do one small thing every day that will make the family more unified. Have everyone write down one specific thing he will do each day.

If you are a couple living alone, you can use this activity, too. Discuss ways you can be more unified as a couple and as members of your extended family. Look at wedding pictures and other pictures and mementos that remind you of your love for each other.

SUGGESTIONS FOR FUTURE HOME EVENINGS

Doing Things Together

Plan an evening of doing something together that everyone will enjoy, such as planting a garden, playing a game, having a picnic or family outing, or visiting grandparents. Make it an activity in which each person can participate, both in the planning and in the activity itself.

Family Unity Demonstration

Attach a small sign that says "Family Unity" to the top of a stick about four or five feet long, such as a broom or mop handle or a yardstick. Cut some strong string or cord into two-yard lengths, one for each family member. Explain that the sign and stick stand for creating unity in your home.

Have each family member tie his string a little above midway up the stick. Then lay the stick in the middle of the floor, and have the family sit around it in a circle. Have a person see if he can raise the stick to a standing position by pulling only his string. He will find that one string does not support it very well; it can fall over easily.

Ask another family member to join him and see if two strings can keep the stick standing. This may be possible, but the stick will still be unsteady.

Then let everyone pull their strings to hold the stick in an upright position. You may have to adjust the places where the strings are tied. Hold the pole upright.

- What can you learn from this exercise? (Family unity depends on everyone pulling together.)

Now have one family member pull the stick toward him with all his strength, while the others pull normally.

- What does this show about family unity? (One person can destroy the balance. His selfishness could soon dispel family unity.)

Use this activity to further discuss how family members can share and support each other and spend more time together. Develop a family calendar of events so that each person can know about times that are special to other family members and plan to share those times.

Learning About Each Other

Use the following activities to help family members to get to know each other better:

1. Ask each person to think of a favorite family experience—humorous or serious. Have him tell it to the others.

2. Tell a fact about a family member that the rest of the family may not know. Have other family members try to match the fact with the person.

3. Ask each family member to tell what he would like the family to do to help make family life happier. There must be no criticizing or defensive replies. Let the family continue until everyone has made as many statements as he wants. Plan ways to put some of these suggestions into practice.

OUR EXTENDED FAMILY

And he shall turn the heart of the fathers to the children, and the heart of the children to their fathers.
[Malachi 4:6]

PURPOSE

Help family members to develop a greater appreciation and love for their extended family and to take steps to strengthen extended family relationships.

FOR THE PARENT

Relationships with members of the extended family can be a great blessing. The extended family includes your children's grandparents, uncles, aunts, and cousins.

It is the Lord's will that we be sealed in an unending chain according to the patriarchal order of the priesthood. If we do all we should together as an extended family, we will be united together after this life in the presence of our Heavenly Father.

PREPARATION

Prepare at least two charts, each showing the families into which the father and mother were born. You may wish to prepare similar additional charts for the grandparents as well. If possible, mount appropriate pictures beside each name.

SUGGESTED HYMN
AND SONG

"There Is Beauty All Around" (*Hymns*, no. 169).
"When Grandpa Comes" (*Sing with Me*, D–17).

SUGGESTED LESSON

Knowing Our Relatives

Tell the following story to lead your family into discussion:

Do You Remember?

Mother and the four children were shopping one afternoon when they bumped into some of their father's relatives.

"Stephen and Kay, these are two of daddy's aunts who live here in town," mother explained as she introduced the two older children to the elderly ladies. "Aunt Nellie and Aunt Elaine are your Grandma Smith's sisters. Remember when we visited them a couple of years ago?"

Stephen and Kay glanced at each other and shrugged their shoulders. They couldn't remember ever meeting Great Aunt Nellie or Great Aunt Elaine.

• Has something like this ever happened to you? Have you ever met distant relatives?

Share experiences of how your feelings toward your relatives may have changed when you got to know them.

Discuss how knowing some of these distant relatives can be interesting and important. You may wish to relate family traditions and history about some of them. Explain that it is even more important to know well the members of your closer extended family.

The Extended Family

Discuss the difference between your immediate family and your extended family. The immediate family includes the father, mother, and children. The extended family includes the grandparents and their children, the aunts and uncles, and their children, the cousins.

- Why is the immediate family so important?

- What are the responsibilities of the immediate family members to each other?

To help answer these questions, read Ephesians 6:1–4.

- Why are family relationships even more important than relationships with friends?

Review your plans for an eternal family, a family that can be together forever. Emphasize your experience of being sealed in the temple if you have had this experience.

- Why is the extended family also important? (Our grandparents made it possible for many of the blessings we now have. Our uncles, aunts,

and cousins can enrich our lives, and we can use our talents to help them in their lives. Our extended family can also be together in the celestial kingdom forever by being sealed in the temple and living worthily.)

Discuss Malachi 4:6.

- Do you know all of your aunts and uncles? How many of them have you met? Which ones are older or younger than father or mother? Do you know all of your cousins? How many of them have you seen? Who are the new ones? When did you last see them? When will you get a chance to see all these relatives again?

Display one by one the charts you have prepared as your discussion progresses. Ask family members to tell anything they remember about each person on the charts. Parents can also tell a story about each person. Discuss any future plans to visit or be visited by these various relatives.

We Can Know Our Extended Family Better

- What are some things we can do to

become closer to members of our extended family?

Allow a free discussion. Often the children will come up with the best ideas. With the aid of the charts, discuss how your family can build a better relationship with each person.

Make both short- and long-range goals to help you draw closer to members of your extended family. You will probably wish to use this year's calendar to help you organize your plans. The following list contains some possibilities:

1. Visit a different family every Sunday, every other Sunday, or regularly on another day that would be convenient.

2. Send birthday and anniversary greetings.

3. Write regularly with cousins of your own age.

4. Help organize a regular extended family meeting. (Due to distance, many may be unable to attend regularly, but those close to each other should meet together.)

5. Help plan an annual family reunion.

6. Organize a family newsletter or newspaper.

7. Set up extended-family traditions.

8. Set up an extended-family photo album.

9. Exchange family histories and family group sheets.

10. Plan to visit relatives who will be having marriage or missionary celebrations.

ADAPTING FOR YOUNGER CHILDREN

An important goal for your children would be for them to be able to identify each member of the extended family on both the father's and mother's side. Point out the pictures on your chart as you discuss your relatives. Perhaps you will want to pause at each picture and tell a story about the person with which the children may be familiar. Emphasize each person's name and that these people are your family even though they do not live in your house.

Conclude by doing something to associate with your extended family members, such as making a visit, calling on the phone, or writing a card.

ADAPTING FOR TEENAGERS AND ADULTS

By telling the story "Do You Remember?" and using the prepared charts, ask the older children and adults how many members of the extended family on both sides they can name. Include the aunts, uncles, and cousins of the parents.

Read together the following statement by President Ezra Taft Benson:

"Our responsibility to organize our families at the immediate family level begins when a couple is married. The grandparent family organization develops as children from the immediate family marry and have children. Through such family organizations, every family in the Church should become actively involved in missionary work, family preparedness, genealogy and temple work, teaching the gospel, and cultural and social activities." (In Conference Report, Oct. 1978, p. 41; or *Ensign*, Nov. 1978, p. 30.)

• What can we do to help establish an extended family organization?

• What kind of activities would our extended family organization enjoy?

• What goals should our extended family organization have?

FOR GRANDPARENTS

Elder Marvin J. Ashton suggested one activity that grandparents could use to help strengthen the extended family organization:

"I challenge grandparents to foster reading programs with your grandchildren. If you are close enough to be with them, read the books to them that will help develop character and ideals. If you're a distance away, send them books, old or new, with a personal invitation to read them and report how they like them." (In Conference Report, Oct. 1977, p. 109; or *Ensign*, Nov. 1977, p. 72.)

• What other things can you do to aid your children's children? What restrictions should you place upon yourself so that you do not take over the proper role of the parents?

Use the conclusion of the family lesson to set goals to become closer to members of your extended family.

SUGGESTIONS FOR FUTURE HOME EVENINGS

Learning Who's Who in Your Extended Family

Find pictures of grandparents, aunts, uncles, and cousins as far removed as you care to extend family knowledge. If possible, get two pictures of the same family member at different ages. Show a picture, and see who can give the correct name first. Or display four or five pictures and challenge family members to name all of them.

When family members have learned to identify the pictures, try a memory game. Display five pictures for ten seconds. The players study them, then look away. Remove one picture and ask, "Who is missing?" As players become more skilled, increase the number of pictures displayed, and rearrange the pictures while they are looking away.

If you have two pictures of each person, you can play "Concentration." Each player gets a turn to try to match a pair by turning up two pictures, one after the other. If they match, he removes them to his pile. If they do not, he turns them face down again. Players watch and try to remember where those that match are located. The player who finds the most pairs wins. To make the game harder, use pictures taken at different ages. Thirty pictures or more (fifteen pairs) makes a good game. You can also challenge family members to arrange the pictures in family trees to show knowledge of family relationships.

Getting to Know Grandparents

Grandparents can enrich your children's lives many times during family home evening through personal visits, tapes, or letters. Help grandparents to prepare by asking them to supply specific information for a given evening, such as what kinds of games they played when they were little, what their earliest memories are, or how they joined the Church. If possible, ask them to supply pictures and objects from their past.

Honoring Our Ancestors

Visit a cemetary where some of your family is buried. You could—

1. Explain the separation of the spirit from the body at death.

2. Notice dates and figure ages.

3. Compare the dates to historical events.

4. Note family relationships.

Tombstone rubbing can be an interesting project. To do this, place a piece of paper over the writing on the tombstone, and rub it carefully with a pencil, crayon, or piece of colored chalk. In this way the writing is transferred to the paper.

You may wish to make a special family project of decorating the graves of grandparents or great-grandparents with flowers.

Getting to Know Our Cousins

Use your family home evening to plan and invite cousins to join. Plan some activities that might be held. Family members might plan to get together three or four times a year for special activities, to encourage each other about missions and temple marriages, to write to missionary cousins, or to do service projects for grandparents and other family members, such as giving a shower for a bride, tying a quilt for each cousin, or having graduation parties or birthday parties. If this is not practical due to distance or for other reasons, family members could plan to write letters regularly back and forth.

Deepening Family Relationships

Consider what you already have in common with different family units in the extended family. Consider what interests you might develop with other families. A variety of activities and experiences with other family units will strengthen your family relationships. Plan activities, such as showing family slides of vacations and travels, playing a game of soccer or baseball, making ice cream, hiking together, collecting minerals or seashells, or going on a temple excursion. You can use a family home evening to plan how to organize and carry out one or two such activities with other family units in your extended family.

LOVING OUR NEIGHBORS

Thou shalt love the Lord thy God with all thy heart, and with all thy soul, and with all thy mind.

This is the first and great commandment.

And the second is like unto it, Thou shalt love thy neighbour as thyself.

On these two commandments hang all the law and the prophets.
[Matthew 22:37–40]

PURPOSE

Help family members love all of our Heavenly Father's children.

FOR THE PARENT

The Lord tells us that if we obey the commandment to love our fellowman, men will know that we are true followers of Jesus Christ (see John 13:35). It is also on this commandment that we will be judged of God. We are told in a parable that when we come to be judged of God we will be divided into two groups—those who loved and served others and those who did not. (See Matthew 25:31–46.) Jesus will say, "Inasmuch as ye have done it unto one of the least of these my brethren, ye have done it unto me" (Matthew 25:40).

Teaching our children and training ourselves to look out for our neighbor's welfare is second only to loving the Lord. If we claim to be followers of Jesus Christ, then we must learn in our families to do his work. We must help, forgive, teach, and love his brothers and sisters, for he gave his very life for them, and he loves them even as he loves us.

PREPARATION

1. Cut a small heart for each member of the family.

2. Make a double dessert that you can share.

SUGGESTED HYMN AND SONG

"Have I Done Any Good?" (*Hymns,* no. 58).

"Love One Another" (lesson 36, "He Is Risen!")

SUGGESTED LESSON

Show the picture of the cows in the lesson, and tell the following story:

We Can Be Friends

Mr. Martin moved to a farm that joined the farm owned by Mr. Thomas, an old-timer in the area. A short time later, one of Mr. Thomas' cows found a hole in the fence and went into Mr. Martin's field. Mr. Martin was angry and demanded the top price for his damages. Mr. Thomas promptly paid him.

A few months went by. Then one day several cows belonging to Mr. Martin got through the fence into Mr. Thomas's property and remained there an entire day before they were discovered. Mr. Martin expected an angry visit from his neighbor but to his surprise, Mr. Thomas was not angry when he called. Instead he said, "We are living side by side as neighbors. It is only natural that some problems arise. I have lived long enough to

know that these problems will make us enemies if we let them. If we decide we want to be friends, we will be. It all depends upon what we want. I value your goodwill. Let's work together and repair the fence between us and make it strong enough that the stock can't get through."

After that the two men became good friends.

The Second Greatest Commandment

Ask your family to think about Mr. Martin and Mr. Thomas while they listen to something very important that Jesus said. Have someone read Matthew 22:35–40.

• What did Jesus say is the first great commandment?

• What did Jesus say is the second greatest commandment?

• How is the second great commandment like the first?

• What did Mr. Thomas do to show that he loved his neighbor?

Who Is My Neighbor?

Remind your family that Mr. Martin and Mr. Thomas were neighbors because they lived next to each other. Another definition of *neighbor* is "a human being like oneself; a fellow man."

You may want to briefly tell the story of the Good Samaritan in Luke 10:25–37.

Have family members raise their hands whenever you name a neighbor. Begin by naming those who live closest to you. Then mention friends that live a little farther away and acquaintances. Be sure they understand that all of Heavenly Father's children are our neighbors and that he wants us to love them all.

Love Is an Action Word

Share the following story:

In Primary, Marilyn was learning about the children who live all over the world. She thought their differences were very interesting, but she felt close to all of the children because in many ways they were the same. As she learned more, the feeling in her heart for the children from all over the world grew. At the end of sharing time, she leaned over and told her teacher, "I love all of Heavenly Father's children."

In class, just a few minutes later, Anna came over and sat down by Marilyn. Anna was new in town, and she wore the strangest clothes. She talked with a funny accent, and she combed her hair differently. She had moved in from another part of the country. Marilyn had listened and laughed before when her classmates made fun of Anna and when Anna sat down and said "Hi," Marilyn heard some of the others giggle. Suddenly Marilyn felt very embarrassed to be sitting next to Anna. Without saying anything, she got up and moved away.

• Did Marilyn feel love for all of our Heavenly Father's children?

• Did Marilyn show love in her actions toward Anna?

Finish the story:

During class Marilyn had a bad feeling inside. She kept looking at Anna who sat with her head bowed in embarrassment all the rest of the way through the lesson. Marilyn wished she had acted differently. When class was over, she hurried over to Anna and caught her arm. "I'm sorry I moved away, Anna," she said. "I would like to be your friend. Will you meet me for lunch in school tomorrow?"

Anna broke into a happy grin, and Marilyn's bad feeling disappeared.

Explain that love is not just a feeling. It is a way we act, something we do. In fact, many times love doesn't come to our hearts until after we have acted in a loving way.

List together some of the things we can do to keep the second greatest commandment. You may need to ask some questions to get the ideas started, such as—

• What did Mr. Thomas do to show love?

• What did Marilyn do?

• What have people done for you to make you feel the love they have for you?

Your list may include being friendly, forgiving you, being responsible, finding solutions when problems arise, paying compliments, giving little treats or gifts, listening, writing letters, helping, or not judging.

Begin By Doing

Explain that because the commandment to love others is important, you want to do something about it. Pass out the little hearts that you made, and have each family member write on one the name of a person he would like to begin to show love toward. Then have each person choose from the list that you made at least one idea that he can do this week to begin. Have him write that action on the back of the heart. Challenge each person to put the heart where he will see it often until his action is accomplished.

Then invite your family to get in the mood for loving their neighbors by helping you to think of someone they would like to share dessert with. Try to think of someone that they want to love more. Call ahead to make sure your treat will be welcomed. Then go together and deliver your treat.

ADAPTING FOR YOUNGER CHILDREN

Hold up the picture of Jesus teaching the people (included in the lesson), and tell the children about the two great commandments. Tell them that a neighbor is anyone we meet. You may want to do the activity under "Who Is My Neighbor?" in the suggested lesson. Make sure they understand that Jesus wants us to love every one. Then tell the following story:

Loving Isn't Easy

One day, six-year-old Tammy was playing with some of her neighborhood friends when one of the boys snatched the jump rope from her. As he did so, he knocked her down. Tammy went crying into the house and found her father. She quickly told him what happened and begged him to go out and punish the boy.

Tammy's father took hold of her hand and said softly, "Would it do any good if I went out and punished him? If I did that he would feel sad, and he would be angry with me. And he'd even be more angry at you. Wouldn't it be better if we went out and started playing jump the rope again and asked him to come over and play with us? We'd feel better, and I know he'd feel better too. Then both of us would still have him for our friend."

- Is loving everybody always easy?
- What did Tammy and her father do to show their love for the boy? Tell the children that love is more than just a feeling in our hearts. Love is the way we act toward people.

Let the family role-play the story of Tammy. Reemphasize that love is something we do. To keep this second greatest commandment, we must act in a kind way toward all of our Heavenly Father's children.

Your children may enjoy writing, on a little heart, a name and an act of love to do in the coming week as in the regular lesson. Help them carry out their ideas so that they feel good about them. They will enjoy taking dessert to share with another family. Let them choose a family they love or a Primary teacher. Then let them present the treat themselves. Again, be sure you call ahead so that you will be expected.

ADAPTING FOR TEENAGERS AND ADULTS

Introduce your lesson with the story "We Can Be Friends" or a simliar story from real life. Then have them read Matthew 22:35–40.

- Who is our neighbor?

Review the story of the Good Samaritan in Luke 10:29–37 to help answer this question.

- Can you love someone who may not feel it?
- If someone is loved and does not know it, does it do him any good?

Explain that our heartfelt concern for others must be converted into action if we are to keep the second greatest commandment. If we love someone, our thoughts will be for them and their best good, and we will treat them unselfishly (see Matthew 7:12).

Discuss John 13:34–35.

- How can we love as Jesus loves?

Ask the family how the commandments to love their neighbor could be kept in the following instances:

1. A girl is sitting all alone at a dance.
2. Your neighbor's unleashed dog often messes up your yard.

3. Your new employee has been stealing from your other employees.
4. Your boyfriend wants you to show your love by inappropriate moral behavior.
5. Your friend is always borrowing money and not returning it.

Now have each family member make up two or three case studies from what he has seen in real life. Point out that this commandment is not always easy to live and may require fasting and prayer to even know what we should do in some cases.

Conclude your home evening by rereading John 13:34–35 and bearing your testimony to the importance of this commandment as we work toward becoming true followers of Christ. Challenge each family member to set a goal of showing love to someone this week when it isn't easy. You may want to set a family goal, too, especially if you are having a specific problem with someone.

If you think your family would enjoy it, you may want to conclude by sharing family home evening dessert with someone as recommended in the regular lesson.

SUGGESTIONS FOR FUTURE HOME EVENINGS

Welcoming New Families into the Neighborhood

Plan how to welcome a new family into your neighborhood, then role-play the part members of the family will play. You might consider—

1. Preparing lunch or dinner for the neighbors on moving day. Furnish paper or plastic plates and tableware, or collect the dishes and silverware afterward so that they won't have to worry about cleaning up.
2. Offering to babysit younger children while parents and older children put the house in order.
3. Giving them a list of addresses and directions for finding schools, cleaning establishments, laundromats, grocery and clothing stores, and nearby churches. If it seems appropriate, invite them to go to church meetings with you.

Add other ideas that would fit the situation for your family or neighborhood.

Going the Extra Mile

Good feelings toward someone often follows doing something for the person without being asked (see Matthew 5:41). If some resident of your neighborhood seems to have trouble keeping up his yard, you might offer to mow the lawn or weed the flower or vegetable garden for him. If yard work is a source of extra income, you might consider going beyond what you ordinarily contract to do as a service. When cleaning snow from your walk, if you notice your neighbor has not yet cleaned the walks, you might go the extra mile to make a path from his door to the street.

Take time to listen to neighbors who like to reminisce, especially older or housebound neighbors. If they spend time complaining, listen without judgment. Sometimes all they need is a good listener to help them feel better. You might decide how long the visit will last, and announce when you arrive that you can only stay so long. Then give your complete attention while you are there. (See also lesson 25, "Developing Compassion.")

Knowing How to Help in Emergencies

Sometimes the greastest service of love you can offer is to be able to help in an emergency. Plan for a time when the family can learn about and practice first-aid, survival techniques, and water safety skills. Each family member should know where the consecrated oil is kept so that priesthood members can administer blessings when needed. (See "Family Preparedness Activities" in the activities section of this resource book.)

Providing Special Help

Many people need special help that you may be able to provide. Ask your bishop for help in contacting Church or community agencies that will assist you in projects like those listed below. In some cases, he may refer you to the Social Services Department of the Church.

1. "Adopt" a prisoner in a penal institution and share regular family home evening with him or her.

2. Bring an Indian student into your home through the Indian Placement Service.
3. Become a foster parent for a refugee child.
4. Read to the blind regularly.

Any of these projects will require a great deal of advance thought and preparation. However, you can use a family home evening to explore the possibilities and decide if this is something the family wants to do and can do. Even if the decision is not to pro-ceed with the project, the evening should prove to be a valuable experience for family members, during which they will be reminded of the Savior's commandment that we love our neighbors as ourselves. You may also wish to have someone with experience in such a project discuss the pros and cons with your family.

Building Friendships with Neighbors

Plan and hold a neighborhood social, such as a backyard barbecue, a street dance, or an evening of sports or games. Invite the whole neighborhood. Where neighbors offer or are willing to help in the preparation, plan so that different families can work together. Encourage families to come together. Plan events for all ages. Explore the possibilities and begin the planning in your family home evening.

Sharing the Gospel with Neighbors

For a good discussion on how to share the gospel with your neighbors, see lesson 26, "Sharing Our Blessings."

UNDERSTANDING THOSE WHO ARE DIFFERENT

As ye would that men should do to you, do ye also to them likewise.
[*Luke 6:31*]

PURPOSE

Help your family accept and appreciate people who are different.

FOR THE PARENT

All of us on earth are members of our Heavenly Father's family, but we may be very different in looks, temperament, and tastes. As our perfect parent, God loves us all unconditionally. It is his desire that we give each other the same unconditional love.

Little children are curious about those who are different from them, but they are not judgmental. They quickly learn from the adults around them attitudes toward people who may be of a different race or culture, or who may have mental or physical handicaps. Parents have a solemn responsibility not to foster prejudices and negative attitudes in their children. All people want to be treated as children of the same loving Heavenly Father.

The Savior showed us the way when he said, "As ye would that men should do to you, do ye also to them likewise" (Luke 6:31).

PREPARATION

1. Have five or six pieces of different colored paper. Choose your children's favorites.
2. Bring enough blindfolds and earmuffs or earplugs for each person in your family. Collect enough mittens, gloves, socks, or something else you can put over a child's hand for each child.
3. For families with little children provide paper, scissors, and crayons for paper dolls.
4. For families with teenagers have a bowl and the suggested slips of paper ready.

SUGGESTED HYMN AND SONG

"Come, Follow Me" (*Hymns*, no. 14). "Jesus Said Love Every One" (*Sing with Me*, B–51).

SUGGESTED LESSON

Different Doesn't Mean Better or Worse

Spread out the colored papers so that everyone can see all of them.

- Which color do you think is the best?
- Which color do you think is the worst?

Explain that there is no color that is better or worse than the others. They are all just different. Variety in color helps make our world beautiful.

People come in varieties, too. Discuss with your family some of the ways the members of your own family are different from each other, such as the color of hair or eyes, age, size, or personality.

- In what other ways are people different? (Race, culture, mental or physical condition.)

Understanding How It Feels to Be Different

Put the blindfolds on each child, and then ask him to perform some easy task such as getting a book from another room or getting a drink of water. Afterward, let the family members talk about how it felt to be unable to see what they were doing.

Sometimes relatively simple tasks are difficult to master for those with other kinds of problems. Put the mittens or gloves on your children's hands, and ask them to tie their shoes or button their shirt. Ask them how it felt to find such an easy job so difficult to do and how they felt when they were finally able to do it.

Use the earmuffs or cotton earplugs to help your children realize how deaf people may feel. Give them a whispered command such as, "Walk across the room and touch the wall." Say it without looking at them or moving your lips very much. If they don't respond, repeat the command after first getting their attention and speak loudly with clear lip movements. Ask them what this has shown them about communicating with deaf people or people that have difficulty hearing.

Let your family pretend that you have all just arrived in your neighborhood from a country far away. Everything is different for you. Your skin is a different color from your neighbors. You are used to eating different food than you can get here. Everyone speaks a language you cannot understand.

To help your family understand what this would be like, read a short sentence or two in a foreign language, and ask them what you said. Don't worry about your pronunciation as they won't understand it anyway.

You may wish to use the following sentences:

English

We are happy to see you. Please stand up and tell us your name. Where do you live? You may sit down.

German

Wir freuen uns, Sie zu sehen. Bitte stehen Sie auf, und sagen Sie uns wie Sie heißen. Wo wohnen Sie? Setzen Sie sich bitte.

French

Nous sommes heureux de vous voir. Levez-vous, s'il vous plaît. Comment vous appelez-vous ? D'où venez-vous ? Asseyez-vous, s'il vous plaît.

Treating People Who Are Different with Love and Understanding

Now that you have had the opportunity to see some of the problems that face people who are different, discuss with your family how you can show love and understanding for these people. Most neighborhoods have in them people who are different. As a family, consider your own neighborhood and those in it who might need your love and understanding.

Remember that handicapped people usually wish to do as much for themselves as possible. They do not want attention drawn to their handicaps. Don't single them out for special attention, but be friendly, helpful, and supportive.

Making Eddy Happy

Tommy lived with his parents at the student housing center while his father attended the university. Tommy liked to live there because he had so many little boys and girls to play with in the big sandpile and on the swings.

Eddy lived there, too, but he didn't come out to play very often. He thought the children didn't like him because they would point to him and say, "Why don't you have two arms?"

One day, when Tommy's mother came for him, she saw Eddy leave the sandpile and go home crying. Tommy's mother called all the children together and told them about Eddy:

"When Eddy was born he was a beautiful baby just as all of you were. For some reason we don't understand, he had only one arm. Now, do you think that matters to our Heavenly Father? He loves Eddy just as much as he loves each of you, and he wants Eddy to be happy too. You can help make Eddy happy by being kind to him, just as you should be kind to each other. Now that you know about his arm, you don't need to talk to him about it anymore. When you are kind to Eddy, think of all those you make happy— Eddy, our Heavenly Father, Eddy's mother and father, and you."

Explain that people of other races or cultures also need acceptance. Even if language is a problem, a friendly greeting and exchange of names will show you care.

Hans Finds Some Friends

Hans had just moved to America from Germany. He didn't understand the teacher and the children.

The first day at kindergarten, Hans was so unhappy that tears came to his eyes. When choosing time came, Hans just stood there. He felt so alone. The teacher took his hand and said something. Her voice was kind, but he didn't know what she said. Then a little girl took his hand from the teacher's. She gently led him over to the playhouse.

She pointed to herself and said, "Anna." She pointed to him and said, "Hans." She touched herself again and said, "Anna, mother." She touched Hans and said, "Hans, father."

Hans knew what she meant. He smiled. He pointed to her and said, "Anna, *Mutter.*" Then he pointed to himself and said "Hans, *Vater.*"

They both laughed.

Anna picked up a baby doll and put it into Hans's arms. "Baby," she said.

Hans said, "*Ja, baby!*" Here was a word he knew. Her language wasn't so different.

Anna touched the doll's foot and said, "Foot."

Hans said, "*Fuss*"; then he said, "Foot."

Anna said, "Foot, *fuss.*" And they laughed again.

Then other children joined them. One held up the doll's shoe and said, "Shoe."

Han's eyes sparkled. He said, "*Ja, ja, Schuh!*"

And they all said, "*Schuh,* shoe."

When time came to go to the circle, the children were so excited they could hardly wait to tell about their word game and about the German words Hans had taught them.

Hans was happy. He felt important. He had found some friends in America.

Let each family member think of some special person they could help in some way during the following week, perhaps by just watching to open the church door for someone in a wheelchair, or saying hello to a newcomer at school.

Remind each one to keep in mind what Jesus said about doing to others what you would have others do to you. Have each family member report at breakfast or dinner each day any experiences he has had with people who are different.

ADAPTING FOR YOUNGER CHILDREN

Parents are often embarrassed when their young children point or ask questions in a loud voice about someone with a physical or mental handicap. Children are extremely curious and seem to be particularly interested in something or someone who is different. What children need is an explanation rather than a scolding.

Try the following activity:

1. Fold a rectangular sheet of paper in half three times. Draw a doll centered on the outside of the last fold, with arms and feet extending to the paper's edges.

2. With paper fully folded, cut around one-half of the outline. This makes four dolls joined at the hands and feet.

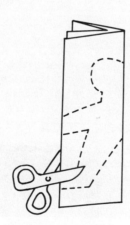

3. Make a set of dolls for each child, and have the children color in their own dolls as they wish. Suggest that they may wish to give the dolls different racial features and ethnic dress. Give them the opportunity to tell about the dolls they have colored.

ADAPTING FOR TEENAGERS AND ADULTS

One of the best ways to try to understand another person is to put yourself in his place. Write one of the following words or phrases on a piece of paper, and place each piece of paper in a bowl: "refugee," "person confined to a wheelchair," "blind person," "deaf person," "mentally retarded person," "new Church member from a

---

foreign land," and "elderly person living alone." You may think of others you wish to add. Let each family member take one slip of paper from the bowl and, after a few moments of thought, tell about the person identified on the slip of paper. Family members should use their imagination to describe what some of the problems are that the indicated person may face every day and how he would like others to treat him. Help each other with these discussions. If you see a problem or a solution that hasn't been mentioned, bring it up. If there are not enough people in your family to each take a role, discuss the roles generally together.

Read the following story from a conference address by Elder Spencer W. Kimball:

A Familiar Spirit

"May I conclude with this experience of my friend and brother, Boyd K. Packer, as he returned from Peru. It was in a branch Sacrament meeting. The chapel was filled, the opening exercises finished, and the Sacrament in preparation. A little Lamanite ragamuffin entered from the street. His two shirts would scarcely make one, so ragged they were and torn and worn. It was unlikely that those shirts had ever been off that little body since they were donned. Calloused and chapped were the little feet which brought him in the open door, up the aisle, and to the Sacrament table. There was dark and dirty testimony of deprivation, want, unsatisfied hungers—spiritual as well as physical. Almost unobserved he shyly came to the sacrament table and with a seeming spiritual hunger, leaned against the table and lovingly rubbed his unwashed face against the cool, smooth, white linen.

"A woman on a front seat, seemingly outraged by the intrusion, caught his eye and with motion and frown sent the little ragamuffin scampering down the aisle out into his world, the street.

"A little later, seemingly compelled by some inner urge, he overcame his timidity and came stealthily, cautiously down the aisle again, fearful, ready to escape if necessary, but impelled as though directed by inaudible voices with 'a familiar spirit' and as though memories long faded were reviving, as though some intangible force were crowding him on to seek something for which he yearned but could not identify.

"From his seat on the stand, Elder Packer caught his eye, beckoned to him, and stretched out big, welcoming arms. A moment's hesitation and the little ragamuffin was nestled comfortably on his lap, in his arms, the tousled head against a great warm heart—a heart sympathetic to waifs, and especially to little Lamanite ones. It seemed the little one had found a safe harbor from a stormy sea, so contented he was. The cruel, bewildering, frustrating world was outside. Peace, security, acceptance enveloped him.

"Later Elder Packer sat in my office and, in tender terms and with a subdued voice, rehearsed this incident to me. As he sat forward on his chair, his eyes glistening, a noticeable emotion in his voice, he said, 'As this little one relaxed in my arms, it seemed it was not a single little Lamanite I held. It was a nation, indeed a multitude of nations of deprived, hungering souls, wanting something deep and warm they could not explain—a humble people yearning to revive memories all but faded out—of ancestors standing wide-eyed, openmouthed, expectant and excited, looking up and seeing a holy, glorified Being descend from celestial areas, and hearing a voice say: "Behold, I am Jesus Christ, the Son of God. I created the heavens and the earth, and all things that in them are. . . . and in me hath the Father glorified his name. . . .

" ' "I am the light and the life of the world. I am Alpha and Omega, the beginning and the end." ' (3 Nephi 9:15, 18.)" (In Conference Report, Oct. 1965, pp. 71–72.)

- How did this story make you feel?
- How do you think the woman on the front row felt?
- What does this story tell about Elder Packer?
- What did he think about the physical characteristics of the child, his color, his clothing, his condition?

Have the family read and discuss 1 Samuel 16:7.

- How do you think the child that Elder Packer held felt?

Discuss ways you might show love and acceptance of those who are different.

- Are there any people living close to you who need your friendship and help?

Usually there are opportunitites in the community to give service to special people. Teenagers who have the opportunity may want to participate in the Special Olympics. Associations for the blind need people to read to the blind and also record books for them. Newcomers in a community, whether they are from foreign lands or not, always need friends. Make a special effort to follow the Savior's direction and treat others as you would like to be treated.

SUGGESTIONS FOR FUTURE HOME EVENINGS

Getting to Know You

Invite someone from a different cultural background to your home for family night, and let him tell you about his country, including its history, customs, dress, and holidays. You could do this with people of several different cultural backgrounds.

Understanding through Service

If there is someone who is elderly or physically handicapped in your neighborhood, arrange a time when your family can help them with housework or yard work or perform some other service. Encourage family members to get to know the person through conversation and working together.

Following the Example of the Savior

Have family members find examples of times when Jesus or his disciples showed understanding and compassion for those who were different. You may wish to select one or two of the following scriptures for them to think about: Luke 19:1–7 (Zacchaeus), Matthew 15:21–28 or Mark 7:25–30 (the Canaanite woman), John 4:5–26 (the Samaritan woman), Acts 10:1–34 (Cornelius and the vision of Peter), Luke 14:12–14 (Jesus teaching about the afflicted), 3 Nephi 17:6–9 (Jesus heals the afflicted among the Nephites). Discuss the chosen examples and how family members might follow them in their own lives.

Different or Alike?

Prepare a two-column chart with "Different" written across the top of the first column and "Alike" written across the top of the second. Have family members suggest ways that people are different and ways that people are alike. Enter these on the chart. Discuss how unimportant the differences are compared with the ways people are alike.

How Does Heavenly Father See His Children?

Prepare beforehand two identical arcs shaped like this:

The arcs must be circular and the same thickness throughout. You can copy these figures from the manual if you wish, or you can make them larger. Put a small 1 in a lower corner of one and a small 2 in the corresponding corner of the other. Arrange the two arcs one above the other like this:

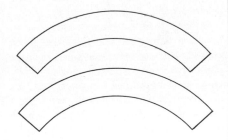

The bottom one will look bigger than the top. Ask the family to pick out the bigger arc. Switch the positions of the arcs, and ask again. Finally put one arc on top of the other to show that they are identical.

Explain that man doesn't always see things the way they really are but that God always does. When he looks at his children, he sees them as they really are. One is as important as another to Heavenly Father, even if they appear different to people. He sees their real values and their real differences, and he is not fooled by appearances. Read 1 Samuel 16:7.

Emphasize that Heavenly Father would like all of his children to accept the gospel.

DEVELOPING COMPASSION

Be ye all of one mind, having compassion one of another.
[1 Peter 3:8]

PURPOSE

Awaken compassionate thoughts and actions by helping family members realize that, like our Savior, they too have compassion for others.

FOR THE PARENT

Have you ever had your children express sympathy and love and a desire to help when a friend has fallen and scraped a knee or gotten a splinter in his finger? Have your children ever ached inside when one of their friends was made fun of at school? Have you ever felt true sorrow at the misfortune of a loved one? These are feelings of compassion—a Christlike virtue that each of us should develop. In fact, we are commanded to be compassionate. However, we should not have compassion simply because we are commanded. It is something we should want to develop. We are each born with feelings of compassion because we are Heavenly Father's children. We have to recognize those in need and develop our compassionate natures.

This lesson will help your family recognize compassionate feelings as they see the needs of others and learn from the example of the Savior.

PREPARATION

1. Obtain a packet of seeds, a mature plant of the same type as the seeds, or a picture of a mature plant or flower of that species.

2. Have pencils and slips of paper for each family member.

SUGGESTED HYMN AND SONG

"Have I Done Any Good?" (*Hymns*, no. 58).
"I Have Two Little Hands" (*Sing with Me*, B–74).

SUGGESTED LESSON

Why Did Christ Feed Four Thousand People?

Tell your family about how Jesus once fed four thousand people with seven loaves of bread and a few small fish. You may want to read the story aloud from Mark 8:1–9.

• Why did Jesus feed the people? (You are looking for the answer *compassion*, but accept all answers.)

If compassion is not mentioned, tell your family that you are thinking of a word that described the good feeling Jesus had for others. If no one says the word, tell family members to hold up their hands when they think they know what the word is, and begin to read Mark 8:1–2 aloud, leaving out the word *compassion*.

• What is compassion? (It is knowing that someone needs help and wanting to help them in any way you can.)

Christ Was Compassionate

• How did Jesus show compassion for people besides feeding the four thousand? (Answers should include various healings, teachings, and acts of kindness.)

• In the last hours of his life, despite the abuse and pain he suffered, for whom did Jesus show his great compassion? (His mother, the Roman soldiers, and the two theives being crucified with him.)

Some family members may be familiar with these events and can give the answers. As an example, you may want to read the account of Christ's compassion for his mother in John 19:25–27. As you do so, ask family members to point out Christ's act of compassion.

We Can Become Compassionate

Explain that our Heavenly Father wants each of his children to become compassionate just as he and the Savior are compassionate (see D&C 52:40).

• Does that mean that compassionate feelings and actions are easy?

Invite the family to pretend to be thirteen years old as Phillip was as you relate the following story:

Phillip

Phillip was a thirteen-year-old retarded boy whose ward boundaries were changed. Most of his friends stayed in his old ward, but his family went to the new ward that went to Church in a different chapel. His mother was concerned about how well Phillip would be accepted.

On his first Sunday in the new ward, Phillip entered his new class. From the back of the room came a question, "Hey, who's the guy with the thick glasses and the weird eyes?"

Phillip had a breathing problem which meant that often he had to stick his tongue out in order to get enough air. Seeing Phillip, one of the boys in the class turned to his friend, stuck out his tongue and said, "Look guys. Guess who I am."

Later that day at home, Phillip told his mother that he did not want to go to church.

• What wrong things did these class members do?

- How might you feel if you were Phillip?
- If you were in this class, what would you do?
- If the class made fun of you, what would you do?
- If Phillip were a friend of yours, would you feel any differently?

Continue the story:

Phillip's mother decided to ask to speak to the class the next Sunday, without Phillip being present. The teacher allowed Phillip's mother to explain: "When Phillip was born, the doctors did not think he would live. He was born with an imperfect body that does not allow him to do as much as some of you are able to do. He may not look like you, but he has the same kinds of feelings you do. He feels alone. He is a little afraid to be here, because he doesn't think he has any friends. I am concerned that without your help, he will never feel that this is his ward or his class."

During the next few weeks there was a decided change in the attitude and actions of the class. One of the girls in the class was slightly sick on a Sunday morning and was told by her mother that she would not be able to go to church. The girl, crying, protested, "But Phillip needs me."

- When have you felt concern, sorrow, and understanding for someone?
- When have you showed compassion for another?

Have your family tell about times when someone treated them with compassion.

How Do We Become Compassionate?
- How do we become compassionate?

Let family members examine a vegetable, fruit, or flower seed. If possible, show the mature plant or fruit or a picture of it. Explain that because we are children of our Heavenly Father, we have within us the seeds, or attributes, of compassion. In order for us to become truly compassionate, we must nurture and work with the seeds, just as we have to water and cultivate the vegetable or flower seeds for them to mature.

Discuss how the following stories relate to developing the seeds of compassion:

Jim Learns Compassion

Jim handed Carol the algebra paper he had corrected. She had missed most of the problems on it. "This stuff is easy," he thought. "Anyone could do it. She isn't that dumb. What's wrong with her?" Then he looked at Carol and saw that she was blinking back tears. "But it must be really hard for her," he admitted in surprise.

- What would you have said to Carol? (Let everyone give an opinion.)
- Jim was experiencing some feelings of compassion as he admitted that algebra was hard for Carol. What could he do to show compassion?

Tim Sees Something Funny

Tim came around the corner just in time to see Larry's bicycle hit a large rock in the street. The front wheel wobbled back and forth, until Larry finally lost control and fell. It looked pretty funny, and Tim wanted to laugh.

- What would you have done if you were Tim?
- Have you ever had an accident when other people were watching? How did you feel?
- How would a truly compassionate person react when Larry fell?

Read and discuss 1 Corinthians 12:26. Make sure that everyone recognizes that in these incidents there is a chance to grow in compassion by trying to understand another person's needs and helping him.

Our Family Members Can Grow in Compassion

Have each family member take a turn sitting in a chair in the middle of the room. As he sits there, have each of the other family members tell one way he could be more compassionate to the one in the chair. Explain that being compassionate means that we care about the problems of the one in the chair and want to help. We can always find something each of us could do to be more compassionate to members of our family.

Read and discuss Matthew 25:40. Then challenge each family member to act on at least one of his own suggestions during the coming week.

Have them write down the suggestion they will work on and keep it as a reminder during the week.

ADAPTING FOR YOUNGER CHILDREN

Often children have compassion for animals. You might want to tell the following story:

What Terry Found

Terry stood at the window watching the rain. Suddenly he heard a sound like someone crying. It was coming from outdoors. Terry listened. He pressed his nose against the glass and tried to see, but all he could see were the wavy shapes of trees and wet grass.

He ran to the front door and opened it. There on the doorstep was a tiny gray kitten, meowing as loudly as a little kitten could. It was soaking wet and shivering with cold.

Something inside Terry swelled up at the sight of the poor little animal. He picked up the kitten very gently. He could feel it shivering. He walked slowly to the kitchen, the kitten cradled against his warm body.

Terry's mother put some clean rags in a box. She dried the kitten, fluffing its fur. Then she set it among the rags and put a saucer of warm milk beside it. Terry sat down beside the box and put his hand on the kitten. It was still shivering, but not so much. Terry felt warm and good. "I'm so glad I heard the kitten crying. Maybe we saved its life."

- How did Terry feel about the kitten? (He felt sorry for it because it was wet and cold. He wanted to help it, and he did. He had compassion for the kitten.)

Tell your children that our Heavenly Father wants them to have compassion for everyone, just as Terry had for the kitten. Ask them to think of each family member—father, mother, a brother or sister—and think of a way they can show kindness or compassion for each one. Help them carry out their ideas during the week.

ADAPTING FOR TEENAGERS AND ADULTS

Use the story of Phillip, and adapt it

107

by using the following questions:

- How do you deal with the situation of other people being made fun of in front of you?

- What if those teasing others are your friends?

Allow the family members some time to share personal experiences of compassion. You may also wish to use the story of the Savior at the time of his crucifixion.

SUGGESTIONS FOR FUTURE HOME EVENINGS

Putting Compassion into Practice

Make plans to help someone outside your home. These plans need not be big or dramatic but should be of value to the person being served. You could visit the sick, relieve those who care for the chronically ill, visit the elderly, help someone who is discouraged, plan a program for shut-ins, or be friendly to your neighbor.

You can use chapter 28, "Service," in *Gospel Principles* [PBIC0245], pages 175 through 180, to help prepare for this family home evening. Many examples and ideas can be found in the *Church News, New Era, Friend, Ensign,* or your international magazine.

Understanding the Feelings of Others

Tell a story about how getting to know someone changes another person's feelings about him. You may find such stories in one of the Church magazines. You may wish to create such a story yourself, or relate an experience that happened in your family.

You may also wish to have family members try walking a short distance in another family member's shoes, using the other person's style of walking and talking to imagine what it would be like to be that person. Or you may wish to have family members act out the story of the Good Samaritan (Luke 10:29–37), Nephi and his brothers (1 Nephi 7:6–21), Joseph and his brothers (Genesis 37:1–35; 44–45), or any other scripture story of conflict between individuals. These stories can also be told with flannel board characters or hand puppets. Then ask each person to tell what he felt like as he was acting the part of the story character. Ask if this changed the way he thinks about the person he was portraying.

Suggest that each family member think of someone they do not like very well and try to imagine themselves to be that person, feeling how that person feels. Suggest that they think about the needs and hopes that might make the other person behave as he does. Then have them review how they feel about that person.

The Difference between Compassion and Tolerance for Sin

Explain that we must be careful that our compassionate feelings do not lead us to excuse or tolerate transgression. To teach this idea, you can read or have family members act out the story of the prodigal son (Luke 15:11–32). The story may also be told using hand puppets or flannel board cutouts. After the story, discuss such questions as the following:

- The prodigal had sinned. Did his father tolerate his sin?

- What was wrong with the attitude of the prodigal's brother?

- How did the prodigal's feelings change?

- What do you think would have happened if he had just gone home and demanded that his father help him out of his trouble?

- What makes the father's behavior righteous and not foolish? (You may wish to remind family members of the scripture from Doctrine and Covenants 1:31, "I the Lord cannot look upon sin with the least degree of allowance.")

Family members may wish to discuss how justice and mercy can exist together, using Mosiah 15:8–12 as an example, and relate these scriptures to the story of the prodigal son.

Showing Compassion for Others Is Serving the Lord

Sing all seven verses of the hymn "A Poor Wayfaring Man of Grief" (*Hymns,* no. 153). You may wish to draw attention to the blessings the narrator receives as he sacrifices for the stranger in each verse.

- Do you know where the inspiration for this song comes from?

Have someone read Matthew 25:31–46.

Ask family members to tell of any times in their own lives when they had an opportunity to serve someone they did not know very well and what the consequences were.

End by having someone read Mosiah 2:16–17. Explain that King Benjamin is speaking to his people in these verses.

Learning Compassion through Example

Assign each family member to find an example of compassionate service in the life of someone—an ancestor, a Church leader, a family member, a famous humanitarian, or some other person. You may want to help young children by directing them to such stories or helping them prepare their presentation.

During the home evening, have each family member tell the story he has found. After each story, have family members express any ideas the story has given them about how they can show compassion for family members or people in the neighborhood or in the ward or branch.

Family members may wish to expand this lesson into compassion service for someone.

Why We Need to Develop Compassion

Read Moses 4:1–4. Note that Lucifer promised to redeem *all* of God's children so that not one soul would be lost.

- Why did he choose the course he did? (Greed, ambition, self-interest.)

Compare Lucifer's plan with that which the Savior chose to follow.

- Which one acted out of real compassion for the souls of men?

Ask family members to name or describe historical events where promises similar to Lucifer's were made.

- What was the result?

Have someone read Doctrine and Covenants 121:36–37 to help answer this question.

Use these examples to discuss the idea that without compassion, man is not capable of becoming like Heavenly Father and can never receive celestial exaltation.

SHARING OUR BLESSINGS

O that I were an angel, and could have the wish of mine heart, that I might go forth and speak with the trump of God, with a voice to shake the earth, and cry repentance to every people!

Yea, I would declare unto every soul, as with the voice of thunder, repentance and the plan of redemption, that they should repent and come unto our God, that there might not be more sorrow upon all the face of the earth.
[Alma 29:1–2]

PURPOSE

Help family members learn how to share the blessings of the gospel with others.

FOR THE PARENT

Imagine what your life would be like if you did not have the blessings of the gospel. Have you ever felt a sense of gratitude for the blessings you enjoy each day and felt as though you wanted to share that gratitude with someone who would listen? Have you ever experienced the warmth that floods your heart when you have shared your feelings with others and could sense their receptiveness? That warmth was the love of Christ burning within your soul and needing to be shared.

Perhaps you have experienced the desire to tell others but have been fearful of rejection. This lesson gives some ideas that may be helpful in sharing the gospel.

PREPARATION

1. Bring to family home evening an envelope, crayon, slip of paper, and pencil for each family member. Also bring two large sheets of paper.

2. Prepare an envelope in which there is a slip of paper with the following scripture written on it: "If you keep my commandments and endure to the end you shall have eternal life, which gift is the greatest of all the gifts of God" (D&C 14:7). Write on the outside of the envelope "Our Heavenly Father's Gift."

3. You may want to get the filmstrip *How Great Shall Be Your Joy* (OF335) from your meetinghouse library.

SUGGESTED HYMN AND SONG

"High on the Mountain Top" (*Hymns*, no. 62).
"I Hope They Call Me on a Mission" (*Sing with Me*, B–75).

SUGGESTED LESSON

Note: If you live in an area where there are few nonmembers, you can help a totally or partially inactive member. These same principles apply in helping either members or nonmembers.

Identifying Our Nonmember Friends
Ask family members to pretend that the names of all the nonmember or inactive families or persons in your neighborhood, at work, or at school are placed in a box. Your family is to pretend that they are given the opportunity to draw a name from the box and give a gift to the family or individual whose name they draw.

Give family members pencils and paper. Have each family member write the name of the family or person whose name he would hope to draw. Have him read the name he has written and explain why he would hope to get that name.

The activity should help the family focus on some of the nonmembers or less active members they know.

If the family has any difficulty in naming someone, you could ask them to tell you the names of nonmember friends with whom they associate. You could give the names of nonmembers you know at work or through other associations in the community.

After several names have been mentioned, decide together on a family or person to whom your family would like to give a gift.

Deciding on the Best Gift

Give each family member an envelope, and ask him to use a crayon to draw a ribbon on the envelope, making it look like a present. On each envelope have him print the name of the family that has been chosen.

Next, have each family member write on a slip of paper what he feels would be the greatest gift he could give to the other family. Have him place the slip in the envelope. Collect the envelopes, and read and discuss the responses.

AMMON GOES ON A MISSION

Ammon   Lamanite   servant   teach   flocks   wicked men

[Ammon] had gone into the [Lamanite] country to serve a mission for the Church. He became a [servant] to King Lamoni so that he might seek opportunities to [teach] the gospel to the [Lamanite] people. One of [Ammon]'s duties was to tend the [flocks] of King Lamoni.

One day some [wicked men] scattered the [flocks]. [Ammon], upon seeing the scattered [flocks] and observing the fear of the other [servant]s, recognized his opportunity to [teach] the gospel.

The [servant]s wept because of fear they would be killed. When [Ammon] saw this, his heart filled with joy. He said, "I will show forth my power unto these my fellow-[servant]s, or the power which is in me, in restoring these flocks unto the king, that I may win the hearts of these my fellow-[servant]s that I may lead them to believe in my words" (Alma 17:29).

Then, acting under the inspiration of the Lord, [Ammon] encouraged the [servant]s to stop their weeping, to gather the [flocks] once more. When this was done, the same [wicked men] came again to scatter the [flocks]. [Ammon] said: "Encircle the [flocks] round about that they flee not; and I go and contend with these men who do scatter our [flocks]" (Alma 17:33).

The [servant]s obeyed [Ammon]. [servants] then went to the watering place to protect the [servant]s and the [flocks] from the [Lamanites] who delighted in killing. At first they fought with slings and stones. [Ammon], in mighty power from the Lord, threw his stones among the [Lamanites] and killed six of them. Not one of the [Lamanites] was able to hit [Ammon], so they threw down their slings and stones and came toward [Ammon] with clubs. As they came near him, [Ammon] raised his sword and cut off the arms of the [Lamanites] who raised their clubs against him.

[Ammon] was able to defend himself, the [servant]s, and King Lamoni's [flocks]. After the battle was over, the [servant]s ran to the king and excitedly told their story of how [Ammon] had saved the king's [flocks]. King Lamoni sent for [Ammon]. He could not understand how [Ammon], a Nephite, could be so loyal to the [Lamanite] people when the Nephites and [Lamanite]s had been bitter enemies for many years.

[Ammon] had been faithful in his duties as a [servant]. Because of this he was able to [teach] King Lamoni, his household, and his court the gospel. He was able to do this because he had first won their hearts with his love, friendship, and example.

WINNING THEIR HEARTS BY EXAMPLE

There have been instances when a person has been turned away from the gospel truths because of the actions of some of the members of the Church. We can win hearts and teach the gospel if we ourselves are good examples of believers.

1. Are you always careful to be honest and fair? For example, do you return extra change a clerk gives you by mistake? Do you speak up when someone else is blamed for something you did? Do you return things you borrow? Do you give an honest day's work for a day's pay?

2. Is there anything you could do to make your home and yard more tidy and thus make the neighborhood more beautiful?

3. Are you always obedient to parents, teachers, and Church leaders?

4. Are you considerate of your neighbors? For example, are you careful not to be noisy late in the evening or early in the morning? Do you keep your pets from being an annoyance? Do you respect rules neighbors have for their children? Do you keep your children from annoying the neighbors? Do you put your outside toys away when not in use so that no one will stumble over them?

5. Are you careful not to gossip or talk about other people? Do you try to say something good about a person who is being talked about negatively in your presence?

6. Are you always courteous? For example, do you wait your turn in line? Do you speak to those who live across the street? Do you always remember to say please and thank you?

7. Are you careful about obeying the law? For example, do you obey traffic signals even though no one else is around? Do you refrain from scattering litter in public places?

8. Do you always keep your word? For example, when you say you will do something, do you do it at the time you said you would, at home, at school, at work, at Church, and in the neighborhood? Do you let the proper person know if you cannot keep an appointment or fulfill an assignment?

WINNING THEIR HEARTS WITH FRIENDSHIP

Accept people for what they are and who they are. Acknowledge from the beginning that life-styles differ, but all are children of our Heavenly Father and need to have the blessings of the gospel. Remain their friend even though they may not accept the gospel at the present time.

1. Is there a nonmember family in your neighborhood with whom you are not well acquainted? Could you pay them a short visit, and tell them you would like to know them better and perhaps invite them to a dinner at a future date?

2. Could you chat with your neighbors about gardening, exchange produce or recipes, in an effort to become more neighborly and to win their hearts?

3. Do you have a nonmember friend you could invite to go with you to Primary, a fireside, or an activity night at Church such as a play, roadshow, carnival, seminary function, or ball game?

4. Could you be a friend to persons at school or work who seem left out? Invite them to eat lunch with you, write a complimentary note to them, or express appreciation for them.

5. Could you make an opportunity to refer to a Church event in your conversations with nonmembers? For example, "I started learning to crochet in Primary yesterday," or "We are learning to make tie quilts in Relief Society next week." Follow with an invitation to have them join you.

6. Is there a new family moving into your area? Acquaint them with the location of the school, the grocery store, and the location of churches in your area; and perhaps tell them of neighborhood customs and group activities of common interest to all.

7. If the opportunity arises, could you explain the family home evening program to your nonmember friends? Is it possible to have them share a family home evening with you and your family?

8. Could you sponsor a "getting-to-know-you" party to welcome people into the neighborhood or to get to know a family or individual with whom you are not well acquainted?

It will be interesting to see what the suggested gifts are. Perhaps some will be material things. Comment on how much fun it would be to give such gifts. Some gifts may be spiritual. Point out how much more lasting such gifts are.

In conclusion, show the envelope marked "Our Heavenly Father's Gift." Have the family pretend that Heavenly Father has named the gift he would offer and placed it in the envelope. Open the envelope and read:

"If you keep my commandments and endure to the end you shall have eternal life, which gift is the greatest of all the gifts of God" (D&C 14:7).

Explain that our Heavenly Father really does offer the glorious gift of eternal life to all of his children.

- Can Heavenly Father just give us the gift of eternal life?

- What must his children do to have this gift? (Accept his gospel, be baptized into his Church, live his commandments, and be married for time and all eternity.)

Point out that each person has to do something to accept the gift. He has to do something for himself to earn eternal life.

- Can our family offer the gift of eternal life to the family we have chosen to present a gift to? Why not?

- What can we give?

Redistribute the envelopes, and ask each person to write on it some blessing that the chosen family would receive if our family could help them become members of the Church. You might make a chart of these blessings as they are mentioned. Some of these things might be included:

1. A true knowledge that God is our Heavenly Father.

2. A prophet to guide us.

3. Opportunities for service to others.

4. Sunday School.

5. Relief Society.

6. Temple marriage and sealings.

7. The full gospel of Jesus Christ.

8. Primary.

9. The Book of Mormon.

10. Spiritual growth.

11. The priesthood.

12. Family home evenings.

13. Opportunity to become a family forever.

- Which of these gifts do you feel we could give first? (Answers may include family home evening, Primary, Relief Society, Sunday School, a recreational activity.)

Talk about how these gifts could be offered. Summarize by stating that if we could give the chosen family the opportunity to become members of The Church of Jesus Christ of Latter-day Saints, we would give them the opportunity to enjoy all these gifts on the list plus many more.

Winning Their Hearts

- Why do we want to give these gifts of the gospel to the family we chose? (So that they can have eternal life.)

- How can we help them to truly desire the gospel? (By allowing them to see the teachings of the gospel in our lives.)

Remind the family of the story of Ammon who wanted to give the gift of the gospel to the Lamanites. He understood that he would first have to do something to make them want to receive the gospel.

Either briefly retell the story of Ammon and King Lamoni (Alma 17:20–19:36), or use the story told in the pictures and words in this lesson for your younger children.

- Why was Ammon able to teach the gospel to the Lamanites?

- What must we do before this family can be taught the gospel? (Win their hearts.)

- How do we win their hearts? (We must become their friends.)

- What is the first gift we must offer? (Love.)

Illustrate by showing the filmstrip *How Great Shall Be Your Joy* or by relating the following story or one from your own experience that will teach the same ideas.

Sharing the Gospel

The Grant family were members of

the Church. They did not know anyone in the neighborhood they had just moved into, so they invited the entire neighborhood to a party.

Among the families who came were the Montgomerys, who had eight children as did the Grant family. Both families liked each other immediately. It seemed natural for them to want to do things for each other.

The Montgomerys came and enjoyed warm and wonderful family home evenings with the Grants. The Grants were invited to dinner at the Montgomerys. The families went sleigh riding together. The children played ball in the Grant's yard and played on the trampoline in the Montgomery's yard. The parents of both families enjoyed watching the children and visiting together.

One day while the two families were together, Sister Grant said to the Montgomerys, "Why don't we invite the missionaries to come over and tell you about The Church of Jesus Christ of Latter-day Saints?" The Montgomerys agreed.

In the weeks that followed, the missionaries taught the Montgomerys, but because of their long family heritage in another church, they did not feel they could accept the gospel.

- Do you think that the Grants were a failure in their missionary efforts because the Montgomerys did not become members of the Church? Why not?

- What blessings did the Grants share with the Montgomerys? (Family home evenings, friendship, knowledge about the gospel.)

- Did the Montgomerys give anything in return? (They gave love and friendship to the Grants.)

Explain that in order to teach the gospel, you do not always have to ask the questions, "What do you know about The Church of Jesus Christ of Latter-day Saints?" and "Would you like to know more?" These questions may be appropriate at times, but they are generally more effective if we first win the hearts of our friends and neighbors. We can share the gospel only as people are willing to receive, a little now and more later. Sometimes a little of the gospel principles now will open their hearts for more later on. Acts of interest and kindness will win their hearts. We must let them see us live the gospel and know we are their friends, then we are better able to share the gospel.

Planning to Give the Gift

Talk about the family you have chosen to receive your gift of friendship. Pray about the family, asking the Lord to help you approach them at the right time and in the right way. Consider the questions and ideas listed on the chart included in the lesson. Read and discuss the suggestions and their possibilities in your missionary efforts. Do those things that you can do sincerely.

As you plan the activities, pray about your plan, and then get started. When you have won the hearts of your friends, give them the opportunity to hear about the gospel. Remain friends whether or not they accept the gospel.

ADAPTING FOR YOUNGER CHILDREN

Little children would enjoy drawing a colored ribbon on the envelope. They could name a child who does not go to Primary. They could tell what they do in Primary and why they think their friends would like to go to Primary with them.

They will like looking at the pictures in the story "Ammon Goes on a Mission" inlcuded in the lesson and hearing the story.

You might also want to tell the following stories:

Primary Day

It was Sunday morning. Judy and Dwight were getting ready for church. There was a knock on the door. Judy ran to open it. Her friends Rachel and Walley were there and wanted to know if she could play. Judy said, "No, it's Sunday, and I'm going to Primary. I don't want to miss it."

"What's Primary?" asked Rachel.

• How would you have answered Rachel? (Allow time for answers.)

Continue the story:

"Why do you like Primary?" Wally asked.

• What would you say to Wally?

Continue the story:

Then Judy said, "Why don't you ask your parents if you can go with us?"

"We will," said Rachel and Wally, and they ran home.

• Do you think the parents of Wally and Rachel would let them go? (Sometimes parents say yes, and sometimes they say no. But it doesn't hurt to ask.)

Mary and Mrs. Johnson

"Mommy," Mary asked as she came in the house, "who lives in the big house down the street? We don't ever see anyone there."

Mother replied, "An older lady. Her name is Mrs. Johnson. She isn't able to get around very well so she stays at home a lot. Would you like to meet her?"

"I don't know," said Mary. "Is she nice?"

"Oh, yes," said mother, "and she loves children. Maybe we could make some cookies to take to her."

The next day Mary helped her mother make some cookies. They took them down the street to Mrs. Johnson's house. Mary was excited to give the cookies to Mrs. Johnson. When Mrs. Johnson answered the door, she had a sad, tired look on her face, but she started to smile when Mary gave her the cookies.

"Oh, thank you," said Mrs. Johnson. "These look delicious. Did you help make them?"

"Yes," said Mary.

The next day Mary was walking down the sidewalk, and Mrs. Johnson was sitting on her porch. Mary waved, and Mrs. Johnson called for her to come. Mary skipped over to where Mrs. Johnson was sitting. Mrs. Johnson again thanked her for the cookies. Then she told Mary some stories about when she was a little girl. Mary loved to listen to her. Each day she would go to see Mrs. Johnson, often taking some pictures she had colored and some fresh peas or corn from the garden. Mary soon grew to love Mrs. Johnson, and Mrs. Johnson loved to have Mary come. They talked about many things.

Then one day Mary asked Mrs.

Johnson to come to family home evening at her house. The whole family planned a special night. They had a good time. Mrs. Johnson felt so good to be involved, and Mary had a new friend.

• How was Mary a missionary? (She showed love and kindness for a neighbor. She invited Mrs. Johnson to family home evening.)

• Is there someone who lives by us that we could show love for?

Explain that all through our lives, we should tell people about the Church. Sometimes they will listen and sometimes they won't. But we should always try to give them the great gift of happiness and kindness. They can be good friends.

ADAPTING FOR TEENAGERS AND ADULTS

In addition to the suggested lesson, your family might enjoy reading and discussing the following scriptures about the responsibility and privilege we have of sharing our blessings of the gospel with others:

1. Doctrine and Covenants 123:12.
2. Doctrine and Covenants 18:10–16.
3. Doctrine and Covenants 4:1–7.
4. Doctrine and Covenants 88:77–83.
5. Alma 39:10–12.

SUGGESTIONS FOR FUTURE HOME EVENINGS

Getting Ready to Share

Prepare a chart with four headings: "My Rewards for Sharing," "What Sharing Does for Others," "Things to Share," and "Preparation for Sharing." Have someone read or tell the story in Mosiah 28:1–9.

• Why share the gospel?

Have family members think of as many reasons as they can. List these under one of the first two headings. If someone does not mention *duty*, read to them the following statement by President Spencer W. Kimball:

"No person who has been converted to the gospel should shirk his responsibility to teach the truth to others. This is our privilege. This is our duty. This is a command from the Lord."

("It Becometh Every Man," *Ensign*, Oct. 1977, p. 3.)

• What can we share?

Again family members can suggest items for sharing with nonmembers. These can be listed under the heading "Things to Share."

• Am I ready to share?

Have family members suggest the qualities that one needs to have in order to share effectively, and list their suggestions under the heading "Preparation for Sharing." Have someone read Doctrine and Covenants 4, and compare that list with those suggested by the family. Suggest that family members can use these suggestions as checklists to see how well they are following the advice of the prophet that we should each be sharing the gospel with others.

Doing Missionary Work

You can build a family lesson on doing missionary work and the reasons for doing it from the material in chapter 33, "Missionary Work," of *Gospel Principles* [PBIC0245], pages 201 through 207. Perhaps family members can read and discuss the chapter. Or you may wish to use the chapter as a lesson outline and present the material to the family.

Bearing Testimony of the Gospel

Ask family members to share ideas about what is the strongest, most convincing way of sharing the gospel with others. If no one suggests testimony bearing, add this on your own. Ask why bearing testimony is a powerful tool in sharing the gospel. Point out that both members and nonmembers need to hear the testimonies of others. You may wish to read and discuss the following incident:

A Scientist Finds a Testimony

A missionary once sat in the home of a learned scientist. The missionary tried in every logical way to convince him that The Church of Jesus Christ of Latter-day Saints was true. The scientist toyed with the missionary as a cat with a mouse, riddling the missionary's message with his superior learning. But then the missionary said something that changed the whole course of the discussion.

He said, "I know the message I am trying to bring you is true. I know it as surely as I'm here with you in this room."

The scientist was silent. He was affected by the spirit he felt in this testimony. His attitude changed. The missionary became the teacher and the scientist the learner.

Three months later the scientist knew something he had never known before. He knew that the Church was true. He was baptized and began to bear his testimony to others.

Book of Mormon Placement Project

Spend an evening preparing copies of the Book of Mormon for a family Book of Mormon placement project. First you will need to obtain several copies of the Book of Mormon that you want to give as gifts. Then together write up a family testimony, and have a friend take a picture of all of you in a group. Glue copies of the picture and testimony inside the front cover of each copy of the Book of Mormon.

Give the copies of the Book of Mormon to nonmember friends, or offer them to local missionaries for them to distribute. If your family wishes to place larger quantities of the Book of Mormon, write to Family-to-Family Book of Mormon Program, LDS Church Missionary Department, 50 East North Temple Street, Salt Lake City, Utah 84150.

The Joy Is in the Doing

Family members may never be really convinced that sharing the gospel can be rewarding until they try it firsthand. Here are some suggestions for activities in which your family can participate that will help them to experience these rewards:

1. If you have a returned missionary in your family, have him tell about his missionary experiences. If not, you might invite a recently returned missionary to share an evening in your home with your family.

2. Invite a family into your home to participate in a family home evening activity. Sincerely try to win their hearts. This can be either a nonmember family or one that is inactive.

3. Read and discuss this statement by President Spencer W. Kimball, "It should be clear to us that usually we must *warm* our neighbors before we can *warn* them properly" ("Report of the Regional Representatives' Seminar," *Ensign*, Nov. 1976, p. 140). Discuss what family members can do to become more friendly and the ways they can go about winning hearts. Point out that it is much more effective to share the gospel with friends than with strangers.

Pray to Find an Investigator

Read the following statement by President Spencer W. Kimball: "Think, brothers and sisters, what would happen if each active family were to bring another family or individual into the Church: . . . We would be joined by several hundred thousand new members of the Church" (in Conference Report, Apr. 1979, p. 114; or *Ensign*, May 1979, p. 82).

Then read or tell the following experience:

One family was inspired by President Kimball's remarks to accept the challenge. They began by going to Heavenly Father for guidance on what to do. After the family had knelt in prayer, the mother said, "Let's invite a refugee family into our home." The next day they made an inquiry, and that evening the family became sponsors and picked up a refugee family from the airport. After learning how to turn on lights and water taps and receiving a lot of love for several days, the refugee family was asked if they would like to go to Church, and they said yes. A Sunday School class was arranged, taught by a returned missionary. Soon several refugee families were attending, and those interested were invited to hear the missionary discussions. Twenty were interested and heard the discussions in the home of the sponsoring family. Fourteen joined the Church.

Discuss with your family the many different ways in which one can find and fellowship investigators. Then make it a matter of prayer. If family members are willing, put your own missionary plan into action.

A CHILD FROM GOD

(To be used when a new baby joins your family)

They shall also teach their children to pray, and to walk uprightly before the Lord.
[D&C 68:28]

PURPOSE

Help your family meet the needs, both physical and spiritual, of the new baby who has become a part of your family.

FOR THE PARENT

This lesson is especially geared to a family with young children. Involve each member of the family in the preparation of this home evening.

PREPARATION

1. Make a special box containing the following articles (or other items of your choosing): a bottle of baby food, a folded diaper, a baby blanket, a bar of soap.

2. Also include the following four labels: "Baby-Food Store," "Tiny Tot Clothing Store," "Lullaby and Goodnight Land," and "Baby Bubble Bath."

3. You will also need a doll approximately the size of a newborn baby.

4. Have a chalkboard and chalk ready, or bring a large piece of paper and a marker to make a list.

SUGGESTED HYMN
AND SONG

"There Is Beauty All Around" (*Hymns*, no. 169).
"A Happy Family" (*Sing with Me*, D–1).

SUGGESTED LESSON

"He Has Sent Me Here"
Begin your home evening by having

the family gather around holding the baby. Then sing the song "I Am a Child of God" (*Sing with Me*, B–76).

Ask some of the family members what they were feeling as they sang the song. Ask one of the children to read the words of the first verse of the song, and have the others listen carefully.

"I am a child of God,
And he has sent me here,
Has given me an earthly home
With parents kind and dear."

Discuss the following questions with your family. (You might try to get the family members to discover some deeper insights by asking, "And what else?" where appropriate when the person finishes giving his first response to the question.)

• What does being a child of God mean to you?

• In what ways is our earthly family like our heavenly family?

• Why would Heavenly Father want us to have "parents kind and dear" here on earth?

Now is a good time for you as parents to tell each of your children how much he means to you. Tell each child how precious he is to you and how special each one was when he was born.

Tell each child about the day he was born: what you did that day, what time you went to the hospital, how long it was before he was born, what he looked like, how long he was, how much he weighed, why you selected the name you did for him, and how father and mother felt. Begin with the oldest and end with the newborn. Conclude this part by having each child express how he feels about the new baby who has come to be part of your family.

"My Needs Are Great"
Have one of the children read the second verse of the song:

"I am a child of God,
And so my needs are great;
Help me to understand his words
Before it grows too late."

Point out that when a new baby becomes a part of a family on earth, like each other member of the family, he has many needs. Each child can help care for the new little brother or sister and help to meet those needs.

Ask the family to help you make a list of things you might want in order to care for the physical needs of the new baby.

The list might be arranged to include the following:

Foods and Utensils	Clothing	Shelter	Bath
milk	diapers	home	powder
water	pins	bassinet or crib	cotton balls
fruits	undershirts	blankets	washcloth
cereals	plastic pants		towel
vegetables	pajamas		small tub
juices	socks		cotton-tipped sticks
baby bottles	booties		soap
dish and spoon			

Let each person know you appreciate his help in compiling the list of the baby's needs. You may want to add to the list when the children are through.

Explain to the children that just knowing what the baby needs is not enough. To take care of the baby's physical needs, we must know where to find those things that the baby needs. Tell the family you have planned a tour to help them know where to find those things. Open the special box, and give each of the family at least one article or label. Then begin the tour. (Note: The tour guide should point out where all of the baby's articles are at each stop on the tour.)

1. "The Baby-Food Store." Enter the kitchen, and have the person carrying the baby food put it on the appropriate shelf. Have the person carrying the label place the label on the appropriate cupboard.

2. "Tiny Tot Clothing Store." Enter the room where the baby sleeps, and have the person carrying the diaper place it on the shelf or in the drawer where it belongs. Have someone else place the label on an appropriate surface.

3. "Lullaby and Goodnight Land." While in the bedroom, have the person carrying the baby blanket place it carefully on the baby's bed. Place the label on the door, wall, or bed.

4. "Baby Bubble Bath." Enter the bathroom, and have the person carrying the bar of soap place it on the counter top or other surface where the baby is bathed. Place the label on an appropriate surface.

After you return to the place where you are holding your home evening, ask the children why they had the tour. Help them to see that now, when mother needs something for the baby, they will be able to help because they know where to get the things that the baby needs.

Now help the children understand that the baby has needs other than the physical ones.

• What are some of the baby's other needs? (Affection, guidance, attention.)

• What does each of us have to give to the baby that will let him know we really care? (Love.)

Tell the family that one way a little baby knows it is loved is by the way family members hold and respond to it.

• How many would like to hold the new baby for a minute?

Tell the children they may hold the baby, but before they do you want each of them to practice by holding a doll.

Demonstrate to each one how to properly hold the baby, using the doll. Show each child how to support the body and head when he is holding it in different positions. You may want to give guidelines at this time about when and under what cirucmstances the baby is to be held. You may also want to give some instructions about feeding the baby.

When all the children have practiced with the doll, let each child hold the new baby in his arms. When all have had a turn, ask each one how he felt toward the baby while he held it. Tell them the baby could also feel their love as they held it.

"Rich Blessings Are in Store"
Read the third verse of the song:
"I am a child of God.
Rich blessings are in store;
If I but learn to do his will
I'll live with him once more."

• Who are the rich blessings for? (Lead the family to answer that they are for all family members.)

• In what ways might each of us receive rich blessings by having this new child of God come into our home?

• How might our baby receive rich blessings from being part of our family?

"Help Me Find the Way"
Now read the chorus of the song:
"Lead me, guide me, walk beside me,
Help me find the way.
Teach me all that I must do
To live with him someday."

• What can we do as a family to lead the baby, guide him, walk beside him, and help him find the way? (Allow plenty of time for the children to respond. Listen carefully to the responses given.)

Make a list, and compliment each person on his good ideas as you write them down. Point out that our Heavenly Father has given us the following guides to help us find the way:

1. Family prayers each day.

2. Individual prayers each day.

3. Scriptures to live by each day.

4. Family home evenings each week.

After the family members have looked at the list, ask each person what he is willing to do to help the baby find the way back to Heavenly Father.

• Can a person lead someone someplace if he is not going there himself? (No.)

• If our family is going to lead the baby back to our Heavenly Father, what must we do? (We must be striving to go back to our Heavenly Father ourselves.)

Assure the family that if each one will remember the words of the song and if all will work together, the family will have the blessing of living with Heavenly Father someday. End the home evening by singing again the entire song "I Am a Child of God."

117

A NAME AND A BLESSING

(To be used before you bless your new baby)

He took them up in his arms, put his hands upon them, and blessed them. [Mark 10:16]

PURPOSE

Inspire family members to become involved in the naming and blessing of your baby.

FOR THE PARENT

One of the parents should conduct this home evening. The other parent could hold the new baby so that all the family can see their new brother or sister.

PREPARATION

Have a sheet of paper and a pencil or a chalkboard and some chalk.

SUGGESTED HYMN AND SONGS

"There Is Beauty All Around" (*Hymns*, no. 169).
"A Happy Family" (*Sing with Me*, D–1).
"The Priesthood Is Restored" (*Sing with Me*, B–58).

SUGGESTED LESSON

The Meaning of Your Name

Discuss with your family the meaning of each of their names if you know it. Discuss with them also why you gave them their names.

Blessing the Little Children

Explain that the ordinance of giving a name and a blessing is a sacred and happy experience for the family.

Have someone read the accounts in Luke 1:5–14, 26-33, of how John the Baptist and Jesus received their names. Point out that these verses tell us the importance of a name for a new baby.

Show your family the picture of a baby being blessed, which is included in the lesson, and read Mark 10:16.

• In what way is the blessing of this baby like the blessing that Jesus gave to the little children?

Express the happiness that the new baby has brought to you and the joy you feel about blessing him or her.

Priesthood Authority for Blessings

Explain that when Christ blessed the little children, he did it with authority from our Heavenly Father. We have the same authority in the Church today.

- What is this authority called? (The Melchizedek Priesthood.)

- When is the baby usually blessed and given a name? (During fast meeting.)

- As the priesthood bearers stand in a circle holding the baby, which one gives the blessing to the baby? (Generally the father, if he holds the Melchizedek Priesthood and is worthy; or, if he does not hold the priesthood, someone whom he asks.)

Help the family understand what a great privilege it is for this new baby to be held and given a blessing by someone who holds the priesthood. This means that the blessing given to this new brother or sister is recognized by God.

- When are we going to have our baby blessed and given a name?

Making the Baby a Member of Record in the Church

You may want to have all the children show their certificates of blessing if they have them.

Mention that the certificate of blessing is an official Church record and will be properly filled out and signed by the ward clerk and the bishop. The ward clerk will, at the time he fills out the certificate of blessing, make up a membership record card with the name of the baby, date of birth, date of blessing, name of the one who blessed the baby, names of mother and father, and other information. Your new baby will then be on the official membership records of the Church.

Now that family members have discussed the reasons for blessing and naming the baby, have them prepare for the event by discussing the following plans for your new baby:

- What relatives should be invited to come to the blessing?

- Who should be in the circle?

- Who will invite the home teachers to be in the circle also?

- What clothes will the baby wear?

- Who will bless the baby?

Conclude by asking each family member to comment on how he feels about the baby and what the chosen name means to him.

ADAPTING FOR YOUNGER CHILDREN

Study carefully the material given, and use what you think will be meaningful to your children.

Tell a story about the time each child was given a name and a blessing. You might keep secret the name of the child you are talking about and let the children guess who the child is. If you have a picture of each child when he was very young, show the picture after telling the story. A child loves to hear about what happened to him when he was a baby.

You may also want to tell the following story:

A Name and a Blessing

At last, Rachel and Stephanie had a new baby brother. A boy! He had a round, pink face; two big, blue eyes; two little hands; and two wiggly feet. But he didn't have a name. What would baby's name be?

"We'll discuss it in our home evening," said father.

And they did. Father showed the little girls a picture of a baby being blessed in fast meeting and explained about how the father was giving the baby a name and a blessing.

Father said, "Next Sunday will be a special day for us. That's the day our baby will be given a name and a blessing. Let's decide on a name for him."

Rachel mentioned all the boys' names she liked. Stephanie gave all the boys' names she liked. Mother and father both suggested names they liked. Then mother said, "We decided on a boy's name for a baby five years ago, only that baby was a girl."

"That's right," said father. "If either of you had been a boy, your name would have been Michael."

"Michael," repeated Rachel and Stephanie.

"I still like it. It's a good name," said mother.

"Yes," said father, "Michael is a good name."

Then mother said, "But it is rather nice for the first boy to carry his father's name, isn't it?"

"Michael Christopher?" asked father.

Rachel and Stephanie agreed, "Let's name our baby Michael Christopher."

"Agreed," said father.

When Sunday came, Rachel and Stephanie helped mother get the baby ready to take to fast meeting. Rachel brought the baby's diapers and pretty blue knit suit while mother bathed him. Stephanie put the baby's tiny, white socks on his wiggly feet.

When they were all ready to go, father said, "Let's have family prayer before we leave."

They all knelt around the baby's crib, and father thanked Heavenly Father for their baby and asked him to bless the family that all would go well on this important day.

When they arrived at the meetinghouse, grandparents, uncles and aunts, and even cousins were already there. They had come for this special occasion.

In the meeting, Rachel and Stephanie sat very still during the song and prayer. Then they heard the bishop say that their baby would be blessed. Their eyes opened wide as father took the baby from mother's arms and walked to the front of the chapel. Both grandfathers and two uncles and their home teacher went up, too. Then the bishop came over and stood with the group.

Rachel and Stephanie bowed their heads and closed their eyes as father began to speak. Everyone bowed their heads and closed their eyes.

Rachel and Stephanie heard father thank Heavenly Father for the baby and say that his name would be Michael Christopher. Then he blessed Michael. When he finished, Rachel and Stephanie and everyone said, "Amen."

Father held Michael up so that everyone could see him. Rachel and Stephanie were so proud they could hardly sit still.

When father brought the baby back and laid him in mother's arms, Rachel and Stephanie reached over and touched him. "Michael," they whispered.

Now the baby had a name, a beautiful name. And they knew Heavenly Father would bless him.

PREPARING FOR BAPTISM

(To be used when a member of your family is baptized)

If this be the desire of your hearts, what have you against being baptized in the name of the Lord, as a witness before him that ye have entered into a convenant with him, that ye will serve him and keep his commandments, that he may pour out his Spirit more abundantly upon you?
[Mosiah 18:10]

PURPOSE

Review the meaning and importance of baptism as you honor a member of your family who is to be baptized.

PREPARATION

Review the four pictures included with this lesson, and prepare to discuss them with your family.

SUGGESTED HYMN AND SONG

"Lord, Accept into Thy Kingdom" (*Hymns*, no. 100).
"Baptism" (*Sing with Me*, B–4).

SUGGESTED LESSON

Honoring the Family Member to Be Baptized

Tell your family to listen carefully as you mention some dates. Have them tell why each date is important to some member of your family. Mention such dates as those on which family members were born, baptized, married, or engaged to be married. Give the birth date and planned baptismal date of the person to be baptized as the last two dates.

State that this baptismal date will be one of the most important days in this person's life. Tell your family that because this is such an important event you will honor him during this family home evening. You might want to display the certificate of baptism of a family member. Explain to the person you are honoring that he will receive a certificate that will be an official record of his baptism. You might also want to show your family group sheet, and point out the space where this date will be recorded.

Learning about Baptism

Turn to the picture of Christ being baptized, and explain that this picture and the others that follow suggest reasons why you, as a family, should honor this person and rejoice with him. The pictures will help the whole family better understand the meaning and importance of baptism. Ask family members to look at the pictures one at a time and discuss the following text and questions.

The Baptism of Jesus

• What important facts about baptism does this picture suggest, which the person being baptized needs to remember? (Baptism is so important that even Jesus was baptized.)

Explain that the person you are honoring will be following Jesus' example. He will be baptized as Jesus was, by immersion.

• What does immersion mean? (To be completely covered by water.)

Bring out that we are baptized by the same authority as Jesus was—the priesthood of God.

To help your family understand what will happen at baptism, read Mosiah 18:10 together.

• What do the words "as a witness before him" mean when you think of your baptism? (I will show by the act of being baptized how I feel in my heart. I witness, or show, that I believe in Heavenly Father, that I loves him, and that I want to obey his commandments.)

• What is a covenant? (An agreement or promise between two persons that each will do certain things.)

Stress that the baptismal covenant is a sacred agreement.

• Who are the persons involved in the covenant or promise when the person we are honoring is baptized? (He will be one. Our Heavenly Father will be the other.)

• What is the promise that the person being baptized will make to Heavenly Father at baptism? (He will promise to keep Heavenly Father's commandments and to serve him.)

You may wish to reread Mosiah 18:10.

• What will Heavenly Father promise when our family member is baptized? (To forgive him of his sins if he repents [see D&C 33:11], to accept him as a member of the Church [see D&C 20:37], to give him the gift of eternal life if he is faithful [see 3 Nephi 11:33].)

The Way to the Kingdom of God

• What does the chart (at right) suggest about the commandments that Heavenly Father has given us? (If we follow them, we will return to our Heavenly Father and inherit a

place in his kingdom. In fact, only by obeying the commandments can we receive these great blessings.)

• Why do you think that our Heavenly Father has asked us to make a sacred covenant or promise to obey his commandments when we are baptized? (Because he loves us, he wants us to be happy, and he wants us to be with him in the kingdom of heaven.)

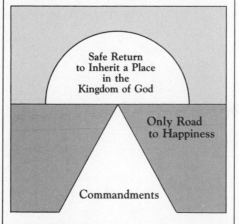

Safe Return
to Inherit a Place
in the
Kingdom of God

Only Road
to Happiness

Commandments

Jesus Paid for Sin and Death

• How is it possible for all of our mistakes or sins to be forgiven when we are baptized? (Because Jesus loved us so much that he was willing to suffer in the Garden of Gethsemane and upon the cross. He had the power to save himself from suffering and death, but he did not use it because he wanted to make it possible for our sins to be forgiven.)

• Does our Heavenly Father expect those who are baptized to keep all of his commandments perfectly from now on? (No. He knows that we need to learn how to keep these commandments and that we will make some mistakes while we learn. Heavenly Father expects us to try to live the commandments as completely as possible. But if we make a mistake, we can repent and do better next time. This is how we will learn. The Savior has given us the great gift of forgiveness for our mistakes when we repent.)

Being Confirmed a Member of the Church

Explain that after your family member has been baptized, he will be confirmed at sacrament meeting and receive two wonderful blessings.

• What are these two blessings? (First, he will be accepted as a member of the church and kingdom of God here upon the earth. He will share in all of the privileges and blessings of this great kingdom. This kindgom is different from any other organization upon the earth because Jesus stands at its head, and its leaders act for him. Second, the person being baptized will also receive the gift of the Holy Ghost and have the right to the companionship of the Holy Ghost if he is faithful.)

Plans for the Day of Baptism

After the discussion, plan ways to make your family member's baptism day a special day for him and for your whole family. You could make plans like the following:

1. Have the entire family attend the baptismal service. Plan transportation and other details.

2. Eat dinner at a special place together, or enjoy a special treat. You might choose to have a special meal at home, serving favorite foods of the person you are honoring.

3. Have this person write the date of his baptism on your family group sheet. To emphasize the importance of this date, your entire family could be there when he does this. You could do this after you return home from the baptismal service or during your next home evening.

4. You may want to give this person a small gift after his baptism, such as his own copy of one of the standard works.

5. To help this person feel more secure when he goes into the water to be baptized, his father or an older brother could show him how he will be held by the one who will baptize him. Time could be taken to let him actually practice the way he will place his hands, bend his knees, and so forth.

A Sacred Experience

Explain that the person you are honoring should go to his baptism with a desire to show Heavenly Father and Jesus that he loves them and wants to make a covenant that he will serve them all of his life. If he does this, he will know that he is doing what they want him to do and that they are pleased with him.

Have someone read President Joseph F. Smith's description of the time when he was baptized:

"The feeling that came upon me was that of pure peace, of love and of light. I felt in my soul that if I had sinned—and surely I was not without sin—that it had been forgiven me; that I was indeed cleansed from sin; my heart was touched and I felt that I would not injure the smallest insect beneath my feet. I felt as though I wanted to do good everywhere to everybody and to everything. I felt a newness of life, a newness of desire to do that which was right. There was not one particle of desire for evil left in my soul. I was but a little boy, it is true, when I was baptized; but this was the influence that came upon me, and I know that it was from God, and was and ever has been a living witness to me of my acceptance of the Lord." (In Conference Report, Apr. 1898, p. 66.)

Have family members who have been baptized tell about their feelings at the time of their baptisms. You may also want to tell how you feel about your child's baptism, and explain the responsibility you have to prepare him for baptism (see D&C 68:25–28). If the person being honored is an older person, a family member or missionary may want to express his feelings about the baptism. Allow the person himself to tell how he feels.

You may want to serve favorite refreshments for the person you are honoring.

A PRIESTHOOD ORDINATION

(To be used when one of your family is to be ordained)

Again I say unto you, that it shall not be given to any one to go forth to preach my gospel, or to build up my church, except he be ordained by some one who has authority.
[D&C 42:11]

PURPOSE

Honor a son or father who will be ordained to an office in the Aaronic or Melchizedek priesthood. Help him and other family members realize the power, responsibility, and opportunities his ordination will bring.

FOR THE PARENT

Use this lesson for anticipated ordinations in both the Aaronic and Melchizedek Priesthoods. Adapt it to the appropriate age of the person being ordained.

SUGGESTED SONGS

"The Priesthood Is Restored" (*Sing with Me*, B–58).

"The Priesthood" (*Sing with Me*, B–22).

"I Want to Be a Deacon" (*Sing with Me*, B–88).

SUGGESTED LESSON

Honoring the Family Member to Be Ordained

Explain that you are holding this home evening in honor of a member of your family who will be ordained to an office in the priesthood. Announce the day and place of the ordination, and make plans for all of the family to be present.

Priesthood Power

Ask the following questions:

• When the family member we are honoring is ordained, men will place their hands on his head. Whom do these men represent? (The Lord.)

Explain that the Lord said to Edward Partridge, "I will lay my hand upon you by the hand of my servant" (D&C 36:2).

• What will these men give to him? (Power from God. This power is called the priesthood.)

Explain that God gives his power to men here on earth so that they can bless themselves, their families, and all the people of the world.

• What are some of the ways in which the priesthood blesses us? (Men who hold the priesthood can baptize us and give us the gift of the Holy Ghost. They can organize and carry out the programs of the Church. They can bless and pass the sacrament. They can perform eternal marriages. They can administer to us when we are sick and give us blessings of comfort and counsel. The prophet, through his priesthood power, can tell us the things God wants us to do. All of these things are great blessings in our lives.)

Tell the family member who is soon to be ordained that as long as he honors his priesthood, he will be able to use its power to bless others in his priesthood callings and in his own home within the guidelines the Church has established.

Priesthood Offices

Explain that when a man receives the Aaronic or Melchizedek Priesthood, he receives all the power of that priesthood. But because there are so many responsibilties for priesthood holders to perform, there are offices within each of these priesthoods that have certain tasks assigned to them.

• What are the offices within the Aaronic Priesthood? (Deacon, teacher, priest.)

• What are the offices within the Melchizedek Priesthood? (Elder, seventy, high priest.)

Ask the person you are honoring to tell the duties of the office to which he will be ordained. You may want to consult with your bishop and the scriptures, especially Doctrine and Covenants 107, to learn what the duties are.

Priesthood Service

• Can anyone remember the first words spoken by John the Baptist as he ordained Joseph Smith and Oliver Cowdery? ("Upon you my fellow servants" [see D&C 13].)

• Why did he call himself as well as Joseph and Oliver "servants"?

Explain that the priesthood is given to men so that they can bless the lives of others.

Tell how Jesus, who is the head of the priesthood on earth, was always concerned with those about him who were suffering hunger, thirst, sorrow, sickness, and need.

How does the priesthood help men to serve others? (It gives them opportunities to provide food, clothing, and other necessities to those in need; to bless and care for the sick; to give help to widows, older persons, and others who need help; to assist and

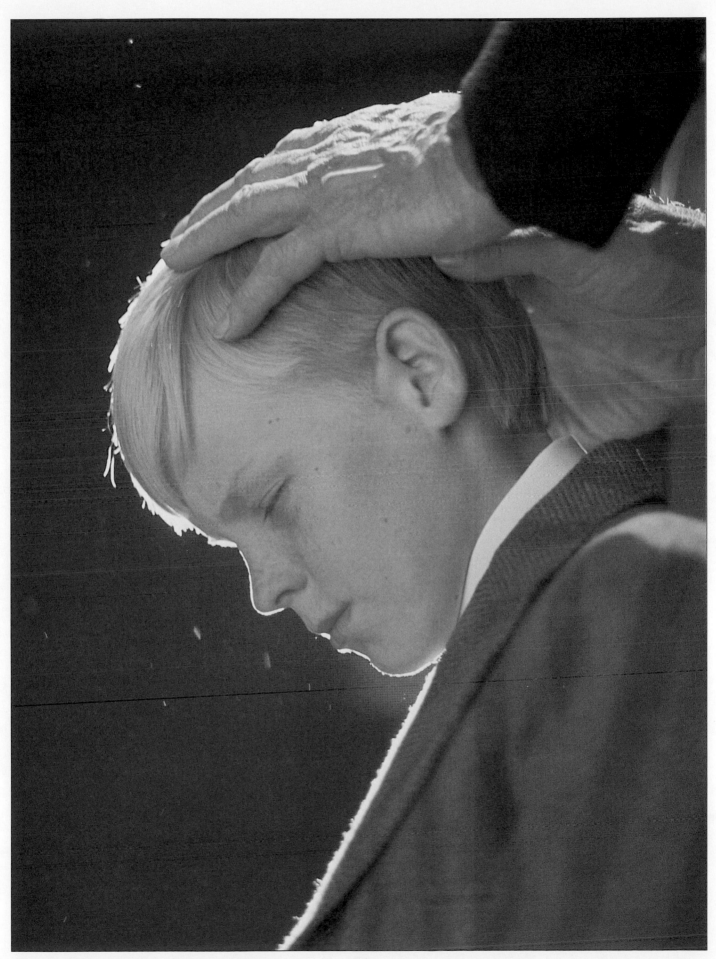

encourage families through home teaching.)

Have the person soon to be ordained tell of ways in which he would like to use his priesthood in giving service. Let family members also give suggestions.

Tell the following story of a young boy in England, and ask the family to notice how his ordination so impressed him that it became a guiding influence in his life. This young man, James E. Talmage, became an Apostle and one of the Lord's mightiest servants. This story occurred at a time when there was much persecution of the Church.

"I was called and ordained one Sunday morning, without any previous notice; and that afternoon was placed as a sentinel at the door of the house in which the Saints had met for worship. As soon as I had been ordained, a feeling came to me such as I have never been able to fully describe. It seemed scarcely possible, that I, a little boy, could be so honored of God as to be called to the priesthood. I had read of the sons of Aaron and of Levi who were chosen for the sacred labors of the Lesser Priesthood, but that I should be called to do part of the service that had been required of them was more than my little mind could grasp. I was both frightened and happy. Then, when I was placed on duty at the door, I forgot that I was but an eleven-year-old lad; I felt strong in the thought that I belonged to the Lord, and that he would assist me in whatever was required of me. I could not resist the conviction that other sentinels, stronger by far than I, stood by me though invisible to human eyes.

"The effect of my ordination to the deaconship entered into all the affairs of my boyish life. I am afraid that sometimes I forgot what I was, but I have ever been thankful that oft-times I did remember, and the recollection always served to make me better. When at play on the school grounds, and perhaps tempted to take unfair advantage in the game, when in the midst of a dispute with a playmate, I would remember, and the thought would be as effective as though spoken aloud—'I am a deacon; and it is not right that a deacon should act in this way.' On examination days, when it seemed easy for me to copy some other boy's work or to 'crib' from the book, I would remember again, 'I am a deacon, and must be honest and true.' When I saw other boys cheating in play or in school, I would say in my mind, 'It would be more wicked for me to do that than it is for them, because I am a deacon. . . . ' "

• How do we know that Brother Talmage felt that the priesthood was important all the time and not just on Sunday?

Continue with the story:

"The impression made upon my mind when I was made a deacon has never faded. The feeling that I was called to the special service of the Lord, as a bearer of the priesthood, has been a source of strength to me through all the years. When later I was ordained to higher offices in the Church, the same assurance has come to me, on every such occasion,—that I was in truth endowed with power from heaven, and that the Lord demanded of me that I honor his authority. I have been ordained in turn a teacher, an elder, a high priest, and lastly an apostle of the Lord Jesus Christ, and with every ordination there has come to me a new and soul-thrilling feeling which first I knew when I was called to be a deacon in the service of the Lord." (*Incidents from the Lives of Our Church Leaders* [Course of Study for the deacons quorums, 1914], pp. 135–36.)

Review with the family three things about his ordination that especially impressed Elder Talmage. He said, (1) "I was called to the special service of the Lord," (2) "I was in truth endowed with power from heaven," and (3) "the Lord demanded of me that I honor his authority."

Conclusion

Explain that this ordination is one of the important milestones in the life of the person you are honoring. Like Elder Talmage, he too may find new goals in life and receive help in improving his daily habits and actions so that he can reach those goals.

Invite family members, especially parents, to express what this ordination means to them.

Because this is such an important milestone to the family, plan to have a family activity during the week as a special honor for the person to be ordained. This activity could be a family dinner, a visit to the ice cream store, or family participation in some activity chosen by the one being honored.

RECEIVING A PATRIARCHAL BLESSING

(To be used before a family member receives a patriarchal blessing)

Patriarchal blessings contemplate an inspired declaration of the lineage of the recipient, and also, where so moved upon by the Spirit, an inspired and prophetic statement of the life mission of the recipient, together with such blessings, cautions, and admonitions as the patriarch may be prompted to give. [*Statement of the First Presidency, 28 June 1957*]

PURPOSE

Help family members understand what patriarchal blessings are and why they are important. Help the person who is to receive his blessing to prepare for it.

FOR THE PARENT

Often young people are confused about the purpose of a patriarchal blessing. Identify what is not clearly understood by your children as they prepare for this experience, and answer their questions.

PREPARATION

1. Ask family members who have already received their patriarchal blessings to prepare to share their feelings about their blessings.
2. Have a piece of paper and a pencil for each family member.

SUGGESTED LESSON

A Personal Revelation

Remind your family that their Heavenly Father loves them very

much and wants them to return to live with him. So he has given many guidelines to help them.

- Where can we find these guidelines? (The scriptures, messages of living prophets, and teachings of parents.)
- Have you ever wished you could

have guidelines for your own personal life?
- Have you ever wondered what your mission in life is?
- Would you like the Lord to help you understand what you might be able to accomplish in life?

GENESIS 17:5, 7:

"Thy name shall be Abraham; for a father
of _____ nations have I made thee.

"And I will establish my _____
between me and thee and thy seed after thee in their
generations for an _____
covenant, to be a _____ unto thee,
and to thy seed _____ thee."

GENESIS 22:17–18:

"I will multiply thy seed as the _____ of the heaven,
and as the _____ which is upon the sea shore; . . .

"And in thy seed shall all the _____
of the _____ be blessed; because
thou hast _____ my voice."

ABRAHAM 2:9:

"I will bless thee above _____ , and

make thy name great among all nations, and thou
shalt be a _____ unto thy seed after
thee, that in their _____ they shall
bear this _____ and
_____ unto all nations."

ABRAHAM 2:10–11:

"And I will bless them through
thy _____ ; for as many
as receive this _____ shall
be _____ after thy name. . . .

" . . . I give unto thee a promise that this right shall
continue in thee, and in thy _____
after thee (that is to say, the literal seed, or the seed
of the body) shall all the families of the earth be
_____ , even with the blessings of
the Gospel, which are the blessings of
_____ , even of life eternal."

- Would you like some guidelines to help you make decisions and to motivate you to do your best in everything you do?
- What way has the Lord provided for us to receive a personal revelation from him that will motivate, comfort, and guide us? (A patriarchal blessing is available to every worthy member.)

Explain that a patriarchal blessing is a priesthood blessing given to a worthy member by a patriarch. Tell your family that a family member has arranged to receive his patriarchal blessing and that this home evening is to help him prepare to receive it.

Ask this family member to tell what he has done to make arrangements so that he can receive this blessing. He should mention that he has had an interview with the bishop or branch president and has received his recommend, which he will give to the patriarch. If he lives in the mission field outside the boundaries of a stake, he has also contacted the mission president for the approval and signature of a member of the mission presidency. He has contacted the stake or mission patriarch for an appointment.

Sometimes members of the immediate family are allowed to be present at patriarchal blessings. If your family member would like this, he should arrange it with the patriarch.

Blessings by Right of Lineage

Explain that the patriarchal blessings usually have several parts. The Lord, through the patriarch, declares the person's lineage; tells him about his life mission as inspired by the Lord; and gives other blessings, cautions, and advice.

Explain that the patriarch will tell you which tribe of Israel you are descended from. Israel was a great prophet of the Old Testament and was also known as Jacob. He had twelve sons, and most of the tribes of Israel are named after his sons. The descendents of Israel have been designated by the Lord as his chosen people. Most people who accept the Lord and become members of his church are already descendents belonging to the house of Israel. Those who are not are adopted into his family.

Great blessings were promised to Abraham, Isaac, and Jacob and to their posterity. Since we are their posterity, these blessings are also available to us if we are righteous. When Elias appeared to Joseph Smith and Oliver Cowdery in the Kirtland Temple, he committed to them the dispensation of the gospel of Abraham, stating that through the members of the Church all future generations would be blessed. (See D&C 110:12.)

To help family members understand the blessings the Lord gave to Abraham, Isaac, Jacob, and their posterity, have family members fill in the blanks for the chart "Blessings to Abraham and His Descendants" by looking up the scripture references. Have them write their answers on a separate sheet of paper so that you can save the chart for future home evenings.

Explain that when family members receive their patriarchal blessing, they will be told the name of the tribe of Israel through which they can receive these blessings.

What must we do to obtain the blessings pronounced upon Abraham and his posterity? (Live to be worthy of them.)

Blessings of Comfort and Guidance

Explain that patriarchal blessings are sacred and personal blessings, and we should talk about them only at special times. We may, however, discuss our blessings with each other in the family if we feel that we want to.

Share how you feel about the promise, the warning, the comfort, and the guidance your blessing has given to you. Ask other family members to do the same. If no one in the family has received a patriarchal blessing, you may want to review the blessings of your ancestors, and tell about some of the instructions or guidance they received. If possible, show how some of the promises were fulfilled.

Keeping an Eternal Perspective

- What do you think it means to keep an eternal perspective as you try to understand a patriarchal blessing?

During the discussion, read the following:

"It should always be kept in mind that the realization of the promises made may come in this or the future life. Men have stumbled at times because promised blessings have not occurred in this life. They have failed to remember that, in the gospel, life with all its activities continues forever and that the labors of earth may be continued in heaven." (John A. Widtsoe, *Evidences and Reconciliations*, 3 vols. [Salt lake City: Bookcraft, 1943], 2:75.)

- Should the family member expect the patriarch to answer all the questions he has about future events in his life? (No, he should not. A patriarchal blessing may contain mostly general guidelines, or it may be quite specific in some areas. He should use his blessing to help him work out his future plans.)
- Why should a patriarchal blessing be read often? (As a person grows older and matures, he will probably discover new meanings, motivations, and insights in his patriarchal blessing.)

To illustrate how the meaning of parts of a blessing may change as the years go by, tell the family you would like them to do the following exercise. Give each one a piece of paper and a pencil and ask them to write on the top, "You will do important work in the temple." Have them write the numbers *15*, *30*, and *60* in a vertical line below this sentence. Have each person write the different meanings that this promise might have to a person aged 15, 30, and 60. After they have taken a few minutes to do this, ask each one to read what he has written. (Possible answers could be at 15—being baptized for the dead, at 30—doing endowment and sealing work in the temple, at 60—giving time and energy to genealogical research.)

Preparing for a Memorable Day

- What can a person do to be prepared to hear and understand the Lord's message to him?

Have the person preparing to receive the blessing answer this question. He will likely mention fasting and prayer. Then ask family members to add their suggestions.

LEAVING ON A MISSION

(To be used before a family member goes on a mission
or leaves home for an extended period)

Go ye therefore, and teach all nations.
[*Matthew* 28:19]

PURPOSE

Honor your family member who has been called to serve a mission or who is leaving home for an extended period to work or to go to school.

FOR THE PARENT

This home evening needs preparation ahead of time to be most effective. The more participation by members of the family, the more love and unity the family will feel. The optional activities at the end are suggestions to help make this home evening a more memorable one for your departing missionary or other family member. It is not intended that all the suggestions be used, only those that will appeal to your family. Adapt the activities to your own situation if you are honoring someone who is leaving home for school or work.

PREPARATION

1. Enough slips of paper for the family dinner activity.
2. Ask family members to prepare to tell about an experience they have had with the person about to leave on a mission, something that has happened to him, or something memorable that he has done.

SUGGESTED HYMNS AND SONG

"It May Not Be on a Mountain Height" (*Hymns*, no. 75).
"Ye Elders of Israel" (*Hymns*, no. 344).
"I Hope They Call Me on a Mission" (*Sing with Me*, B–75).

SUGGESTED LESSON

A Family Dinner

Start your home evening with a special family dinner. Invite extended family members if possible. Include some of the missionary's favorite foods in the meal. You could also serve dishes typical of the area or country to which the missionary has been called.

Before the dinner, assign family members to compile some information about the particular area or country in which the missionary will serve. This information could include such things as interesting places in the mission area, customs, eating habits, and climate. Write these facts on separate slips of paper. Tape one slip on the bottom of the seat of each chair.

During the dinner, ask family members, one at a time, to find the slips of paper under their chairs and read aloud the facts about the country or area to which the missionary will be going.

The missionary could then add things he has learned about his mission area since receiving his call.

Honoring Your Missionary

After dinner have each person tell briefly about an experience he has had with the missionary, something that has happened to the missionary, or something memorable that the missionary has done.

Family Conversion Story

Have a family member tell the conversion story of one of the first people to join the Church in your family. This story will point out the far-reaching effects of a single baptism

and show how much a baptism has meant to all of you. If you do not know or do not have access to a family story, you can use the following:

Georg Salzner was a Protestant who lived in Hambach, Germany, in the late 1800s. His wife, Anna, was a Catholic. Georg consented to allow his children to attend the Catholic church with their mother, which they did regularly, but Georg had his own convictions. For years he had treasured a pamphlet written by a Protestant minister. Among other things, this pamphlet said that the pure gospel as taught by Christ was not upon the earth but would be brought back some day. Georg was much impressed by this writing and carried it around with him for many years wondering if he would live to hear the true gospel of Christ.

In 1880 Georg lost his job as a screen maker. He left his family in Hambach for a time and took a job in a town twenty miles away. One evening his landlady called him out of his room and introduced him to some men from America, saying that he might be interested in their message. Away from home and lonesome, Georg sat down and listened to their story. He heard how the gospel had been restored. He heard passages of scripture quoted that he had read in his pamphlet many times. After these men, who were missionaries of the Church, finished their message, Georg exclaimed with great joy, "Gentlemen, I have been searching for this message for many years! I know it is the truth!" Soon after this he was baptized, and his family was baptized not long afterward.

In 1883, Georg sold his home and left with his wife and two children to join the Saints in America. His life was completely changed because two young missionaries were serving the Lord. The lives of a great many other people are also different because of the conversion of this one man. His posterity now numbers approximately 150 people, all of whom are members of the Church. Many others have been given the blessings of the gospel through the efforts of members of his family who have served as missionaries and mission presidents.

At the conclusion of the story or stories, emphasize the difference the gospel has made in your lives. Ask family members to list ways their lives would be different if their ancestor had not joined the Church.

Point out that your missionary is going to have the opportunity and responsibility to help the Lord bring blessings of the gospel into the lives of other families. Each conversion can have far-reaching effects.

To conclude this discussion, family members, including the missionary, may want to bear their testimonies.

A Father's Blessing

The father may want to close this home evening by giving the missionary a father's blessings.

Optional Activities

Have each member of the family write a note of appreciation to the missionary, mentioning some of the traits he has that will make him a good missionary. You could also ask the bishop, a seminary teacher, Sunday School teacher, quorum president, or special friends to do the same thing. Put these tributes together in a notebook or large envelope and give them to the missionary at home evening.

Have members of the family make useful small gifts ahead of time to give the missionary at home evening. These might include a first-aid kit, an apron, or a small collection of simple recipes.

Take a family picture during this home evening, or during an earlier one if possible, and have small copies made of it. Write a family testimony, and put a copy of it with each picture. Your missionary can glue these in the front of copies of the Book of Mormon he leaves with investigators. If you do this early enough, you could present these to the missionary at this home evening. This will help both the missionary and the family members feel you are all sharing in his work.

Get a map of the area or country in which your missionary will be serving, and mount it on corkboard or similar material. Hang the map in a place where it can stay throughout his mission. Have your missionary put a pin in the city in which his mission home is located. Tell him you will add a pin each time he is transferred to a new city. This will help the family keep track of where he is serving. If the missionary is taking a camera with him, suggest that he send you a picture of his companion and his living quarters each time he is transferred. These could be pinned to the corner of the map. Travel agencies and automobile clubs often have maps. Oil companies and the tourist bureau in the capital city of each state have state maps. Encyclopedias and atlases also have maps.

If there are young children in your family, they might enjoy playing a game similar to "Pin the Tail on the Donkey," using a map of your missionary's mission. Have family members take turns trying to pin a marker on the city of the mission headquarters while they are blindfolded. (A map for this purpose could be roughly outlined from one in an encyclopedia or atlas.)

Decorations for the dinner table could include small flags of the area or country to which the missionary is going. These can be drawn from illustrations in an encyclopedia or sometimes can be purchased at novelty shops. You could aso make pennants with the initials of the mission on them. These can be made of felt or colored paper and laid on the table, or they can be made of cardboard and glued to a dowel and a base so they will stand up.

President David O. McKay suggested that every member ought to be engaged in missionary work. Those who are going away from home where they will meet new people will have new opportunities to tell those people about the gospel. Family members can each present the one leaving home with a Book of Mormon for him to lend or give to others. They may wish to insert their testimonies in the book. Or, during the dinner, the family can discuss other opportunities for missionary work that the missionary's new circumstances will provide.

THEY TWAIN SHALL BE ONE

(To be used when a family member is to be married)

[Marriage is] *without beginning of days or end of years. . . . It lays the foundation for worlds, for angels, and for the Gods; for intelligent beings to be crowned with glory, immortality, and eternal lives. In fact, it is the thread which runs from the beginning to the end of the holy Gospel of Salvation; . . . it is from eternity to eternity.* [Brigham Young, Discourses of Brigham Young, sel. John A. Widtsoe (Salt Lake City: Deseret Book Co., 1941), p. 195.]

PURPOSE

Honor a family member who is soon to be married, and teach family members the importance of the marriage covenant.

FOR THE PARENT

If possible, make this one of the last home evenings before the wedding. Make this a time to honor the bride or groom and to remind her or him of the sacred nature of marriage.

PREPARATION

Ask family members to think of qualities of the person to be married that will contribute to a happy marriage. They should be prepared to share these qualities at home evening.

SUGGESTED HYMNS AND SONGS

"There Is Beauty All Around" (*Hymns*, no. 169).
"How Beautiful Are Thy Temples" (*Hymns*, no. 65).
"Families Can Be Together Forever" (*Supplement to More Songs for Children*, p. 1).
"I Love to See the Temple" (*Supplement to More Songs for Children*, p. 4).

SUGGESTED LESSON

Marriage Ordained of God

Explain that the family member you are honoring will soon be leaving the family circle to begin a new family of his or her own, and this is as it should be. Getting married and raising a family is an important part of the Lord's plan for us.

Invite each family member to tell of a quality the person to be married has that will contribute to a happy marriage. For example, a person might say, "I think the person being married will be a good mother because she knows how to make us feel better when we are hurt, like the day I fell and hurt my knee," or "I think the person being married will be a good father because he is so kind to children."

Remind the family that there are some basics that are essential if any marriage is to be successful. Ask them to tell what things they feel are necessary if a marriage is to be successful and happy. Show the pictures included with this lesson one at a time, and have the family decide what is depicted in each one.

Then have someone read the statements that accompany each of the pictures. The eight pictures represent love, trust, appreciation, communication, children, financial security, spirituality, and a sense of humor.

Record Keeping—Another Essential

Explain that another essential for a new family is record keeping. Give a blank family group sheet to the person about to marry during home evening, and suggest that he fill it out while the information is fresh in his mind. Parents should remember to update their own family group sheet also. Emphasize that the new family should keep records current as other milestones are reached in their family.

Gifts for the Newly Married (Optional)

Before this home evening, you may want to prepare small inexpensive gifts that the newly married couple will need. You could select an appropriate scripture verse and attach it to each package. Following are a few ideas:

Item	Scripture
1. Box of salt	Luke 14:34: "Salt is good: but if the salt have lost his savour, wherewith shall it be seasoned?"
2. Measuring spoons or a measuring cup	1 Chronicles 23:29: "For the unleavened cakes, and for that which is baked in the pan, and for that which is fried, and for all manner of measure and size."
3. Book of scripture	Matthew 4:4: "Man shall not live by bread alone, but by every word that proceedeth out of the mouth of God."
4. Alarm clock	Doctrine and Covenants 88:124: "Cease to sleep longer than is needful; retire to thy bed early, that ye may not be weary; arise early, that you bodies and your minds may be invigorated."
5. Favorite bread recipes	Ruth 2:14: "At mealtime come thou hither, and eat of the bread."
6. Small jar of honey	Proverbs 24:13: "Eat thou honey, because it is good."
7. Pitcher, cups, or glasses	Proverbs 5:15: "Drink waters out of thine own cistern, and running waters out of thine own well."
8. Soap, detergent, towels, shampoo, toothpaste, wash cloths, dish towels, paper towels	Isaiah 1:16: "Wash you, make you clean."

During home evening, instruct the one being married to read the accompanying scripture, try to guess from the words what the package contains, and then open the package and show the gift to the family.

A Family Meal

You may want to have a family dinner to honor the person being married. To give advice to this person, you may want to place pieces of paper with scriptures written on them under each plate and read them as the meal progresses. You could use scriptures such as the following or other pieces of advice:

1. Proverbs 16:24
2. Proverbs 16:8
3. Proverbs 14:29
4. Proverbs 15:13
5. Proverbs 15:17
6. Proverbs 3:9–10
7. Proverbs 4:26
8. Proverbs 3:5–6
9. Proverbs 15:1
10. Proverbs 17:1

A Father's Blessing

You may want to make arrangements to give a father's blessing to the family member getting married. It could be given at the end of this family night, on the day of the wedding or at another appropriate time.

Love

"There is something besides instinct which is far more beautiful and that something is Love, the divinest attribute of the human soul. There is no difficulty, there is no sorrow, there is no success, there is no fame, there is no wealth, there is nothing in the world which can separate two hearts that are bound by the golden clasp of love." (David O. McKay, *Secrets of a Happy Life* [Salt Lake City: Bookcraft, 1960], pp. 36–37.)

Children

"The command to multiply and replenish the earth and subdue it comes from the Lord also. To refuse to bear or refrain from the bearing of children is an error of omission. Of course, the mere bringing of children into the world does not fulfill the obligation. Nor have parents met all their responsibilities when they feed and clothe and give schooling and entertainment to their offspring. The great parental responsibility is not met unless fathers and mothers do all in their power to train their children to pray and walk uprightly before the Lord, giving proper example and positive verbal teaching." (Spencer W. Kimball, *The Miracle of Forgiveness* [Salt Lake City: Bookcraft, 1969], p. 97.)

Spirituality

"Let us live so that the spirit of our religion will live within us, then we will have peace, joy, happiness and contentment, which makes such pleasant fathers, pleasant mothers, pleasant children, pleasant households, neighbors, communities and cities. That is worth living for, and I do think that the Latter-day Saints ought to strive for this." (Brigham Young, *Discourses of Brigham Young*, sel. John A. Widtsoe [Salt Lake City: Deseret Book Co., 1941], p. 204.)

Trust

"I beg of you to lay the foundations of the home on a solid, firm foundation of love, trust, and faith. Start the day with family prayer. Kneel together before you retire. There may have been some rough edges through the day, and a good way to smooth them out is by kneeling together in prayer." (Harold B. Lee, *Strengthening the Home* [pamphlet, 1973], pp. 7–8.)

Communication

"Marriage counselors report that one of the major family problems today is the inability of mates to talk things over. . . . Just living together does not weld two persons into a loving, understanding oneness; this may materialize only as husband and wife open their hearts and minds to each other, so that a two-way street is paved for sharing hopes and aspirations as well as problems, so that plans may be democratically and wisely made.

"What can be done to help lubricate the wheels of communication between husband and wife?

"1. Develop a desire to share ideas with one's mate. . . .

"2. Try to talk *with* rather than *to* or *at* each other. . . .

"3. Be a good listener. . . .

"4. Learn to accept each other's opinions and feelings. . . .

"5. Keep confidences." (Rex A. Skidmore, *I Thee Wed*, rev. ed. [Salt Lake City: Deseret Book Co., 1964], pp. 41–43.)

Financial Security

"Brethren and sisters, plan and work in a way that will permit you to be happy even as you do without certain things that in times of affluence may have been available to you. Live within your means and not beyond them. Where you have a plot of land, however small, plant a garden. Staying close to the soil is good for the soul. Purchase your essentials wisely and carefully. Strive to save a portion of that which you earn. Do not mistake many wants for basic needs.

"Teach your children these basic principles in your family councils." (Spencer W. Kimball, in Conference Report, Apr. 1981, pp. 107–8; or *Ensign,* May 1981, p. 80.)

Appreciation

"May you young husbands realize that the home is your wife's castle where from morning till night she toils to build. . . . For you to fail to appreciate her efforts or to disregard the sanctity of her home and its orderliness by your careless habits, would be to put into her mind the dangerous thought that her husband doesn't appreciate her efforts. You young wives must realize that as your companion comes home from his day's labor, he comes sometimes with nerves that are taut with the tensions of that day's efforts, hoping to find in you someone to give him the strength and the courage to go back inspired and better prepared to meet the problems of the next day. To nag and to scold and to fail to appreciate his problems is to fail in being the companion that he needs." (Harold B. Lee, *Youth and the Church* [Salt Lake City: Deseret Book Co., 1970], p. 178.)

Sense of Humor

"A sense of humor may save numerous difficult or awkward situations, turning them into pleasant experiences. . . .

"In addition to making life more pleasant for all concerned, a sense of humor also helps cushion the bumps along the road of living together. Every situation has at least two sides, and what is emphasized may bring entirely different results. It is important to look at the good side of people and experiences." (Rex A. Skidmore, *I Thee Wed*, pp. 53–54.)

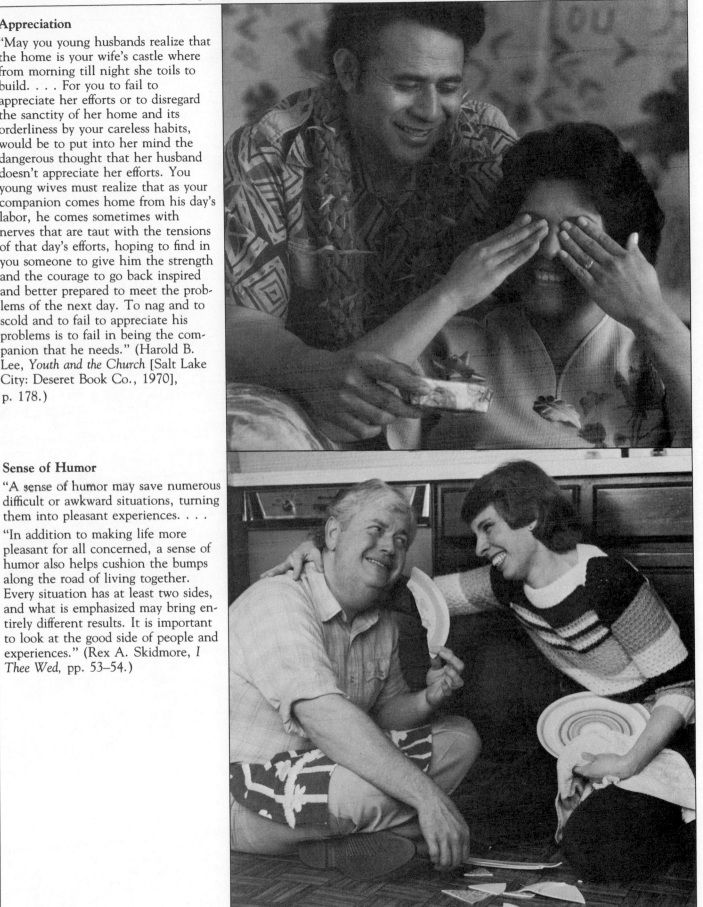

WHEN ILLNESS STRIKES

(To be used when someone in your family becomes
seriously, chronically, or terminally ill)

*Let not your heart be troubled, neither let
it be afraid.*
[John 14:27]

PURPOSE

Help your family face illness with
greater understanding and unity.

FOR THE PARENT

Extended or terminal illness in a family can be more difficult to face than
almost any other adversity. It can be
turned into a faith promoting and
strengthening experience if the family
faces it with the right attitudes and
actions. This lesson will help your
family grow from such an experience if
you approach it prayerfully and wisely,
adapting your discussions to the specific problems and needs of your
situation.

PREPARATION

Fill a box, sack, or pillowcase with
books or other unbreakable objects,
one or more object for each member
of your family. Make sure there are
enough heavy things in the sack that
it will be too heavy for just one family
member to lift and carry easily.

SUGGESTED HYMNS AND SONG

"How Firm a Foundation" (*Hymns*,
no. 66).
"When upon Life's Billows" (*Hymns*,
no. 202).
"The Lord Is My Shepherd" (*Hymns*,
no. 104).
"When We're Helping" (*Sing with Me*,
D–5).

SUGGESTED LESSON

When You Were Sick

Have the members of your family try
to remember a time when they were
sick or injured and confined to the
home. Have each family member take
a few minutes to tell about his
experience.

- Who helped care for you and comfort you?

- How would you feel if your sickness
were to last for several months or
even several years?

Sharing the Burden

Tell each of the following stories to
the family:

The Carson Family

Brother and Sister Carson had twin
daughters, sixteen years of age, and
two sons, ages twelve and ten. Sister
Carson was an expert homemaker. No
one in the home could equal her
efficiency. Brother Carson and his
family depended heavily upon Sister
Carson's smooth manner of handling
all matters dealing with the home.

One evening at a social gathering, Sister Carson suffered a stroke. She was
paralyzed from the waist down and did
not respond to treatment. She was
very worried about what would happen
to her home now that she could not
do all that she had done. Her family
seemed incapable of maintaining the
order that she expected and this upset
her and her family. The family did not
seem to know where to find things,
what to do, or how to do it.

Brother Carson mourned over the situation and seemed to spend longer
hours at his work. He lacked

resourcefulness in bringing hope, comfort, or encouragement into the home.
The situation became more and more
discouraging until the twins were sent
to live with Brother Carson's sister,
and the boys found a home with
Grandmother and Grandfather
Carson. Brother Carson and his wife
went to her mother's to live.

After the family had gone, a neighbor
made the following observation: "They
were a happy family until trouble
came. They did not know how to
share responsibility. When the mother
had her stroke, the family members
did not know how to help and comfort one another."

The Fosters

The Fosters had five children ranging
in age from six to fifteen. They were a
happy family and enjoyed doing things
together. Each had his own responsibility in the home, and even Susan,
age six, was expected to do her part.

One afternoon while driving home
from shopping, Sister Foster was involved in an automobile accident. She
was seriously injured and lost the use
of both legs.

It was a tragic circumstance, but
Brother Foster and his five children
gathered in prayer and sought the
comforting influence of the Lord.
They put their arms around each other
and began to make plans. Brother
Foster told his family, "Mother can't
walk. The doctors say she may never
use her legs again. We have depended
on her for our meals, washing, and
ironing, but now things have changed.
We will each need to do some of the
things she used to do. What do you
suggest?"

Denton, the oldest son, said, "I'll come home from school as early as I can. I know how to wash clothes."

Joyce, almost fourteen, quickly added, "I'll do the cooking."

Each member of the family told what he would do. Little Susan promised to help keep things off the floor and in their place. Donald and Jane mentioned other things that they could do. The Foster family found comfort in the Lord through their prayers and also in each other. They made plans and took over most of Sister Foster's duties. Despite the unfortunate accident, they were still a happy family.

• Why was the Foster family better able to adjust to their new situation?

Now bring the sack filled with books or other heavy objects into the room. Have each family member take a turn trying to lift the sack and carry it.

• Can you carry the contents of this sack easily?

Remove the books or objects from the sack, and divide them among the family members. Give each member only as many as he or she is able to carry easily.

• Can you carry the contents of this sack easily now?

Explain to your family that when the responsibility of caring for a sick or disabled member of the family is placed upon only one member of the family, the burden of that responsibility becomes very heavy, just as the sack became very heavy for only one of them to carry.

Explain that when that same burden of responsibility is divided and shared among all the members in the family, it becomes lighter and is easy to carry, just as the contents of the sack were easy to carry when they were divided and shared.

Have a family member read Galatians 6:2 and explain what the scripture means to him.

• Are we, as members of this family, ready to share one another's burdens?

A Time For Prayer

• What was the first thing the Foster family remembered to do in the story? (They gathered in prayer and sought the comforting influence of the Lord.)

Explain to your family that sometimes through the blessings of the priesthood and through the fasting and prayers of family members, the sick can be healed. Explain that sometimes the person is not healed, but through the prayers of family members and others, he and his family can feel the comforting Spirit of the Lord. Explain to your family that all of them can receive needed comfort, understanding, and unity from fasting and praying together.

Blessings in Disguise

Have the family find Romans 8:28 and 2 Nephi 2:2 and read the passages aloud.

• What do these scriptures teach us about sickness and adversity?

Explain to the family that the Lord can bless us in many different ways, and sometimes he allows us to experience sickness and adversity so that we can grow. Read the following story told by Bishop H. Burke Peterson:

"We have all been aware of President Kimball's health problems. I remember several years ago when I was called into the Presiding Bishopric that we were invited into a room in the temple where the newly sustained Brethren were to be set apart. Prior to the setting apart the Brethren were going to give a blessing to President Kimball, who was then President of the Quorum of the Twelve, because he was going to have open-heart surgery within a matter of a few days. As they gave him the blessing, many thoughts went through my mind.

"President Kimball had been raised in Arizona, as I had been, and I had paid particular attention to him. I remembered many of the trials that he had experienced, especially the very serious health problems. I knew that he sang in a quartet at one time with members of the Twelve, and I understood he sang beautifully. Then he had cancer and had to have that voice taken away from him.

"I thought as I saw him seated in his chair, with the Apostles' hands on his head, 'Why? Why should a man who has been through what he has endured now have to go through open-heart surgery?' I knew the Lord could heal him in an instant if he chose to, and I wondered why he didn't. But now I understand, as I'm sure you do, that the Lord was preparing a man, an Apostle, to be his prophet. He wanted a prophet and a president who would listen to him, who could receive the promptings of the Spirit and would be open to them.

"These are the reasons for the continual trials with which we are all faced. We need these experiences so that we might draw closer to the Lord and learn to depend on him for everything." ("Prayer—Try Again," *Ensign*, June 1981, p. 72.)

Explain that sometimes blessings can come to us from times of tragedy or sickness. Have your family think of some of these blessings, and then add those they do not mention:

1. A feeling of closeness to the Lord.
2. Greater compassion and charity for others.
3. Appreciation for the most important things in life.
4. A closer family unit.
5. Development of new talents and strengths.

Tell the following story:

Michael's Weakness Becomes a Strength

When Michael was ten years old he was in an automobile accident. His legs were crushed so badly that the doctors told Michael he would probably never walk again. Michael didn't believe them, however. His dad had given him a priesthood blessing. He remembered the words: "Your weakness will become a great strength if you have faith in Jesus Christ."

How could his weakness become a strength unless he could walk and run again? Then maybe he would become a great runner or even a football hero. He pictured himself running to the winning touchdown with the fans going wild! Yes, he knew he would walk again because he did have faith in the Lord. He was brave through all the operations and pain, and he tried to be cheerful. He prayed every day. He *knew* he would walk again.

Michael soon made friends with the other children in the hospital. In fact, they called him "Mr. Friendly" because he was so happy and tried to make everyone else happy, too. That made Michael feel good because he wanted to help. He knew that all the children didn't have the special blessing that he did to keep his spirits up. He especially felt a love for the babies. They were so little and helpless. He loved to make them smile and laugh. Pretty soon even the smallest baby would grin just to see him coming.

Then one day, one of Michael's legs hurt even worse than usual. After the doctors examined his leg, they told him that it was getting worse and not better and that they would have to take it off.

"Take my leg off!" Michael thought. "If they did that, then how could I

become a great football star? They just can't do it!"

But they had to do it to save Michael's life. When it was all over, Michael felt sad and confused. How could his weakness become a great strength now? But Michael didn't quit having faith. He still loved the Lord, and he knew that the Lord loved him. He kept praying, and he tried to be good. He knew that the Lord could perform mighty miracles, and so he would just have to wait.

Meanwhile, as he began to feel better, he spent more and more time trying to keep all of the other children happy. He told them about Jesus and our Heavenly Father and helped them learn to pray. He didn't have time to be too sad or to think about football anymore. He began, instead, to pretend that he was a great doctor that helped little children get well.

Finally, after many months in the hospital, Michael was ready to go home. It was an exciting day but a sad one too as he said good-bye to each of his friends. When he said good-bye to the babies, he almost didn't want to go. He said a special prayer in his heart for each one of them. When his doctor came to say good-bye, he ruffled Michael's hair and said, "Well, Mr. Friendly, you have been a great strength to all the children in the hospital—a very great strength." And then another voice echoed in Michael's mind, "A great strength—your weakness will become a great strength."

Suddenly Michael knew how his prayers were being answered, and he also knew that he would never run again.

After you discuss the story of Michael and the implications it may have in your family, conclude by having a family member read Elder Marion D. Hanks' counsel:

"In your own life realize there will come troubles. God bless you not to be negative or fatalistic in your thinking but to treat trouble as a friend and raise foundations that will permit you to stand steady.

"God does love us and He takes no delight in our sorrows and failures." ("Use Gift of Time," *Church News*, 24 Apr. 1965, p. 6.)

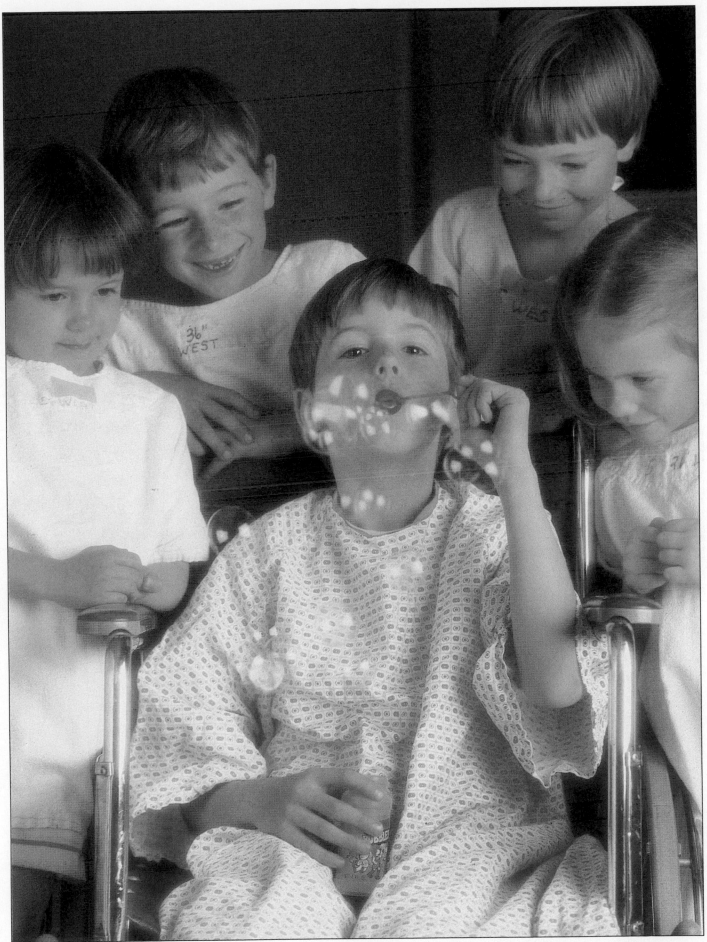

THEY THAT MOURN SHALL BE COMFORTED

(To be used after a loved one has died)

Blessed are all they that mourn, for they shall be comforted.
[3 Nephi 12:4]

PURPOSE

Help members of the bereaved family find comfort in having each other and in being able to trust in the Lord, accepting death as a necessary part of eternal life.

FOR THE PARENT

For this home evening to be most effective and comforting, your family should have it as soon as possible after the death or funeral of the family member. You will need to familiarize yourself with the material and assign the scriptures to be read and discussed well before the home evening.

PREPARATION

You will need a glove.

SUGGESTED LESSON

Missing a Loved One

Ask family members to each share one of their favorite memories of the person who has died. Remind them that this family member is no longer sick or sad or in pain and that he would want them to speak of him often and not forget the things they did together. Stress here that it is natural to miss him and to cry because he is gone. Our Heavenly Father knew it would be this way, for he said, "Thou shalt live together in love, insomuch that thou shalt weep for the loss of them that die" (D&C 42:45).

Enduring the Separation of Death

Have someone read the following words of President Spencer W. Kimball:

"We knew before we were born that we were coming to the earth for bodies and experience and that we would have joys and sorrows, ease and pain, comforts and hardships, health and sickness, successes and disappointments. We also knew that after a period of life we would die. We accepted all these eventualities with a glad heart, eager to accept both the

favorable and the unfavorable. . . . We eagerly accepted the chance to come earthward even though it might be for only a day or a year." (*Tragedy or Destiny* [Salt Lake City: Deseret Book Co., 1977], p. 12.)

If it is appropriate, remind the family that the family member who died had a number of years on earth, and he knew joys and sorrows and had a chance to grow before he died. All of us are having our earthly experiences now. This death is one of the sorrows we share as a family. No one of us has to bear it alone because we have each other and the help of our Heavenly Father. With this support, we will find a way to go on living without him.

A Separation of the Spirit from the Body

The idea for the following presentation comes from a conference talk by Elder Boyd K. Packer in the 1973 April general conference. If you have access to this talk (in Conference Report, Apr. 1973, pp. 78–82; or *Ensign*, July 1973, pp. 51–54), you may want to read it before you present this family home evening.

Using your hand to represent the spirit and a glove to represent the body, tell the following to your family, using your own words:

Pretend that my hand is your spirit (hold it up). Each of you lived as a spirit with your Heavenly Father before you came to this earth. The spirit can live and move by itself (wiggle your fingers). Pretend that this glove is your body (hold it up). Until the spirit enters it, the body cannot move. By itself it has no life. When the time came for you to enter this world, your spirit was clothed in your body (put on the glove), and your body became alive. From your birth to your death, your spirit and your body are together (wiggle your fingers in the glove), and you are said to be alive. At the time of your death, whenever that is—in childhood, the teen years, young adulthood, middle age, or old age—your spirit will be separated from your body (pull off the glove and hold it up). Your body will again become lifeless (drop the empty glove). It will not be able to move because your spirit will be gone from it. Your spirit,

however, will never die (wiggle your fingers). It goes to be with other spirits who have been separated from their earthly bodies.

Explain that this is what happened to the member of your family. His spirit was separated from his body. We all saw his body lying there like this glove. It could not move or speak. There was no life in it. His spirit was no longer there. Although his body is dead, he is not dead. The part of him that looked out through his eyes and allowed him to think and smile and act, to know and to be—that part of him is his spirit and lives on. He is only separated from his body.

The Larger Picture

Invite your family to stand with you at the window. Point out to them how much they cannot see—the other side of the house, down the street, the next block. From the window, their point of view is limited.

Take the family outdoors. Tell them to look around and see that without the walls and ceiling in the way, they can see more than they could from the window—more houses, more street, more sky. They can get a better idea of where they are. After they have looked around a bit and thought about what they have seen, go back inside. When they are assembled indoors

again, explain that this death was something like their going outdoors; the family member went through a door into a bigger and better place.

Read the following statement of President Joseph F. Smith, who in his lifetime experienced the deaths of many loved ones:

"While we are in mortality we are clogged, and we see as through a glass darkly, we see only in part, and it is difficult for us to comprehend the smallest things with which we are associated. But when we put on immortality, our condition will be very different, [for] we ascend into an enlarged sphere." (Joseph F. Smith, *Gospel Doctrine*, 5th ed. [Salt Lake City: Deseret Book Co., 1939], p. 440.)

Tell the family that the family member's spirit, separated from his body, has gone into that larger sphere, and now he can see and understand more than they can, just as they could see more when they went outdoors. Although he cannot come back to us, he will be waiting for us to come where he is, to see what he sees, and to know what he knows. Then the whole family will await the resurrection that will reunite each spirit and body forever. (Pick up the glove and put it on again, wiggling the fingers.) As resurrected beings, they can receive a fulness of joy and have eternal life, which is the greatest gift of all.

A Time of Reunion

Remind your family that they all know something about the plan of salvation. Through this plan, the Savior made it possible for them to be with their family member again, to be together as a family, if they live by the commandments of God and keep themselves holy before him. This family member is hoping that they will be worthy to come where he is, so that they can all be together again. Each of them lived before they were born and will go on living, just as he is, after they die. Have someone read these words of President Joseph F. Smith:

"Our relationships are formed for eternity. We are immortal beings, and we are looking forward to the growth that is to be attained in an exalted life after we have proved ourselves faithful and true to the covenants that we have entered into here, and then we will receive a fulness of joy." (*Relief Society Magazine*, May 1917, p. 316.)

"I cannot express the joy I feel at the thought of meeting my father, and my precious mother, who gave me birth in the midst of persecution and poverty. . . . The thought of meeting her, who can express the joy? The thought of meeting my children who have preceded me beyond the veil, and of meeting my kindred and my friends, what happiness it affords! For I know I shall meet them there. God has shown me that this is true. He has made it clear to me, in answer to my prayer and devotion as He has made it clear to the understanding of all men who have sought diligently to know of Him." (In Conference Report, Oct. 1899, p. 71.)

You may want to add your witness to President Smith's that each member of your family can receive the comforting assurance that the family member who died actually lives and that they can be with him again.

Trusting Our Heavenly Father

Explain to your family that although everything can turn out all right, the time right after the death is very difficult because everyone misses the family member so much. Remind them that Heavenly Father can see and understand even more than the family member can. He loves everyone in the world and is able to know how sad and lonely they feel. Many times he has told us that he loves us and will help us through difficult times in our lives if we stay close to him.

Assign each family member ahead of time to read and think about one of the following scriptures so that he can read it aloud and tell what it means to him. Discuss each scripture verse.

1. "And again, blessed are all they that mourn, for they shall be comforted" (3 Nephi 12:4).

2. "Come unto me, all ye that labour and are heavy laden, and I will give you rest" (Matthew 11:28).

3. "Be still, and know that I am God" (Psalm 46:10).

4. "The Lord gave, and the Lord hath taken away; blessed be the name of the Lord" (Job 1:21).

5. "Be thou humble; and the Lord thy God shall lead thee by the hand, and give thee answer to thy prayers" (D&C 112:10).

6. "For God so loved the world, that he gave his only begotten Son, that whosoever believeth in him should not perish, but have everlasting life" (John 3:16).

7. "In my Father's house are many mansions: if it were not so, I would have told you. I go to prepare a place for you. And if I go and prepare a place for you, I will come again, and receive you unto myself; that where I am, there ye may be also." (John 14:2–3.)

8. "Peace I leave with you, my peace I give unto you: not as the world giveth, give I unto you. Let not your heart be troubled, neither let it be afraid" (John 14:27).

9. "Jesus said unto her, I am the resurrection, and the life: he that believeth in me, though he were dead, yet shall he live: And whosoever liveth and believeth in me shall never die. Believest thou this?" (John 11:25–26.)

Conclude the evening with the reminder that in spite of death, life goes on, and the family member who has died would want the family to meet it bravely. If they remember what he wants them to do, his influence will remain with them. Explain that you are still a family and have each other. You will find out as you go along that you can comfort each other and be comforted by Heavenly Father as you pray to him.

SUGGESTED READING MATERIAL

Joseph F. Smith, *Gospel Doctrine*, 5th ed. (Salt Lake City: Deseret Book Co., 1939), pp. 277–79; see also the chapter "Eternal Life and Salvation," pp. 428–77.

Joseph Smith, "The King Follett Discourse," *Teachings of the Prophet Joseph Smith*, sel. Joseph Fielding Smith (Salt Lake City: Deseret Book Co., 1938), pp. 342–62; see also pp. 196–210.

Heber J. Grant, "The Death of My Last Son," *Gospel Standards*, comp. G. Homer Durham (Salt Lake City: Improvement Era, 1941), pp. 364–66.

HE IS RISEN!

Behold my hands and my feet, that it is I myself: handle me, and see; for a spirit hath not flesh and bones, as ye see me have. [Luke 24:39]

PURPOSE

Help your family develop more love for Jesus Christ as you celebrate Easter together.

FOR THE PARENT

Holiday traditions are fun. Unfortunately we often get so busy with the bustle of the celebrations that we rob them of any real meaning. This is sad because religious holidays provide parents with some very natural teaching moments when they can share with their children those feelings and experiences that will bind them to each other and to the gospel throughout their lives.

Easter celebrates the final triumph of Jesus the Christ at the end of his earthly mission as he overcame both sin and death. But it is hard, especially for children, to find a connection between the common Easter traditions and the Atonement of the Lord. We need to find ways to celebrate Easter that are meaningful and that help them grow in love and appreciation for the Savior. This lesson includes some ideas for celebrating Easter that you may want to make traditional in your family. Before you give it, make sure you prepare spiritually so that your family will feel your appreciation for Jesus Christ and testimony of the Atonement. Review the story of the first Easter from the scriptures. You may also want to read chapter 12, "The Atonement," in *Gospel Principles* [PBIC0245], pages 65 through 72, to help you be able to talk about the Atonement in simple, understandable terms.

If you approach the Easter lesson with enthusiasm and thankfulness, your children too will learn to love this holiday for the right reasons. Celebrate it together in a spirit of love for the Savior and the wonderful gifts he has given us.

You will want to give this family home evening in two sessions: the preparation and the program.

PREPARATION

1. Bring a picture of someone you love that has died.
2. Prepare three wordstrips that say "Suffered for our sins," "Resurrection," and "Atonement."
3. You may want to make word charts of unfamiliar songs.

SUGGESTED HYMNS AND SONGS

Use the hymns and songs listed in the suggested lesson.

SUGGESTED LESSON

We Celebrate the Atonement of Jesus at Easter Time

Explain to your family that Easter is a time when we celebrate some important things that Jesus did for us.

• What did Jesus do for us at Easter time?

Explain that first he suffered for our sins so that we may be forgiven if we repent. Show the family the wordstrip "Suffered for our sins." Second, he had the power to live again after he died. We call this the Resurrection. Hold up the wordstrip "Resurrection." Because Jesus was resurrected, all of the people who have ever lived on the earth will be resurrected too.

Explain that we call these two things that Christ did for us—his suffering for our sins and resurrection—the Atone-

A New Commandment I Give Unto You, That Ye Love One Another; As I Have Loved You, That Ye Also Love One Another

JOHN 13:34

LOVE ONE ANOTHER

Luacine C. Fox   With devotion

Luacine C. Fox   Arr. by Jo Marie Borgesen Bray

As I have loved you, Love one a - no - ther.

This new com - mand - ment. Love one a - no - ther.

By this shall men know Ye are my dis - ci - ples,

If ye have love one to a - no - ther. _____

8va

ment. Hold up the wordstrip "Atonement." Talk about the fact that sin and death are a part of mortal existence. They are part of the experience that we came to this earth to have. But we alone could not overcome the effects of either. For this reason our Heavenly Father planned to provide us with a Savior. Jesus lovingly gave us the gift of the Atonement so that we could return to our Father in Heaven and become like him.

At this time you may enjoy singing "Jesus Has Risen" (*Sing with Me*, F–17).

Now take out the picture of your loved one, and share with your family your feelings about your loved one and his death. You may use the following story if you do not want to tell a personal story of your own:

Jamie

When Jamie was born, the doctors knew right away that there was something wrong with his tiny body. They sadly told his mother and father that he would not live very long. But when Jamie's mother was ready to go home from the hospital, Jamie was still alive. So Jamie went home with his mother.

The doctors said that Jamie's brain was very damaged and that he would never even know whether anyone loved him or not. But Jamie did know. Each day he grew and responded a little bit more. Soon he began to smile at his family, and sometimes he would even laugh. Jamie's family knew that he was a very special baby, and they loved him very much.

Jamie needed more care than most babies, but everyone in his family was glad to help care for him. Still, despite, all their loving care, Jamie grew weaker. Finally when he was nine months old, he died.

Jamie's family was comforted because they knew that he would live again and that his little body would be made perfect. Their appreciation for the Savior and the Resurrection was greatly strengthened.

Jamie's father and mother and brothers and sisters wanted to be with Jamie again, so they all tried hard to keep Heavenly Father's commandments.

Sometimes they made mistakes and did things that were wrong. Because of this, they wanted to repent, and the suffering that Jesus went through for their sins became very meaningful to them. They knew that as they truly repented, their sins would be forgiven and they could someday be with Jamie. They knew that all of them could live with Heavenly Father again.

The Atonement Is Important to Our Family

• Why do we as a family need the Atonement?

Help your family understand that without the Atonement, it wouldn't matter how good we tried to be; we would not be able to return to our Heavenly Father or regain our bodies. We would all be lost.

Bear your personal testimony of the Atonement, and tell why it is important to you. Then discuss with your family how you want Easter to be a special day this year, and to make it that way you are going to plan together tonight.

Preparing for Easter

Look over the pictures and program ideas. Decide how you will use the program. If it is too long you may wish to give parts of it on different days. Make assignments for narrators, scripture readers, and song leaders. Try to involve everyone. You may wish to use the program as a sunrise or Easter evening service. Arrange to learn the songs, or choose others that you are familiar with.

As you end your family home evening, challenge your family to strive to bring the Spirit of Christ into your home for Easter. Ask them to remember the great sacrifices that Jesus made to give us the gift of the Atonement. Suggest that they prepare for Easter by working extra hard to be unselfish and loving.

Encourage your family to make sacrifices to bring each other happiness. Let them name some sacrifices they could make such as giving up some of their playtime to help someone, sharing their toys, saying a kind thing to someone who has been unkind to them, or doing their chores without being reminded. Look up John 13:34,

and read it together. Then show the chart of it included in this lesson. Use it to remind your family of the challenge during the week.

Easter Program

Read John 3:16.

Have a narrator read or discuss the following: Even though he knew that Jesus would be cruelly treated, our Heavenly Father sent him to earth. He sent Jesus because he loves us. And Jesus loves us so much that he wanted to come. They both wanted every one of us to have the chance to go back and live with them. Is it any wonder that the angels sang for joy over this miracle of love, the gift of the Savior's birth?

Sing "Silent Night" (*Hymns*, no. 160).

Read Matthew 19:13–14.

Have a narrator read or discuss the following: When Jesus grew up, he spent his time teaching the people how to live and how to be happy. He preached the gospel, healed the sick, and blessed the children. He loved everyone, and many of the people loved Jesus, too. He lived a life of service and provided us with a perfect example to follow. Never thinking of himself, he lived his life giving to others

Sing "I Think When I Read That Sweet Story" (*Sing with Me*, B–69).

Read Luke 22:44.

Have a narrator read or discuss: Jesus knew that the time had come for him to suffer for our sins and die. He gathered his Apostles around him for the Passover feast, which was to be his last supper with them. There he taught them about the sacrament so that they would remember him and what he was about to do for them. He said something very important to them, "A new commandment I give unto you, That ye love one another; as I have loved you" (John 13:34). Later that same night, he prayed in the Garden of Gethsemane, and there he suffered for our sins to show his great love for all of us.

Sing "Love One Another" (included in this lesson).

Read John 19:17–18.

Have a narrator read or discuss: On

Friday, after a long night of illegal trials, Jesus was sentenced to death. He was beaten and laughed at and spit upon. Then he was hung on a cross, with nails piercing his hands and feet, and left to die. Still, he never stopped loving. He forgave those who were putting him to death. While he hung there, darkness covered the earth, for men were murdering their Creator.

Sing "There Is A Green Hill" (*Hymns*, no. 201).

Read Matthew 27:57–60.

Have a narrator read or discuss: Jesus was buried in a borrowed tomb on Friday evening, for Saturday was the Sabbath and burying people on that day was not allowed. Some women wanted to put special ointments on Jesus' body to prepare it for burial, but they didn't have time, so they planned to come back as soon as the Sabbath was over to finish preparing his body. The Sabbath was a long, sad day. Jesus was dead, and his followers could only wait and weep and think about him.

Sing "To Think About Jesus" (*Sing with Me*, B–55).

Read Luke 24:1–9.

Have a narrator read or discuss: The great rock was rolled, away and an angel declared that Jesus had risen. Mary Magdalene was the first to see him and she told his Apostles, but they did not believe her. Soon he appeared to others.

Then, as the Apostles were gathered together, "Jesus himself stood in the midst of them, and saith unto them, Peace be unto you.

"But they were terrified and affrighted, and supposed that they had seen a spirit.

"And he said unto them, Why are ye troubled? and why do thoughts arise in your hearts?

"Behold my hands and my feet, that it is I myself: handle me, and see; for a spirit hath not flesh and bones, as ye see me have." (Luke 24:36–39.)

At last they believed, though they were filled with wonder and joy. Jesus had risen from the dead and was with them again.

Although the events of the first Easter happened almost two thousand years ago, the story of Jesus does not end there. Still he lives, and still he loves us. He has again set up his Church on the earth so that we can have the blessings of the gospel. And that is the miracle of Easter. Jesus the Christ has triumphed over sin and death. He lives.

Sing "Jesus Has Risen" (*Sing with Me*, F–17).

Bear your own testimony to your family that Jesus lives today, that he is directing the prophet and guiding his Church. Allow each member of your family to express his feelings and appreciation for the Savior and the Atonement at this time.

Sing "He Is Risen" (*Hymns*, no. 61).

Close with a prayer.

For teenagers or adults, you may want to add more depth by reading some of the following scriptures:

1. Mark 16:2–8
2. John 20:11–17
3. Mark 16:10–11
4. Luke 24:36–39
5. John 10:16
6. 3 Nephi 11:3–11
7. Doctrine and Covenants 76:22–24

Add any hymns, songs, or musical numbers that are favorites of your family members.

SUGGESTIONS FOR FUTURE HOME EVENINGS

"Could Ye Not Watch with Me One Hour?"

Read aloud Matthew 26:36–45. Then discuss Doctrine & Covenants 19:16–18.

Assign a family member to read the following aloud:

Orson F. Whitney, an Apostle during the early days of the restored Church, dreamed that he saw the Savior in the Garden of Gethsemane. He wrote:

"I seemed to be in the Garden of Gethsemane, a witness of the Savior's agony. . . .

"As He prayed the tears streamed down his face, which was toward me. I was so moved at the sight that I also wept, out of pure sympathy. My whole heart went out to him; I loved him with all my soul, and longed to be with him as I longed nothing else.

"Presently He arose and walked to where those Apostles were kneeling— fast asleep! He shook them gently, awoke them, and in a tone of tender reproach, untinctured by the least show of anger or impatience, asked them plaintively if they could not watch with him one hour. There He was, with the awful weight of the world's sin upon his shoulders. . . .

"Three times this occurred, until I was perfectly familiar with his appearance—face, form and movements. He was of noble stature and majestic mien." (*Through Memory's Halls* [Independence, Mo.: Zion's Printing and Publishing Co., 1930], pp. 82–83.)

You may wish to use a flannel board with cutouts representing the Savior, the Apostles, the garden trees, and other things as Elder Whitney's dream is told.

Repeat Jesus' question: "Could ye not watch with me one hour?" Then ask family members how they can especially remember the Savior on Easter and "watch with him." You may wish to take this opportunity to plan a special family home worship or prayer service in memory of his atonement and resurrection to be held on Easter Sunday if you do not plan to use the suggestions given in the lesson.

The Savior's Work Continued after His Crucifixion

During the short time between his death on the cross and his resurrection, the Savior performed another great work. Explore with your family the great message of section 138 of the Doctrine and Covenants. Read the section together, and discuss its meaning for those in the spirit world and for us. For young children, you may wish to tell the story of how Jesus went to the spirit world and organized missionary work there.

The Other Sheep

Have a family home evening in which you compare events during Christ's ministry in Palestine with events going on in America at the same time. Give special attention to the Crucifixion, Resurrection, and the Savior's visit to the Nephites (see 3 Nephi 8 and the following chapters). You may wish to have family members act out portions of the story. Or you may wish to prepare a chart showing the parallel history of the two places.

"COME LET US ADORE HIM"

For unto you is born this day in the city of David a Saviour, which is Christ the Lord.
[Luke 2:11]

PURPOSE

Plan and prepare as a family to celebrate Christmas by enjoying the true spirit of the Savior's birth during the holiday season.

FOR THE PARENTS

"If Christmas could just happen without so much bother." "I can't wait to see what I get." "By the time Christmas arrives I am so exhausted I hardly feel anything but relief." Many of us—adults and children—go through the whole holiday season with thoughts like these foremost in our minds. How many times have you had such feelings or thoughts yourself? But Christmas is actually one of the most sacred of holidays, and enjoying its true spirit, which is the Spirit of Christ, can bring us closer to the Savior.

You may wish to take two separate home evenings to accomplish the objectives of this lesson. The first part should be given early in December, the second part during the week of Christmas.

PREPARATION

1. Prepare simple Christmas priority charts for each member of the family.
2. Assign parts for the Christmas program.

SUGGESTED HYMNS AND SONGS

Use the hymns and songs listed in the suggested lesson, parts 1 and 2.

SUGGESTED LESSON
PART 1: PLANNING

Examine Your Christmas Priorities

On standard sized paper, prepare a Christmas priorities chart for each family member. See the example:

Christmas Priorities

	Most Exciting	Most Important
Gifts		
Decorations		
Food		
Friends		
Family		
Christ		

In the column labeled "Most Exciting," have each person put down his first, second, and third choices of what is personally most exciting about Christmas to him. Discuss why each person made the choices he did.

Your little children will not be able to write, but parents or older children could help them. They will enjoy having a list of their own.

In the column labeled "Most Important," have family members write what they think should be most important, again indicating their first, second, and third choices.

- Why is it that at Christmastime the things that are most exciting and take the most time are not necessarily the most important?

- What can we do to make our Christmas more meaningful and to spend more time considering those things that are most important? (Cut down on some activities and preparations that are not important; then spend more time on things that are.)

- How can we make Christ the center of our Christmas?

Have family members place their lists where they can see them during the weeks preceding Christmas.

Plan to Put Christ in the Center of the Christmas Season

Have your family sing "Joy to the World" (*Hymns*, no. 89). Then discuss each part of your Christmas celebration, and decide how you can honor Jesus more. Help your family to have the courage to make necessary cuts and changes. The answers given are for your consideration. You should make the decisions that fit your own family.

Gifts

- How can we plan our Christmas gifts so they will help us to honor the Savior and feel the true spirit of Christmas?

Remind your family that our gifts should reflect the same spirit of love and concern as did those of the Wise Men who presented the first gifts to the baby Jesus. Explain that gifts will contribute to the spirit of Christmas only when they pass these three tests:

1. Is the gift given in the spirit of love?
2. Is it a reasonable choice and not too expensive or time consuming for the giver?
3. Will it be ready before Christmas so that it will not take last minute preparation that should be spent on more important activities?

Your family may think of alternatives to material gifts, such as the following:

1. Gifts of time and service. For example, one teenager wrapped a card for his sister that read, "I will take your turn doing the dishes three times when you need me." Suggest that each person give at least one such gift of service to each family member.
2. Gifts of ideas. For example, personal ideas, recipes, genealogical information, and personal histories

make gifts that will be deeply appreciated.

If gifts are purchased, they should be chosen especially for the one who will receive them. A good gift need not be expensive, but it must let the person who receives it know that he is loved.

Perhaps you should consider cutting down on your list of those to whom you give gifts. The mere exchanging of gifts does not necessarily reflect the true spirit of Christmas and may contribute to your putting material things at the center of your Christmas season rather than the Savior.

Decorations

• How can our Christmas decorations add more to the spirit of Christmas?

If Christmas decorations are too time consuming and expensive, they can detract from the spirit of Christmas. If left to the last minute, they often add haste and confusion to Christmas observance.

As you plan your decorations, discuss the idea that traditional decorations can remind us of Jesus because of their symbolism. For example:

Decoration	Symbolism
Bells	Sheep bells
Candy canes	Shepherd's staff
Lights, candles, star	The star that appeared on the night of Jesus' birth
Holly	The crown of thorns
Evergreen tree	Eternal life
Green, ivy	Life and hope
Red, holly berries	The blood of Christ

Food

• How can we enjoy preparing Christmas food so that it will add to the spirit of Christmas?

If Christmas food is kept simple, it can be an enjoyable part of Christmas. Make up menus and shopping lists weeks before Christmas, and purchase the items when it is convenient. This takes planning. Making cookies, candies, and cakes can be a family project that will bring you closer together and add to the real meaning of Christmas. Be sure to include your young children in these projects.

Family and Friends

• Which of our traditional Christmas activities add to the spirit of our celebration and bring us closer to the Savior?

Your family should honestly evaluate such activities as Christmas parties or the sending of Christmas cards and omit those that take away time from more important activities you want to plan.

You may wish to begin Christmas traditions that put service and love first in your plan by visiting long neglected relatives, lonely persons, or neighbors with whom you are not well acquainted. By sharing food, toys, and gifts with families who are in need, you may find new meaning in your celebration of the birth of the Lord. Remind your family that the Savior taught, "Inasmuch as ye have done it unto one of the least of these my brethren, ye have done it unto me" (Matthew 25:40).

Jesus Christ

- How can our family center our thoughts more upon Jesus Christ?

Following are some suggestions to help your family center their thoughts upon the Savior in the weeks preceding Christmas. Discuss them with your family, and together determine which ones you plan to use. You may think of other activities that you will want to plan.

1. Read the scriptures about the Lord's birth. Suggest a "Scriptural Twelve Days of Christmas." Beginning twelve days before Christmas, have a daily scripture reading using one of the following scriptures:

Luke 1:26–38	Matthew 2:1–12
3 Nephi 1:4–9	Helaman 14:2–6
Luke 1:39–45	Luke 2:1–7
2 Nephi 9:19–22	Isaiah 9:6–7
Matthew 1:18–25	Luke 2:8–20
3 Nephi 1:12–21	Isaiah 7:14

2. Ask each family member to give the Savior a special gift by trying to live the law of love in some special way during the Christmas season.

3. Plan to hold a special family home evening during Christmas week to celebrate the birth of the Savior. A program is suggested as part 2 of this lesson, or you could plan one of your own.

4. Listening to sacred Christmas music will also help you think about Jesus. Plan times when you can sing carols together and talk about the meaning of the words.

End this home evening by singing a favorite Christmas carol.

SUGGESTED LESSON
PART 2: CELEBRATION

Preparation for a Christmas Program

This family Christmas program is simple and will need no extensive preparation, but it will be much more effective if it can be presented without interruption. Use the following suggestions to help you make this a spiritual experience for your family:

1. Plan to let all family members participate on the program. Tell, rather than read, the story of the birth of the Savior.

2. The program will run more smoothly if each reader on the program has his own Bible and has marked where his part begins and ends. If younger children are reading some of the scripture verses, let each one practice his part privately with you.

3. If you plan to use an accompaniment, the person playing should begin the prelude music for the next song as soon as each scripture reading is finished.

Program: "Come Let Us Adore Him"

Prayer: Perhaps a child could offer the opening prayer.

Song: Sing the first two verses of "Oh Come, All Ye Faithful" (*Hymns*, no. 129). If you have accompaniment for the singing, it would be effective to continue playing this song softly after the first two verses while the following scripture is read. Then the family can join in singing the third verse when the scripture is finished and when the accompanist returns to the beginning of the song. If you do not have musical accompaniment, the group may want to hum softly while the scripture is read.

Scripture: Have someone read Matthew 1:18–23. Do not attempt to explain the hard words or the meaning of this passage. Let the family feel the spirit of what is read and go on with the program.

Song: Sing the third verse of "Oh Come, All Ye Faithful."

Scripture: Have someone read Luke 2:1–7.

Song: Sing one verse of "O Little Town of Bethlehem" (*Hymns*, no. 165). This carol would be a good one to use as a solo.

Scripture: Continue reading Luke 2:8–14. Perhaps this passage could be recited together as a choral reading by all the family.

Song: Have your family sing at least the first two verses of "Far, Far Away on Judea's Plains" (*Hymns*, no. 33). Some families may want to sing all four verses because of their message.

Scripture: Finish reading the story of the Savior's birth found in Luke 2:15–20.

Song: Sing both verses of "Hark! The Herald Angels Sing" (*Hymns*, no. 60).

Narration: Have someone read the following paragraphs or give the message in his own words.

The Wise Men did not come the night Jesus was born as the shepherds did. They saw the star in the East and traveled far to see him. They arrived in Palestine from the East sometime later, perhaps even months later.

There is no account that tells us just how many Wise Men came to worship the Savior. There may have been three; there may have been seven; there may have been ten. But how many came is not so important. What is important is that they were wise men who came to present their gifts and worship this wondrous child. We today should remember that wise men still seek him.

Song: "With Wondering Awe" (*Hymns*, no. 209) would be a good song to have a small group in your family sing as a duet or trio. If you prefer, have the entire group sing it. The first two verses are the most important for the program.

Scripture: Have someone read Matthew 2:1–11.

Song: Sing the first two verses of "Joy to the World" (*Hymns*, no. 89).

Testimony: This would be a good time for the parents to bear their testimonies of Jesus Christ. They may want to encourage their family to make this Christmas a time of tenderness, peace, and appreciation by showing love for each family member, not by the gifts they give, but by the way they treat and feel toward each other.

Song: Close by singing all the verses of "Silent Night" (*Hymns*, no. 160).

Prayer: Have a family member give the closing prayer.

After the Program

You may want to have some special refreshments after the program, perhaps some treat that is traditional in your family at Christmastime. The family may also want to sing some more carols together. For this special night, it would be best to sing hymns about the birth of the Savior and to avoid songs about Santa Claus, Christmas trees, and other traditions not related directly to this event. These songs may be sung at another time.

SUGGESTIONS FOR FUTURE HOME EVENINGS

The Other Sheep

The signs of the Savior's birth were given to the people in America as well as to those in Palestine. You may wish to present a family program similar to "Come Let Us Adore Him" but using the scriptures and story given in the Book of Mormon.

Begin with the vision of Nephi (1 Nephi 11:12–21) and the words of Samuel the Lamanite (Helaman 14:2–13). Then continue with 3 Nephi 1:1, 4–21. You may wish to end with Christ's first appearance to the Nephites after his resurrection (3 Nephi 11:1–11).

What Kind of Gifts Shall I Give Him?

Devote one evening to discussing the gifts we can give to Jesus. You may want to begin by having someone read the account of the visit of the Wise Men (Matthew 2:1–12). Or the family members may enjoy acting out the story.

Use the story as a key for discussing your family's own gifts to the Savior. Have each family member plan a gift he will give the Savior over the Christmas season. The family can write out their gifts, place the slips in a box, and decorate the box. The box can be opened on Christmas, and family members can tell what they have given or are going to give to the Lord.

We Celebrate the Lord's Birth in Song

Plan an evening of carols with family members singing together or as groups or soloists. Choose carols that deal with the birth of Christ. Some family members may enjoy telling about the origins of the carols they sing or about why the carol they have chosen is special to them.

Younger children can dress up in costumes representing shepherds, Wise Men, or angels, as they sing their carols. Be sure to portray the angels without wings.

You may wish to go caroling on another evening after this family home evening.

Christmas—A Family Affair

If you have no particular family Christmas traditions, you may want to spend an evening talking about and choosing some Christmas activity that can become a tradition in your family. Plan it so that all family members can participate. Choose an activity that you can repeat year after year. You may want to appoint or elect one family member to remember the tradition and remind everyone the next year.

Serving Others at Christmas

Plan and carry out a Christmas service project in which you carry the spirit of Christmas and the love of Christ to someone who is ill, lonely, unfortunate, friendless, or afflicted.

For example, you may wish to have a "Twelve Days of Christmas" remembrance in which you present some small gift or service to a person on each of the twelve days. Or you may wish to adopt a family for Christmas to share with you in the joyous season. You might consider giving a gift of the gospel—an *Ensign* or international magazine subscription, a copy of the scriptures, or a recent book by a General Authority.

You may wish to coordinate your family project with the bishop or branch president to avoid duplication.

'Tis the Season to Remember

The December issue of the *Ensign*, *Friend*, *New Era*, or your international magazine will contain inspirational stories and messages about Christmas. Build a family home evening around reading Christmas stories and articles from your Church magazine.

Suggestions

*for improving your
home evenings*

Contents

MAKING HOME EVENINGS SUCCESSFUL

Participation—an Important Part

One key to a successful family home evening is participation by all family members. This doesn't mean just assigning various responsibilities, such as prayers, singing, or reading, to different members. It means freely sharing thoughts, ideas, and feelings that pertain to the lesson. The only way you can tell if family members understand what you present is to allow them to respond. Family home evening lessons were never intended to be given as lectures; they were designed to promote discussion and participation by everyone. If family members feel free to express themselves, you will be more aware of their feelings and concerns. This information will help you plan your home evening lessons to fill the needs of your family.

Having an open discussion does not mean that everyone talks at once. In fact, proceeding in an orderly way, allowing each person his turn to talk while others listen, can in itself be a good lesson in communication for your family. Each should have the opportunity to talk, but he must also listen while others are speaking. If a child realizes that what he says is valued, he will be more attentive and involved in the lesson.

One way to stimulate participation is to ask questions. The kind of questions you ask will determine the kind of responses you will get. Often questions are asked to get a specific answer, such as *yes, no,* or a date, name, or some other fact. Although these questions may help to get family members to participate, some may hesitate to respond because either they are afraid of giving the wrong answer or they feel the answer is too obvious for a response. Questions that help people express themselves are those that ask, "What do you think about this?" or "How do you feel about this?" or "Do you remember an experience like this?" There are no wrong answers to questions like these.

It is very important to listen carefully to the answers and to let your family know that you appreciate whatever contribution they make to the discussion. Children should feel comfortable about expressing themselves to the family.

Another good way to invite comments is to use your own family's experiences to illustrate ideas in the lesson. Children enjoy remembering and talking about their past experiences. Many good lessons can be learned and important feelings of love and belonging can be reinforced this way. Be careful, however, to avoid using examples that might embarrass or draw negative attention to anyone.

Family home evening lessons should involve the whole family.

It is more important for your children to enjoy participating in the discussion than it is for you to finish the lesson, or cover every point you planned to make. If you can conclude the lesson with one good thought, idea, or gospel principle that each family member can remember, think about, and apply in his life, you have succeeded.

Using a Planning Wheel for Assignments

Many home evening discussions must be prepared well before they are given. There is no substitute for good preparation, and home evenings are more effective and enjoyable if all family members participate in their preparation.

Making a planning wheel similar to the one in the illustration can be an enjoyable family project and can help you make assignments. This sample planning wheel is for a family of two adults and six children. However, make your wheel to fit your own family.

Begin by using a piece of heavy paper or poster board to make the background chart. Out of heavy paper, make a wheel that you will attach to the chart. On the chart, outside the borders for the wheel, write all the assignments you normally have as part of your home evening (see the illustration). On the wheel write the name of each family member, as illustrated. Attach the wheel to the chart by pushing a round-headed prong fastener through the center (see illustration). This will allow the wheel to turn freely. Children too young to accept responsibility on their own should be paired with a parent or an older child.

Rotate the assignments each week. For example, if Mother and Kirk have the assignment to plan an activity this week, then next week they will take care of the musical numbers for the home evening.

Making a planning wheel would be a good family project to start off the new year of family home evenings.

1

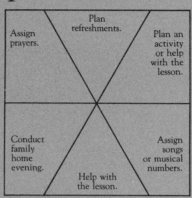

2

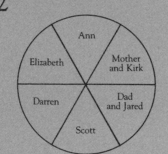

3

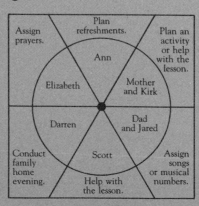

Meeting Adult Needs

Each of us has several basic needs, regardless of our age. For instance, everybody needs to love and be loved. And all of us, children and adults, become frustrated when our basic needs are not met.

The need to overcome inner weaknesses and to grow spiritually is just as basic as our need for love or for food and shelter. However, we may not realize this. President Harold B. Lee said:

"Conversion must mean more than just being a 'card carrying' member of the church with a tithing receipt, a membership card, a temple recommend, etc. It means to overcome the tendencies to criticize, and to strive continually to improve inward weaknesses and not merely the outward appearances." (Harold B. Lee, *Church News*, 25 May 1974, p. 2).

Home evening can help us meet this need to grow spiritually and overcome inner weaknesses. A family, a couple, a group, or someone by himself can plan home evenings to meet the need for greater spirituality.

Overcoming faults and weaknesses is one of the important objectives of the home evening program. *Knowing* is only part of the goal. It means little without *doing*. Just saying to ourselves, "I am going to overcome my inner weaknesses" does little to help us change. We first need to decide what our faults and weaknesses are, and then we need to work on them prayerfully one at a time. The home evening manual can be of great service as a guide for gradually overcoming our problems, one by one, year by year.

Since no two families, groups, or individuals have all the same needs or problems, the home evening manual cannot be used line by line and paragraph by paragraph in all situations. It can, however, be an inspirational guide to anyone trying to follow President Lee's counsel to improve.

Adults living alone, whether single or widowed, often find their needs for companionship and social relations unmet. For such people, meeting for a weekly home evening with a small group can help solve feelings of loneliness. Any adult who feels lonely, discouraged, or that life is passing him by may find a better outlook on life by participating in such a home evening group.

"With the approval of priesthood leaders, home evening groups may be organized for single adult members who have no children in the home and who do not live with their parents.

"Ward home evening groups may be organized under the direction of the bishopric, with one single adult appointed as the leader. When sufficient numbers are not available in a ward, home evening groups that cross ward boundaries may be organized under the direction of the stake presidency.

"Material for the home evening lessons should be taken from the Family Home Evening manual,

the scriptures, or other approved Church sources." (*Guidelines for Single Adult Activities*, p.3.)

Whatever the group decides, their purpose should be to meet the needs of that group, to help members solve their problems.

For example, consider the increased benefits to a group that studies the scriptures to meet individual needs rather than studying them with no specific purpose in mind.

Involving Your Teenagers

Because teenagers often want freedom from parental and adult authority, they present a special challenge in holding successful home evenings. To involve a teenager more meaningfully in home evenings you need to understand his needs. The teen years are an important part of the training ground for responsible adulthood, and good family relationships will add strength to your teenagers chances for success in their adult years. Home evenings that involve teenagers can be fun but challenging to parents. The ideas that follow may help you understand how to have better home evenings, with your teenager participating in rather than complaining about them.

1. Provide your teenagers with meaningful opportunities to share in planning home evenings. (This means that his suggestions be given as much careful consideration as any family member's suggestions. It also means that as a parent you may need to be more receptive to trying new ideas for home evenings.)

2. Select projects and activities the whole family can take part in. (All children need to learn to serve others, and teenagers can be particularly receptive to the joy of helping others. Teenagers, especially, need worthwhile and *active* participation in any project or activity. You may need to give them more responsibility than in the past.)

3. Let your teenager lead home

evening discussion as he wishes; don't expect or try to force him to do it your way.

4. Provide opportunities for your teenagers to ask questions and challenge ideas. (Accept his questions as seriously as you would an adult's. And invite him to join you in finding any answers you may need to seek.)

5. Don't be defensive about questions and comments; he may be seeking security in your strength, not challenging you.

6. Encourage discussion of problems important to your teenager. (Ask his help in choosing discussion topics, particularly as you plan them.)

7. Although teenagers may challenge adult authority, they like and expect parents to be strong in their convictions, especially in matters of morality.

8. A teenager's rejection of authority is usually only temporary. Don't force him to participate in home evening but be sure he attends.

9. Base communication on mutual respect.

10. Teenagers respond to genuine emotional warmth and understanding.

11. Be well prepared and let your teenagers' interest help determine the length of discussions.

12. Keep your teenager involved in home evenings by consistently holding them.

Family Home Evening with Younger Children

Each day you are teaching your children through your example; family home evenings are to help you teach in a more structured way. You should not wait until your children are school age to hold them. Successful family home evenings can help younger children learn gospel principles and learn to enjoy being together. In fact, young children soon reach a point when they will not let you forget to hold home evening.

Most lessons in this manual have an adaptation for younger children that will help you in preparing your family home evenings. Some additional helps for families with younger children follow.

If you follow a routine each week, your children will know what to expect. Let them help prepare. Involve them in every aspect of family home evening. You may, of course, need to help your younger children with most things, but the effort will be worth it. Give each a chance to say the prayers, lead the singing, choose the songs, and give parts of the lessons. They will learn more, for instance, if they tell the story meant to illustrate the lesson. Let them choose a game to play, pick refreshments, or help in their preparation. When the time comes to enjoy refreshments, children love to help serve them. Make sure that each child

has a responsibility each week. Because the attention span of young children is not very long, your entire family home evening may need to be relatively short; however, children can learn a lot in a short time. If you have both teenagers and very young children, consider the increased needs of the teenagers when deciding how long home evening should be. Keeping separate activities varied and short will help you keep the attention of the younger children.

When you or an older child tell a story, use visual aids, if possible, such as pictures or flannel board figures that the younger children can display. Explain the meaning of stories and let the younger children retell the story or play with the flannel board figures. You may want to leave the pictures out during the week where children can play with them. This will reinforce the learning.

After a short lesson, you could play a game with your children. Involve everyone and don't worry if the game lasts longer than your lesson. Enlist the aid of older children to either lead the games or to help the younger children.

Young children are very receptive to new ideas and thoughts, and if you teach them correct principles at this age, those teachings will more likely become part of their lives. Make your family home evenings fun for all, and it will become a time of family growth.

Reading Scriptures with Children

Because the scriptures are sometimes difficult to understand, we often avoid reading them with children, particularly younger children. But children need and can be helped to understand and love the word of God. Many Bible stories are exciting and have all the elements of stories that children love. However, you cannot just sit down and read long passages to young children and expect them to understand. They can benefit from reading the actual words, and this should be included when you teach your children about the scriptures, but you also need to adapt the scriptures to the level of your children's understanding.

All of us benefit from a study of the scriptures, not just a reading of them. Questions and discussion will help both younger and older children to gain a better understanding of scriptures.

The following are some different ways to help your children understand the scriptures:

1. **Tell scripture stories to your children in simple terms.** Use the names of people and places in the story. These may be written on small cards, posters, or prepared for a flannel board. Have your children repeat the names to help them remember them, and let them place the names on the flannel board. You should explain the meaning of the story to the children. For example: Noah tried to teach the people about Heavenly Father and about how they should live, but they did not listen to him. They were very bad and did not do what Heavenly Father wanted them to do, so he sent a flood, and all the people that were bad, the wicked people, died. After telling the story, read the actual scripture story to your children. You may need to stop and explain some of the words to help your children remember the easier version you have just told them. If necessary, skip some verses that do not add to the meaning of the story and read only the parts that tell the story. Your children will enjoy hearing verses read to them, and it is good for them to become familiar with the language used in the scriptures.

2. **Let children have their own scriptures.** Get each child an inexpensive set of scriptures, even though they are too young to read. They will love to have their own books, and you can help them mark some of the stories you read. As they learn to read, help them ahead of time with scripture assignments so that they can read them during family home evening. Older children and teenagers often enjoy being able to explain terms or give background information for assigned scriptures. Be prepared to help with these assignments, to offer suggestions and sources of information.

3. **As a family, study the new LDS editions of the scriptures to learn what aids to scripture study these contain.** For instance, help children understand what the footnotes mean and how the Topical Guide and Bible Dictionary can help them understand passages. Short assignments and exercises for family home evening can help each family member gain a greater understanding of how he can be helped in his study of the scriptures.

4. **Use the Church's excellent books:** *Book of Mormon Stories, Old Testament Stories, New Testament Stories,* and *Doctrine and Covenants and Church History Stories* (each for beginning readers), as well as *Scripture Stories*. These have cassette tapes that children can listen to while looking at the pictures in the books. These teaching aids can help your children learn the stories from the scriptures. Be sure, however, that your children also hear the actual stories read from the standard works.

5. **Set up a regular time, in addition to family home evening, when you can read and study the scriptures together.** This could perhaps be each Sunday or at bedtime. Make it a time your children will look forward to.

Avoiding Putting Children in Corners

Even the tamest small animal will fight to preserve its life if it is backed into a corner. No family can hope for successful home evenings if the children feel threatened or pushed into a corner. Some parents, in trying to teach their family, sometimes use family home evenings to talk about personal problems of individual family members, thus embarrassing them and forcing them into corners. As a result, instead of confiding in their family and resolving problems, a child may withdraw, become angry, and possibly fear future home evenings. As parents, you should tactfully direct home evenings toward the solution of problems that affect the whole family, but never tear down or criticize individuals.

For example, during one home evening six-year-old Marie told how her brother David had giggled when she tripped and fell on the front step. Both parents immediately became angry with David, telling him that it was wrong to laugh at mistakes, that he should try to understand others and always make them feel better, and so on. Although the ideas were good, without realizing it the parents were committing the same errors they were criticizing in their son. They had backed him into a corner and embarrassed him. Feeling angry and unfairly treated their son refused to participate during the rest of the home evening, and the experience was unpleasant for everyone.

You cannot remake your children's characters in one evening. And a direct attack often produces only resentment and anger. If your children learn to expect a lecture or reprimand whenever they disagree with you, they will soon stop expressing their real feelings. For example, one couple noted that their only child, five-year-old Jess, became unusually quiet every week during home evening, often early in the presentation. Only when they realized that everything they said was directed at him, that he was the target for each probing question, or was used as an example in each story, were they able to change. When they were finally able to make home evenings relaxed, with an open atmosphere, Jess began to enjoy and participate in the evenings.

At the end of a home evening on service and sharing, another family tried to apply what had been discussed. Earlier in the day sixteen-year-old Marilyn had asked her older sister Teresa if she could borrow her formal for a dance the next Friday. Teresa had refused. To bring the lesson to a practical focus, the father directed a question to Teresa:

"Teresa, do you have anything you could share?"

Knowing what her father was trying to get her to say, Teresa said, "No. I don't have anything to share!"

"What about your formal dress that Marilyn wants to borrow?" her father persisted.

"Well, what about it?" Teresa shot back, her annoyance showing in her voice.

"You should let your sister wear it," her mother commented; "you're being very selfish, and that's just what our home evening was about—sharing."

Teresa was then completely cornered. "Now look," she said, "I worked and saved to buy that dress with my own money. I've only worn it once, and I just don't feel like lending it yet."

Thinking only of the evening's lesson and not of his daughter's feelings, the father said, "You haven't learned a thing from home evening. You're staying home from dances until you learn to share."

"All right, all right," Teresa said sarcastically, "she can wear my dress. Should I give her my shoes and everything else too?"

The parents might think they have solved the problem: Teresa has shared her dress, and they do not have to buy a dress for Marilyn. However, Teresa, who was pushed into a position where she had to fight or surrender, has feelings of anger and resentment toward both her parents and her sister. This type of personal conflict should not have been introduced into the family home evening. Such personal problems can be handled more effectively in private, with the parent giving each girl a chance to openly state her feelings.

Home evenings must not become a time to check or report on whether children's bedrooms are clean, toys are picked up, or chores are completed. Neither is it a time to determine whether one has really earned his allowance, or has been good enough to go out on a date the coming weekend. Wise parents will plan each home evening to avoid these personal conflicts. Family problems should be discussed, but not those that single out one family member, embarrassing him and pushing him into a corner. Corners are not comfortable!

Creating Your Own Lessons

No one knows your family better than you do. You live with them every day—work, play, struggle, laugh, grow, and learn with them. You are in the best position to know their needs and abilities, their weaknesses and strengths. You are probably the best teacher your family could have.

Although this manual contains enough lesson ideas to last for many years, not all of them are expanded into complete lessons. Once you learn to put together a simple lesson, you will be able to adapt these ideas to teach your family just what they need. Use the full lessons as models or examples of a good lesson. They contain stories, thought questions, personal experiences, games, and activities—elements of a well-balanced lesson. Remember that there is no one right way to present a lesson. What matters most is your sincere desire to help your family understand and live the truths of the gospel. With that desire, and with prayerful study, you can develop your own lessons. Some suggestions and steps to help you create your own lessons follow.

First, choose a lesson topic. Think about any special needs, events, and interests your family may have right now. If you have just moved to a different city, a lesson on how to make new friends might be in order. If you are helping a child prepare for baptism, you may want to teach a lesson on the gift of the Holy Ghost. If someone in your family is suffering from low self-esteem, you might want to have an

appreciation night for that person. Or, if someone in your ward or neighborhood has a special need, a lesson on serving others might be most helpful.

If you can think of no special need or event, look for ideas in the manual. You may want to use some of the topics listed there, or, you may want to share something you have learned in a Relief Society or priesthood lesson with your family. Perhaps an event in the news or in your community will give you an idea for a lesson.

Be realistic when you choose your topic. You can't hope to completely cover a gospel principle in one home evening. If you try, your lesson will probably be superficial and confusing. By focusing on one specific aspect of a principle, you can teach it more clearly and in some depth. For example, if your lesson is on prayer, focus on one specific idea, such as how praying with and for each other can unify family members.

After you have selected a topic, choose materials to make a full lesson. Consider the following resources: this manual, the scriptures (including illustrated children's versions), the *Gospel Principles* manual, Church magazines and the *Church News*, *Teaching—No Greater Call* (prepared for teachers of Church classes but with many principles adaptable to home evening), current events, and personal experiences. The last one could be the most important. Sharing your own experiences will make your lessons more interesting and relevant to your children and will also help your family draw closer to one another. Your family will learn that the gospel is something to live, not just something to know.

Your chosen topic should be the central part of your lesson. But how do you actually plan a full lesson around it? After you have studied the topic, you may want to make a simple outline of the points you think are most important. You will need to support each of these points with specific details—stories or examples to show what you mean; get them from the scriptures if you can. If you want your family to understand how repentance works, for example, you might tell a story to show repentance in action.

Keep in mind that a good lesson usually has a variety of elements to support the main ideas. For instance, you may wish to use some of the following elements:

1. Start with an attention-getter—a game, story, picture, or activity that will create immediate interest in your topic.

2. Choose one or two key scriptures that are central to the gospel topic you have chosen. (You may wish to write these on a poster that can also be displayed throughout the coming week. Some families memorize these scriptures as part of their weekly assignments.)

3. Use an occasional game, role play, or other activity within the lesson to support the main idea. (This is also one way to involve children of all ages in one activity.)

4. Use visual aids to create interest. A picture or poster can make your ideas more vivid and memorable. (Very young children can also participate by holding the visual aids or by placing them on a flannel board.)

5. Ask questions that will cause thought. Avoid questions that can be answered yes or no. Questions that have more than one right answer, for instance, will cause more response. Help your family share their real feelings through thoughtful questions.

6. Use personal experiences, scripture stories, and actual examples to illustrate your main points.

7. Plan to inspire feelings and not just teach facts about the gospel. Family home evening is a time for sharing feelings, bearing testimony, and determining to do better together. It can help you draw closer together in a special way.

8. Help the family apply the gospel principle in their lives by giving them something to think about or do during the coming week that applies the main idea.

Adapt and plan your lessons to interest each member of your family. If most of your children are teenagers or adults, stimulate them with ideas and activities that excite them. If your children are younger, select materials that will help them understand and appreciate the principle you are teaching. If you have a range of ages in your family group, be sure to include activities, questions, and lesson ideas that suit the level of every family member.

You do not have to know everything about a topic to teach it. Nor do you have to be perfect in a gospel principle to help your family understand it. In fact, pretending to know all about a topic or acting as if we are perfect in living the gospel can actually be discouraging to our families. But if we honestly and humbly try to live the principles of the gospel better ourselves, we can learn with our families. And they, seeing our efforts, will trust our teachings and want to try also.

May the Lord bless you in this great opportunity and responsibility.

IDEAS

Ideas
for home evening lessons,
covering
thirty-seven topics

CONTENTS

ADVERSITY

Know thou, my son, that all these things shall give thee experience, and shall be for thy good.
—Doctrine and Covenants 122:7

GOSPEL TRUTH

Adversity is part of our Heavenly Father's plan for us here upon the earth. We are here to be proven—to see if we will do whatever God commands us to do (see Abraham 3:25). As we struggle to meet trials, we grow and develop qualities that we can attain in no other way. When we seek his help, our Heavenly Father will strengthen us and make us equal to the trials that come to us.

IDEAS FOR LESSONS

Lesson 1: Understanding the Blessings of Adversity

Tell the following story:

Sister Bates loved music; she played the piano and the organ. She also enjoyed reading. But she became blind in both eyes.

• How might have Sister Bates reacted to her tragedy?

Continue the story:

Sister Bates decided she couldn't give up reading, so she learned to read Braille. She kept practicing the piano and learned to play by touch. She also devised a way to teach beginning piano students even though she was blind.

Have your family discuss the growth that she received in enduring and overcoming this trial.

Review our Heavenly Father's plan for us to be tried and tested as part of our mortal experience (see *Gospel Principles* [manual, 1979], p. 11, and 2 Nephi 2:11). Emphasize that as we cope with our trials and adversity we

can develop God-given strengths.

Lesson 2: Growing from Adversity

Discuss the Prophet Joseph Smith's experience in Liberty Jail as found in Doctrine and Covenants 121 and 122.

• What are some of the blessings that came to the Prophet and which, as a consequence of the Doctrine and Covenants record, have come to all of us as a result of this experience? (He studied and increased in knowledge and understanding while there. He continued to receive revelations and, through his writings, direct the Church. He grew in compassion.)

Read his statement, "I think I could never have felt as I do now if I had not suffered the wrongs I have suffered. It has awakened my soul to the love of God" (*History of the Church*, 3:290).

Read Doctrine and Covenants 121:7.

• What can we learn from the fact that the Prophet Joseph Smith received the blessing of peace in the midst of his afflictions in Liberty Jail? (We can pray for and receive peace of mind in any adversity that may come to us.)

Choose from among the following activities those you would like to do with your family:

1. List everyday problems on word-strips and place them in a bowl. Have each person draw one and identify blessings that could come from such adversity. (Sickness, for example, can increase our compassion for the sick and our appreciation for the blessing of good health.)

2. Tell of a trial (either from your own life or from one of your ancestors) that has strengthened and blessed you.

3. Ask each one to say how some difficult experience he has had has been helpful to him—what he has learned from it, or how he has been blessed from it.

4. Encourage family members to recognize trials as challenges. Remind them to seek the Lord's help in overcoming them.

Lesson 3: Learning to Cope with Adversity

Help your family recognize that we can take positive steps to climb out of adverse situations. Review the Prophet Joseph Smith's experience (Doctrine and Covenants 121 and 122) to discover step by step what he did to overcome his discouragement.

Draw steps and label each with the action we can take to lift ourselves. Your completed chart should look something like this:

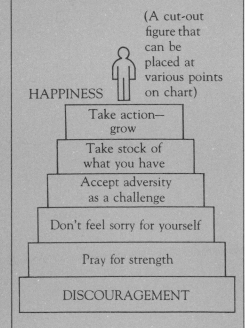

(A cut-out figure that can be placed at various points on chart)

HAPPINESS

| Take action—grow |
| Take stock of what you have |
| Accept adversity as a challenge |
| Don't feel sorry for yourself |
| Pray for strength |
| DISCOURAGEMENT |

Using your own problems or those of family members, discuss step by step how you could "climb out" of your discouragement. Emphasize that seeking the Lord's help is the first step.

Encourage members to think of ways to act to diminish ongoing problems (the fifth step). List their suggestions and have them consider how doing the following could help:

1. Serving others
2. Working
3. Recognizing past victories

Lesson 4: Likening Our Lives to Kites in the Wind

Compare life to a kite. The following parallels may help in your discussion:

Kite
   Each one of us is like a kite.

Wind
   Trials, like the wind, push against us each day. The resistance they provide, like the wind, keeps us, like the kite, up and going.

String
   We have the gospel which, like the string of a kite, directs, controls, and anchors our lives.

Have each family member do the following:

1. Cut a small kite out of paper and attach a tail made of string, twine, or yarn.
2. Write on small pieces of paper some of the major trials you have undergone in life. Generally these would be situations that have required endurance, patience, and persistence—such as serious illness, a death, a handicap, a failure, a new job, a challenging Church assignment. Small children could draw things they have learned to do, like buttoning clothes and tying shoes.
3. Glue these papers on the kite's tail.

Invite each person to look at the victories represented on the tail of the kite and recognize that he has already overcome a good deal of adversity.

Explain that we can gain courage and strength to meet future adversity if we recognize our past trials as a refining process that we have grown from (see Job 23:10). We should also remember that even though we have many problems, the Lord has blessed each one of us abundantly.

Lesson 5: Avoiding Bitterness from Adversity

Relate the following story and ask family members to contrast the attitudes and the results:

"When my great-great grandparents joined the Church in Sweden, they were faced with a long ocean voyage to America, a train trip from New York to Omaha, and then a trek by wagon to Salt Lake City. But when they boarded the train in New York, they discovered that they were to ride in stock cars that had been used to haul hogs to market—and the cars were filthy and filled with hog lice.

"Grandmother accepted the inconvenience, but the humiliation was almost more than grandfather could bear. 'To think we are no better than hogs,' he grumbled. Reluctantly he made the trip anyway.

"Grandmother was expecting another child. . . .

"Somewhere on the plains of Nebraska, a healthy baby was born. But a few days later, the three-year-old son contracted cholera. . . . The boy died that night.

"The next morning the wagon master said they would hold a short funeral service and bury the boy in a shallow grave, apologetically explaining that they were in Indian country and didn't have time to do anything more. But grandfather couldn't accept this, and insisted on staying behind and digging a grave deep enough so the animals wouldn't get the body.

"Throughout the day and into the night he worked, building a strong wooden coffin and digging a grave five feet deep in the hard soil. Finally, exhausted and sobbing, he buried his son and then walked all night to catch up with the wagon train. He was heartbroken and mad—mad at the wagon master for not waiting to give his son a proper burial, and mad at God for 'allowing' his son to die. . . .

"This wasn't the end of their difficulties; they continued to suffer serious hardships and adversities throughout their lives. But although they both went through identical experiences, each was affected differently by them. Grandfather became withdrawn, cantankerous, and bitter. He stopped going to Church and found fault with Church leaders. He became caught up in his own miseries, and the light of Christ grew dimmer and dimmer in his life.

"On the other hand, grandmother's faith increased. Each new problem seemed to make her stronger. She became an angel of mercy—filled with empathy, compassion, and charity. She was a light to those around her. Her family gravitated toward her and looked to her as their leader." (Steve Dunn Hanson, "What to Do with Adversity," *Ensign*, Feb. 1981, pp. 54–55.)

Explain that those who yield to adversity become weaker. To the valiant it is a stepping-stone to increased power (see 1 Corinthians 10:13). One way to overcome adversity is to make our problems into stepping-stones by finding out some good that can come from them.

Make some lemonade without sugar. Have each family member taste the drink. Add the sugar and have your family taste the difference. Explain that the bitter lemon juice is still present but by adding sugar you have made something that tastes good.

Suggest that each of us can do the same thing with the problems we face.

AUTHORITY

We can complain bitterly, "Why me?" or we can use the principles of the gospel to sweeten our lives.

During the coming week, help family members remember this principle by reminding complainers to make lemonade out of their problems. You may want to post a sign such as "When life hands you a lemon—make lemonade."

RESOURCES

Scriptures

Job (The story of one who withstood adversity with faith.)

John 9:2–3 (Trials do not always come because of sin.)

2 Nephi 2:11 (Opposition in all things.)

2 Nephi 2:27 (In spite of all trials we are free to choose liberty and eternal life.)

Ether 12:6 (Receive no witness until after the trial of faith.)

Doctrine and Covenants 50:5 (Blessed are they that endure.)

Doctrine and Covenants 122:5–7 (All these things shall give thee experience.)

Doctrine and Covenants 136:31 (Must be tried in all things.)

See also "Adversity" in the Topical Guide, Latter-day Saint edition of the King James Version of the Bible.

Songs and Hymns

"Let Us All Press On," Hymns, no. 98.

"When upon Life's Billows," Hymns, no. 202.

"Though Deepening Trials," Hymns, no. 285.

Other

John Baker's Last Race, Dream Big, and The Emmett Smith Story, available through your meetinghouse library in either 16mm film or videocassette versions.

We believe that every man should be honored in his station.
—Doctrine and Covenants 134:6

GOSPEL TRUTH

God gives man authority for his guidance and protection. Without it there would be no order or freedom. God has commanded us to respect the authority of home, church, and community.

IDEAS FOR LESSONS

Lesson 1: How Those in Authority Help Us

You may wish to tell the following story:

As one family was traveling late at night, they were followed by a car that repeatedly tried to run them off the road. The father succeeded in reaching the next town where he pulled into a service station, called the police, and explained what was happening.

The police suggested that the family start out again. They said they would have officers follow and arrest the offenders if they repeated their attempts. The family dreaded to start out into the lonely desert with someone following with intent to harm them, but they trusted the police to protect them. A few miles out of town the same car attempted to run them off the road, but this time a police car appeared out of the darkness with its flashing lights and sirens.

The officers arrested the men in the car, who had been running many tourists off the road and robbing them. The family gratefully and peacefully went on their way.

After telling the story, divide a large sheet of paper into three columns (see chart below). In the first column list people who have some kind of authority (such as parents, bishops, principals, and mayors). Ask your family where each of those listed gets his authority, and write the answers opposite the appropriate name in column two (parents are authorized by God, bishops are called of God by those having authority, principals are hired by school boards, mayors are elected by the people).

• According to the Lord, how should we treat those in authority?

For answers to column three, (1) Parents: read Exodus 20:12 and place the word "honor" opposite parents, (2) Church leaders: read the following by President Joseph F. Smith: "If you will honor the Holy Priesthood *in yourself first, you will honor it in those who preside over you*" (Gospel Doctrine, 5th ed. [Salt Lake City: Deseret Book Co., 1939], p. 165), (3) Other leaders: read Doctrine and Covenants 134:6.

Explain to your family that to honor means to obey, esteem, support, and sustain. Discuss some specific ways that we can honor each of the groups of leaders listed on this chart.

Ask family members to list things that each of the groups of people in au-

Person in authority	Source of authority	Lord's instructions
Parents	God	Honor
Bishops or church leaders	God	Honor
Principal or school leaders	School board	Honor
Mayor or community leaders	The people	Honor

175

thority on the chart do to help us. Encourage them to tell experiences of times when those in authority helped them.

Lesson 2: How We Can Respect Authority

Have the family describe what a day would be like without the leaders listed on the chart presented above in lesson 1. Consider the chaos of one day in your home without parental guidance, one Sunday without ward leaders, one day at school without teachers or a principal, and one day in your community without police or firemen. Contrast it with the peace and order that results when authority is present and is respected.

Conclude that Heavenly Father has given us leaders with authority to protect, guide, teach, and bless our lives.

Lesson 3: Learning More about Those in Authority in Your Community

Prepare your family to attend a meeting of your city council, a session of a court, or a session of some other governmental body. Before the visit ask your family to notice how those in authority interact with the other participants. Afterward discuss how those involved in the council meeting or trial seemed to feel about authority—how they did or did not respect it.

Lesson 4: Resisting Pressures to Disrespect Those in Authority

Invite a community, school, or church leader to your home to explain his responsibilities and duties. Have him tell how he can be more effective when people respect his authority.

Role-play some situations that members of your family may encounter when they are being pressured to disobey teachers, priesthood leaders, and others in authority. Help them plan ahead to have the courage to respect the authority of their leaders.

Lesson 5: Respecting Leaders, Even When They Are Not Perfect

Relate the following story by Elder Boyd K. Packer and ask family members what it teaches about authority.

"On one occasion he [Karl G. Maeser] was going with a group of young missionaries across the alps. They were crossing a high mountain pass on foot. There were long sticks stuck into the snow of the glacier to mark the path so that travelers could find their way safely across the glacier and down the mountain on the other side.

"When they reached the summit, Brother Maeser wanted to teach the young elders a lesson. He stopped at the pinnacle of the mountain and pointed to those sticks that they had followed. And he said, 'Brethren, behold the priesthood of God. They are just common old sticks, but it's the position that counts. Follow them and you will surely be safe. Stray from them and you will surely be lost.' And so it is in the Church. We are called to leadership positions and given the power of the priesthood. And we are just common old sticks, but the position we are given counts. It is separate and apart from us, but while we hold it, we hold it." ("It Is the Position That Counts," *New Era*, June 1977, p. 51.)

Discuss with your family whether we are obligated to respect the authority of someone we do not like as a person. As you discuss this question, help your family recognize that our leaders, who are not perfect, will be more successful when we respect and support them. Talking against them and failing to sustain them only makes them less effective.

Tell the following story:

Brother Taylor was a shy man. He had a strong testimony of the gospel, but he was not very confident about discussing it with others. He had never finished high school and felt embarrassed that his knowledge of the

scriptures was lacking. He was assigned as home teacher to several families. He visited them faithfully every month and made extra visits at birthdays, in times of illness, and whenever he felt he could be of help.

Then Brother Taylor was assigned to visit a new family in the ward. After his first visit, the family discussed their new home teacher.

"What a strange man," remarked Sister Brown.

"Yes," laughed the oldest son. "I thought I'd die when he kept mispronouncing words in that scripture he read."

"I can even read better than that," added nine-year-old Susan.

"I doubt we can expect much help from him," concluded Brother Brown.

Ask the following questions:

• How will this family's attitude weaken Brother Taylor as a home teacher?

• What are some ways they could sustain him that would also strengthen him?

Discuss possible ways of handling the following situations:

1. Your parents have asked you not to do something that you want to do very much. They think it is unsafe, but many of your friends have done it.

2. You do not enjoy your present priesthood adviser. He is never well prepared and is not an interesting teacher.

3. Your new bishop isn't easy to talk to. You wish he were more like your former bishop who was friendly to everyone.

CHASTITY

Have someone read the following quotation and discuss why we need to learn respect for authority at home:

"Disregard of law and authority under the parental roof, leads inevitably to utter disregard and contempt for all law, authority, and restraint" (*Millennial Star*, 5 Apr. 1868, p. 258).

For help with respecting parental authority, see lesson 19, "The Priesthood in Our Home," and lesson 20, "A House of Order," in the "Lessons" section of this manual.

RESOURCES

Scriptures

Matthew 5:44 (Love your enemies and pray for them.)
Doctrine and Covenants 134 (A declaration of belief regarding governments and laws.)
See also "Authority" in the Topical Guide.

Songs and Hymns

"Kindness Begins with Me," *Sing with Me*, B–49.
"Jesus Said Love Everyone," *Sing with Me*, B–51.
"Nay, Speak No Ill," *Hymns*, no. 116.

Other

The Trophy Case, available through your meetinghouse library in either a 16mm film or videocassette version.

Thou shalt not commit adultery.
—Exodus 20:14

GOSPEL TRUTH

God has given his children on earth the power to provide physical bodies for his spirit children. When we use this sacred power only within the bonds of marriage and when we think and speak of it with reverence, we are keeping the law of chastity.

IDEAS FOR LESSONS

Note to parents: Some parts of this lesson may be more effective if discussed privately with individual family members.

Lesson 1: The Power of Procreation

- What is the power of procreation? (We, along with our Heavenly Father, create bodies for his children. We can have children. See Genesis 1:28.)

Discuss how having children helps prepare us for godhood. Talk about learning the value of sacrifice, becoming unselfish, giving unconditional love, learning self-control, being organized, teaching, and disciplining others. These are all skills we need to become like our Father in Heaven.

- How does parenthood give us an opportunity to learn these skills?

Explain that parenthood is not only a learning time for parents but it is an act of service to Heavenly Father's other children. Parenthood allows us to provide bodies for our spirit brothers and sisters, love them, and pass on to them the things that we have already learned from our experiences on earth.

Let your children talk about what kind of parent each wants to be and some of the things each hopes to teach his children.

Share your feelings about parenthood. Talk about things you have learned, how you've grown in appreciation,

and the joys and sorrows you have felt. Express your thankfulness for the wonderful blessing of procreation. Explain that no other experience helps us to understand our Heavenly Father as well as the sacred opportunity of becoming parents ourselves. Challenge your children to think about and prepare for this wonderful blessing.

Lesson 2: The Law of Chastity

Relate the story of Corianton, one of Alma's sons, in Alma 39:3–4. Discuss how he sinned by forsaking his ministry and going after Isabel. Point out that he broke God's law of chastity.

Read together what Alma said to Corianton in Alma 39:5.

- Why are fornication and adultery such serious sins?

Make a list of some of the destructive effects of these sins, such as the following:

1. They make our procreative power a thing of cheap and selfish pleasure, instead of an unselfish act of lasting joy.
2. They destroy our character.
3. They destroy the character of the partner in sin.
4. They bring babies into far from ideal circumstances.
5. Fornication can force early and unplanned marriages; adultery can break up marriages and families in divorce.
6. They encourage abortion, itself a grave sin.
7. They drive the Spirit of the Lord away from us.
8. They destroy Heavenly Father's plan for families.
9. They destroy self-respect.

Discuss how every baby has a right to be born into a family where he is wanted and loved. This is possible only when the law of chastity is obeyed.

Remind your children that our power to become parents is one of the most sacred and special blessings given to us by our Heavenly Father. It can bring us the greatest of joys if we use it in the right way or the greatest of sorrows if we misuse it.

Read and discuss the following quotation: "Much of the happiness that may come to you in this life will depend on how you use this sacred power of creation" (Boyd K. Packer, *Teach Ye Diligently* [Salt Lake City: Deseret Book Co., 1975], p. 259). Challenge family members to think of their future children whenever they are faced with a moral decision.

Lesson 3: Blessings of Obedience
Have your children write down the characteristics of the man or woman they would ideally like to marry. Be sure to have them emphasize moral qualities, not just physical.

• If you met this wonderful person, what kind of partner do you think he or she would be looking for?

Have them list these qualities too. Explain that we must become worthy of the one that we hope to marry. We must stay morally clean and develop these qualities. Talk about the dangers of trying to impress our peers at the expense of losing our ability to impress that certain someone someday. Discuss how we need to begin very early in our lives to build the habits and form the character that will give us the blessing of someday creating our own ideal home.

Assure your children that there are others in the world that are holding to their standards and standing up for the right, and that if your children stay worthy Heavenly Father will bless them that they will be able to marry someone just as wonderful as they imagine.

Discuss the great blessings of starting a family with the right person (someone with these important qualities) at the right time (when we are sufficiently mature) and in the right place (in the temple). Remind family members that much of their future happiness will rest on these decisions. Challenge them to live worthy of these ideals.

Lesson 4: Keeping the Law of Chastity
Read Doctrine and Covenants 121:45–46. Discuss what virtue (being morally clean) means and the blessings that come from it.

• Is a person morally clean who thinks and talks lustfully but doesn't *do* what he talks about? Read together 3 Nephi 12:27–29.

• Is a person morally clean who consciously arouses unclean thoughts or desires in another?

List together some of the things Satan tempts us to do that encourage us to begin to break the law of chastity. Some of them might be:

1. Dressing immodestly.
2. Watching unclean movies or television shows.
3. Telling or listening to dirty jokes.
4. Staying out late on dates.
5. Dating too young.
6. Listening to bad music.

Make the list as extensive as you can. Then discuss each item on your list.

• What thoughts will these put in our minds or in the minds of others?

• How is this a beginning to breaking the law of chastity? (See Proverbs 23:7.)

• What steps can you take to resist this temptation?

Play a game of "What would you do if . . . ?" making up realistic situations that your children, at their ages, might face. See if your children can think of graceful ways out of bad situations. Sometimes there will be no graceful way out.

Next tell the story of Joseph and the wife of Potiphar (Genesis 39:1–13). Explain that it is much better to look foolish or displease someone else (no matter who it is) and run away than to compromise on the law of chastity and lose out on the glorious blessings that come from staying truly clean.

Challenge family members to be careful in all that they do to stay clean in thought as well as action.

RESOURCES

Scriptures
Genesis 39:1–18 (Joseph fleeing from Potiphar's wife.)
Psalm 24:4 (Have clean hands and a pure heart.)
1 Corinthians 6:19 (Our bodies are temples.)
James 1:27 (Unspotted from the world.)
Alma 38:12 (Control our passions so we may be filled with love.)
Doctrine and Covenants 121:45 (Let virtue garnish our thoughts unceasingly.)
Doctrine and Covenants 88:86 (Avoid sin.)
See also "Chastity, Chaste" in the Topical Guide.

Songs and Hymns
"I Am a Child of God," *Sing with Me*, B–76.
"The Still Small Voice," *Sing with Me*, B–92.
"Firm as the Mountains around Us," *Hymns*, no. 42.
"Choose the Right," *Hymns*, no. 110.
"Shall the Youth of Zion Falter?" *Hymns*, no. 157.

Other
Gospel Principles, "The Law of Chastity," chapter 39.

Morality for Youth, available through your meetinghouse library in either a 16mm film, filmstrip, or videocassette version, and *The Very Key*, available in a filmstrip version only.

CITIZENSHIP

We believe in being subject to kings, presidents, rulers, and magistrates, in obeying, honoring, and sustaining the law.
—Twelfth Article of Faith

GOSPEL TRUTH

Being a good citizen means more than just obeying the laws of the land. It also means being actively involved in making our community the best possible place for all to live. As we become good citizens of our community, we are doing the will of our Heavenly Father in that regard.

IDEAS FOR LESSONS

Lesson 1: Are Laws Necessary?

Discuss with your family what it would be like to live in a country where citizens do not obey the laws of the land.

Use the following questions and include your own to help in the discussion:

- What would happen if no one obeyed the traffic laws?
- Would the people be safe on the streets at night or in the parks? Why?
- What would happen without laws to protect people's possessions and property?
- How would you feel about living in such a country?

Explain to your family that without law-abiding citizens, your country would not be a safe place to live and only the strongest would survive.

Contrast this imaginary country without obedient citizens with a real city where everyone cared for each other and all obeyed the law. Let a family member read Moses 7:18–21, or tell the story of the city of Enoch in your own words.

- How would you feel about living in this city? Why? Is there anything you as a family can do to make your city or country a better place to live? Read the twelfth article of faith and discuss why you think our Heavenly Father wants us to be good citizens.

Lesson 2: What Is a Good Citizen?

Review some of the laws that affect you and your family such as traffic laws, school laws, city laws, tax laws.

- What is the role of a good citizen in relationship to these laws?

Have your family read aloud Doctrine and Covenants 58:21, and discuss it. Explain that being a good citizen is more than just obeying the law. It means taking an active part in the community and working to make it the best possible place for all to live. (See Mosiah 2:17.)

- What are some of the ways we can do this? (Finding and voting for good leaders, supporting improvements in laws, volunteering to help on local civic boards and committees, serving in civic groups, helping to improve the community in different ways. See D&C 98:8–10.)

Have family members find examples of good citizens in the newspaper or magazines or think of someone in your city, at work, or in school who would qualify as a good citizen. Have them explain why the person they chose is a good citizen.

Plan a trip to a meeting of a local school board, city council, or planning commission. Learn in advance who the members of the governing body are. Get a copy of the meeting agenda. Discuss the procedures the body will follow in conducting the meeting and how they hear from citizens like you. Discuss why some of the business items on the agenda have been placed there.

Think of a family project to help your own community in an active way (such as a neighborhood clean-up campaign). You could have a contest to see who could pick up the most cans, paper, etc. You may want to coordinate this activity with local offi-cials. (They may suggest a particular place or job area where your family could be of the most service.)

Lesson 3: Loving Our Country

Present a story or skit about the early days of your country or learn together about some of your country's early leaders. Tell what motivated them to do what they did.

Read Alma 46 and discuss Moroni and his title of liberty. Show your country's flag or a picture of it. Have someone tell what the design on the flag means.

You might plan to let your family see the swearing in of a new citizen. If possible, have one of these new citizens talk to your family and tell what it means to become a citizen.

Plan a trip to a site important in the history of your country, state or province, or city (such as a battlefield, a fort or outpost, early homesite or settlement, home of distinguished person, or government building). Discuss what took place there. Try to learn something about the men and women who contributed to the event that gave historical significance to the site. What kind of people were they? Discuss the sacrifices that are necessary to make possible the comforts we enjoy today.

Learn the words of and sing your national anthem for a closing song.

RESOURCES

Scriptures

Matthew 7:12 (The Golden Rule.)
Doctrine and Covenants 58:22 (Be subject to the powers that be.)
Doctrine and Covenants 134 (Statement of belief on governments and laws.)
See "Citizenship" in the Topical Guide.

Songs and Hymns

Patriotic songs of your land.

CONTENTION

He that hath the spirit of contention is not of me, but is of the devil, who is the father of contention.
—3 Nephi 11:29

GOSPEL TRUTH

Contention brings unhappiness into our homes and into our lives. Satan is the father of contention and all the misery that it brings. Our Father in Heaven wants us to fill our lives with love and eliminate contention.

IDEAS FOR LESSONS

Lesson 1: Why We Need to Eliminate Contention

Read the following true statement by a seventeen-year-old girl who left home:

"I have had all I can stand of the hassle back home. There is always fighting. I can never remember when it was different. Everyone in the house, including my parents, takes delight in bad mouthing each other."

What was wrong in this family?

To help your family understand the great importance the Lord has placed on eliminating contention, have them read aloud the following scriptures: 3 Nephi 11:29–30, Doctrine and Covenants 136:23, Mosiah 4:14–15. Discuss why the Lord wants us to avoid contention and why Satan desires to have us contend one with another. Help family members to recognize how contending drives us away from the Spirit of the Lord.

To illustrate how we choose whether we are "of the Lord" or "of Satan," divide a sheet of paper or a chalkboard into two columns and put *of the Lord* at the head of one column and *of Satan* at the head of the other. Have your family name some typical actions and responses to daily situations to see if such reactions are of the Lord or of Satan. Check the appropriate column as your family responds. Emphasize that Satan has power over us only when we allow it. Being contentious invites him in, but we have agency and can choose our behavior.

Discuss this statement: "Contention builds walls and barriers. Love opens doors."

• How does contention keep us from building a strong family?

Name some of the destructive results of contention, such as bitterness, sorrow, and unhappiness.

You may want to have your family repeat together: "He that hath the spirit of contention is not of me" (3 Nephi 11:29) and resolve to be of the Lord. A family member could be assigned to make a wordstrip with this scripture on it and place it where the family can be reminded.

Lesson 2: Recognizing the Causes of Contention

Help your family to recognize that there are many reasons for contention, but if we recognize what some of the most common problems are, we can work toward overcoming them.

Have family members take turns reading the following situations, then help them identify the basic reason for the contentions such as selfishness, conflict of scheduling, need to repent, need to listen.

1. Bart had asked for the car on Friday night. It was agreed that he could have it, but Jim said Bart had had it for the last three Fridays and he should now have a turn.

2. Guests were coming, and Anna was asked to give up her bedroom for the duration of their visit. She refused because, she said, "I've just cleaned it and arranged it the way I wanted it."

3. Jim had not been keeping the Word of Wisdom. He refused to come to family home evening because he felt guilty.

4. Jose was proud of his knowledge of the scriptures and loved to argue with ministers of other faiths about the gospel.

Name specific things that cause contention in your home. Identify the cause and discuss ways to avoid these problems.

Discuss "Only by pride cometh contention" (Proverbs 13:10).

Review the Lord's counsel in 3 Nephi 11:29–30, Doctrine and Covenants 136:23, and Mosiah 4:14–15 and help family members resolve to avoid the destructive nature of contention. They might ask themselves, "Why do I participate?"

Lesson 3: Learning to Settle Conflict in a Fair and Loving Way

Tell of the boy who returned home after running away because his father's parting remark that he loved him and wanted to be a better father kept ringing in his ears. Ask your family to discuss how this was a loving way to settle their problem.

Ask your family to consider ways that our Heavenly Father would have us settle our differences, such as the following (see 4 Nephi 1:2, 15):

1. One family stopped children who were quarreling and reminded them "there is a better way to settle this." They were taught to work out their differences according to what Heavenly Father expected.

2. One mother found that when she stopped and listened with full attention her children's frustrations were lessened.

3. One father listed the things he loved about his wife, and the little annoyances dwindled and disappeared.

4. One daughter answered softly even when she was addressed in an angry, contentious way.

5. The members of one family practiced controlling their tongues by adopting as their motto, "Think twice before you speak."

6. One family prayed to have the love of God in their hearts and home.

COVETOUSNESS

Lesson 4: Avoiding Contention with Nonmembers

Tell the following true experience of Elder Marvin J. Ashton:

When he visited one mission, the elders asked him how they could best respond to some anti-Mormon publications in their area. He answered: "We do nothing. We have no time for contention. We only have time to be about our Father's business." (In Conference Report, Apr. 1978, p. 9; or *Ensign*, May 1978, p. 7.)

• Why is it important for us to live the gospel as we should and not argue or contend with nonmembers?

Help your family recognize that we offend people and drive them away when we do more than govern ourselves. We can express our beliefs without clenching our fists or raising our voices. Discuss this comment by Elder Ashton: "Ours is . . . to plow our own furrow, plant our own seeds, tend our crops, reap the harvest. This can best be accomplished not only by plowshares rather than by swords, but by appropriate commitment rather than contention." (In Conference Report, Apr. 1978, p. 12; or *Ensign*, May 1978, p. 9.)

Role-play situations where you may be misunderstood, accused, or misquoted by others. Help your family learn to respond quietly, accurately, and with love.

RESOURCES

Scriptures

Matthew 5:25 (Agree with our adversary quickly.)
2 Corinthians 13:11 (Be perfect, of one mind.)
Doctrine and Covenants 10:63 (Satan causes contention.)
Doctrine and Covenants 121:41–44 (How to influence others.)
See "Contention" in the Topical Guide.

Songs and Hymns

"Love One Another," in lesson 36, "He is Risen," in the "Lessons" section of this manual.
"Let Us Oft Speak Kind Words," *Hymns*, no. 94.
"Should You Feel Inclined to Censure," *Hymns*, no. 159.
"Let's Be Kind to One Another," *Sing with Me*, B–68.

Covet not that which is thy brother's.
—Doctrine and Covenants 136:20

GOSPEL TRUTH

Coveting is an ungodly desire for something that belongs to another. It can lead to greed, stealing, jealousy, envy—even murder. Our Heavenly Father wants us to be grateful for those things we have and to work for what we desire, rejoicing with others in what they possess.

IDEAS FOR LESSONS

Lesson 1: Understanding Why Our Heavenly Father Wants Us to Avoid Coveting

Relate briefly one or both of the following stories from the Bible, asking your family to listen to be able to tell what caused the problem: Ahab coveting someone's field (1 Kings 21:1–19) and David coveting someone's wife (2 Samuel 11). Discuss with the members of your family the basic problem, making sure they realize it was covetousness which led to even greater sins.

Have a family member read Exodus 20:17. Discuss the meaning of this commandment of the Lord and of the word *covet*. Be sure they understand that coveting is wanting something that belongs to someone else. Point out the difference between coveting something and having the desire to work to acquire something similar.

Have your family list some things which are often coveted such as wealth, possessions, talents, and opportunities. With this list before them, let them name and discuss other sins that coveting these things can lead to such as greed, stealing, jealousy, envy, and harming others. If you used the story of David, point out that he, though once highly favored of the Lord, lost his eternal blessings because he desired and took another man's wife and even murdered to keep her (see D&C 132:39).

Ask your family to listen to the contrast as you read or tell the experience of Paul in Acts 20:33–37. Let your family talk about the feelings of Paul toward his fellow Church members and their feelings toward him. Emphasize the great love they had for one another, which they would not have had if Paul had been covetous.

Help the members of your family realize the blessings that can come to them as they work to earn their own possessions and to develop their own talents instead of coveting what others have.

Encourage them to think of one thing they may be coveting that belongs to another and challenge them to overcome this desire.

Lesson 2: Counting Our Blessings Helps Us to Avoid Coveting

Have your family sing "When upon Life's Billows" (Hymns, no. 202).

Get a small ball or roll up a pair of stockings. Toss the ball to one member of your family. Have him name a blessing your family enjoys such as food, clothing, or home. Have him toss the ball back to you. Then throw it to another member. Continue until your family has named your most important blessings. You may want to express your gratitude for these blessings.

Repeat the game, this time having the person with the ball name one talent or outstanding quality possessed by the person on his right. Continue until one or more qualities have been named for each person.

Help the members of your family realize and appreciate the many blessings they have, both individually and as a family (see 1 Thessalonians 5:18). Point out that as they work, they can achieve additional blessings and develop other talents. Help them feel that they have no need to covet what others have; Heavenly Father has blessed them in many ways.

You may wish to plan a service project where the members of your family can share their talents or possessions with others. You might present a program at a nursing home, volunteer to read or write for the blind or handicapped, visit the sick, or invite an elderly person to dinner.

Lesson 3: Rejoicing with Others in What They Have Helps Us Avoid Coveting

Discuss qualities, talents, or possessions that others have that family members have been able to enjoy. Talk about which of these your family would like to acquire. Point out that working toward these goals is not coveting.

Arrange to have one or more members of your family display a talent (musical, artistic, sewing, reciting, or others).

Discuss with the members of your family whether they coveted these talents or admired them. Help them to understand the difference. Emphasize that when we admire someone's talent, we can enjoy it, and it can inspire us to work harder to develop our own talents. (See 1 Corinthians 12:26.) When we truly admire someone's accomplishments, our love for that person grows.

You may want to let each family member draw the name of another family member and write a letter to that person, expressing love, appreciation, and genuine admiration of his talents and abilities.

You may also want to have "spotlight" nights in which different members of the family are honored—each on a different night, using pictures, stories, and other methods.

RESOURCES

Scriptures

Exodus 20:17 (Do not covet.)
Proverbs 21:26 (Difference between wicked and righteous.)

Matthew 6:19–20 (Do not lay up treasures on earth.)
Matthew 6:33 (Seek first the kingdom of God.)
See "Covet, Covetousness" in the Topical Guide.

Songs and Hymns

"Give Said the Little Stream," Sing with Me, G–24.

DEPENDABILITY

I will go and do the things which the Lord hath commanded.
—1 Nephi 3:7

GOSPEL TRUTH

Being dependable means that we *do* what we have said we would do, *when* we said we would do it, and in the *best way* we can. Being dependable brings us a feeling of success and self-respect, and it helps others trust us. Our Heavenly Father wants us to be dependable.

IDEAS FOR LESSONS

Lesson 1: Is Dependability Important?

Discuss the following questions with your family:

- What if a sky diver's parachute didn't open?
- What if the brakes on a car didn't hold?
- What if dad didn't go to work?
- What if the bishop didn't go to church?

On two large sheets of paper, place the headings *Dependable* and *Undependable*. Have someone read the gospel truth above, then ask the family to describe a day in the life of a dependable person and of an undependable person. List the actions of both kinds of people and discuss the results. Stress the positive results of being dependable.

Discuss the following or similar problems and how the participants in each situation might feel:

1. Several boys have accepted a quorum assignment, but only the leaders show up.
2. It was Mary's turn to do the dishes, but she ran off to play with a friend instead.
3. A father puts off his home teaching until the end of the month, then becomes ill.

Have family members list some of their responsibilities at home, school, and Church. Then have them list opposite each responsibility, the names of those who are depending on them. Have them consider what will happen if they do not fulfill these responsibilities.

Help family members understand that the Lord wants us to be dependable. Use the example of Nephi in 1 Nephi 3:7, of the stripling warriors in Alma 53:20–21, or of any other similar story from the Book of Mormon.

Lesson 2: Making Promises You Can Keep

Ask your family to identify the problem in each of the following situations:

1. Sister Thomas agreed to help with a community fund-raising drive. But she is so busy with her Church callings and family responsibilities that she has to back out.
2. Sarah agreed to help her brother Greg with his math lessons. But she didn't realize he would need more than a few minutes' help each week. Now she avoids being at home when he starts his homework. Dad usually has to help him instead.

Hold up a paper with the word *dependability* on it and discuss what this word means. Explain that in order to be dependable we must (1) know what is expected (2) know when we are to do it (3) know how well we should do it.

Help your family members see that before they promise to do something, they should find out what, when, and how, and agree to do it only if they can meet those requirements.

Role-play some situations where assignments are given in a vague way (such as, "Will you take care of the front lawn please?") Have family members ask for a clear assignment before agreeing to do it.

Lesson 3: What to Do When Promises Are Not Kept

Tell the following true experience of President N. Eldon Tanner:

"I remember another thing [my father] taught me which was very important. As a bishop he was not able to spend the time at home that some men can who are not bishops. He left us one afternoon while he was going out to look after his flock in the ward, and my brother and I were assigned to do certain things. He came back a little sooner than he had intended, or than we had expected him to come back anyway, and we hadn't accomplished what he had asked us to do. We had some calves in the corral we thought needed riding, and so we went about to accommodate those calves.

"I will never forget the whipping my father gave me when he came in and found we had not done the work which we had been assigned. He called me over to him and he said, 'My boy, I thought I could depend upon you.' That is all he said." (In Conference Report, Apr. 1964, p. 51; or *Improvement Era*, June 1964, p. 481.)

- What should you do when you have disappointed someone by failing to keep your word?

Discuss the need to apologize and to try to find a way to make up for our failure.

Read the following case studies and discuss what each person should do at this point.

1. A teenager promised his parents he would be home at 10:00 P.M. He got so involved in a game at a friend's house that he didn't notice the time until almost 10:30 P.M.

FASTING

2. The high priests group was assigned to clean a widow's yard. Brother Brown signed up to help before he remembered that he had promised to take his son fishing that morning.

3. Jane, a talented artist, had agreed to make some posters for a Relief Society lesson. Now it is late Saturday night, and Jane hasn't done it yet. She also needs to finish preparing her own Sunday School lesson for tomorrow.

Discuss the need to make sacrifices at times in order to keep our word and the need to apologize when we have planned poorly and will not be able to do what we have promised. Sometimes we can call on others to help us or offer to fulfill our obligation at another time.

Lesson 4: Rewarding Dependability

To reward dependability, try one or more of the following activities with your family:

As family members grow in dependability, spotlight them in a family home evening by telling of their dependable behavior.

Have family members write up experiences of the dependable behavior of other family members. Place these experiences in a box or bowl, draw them out one at a time, and read them aloud.

Have the family make a poster to encourage dependable behavior and place it in a predominant place where all can see it.

RESOURCES

Scriptures

1 Timothy 6:20 (Be trustworthy.)
Alma 53:1–23 (Story of the stripling warriors.)
See also "Dependability" in the Topical Guide.

Songs and Hymns

"Dare to Do Right," *Sing with Me*, B–81.

I give unto you a commandment that ye shall continue in prayer and fasting from this time forth.
—Doctrine and Covenants 88:76

GOSPEL TRUTH

To fast is to go without food and drink. Proper fasting, with prayer as its companion, increases spirituality, fosters a spirit of devotion and love of God, increases faith, encourages humility, teaches man his dependence upon God, and provides an opportunity for the spirit to take control over the body. (See Bruce R. McConkie, *Mormon Doctrine*, 2nd ed. [Salt Lake City: Bookcraft, 1966], p. 276.)

IDEAS FOR LESSONS

Lesson 1: Fasting Prepares Us to Pray with Greater Power

On one half of a chalkboard or large paper write the word *prayer*. Explain that this is one way we can receive the guidance of the Holy Ghost, but Heavenly Father has told us of something else we can do to help us feel even closer to him when we pray. To find what this is, have your family read Doctrine and Covenants 88:76. Write *fasting* on the other half of the chalkboard or paper.

Read or tell the story in Mosiah 27: 8–37; 28:1–8. Discuss the importance of fasting in the conversion and spiritual growth of Alma the Younger and Mosiah's four sons. (See Mosiah 27:22, 23; Alma 17:1–3.)

Read what President Marion G. Romney said about fasting:

"We haven't really called on the Lord so that we can reach him intimately if we don't fast occasionally, and pray often. Many of our personal problems can be solved by so doing." ("The Blessings of the Fast," *Ensign*, July 1982, p. 4.)

Discuss how fasting can help the following people:

1. Sister Fletcher fasted so she could accept her husband's untimely

death without bitterness and raise her three small children alone.

2. Jan, a young woman, began to doubt the Church was true. She fasted for a testimony.

3. A missionary, Elder Thomas, fasted and prayed for help in teaching a fine family that was having difficulty understanding the gospel.

• Why did Heavenly Father command us to fast as well as pray?

Be sure the following points are discussed: By going without food, we humble ourselves and show our desire to be close to him; we better understand our complete dependence upon him to supply our needs; and we make our spiritual needs more important than our physical needs.

Talk about how fasting can help your family.

Lesson 2: Learning How We Should Fast

Have part of your family read Matthew 6:16–18 and the others read Doctrine and Covenants 59:13–16 to discover how we should fast. Answers should include the following: in secret, joyfully, with thanksgiving, with cheerful hearts and faces.

Then have family members read the same verses to find the blessings that come to those who fast properly. Answers should include the following: we will be rewarded openly, we will receive fulness of joy and fulness of the earth.

Discuss how the scriptures relate to your own family's fasting experiences. As you discuss with your children the spiritual feelings that come from fasting, be sure they understand that they may experience feelings of hunger and thirst, but they can grow in spirituality as they continue to cheerfully obey the commandment to fast.

To help your family understand that wisdom should be used in deciding how long to fast on Fast Sunday, discuss the following statements:

"The law to the Latter-day Saints, as understood by the authorities of the Church, is that food and drink are not to be partaken of for twenty-four hours. . . .

" . . . The Lord has instituted the fast on a reasonable and intelligent basis, and none of his works are vain or unwise. His law is perfect in this as in other things. Hence, those who can, are required to comply thereto; it is a duty from which they cannot escape; but let it be remembered that the observance of the Fast Day by abstaining twenty-four hours from food and drink is not an absolute rule, it is no iron-clad law to us, but it is left with the people as a matter of conscience, to exercise wisdom and discretion. Many are subject to weakness, others are delicate in health, and others have nursing babies; of such it should not be required to fast. Neither should parents compel their little children to fast. I have known children to cry for something to eat on fast day. In such cases, going without food will do them no good. Instead, they dread the day to come, and in place of hailing it, dislike it; while the compulsion engenders a spirit of rebellion in them, rather than a love for the Lord and their fellows. Better teach them the principle, and let them observe it when they are old enough to choose intelligently, than to so compel them." (Joseph F. Smith, *Gospel Doctrine*, 5th ed. [Salt Lake City: Deseret Book Co., 1939], pp. 243, 244.)

"Sometimes Latter-day Saints think that if it is good to fast for 24 hours, it is three times as good to fast for 72 hours. Healthwise nothing could be farther from the truth. Missionaries, especially, must have strength to carry out their work and should not over-indulge in fasting anymore than in food-faddism. Let's follow the counsel of our leaders 'that food and drink are not to be partaken of for twenty-four hours. . . . ' If longer fasting is required of us, they will so direct us."

(Lindsay R. Curtis, M.D., "Questions and Answers," *New Era*, Apr. 1977, p. 49.)

Determine as a family how you can improve the quality of your fasting. It might be helpful to make individual commitments to be implemented on the next fast Sunday. The family could meet before beginning the fast, discuss a righteous reason for fasting or a special blessing that is needed, and begin with prayer.

Lesson 3: Fasting to Help the Needy

Discuss the following questions to help your family understand the importance of helping those in need:

- Who supplies all of our physical needs? (Heavenly Father planned the earth to meet our physical needs. Jesus carried out his plans.)
- For whom did they create the earth? (All of Heavenly Father's children. There is enough to supply the needs of all.)
- How did our Heavenly Father intend for the needs of those who cannot provide for themselves to be supplied? (Those who have the means are to share with those in need. Read and discuss Mosiah 4:16–21 and Matthew 25:31–46.)

Read Isaiah 58:6–7 and ask what those who fast should do for the needy.

Teach your family that Heavenly Father commanded us to fast, giving money equal to the price of food we didn't eat and whatever else we can afford to help those in need.

Read what President Joseph F. Smith said about fasting for the needy: "For the benefit of the poor we have the fast instituted, a leading object of which, among other things, is to provide the poor with food and other necessities until they may help themselves" (*Gospel Doctrine*, p. 236).

Discuss the following ideas in relation to your family:

When we are humble, fasting, and prayerful, we are more able to feel love and caring for those in need; we give to the needy regularly every month; and we each give the amount we can afford.

- What promises are given to us if we fast for the needy? (See Isaiah 58:7–11.)
- How well is your family observing the law to fast for the needy? Can you make at least one commitment to improve? Does every family member (even young children) feel a part of giving fast offerings as a family?

RESOURCES

Scriptures

Exodus 34:28 (Moses fasted upon the mount.)

2 Samuel 12:15–23 (David fasted for the life of his child.)

Esther 4:15–17 (Esther asked the Israelites to fast for her.)

Matthew 6:16–18 (Do not appear to fast.)

Matthew 17:14–21 (Apostles needed prayer and fasting to perform miracle.)

Luke 2:37 (Anna fasted and prayed in the temple.)

Alma 5:45–46 (Alma fasted and prayed for a testimony of the truth.)

Alma 6:6 (The righteous gathered to fast and pray.)

Helaman 3:33–35 (The members of the Church fasted and prayed often.)

3 Nephi 27:1–2 (The disciples were united in mighty prayer and fasting.)

Doctrine and Covenants 59:3–14 (Perfect fasting.)

Doctrine and Covenants 88:76, 119 (Continue in prayer and fasting.)

See also "Fast, Fasting" in the Topical Guide.

Songs and Hymns

"Lord, Accept Our True Devotion," *Hymns*, no. 101.

Other

Gospel Principles, "Fasting," chapter 25.

A Generous Fast Offering, available through your meetinghouse library in a filmstrip version only.

FORGIVING

I, the Lord, will forgive whom I will forgive, but of you it is required to forgive all men.
—*Doctrine and Covenants 64:10*

GOSPEL TRUTH

Forgiveness is using the power within us to overcome anger, feelings of revenge, and unhappy and bad feelings. Our Heavenly Father commanded us to forgive everyone, and he will help us as we try to keep this commandment.

IDEAS FOR LESSONS

Lesson 1: Understanding What It Means to Forgive

Print the letters *F, O, R, G, I, V, E* on seven small pieces of paper. Mix them up and give them to family members to make into a word. Give them help if needed. When the word is complete ask each family member to complete the sentence, "Forgiveness is _____ ." Read the gospel truth above and Doctrine and Covenants 64:10.

To help family members understand the principle of forgiveness, read or tell the following experience as told by the late Chief Blue of the Catawba Indian nation:

One day my eleven-year-old son went squirrel hunting with six other Indians. He saw a squirrel run up a tree and climbed up to scare it out on a limb. After he had done this he called to the others to hold their fire until he could get down. One of the Indians in the hunting party had always been jealous of me and my position as chief. He and his son both shot deliberately at my boy. He was filled with buckshot from his knees to his head. The Indians carried my boy towards home and found a spot where they lay him while they ran for the doctor.

A friend came and found me and said, "Sam, run home at once; your boy has been shot." I ran all the way home

and found my boy near death. The doctor was there and said my boy would not live. He was right; the boy died in a few minutes.

The man and son who had done the shooting were in my front yard visiting with members of the crowd that had gathered. They did not appear to be upset at their deed. My heart filled with revenge and hatred. Something seemed to whisper to me, "If you don't take down your gun and kill that man who murdered your son, Sam Blue, you are a coward."

Now I have been a Mormon ever since I have been a young lad and I knew it would not be right to take revenge. I decided to pray to the Lord about it. I walked to my secret place out in the timber where I always have gone to pray alone when I have a special problem, and there I prayed to the Lord to take revenge out of my heart. I soon felt better and started back to the house. But again I heard something inside whisper, again I turned back and prayed until I felt better. On my way back to the house I again heard the voice say, "Sam Blue, you are a coward." I turned again and went back to pray and this time I told the Lord he must help me or I would be a killer. I asked him to take revenge out of my heart and keep it out. I felt good when I got up from praying. I went back to the house a third time and when I reached the house I went out and shook hands with the Indian who had killed my boy. There was no hatred or desire for revenge in my heart. (See Marion G. Romney, *The Power of God unto Salvation*, Brigham Young University Speeches of the Year [Provo, 3 Feb. 1960], pp. 6–7.)

Discuss the story by asking questions such as the following: Was it too much to expect Chief Blue to forgive his son's killers—especially when they did not repent? How did Chief Blue's strong desire to overcome feelings of hatred and revenge make it possible

for him to forgive? Where did he get the strength to forgive? What happened to Chief Blue that showed he had forgiven those who killed his son?

You may want to contrast this experience with the parable of the unmerciful servant (Matthew 18:23–35).

Read Luke 23:33–34. Remind your family that the Savior set a perfect example of forgiveness.

Ask family members to write on a piece of paper the name of someone they need to forgive. As you encourage them to be forgiving, remind them of Chief Blue. Emphasize the importance of *wanting* to forgive, believing we have the power to forgive, praying for help, and receiving the blessing of having hatred and revenge taken from our hearts. Have each family member keep his piece of paper to remind him of this commitment.

Lesson 2: Forgetting Is Part of Forgiving

To help family members better understand how forgiving and forgetting can affect their lives, have them participate in the following activities:

Activity one. Fill a bag or sack with five heavy objects (such as books or rocks) that have each been labeled with one of the following words: *revenge, hurt, hate, resentment,* and *anger.* Have each family member take a turn trying to carry this heavy load. Explain that carrying those feelings in our hearts is an even greater burden than carrying the heavy bag. When we really forgive, we forget all of these feelings and are free from the burden of carrying them.

Activity two. Prepare an easy obstacle course. Have family members try to go through it while looking backwards. After everyone has had a turn, let them go through the same course looking forward. Discuss how looking forward is like forgiveness because when we forgive we can concentrate on our future or what is ahead and forget the hurts of the past.

Discuss how we can tell if we have really forgiven someone and forgotten—by the way we feel about him, by how we treat him, and by our willingness to help him. Encourage your family to use this test in their lives: Is there someone you have not forgiven? What can you do about it?

Lesson 3: Understanding the Importance of Forgiving

To demonstrate the harm we do ourselves when we have ill feelings towards others, leave a small amount of tomato juice in an open can for several days. Show your family how the acid in the juice eroded the can. Explain that when we don't forgive, the feelings we keep in our hearts are like this acid—they eat away at us. Discuss how this might affect our lives in creating a negative attitude and making us resentful and unhappy).

Discuss whether it is a sign of weakness or strength to be forgiving. Why?

Read or tell in your own words the following quotation by President Spencer W. Kimball:

"Bitterness poisons mostly the one who harbors it in his heart. . . .

"Generally, the hated one does not even know how bitter is the animosity leveled against him. . . . The one who hates estranges himself from good folk, shrivels his heart, dwarfs his soul, makes of himself an unhappy pygmy." (*The Miracle of Forgiveness* [Salt Lake City: Bookcraft, 1969], pp. 271–72.)

Have each family member remember from his own experiences a time he found it difficult to forgive and how it affected him.

- Who was hurt the most when we did not forgive? (Us.)
- Why?
- What difference does it make when we do forgive? (We can be happy instead of miserable. We can be forgiven of our own sins.)

Read and discuss 3 Nephi 13:14–15, Matthew 7:1–2, and Doctrine and Covenants 64:10.

- Why do you think the Lord commanded us to forgive everyone—no matter what they do to us? (He wants us to feel the peace that comes from forgiving and escape the misery that comes from feeling hatred and revenge.)

You may want to read or tell the parable of the prodigal son (Luke 15:11–32) and discuss forgiveness in relation to the story.

Ask your family members (1) that they try to be forgiving with each other during the week, and (2) that they watch for the difference the spirit of forgiveness makes in your home.

RESOURCES

Scriptures

Genesis 37–45 (The story of Joseph and his brothers.)
Leviticus 19:17–18 (Do not hate your brother.)
Matthew 5:44 (Love your enemies.)
Matthew 6:12, 14–15 (Forgive men their trespasses.)
Matthew 18:21–22 (Forgive seventy times seven.)
Matthew 18:23–35 (Parable of the unmerciful servant.)
Hebrews 8:12 (The Lord will remember your sins no more.)
Doctrine and Covenants 58:42–43 (The Lord will forgive and forget.)

See also "Forgive, Forgiveness" in the Topical Guide.

Songs and Hymns

"Forgiveness," *Sing with Me,* B–35.
"I Stand All Amazed," *Hymns,* no. 80.

Other

Gospel Principles, "Repentance," chapter 19.

In One Blinding Moment, available through your meetinghouse library in either a 16mm film or videocassette version.

FRIENDSHIP

A new commandment I give unto you, That ye love one another; as I have loved you.
—John 13:34

GOSPEL TRUTH

Friendship is a loving relationship between two people. Friends respect each other, care about each other, remain true to each other, and overlook and forgive each other's faults. Our Heavenly Father wants us to be friends to all his children.

IDEAS FOR LESSONS

Lesson 1: Understanding What It Means to Be a True Friend

Ask your family to listen for some qualities of a true friend as you tell the following incident:

Bill was approached by some kids he knew at school. They were angry, because Jim, a member of the group, said Bill had pushed Jim's brother into the park pond that morning. Bill had not been near the pond.

At this tense moment, Bill saw his friend John walking toward him. He was excited to see John because he had been with John all morning. John could prove his innocence. As John came nearer, the other boys threatened him, but he kept coming. He stood up for Bill and finally convinced the others that he was innocent; they were accusing the wrong man.

- What qualities of friendship were displayed by John?

Read and discuss the description of the friendship of Jonathan, a son of King Saul, and David, the shepherd boy, in 1 Samuel 18:1–4. Ask your family to describe a true friend by completing the sentence "A true friend is a person who _____." Compare the answers with the gospel truth at the beginning of this lesson.

To find one word that describes a true friend, read the first part of Proverbs 17:17, "A friend *loveth* at all times" (italics added). Also, read what Jesus has commanded us to do in John 13:34–35.

Help your family understand that as we truly love others, we become their friends. Discuss the difference this could make in our home, our neighborhood, the Church, our nation, and even the world. Read what the Prophet Joseph Smith said about this:

"Friendship is one of the grand fundamental principles of 'Mormonism'; [it is designed] to revolutionize and civilize the world, and cause wars and contentions to cease and men to become friends and brothers" (*Teachings of the Prophet Joseph Smith*, sel. Joseph Fielding Smith [Salt Lake City: Deseret Book Co., 1938], p. 316).

You might set a goal for each family member to try to be a loving friend to his family and associates during the entire week (or even just one day) and then evaluate the results.

Lesson 2: Making and Keeping Friends

Tell your family that there is a secret to having a friend. Have them listen to the following experiences of Sister Dwan J. Young, general Primary president, to discover what this secret is:

"As I grew older and developed friendships in my neighborhood, I found I had to be a friend in order to have a friend. . . . It took time to show my friends I really loved them. Sometimes just listening to them was what they needed. A call to invite them over to play a game made them happy. I learned I had to do *my* part in order for friendship to grow.

"At school there were many opportunities to be a good friend. I remember how hard it was when I was not chosen to be one of the first in the class on a baseball team or for some other activity. That experience reminded me that when I had a chance to choose, I should look for those who needed a turn.

"A good time to be friendly was when new students joined the class. I found that by helping them feel welcome and happy, I was happy too." ("Friend to Friend," *Friend*, May 1982, p. 7.)

Discuss the secret: to have a friend, you must be one.

List on slips of paper ways to make and keep friends:

Learn to love them.
Be yourself.
Include someone who is feeling left out.
Be interested in what others are doing.
Help others.
Say good things about others.
Share with others.
Invite others to do something with you.

Also list ways *not* to make and keep friends:

Buy friendship by giving treats and expensive gifts.
Lie about others so you will seem to be the only worthwhile friend to have.
Give false praise.
Threaten to desert your friend if he won't agree with you.
Don't be a friend to persons you don't like.

You could display the good ways on a poster entitled "Being a True Friend." Encourage each family member to plan ways he can become a better friend.

Lesson 3: Friendship Starts at Home

Ask your family to listen to what was wrong in the following story: Two boys were delivering newspapers on their bicycles. One of the bicycles hit a rock, and the boy flew off the bike in one direction and the newspapers in another. The second boy rode up laughing and teasing. As a neighbor came to the first boy's assistance, the second boy rode on down the street.

Seeing the boy's pride was hurt more than his body, the neighbor said, "It's kind of a low blow to have your friend laugh when you've had a bad spill, isn't it?" As the boy packed the news-

papers back in place, he replied, "He isn't my friend—he's my brother." (See Marvin J. Ashton, in Conference Report, Oct. 1969, p. 28; or *Improvement Era*, Dec. 1969, p. 51.)

• What was wrong? (The brother should have been a friend and shown love for his brother.)

Discuss why every family member should be a true friend to every other member.

Talk about what can happen in your home if family members practice being friends to each other. Ask each to tell of a time when he has felt one of the family was his true friend. Refer to the poster in the second lesson idea above, and decide ways you can be better friends to one another.

Lesson 4: Maintaining Gospel Standards When Friends Do Not

Discuss the importance of standing for what you believe when friends want you to do something wrong. Talk about how difficult peer pressure can be, but assure each family member he has the capacity to influence his friends for good and be a strong example to them. Tell the following true story:

The parents of one family were concerned about a new friend their children had made in the neighborhood. The boy was not a member of the Church and did not have the same standards of speech and behavior.

In family home evening one night, they talked about the importance of showing this boy their way of living, rather than adopting his way. They welcomed him into their home to play and share in family activities.

Soon other neighbors invited the boy into their homes also, and he grew up in a neighborhood of love and kindness. He eventually joined the Church, but, during his growing up years, he received the love, friendship, and example that he, as a child of God, needed and deserved.

GENEALOGY

Encourage family members to speak freely of problems they may face in being true to their standards and still keeping friends. Let each one know he has the love and support of the family. Parents could tell of their concern and their prayers for each child. Discuss how prayer can help strengthen each family member and give him the courage to do what he knows is right.

RESOURCES

Scriptures

Proverbs 17:17 (A friend's love doesn't end.)
Matthew 7:12 (The Golden Rule.)
1 Corinthians 12:26 (Suffer and rejoice together.)
Doctrine and Covenants 4:6 (Remember brotherly kindness.)

Songs and Hymns

"Jesus Said Love Everyone," *Sing with Me*, B–51.

Other

See also other topics in this section entitled "Forgiving" and "Selfishness," and "Loving Our Neighbors," lesson 23 in the "Lessons" section of this manual.

The Drop Card and *Greater Love*, available through your meetinghouse library in either 16mm film or videocassette versions.

The greatest responsibility in this world that God has laid upon us is to seek after our dead.
—The Prophet Joseph Smith

GOSPEL TRUTH

It is our responsibility and privilege to identify our ancestors so the saving ordinances of the gospel can be performed for them. Genealogy will also help tie us to our ancestors in an eternal family unit.

IDEAS FOR LESSONS

Lesson 1: The Importance of Genealogy and Temple Work

Read chapter 40 in *Gospel Principles* for background information.

Ask one member of the family to move to the far side of the room, away from the others. Discuss how you would feel if one of your family could not be with you in the next life.

If possible, show a picture of the temple nearest you, or write the word *temple* on a piece of paper.

- What blessing can come to your family in the temple? (Being sealed together.)

- What about those of our ancestors who died without being sealed in the temple? Will they always have to be separated from their family?

Point out that Heavenly Father loves all of his children. He made it possible for these people who died without the gospel to receive all of the sacred ordinances. Have the person return to the group.

Read 1 Corinthians 15:29.

- What does this scripture tell us? (Baptisms for the dead were performed in New Testament times.)

Explain that through the temple, the dead can receive all of the blessings

---

and ordinances of the gospel—baptism, endowment, and sealing. In this way, all of our ancestors who accept the Lord's plan can be sealed to our family.

Show and study a pedigree chart from a branch of your family; or, write the names of children, parents, and grandparents on a sheet of paper. Explain that all of the people, plus their parents, grandparents, and so on need to be sealed together in an unbroken chain.

Ask your family to listen to what the Lord revealed through Joseph Smith about this as you read Doctrine and Covenants 128:15.

Tell the following experience:

When President Wood of the Cardston Alberta Temple was sealing a family together around the altar, he felt impressed to ask if the information on the sealing sheet was correct. The mother said it was. As they began the ordinance again, he again felt impressed to ask if there were other children who needed to be sealed. She assured him there were none. The third time, he heard a voice quite clearly say, "I am her child." Again, he asked the mother if she had ever had another child. As she thought back to her early married years, she remembered a baby who had died shortly after birth. The mother rejoiced as her little girl was included as part of their eternal family unit. (See Melvin S. Tagg, "The Life of Edward James Wood, Church Patriot," [Masters thesis, Brigham Young University, 1959], pp. 118–19.)

- How can we make sure that no family member is left out? (By keeping accurate records.)

Point out that accurate records are necessary before temple work can be done. The making of these records is called *genealogy*. Read Doctrine and Covenants 128:24.

You may wish to end the discussion by

bearing your own testimony of the sacred importance of genealogy and temple work, then having the family sing, "The Temple Is a Sacred Place," *Sing with Me,* B–31.

Lesson 2: Knowing and Loving Our Ancestors

If possible, invite grandparents or other close family members to share this evening with you.

Choose one or more ancestors to honor. Show the family any pictures you may have of those people. Note their style of dress, and discuss how their life-styles may have been different from yours. Point out any family resemblances you can see in the pictures.

Have each family member read or tell stories about one of the ancestors. Help your children see your ancestors as real people who actually lived and had feelings and experiences like their own. Try to help your family feel closer to them and realize that they are an important part of your family. Mention physical traits, talents, or other good characteristics you and your children inherited from ancestors (for example, red hair like grandpa's or musical talent like grandma's).

Take several slips of paper and place the name of another ancestor on each. Place them in a bowl or other container and have each family member draw one out. During the coming month, have each person find out all he can about that ancestor by collecting pictures, talking to relatives who know about that person, and so forth. Younger children may work with an older family member. They could draw pictures about important events in the life of the ancestor.

Hold a special family home evening where each family member can present his findings.

Lesson 3: Visiting Important Sites

Visit the homes, places of birth, or burial sites of some of your ancestors. If you cannot do this, you may be able to find pictures and other information about these places.

Lesson 4: Genealogical Forms

Give each family member a blank Family Group Record form to practice filling out. Explain any unfamiliar words or phrases.

Set a goal to complete your own Family Group Record. Plan ways to research any information you do not have. Then fill out sheets for grandparents and great-grandparents.

If you have any names ready for temple work, you may wish to have the family help you fill out the appropriate forms.

Lesson 5: Baptisms for the Dead

Children over age twelve can act as proxy for baptisms for the dead in the temple. If you live near a temple or can take a family vacation in a place where one is located, arrange with local priesthood leaders and the temple to give them this opportunity. It can help them understand the blessings of genealogy and temple work.

Lesson 6: Records Sources

Plan a visit to the Genealogical Department Library in Salt Lake City or a branch genealogical library. If there is not a genealogical library near your home, you may wish to visit a local record repository—a library or government records office. The manual *From You to Your Ancestors* (PBGS0683) can also be helpful.

RESOURCES

Scriptures

John 5:25 (The dead shall hear the voice of Jesus Christ.)
Hebrews 11:40 (They without us cannot be perfect.)
1 Peter 4:6 (The gospel is preached to the dead.)
3 Nephi 25:5–6 (Elijah will come to turn hearts.)

Doctrine and Covenants 124:93 (Ordinances sealed by authority of priesthood are binding after death.)
Doctrine and Covenants 128:17–18 (Malachi 4:5–6 is explained.)
See also "Genealogy and Temple Work" in the Topical Guide.

Songs and Hymns

"I Love to See the Temple," in *Supplement to More Songs for Children,* p. 4.
"When Grandpa Comes," *Sing with Me,* D–17.
"High on the Mountain Top," *Hymns,* no. 62.
"Holy Temples on Mount Zion," *Hymns,* no. 63.
"How Beautiful Thy Temples, Lord," *Hymns,* no. 65.

Other

Gospel Principles, "Temple Work and Genealogy," chapter 40.

GOSSIP

Thou shalt not speak evil of thy neighbor, nor do him any harm.
—Doctrine and Covenants 42:27

GOSPEL TRUTH

When we gossip, we idly discuss someone's weaknesses or problems when that person is not present. Gossip harms not only those who are being talked about, but also those who gossip and those who listen. Heavenly Father wants us to look for and speak of the good in others and eliminate gossip from our lives.

IDEAS FOR LESSONS

Lesson 1: The Bad Effects of Gossip

Invite family members to tell what they think of when they hear the word *gossip*.

- What are some other words that have the same meaning as gossip? (Tale-bearing, evil-speaking, backbiting, bearing false witness.)

Read Exodus 20:16 and Doctrine and Covenants 42:27. You could write either or both of these verses on a poster. Emphasize that these verses are more than suggestions from the Lord. The Lord has actually commanded us not to gossip.

- How many people are always involved in gossip? (Three—the gossiper, the listener, and the victim—but the victim is not usually present.)

Name the following aspects of gossip. As you do, have the family discuss how each aspect of gossip hurts the gossiper, the listener, the victim, or all three.

Gossip—

1. Centers on faults.
2. Is blind to good qualities.
3. Is often untrue.
4. Can't be taken back.
5. Cuts us off—from the Lord's Spirit and from other people.

Help your family understand why our loving Heavenly Father has commanded us not to gossip. Point out that gossip only destroys; it never builds. And Heavenly Father wants us to be free of the problems and sorrow it causes. Read several of these verses, which contain the Lord's promises to those who do not speak evil of others: Psalms 15:1–3, 1 Peter 3:10; Proverbs 21:23; Proverbs 26:20.

Have each member of your family draw an imaginative picture of gossip. For example, it could have a poison arrow for a head, with poison feathers behind and sharp claws. Use these drawings as a reminder of how dangerous gossip is.

Lesson 2: Looking for Good in Family Members

Write the name of each family member at the top of a separate piece of paper. Pass them around in a circle. Have each person write down a good quality of the person whose name is on the sheet or something good that person has done. Continue passing and writing until each person has written on every paper except his own. Then have each person read aloud what is written on someone else's sheet.

- How did you feel when you looked for the good in the rest of the family? When you heard the good others found in you?

Read and discuss the following statement by President Joseph F. Smith:

"Watch constantly for that which is worthy and noble in your fellowman. It makes a person better to see and speak of good in his neighbor; while there is unbounded delight in observing the effect that a few words of appreciation and encouragement have upon men, women, and children with whom we associate." (*Gospel Doctrine*, [Salt Lake City: Deseret Book Co.], p. 112.)

Point out that we often think of gossip as talking about a neighbor or friend

from school. But gossip can be very destructive within a family. Discuss with your family how looking for the good in each other can make your family stronger and more unified.

Lesson 3: Looking for Good in Everyone

- Why do we sometimes want to say negative things about others?

Point out that, if we feel insecure about ourselves, we may think that pointing out another's faults will make us feel better. We may feel threatened or envious about someone else's success. Or, we may fall into a habit of gossiping without realizing it or think that gossip won't really hurt anyone.

Tell the following story to help your family understand that seeing the good in others crowds out gossip:

Two friends found they often criticized another friend when she was not with them. They knew this wasn't good, so they decided to say two good things every time they said one bad thing. It was hard at first, but soon they came to appreciate the qualities of their friend so much that they had no desire to gossip about her.

Together make a list of qualities you admire in others. Name people you know who have each quality. You might write notes to some of these people, telling of your appreciation for them. Or, tell them of your appreciation in person.

Discuss President Joseph F. Smith's description of the effects of eliminating gossip:

"Happiness, beauty of disposition, love and moral cleanliness, would increase among the Saints; the Spirit of God would delight to dwell in their midst, and the best qualities of people would unfold and develop like the rose in the warm sunshine" (*Gospel Doctrine*, p. 113).

Point out that the rewards of building others up are eternal—better relationship with others, the ability to love them, Heavenly Father's approval, and the Holy Ghost's companionship.

Lesson 4: When Others Gossip

• When is it most difficult not to gossip?

Point out that we sometimes feel strong social pressure to gossip among our friends.

• How can we avoid joining in when we hear someone gossip?

Try to think of some tactful ways to steer a conversation in a more positive direction when others begin to gossip. For example, an elderly lady, when asked if she could keep a secret said, "Of course. I can keep it going. Better not tell me." Often, you can change the tone of a conversation by simply saying something good about the victim.

Prepare the members of your family to have the courage to refuse to be a willing listener to gossip. Ask each one to think of a situation where he commonly hears gossip. Ask several people to tell or role-play what they could do.

Lesson 5: When Someone Gossips about You

Point out that everyone is a victim of gossip at one time or another.

• How will you react when you know that others have spoken unkindly about you?

Discuss each of these statements:

1. "My Heavenly Father knows the truth about me. No matter what others may say, I am precious to him."

Have someone read Doctrine and Covenants 18:10, substituting in turn the name of each family member for the word *soul*.

2. "If I don't forgive, my anger and bitterness will hurt me long after the hurt from the gossip has gone."

Read this statement:

"It is reported that President Brigham Young . . . explained that there are two courses of action to follow when one is bitten by a rattlesnake. One may, in anger, fear, or vengefulness, pursue the creature and kill it. Or he may make full haste to get the venom out of his system. If we pursue the latter course we will likely survive, but if we attempt to follow the former, we may not be around long enough to finish it." (Marion D. Hanks, in Conference Report, Oct. 1973, p. 16; or *Ensign*, Jan. 1974, p. 21.)

• How is being the victim of gossip like being bitten by a snake?

Learning to believe in yourself and forgive the person who gossiped about you is the only happy way to cope. For help in learning to forgive, use the home evening lesson ideas in the chapter on forgiveness.

RESOURCES

Scriptures

Psalm 34:13 (Do not speak evil.)
Proverbs 21:23 (Controlling the tongue keeps the soul from trouble.)
Matthew 7:3 (Why notice another person's fault?)
Luke 6:37 (Do not condemn others, and you will not be condemned.)
John 8:7 (Let him that is without sin first cast a stone.)
James 1:26 (If you do not bridle your tongue, your religion is vain.)
Doctrine and Covenants 88:124 (Cease to find fault.)
Mosiah 4:30 (Watch your thoughts and your words.)
See also "Gossip" in the Topical Guide.

Songs and Hymns

"Nay, Speak No Ill," *Hymns*, no. 116.
"There Is Beauty All Around," *Hymns*, no. 169.
"Let Us Oft Speak Kind Words," *Hymns*, no. 94.

GRATITUDE

Thou shalt thank the Lord thy God in all things.
—Doctrine and Covenants 59:7

GOSPEL TRUTH

Gratitude is being aware of and appreciating blessings and kindnesses given to us. We can express it through sincere words of thanks and through actions that show our appreciation. An increased spirit of gratitude will bring increased joy into our lives.

IDEAS FOR LESSONS

Lesson 1: Gratitude Brings Joy

• What does gratitude mean to you?

Compare your answers with the gospel truth above. Also, see Doctrine and Covenants 78:19. Then tell the following story to help family members understand that warm, loving feelings come when we show gratitude.

Laura received many nice gifts for her birthday, but when she opened the package from her grandmother, a deep, warm feeling came over her. The gift was a beautiful handmade doll. As Laura touched the carefully braided hair, the embroidered face, and the lacy dress she thought of the time it must have taken for grandma to make this doll. Grandma's eyesight was failing, and sewing by hand was becoming difficult for her. Laura ran to grandma and hugged her tightly. "Oh, thank you, grandma," she whispered. Grandma hugged her back. She knew Laura loved the doll and that her many hours of work were appreciated. Best of all, she knew that Laura loved her.

Discuss the feelings of love that Laura and her grandmother shared because Laura felt grateful and showed her gratitude. Ask family members to tell how they have felt when someone has expressed gratitude to them.

Tell the story of the ten lepers (Luke 17:11–18).

- How did the one leper show his gratitude? (Reread Luke 17:15–16 if necessary.) Point out that although the nine were no doubt happy to be healed, they did not think of the source of their blessing or go back to thank Jesus.

- What experience did the ungrateful nine miss? (They missed the opportunity of expressing gratitude and love to the Savior.)

Read Doctrine and Covenants 59:7 together. To help your family determine how well they obey this commandment, have each person write down two blessings they have received from Heavenly Father and two kindnesses or gifts they have received from other people. Then have them write by each blessing or gift the name of the person who gave it to them and how they showed gratitude to that person. Discuss how showing gratitude can help us feel closer to the giver of a gift or blessing.

Lesson 2: Showing Gratitude to Heavenly Father and Jesus

Sing "When upon Life's Billows," (Hymns, no. 202). Then have each family member make a list of his blessings. Be sure to include some of the blessings of the gospel. Have each person choose one blessing from the list and tell how life would be different without that blessing.

Read aloud Mosiah 2:19–24 to help your family feel the spirit of gratitude expressed by a great prophet, King Benjamin.

- What blessings did King Benjamin say we should thank our Heavenly Father for?

- What does Heavenly Father want us to do for him to show our gratitude? (See Mosiah 2:22)

Ask your family to think of one thing they have done during the past week to show their gratitude to Heavenly Father and Jesus.

- What more can you do? (Express

thanks through prayer, more often and more sincerely; pay tithes and offerings with feelings of love; study scriptures daily; attend Church and worship reverently, especially during the sacrament.)

Each member of the family might make a commitment to show more gratitude to Heavenly Father and Jesus.

Talk together about what you would like to thank Heavenly Father for in the closing prayer of this home evening.

Lesson 3: Expressing Gratitude for Your Family

To help your family feel grateful to be a part of a family, tell this make-believe story: A boy dreamed he came home from playing baseball and found his home had disappeared. He wandered around forlornly, thinking, "I have no place to eat or sleep, and no one to be with." Then he woke up.

Ask family members to imagine how it would be to have no place to eat, no bed to sleep in, no one to cook their meals or care for them when they were ill. Ask them to name other privileges they may be taking for granted.

Invite family members to name ways they have shown gratitude for the privilege of belonging to your family and what they can do to show more gratitude in the future.

Tell the following story as an example of how one mother expresses gratitude to her family:

A mother with three children had few worldly goods. On birthdays and other special days, the most she could give her children was a small homemade toy. However, she always did something else that was worth more than the most expensive toy. On each child's birthday, she would call him into the bedroom and have him sit in a chair. Then she would kneel down to pray. In her prayer, she would

thank Heavenly Father for blessing her with this child. She would mention the joys the child had given her and pray for his continued health and happiness.

Have family members express their gratitude for each other. Be sure everyone is included. Discuss what family members can do to express gratitude for each other. Family members might relate an instance or two when gratitude was expressed to them. Have them tell what they felt at the time.

Lesson 4: The Habit of Gratitude

Review the story of the nine lepers (Luke 17:11–19). Discuss that the lepers were probably not in the habit of showing their gratitude for a blessing received.

Read Alma 34:38.

- Why is it important to make a habit of feeling and expressing gratitude constantly, not just now and then?

Sing or read the words to "Children All over the World" (More Songs for Children, pp. 23–25) with your children, or sing "I Thank Thee, Dear Father" (Sing with Me, A–8).

After the song, discuss how important it is to thank our Heavenly Father in all our prayers. It does not matter who we are or where we live, we all receive great blessings we should be thankful for.

Here are some suggestions to help your family express gratitude daily:

1. During a meal, invite family members to tell of something they have received from Heavenly Father, other members of the family, or others for which they feel grateful.

2. Keep the list of blessings made during the home evening. Have each person place this list in a drawer or on a mirror where it will be seen often and add to it from time to time.

3. Occasionally, let the family spend a home evening expressing their

HONESTY

gratitude for blessings and kindnesses they have received, as individuals and as a family.

Think of other ways your family can make gratitude a habit.

RESOURCES

Scriptures

Psalm 136:1–26 (Give thanks unto the Lord, for he is good.)

Psalm 147:1–20 (It is good to sing praises to our God.)

Isaiah 12:1–6 (O Lord, I will praise thee.)

1 Corinthians 15:55, 57 (Thanks be to God, who sent his Son.)

1 Thessalonians 5:18 (Give thanks in everything.)

2 Nephi 9:52 (Give thanks to God at night.)

Mosiah 26:39 (Pray always and give thanks in all things.)

Doctrine and Covenants 98:1 (In everything give thanks.)

Doctrine and Covenants 59:20–21 (We offend God when we are ungrateful.)

See also "Ingratitude" in the Topical Guide.

Songs and Hymns

"We Thank Thee, O God, for a Prophet," *Hymns*, no. 196

"Father, Thy Children to Thee Now Raise," *Hymns*, no. 43

"Can a Little Child Like Me," *Sing with Me*, B–86

"My Heavenly Father Loves Me," *Sing with Me*, B–59

Other

The Gift, available through your meetinghouse library in either a 16mm film or videocassette version.

And let every man deal honestly, . . . that ye may be one, even as I have commanded you.
—*Doctrine and Covenants 51:9*

GOSPEL TRUTH

God commands that we be honest in all things. When we lie, cheat, or steal, we open ourselves wide to Satan's influence and close ourselves to God's influence. If we want to have the Spirit to guide and comfort us, we must be honest with God, with ourselves, and with other people.

IDEAS FOR LESSONS

Lesson 1: The Importance of Honesty

Tell this story to your family and discuss it with them.

"Recently, our grandson, Adam, was traveling with Sister Stone and me on a trip. . . . About noontime we stopped for lunch. When the waitress . . . gave me my change, I realized that she had charged me for only two sandwiches instead of three. . . . I felt this was a good time to talk to Adam about honesty, and so . . . I explained what had happened. . . .

"I said we could leave now and keep the extra change and no one would ever know the difference, or we could tell the girl that we still owed her for a sandwich. Our decision wasn't at all difficult to make when we decided that if we kept money that did not belong to us that we would be breaking the commandment, 'Thou shalt not steal.' . . .

"Adam and I approached the girl at the counter, and I explained to her that she had undercharged us. . . . She thanked us for telling her of the mistake. We continued on our way with a good feeling, and I am sure our Heavenly Father approved of what we had done." (O. Leslie Stone, "Be Honest," *Friend*, Jan. 1975, p. 7.)

Have a family member read this statement by Elder Mark E. Petersen and

invite each member to comment on it:

"We come to the point where faith and works meet each other. Here we ask ourselves: Do our works verify our faith? . . .

"Honesty, truth, virtue, and kindness are hallmarks of true Christianity. If we lack them, we can hardly say that we follow Christ.

"Whether it be lying, or cheating, or robbery or deception; whether it is in the home, in business, in sports, or in the classroom; dishonesty is completely foreign to the teachings of Jesus." (In Conference Report, Apr. 1982, pp. 19–20; or *Ensign*, May 1982, p. 15.)

To show what the Lord has said about being honest, look up some of the following scriptures and discuss them: Exodus 20:15, Ephesians 4:25, Doctrine and Covenants 51:9, Doctrine and Covenants 63:17, thirteenth article of faith.

- What are several manifestations of dishonesty? (Lying, cheating, stealing.)

Read Proverbs 6:16–19. Discuss how many of the sins listed are associated with dishonesty. Help your family realize that dishonesty is at the root of almost every other sin and that they cannot receive the blessings of the gospel if they are dishonest.

Ask each family member to recall an incident in his life when he made the decision to be honest. After he shares the experience, have him tell how it made him feel. Express your desire to try harder to be honest in everything you do and challenge your family to do the same.

Lesson 2: Resisting the Temptation to Lie

Ask each member of your family to give a definition of a lie. Then compare your definitions to Elder Marvin J. Ashton's: "A lie is *any* communication given to another with the intent to deceive" (in Conference Report,

Apr. 1982, p. 10; or *Ensign*, May 1982, p. 9).

Discuss Elder Ashton's definition. Explain that we can effectively communicate a lie without ever speaking a word. A nod of the head or just keeping silent can deceive.

• What are some ways we can deceive? (Recommending a questionable business investment, pretending not to hear mother call, using flattery to get our way, or withholding important facts.)

For the next activity, you will need to have asked one member of your family in advance to answer each question you will ask falsely. Ask that member a simple question—for example, "Where were you just before we began family home evening?" As he answers falsely, wrap a long string or yarn around him once. Then ask him a follow-up question—for example, "Why were you there?" As he answers falsely again, wrap the string around him once more. Continue to ask him follow-up questions, wrapping the string around him each time he gives a false answer. Explain that you asked the person to give wrong answers to show how one lie leads to another and how quickly we can become trapped by lies.

Have each person describe one or more situations where it is easy to tell a lie. As each situation is given, list reasons why it might be tempting to lie. Your list may include such reasons as to avoid embarrassment, to flatter, to gain advantage, to destroy others, and to excuse poor performance.

Discuss how easy it is to tell a lie. Point out that some lies seem bigger than others, but even the smallest lie is a sin.

Read Doctrine and Covenants 42:21 to show how serious a sin lying is. Be sure the members of your family understand that they can repent of any lies they may have already told. Encourage them to watch for situations where they might be tempted to lie, and to be sure they choose to tell the truth.

Lesson 3: Resisting the Temptation to Cheat

Relate to your family the following experience of a seminary teacher:

"I had stressed the need for honesty, explaining to my students that many times we don't even know our integrity is being tested. . . .

"So my class should have been prepared for the snap quiz I gave them that Thursday afternoon. It was a twenty-question, true-or-false test covering material we had discussed during the week. They finished the test just as the bell rang for dismissal.

"Later that evening I very carefully graded each paper, recording the score in my grade book but leaving no marks on the papers.

"When the class assembled the next morning, I passed the papers back and, as usual, asked that each student grade his own paper. . . .

" 'Please count five off for each one missed and subtract the total from one hundred,' I instructed. 'Your scores please.'

" 'John?'

" '85.'

" 'Susan?'

" '95.'

" 'Harold?'

" '80.'

" 'Arnold?'

" '90.'

" 'Mary?'

"The response could hardly be heard: '45.'

"I went on, putting the grades in my grade book, carefully recording each oral report next to the grade I had recorded the night before. The comparison was revealing.

"A stillness settled on the class when I explained what I had done. . . .

" 'This was a different kind of test. This test was a test for honesty. Were you true or false? I noticed that many of you looked at Mary when she announced her score of 45. Mary, if you don't mind, would you please stand up? I want each of you to know that in my book Mary just achieved the highest score in the class. You make me feel very proud, Mary.'

"Mary looked up rather timidly at first, then her eyes glistened as she broke into a smile and rose to her feet. I had never seen Mary stand so tall." (Wayne B. Lynn, "True . . . or . . . False," *New Era*, Sept. 1978, p. 11.)

Discuss what the seminary students who cheated lost or gained and what Mary lost or gained.

Prepare a slip of paper with one of these phrases written on each one: *at home, at school, at church, in the neighborhood, at work, at the store, at play.* Let each person draw a slip, read the phrase, and lead a discussion on how cheating occurs in that situation. Help your family members realize that anything they might gain by cheating is always outweighed by what they will lose by cheating. Challenge your family to be honest at all times.

Lesson 4: Resisting the Temptation to Steal

Write the word *Stop* on a large piece of paper and attach it to a door in the room. Ask your family to pretend that eternal life with Heavenly Father is beyond that door. Ask them to name some of the actions that could keep them from going through that door.

Read Doctrine and Covenants 42:20 to discover one of these actions. Discuss why stealing is so serious.

Discuss whether stealing once will keep them from going though the door. Be sure they understand that, if a person repents and stops stealing, he will be able to go through.

Write, "Thou shalt not steal," (Exodus 20:15) on a paper. Place it

HUMILITY

inside an envelope. Tell your family that you have a message from the Lord to them. Have someone read the message. Point out that, though given long ago, this commandment is intended for each person in your family now.

Consider the following situations together. Point out how easy it may be to think of reasons or excuses that keep us from realizing that we are stealing.

1. Mr. Watson brings home stamps, pencils, and paper clips from the office. He reasons that he is underpaid anyway, and no one will ever miss them.

2. A woman does not pay an honest income tax. She feels the tax laws are unfair.

3. Renee takes change from her mother's purse to buy treats for her friends. She reasons that her mother wants her to make friends.

Have your family name a few other ways that we might be tempted to steal, even though we do not consider ourselves thieves.

RESOURCES

Scriptures

Alma 7:19-20 (God is honest and just in all things.)
Ether 3:12 (God is a God of truth.)
Moses 4:4 (Satan is the father of lies.)
2 Nephi 28:8 (Satan tries to make us think there is no harm in lying a little.)
2 Corinthians 4:2 (Paul renounces dishonesty.)
Doctrine and Covenants 136:20 (Keep all pledges.)
Doctrine and Covenants 136:25 (Return what you borrow.)
Doctrine and Covenants 136:26 (Return what you find.)
Proverbs 12:22 (They that deal truly are God's delight.)
See also "Honesty" in the Topical Guide.

Songs and Hymns

"Shall the Youth of Zion Falter?" *Hymns*, no. 157.
"Dare to Do Right," *Sing with Me*, B–81.

Other

Gospel Principles, "Honesty," chapter 31.

Be thou humble; and the Lord thy God shall lead thee by the hand, and give thee answer to thy prayers.
—Doctrine and Covenants 112:10

GOSPEL TRUTH

Humility is a feeling that comes when we realize how much we depend on our Heavenly Father. We show humility by being teachable and by serving our fellowmen. Great blessings come to us when we are humble.

IDEAS FOR LESSONS

Lesson 1: What Is Humility?

Make wordstrips describing what humility is and is not. For example, humility is: teachable, loving, dependent on the Lord, obedient to God, gracious. It is not: proud, arrogant, boastful, self-depreciating, weak, lacking confidence. Prepare a chart as follows:

Humility Is	Humility Is Not

As each person chooses a wordstrip, discuss what each means and place it in the appropriate column. Discuss the differences between being truly humble and belittling oneself.

Read Mosiah 4:19.

• In what way are we all beggars?

Explain that real humility begins when we understand our true relationship to Heavenly Father. When we know that we owe everything to him, we realize that our achievements and possessions are not our own.

• Does this mean we should belittle ourselves or feel worthless?

Point out that, knowing that we are important to our Heavenly Father and that he is willing to help us, we can be confident.

Together make a list of achievements and successes of the members of your family, including at least one for each person. For example, one child might have a musical talent or a gift for making friends. Perhaps someone has won a place on a sports team or written a beautiful poem. After you have finished this list, give a word of praise for each item on the list. You might mention how hard each person had to work for each achievement listed.

Ask each person to tell who is responsible for his achievement or ability. For example, a child might tell how he worked for the achievement he listed (for example, "It took a lot of time to learn how to play soccer well enough to make the team, and I had to miss out on a lot of other activities to practice").

Then have him talk about other people who helped make his success possible (for example, "Dad taught me the rules of the game, and Mark practiced with me on Saturdays. Mom let my chores wait whenever I had a game"). Last, have him tell how Heavenly Father is ultimately responsible for this achievement (for example, "I can play soccer because Heavenly Father blessed me with a strong, healthy body. And our family has enough material blessings that I can afford to spend some time in such an enjoyable way").

Point out that being humble does not mean denying our achievements. But it does mean acknowledging the source of our blessings. Challenge your family to develop a humble spirit by remembering that all good things in our lives come from Heavenly Father.

Lesson 2: The Savior's Example of Humility

To help your family understand how the Savior showed humility, discuss these:

• Whom did he honor in all his actions? (See John 6:38 and John 5:30.)

• How did he treat everyone, including the poor, the sick, the lonely, the repentant sinner? (See Luke 4:18; Matthew 14:14; John 8:11.)

Have your family name other specific times when the Savior showed humility. (See Luke 23:1–9.)

Read the parable in Luke 18:9–14 and discuss how the differences between the Pharisee and the publican can help us define humility.

List things family members can do to develop Christlike humility. Set a goal and work on one thing at a time, individually or as a family.

Lesson 3: Blessings of Being Humble

To discover the great blessings the Lord has promised the humble, have each person read one or more of the following scriptures and tell what blessings the humble will receive: Doctrine and Covenants 112:10, 136:32, 67:10, 12:8, and 1:28; 3 Nephi 12:2; Ether 12:26–27.

Have each person choose his favorite scripture, write it on a card, and decide at least one way he will practice humility during the coming week. Family members may wish to memorize their scripture.

RESOURCES

Scriptures

Psalm 34:18 (The Lord is near those with broken hearts and contrite spirits.)
Isaiah 57:15 (The Lord dwells with those with humble spirits.)
Mosiah 4:11 (Humble yourselves and be steadfast in the faith.)
See also "Humility, Humble" in the Topical Guide.

Songs and Hymns

"Father Up Above," Sing with Me, A–14.
"More Holiness Give Me," Hymns, no. 114.
"In Humility, Our Savior," Hymns, no. 49.

SENSE OF HUMOR

A merry heart doeth good like a medicine.
—Proverbs 17:22

GOSPEL TRUTH

Good humor truly is medicine to the soul. Humor can ease tension, relieve uncomfortable or embarrassing situations, change attitudes, generate love and understanding, and add sparkle to life. A properly developed sense of humor is sensitive to others' feelings and is flavored with kindness and understanding.

IDEAS FOR LESSONS

Lesson 1: Humor Helps Us Face Problems

Discuss the following examples:

In January of 1847 the Saints endured severe trials at Winter Quarters. They had been brutally forced from their homes and were suffering from cold, starvation, and the loss of loved ones. In the midst of their sorrow came a revelation to help prepare them for their journey west. Read Doctrine and Covenants 136:28–29. Explain that the Lord wants us to feel joy even during hardships and trials.

Describe how a pressure cooker works. (The sealed pot builds up a tremendous amount of steam inside it in order to speed up the cooking process. As a safety measure, however, it releases excess steam through a safety valve, which keeps the cooker from exploding.) Point out that pressures and problems can build up in all of us until we feel like exploding in anger or tears. One safety valve the Lord has given us is a sense of humor. Discuss how humor can release frustrations and put problems in a different light. Tell the following experience or share one of your own:

A family had worked and saved for a long time for a family vacation at a beautiful seaside resort. After they had arrived, three of the children became very ill with chicken pox, making it impossible to sightsee, spend time at nearby beaches, or return home on schedule. The family spent most of the vacation in a hotel room, missing many places they had hoped to see. Instead of letting this ruin their vacation, they saw the humor in their plight. The boys decided they were probably the only children there with a lumpy sunburn. Another child joked that he was awfully young to have such a terrible case of acne. They also discovered that they could learn many interesting things about the place from their hotel window.

Discuss how this family might have been miserable without a sense of humor to relieve the pressure of their experience.

• How did Proverbs 17:22 apply in this situation? As a family, try to find humor in a problem you are facing now. Encourage family members to help one another see the humor in future problems.

Lesson 2: An Appropriate Sense of Humor

Help family members understand that humor must be appropriate to fulfill its proper purpose.

Read the following from Elder Richard L. Evans: "There is both dignified and undignified humor. There is raucous, loud-mouthed humor, uncouth humor. There is evil, offensive humor. And there is high-minded, delightful humor." (*Richard Evans' Quote Book* [Salt Lake City: Publishers Press, 1971], p. 221.) Discuss this and determine what your family considers appropriate humor. Stress that humor that degrades, embarrasses, or is based on sarcasm or indecent situations is inappropriate. We should never make fun of another's physical infirmities or handicaps, ethnic or racial differences, the sanctity of the body, or sacred things.

Help family members understand that even people in important positions in the Church see humor in serious

matters without making light of spiritual things. Explain that we, too, can be light-hearted without being light-minded or silly. Tell the following experience:

"On one occasion, President [Spencer W.] Kimball spoke for the First Presidency in giving a certain difficult assignment to Elder [Neal A.] Maxwell and Elder James E. Faust. Elder Maxwell responded, 'President Kimball—surely you can find better men than the two of us for such a challenging task.' With a gentle smile, President Kimball replied, 'Well, while we're looking for two better men, would you two mind going ahead with the job?'" (Bruce C. Hafen, "Elder Neal A. Maxwell: An Understanding Heart," *Ensign*, Feb. 1982, p. 13).

Give each family member a sheet of paper divided into two columns with the following headings:

Appropriate Humor	Inappropriate Humor

During the coming week have them evaluate humor they observe at work, school, on television, and among family members. Have them generally describe what they observe in either the appropriate or inappropriate column. The following week, discuss their observations, evaluating the effect the humor had on those involved. Challenge each family member to strive to use only appropriate humor.

Lesson 3: Humor Can Create Happy Family Memories

Plan a "The Funniest Thing That Ever Happened to Me" party. Make

an invitation or poster decorated with a smiling face or cartoons cut from magazines or newpapers. Instruct family members to be prepared to tell about the funniest thing that ever happened to them. Make it an evening of fun by sharing the experiences, singing activity and nonsense songs, and playing a game or two if desired.

Lesson 4: Humor Can Ease Embarrassing Situations

Tell the following: Entertainer Will Rogers' lariat once fell around his legs as he performed before a large audience. Instead of being embarrassed, he said, "A rope isn't so bad to be tangled up in if it isn't around your neck!" (Spencer Johnson, *The Value of Humor: The Story of Will Rogers* [San Diego, California: Value Communication, Inc., 1977], p. 41.) Discuss how this embarrassing situation was eased because Will Rogers was able to recognize the humor in the situation and laugh at himself. Will Rogers said on another occasion: "When people see the funny side of what they are doing they aren't afraid to make a mistake. They think more clearly and they like themselves a lot better." (*The Value of Humor*, p. 45.)

Discuss experiences you and other family members have had where humor eased an embarrassing situation.

Role-play some possible embarrassing situations, and let family members practice responses that find humor in the situations. For example: At a party someone points out that you have on one brown shoe and one black shoe. Possible response: "I have another pair at home just like them."

Discuss Proverbs 17:22 and tell how being able to laugh at yourself can ease embarrassment. The family could make a poster to remind them of this.

JOURNALS

Lesson 5: Record Humorous Experiences

Read a humorous experience from your journal or someone else's. Discuss how remembering this experience has brought you happiness and helped you understand yourself or the other person better. Encourage family members to record humorous experiences in their journals.

You might obtain a special journal or notebook and start a family humor book to record the family's humorous experiences for all to enjoy. Young children could draw pictures or cartoons to illustrate. Invite family members to record past humorous experiences they feel should be remembered. Leave the journal where it can be written in and read from often. Occasionally, you may read from it during family home evening.

RESOURCES

Scriptures

2 Nephi 2:25 (Men are that they might have joy.)
See also "Laughter" in the Topical Guide.

Song and Hymns

"Smiles," *Sing with Me*, D–5.

Every person should keep a journal and every person can keep a journal.
—President Spencer W. Kimball

GOSPEL TRUTHS

A journal is a continuing record of meaningful experiences that affect our lives. Through his prophets, the Lord has commanded each of us to keep a journal. As we record our activities and feelings, we can more clearly see the Lord's influence in our lives.

IDEAS FOR LESSONS

Lesson 1: Why Keep a Journal?

Help each family member understand how a journal can bless his life by relating an experience from your journal, by inviting a grandparent or other family member who keeps a journal to share an experience, or by reading the following entries.

Journal Entry One. "My mother had a serious heart condition. She was told if she ever had a baby, she would probably die. But mother felt strongly she should have a baby. When I was only nine weeks old, my mother died. She loved me enough to willingly give her life for me. Those who knew mother best found it painful to talk about her, so I never learned much about her. When I was seventeen, my father gave me one of my dearest possessions. It was a journal my mother had written. She had kept it each day for one short year of her life. I had in my hands one year of my mother's life! She had been a school teacher in Wyoming that year, and through her own words she became for me a real person at last. She cried, she struggled, she laughed, she grumbled, she learned of her heart condition, she met and fell in love with my father, and I shared it all with her! That record, that precious, loved record—it seemed to me at that time that it was all I had of her." (See "For Your Remembrance: A Presentation on Record Keeping" [audiovisual presentation,

1975 MIA June Conference].)

Journal Entry Two (from a child's journal). "Uncle Bart conducted Grandpa's funeral. He read some words Grandpa had written to his grandchildren. Grandpa said he knew the Church is very true. I love Grandpa very much. I know he is living with Heavenly Father. Grandpa is very busy and happy. I know I will live with him someday."

The Savior chastised those who failed to record spiritual events (see Spencer W. Kimball, "The Angels May Quote from It," *New Era*, Oct. 1975, p. 5).

Each family member should understand that he or she has a responsibility to keep a journal. President Spencer W. Kimball said:

"Those who keep a personal journal are more likely to keep the Lord in remembrance in their daily lives" ("President Kimball Speaks Out on Personal Jounals," *New Era*, Dec. 1980, p. 27).

To help family members understand why the Lord and his prophets have asked us to keep records, read and discuss 2 Nephi 25:23.

Allow family members to express their feelings about some special personal experience that will be of value to them and their children. Distribute papers and pens, and suggest they write it down as a possible journal entry. During the week you might remind family members to think of what things they should write about in their journals.

Lesson 2: How Do I Begin a Journal?

Help each family member obtain or make a journal. This may be a special purchased journal, a three-ring binder with paper, or a spiral notebook. Journals may be personalized by decorating the cover or putting photographs in them. Let each family member personalize his journal in his own way.

Ask each family member to set aside a

LEARNING

certain time each week, each day, or every other day to write in his journal. Or, set aside time as a family to write in journals. Sundays or early weekday mornings may be good times.

Suggest that family members begin by writing a brief description of themselves—including age, grade, physical traits, and feelings about beginning a journal.

Lesson 3: What Should I Write?

Share ideas about what should be included in a personal journal. Encourage discussion by asking questions like these: What would you like to remember about yourself? What has the Lord done for you? What would you like to tell your children or grandchildren about yourself?

Discuss the following suggestion by President Spencer W. Kimball:

"Your journal should contain your true self rather than a picture of you when you are 'made up' for a public performance. . . . The truth should be told, but we should not emphasize the negative." ("The Angels," *New Era*, Oct. 1975, p. 5.)

To help family members understand how to write in their journals, read the following from the journal of Elder Parley P. Pratt, one of the Council of the Twelve in the early days of this dispensation:

"When I first entered the dungeon there were some twenty men, mostly heads of families, who had been torn from their families in those awful times, and thrust into prison. It was not only crowded to suffocation, without a chair, stool, bench, bed, furniture or window light, but just then completely filled with smoke from a fire which was lighted in a stove without a pipe, or any conductor for the smoke to pass out, except at the crevices between the timbers, where the winter storm was passing in. When my guard conducted me to the door of this miserable cell it grated on

its huge hinges and opened like the pit yawning to receive me; a volume of thick smoke issued forth and seemed to forbid my entrance; but urged . . . by bayonets and loaded pistols in the hands of savage beings, I endeavored to enter." (*Autobiography of Parley P. Pratt*, 5th ed. [Salt Lake City: Deseret Book Co. 1961], pp. 233–34.)

Discuss what makes this entry seem vivid and real (details, descriptions using the senses and feelings).

Encourage family members to faithfully record their experiences and feelings in their journals.

RESOURCES

Scriptures

3 Nephi 23:6–13 (Jesus saw and added to the records of the Nephites.)
Doctrine and Covenants 128:7 (Records are kept in heaven.)
Moses 1:40 (Moses was commanded to write the Lord's words.)
Moses 6:5 (Book of remembrance was kept by Adam's descendants.)
See also "Record Keeping" in the Topical Guide.

Songs and Hymns

"The Golden Plates," *Sing with Me*, B–57.

Whatever principle of intelligence we attain unto in this life, it will rise with us in the resurrection.
—Doctrine and Covenants 130:18

GOSPEL TRUTH

Our purpose on earth is to gain the knowledge and experience that will prepare us for godhood. Great joy comes as we learn to discern good from evil and gain mastery over ourselves and the earth. In this way, we can gain a deep appreciation for the beauties and intricacies of creation.

IDEAS FOR LESSONS

Lesson 1: Learning Is Important

Discuss the following ideas to show the importance of gaining knowledge:

1. Perfect knowledge is one of God's attributes (see 2 Nephi 9:20).

2. The commandment to study and learn is repeated many times in the Doctrine and Covenants (D&C 88:118, 130:18–19, and 131:6).

3. Peter said knowledge was necessary to become like Heavenly Father (2 Peter 1:5–9).

Discuss how learning can help us become more like our Father in Heaven.

Lesson 2: Priorities in Learning

Teach family members that the greatest joy and growth come from learning and obeying gospel truths.

Have two children get under separate blankets, each with a flashlight. Ask one child to find his way to another room or to another place in the room. The only person he can ask for help is the child under the other blanket. Point out that this is what it is like to go through life without the help of Heavenly Father and the gospel to guide us. This is what Jesus meant when he referred to "blind leaders of the blind" (Matthew 15:14). Contrast the darkness of finding our own way with the security of being led by someone who sees and understands. Let someone in the light guide the child under the blanket to the goal. When we walk in the light, we learn faster and avoid many painful mistakes.

Teach that the principles God reveals never change, but what man discovers is subject to constant change. Read 2 Nephi 9:28-29. Discuss why it is important to learn and obey gospel truths and then place all other knowledge in that framework. Read Mosiah 4:9. Discuss what could happen if a scientist suddenly had God's power without God's love and wisdom.

You may wish to share an experience where you learned to trust the gospel truths when they conflicted with the teachings of men. Bear testimony that holding fast to gospel principles heightens our power to learn, our ability to discern the value of what we learn, and our appreciation of those truths.

Lesson 3: Learn to Enjoy Learning

Help family members enjoy learning by teaching the power of careful observation. No other single skill has produced more scientific discoveries than this one. Use one or more of the following activities:

1. Take your children on a nature walk or to a farm or zoo. Or go bird-watching. Ask them to observe closely. How are two leaves, plants, or trees alike? How are they different? How are two animals or birds alike? Different? Encourage family members to sharpen every sense, noting differences in what they see, hear, feel, and smell. Challenge older children to discover why differences are important. For example, what can a giraffe do that a horse can't? What can a duck do that a sparrow can't?

2. Have each member of the family mark off one square foot of ground. Have a contest to see who can find

the most insects, rocks, leaves, and so forth in that small area.

3. Select a book from the library that explains the parts of insects or flowers. During a family home evening, have family members observe flowers or insects under a microscope or magnifying glass. Make a game of seeing how many parts each family member can identify. Tell why each part is important and how it functions.

Conclude the activity by inviting family members to share their feelings of delight and reverence for God's creations. Encourage them to develop observation skills in every aspect of their lives.

Lesson 4: Sharing What We Know

Plan one or more family home evenings where children can demonstrate something they have learned from their studies. They might act out a historical event, describe a character from a novel, recite a poem, perform and explain a scientific experiment, or describe a famous person or place they are studying. Praise each family member for his contribution and accomplishments.

Lesson 5: The Classics

Note: This activity may require more than one evening to complete.

As a family choose one of the world's masterpieces of art, music, or literature to learn about. Then do the following:

1. Find out about the life of the writer, composer or artist, and report on it in family home evening. Note the creator's years of preparation.

2. Study the work itself. What patterns can you find? Are melodies, colors, textures, or messages repeated? See if you can discover why the work is considered a masterpiece. Study what others have written about the work. Memorize lines from the play, story, or poem.

Act out parts of the play. Learn to play or sing the musical themes. If possible, find an inexpensive print of the painting and display it in your home. Try to draw a picture like the one you're studying.

3. If possible, attend a concert, performance, or showing of the work you are studying. Make the experience as creative and rewarding as possible.

Prepare a special treat to eat after studying the work. Share your excitement about what you are learning as a family.

Lesson 6: Learning Despite Handicaps

The following experience can be used as the basis for a discussion about learning and handicaps:

Helvi Temiseva, a Finnish girl, was struck with polio at age eight. She read many books at home and kept up with her studies. At age eleven, she suffered a severe attack of rheumatoid arthritis that stiffened the joints of her already crippled body. Helvi struggled through long months of illness and operations to keep up in school.

At age twenty-one, Helvi joined the Church and realized that she was a daughter of God with limitless potential. With a thirst for knowledge, Helvi continued studying and became a translator. Her work brought her to Utah, where she tried to enroll in college. But since she had never graduated from high school, she had to return to Finland for two years to finish her education. She finally passed the rigorous graduation examinations, doing well in all thirteen subjects.

At BYU she studied English, Hebrew, Greek, and religion, and went on to earn a master's degree in linguistics. With the help of many friends, Helvi proved that even someone with a severe handicap could experience the joy of learning. "Who would expect an almost totally helpless arthritic to graduate from high school without the

LISTENING

aid of teachers, to attend college, to speak several languages, to travel across oceans and continents, and to earn a living as a professional translator?" (Adapted from Paul C. Richards, "Helvi Temiseva—Victor in a Wheelchair," *New Era*, Oct. 1973, p. 27.)

RESOURCES

Scriptures

John 5:39 (Search the scriptures.)
John 14:26 (The Holy Ghost will teach all things.)
1 Corinthians 2:11–14 (The natural man cannot understand the things of God.)
1 Nephi 19:23 (Scriptures are for our profit and learning.)
2 Nephi 9:42 (Do not be puffed up because of learning.)
Alma 26:21–22 (The righteous will learn the mysteries of God.)
Doctrine and Covenants 19:23 (Learn of God and have peace.)
Doctrine and Covenants 90:15 (Study and learn.)
Doctrine and Covenants 130:18–19 (What we learn here helps us in the hereafter.)
See also "Learn, Learning" in the Topical Guide.

Songs and Hymns

"Truth Reflects upon Our Senses," *Hymns*, no. 188.
"Oh Say, What Is Truth?" *Hymns*, no. 143.

He that hath ears to hear, let him hear.
—Matthew 11:15

GOSPEL TRUTH

Listening with love involves trying to understand what a person is feeling, as well as what he is saying. With constant practice, we can learn how to listen with love, thus improving family relationships.

IDEAS FOR LESSONS

Lesson 1: The Importance of Listening

• Why is every person worth listening to?

Read the following scriptures: Doctrine and Covenants 18:10; Mosiah 27:4; and Doctrine and Covenants 38:24–25.

• How does listening to another person show love and respect for him? (It lets him know that we want to know what he thinks—that we value his opinion.)

Help your family realize the need to listen to one another by doing the following: Have a family member come forward, stand directly in front of you, and tell something that happened to him that day. As he begins to talk, put your hands over your ears. If he stops talking, say, "Keep talking; I'm listening." Then hum or walk away from him as he continues to talk.

Discuss the feelings of both individuals in this situation. Point out that hearing is not the same as listening. Then discuss how people can tell when they are listening to one another. Have family members list the signs of real listening. Let them tell how they felt when someone really listened to them.

Lesson 2: Learning to Listen

Use one or more of the following activities to help your family learn to listen:

To help family members realize that

---

real listening means understanding a person's feelings, as well as his words, do the "I Feel" pantomime: Have each family member pantomime a particular feeling—happiness, sadness, anger, shyness, and so forth. Then have the other family members guess the feeling being pantomimed. Explain that looking at the speaker helps us understand his feelings through facial expressions, hand gestures, or other nonverbal means. Encourage family members to use their eyes as well as their ears this week to listen to each other.

Explain that you are going to read a verse from the Bible and then ask questions about it. Read Mark 4:1 aloud to the famly, making sure they know the pronoun *he* refers to Jesus. Then ask:

• Where was Jesus teaching?

• Had he taught there before? How do you know from this verse?

• Were there few or many people there?

• What use did he make of a ship while he taught?

• Where were the people?

If necessary, reread the verse, encouraging family members to listen more carefully for details.

Read the following:

"1. Listen to your child . . . with all of you. Rather than thinking of what to tell him, listen to what he is telling you. Listen patiently to the end, until he has emptied his heart. Encourage him, looking directly into his eyes, with 'I see,' 'Um-hum,' 'Is that right?' 'And then what?' Listen, and savor the joy of having this child.

"2. Listen to your spouse . . . with all of you. Not while pondering a business problem or tonight's dinner or what is wrong. Look into his/her face, see the beauty there, cherish the expression, the eyes, the mouth; feel the care, the concerns. Listen with understanding and love. Listen.

"3. Listen to your parents . . . with all of you. Listen to their direction, their counsel, their remembrances and reflections. Listen to the wonder of their age, and respect and honor them. Listen to them. It is your sweetest gift.

"4. Listen to a friend . . . with all of you. Listen to his worries and his frustrations, to his thoughts and joys. Feel with him, ache with him, be excited with him. Be the receptacle for his pent-up emotions. Just listen." (Winnifred C. Jardine, "Listen with All of You," *Ensign*, Feb. 1974, p. 51.)

Discuss what it means to "listen with all of you." Ask a family member to tell of a personal experience that has special meaning to him. Ask the rest of the family to practice listening with all of themselves—their ears, their minds, their hearts.

Record the voices of your children and play them back to allow them to listen to their own voices.

Lesson 3: Learning to Understand One Another

Several exercises can help your family members become more effective listeners. (See *Love Makes Our House a Home* [family home evening manual, 1974], pp. 163–69 or *Delight in the Law of the Lord* [family home evening manual, 1982], pp. 44–45, if they are available.)

Exercise One—Parroting—listening to hear exact words: Divide into pairs. Have one person make a statement, and have the partner repeat what he said. Example—Johnny: Ice cream is my favorite dessert; Sarah: Ice cream is your favorite dessert.

Practice parroting for several minutes. Then ask if family members listened well enough to catch every word their partner said.

Exercise Two—Paraphrasing—restating the message in different words: Example—Marie: At first the party looked like a bore, but it turned out

to be a lot of fun. Jacob: So you really didn't think you would have a good time at the party, but afterwards you were glad you went. Right?

Again, divide into pairs and take turns paraphrasing.

Exercise Three: Explain that when we listen to someone, we would not usually parrot or paraphrase everything that person says. But these two exercises can make us more aware of what others say. Now the family is ready to practice listening with love and understanding. In pairs, have one person make a statement on something he has strong feelings about. The second person tries to understand how the first person feels about what he said. Do this several times.

Lesson 4: Listening with the Heart

Read and discuss James 1:19. Explain that, when someone is upset or feeling other strong emotions, he is often unable to listen to counsel. At times like this, we need to be especially understanding. For example, imagine that mother has had a terrible day. Everything has been going wrong. If her husband listens to her problems sympathetically and says something like "It has been a tough day for you, hasn't it?" her negative emotions may disappear. But if he says, "For Pete's sake, can't you see that you need to get better organized?" or, "When will you learn to handle the kids without getting so upset?" her problem and her bad feelings will probably increase. Have each person recall a time he was upset and needed a listening ear. Discuss what responses he might have needed at that time.

Lesson 5: Listening in Church Meetings

Help family members understand what it means to listen by the Spirit by reading 3 Nephi 11:3–6. Note that the Saints heard the voice twice without understanding it. Then, the third time, they "open[ed] their ears to hear it" and finally heard and understood.

We, too, must open our ears and listen by the Spirit to hear what the Lord has for us in Church.

Tell this experience:

Brother Green was having trouble listening to an inexperienced counselor in the bishopric speak. The counselor read slowly and haltingly. But, as Brother Green prayed for help to listen by the Spirit, he heard an answer to a gospel question that he had never understood before. He knew the Lord had blessed him for listening with his heart. (See John A. Green, "A Lesson from My Conscience," *Ensign*, Apr. 1981, p. 43.)

Assign family members to listen closely during the next sacrament meeting and write a sentence or two telling what each speaker was trying to say. Compare results at the next family home evening.

RESOURCES

Scriptures

Proverbs 1:5 (A wise man will hear, and will increase learning.)
1 Nephi 19:24 (Hear the words of the prophet.)
2 Nephi 9:31 (Woe to the deaf who will not hear the things of God.)
Doctrine and Covenants 1:14 (Those who will not listen will be cut off.)
See also "Communication" in the Topical Guide.

Songs and Hymns

"Come, Listen to a Prophet's Voice," *Hymns*, no. 46.
"The Still Small Voice," *Sing with Me*, B–92.

Other

Are You Listening? available through your meetinghouse library in either a 16mm film or videocassette version.

MANNERS

Courtesy is a natural outgrowth of the refining influence of the Spirit of the Lord.
—Elder Bruce R. McConkie

GOSPEL TRUTH

We practice good manners when we show love, respect, and gratitude to those around us. Our Heavenly Father is pleased when we use good manners in our associations with all of his children.

IDEAS FOR LESSONS

Lesson 1: The Importance of Good Manners

Write a list of polite, courteous words and phrases on a chalkboard or a piece of paper. Discuss with your family why they are words which show courtesy, politeness, and good manners. You may use the following examples or any which apply in your area:

Please.
May I?
You are welcome.
Thank you.
Take my seat.
Let me share.
Excuse me.
You go first.
Let me help.

Use questions such as the following to help your family discuss why good manners are so important in our lives:

- What are some qualities of people you know who show good manners? (Thoughtful, kind, loving, respectful, grateful.)
- Why are good manners more than just words? (They come from feelings in our hearts.)

Point out that the words on the list actually say something more important than they appear to be saying. They say "I like you;" "I care about you;" "I respect you;" "I am grateful to you." (See 1 Peter 3:8.)

Ask family members to describe situations in which they can use the words on the list.

- Why do these words, if spoken sincerely, always create good feelings?

Read and discuss the statement by Elder Bruce R. McConkie found at the beginning of this lesson.

To help your family understand the difference that good manners can make in their lives, write the statements below on slips of paper and place them in a hat or bowl. Have each family member in turn draw one out and give his ideas of how good manners could bring about that result. Invite family members to add more statements of their own.

Create a loving atmosphere at home.
Improve relationships with other people.
Make a business organization run more smoothly.
Make a better community (or country or world).
Strengthen priesthood quorums or Church classes.
Help Church activities and projects to succeed.

Lesson 2: Practicing Good Manners at a Family Dinner

Plan a special dinner at which your family can practice good table manners. Make assignments as needed. Plan a menu of favorite family foods (they need not be expensive). Plan to set the table using proper rules for table setting, your best tablecloth, dishes, and decorations.

Explain and demonstrate the good manners that you want your family to learn. Have all family members practice them during the dinner.

You could repeat this kind of dinner as many times as you wish to help your family make good table manners a habit.

Lesson 3: A Good Manners Quiz

Write down some situations your family members might face which would require them to use good manners,

along with three or four possible solutions to the situations.

Go over the situations with your family and choose which of the answers show good manners. (More than one answer may be right.)

The following are examples:

1. Mary is supposed to clear the dishes after dinner every evening. Usually she forgets. One night she does a good job without a reminder. Her parents should (a) remark to each other that Mary finally remembered, (b) avoid compliments because it's just a job she's supposed to do, (c) make special notice, calling Mary's actions to the attention of the family, (d) tell Mary they are very pleased with what she has done.

2. You are on a bus or streetcar. After you take the last seat, an elderly woman gets on the bus. You should (a) get up and offer her your seat, (b) hide your face in a magazine or newspaper, (c) let her stand because she'll soon find a seat, (d) rationalize by thinking, "First come, first serve."

3. Mother has fixed your favorite dinner dish. You are the first to serve yourself. You should (1) take the biggest piece, (2) take a medium piece and hope there is some left, (3) leave the biggest for someone else because others like the dish also, (4) decide that someone should have the largest piece, so why not you.

Encourage family members to think of other situations that may be a problem to your family and decide what would be the courteous thing to do. If you do not have the answer to a situation, assign a family member to find it.

Lesson 4: A Good Manners Week

Ask a family member to knock at the door and come in as a visitor. Ask family members to treat this person as if he is a visitor to your home. Afterwards discuss this question: Do we

MARRIAGE

treat visitors in our home with more courtesy than we treat each other?

Ask family members to discuss why the home is the best place to practice good manners. You may want to summarize the discussion by pointing out that courtesy is often hardest to practice at home because family members are so familiar to us and because we are in so many types of situations with family members. It is at home, therefore, that we show whether we are truly courteous or not.

Set the following week as a Good Manners Week for your family. During this week, try to use good manners continually in your home. Encourage your family to make posters, wordstrips, table decorations, clever messages on bathroom mirrors, or other reminders to family members to be courteous.

RESOURCES

Scriptures

Matthew 7:12; 3 Nephi 14:12 (The Golden Rule.)
1 Corinthians 13:4; Moroni 7:45 (Charity suffereth long and is kind.)
Ephesians 4:31–32 (Be ye kind one to another.)
Galatians 5:22 (Fruit of the Spirit is love.)
See also "Courtesy" in the Topical Guide.

Songs and Hymns

"Be Polite," *Sing with Me,* D–6.
"Kindness Begins with Me," *Sing with Me,* B–49.
"Let Us Oft Speak Kind Words," *Hymns,* no. 94.

Marriage is ordained of God.
—*Doctrine and Covenants 49:15*

GOSPEL TRUTH

Marriage is designed of the Lord to allow men and women to create strong, happy homes for themselves and their posterity. All young people should plan and prepare for eternal marriage early in life so they can enjoy the blessings of this sacred covenant.

IDEAS FOR LESSONS

Lesson 1: Deciding Who and Where to Marry

- What happens to the surface of a still pond when you cast a pebble into it? (It ripples.)

Point out to family members that many of the decisions they make in their lives will have an effect similar to the effect of the pebble on the water. The effects of these decisions will continue on and on, touching other people's lives besides their own.

- What are some of these decisions? After discussion, read the following quotation:

"Probably the most consequential event in your lives takes place when you are united in marriage. It will have a far reaching effect upon your future. Like the ripples caused by a pebble cast upon a placid pool, the decision you make in regard to where, with whom, and by whom this event will take place will affect not only you, but the lives of many others, especially your children." (ElRay L. Christiansen, in Conference Report, Apr. 1974, p. 34; see also *Ensign,* May 1974, p. 25.)

- Why is temple marriage so important?
- How will it affect your life now and in the future?

Discuss how deciding early in your life that you want a temple marriage could help you make many correct decisions in the future.

Lesson 2: Blessings of Eternal Marriage

To help family members understand the blessings of eternal marriage, have them compare temple marriage and civil marriage.

To do this, you could write questions like the following on a chalkboard or on wordstrips. You could have two columns under the questions, one labeled "Temple Marriage" and one labeled "Civil Marriage." Have the family answer each question for both a temple and a civil marriage and put their answers in the appropriate column.

- What preparation is needed?
- Where will this marriage take place?
- Who performs the ceremony?
- How long will the marriage last?
- What will the people married in this way be doing throughout eternity?
- What will happen to the family after this life?

Compare the answers on each side of the chart.

Discuss the meaning of the statement, "Temple marriages make better marriages."

Lesson 3: Preparing for Eternal Marriage

To help family members understand that they must obey the specified law before they can receive any blessing, point out an important accomplishment of a family member such as graduation from school or college, a special award in Scouting, or ability to play a musical instrument. Ask the family member the following questions:

- Why did you want this accomplishment?
- What plans did you make to get it?
- What did you do to get it?

Display a picture of a temple and a sealing room. Discuss how obtaining the blessings of eternal marriage is similar in principle to obtaining anything worthwhile. We must desire it and plan and work for it. Emphasize that eternal marriage is far more precious and worth working for than almost anything else we do in life. Read the following statement of President Spencer W. Kimball on the doctrine of eternal marriage:

"Marriage by civil officers or local leaders is 'til death do you part,' and terminates with death. Only celestial marriage extends beyond the grave. . . .

"There is no bias nor prejudice in this doctrine. It is a matter of following a certain program to reach a definite goal. If you fail in following a program, you fail in attaining the goal. Even in college work, if you never registered properly, never attended your classes, never did the things which are required by the college, you would never receive your degree. Certainly you cannot expect the eternal program to be less exacting." ("The Importance of Celestial Marriage," *Ensign*, Oct. 1979, pp. 4–5.)

Discuss specific ways in which family members could prepare for an eternal marriage. (Do the things that will make them worthy to receive a temple recommend—pay tithing, support Church leaders, keep the Word of Wisdom.)

You could summarize these points under two headings on a chart: "What I Will Do," and "What I Won't Do." You could post this chart in a prominent place.

Each family member may want to have a picture of a temple in his room with the words "I want to be married in the temple" printed beside the picture.

Lesson 4: Visiting a Temple

If possible, your family could visit the grounds of a nearby temple, and family members could share their testimonies about and goals for temple marriage. Each member may want to

make a personal commitment there and record it in his journal.

If the parents have not yet been sealed, they may wish to set goals along with their children.

Lesson 5: Intelligent Dating

Discuss with your family some reasons for dating, and make a list of the reasons. They may include learning to get along with others, becoming better acquainted with other young people, spending leisure time in a fun way, learning about the person you might be considering marrying, and finding someone to marry.

Explain that Church leaders have told us that young people should wait until they are sixteen years of age to start dating. However, many young people are not ready or do not have the opportunity to date until some years later. This should not cause unnecessary worry or concern to parents or young people. Sooner or later, most everyone will have the opportunity to date.

- Which of the reasons for dating that you have listed would apply to young people between the ages of sixteen and nineteen?
- Which reasons would apply to those over nineteen?

Discuss what kinds of activities would best help people in each age group to accomplish their reasons for dating.

Point out that it has been said that you marry those you date. Since every member of the Church should be planning on a temple marriage, have your family decide on their own dating standards. These standards may include ideas such as dating only members of the Church, dressing modestly, never necking, and staying active in the Church. After your family has decided on the standards they wish to maintain, have family members write them in their journals or some other permanent place where they can be referred to often.

Lesson 6: Preparing to Become an Eternal Companion

Explain that being married in the temple does not guarantee that a couple will have a happy life together. A happy marriage requires preparation before the ceremony and work and commitment afterwards.

Discuss with your family some of the responsibilities that come to a man and to a woman when they are married.

- How could you prepare yourself before marriage for these responsibilities?

Think about and list some of the personal characteristics a person should bring to marriage, such as unconditional love, unselfishness, willingness to work, ability to take responsibility and be dependable, willingness to sacrifice. Discuss each of these characteristics and some reasons why they are necessary to a happy marriage.

- What could you do before marriage to develop these characteristics?

Suggest to your family that each person choose a specific characteristic to work on. For example, in order to develop an attitude of sacrifice which allows you to be more concerned for another's happiness than for your own, perhaps you could try to put certain needs of a family member or friend before your own. This will help you to better understand the kind of sacrifice that is necessary in an eternal marriage.

RESOURCES

Scriptures

Matthew 16:19 (Binding on earth and in heaven.)
Titus 2:4 (Teach young women to love their husbands.)
Doctrine and Covenants 42:22 (Thou shalt love thy wife.)
Doctrine and Covenants 49:15 (Marriage is ordained of God.)
Doctrine and Covenants 132:14–21

(Importance of the marriage covenant.)

See also "Marriage" in the Topical Guide.

Songs and Hymns

"Families Can Be Together Forever," *Supplement to More Songs for Children,* p. 1.

"I Love to See the Temple," *Supplement to More Songs for Children,* p. 4.

"There Is Beauty All Around," *Hymns,* no. 169.

Other

Gospel Principles, "Eternal Marriage," chapter 38.

Johnny Lingo, available through your meetinghouse library in a 16mm film, filmstrip, or videocassette version.

MEDIA

If there is anything virtuous, lovely, or of good report or praiseworthy, we seek after these things.
—*Thirteenth Article of Faith*

GOSPEL TRUTH

The word *media* as used here means public communication such as newspapers, magazines, radio and television broadcasts. The media offer much education and wholesome entertainment. Frequently, however, they also offer encouragement to sin. We can be happier and serve our Heavenly Father better if we choose to read, see, and hear only that which encourages virtue, purity, and kindness.

IDEAS FOR LESSONS

Lesson 1: Controlling the Media in Our Lives

Ask each family member to name someone he admires and wishes to be like. Discuss the idea that we tend to become like those we admire. We also tend to become like those we spend time with and watch closely.

Talk about some of the people your family watches and spends time with through television, movies, books, and other media.

- Would you want to become like them?

Discuss the influence that various types of media have on people. Point out the good that is available through them and also the bad.

Help your family understand that through these media they can be cheered up or depressed, calmed or made aggressive, uplifted or degraded. If they let evil thoughts and acts pour into their minds, they can even be influenced to sympathize with sin and to accept it.

Read and discuss the first part of Proverbs 23:7: "For as he thinketh in his heart, so is he."

To help your family decide how they can avoid the harmful effects of media

in their lives, read the following and decide as a family which of these people are likely to be influenced for good by the media:

1. Sister Anderson turns on the television as soon as she gets up and leaves it on all day. The children watch it after school until bedtime. The family frequently quarrels about which programs to watch.

2. Bill and Sherrie decided to go to a movie that had won many prestigious awards. They knew that it had some profanity and nudity, but their friends said it was too good to miss.

3. The Johnsons carefully select the shows they watch on television and discuss any important messages in the shows.

4. Marvin's friends sometimes give him pornographic magazines. He hides them in his room to look over in private.

5. Susan goes to the library often where she chooses books about people and events in history, different cultures, and poetry to fill her spare time.

Set some family standards and guidelines to help family members choose only quality media entertainment. Also plan some fun substitutes to use when such entertainment is not available.

Lesson 2: Recognizing What Is Good and What Is Evil

Show your family the scriptures in a plain box or bag, and a package of garbage that has been attractively wrapped. Allow them to choose which package they would like. Let them open both packages. Discuss why they chose as they did.

- Why does evil sometimes seem attractive?

Discuss how movies, books, and television programs could be compared to these packages.

- What kind of garbage might we find

MISSION PREPARATION

in these sources of entertainment?

- How can you tell what is good and what is evil?

Read together Moroni 7:12–19 and discuss the standard for judgment presented in these scriptures.

Ask family members to make a list of television programs and movies they have seen lately as well as books and magazines they have recently read. Ask them to compare the items on this list to the standard outlined in Moroni and see if the items invited them to do good and love God.

On a piece of paper or a poster, write down the things that you will do as a family to control the contact that family members have with undesirable programs or ideas in the media.

Lesson 3: Sharing the Good in the Media

Occasionally take an evening to let family members review their favorite books or movies, sharing insights and feelings about them. Keep a list of best books or best movies that you each discover so that others in the family will be aware of them.

Review new television shows, including those on the public television channels. Then discuss what you find, and decide what will and will not be appropriate for your family to watch.

RESOURCES

Scriptures

Psalm 97:10 (Ye that love the Lord, hate evil.)
Isaiah 5:20–21 (Woe to those who call evil good, and good evil.)
Amos 5:14 (Seek good, and not evil.)
Alma 41:10 (Wickedness never was happiness.)
Thirteenth article of faith (We seek that which is lovely and of good report.)
See also "Agency," "Evil," and "Good" in the Topical Guide.

Songs and Hymns

"Choose the Right," *Hymns*, no. 110.

And faith, hope, charity and love, with an eye single to the glory of God, qualify him for the work.
—*Doctrine and Covenants 4:5*

GOSPEL TRUTH

Our Heavenly Father wants all of his children to hear the gospel. It is the responsibility of those who have the gospel to share this important message. In order to do so effectively, we must prepare family members to experience the great joy of missionary work. (See Matthew 28:19–20, D&C 12:6.)

IDEAS FOR LESSONS

Lesson 1: Developing Love for Others

Explain that before we can effectively share the gospel with anyone, we must love them. By learning to have greater love for others, we can prepare ourselves to be better missionaries.

To help your family members understand what the Lord has taught about the importance of love in missionary work, have them read and discuss the following scriptures: Doctrine and Covenants 12:8; 18:15; and 121:41.

- How can we get love for others if we don't already have it?

Read and discuss the first part of Moroni 7:48: "Pray unto the Father with all the energy of heart, that ye may be filled with this love."

You may want to relate experiences you or someone you know may have had with being a missionary and developing love for the people with whom you worked.

You might also tell stories about how people change and learn to love others as the missionaries work with them.

You may wish to invite a returned missionary to tell how he was able to successfully teach people the gospel because he loved them.

Assign each family member to choose someone with whom they have

difficulty getting along and show this person more love than usual. This could be done in secret. Have family members set a goal to try Moroni's counsel and ask Heavenly Father to help them love one another.

Have family members make small cards that say something like the following:

"I will share the gospel of love."

"Love one another, as I have loved you."

Put the cards up where your family will see them and be reminded to love others.

Lesson 2: Taking the Gospel to All the World

Have your family look at maps of the world and of your own country. Discuss the nationalities and cultures of people the missionaries meet. List ways in which people are similar worldwide. (They want to be happy, they care for their children, they work to earn a living.)

Help your family conclude that all of these people are God's children and that their needs and desires are similar to ours.

Challenge family members to prepare to help the kingdom of God roll forth to fill the whole earth (see Daniel 2, especially verses 44–45).

If possible, invite a convert to the gospel from another nation or culture to come to your home and share his conversion experiences with your family.

Lesson 3: Doing Missionary Work Now

Discuss who is basically responsible for doing missionary work. The following sources might help you in your discussion:

Doctrine and Covenants 88:81. (The responsibility for doing missionary work rests with every member of the Church.)

"Every member a missionary!" (David

O. McKay, in Conference Report, Apr. 1959, p. 122).

"Think, brothers and sisters, what would happen if each active family were to bring another family or individual into the Church before next April conference: We would be joined by several hundred thousand new members of the Church" (Spencer W. Kimball, in Conference Report, Apr. 1979, p. 114; see also *Ensign*, May 1979, p. 82).

For a complete lesson on this topic, see lesson 26, "Sharing Our Blessings" in the "Lessons" section of this book.

Lesson 4: Motivation to Serve a Mission

Arrange to see the filmstrip *Preparing Missionaries* (OF121) or the film *Go Ye into All the World* (MP162) from your meetinghouse library if they are available.

Lesson 5: Preparing Spiritually to Do Missionary Work

Discuss how important it is for missionaries to know the scriptures and understand the organization and history of the Church. One young man tells the following story about himself:

"It was about the third day of heavy tracting when I decided that I had better straighten things out with my companion. After all, what was he doing telling everyone that the Book of Mormon took place in America and that the Book of Mormon was a history of the people on the American continent? During our talk, my companion got *me* straightened out, and I realized that somewhere in my 'learning' I had neglected to get understanding. You may find this hard to believe, but I really didn't know the background of the Book of Mormon."

Make a list of ways in which family members can learn more about Church history and organization. These may include listening attentively in Sunday School classes, participating in seminary programs,

talking with people about their Church callings, and reading books.

To help your family become familiar with the scriptures and better understand the principles of the gospel, you may wish to do some of the following:

1. Provide each family member with his own scriptures for study and marking.

2. Obtain a list of the scriptures that full-time missionaries memorize, and systematically become familiar with them or memorize them as a family.

3. Share testimonies in your home on Christmas Eve, Easter, or another special occasion.

4. Discuss the things that a full-time missionary would need to know about the gospel. Then ask family members to identify some of the areas in which they need to learn more. Set family or individual goals to learn more about the gospel. These goals might include establishing a more regular and effective scripture study program, having family prayer more regularly, paying more attention in Church meetings, and studying books on Church history and doctrine. Consider using films, filmstrips, and tapes from your meetinghouse library.

5. In advance, assign each family member a topic or problem of interest to them, and have them use the Topical Guide to find scriptures that provide suggested solutions to the problems. Help family members see the value of using the scriptures in all of life's experiences.

6. Arrange to have a recently returned missionary present a missionary discussion to your family.

Lesson 6: Learning to Organize Your Time

Plan activities to help family members learn to set priorities and organize their time. (Activities are suggested under the topic "Priorities," in this

section of this book.) Explain that they will need to be able to do this well as missionaries. You might ask a returned missionary or mission president to come and tell how a missionary plans and organizes his time. Have family members plan ways in which they will better manage their time.

Lesson 7: Practical Preparation for a Mission

1. When family members are asked to give talks in Church, have them practice in your family's home evening. You might also have a speech contest within your family and give awards for the most humorous, most interesting, and most original talks.

2. Plan an evening in which you teach proper care of clothing. Discuss the kinds of things a missionary needs to do on preparation day. Have family members demonstrate or teach how to polish shoes, sew on buttons, press clothes, and wash and iron as needed.

3. Teach principles of proper food selection and nutrition. Use a poster showing the four basic food groups. Plan a week in which each family member takes a turn planning a meal and then shopping, preparing, and serving that meal. Stress the importance of cleaning up after meals as well.

RESOURCES

Scriptures

Matthew 28:19–20 (Go, teach all nations.)

Revelation 14:6–7 (Gospel to be preached to every nation and people.)

Mosiah 18:9 (Those who are baptized are to be witnesses for God at all times.)

Mormon 9:22–25 (Preach the gospel to every creature.)

Doctrine and Covenants 1:4–5 (None shall keep missionaries from doing their work.)

MONEY MANAGEMENT

Doctrine and Covenants 4 (Advice to missionaries.)

Doctrine and Covenants 11:21–22 (Seek to obtain my word.)

Doctrine and Covenants 62:5 (Declare glad tidings.)

See also "Missionary Work" in the Topical Guide.

Songs and Hymns

"I Hope They Call Me on a Mission," *Sing with Me*, B–75.

"High on the Mountain Top," *Hymns*, no. 62.

"It May Not Be on the Mountain Height," *Hymns*, no. 75.

Other

Go Ye into All the World, available through your meetinghouse library in either a 16mm film or videocassette version.

Better is a little with righteousness than great revenues without right.
—Proverbs 16:8

GOSPEL TRUTH

We should use the financial resources with which we are blessed to perfect ourselves and build up the kingdom of God.

IDEAS FOR LESSONS

Lesson 1: A Practical Experience in Budgeting

This unique way to help family members understand their part in helping with the family budget was suggested by Dr. Dwayne Belt of the Brigham Young University faculty. You may wish to use some of his ideas or adapt them to the needs of your family:

"I had told the children to sit in a circle on the floor to prepare for a special activity during our family home evening. To their astonishment, I gave each one a large bundle of one-dollar bills. My wife and I also had a bundle.

" 'All of this money together is the amount earned each month in our family,' I said. 'Tonight you are all going to help Mom and Dad spend it.' . . .

[Note: It might not be practical to have this much real currency in your home. You may want to make paper bills the same size and color as your currency, and if possible place at least one real bill on the top of each bundle.]

"For some time my wife and I had felt that one of the important things we should teach our children was the wise use of money. Although we felt the children should not be overburdened with concern about the family budget, we believed that a better understanding of our financial responsibilities and goals would contribute to the harmony we desired in our home.

" 'You need to know that there are some things we are required by law to pay and some that we have promised to pay,' I explained. 'After these things are paid, there will be other things we need and must pay for, and then we can use the rest of the money as we wish.' . . .

"Tithing was quickly agreed upon as the most important thing we have promised to pay, followed by other Church donations. Each person counted out his share and handed it to me.

" 'We have always paid our tithing first, even when we "owed" only $9.00 a month, and we have always been blessed for it,' I reported to the family.

"So we continued on down the list—taxes, social security, insurance, house payment, utilities, and many others. The children looked distressed as their piles of money began to get smaller.

"Occasional questions arose about things such as retirement funds. These were discussed in an attempt to help each one see the reason for these kinds of programs.

" 'In our family,' I said, 'savings comes under the list of things we have promised to pay. We have promised ourselves that we would save regularly to prepare for missions, college, or family emergencies. To help us keep that promise to ourselves, my employer pays some of our money to our savings account each month.'

"When we had exhausted the list of things required by law and promises, we moved to other things we needed. Food was mentioned first, followed by clothing and medical care.

"Soon we began to mention a few things we would like to do or to have, and as families often do we found that we had too much *month* left at the end of the *money*. Long before our list of needs and wants was exhausted, the piles of one-dollar bills had disappeared.

"The children stared in disbelief. My wife and I smiled knowingly.

"Some of the comments were:

" 'I'm sick!'

" 'What do you do at Christmastime?'

" 'I didn't realize how fast we spend the money you make, Dad.'

" 'Boy, it must take a lot of time to figure out the budget and pay the bills each month.'

" 'It's all the dozens of little things that really add up.' . . .

" 'You sure have to plan ahead.' . . .

" 'Is it wrong to buy things we don't actually need?' one of the children asked.

" 'It is not wrong to have and to enjoy many of the beautiful and wonderful things in the world,' we told her, 'as long as we keep two things in mind: First, our desire for material possessions should always be secondary to our desire to serve the Lord and our fellowmen. Second, acquiring luxuries should always be secondary to acquiring necessities.'

" 'That was fun,' one of the children said, 'but what does money have to do with the gospel?'

" 'We have been told that our Heavenly Father gives us no temporal commandments,' answered Mother. 'Everything he tells us to do is for our eternal good. And every part of our life, including handling the family income, is part of living the gospel.

" 'We hoped that this activity would remind each of us that we should use our resources toward perfecting ourselves and building up the kingdom of God.'

" 'Now, what can each of you do that will help you or our family to make better use of the financial resources with which we are blessed?' I asked.

"That evening the following commitments were made:

"*I will keep track of what I spend for an entire month and then make a priority list for using my allowance.*

"I am going to be more careful about the little things I buy that I could get along without.

"I'm going to try to save $100 from my allowance and baby sitting by the time school starts next fall.

"I'm going to pay my tithing the very first Sunday after I get my allowance, without fail.

"I'm going to make a plan for saving enough from my allowance so that I can buy a new dress every three months.

"I will try even harder to make only one trip a week for the family groceries.

"With an occasional reminder, our family have noticeably made sincere attempts to use our financial resources more wisely since this experience.

"We will never forget the night we helped 'spend' the family income." ("They All Held the Money," *The Instructor*, May 1970, pp. 158–59.)

Lesson 2: Adult Adaptations

It is generally recognized that one of the leading causes of friction in marriage, often leading to divorce, is the inability of the couple to wisely handle the family income.

In order to use family finances wisely, the husband and wife must each understand their own responsibilities for the finances and be committed to living within a budget they have both agreed upon. If a couple has not already done so, they could spend an evening planning a detailed budget and outlining the responsibilities they will each have for their finances.

Any married couple can profit from an evaluation of their financial practices. Even if they have already established a budget, they could take an evening to review it and make necessary adjustments.

RESOURCES

Scriptures

Matthew 6:19 (Lay not up for yourselves treasures upon earth.)
1 Timothy 5:8 (If any provide not for his own.)
Doctrine and Covenants 75:28 (Obliged to provide for own family.)
Doctrine and Covenants 88:119 (Prepare every needful thing.)

See also "Family, Managing Finances in," and "Money" in the Topical Guide.

Songs and Hymns

"Count Your Many Blessings," *Hymns*, no. 202.

MUSIC

For my soul delighteth in the song of the heart; yea, the song of the righteous is a prayer unto me.
—Doctrine and Covenants 25:12

GOSPEL TRUTH

Good music—music that elevates and inspires—can both enhance our worship and enrich our lives. It can help us to grow closer to our Father in Heaven and to be more receptive to his Spirit.

IDEAS FOR LESSONS

Lesson 1: Music Can Be a Form of Worship

Begin the evening by singing two or three of the family's favorite hymns. After an opening prayer, discuss how these hymns made family members feel. Make a list of feelings we should have when we worship—love, reverence, faith, respect, etc. Discuss why music is important in helping us have these feelings in our worship services.

You might tell a story like the following:

A pianist who played regularly for Primary had become discouraged. It seemed that although she took the time to prepare prelude music that would set a reverent tone for the rest of the meeting, no one listened. Many people arrived late, and those that arrived on time often spent the minutes before the meeting in talking or in last-minute lesson preparation.

When she expressed her dissatisfaction with such irreverent behavior, the Primary leaders and teachers agreed to be more reverent out of respect for her wishes. To their surprise, they found that when they were reverent and listened to the prelude music, they were able to be much more in tune with the Spirit when the meeting actually began. Such mental and spiritual preparation helped them not only to present their lessons more effectively but also to learn more from the lessons of others.

Discuss how we can show our love and respect for the Lord through music (see D&C 25:12; 138:24).

Play or sing some quiet, reverent music, and, if your children are young, practice sitting reverently as you would in a Church meeting.

- Did listening to such quiet music help you to feel in tune with our Father in Heaven's Spirit? (See also "Sing Praises: Learning Our Hymns and Children's Songs," in the "Family Activities" section of this book.)

Lesson 2: Music Has Great Power to Affect Our Lives

Play, sing, or have family members name several of their favorite songs. These may range from hymns to classical selections to currently popular songs.

Point out that music has great power over us; some music makes us want to dance, some makes us want to march, some makes us want to sit and think. Have the family participate by marching to some marching music and dancing to some dancing music.

Point out that music has great power to inspire us and to bring us closer to our Father in Heaven and that it also has the power to encourage evil thoughts and acts.

Have family members analyze how each of the songs they have named makes them feel. Which of the pieces make them feel closer to our Father in Heaven, and which ones would not make them feel close to him? Are there any that would not be pleasing to him? Suggest that your family adopt a standard of singing, playing, or listening only to music that is pleasing to the Lord.

Lesson 3: Music Can Teach the Gospel

Tell the following true experiences to help your family understand how music not only teaches us the truths of the gospel but also helps us to recall them when we need to:

A mother was called to the home of her oldest daughter who had recently given birth to a beautiful baby boy. There had been a dramatic call: "Mom, come quick—the baby!" When the mother arrived at the apartment, the baby was lying lifeless on the couch. He had been well when the daughter put him to bed, but from unknown causes, he had slipped silently into death during the night. The mother felt as if her heart would break. "Why, Lord, why?" she cried. Then, as if in answer, strains of music and the accompanying words came to her mind: "Hold to the rod, the iron rod; 'Tis strong, and bright, and true; The iron rod is the word of God, 'Twill safely guide us through." (See Connee Garrett, "A Song of the Heart," *Ensign*, June 1982, p. 37.)

A young girl was often so frightened at night by strange sounds and an active imagination that she couldn't sleep. Then, to her mind would come the words: "The Lord is my light; then why should I fear? By day and by night his presence is near." She would soon relax and go to sleep. (See Garrett, "A Song of the Heart," p. 37.)

Share similar experiences that members of your family may have had.

Sing some songs that teach a truth of the gospel. Talk about what the words mean. You might choose songs like "I Am a Child of God," *Sing with Me*, B–76; "The Still Small Voice," *Sing with Me*, B–92; "I Stand All Amazed," *Hymns*, no. 80; "It May Not Be on the Mountain Height," *Hymns*, no. 75.

Lesson 4: Making Music Together

(Each of these ideas could be a separate family home evening.)

Form a family orchestra, using the instruments the various family members play. If family members do not play traditional instruments, form an orchestra using such things as kitchen utensils, kazoos, and tissue-paper combs.

Have a family make-believe orchestra. Assign each child to pretend he is playing an instrument while a record is being played, for example, moving fingers on a piano, fingering a violin, or playing a flute or drum.

Organize a sing-along with piano or guitar. Sing or play a variety of favorite family songs. Have a family singing time in which family members draw songs out of a hat or choose songs in some other interesting way.

Select a hymn or choral arrangement of a folk song and form a family duet, trio, quartet, or choral group (depending on the numbers available). Learn the parts; then sing the hymn or folk song in parts. If members cannot sing parts, try a round song in which everyone sings the same melody but starts at a different time.

Plan a family recital or musical program for friends, relatives, and neighbors. Include a variety of numbers such as solos, duets, group numbers, and musical skits. Encourage family members to try writing their own music, lyrics, or both to present on the program. Set a definite date and work toward it. You might want to print programs, send invitations, and serve refreshments to those who attend. Or take your program to those who cannot get out—those who are confined in hospitals, nursing homes, or at home.

Lesson 5: Becoming Acquainted with Good Music

See "Appreciating Music," in the "Family Activities" section of this book.

RESOURCES

Scriptures

Doctrine and Covenants 45:71 (Righteous shall come to Zion singing songs of joy.)

Doctrine and Covenants 136:28

(Praise the Lord with singing.)

Matthew 26:30 (Christ and his Apostles sang a hymn after the Last Supper.)

See also "Music" and "Singing" in the Topical Guide.

Songs and Hymns

You can use any of the hymns. Musical accompaniments for many of the hymns and songs are recorded on *Hymns and Children's Songs: Cassettes of Music for Worship Service (VVOT0529). The cassettes are available through your local Church distribution center.*

Other

Gospel Principles, "Developing Our Talents," chapter 34.

Most public or school libraries have books which contain explanations of different types of music, descriptions of the musical instruments, and stories of famous composers. Many public libraries will also have recordings available for loan.

Worthy Music, Worthy Thoughts, available through your meetinghouse library in a filmstrip version only.

PRIORITIES

Seek ye first the kingdom of God, and his righteousness.
—*Matthew 6:33*

GOSPEL TRUTH

Our Heavenly Father has told us to seek first to build up the kingdom of God and establish his righteousness. The activities of our lives should be centered around this priority.

IDEAS FOR LESSONS

Lesson 1: Our First Priority

Give each family member a piece of paper. Have him leave some space at the top of his paper and write on it two things he would like to accomplish in this life. Set the papers aside to be used later.

Remind family members that they are each children of our Heavenly Father and that they used to live with him.

To help your family understand this concept, you might lead them into another room. As you stand together, tell them that this room represents the place where they all lived together before this life. One by one they left the presence of Heavenly Father and came to earth. Try to help them understand how much our Heavenly Father loved each of them as he sent them to earth to have experiences that would help them become like him. Try to help them realize how much he wants each one of his children to return safely to him. (See Moses 1:39.)

Return to the room you left, which represents your life now.

- What is the most important thing our Heavenly Father wants us to do here upon the earth?

Read Matthew 6:33. You might underline the word *first* in this Bible verse. Explain that the word *priority* means something that we do first before other things. Our first great priority is to do those things that will enable us to return to our Heavenly Father.

Ask family members to write their first priority in the space they left at the top of their papers. Their statement will probably say something like "My first priority to to do those things that will help me get back to my Heavenly Father."

Discuss how an understanding of this priority helps them evaluate the importance of everything they do in their lives. Ask each family member to look at his written statements of things he would like to do in this life. Have them ask themselves, "Will doing this thing help me get back to my Father in Heaven?" Ask family members if they would like to change their statements.

Ask the family to suggest things they could be doing individually or as a family that would show that they were putting the Lord first in their lives.

You may want to make a poster of Matthew 6:33 or one that reads, "Do not let the least important things get in the way of the most important things."

Lesson 2: Managing Time Using Righteous Priorities

Ask your family to pretend they are in the following situation:

Someone calls, "Help, the neighbor's house is on fire!" As you rush to help the neighbors, which of the following would you do first? Carry out the furniture, call for help, save members of the family, or get the car out of the garage? Why did you choose as you did?

Discuss with the family the fact that all of these things are important, but saving the family members is the most important, so it is the thing you should do first.

Explain that in this situation it is very easy to see that one thing is more important than other things and so must be done first. But every day we must decide which are the most important things for us to do that day,

and often we have a hard time making the right decisions.

Ask family members to list, in as much detail as possible, the things they did during the last two days. Have them set these lists aside for a few minutes.

Explain that our first priority in this life is to do the things that will help us return to our Father in Heaven. We are commanded to seek first to establish the kingdom of God (see Matthew 6:33).

• What are some things that you do each day that help you or other people to return to our Father in Heaven?

They may name such things as serving other people, spending time with family members, working hard at school or job, making home a clean and pleasant place to be.

Ask family members to look at the list of things they did during the last two days and decide what this list says about their priorities. Have they been doing the things that are most important or have they been spending much of their time doing things that do not really matter?

You may want to have family members make a list of the things they want to do to help themselves and others return to our Father in Heaven. They could then make a plan for how they will use their time during the next week, making sure that they plan to get the things they have listed done.

You may want to spend another evening evaluating the effectiveness of the family's plans for using their time.

RESOURCES

Scriptures

Joshua 24:15 (Choose you this day.)
John 14:15, 21 (He that loveth me keepeth my commandments.)
2 Nephi 2:27 (We can choose.)

See also "Objectives" in the Topical Guide.

Songs and Hymns

"Do What Is Right," *Hymns*, no. 27.
"Guide Us, O Thou Great Jehovah," *Hymns*, no. 56.
"I Need Thee Every Hour," *Hymns*, no. 79.
"Choose the Right," *Hymns*, no. 110.

Other

Gospel Principles, chapter 15, "The Lord's Covenant People."

PROFANITY

Thou shalt not take the name of the Lord thy God in vain.
—Exodus 20:7

GOSPEL TRUTH

Profanity is the disrespectful use of the names of Deity, or the use of offensive or indecent language. Profanity separates us from our Heavenly Father while clean, reverent language brings us closer to him.

IDEAS FOR LESSONS

Lesson 1: Proper Use of the Lord's Name

Relate and discuss with your family the following story:

"[Spencer W. Kimball] was put under total anaesthesia and operated on, then wheeled on a table back toward his room. Still drugged, Spencer sensed his table stop by an elevator and heard the orderly, angry at something, profaning the Lord's name. Half-conscious, he pleaded with labored sounds: 'Please don't say that. I love Him more than anything in this world. Please.' An absolute silence. Then the orderly aswered softly: 'I shouldn't have said that. I'm sorry.' " (Edward L. Kimball and Andrew E. Kimball, Jr., *Spencer W. Kimball* [Salt Lake City: Bookcraft, 1977], p. 264.)

Have someone read aloud what the Lord has commanded in Exodus 20:7.

• What does it mean to take the Lord's name in vain?

To help answer this question, read and discuss Doctrine and Covenants 63:60–64. Be sure your family members understand that we only use the names of Deity in a worshipful, respectful way.

Remind your family that as they learn to love Heavenly Father and Jesus in the way that President Kimball does, they will not be tempted to use the names of Deity in a disrespectful way.

Lesson 2: Swear Not At All

Show your family a dictionary. Talk about all the good words that are available to use when we speak. Point out that even though we have so many good words to select from, we sometimes choose words which are not good—words which have vulgar and impure meanings. Using these kinds of words is called swearing.

Read what Jesus said about swearing in the first part of Matthew 5:34, "But I say unto you, Swear not at all."

Then read and discuss Matthew 15:18 where Jesus explained why we should not use vulgar language.

Show a picture of a garbage can, and tell your family that you want them to throw away any vulgar words they may be inclined to use. You may wish to have a variety of words written on slips of paper—some good and some bad (those that any member of your family may be having a problem with). Have family members take turns drawing a word and deciding if it is a good word or a "garbage can" word.

Discuss what family standards you want to establish for words you will and will not use. You may want to make a poster using the garbage can and one of the scriptures used in the lesson to remind the family of these standards.

Lesson 3: Eliminating Profanity

Relate and discuss the following story by Elder A. Theodore Tuttle:

" 'When I was growing up in our town my friend and I used to hear lots of the boys swearing and taking the name of the Lord in vain. This offended us. Our parents had taught us not to swear. We knew that we should not take the name of the Lord in vain. One day as we were talking about this, my friend and I promised each other—we made a covenant—that we would never take the name of the Lord in vain. During the inter-

vening years, each of us kept the vow which we had made.

" 'A few years later, . . . I moved away from our home town to a farm in another valley. It was there that I met head on with trouble. We were hauling hay one hot summer day and had taken a break for lunch. After we unhitched the horses, my father sent me down to the well with a gallon jug to bring back some cool water. I mounted one of our work horses and loped down to the well. After filling the jug I put my finger through the handle, threw the jug over the back of the horse, and tried to jump up on its back. But before I could get completely on the horse, he wheeled around and started off on a trot back to the hayrack, jogging me on his back. There I was, half on and half off, bouncing along on the bony withers of that horse. My finger was so twisted it was about to break with the weight of that jug of water. I tried to jerk on the reins to stop the horse with the other hand, but he would not stop.

" ' . . . With everything going all wrong I got so angry that I swore at the horse and took the name of the Lord in vain. At the very moment I did this, I realized what I had done. A great wave of guilt swept over me because I had broken my covenant with my friend. But worse, I knew that I had offended the Lord, and I had failed to be true to the standard I knew. As I finally managed to fall off the horse, I kneeled immediately—right there in the stubble of the field—and asked the Lord to forgive me. I vowed again, this time with repentant fervor, that I would never again break the pledge which my friend and I had made about swearing.' " (In Conference Report, Oct. 1965, pp. 30–31; or *Improvement Era*, Dec. 1965, p. 1117.)

Decide on some ways in which family members can improve the language

REVERENCE

they use and ways in which they can lovingly encourage others to eliminate profanity, for example:

1. Promise to repent immediately of profanity. If anyone forgets and uses profanity, he will apologize immediately to anyone who heard him and ask the Lord's forgiveness and help in overcoming the problem.

2. Decide that offensive or obscene words will be considered "garbage can" words. Post a picture of a garbage can in your house to remind family members that they must mentally dispose of such words.

3. Make it a practice to refuse to listen to or laugh at dirty stories. Forget the stories, and do not repeat them to others.

4. Promise to pay someone a sum of money for each profane word you speak.

5. If a family member is having a serious problem with profanity, have him fast, pray, and, when appropriate, ask for a priesthood blessing to help him make his language pure and acceptable to the Lord.

6. Little children sometimes use bad words without knowing their meaning. When this occurs, the parent or older brother or sister who hears the words should kindly explain to the child that we do not use those words in our family.

Lesson 4: Choosing Good Language

Have family members read aloud the following case studies and discuss which ones show the use of respectful, wholesome language or ways of avoiding profanity.

1. The man said the name of the Lord in a loud, angry voice when he saw that his tire was flat.

2. The priest read the sacrament prayer in a reverent voice.

3. Though the bump on her knee hurt very much, Jill didn't say any angry words.

4. Lyle turns off the television when he notices that the performers are using profanity.

5. Clyde knows that he should not use profanity, so he uses it only at work.

6. Alice feels uncomfortable every time she hears her friends swear, but she says nothing because she doesn't want to hurt their feelings. She uses profanity occasionally so that her friends won't think she is being self-righteous.

Encourage your family always to use good, wholesome language and to avoid situations in which they are exposed to profanity.

RESOURCES

Scriptures

Leviticus 19:12 (Thou shalt not profane the name of God.)

Matthew 12:36 (We will be judged by every idle word.)

Matthew 15:11 (A man is defiled by what comes out of his mouth.)

Ephesians 4:29 (Let no corrupt communication proceed out of your mouth.)

Colossians 3:8 (Put off filthy communication out of your mouth.)

James 1:26 (If any man bridleth not his tongue.)

Moses 6:57 (No unclean thing can dwell with God.)

See also "Profanity" in the Topical Guide.

Songs and Hymns

"More Holiness Give Me," *Hymns*, no. 114.

Latter-day Saints should be the most reverent people in all the earth.
—*President Spencer W. Kimball*

GOSPEL TRUTH

Reverence is a feeling of love and respect for all that is sacred. We show this feeling in our words and actions. When we are reverent, we draw closer to Heavenly Father and Jesus.

IDEAS FOR LESSONS

Lesson 1: What Is Reverence?

Help your family understand the meaning of reverence by telling the story of Jesus' first appearance to the Nephites. (See 3 Nephi 11:1–17. For background information, read 3 Nephi 8, 9, and 10.)

Be sure family members understand that many people had been killed and that those remaining were frightened. They knew that the terrible storms and darkness were signs of Jesus' death. Help your family imagine how the Nephites felt as they gathered around the temple and Jesus appeared to them. Read 3 Nephi 11:16–17. Let them discuss why they think the people fell to the earth. Point out the awe and reverence they must have felt.

Discuss with your family the meaning of reverence. Help them realize that it is more than being quiet. It is a feeling of love and respect for Heavenly Father, Jesus, and their creations, as well as for sacred places. It grows as we learn about Heavenly Father and Jesus and their love for us.

Read President Kimball's definition of reverence: "We must remember that reverence is not a somber, temporary behavior that we adopt on Sunday. True reverence involves happiness, as well as love, respect, gratitude, and godly fear. It is a virtue that should be part of our way of life. In fact, Latter-day Saints should be the most reverent people in all the earth." (*We Should*

Be a Reverent People, [pamphlet, 1976], p. 4.)

Help family members to remember times when they have felt reverent. Remind them of situations such as thinking about Jesus during the sacrament, watching a beautiful sunset, walking through a quiet garden, seeing our prophet or listening to his voice, holding a tiny baby, listening to peaceful music, praying sincerely to Heavenly Father.

Be sure they understand that the feelings they have in such situations are part of being reverent. When we are quiet and respectful because we feel love for Heavenly Father and Jesus, we are being reverent.

Challenge family members to be especially reverent next Sunday in their Church meetings. Discuss this challenge before you go to Church, and also spend a few minutes when you return home to discuss how being reverent made you feel.

Lesson 2: Why Our Family Wants to Be Reverent

Discuss with your family why they want to be reverent, using the first part of Doctrine and Covenants 88:63: "Draw near unto me and I will draw near unto you."

Have your family list the blessings that come to them when they are reverent in Church, for example—

We can communicate with Heavenly Father.
We can learn about Heavenly Father and Jesus.
We can renew our covenants during the sacrament.
We can feel the Spirit of the Lord.
Help them to realize that these blessings are denied to them when they are irreverent.

Lesson 3: Creating Reverent Situations

You might hold an early morning devotional in a secluded place such as the mountains, seashore, or nearby park. After watching the sunrise, sing a hymn, read the scriptures, and have family prayer. Express your feelings of love for Heavenly Father and Jesus and all their creations. You could plan a similar experience after watching the sun go down on a summer evening and watching the stars fill the sky.

Lesson 4: Showing Reverence in Sacred Places

Discuss with your family the difference between Church buildings (temples and meetinghouses) and other buildings (office buildings, stores, schools). Church buildings are dedicated with special prayers and are often called Heavenly Father's house or the house of the Lord.

Have the family list the sacred events that take place in meetinghouses and temples. Help them understand why we conduct ourselves differently in these places. Remind them that they are guests of Heavenly Father and Jesus.

Show how Jesus felt about being reverent in sacred places by reading or telling the story in John 2:13–16.

Print or write the following sentences or ideas of your own on small strips of paper and place them in a paper bag:

Running in the halls.
Thinking about Jesus during the sacrament.
Closing my eyes during the prayers.
Tearing or writing on pages of the hymnbook.
Whispering during the sacrament.
Listening to and trying to understand the speakers in meetings.
Wrestling or playing games with someone anywhere in the meetinghouse (except during organized games in the cultural hall).
Wiping my feet before entering the meetinghouse.
Teasing my little brother or sister during sacrament meeting.
Dropping paper towels on the floor of the restroom.

Have family members take turns selecting a paper and determining if the action is reverent or irreverent. Tell the family that you would like them to discard all irreverent actions. Put the papers with irreverent actions on them in a separate bag and discard.

Discuss the reverent actions and how they can help you express love for Heavenly Father and Jesus. Have each family member decide on a reverent action he would like to improve on. Have him write it on a slip of paper and commit to making it a serious goal.

Before leaving for Church meetings on Sunday, have family members read their commitment slips to remind them of what they are going to do. After the meeting, have them share how their actions helped them to feel more reverent.

If there is a temple nearby, plan to visit the grounds and visitors' center. If you are a recommend holder, stop and think each time you enter the temple, "This is the Lord's house."

Especially for Young Children

Help your children understand that we show our love for Heavenly Father and Jesus by using our hands, arms, feet, eyes, lips, and heads in a reverent way when we are in sacred places and when we pray. It is easier to think loving, reverent thoughts when we are quiet. Draw from the children how each part of our body can help us to be reverent.

Hands and arms—Fold during prayer, keep quiet in our laps, raise to take part.
Feet and legs—Walk quietly, remain still.
Ears—Listen to what is said, listen to the sacred music.
Heads—Bow when prayers are being said and think about Heavenly Father and Jesus.
Eyes—Watch the teacher, bishop, or anyone who is speaking.
Lips—Speak quietly, smile, sing songs, pray, remain closed when someone else is praying.

SABBATH

Remember the sabbath day, to keep it holy.
—Exodus 20:8

GOSPEL TRUTH

The Sabbath provides us with rest for mind and body, with opportunities for worship, and with time to give loving service to our fellowmen. By using the Sabbath wisely to rest, worship, and serve, we can receive temporal blessings and develop great spiritual strength.

IDEAS FOR LESSONS

Lesson 1: The Importance of Keeping the Sabbath Day Holy

Have family members read and compare Exodus 20:8–11 and Mosiah 13:16–19. Point out that the commandment to keep the Sabbath day holy is found in both the Bible and the Book of Mormon and has always been part of the gospel. The Lord consecrated the Sabbath as a day for remembering the great work of the Creation.

Explain that the Lord commanded the children of Israel to keep the Sabbath day holy in commemoration of his mighty power, which delivered them from the bondage of Egypt. Read Deuteronomy 5:12–15.

Point out that we observe the Sabbath on Sunday because Jesus was resurrected on Sunday, "the first day of the week" (see Acts 20:7; 1 Corinthians 16:2).

To help your family members understand that in our day we have also been commanded to keep the Sabbath day holy, read and discuss Doctrine and Covenants 59:9–19. Ask them to identify what is being asked of them and what blessings are promised in return.

- What are you asked to do? (See verses 9–15.)

- What temporal blessings are promised? (See verses 16–19.)

- What spiritual blessings are promised? (See verse 9: "Keep thyself unspotted from the world.")

Discuss how keeping the Sabbath day holy can keep us unspotted from the world.

Bear your testimony of the blessings that come from keeping the Sabbath day holy. Relate the following incident or a personal experience like it:

John and Mary had been married fourteen years and still didn't have a home of their own. They had just gone through a particularly difficult business year, and had been turned down on a loan application for a modest house. John was brokenhearted.

Then he happened to read in Doctrine and Covenants 59 where the Lord promises to all those who keep the Sabbath day holy:

"The fulness of the earth is yours, ...

" . . . whether for food or for raiment, or for *houses*, or for barns" (verses 16–17; italics added).

He resolved to put this scripture to the test, and asked the Lord to help him and his family keep the Sabbath day holy and to help them buy their own home. Thirteen months later they were led by inspiration to visit their old neighborhood, where they saw a "For Sale" sign on one of the houses. They called the owner, who knew them, and he offered to let them move into the home, buy it on a contract, and pay the down payment when their business improved. They knew the Lord meant what he said when he promised them "the fulness of the earth" for keeping the Sabbath day holy.

Lesson 2: How Can I Keep the Sabbath Day Holy?

Ask your family to suggest ways to observe the Sabbath day.

Help them understand that a balance of rest, worship, and service is necessary to keep the Sabbath day holy. To determine whether a specific activity is

RESOURCES

Scriptures

Psalm 111:9 (Holy and reverent is his name.)

Doctrine and Covenants 76:92–93 (All things bow in reverence before God.)

Doctrine and Covenants 133:38–39 (Worship him who made heaven and earth.)

See also "Reverence" in the Topical Guide.

Songs and Hymns

"Father, We Will Quiet Be," *Sing with Me*, A–15.

"Reverently, Quietly," *Sing with Me*, A–9.

"The Chapel Doors," *Sing with Me*, B–56.

"O My Father," *Hymns*, no. 139.

"Praise God from Whom All Blessings Flow," *Hymns*, no. 214.

"Precious Savior, Dear Redeemer," *Hymns*, no. 109.

appropriate, ask, "Does it bring me closer to my Heavenly Father?"

Read Doctrine and Covenants 59:12–13. Note the footnote on the word *oblations* in verse 12; *oblations* means "offerings, whether of time, talents, or means, in service of God and fellowman."

Read the following quotation by President Spencer W. Kimball:

"The Sabbath is a holy day in which to do worthy and holy things. Abstinence from work and recreation is important, but insufficient. The Sabbath calls for constructive thoughts and acts, and if one merely lounges about doing nothing on the Sabbath, he is breaking it. To observe it, one will be on his knees in prayer, preparing lessons, studying the gospel, meditating, visiting the ill and distressed, writing letters to missionaries, taking a nap, reading wholesome material, and attending all the meetings of that day at which he is expected." ("The Sabbath—A Delight," *Ensign*, Jan. 1978, p. 4.)

List the three aspects of keeping the Sabbath day holy defined in these passages:

1. Rest from labors
2. Offerings of service
3. Worship

Considering the activities family members mentioned earlier as being appropriate for the Sabbath, have them list those and other Sabbath activities under each category—rest, service, and worship. You might include the following:

Eat light meals
Cook on Saturday
Clean on Saturday
Take a nap
Write letters to loved ones and missionaries
Visit family members
Visit a sick friend
Ponder the sacrament prayer more reverently

Ponder the mighty power and works of God
Read the scriptures
Try in every way to feel closer to Heavenly Father

Discuss how a wise Heavenly Father showed his love for us by giving us a day we could devote to rest, service, and worship.

Invite each family member to choose one activity from each category to concentrate on during the next Sabbath.

Discuss with young children the difference between holy days and holidays, and list appropriate activities for each. Ask them to choose a holiday activity the whole family can participate in during the coming week. Then decide how the family can keep Sunday a holy day, not a holiday.

RESOURCES

Scriptures

Genesis 2:1–3 (God blessed the seventh day.)
Isaiah 56:1–8 (All are expected to keep the Sabbath day holy.)
Isaiah 58:13–14 (Those who keep the Sabbath holy receive a promise.)
Jeremiah 17:19–27 (Importance of the Sabbath in ancient Israel.)
Nehemiah 13:15–22 (Ancient Israel told to honor the Sabbath.)
Mark 2:27 (The Sabbath is made to help us.)
Doctrine and Covenants 68:29 (We are to keep the Sabbath day holy.)
See also "Sabbath" in the Topical Guide.

Songs and Hymns

"Saturday," *Sing with Me*, D–10.
"Gently Raise the Sacred Strain," *Hymns*, no. 92.
"Welcome, Welcome Sabbath Morning," *Hymns*, no. 190.

Other

Gospel Principles, "The Sabbath Day," chapter 24.

SACRIFICE

And verily it is a day of sacrifice.
—Doctrine and Covenants 64:23

GOSPEL TRUTH

The greatest sacrifice ever made was that of our Savior, Jesus Christ, when he took upon himself our sins and laid down his life for us. Anciently people were commanded to worship the Lord by offering their choicest animals as a sacrifice, in similitude of the Savior's yet-future sacrifice. As part of his gospel, the Savior instituted a different sacrifice—the sacrifice of a broken heart and a contrite spirit, commemorated at the sacrament table. And in this dispensation, the Lord has added to the law of sacrifice and gospel law, revealing the law of consecration. When we receive the law of consecration, we covenant to give our time, our talents, and our possessions as needed for his work, and to offer ourselves—our hearts filled with gratitude, love, and humility.

IDEAS FOR LESSONS

Lesson 1: We Are Blessed As We Sacrifice

Briefly discuss the following experiences:

Experience One. When Gordon was a small boy, his father turned away from the Church and refused to have anything to do with it. His mother continued to be active, however, and took Gordon to Church meetings with her. As Gordon grew, he gained a testimony of the gospel and, when he was old enough, decided to go on a mission. The day before he was to leave, his father said, "Gordon, I am sorry you have decided to leave our family by going on this mission. I am planning to move the rest of us while you are gone, and I probably won't let you know where we are."

Gordon loved his family, but he had promised to serve the Lord; he left on his mission despite his father's threat. While Gordon was serving his mission, his father's feelings gradually softened, and he finally agreed to let his son return home.

Discuss how Gordon must have felt as he left to go on his mission, thinking that it might mean giving up his family. Talk about other kinds of sacrifices missionaries make to serve the Lord—money, time, delays in education, and forfeiting of scholarships, for example. Point out the blessings that come to missionaries and to the people they teach because of their willingness to sacrifice.

Experience Two. While getting ready for baseball practice, David overheard his mother on the phone trying to get a baby-sitter so she could visit her sick mother. After two neighborhood girls said they were busy, David volunteered to stay home from baseball practice and tend the baby. During the hours he was with his baby sister, he felt more love for her than he ever had before.

• What made David happy?

Point out that David's sacrifice was really a blessing to him.

Read and discuss Matthew 10:39. Emphasize that we will be blessed as we think of others and sacrifice to serve them.

Lesson 2: The Gospel of Christ Requires Sacrifice

Discuss Christ's atoning sacrifice.

• What does Christ's sacrifice make possible for you and for all people? (See Moses 5:9.)

Read Moses 5:5–8 and discuss why Adam was asked to make sacrifices.

• How do we remember the sacrifice of Jesus today? (See Matthew 26:26–28; 3 Nephi 9:19–22.)

Help family members understand what it means to sacrifice by listing some of the sacrifices we are required to make for the Lord and his Church (paying tithing and fast offerings, fulfilling Church callings, serving a mission, and doing genealogy and temple

work). Ask each family member how he or she feels about making these sacrifices. Point out that as we make these sacrifices willingly, we will be greatly blessed.

Relate the following incident to your family:

A whole family gave up its comfortable life in a fine city and spent approximately ten years traveling to a new continent where they prospered and found freedom to worship Heavenly Father and Jesus Christ. (See 1 Nephi 2:1–7.)

• Who were they? (The family of Lehi.)

• What sacrifices did they make? (Gave up home, wealth, and country.)

• Why did they leave their home? (They followed the direction of Heavenly Father.)

One man showed he was willing to sacrifice everything he had—even his son—for the Lord.

• Who was he? (Abraham.)

Describe how Abraham was blessed because of his willingness to give all that was asked of him.

Read Matthew 19:16–22.

• What did Jesus require of the rich man in addition to following the commandments? Why did the rich man leave in sorrow?

Challenge family members to make at least one sacrifice for another member of the family, relative, or close friend during the next week. Ask them to record their experiences in their journals and to share them with each other during the next family home evening.

RESOURCES

Scriptures

Doctrine and Covenants 59:8 (Offer sacrifice of a broken heart and a contrite spirit.)
Doctrine and Covenants 97:10–15

(Sacrifice to build the Lord's house.)
Doctrine and Covenants 98:13 (Those who sacrifice their lives in the Lord's cause shall receive eternal life.)
See also "Sacrifice" in the Topical Guide.

Other

Gospel Principles, "Sacrifice," chapter 26.

Greater Love, available through your meetinghouse library in either a 16mm film or videocassette version.

SELF-CONTROL

See that ye bridle all your passions, that ye may be filled with love; see that ye refrain from idleness.
—Alma 38:12

GOSPEL TRUTH

Self-control is the ability to govern ourselves in righteousness. When we are able to control ourselves, we increase our self-esteem and our ability to help build God's kingdom on earth.

IDEAS FOR LESSONS

Lesson 1: How We Exercise Self-control

Explain that one of Heavenly Father's greatest gifts to us is our freedom to act for ourselves (see 2 Nephi 2:27). Without that freedom, we could never develop self-control; instead, we would be controlled by forces outside ourselves. Although we cannot change other people nor always control circumstances, we can control the way we react to people and circumstances. We decide our own emotional responses, and we can change and control them. The following tells how one man was able to put this principle into practice.

Almost every day on his way to work, a man gave a cheery greeting to his neighbor. The neighbor either did not respond at all or did so sullenly, with a scowl. One day a friend asked the first man why he continued to be courteous to the neighbor. "Why aren't you as rude to him as he is to you?" the friend asked.

"Why should I let him decide how I am going to act?" the cheerful man responded.

Discuss ways family members could react to each other as this man did to his neighbor. If someone shouts angrily at them, what can they do instead of shouting back? If someone hits them, what can they do instead of hitting back? Discuss other areas where self-control is important, such as going to bed and getting up on time, deciding to do chores or homework rather than to play.

Discuss the fact that just as the body gains strength from exercise, the spirit gains strength from discipline. This strength allows us to feel good about ourselves and to accept and deal patiently with the everyday irritations and problems.

Have each family member identify one area he wants to work on to improve his self-control. In a few weeks, discuss the progress that has been made and how developing self-control in that area has helped other areas of the person's life.

Lesson 2: Why Self-control Is Important

Write the following scripture references on wordstrips and put them in a bowl. Have family members draw them out, and then read and discuss each scripture as it relates to self-control.

Proverbs 14:29
Proverbs 15:1
1 Corinthians 13:4–5
2 Nephi 4:27
Doctrine and Covenants 121:41

Drop a small handful of toothpicks (or regular "pickup sticks") in a small pile on the table or floor. Let each family member take turns picking up a toothpick with his fingers or with the end of another toothpick. Only one toothpick may be picked up each turn. If, in the process of picking up a toothpick, a player jostles another toothpick, he must put his toothpick back and wait until his next turn to try again. After the toothpicks are all picked up, the one with the most is the winner.

Discuss the game you have just played.

• What enabled the winner to win? To what degree was self-control involved in winning? How is "winning" in life dependent upon controlling our actions, thoughts, and words?

Read and discuss the meaning of Proverbs 25:28.

Name some of your goals as a family, as individuals. Decide how you can use self-control to achieve those goals.

Lesson 3: Practicing Self-control

Point out that some people become so obsessed with a desire for revenge after a real or imagined wrong that the desire takes control of their lives. Read and discuss the following story:

In the early part of this century, a man living on an isolated cattle ranch discovered he did not have enough hay to feed his cattle through the winter. The closest source of help was a neighboring rancher who lived several miles away.

The man went to his neighbor, explained his need, and asked to buy hay. "Yes, I'll sell you some hay," the neighbor answered. Then, knowing there was no place else to get hay, added, "but it will cost you double the price."

The rancher said nothing, paid the price, and made the long haul by wagon and horse team back to his own ranch.

Several years later the neighbor found himself in the same predicament—no feed for his cattle. He had no choice but to approach the man whom he had treated so shamefully with the request to buy some hay.

"No," said the rancher, "I will not sell you any hay." The neighbor had begun to walk dejectedly away, when the rancher stopped him. "But I'll tell you what I *will* do. I'll give you hay—all you want—and my sons and I will haul it to your place for you."

Read Psalm 37:8–9 and Matthew 5:38–48.

• Why was the rancher able to live up to these laws? (Because he had developed self-control. He could control his feelings and do what was right.)

Discuss how each man must have felt during the two episodes of the story. Identify the gospel principles involved.

SELFISHNESS

Have your family suggest situations in your home when someone might give in to negative emotions such as anger, laziness, revenge, or lying.

Discuss the following ways to control or change such emotions (then role-play the above situations, using one or more of these solutions):

1. Delay an expression of anger until you find a constructive way to deal with the situation.

2. Get involved with a physical activity to help release tensions and drain off the poisons they produce.

3. Recall a motivating poem, scripture, or thought. Two good ones are, "Master yourself and you can master anything" (old proverb), and "No Man is free who cannot command himself" (Pythagoras, in *The Home Book of Quotations*, sel. Burton Stevenson [New York: Dodd, Mead and Co., 1956], p. 722).

4. If another person is involved, express your feelings to him without condemning, labeling, name-calling, or accusing.

5. Pray for help in controlling your feelings or for strength to do the difficult task.

Discuss the rewards that come from learning self-control. Some of them include enjoying the guidance and direction of the Spirit, gaining self-esteem, and increasing harmony in the home.

RESOURCES

Scriptures

Matthew 5, 6, 7 (The Sermon on the Mount.)
Matthew 7:12 (The Golden Rule.)
John 18:1–12 (Jesus set an example in self-control.)
Alma 34:32 (Now is the time to prepare to meet God.)
Alma 38:1–5 (Alma's advice to his son.)
Doctrine and Covenants 10:5 (Pray always to conquer Satan.)
Doctrine and Covenants 88:121–125 (Cease from evil doings.)
Doctrine and Covenants 124:116 (Cease to do evil.)
See also "Self-mastery" in the Topical Guide.

Songs and Hymns

"Do What Is Right," *Hymns*, no. 27.
"Ere You Left Your Room This Morning," *Hymns*, no. 31.

For what is a man profited, if he shall gain the whole world, and lose his own soul?
—*Matthew 16:26*

GOSPEL TRUTH

Our Savior is the perfect example of unselfishness. If we are to follow his example, we must be concerned with the needs and feelings of others. We must be able to put our own wants and needs aside to show love and concern for others.

IDEAS FOR LESSONS

Lesson 1: The Importance of Becoming Unselfish

Tell the story of the rich young man (see Matthew 19:16–22), and have your family identify why the young man was unable to do what the Lord asked him to do.

Ask your family members to each define selfishness as they understand it and to give an example from personal experience or from the scriptures. One definition of selfishness is "clinging to your own comfort, advantage, or position at the expense of others." Elder Theodore M. Burton has said that true love is the exact opposite of selfishness (see Conference Report, Apr. 1979, p. 100; or *Ensign*, May 1979, p. 72).

Discuss and list the ways that Jesus demonstrated unselfishness. Conclude that the Atonement was the most unselfish act of all.

Write the following teachings of Jesus (and any others of your choice) on wordstrips, and put them in a bowl. Have family members draw them out and explain how they relate to unselfishness.

1. "Love one another" (John 13:34).

2. "Whosoever will lose his life for my sake shall find it" (Matthew 16:25).

3. "Seek ye first the kingdom of God" (Matthew 6:33).

4. "Let every man esteem his brother as himself" (D&C 38:24).

5. "Love thy neighbour as thyself" (Matthew 22:39).

Discuss why the Lord has placed such emphasis on our learning to become unselfish. Point out that selfishness comes naturally and easily, and it takes struggle and growth to rid ourselves of self-centeredness. But one of the purposes of this life is to overcome our weaknesses and become Christlike.

Have each family member name a blessing that comes from being unselfish and explain why unhappiness results from continued selfishness.

Lesson 2: Evaluating Our Own Selfishness

Observe your family for a week, and write down any unselfish acts you notice. Share these at family home evening and tell your family how proud you are of them. Have them discuss possible reasons behind selfish behavior and suggest some strategies for overcoming it. Make sure that each person deals with his own attitudes, not someone else's. Ask questions such as these:

- Think of a time when you were selfish. How did you feel?

- Think of a time when you were unselfish. How did you feel?

- What happens to us spiritually when we are selfish?

- How does our selfishness affect our relationships with others?

Share Elder Gordon B. Hinckley's thought that selfishness is a canker that drives out peace and love (see Conference Report, Apr. 1971, p. 83; or Ensign, June 1971, p. 72).

Allow each person to resolve to become less selfish. Ask them to report their progress next week.

Lesson 3: Learning to Be Unselfish at Home

Role-play the following situations and any others that apply to your family, adding unselfish endings:

1. Johnny asked dad to help him with his homework, but dad said he was too tired.
2. Adam wanted to play with his truck, but his younger brother was having a good time with it. Mother asked, "Couldn't he play with it just a little longer?"

Discuss what happens when family members are unselfish with each other. Put the name of each family member on a slip of paper. Have each one draw someone else's name, without revealing whose name they have. Encourage them to be particularly unselfish toward that person throughout the coming week, and to notice how it makes them feel.

Lesson 4: Unselfishness toward Others

Using the following story, discuss the results of unselfishness:

When Elder Thomas S. Monson was a young boy, he received an electric train for Christmas. His mother had purchased a smaller wind-up train for Mark, a needy boy in the neighborhood. She allowed young Tom to keep an oil tanker out of the wind-up train set to use with his own train. But when he saw how happy Mark was with the wind-up train, he ran home, got the oil tanker, plus another car from his own train, and gave them to Mark. (See "Mark's Train," Friend, Oct. 1977, p. 16.)

As a group, suggest ways your family could practice being more unselfish toward those outside your family. Consider the following ideas:

1. Remembering others in our prayers
2. Serving others
3. Paying more fast offerings
4. Helping in community volunteer programs
5. Helping neighbors
6. Supporting missionaries with letters, copies of the Book of Mormon, money, and prayers

Decide on and plan a project to unselfishly serve someone outside your family, and make appropriate assignments.

Lesson 5: Resolving to Be Unselfish

Show and discuss some pages from a newspaper, pointing out or having family members circle each news item that is a result of selfishness; examples would include wars, theft and other crimes, and civil disputes.

Relate the account of the people of Enoch (see Moses 7:18) or of the Nephites after the Savior's visit (see 4 Nephi 1:2–3, 15–16), explaining the great happiness that existed because there was no selfishness and they were able to have "all things common among them; therefore there were not rich and poor."

Assign a family member to be a reporter. Ask him to observe family members during the coming week and prepare to report on their acts of unselfishness.

RESOURCES

Scriptures

Isaiah 56:10–12 (The results of selfishness.)
Matthew 20:25–28 (The greatest is a servant to all.)
Acts 8:18–24 (Simon wanted to use the priesthood for selfish purposes.)
1 Timothy 6:10 (The root of all evil.)
Mosiah 11:1–10 (The story of the selfish King Noah.)
Helaman 7:20–22 (Nephites admonished to repent of selfishness and wickedness.)
See also "Selfishness" in the Topical Guide.

Songs and Hymns

"Jesus Said Love Everyone," Sing with Me, B–51.
"Shall the Youth of Zion Falter?" Hymns, no. 157.
"Who's on the Lord's Side?" Hymns, no. 175.

Other

Gospel Principles, "Service," chapter 28.

SELF-RELIANCE

For behold, it is not meet that I should command in all things. . . . Men should . . . do many things of their own free will, and bring to pass much righteousness.
—Doctrine and Covenants 58:26–27

GOSPEL TRUTH

We are self-reliant when we take responsibility for our own physical and spiritual welfare. Through our own efforts and with guidance from our Heavenly Father, we can experience the feeling of self-worth that comes from being truly self-reliant.

IDEAS FOR LESSONS

Lesson 1: We Grow from Being Self-reliant

Help your family understand the value of self-reliance by telling the following story:

The owners of a Rocky Mountain resort lodge kept an eagle in a large cage for their guests' entertainment. The eagle was well cared for and grew into a healthy, noble bird. But one day a group of visitors expressed resentment that so wild and beautiful a creature should be confined. The lodgekeeper opened the door of the cage, but the bird would not leave. Eventually the eagle left, but he died soon after that. He had long since forgotten how to hunt for his own food, and with no one to feed him, he could not survive.

Discuss the story of the eagle. Contrast the strengths of a person for whom everything is done with those of a person who must work, make his own decisions, and solve his own problems.

Help your family members evaluate their own self-reliance by asking them to silently answer these questions:

• Do I adhere to my standards when I am with friends, or do I go along with the group's?

• When I am faced with a difficult job, do I try to get others to do it, or do I do it myself?

• Do I have to be reminded to do my chores and other duties, or do I do them on my own?

Ask similar questions that apply to your family.

Lesson 2: Self-reliance Is Learned in the Home

Have your family think of the pioneers who settled in the Salt Lake Valley when it was a wilderness. List some of the ways they were self-reliant (examples could include growing their own food, making their own soap, weaving their own fabrics, and sewing their own clothing). Contrast their situation with ours.

Tell the following story.

When twelve-year-old David broke his arm, his father insisted that he could still do his chores and homework for himself. Although the first few days of milking the family cow with one hand produced very little milk and a very unhappy cow, David was soon bringing in buckets of milk. He learned to write with his left hand well enough to complete his term paper, and by the time Scout camp came, David had learned self-reliance. He earned six merit badges. (See Ron and Sherri Zirker, "Teaching Teens Self-discipline," *Ensign,* Apr. 1982, pp. 17–21.)

Explain to your young children that they are being self-reliant when they dress themselves and put away their toys without being told. Help them make a chart by drawing things they can do for themselves. Help them choose one thing they will work on learning to do for themselves. When they have shown self-reliance in doing it for one week, have them add it to their chart.

Lesson 3: Each Family Should Be Self-reliant

Read the following quotation:

"The responsibility for each member's spiritual, social, emotional, physical, or economic well-being rests first, upon himself, second, upon his family, and third, upon the Church. Members of the Church are commanded by the Lord to be self-reliant and independent to the extent of their ability. (See D&C 78:13–14.)

"No true Latter-day Saint, while physically or emotionally able, will voluntarily shift the burden of his own or his family's well-being to someone else. So long as he can, under the inspiration of the Lord and with his own labors, he will work to the extent of his ability to supply himself and his family with the spiritual and temporal necessities of life. (See Gen. 3:19, 1 Tim. 5:8, and Philip. 2:12.)" (Spencer W. Kimball, in Conference Report, Apr. 1978, p. 120; or *Ensign.* May 1978 p. 79.)

Discuss how this specifically applies to your family. List ways your family is striving to be self-reliant.

Examples: We grow our own vegetables. We work to earn money to pay our bills. We are assembling our food storage.

Examine areas where your family could become more self-reliant. Perhaps your family could produce more of their own food or clothing or learn to do their own car repairs. Set goals and make definite plans to accomplish them.

Lesson 4: We Are Responsible for Our Own Salvation

Read or summarize 1 Nephi 15:1–11. Contrast Nephi's attitude with the attitudes of Laman and Lemuel.

• How could Laman and Lemuel know these things for themselves? (See verse 11.) Explain that even though their father was a prophet, they could not gain the celestial kingdom through his testimony. Each brother had to develop his own testimony.

Read the following:

"This Church relies on individual testimony. Each must earn his own testimony. It is then that you can stand and say, as I can say, that I know that

God lives, that He is our Father, that we have a child-parent relationship with Him. I know that He is close, that we can go to Him and appeal, and then, if we will be obedient and listen and use every resource, we will have an answer to our prayers." (Boyd K. Packer, "Self-Reliance," *Ensign*, Aug. 1975, p. 89.)

Illustrate the idea that we cannot live on borrowed light: Darken a room and give one person a flashlight. Instruct everyone to draw a picture of something. The person holding the flashlight can help, but if he is not always near, the others will flounder. Discuss how everyone needs to have his own light. Liken this to the strength of a testimony and the need to know for oneself that the gospel is true.

Explain that as we learn, grow, and live the gospel, it is as if we climb higher and higher up a ladder. Each of us has his own ladder to climb. We can encourage and help one another, but each must do his own climbing. Reread 1 Nephi 15:11. Bear testimony that, if we are trying, the Lord will help and bless us so that we will be able to achieve salvation.

Have family members select and work on an area of the gospel in which they would like to become more self-reliant, such as gaining a testimony of the Book of Mormon, doing the right thing when friends are not, learning to fast, or completely reading a book of scripture.

Lesson 5: With the Lord's Help We Can Solve Our Own Problems

Read 1 Nephi 3:7. Discuss how the Lord has prepared the way for us to keep his commandments. Explain that, along with the scriptures, the prophets, and other helps, the Lord has given us ourselves. Each of us came to earth possessing many talents and abilities, and the Lord expects us to use these talents and abilities to accomplish many things.

Read Doctrine and Covenants 58:26–

28 and discuss what the Lord expects us to do for ourselves. For example, a Primary teacher is called to teach a class each week. What could he or she do to enrich this calling, without having to be asked by the bishop or Primary president? Ask your family to suggest situations which apply to them.

Tell the story of the Brother of Jared (Ether 1:33–3:6), emphasizing that while the Lord gave the Brother of Jared many instructions, the Lord expected him to also show self-reliance. He did what he could before asking the Lord to provide the light for the stones. (See Ether 2:23, 3:3–4.) Emphasize that, like the Brother of Jared, we must do our part first.

RESOURCES

Scriptures

Acts 20:32–37 (Paul worked to supply his own personal needs.)
Galatians 6:7–9 (As we sow, so shall we reap.)
2 Nephi 5:17 (Nephi taught his people to labor.)
2 Nephi 10:23 (Ye are free to choose.)
Mosiah 27:4–5 (People of Mosiah were self-reliant.)
Alma 1:26–27 (People of Alma were self-reliant.)
Doctrine and Covenants 46:7–8 (Ask God in all things.)
Doctrine and Covenants 58:26–28 (Not to be commanded in all things.)
See also "Accountability" in the Topical Guide.

Songs and Hymns

"I Pledge Myself to Love the Right," *Sing with Me*, B–47.
"I Want to Live the Gospel," *Sing with Me*, B–65.
"Dare to Do Right," *Sing with Me*, B–81.
"Do What Is Right," *Hymns*, no. 27.
"Choose the Right," *Hymns*, no. 110.

Other

"Gaining a Testimony through the Holy Ghost," lesson 16 in the "Lessons" section of this manual.

TALENTS AND GIFTS

Well done, thou good and faithful servant: thou hast been faithful over a few things, I will make thee ruler over many things: enter thou into the joy of thy Lord.
—Matthew 25:21

GOSPEL TRUTH

We are given talents and gifts to help us fulfill our missions on this earth and to help us bless the lives of others. We have a responsibility to Heavenly Father, to ourselves, and to others to develop our talents and gifts as completely as we can. The development of talents and gifts requires persistence, courage, and patience, but brings great joy.

IDEAS FOR LESSONS

Lesson 1: The Importance of Developing Talents and Gifts

Read or tell the parable of the talents found in Matthew 25:14–30.

The word *talent* in this parable means a piece of money. Discuss the fact that abilities are given to us by the Lord much as the money was given to each of the three servants in the parable. We each have the responsibility for developing our own abilities. Have each family member tell what his or her best talent or gift is, and then invite other family members to comment.

If older children have had patriarchal blessings that declare their gifts and talents, they may want to share these. Encourage family members to search for talents they would like to develop. Invite them to suggest ways they can help one another fulfill the responsibility of developing their talents and gifts.

Lesson 2: Talents and Gifts Are Given to Us to Bless Others

Before family home evening, ask each family member to be prepared to tell about someone who blessed his life by sharing his gifts and talents. Ask family members to report at the beginning of family home evening. Discuss how your family's talents and gifts could be used to help a friend or neighbor. Create a workable plan and carry it out.

Challenge each family member to watch for opportunities to use his or her talents and gifts to bless another family member.

Lesson 3: Developing Talents and Gifts Requires Time and Patience

Show a picture of each parent as a tiny baby. Discuss whether or not these babies had talents and gifts. Have each parent then demonstrate a talent or gift he or she has worked hard to develop, and tell of the time and effort involved. Show pictures of each child as a baby, and ask these questions:

• What talents and gifts did you have as babies?

• What talents did you demonstrate at a young age?

• What talents and gifts have you developed?

• What talents and gifts would you like to develop this year? In ten years?

Discuss specific steps each person can take to develop his or her talents and gifts.

Lesson 4: Discovering and Developing Talents and Gifts

Note to Parents: Give constant, positive support to family members as they develop their talents and gifts. Make lessons, books, and other resources available as you can. Attend school and Church performances as a family. Give special recognition for talks, performances, or other displays of talent by having special days or meals in which the performer gets a special treatment for one day or his favorite meal for dinner.

Plan family activities that will help family members discover new talents and develop old ones. Be creative in involving family talents in every family home evening and gathering. Act

out stories; let everyone lead the singing; recognize special achievement. Set the example by developing your own talents.

Build a family home evening around the following ideas:

1. Plan an art outing and spend an hour sketching details of nature or buildings.

2. Design your dream house.

3. Plan a family talent show.

4. Carve soap animals.

5. Write essays, short stories, or poems.

6. Invite the children to plan and present a play to parents and grandparents. Offer to help write the script or make costumes.

7. Play with clay.

8. Write a family song.

9. Organize a family band with simple instruments like harmonicas, wooden recorders, or kitchen utensils. Learn one or two fun songs, and practice until you enjoy playing them as a family.

10. Build a tree house or playhouse.

11. Spend an evening teaching your children dances from your youth.

12. Have a cupcake- or cookie-decorating contest.

13. Do something new!

Lesson 5: Overcoming a Handicap or Fear That Prevents Us from Developing or Using Our Talents

Relate a personal experience of how you developed a talent despite a weakness or fear, or tell an inspiring story about someone who overcame a handicap to develop a talent.

Read Ether 12:27. Ask family members to write down one talent they are afraid to develop or a handicap they would like to overcome. Let other family members discuss how they can help that person develop that talent.

Ask each person to list specific steps he will take to develop that talent

during the week. Report on the progress at the next family home evening.

RESOURCES

Scriptures

Luke 12:48 (Where much is given, much is expected.)

1 Timothy 4:14 (Neglect not the gift within you.)

2 Nephi 2:27 (Man is given all things he needs.)

Moroni 10:8–18 (Every gift comes from Christ.)

Doctrine and Covenants 6:11 (Use gifts to teach the gospel.)

Doctrine and Covenants 46:8–12 (Every person has a gift.)

Doctrine and Covenants 60:2–3 (It is wrong to hide talents.)

Doctrine and Covenants 82:18 (Talents increase when used to serve.)

See also "Talents" in the Topical Guide.

TITHING

No person knows the principle of tithing until he pays tithing.
—President Harold B. Lee

GOSPEL TRUTH

The Lord has asked that we pay tithes and offerings; by doing so, we show our love for him and help to build his kingdom.

IDEAS FOR LESSONS

Lesson 1: Why Pay a Full Tithing?

On separate pieces of paper, make a copy of the following for each member of your family:

Alma 13:15 — Israelites
Genesis 28:20–22 — Abraham
2 Chronicles 31:5 — People of Judah
Nehemiah 13:12 — Jacob

Have the members of your family look up the scriptures and match each scripture with the person or persons to whom it pertains. Then ask each one to write on his paper the one thing all of these people had in common. (Each paid tithing.)

Read Leviticus 27:30, 34. Explain that the law of tithing has always been part of the gospel. To help your family understand that it is a commandment for us as well as it was for God's people anciently, read Doctrine and Covenants 119:4.

Discuss how paying our tithing is one way we can acknowledge what our Heavenly Father has given us and show our love and appreciation to him.

On a chalkboard or large piece of paper, have family members make a list of possible reasons for paying tithing. Highlight those that demonstrate our love and appreciation for our Heavenly Father.

Discuss the following attitudes and decide on the right solution:

1. A man once said, "I pay tithing on all my salary after deductions, since I don't get the money that is taken for taxes." Is he correct? (Tithing is one-tenth of *all* our interest or increase, before anything else is taken out. See D&C 119:4.)

2. Another person made this statement: "I don't know why I should pay tithing. The Church is rich enough, anyway." (The Church does need everyone's tithing to build buildings and operate its many programs. But even if it did not need our money, tithing is still a commandment and will bring us many blessings. See Malachi 3:10.)

Help your family members realize that paying a full tithing can be a blessing in their lives. Encourage them to make a commitment to always obey this commandment.

Lesson 2: Spiritual Blessings of Paying Tithing

Read and discuss Doctrine and Covenants 29:34–35.

• In what way is tithing a spiritual commandment? Why did Heavenly Father give us this commandment?

Discuss the following:

"I think it is not well known in the Church that payment of tithing has very little to do with money. Tithing has to do with faith." (A. Theodore Tuttle, in Conference Report, Apr. 1970, p. 86; or *Improvement Era*, June 1970, p. 80.)

• What does Elder Tuttle mean when he says that tithing has "very little to do with money?"

Read the following experience of a sixteen-year-old girl:

" 'My dad and mother are good people, and I love them very much. We have family prayer but not very often any more because Mom and Dad are always fighting about money. We have lots of bills to pay each month, and my dad is working two jobs to make more money. I am wondering if it is all right for me, since I have a job at a drive-in, to give my money to my mother and skip tithing for a while?' " (John H. Vandenberg, in Conference Report, Oct. 1966, p. 66; or *Improvement Era*, Dec. 1966, p. 1123.)

Discuss the following questions:

• What counsel would you give to this sixteen-year-old girl? (Pay your tithing first, and you will be blessed in helping your family.)

• What suggestions would you give to this family? (Realize the spiritual blessings that come with paying tithing, and trust the Lord to help you better manage the 90 percent that is left.)

• Should they begin paying tithing now, or wait until they get caught up financially? (Begin right now.)

Ask family members to list the potential blessings this family could enjoy by paying their tithing first.

Relate the story of the widow's mite found in Mark 12:41–44.

• Do you think the poor widow was blessed? In what ways?

Bear your testimony of the blessings which come from paying a full tithing.

Lesson 3: Budgeting for Tithing and Offerings

Help family members understand that we pay our tithing first by conducting the following experiment: Give each member of the family ten small pieces of fruit. Ask one family member to give back one piece and keep the rest. Ask another to eat nine pieces and then give back the only one left. Discuss the results of the experiment.

• Which was the easier way to give? How does this apply to paying tithing?

Read and discuss the following statements:

"Wise family budgeting begins with obeying the law of tithing, for the payment of tithing puts the mind at ease and alert to cope with other essentials of family financial matters" (John H. Vandenberg, in Conference Report, Oct. 1966, p. 69; or *Improvement Era*, Dec. 1966, p. 1124).

WORD OF WISDOM

"We can't make the family budget stretch far enough on our own, so we had better form a partnership with the Lord by giving ten percent to him" (Robert L. Simpson, in Conference Report, Apr. 1966, p. 53; or *Improvement Era*, June 1966, p. 518).

The following game can stimulate discussion on the law of tithing.

Have one of the children leave the room and remain out of hearing range until called. Have the rest of the family make paper signs as follows:

Tithes and offerings
Rent or house payment
Groceries
Service station
Insurance
Car payment

Members of the family or empty chairs can represent these various businesses or expenditures. Prepare play money totaling $550 and give it to the child when he returns to the room.

Give him a list of monthly payments to be made, as follows:
Rent or house payment, $300
Groceries, $60
Service station, $40
Insurance, $30
Car payment, $76
Tithes and offerings
   (Tithing, $55;
   Fast offering, $7;
   Budget, $10)

Tell him to pay his bills as fast as he can. Observe what happens, and discuss the situation. There is not enough money to pay all of the bills and still pay a full tithing. What should he do?

Point out that you pay tithing first, and then you pay a portion of what you owe on each other bill. Talk about which areas you might be able to cut expenses in so that you can live within your budget. Paying the Lord first ensures his help and blessings in being able to budget the rest of your money successfully.

RESOURCES

Scriptures

Malachi 3:10–12 (Blessings from paying tithes and offerings.)
Mark 12:33 (Loving God is most important.)
2 Corinthians 9:6–7 (Paying tithing cheerfully.)
Hebrews 7:1–2 (Abraham paid tithes.)
Doctrine and Covenants 64:23–24 (He who is tithed will not be burned.)
Doctrine and Covenants 97:10–12 (House of the Lord to be built by tithing.)
Doctrine and Covenants 119:3–6 (Law of tithing as we know it was given.)
See also "Tithing" in the Topical Guide.

Songs and Hymns

"I'll Pay My Tithing to the Lord," *Sing with Me*, B–44.
"I Want to Give the Lord My Tenth," *Sing with Me*, B–47.

Other

Gospel Principles, "Tithes and Offerings," chapter 32.

Windows of Heaven, available through your meetinghouse library in either a 16mm film or videocassette version.

All saints who remember to keep and do these sayings . . . shall find wisdom . . . and shall run and not be weary.
—Doctrine and Covenants 89:18–20

GOSPEL TRUTH

One of the greatest gifts from our Heavenly Father is the physical body each of us has. He has given us a law of health to help us care for the body, because it is a temple to house the spirit. Great blessings are promised if we obey this law.

IDEAS FOR LESSONS

Lesson 1: Why Is It Important to Take Good Care of Your Body?

If you have small children, you can play "Simon Says" for a few minutes or sing "Hinges" (*Activity Songs and Verses*, p. 6) to illustrate how many things our bodies can do.

Have the family sit in a circle and play the following game. Each person, in turn, tells of one thing his body can do. For example: "I can *blink* my eyes like an owl," or "I can *swim* like a *fish*," or "I can *eat* like a *horse*." Go around the circle; if a person cannot think of a statement in ten seconds, he is out of the game and must leave the circle. Continue taking turns until only one person remains.

Discuss what an amazing creation our body is. Point out the fact that we were created in the image of God and that we have the potential to someday do all the things he can do.

Have someone find the following scriptures and read them aloud. Discuss what the Lord is saying in each one of them:

Deuteronomy 14:3 (Be careful of what you eat.)
Doctrine and Covenants 88:124 (Allow your body enough rest.)
Doctrine and Covenants 89:7–9 (Don't take harmful substances into your body.)

Ask why the Lord has said these

things to us. To help answer this question, have a family member read 1 Corinthians 3:16–17. Discuss as a family how important it is to take care of these temples that house our spirits. Sing "The Lord Gave Me a Temple" (*Sing with Me*, B–48).

Lesson 2: What Does the Lord Really Say in the Word of Wisdom?

As a family, study the Word of Wisdom in Doctrine and Covenants 89. Write the following questions and references on one side of cards, and draw a large question mark on the opposite side. Have each family member draw a card and answer the question by referring to the verses indicated:

- Why did the Lord give us this law of health? (See verses 1–4.)
- What should we avoid putting into our bodies? (See verses 5–9; see also the "Note" below.)
- What has the Lord made for the use of man? (See verses 10–11, 14, 16–17.)
- When should we use animals and birds for food? (See verses 12–15.)
- Who will run and not be weary? (See verses 18–21.)

Note: The Word of Wisdom warns against the use of tobacco, wine and strong drinks (alcohol), and hot drinks (which the prophets have interpreted as tea and coffee). More recently, President Spencer W. Kimball warned that drugs can also be harmful (see Conference Report, Apr. 1974, p. 8; or *Ensign*, May 1974, p. 7).

Have each family member tell what he might do to better live the Word of Wisdom. Challenge each family member to implement the suggestion during the coming week and report on progress at the next family home evening.

Lesson 3: How Can Keeping the Word of Wisdom Bless Our Lives?

Relate the story of Daniel, Shadrach, Meshach, and Abed-nego found in

Daniel 1. Tell how these young men were blessed by keeping the Lord's law of health.

Have family members compare Daniel 1:17–20 with Doctrine and Covenants 89:18–19. Explain that these men were blessed both spiritually and physically by their adherence to the Lord's law of health. Emphasize that we can obtain these same blessings if we follow the Lord's advice.

Relate the following story:

Creed Haymond, a Mormon boy, was representing his Pennsylvania college in an annual athletic meet involving 1,700 men. The night before the big event, Creed's coach said, "Creed, I'm having the boys take a little sherry wine tonight. I want you to have a little."

"I can't do it, Coach."

"But, Creed, I'm not trying to get you to drink. I know what you Mormons believe. I'm giving you this as a tonic."

"It wouldn't do me any good. . . . I can't take it."

The coach continued trying to coax Creed into taking some of the wine, but Creed refused.

Supposing, Creed thought, he made a poor showing tomorrow; what could he say to the coach? He was to go against the fastest man in the world. Nothing less than his best would do. His teammates were doing as they were told. They believed in their coach. What right had he to disobey? Only one right, one reason, this teaching he had been following and believing all his life, the Word of Wisdom! He knelt down and earnestly, very earnestly, asked the Lord to give him a testimony as to the source of this revelation which he had believed and obeyed literally. Then he went to bed and slept the sound slumber of healthy youth.

The next morning, all the boys on the team except Creed were sick.

"Maybe it's the tonic you gave them," Creed volunteered.

"Maybe so," the coach answered.

As the events got underway, it became plain that something was wrong with Creed's team. One after another, their entrants fell far below their own records. The 100-yard dash was announced: it and the 220-yard dash were Creed Haymond's races.

The pistol shot—and every man sprang forward into the air and touched earth at a run—that is, all except Creed Haymond. The earth gave way because of a hole made by a previous runner and he came down on his knees. In a flash he was up and running. Creed swept in a whirlwind past the leader to victory.

Through some mistake in arrangement, the finals of the 220 came immediately after the semifinals. He had already run three races and was panting for breath.

The starter ordered the breathless men to their marks and raised his pistol. This time Creed literally shot from his marks. Later, Creed's coach laid his hand on his shoulder and said, "You just ran those 220 yards in the fastest time ever run by any human being." (See "I Can't Do It, Coach," in Leon R. Hartshorn, comp., *Inspiring Stories for Young Latter-day Saints* [Salt Lake City: Deseret Book Co., 1975], pp. 123–28.)

Discuss with your family the blessings that Creed Haymond received because he kept the Word of Wisdom.

Have your family list the promises made to those who keep the Word of Wisdom (see D&C 89:18–21). Discuss how these promises can bless our lives.

Lesson 4: How to Gain Strength to Say No

Tell the following story from the life of Spencer W. Kimball and discuss how deciding in advance can help us withstand temptation.

"I made up my mind while still a little

boy that I would never break the Word of Wisdom. . . . I wanted to . . . please my Heavenly Father. And so I made up my mind firmly and solidly that I would never touch those harmful things. . . .

"I remember once in later years . . . that I went to Nice, France, to [an] international convention. As a part of that celebration there was a sumptuous banquet . . . , and the large building was set for an elegant meal. . . . I noted that at every place there were seven goblets. . . .

"As the meal got underway, an army of waiters . . . poured the wine and liquor. Seven glass goblets were filled at every plate. The drinks were colorful. I was a long way from home. . . . The evil one seemed to whisper to me, 'This is your chance. You are thousands of miles from home. There is no one here to watch you. No one will ever know if you drink the contents of those goblets. This is your chance!' And then a sweeter spirit seemed to whisper, 'You have a covenant with yourself; you promised yourself you would never do it; and with your Heavenly Father you made a covenant. . . .' Suffice it to say that when I got up from the table an hour later, the seven goblets were still full of colorful material that had been poured into them but never touched." (In Conference Report, Apr. 1974, pp. 127–28; or Ensign, May 1974, pp. 88–89.)

Put words such as the following on small pieces of paper:

Tea	Coffee
Alcohol	Tobacco
Harmful Drugs	

Make enough so that each family member can draw at least one from a sack or bowl. Have everyone draw a slip and role-play how he or she would respond to peer-group pressure to indulge in that item. Encourage all family members to suggest additional ways of responding to people who try to

pressure others to break the Word of Wisdom.

Encourage each family member to commit or recommit himself to keep the Word of Wisdom. Some may find it helpful to put the commitment on paper; others may prefer to make it silently to the Lord in prayer. Emphasize that having once made the decision and commitment, it is not necessary to redecide it later. Suggest that such a commitment will offer protection and comfort when faced with these temptations.

Lesson 5: Withstanding Advertising Pressure to Break the Word of Wisdom

Show your family a baited mousetrap, set and ready to spring closed. Then have a child use a stick to touch the bait and spring the trap. Ask what the mouse would do if it understood how the trap worked and that touching the bait was sure to bring disaster.

Read Doctrine and Covenants 89:4 and Jeremiah 5:26. Explain these scriptures to small children as necessary. Discuss how advertisements are like the trap—they attempt to persuade us to use products that are harmful to us.

Help your children identify the "bait" by giving the children each a magazine or newspaper. Have them cut out the advertisements that are urging us to break the Word of Wisdom. Have the children explain how these ads are like the baited trap.

You may wish to help your small children recognize and avoid these attractive traps by suggesting that they say aloud "It's a trap!" whenever they see these ads in magazines, on billboards, or on television. Throw all of the cut-out ads into the garbage can.

You may also want to alert your teenagers to the frequency of subtle pressure from television shows that make drinking and smoking look attractive: have them count the instances of drinking and smoking during the typical half-hour or hour television show.

Lesson 6: Special Helps in Overcoming Problems

If a member of your family has a Word of Wisdom problem, consider some of the following ideas, which other families have found helpful.

1. We first tried to put our own lives in order, and as our son saw our example, he decided he wanted to change.

2. We approached our daughter with increased unconditional love to let her know that we loved her in spite of the problem. She decided to move home again, and in that atmosphere she is finding the strength to change.

3. We fasted and prayed often for our brother. When he learned that we had added his name to the prayer roll at the temple, he knew that we really cared. He is trying to change his life and habits.

If you have a Word of Wisdom problem that you would like to master, but feel that you cannot win the battle over your body and mind, you may want to consider the counsel of Elder Theodore M. Burton:

"The spirit within us is more powerful than the body, and we can use that spirit to commit ourselves to righteous actions. We *can* control the body and its bodily appetites. It is fallacious to say that we were created with propensities and appetites we cannot control. It is simply not true that people are born with such powerful appetites and passions that they are powerless to control them. God would not be a righteous God if man were created with drives he could not control." (In Conference Report, Apr. 1981, p. 39; or Ensign, May 1981, pp. 30.)

RESOURCES

Scriptures

Exodus 20:9–10 (Rest bodies on the Sabbath.)

Proverbs 23:20–21 (Do not be a

WORK

drunkard or a glutton.)
Daniel 1:4–21 (Daniel and his brethren proved the wisdom of eating good food.)
1 Corinthians 3:16–17 (Our bodies are temples of God.)
Doctrine and Covenants 10:4 (Do not labor more than you have strength.)
Doctrine and Covenants 59:16–20 (Use food with judgment, not in excess.)
Doctrine and Covenants 88:124 (Do not sleep longer than is needful.)
See also "Word of Wisdom" in the Topical Guide.

Songs and Hymns

"In Our Lovely Deseret," *Sing with Me*, B–24.
"How Gentle God's Commands," *Hymns*, no. 67.

Other

Gospel Principles, "The Lord's Law of Health," chapter 29.

Uncle Ben, available through your meetinghouse library in either a 16mm film or videocassette version.

In all labour there is profit.
—Proverbs 14:23

GOSPEL TRUTH

Work, our primary means of both growth and happiness, is ordained of God. A family will be strengthened by working together, and individual members will gain self-esteem by realizing they can make a worthwhile contribution to the family.

IDEAS FOR LESSONS

Lesson 1: The Value of Work

Discuss what life would be like if no one worked. List ways work helps people (provides food, clothing, shelter, entertainment).

• How does the work of each family member help the individual and the whole family?

In your discussion, share the following quotation:

"Thank God every morning when you get up that you have something to do that day which must be done, whether you like it or not. Being forced to work, and forced to do your best, will breed in you temperance and self-control, diligence and strength of will, cheerfulness and content, and a hundred virtues which the idle will never know." (Charles Kingsley, quoted in *Liahona: The Elders' Journal*, 12 May 1914, p. 761.)

Read Moses 5:1 and Genesis 3:19.

• How was Adam's curse—to eat "by the sweat of his brow" (Moses 5:1)—a blessing?

Draw attention to skills and talents each individual in the family has worked to develop in the past few months, or year. (Mention skills such as tying shoes, making the bed, reading, playing an instrument, or cooking.) Ask each person how he felt when he accomplished that skill or developed that talent. Discuss how these new skills improve the individual, the family, and the

community.
Discuss as a family the good feeling that can come while working to accomplish a chore or a job and the satisfaction that comes when that job is completed. Point out that this satisfaction is part of the reward.

• Would there be growth if we were rewarded first?

Read the following from Ether 12:6: "Dispute not because ye see not, for ye receive no witness until after the trial of your faith." Discuss how this relates to work.

Note to parents: You might decide upon some rewards for jobs well done. Hide a coin on a shelf to be dusted as a reward for the person who dusts it. Hang a homemade award badge on the door of a well-cleaned bedroom.

Lesson 2: Work Can Be Fun

Make a poster of the following quotation, and place it in a prominent place following the lesson:

"Let us realize that the privilege to work is a gift, that power to work is a blessing, and that love of work is success" (David O. McKay, *Pathways to Happiness* [Salt Lake City: Bookcraft, 1957], p. 381).

Ask family members to tell some of the jobs they enjoy most, some they enjoy least, and why. Discuss ways tasks can be done easier, faster, and more enjoyably. Discuss specific ways family members can help and encourage each other in the tasks they have to do.

To start them thinking, tell about Margaret, who learned the multiplication tables while doing the dishes, practiced adding prices and counting change when she was sent to the store, and added and subtracted stairs while sweeping (see *Walk in His Ways: Basic Manual for Children, Part B*, p. 11). Tell them also of President Spencer W. Kimball, who sang, counted, and memorized the Articles of Faith while milking cows (see

Edward L. Kimball and Andrew E. Kimball, Jr., *Spencer W. Kimball* [Salt Lake City: Bookcraft, 1977], p. 36).

Discuss the following quotation: "When man is industrious and righteous, then is he happy" (Brigham Young, in *Journal of Discourses,* 9:244).

• Why does our joy in work depend on how well we do our job?

Lesson 3: Learning By Working

Organize a family work project. You might consider one of the following:

1. Clean up and reorganize a problem area in your home.

2. Build a tool shed, build a playhouse, or do some remodeling.

3. Plant and care for a family garden.

4. Clean up, repair, or build something for a needy neighbor.

Lesson 4: Career Planning

Spend a family home evening discussing individual career plans. Parents could tell about their own careers, the preparation involved, and the satisfactions (or regrets).

Encourage teenagers to find summer or other employment to help them develop skills and learn what types of work suit them. Discuss their career goals and what will be necessary to achieve them. Help them with ideas for careers especially suited to their interests and talents; discuss the possibilities of job opportunities in these areas.

Be careful not to dictate your children's career plans. You may suggest, but then support and encourage their own ideas. Plan a field trip to observe the types of work they are interested in, or arrange to talk to someone in that profession.

Lesson 5: Work in the Home

For background materials, see "A House of Order," lesson 20 in the "Lessons" section of this manual, plus the additional ideas following it. Also see the work chart and organization

ideas in "Making Work Fun" in the "Family Activities" section of this manual.

RESOURCES

Scriptures

2 Chronicles 15:7 (Your work shall be rewarded.)

Proverbs 14:23 (In all labor there is profit.)

1 Thessalonians 4:11–12 (Work with your own hands.)

1 Timothy 5:8 (All to work to supply their own needs.)

2 Nephi 5:17 (Nephi taught his people to work.)

Doctrine and Covenants 42:42 (Do not be idle.)

Doctrine and Covenants 58:26–28 (Men should be actively engaged in a good cause.)

Moses 1:39 (The work of the Lord is to help us.)

Moses 4:23–25 (Adam to work for his food.)

See also "Work" in the Topical Guide.

Songs and Hymns

"A Happy Helper," *Sing with Me,* D–1.

"When We're Helping," *Sing with Me,* D–5.

"Have I Done Any Good?" *Hymns,* no. 58.

"The World Has Need of Willing Men," *Hymns,* no. 206.

Other

Gospel Principles, "Work and Personal Responsibility," chapter 27.

BUILDING A STRONG FAMILY

Examples
and ideas to help you
solve problems
and develop a strong
family

Contents

Introduction

As we strive to improve ourselves and our families, we need to remember that the Lord wants us to have joy and happiness in our lives. One of Satan's most effective tools is discouragement. Sometimes in our efforts to improve we forget that change and growth take time. We should not expect overnight perfection from either ourselves or other family members. Enjoying our families is one of the joys we should accept.

The Prophet Joseph Smith said, "Happiness is the object and design of our existence; and will be the end thereof, if we pursue the path that leads to it; and this path is virtue, uprightness, faithfulness, holiness, and keeping all the commandments of God. But we cannot keep all the commandments without first knowing them, and we cannot expect to know all, or more than we now know unless we comply with or keep those we have already received." (*Teachings of the Prophet Joseph Smith*, sel. Joseph Fielding Smith [Salt Lake City: Deseret Book Company, 1976], pp. 155–56.)

This section of the manual has been prepared to help us better apply those principles that we teach and learn during home evenings. It was written generally to parents with children; but whether we are single or married, parents or not, living alone or with family or friends, we can adapt material from this section to meet the challenges of our own circumstances.

BUILDING A STRONG FAMILY

"*We continue to stress the urgent need for couples, for parents and children, and for single adults living alone to study and live the principles of truth, with special attention to nurturing love and harmony within their family circles*"

(Spencer W. Kimball, "Therefore I Was Taught," Ensign, Jan. 1982, p. 3).

As you study the suggestions, select one idea or area to work on at a time. Don't expect instant perfection or try to improve in more areas at the same time. Smile and be happy. Tell your spouse and children that you love them, and hug and kiss them regularly. Each of us needs the blessings that come from giving and receiving love.

Although creating love and harmony within our families is not always easy, it is vital, especially today when we and our children must withstand the growing evil influences around us.

Everyone faces challenges and choices. We and our children have many voices calling us away from gospel principles and the counsel of the Brethren. But when we make our homes places of safety for us and our children, we can more easily grow and develop in righteousness.

Turning a home into a righteous haven and making our family relationships ideal takes more than merely being active in the Church and participating in its programs, important as these are. It takes a strong, honest commitment to live gospel principles and to teach these principles in our homes.

Many parents feel inadequate as they face the challenges of marriage and parenthood. Many worry about the temptations of the world that daily confront them and their children. Some worry that they may already have "lost" their children.

Fortunately, we do not need to face our problems alone; Heavenly Father wants us to succeed as individuals and as parents and families. To help us, he has provided important guides, such as the scriptures, a living prophet, other Church leaders, and the Holy Spirit. These can help us understand and apply the gospel principles that will bring joy to us and our families.

This section of the Family Resource Book highlights three fundamental gospel principles: integrity, agency, and love. As you read and ponder this section, you will read about husbands and wives, parents, children, and single adults who face much the same everyday challenges you do. The principles needed to help them solve their problems are the same that will help you.

Helping Family Members Live the Gospel

Sometimes we think that some five-second formula or recipe will effectively change a family member's behavior. Long-term change, however, comes only from living correct principles. The Lord told priesthood bearers how the power and influence of the priesthood should be used (see D&C 121:41–46). We can use some of the things he mentioned, such as persuasion, long-suffering, gentleness, meekness, and love unfeigned to teach and guide our children and others. In contrast, using sarcasm, intimidation, force, impatience, irritability or anger, harshness, and pride will neither teach children proper values nor help them change their behavior. In fact, we know that it is Satan, not Heavenly Father, who wants us to use force and hostility.

We can learn to be better parents by studying the scriptures to see how Heavenly Father deals with his children. We can also learn how not to act by observing Satan's methods. What can you learn from the following chart to help you be a better parent and spouse?

The Lord's Way	Satan's Way
Love unfeigned—charity, caring for others' welfare despite any wrongdoing.	Physical force—being hostile and unfairly using physical strength.
Acceptance—seeing others in eternal perspective, judging with compassion.	Blame—condemning others' faults without compassion.
Integrity—being honest, a personal commitment to righteousness.	Accusation—provoking guilt, reminding people of their mistakes to punish them and justify oneself.
Persuasion—teaching with compassion, kindly pointing out advantages and disadvantages of situations.	Intimidation—ruling by fear because others are afraid of one's power.
Gentleness—soft, not treating others harshly.	Threat—expressing an intent to physically or emotionally harm someone.
Trust—lovingly allowing others to exercise their agency to choose right or wrong and to accept the consequences.	Pride—self-righteously preaching moral truths and condemning others.
Responsibility—acknowledging and assuming your role in any situation including repenting for past wrongdoing.	Self-centeredness—refusing to accept responsibility for your actions.
Meekness—humility, uncomplaining, and teachable	Hautiness—being unteachable, proud, and pessimistic.

Personal Integrity— The Key to Example

The foundation of a righteous home is the parents' righteousness. If we desire others, especially our children, to be obedient to gospel principles, we must first look to our own integrity and obedience. When we live by correct principles, our children will be more likely to follow our example.

Our obedience, however, does not assure us an easy life free of problems nor that our children will automatically follow our example. However, by earnestly seeking the Lord's help and striving to be good parents, our chances for success will be greatly increased.

The example of an honest parent humbly struggling to live the gospel can greatly influence children. Despite what we might think, children are not discouraged by imperfect parents. In fact, parental honesty, along with parental repentance, is important. A parent who admits his own wrongs and honestly strives to overcome them is trying to become perfect. His honest behavior invites his children to be honest. Parents who honor the covenants and promises they make with God and men teach integrity to their children.

Richard Repents

Richard had been searching for a late night snack and found an uneaten sweet roll in the bread drawer. After having the roll and a cold glass of milk, he went satisfied to bed. About 7:15 A.M.,

Agency–The Key to Growth

the quiet morning was interrupted by the obviously irritated voice of his four-year-old daughter: "Who ate my roll?"

"I did, sweetheart," Richard answered. "I'm sorry; I didn't know it was yours."

She appeared in the doorway of the bedroom, one hand on her little hip. Richard humbly said, "Next time, I'll ask, ok?"

"Ok," she replied forgivingly, "but don't forget!"

That afternoon, Richard brought home another sweetroll for his little daughter. His repentance taught more than the value of honesty; Richard's daughter also learned that her father respected her rights.

Agency is the power and freedom to make choices, right or wrong. Children are able to grow the most when they can exercise their agency. However, when they use their agency to choose the wrong, they limit their future happiness. To make choices properly, children need knowledge. They need to understand the alternatives, and they need the freedom to choose. As a parent, allowing your children to exercise their agency and choose for themselves is one of the greatest challenges you may face. Some parents force their children to do right, denying them the right of agency. Consider the following different responses to the same situation:

Natalie Chooses New Clothes
Thirteen-year-old Natalie's parents gave her some money to buy clothes for school. So she and her mother went shopping for the clothes.

Possibility One: With her mother by her side, Natalie first looked through a dress rack and then through a large selection of jeans. Unfortunately, she had never been taught nor allowed to make choices. Finally, she found something she liked and turned to her mother for approval.

"Mom! Look at this dress! Isn't it beautiful!"

"Now Natalie," her mother replied, "you know you aren't very tall, and this dress has lines that go around the middle. It will make you look even shorter and fat. That will never do. You

need to pick something more appropriate."

Natalie's voice showed her disappointment as she held up another dress. "How about this one? It doesn't have lines around the middle. I really like it."

"Well," her mother admitted, "it's nicer than the other one, but it has a large turtle neck. We couldn't purchase one with a roll-over neck like that; your neck is very short, sweetheart. You want one that will accent your good features, don't you? How about this one?"

Natalie's enthusiasm was noticeably decreased by the time she held up a brightly colored pair of jeans. "Are these ok?" she asked her mother.

"The colors certainly are bright, aren't they! I really doubt that you'll have much to wear with them. Besides, the way styles change so much, don't you think you'd better pick something more basic. What about these?" Natalie's mother held up a plain, traditional pair.

Natalie and her mother left the store with the necessary purchases made.

- Who made the selections?
- How might Natalie feel toward her new clothes?
- How do you think Natalie feels about herself?
- How might she feel toward her mother?
- What might she say to her friends if they criticise her new clothes?

- How could Natalie's mother have helped more appropriately?

Possibility Two: Natalie, from the time she was a toddler, has been encouraged to think things through, to consider each choice, and to make her own decisions. Some of her early choices were not as wise as they might have been, but she learned much from her experiences. Before the shopping trip, Natalie thought about the clothes she needed and discussed these with her mother. Among other items, Natalie decided she needed a dress and two pair of jeans. Her mother asked if she had decided how much she wanted to spend on each. Natalie said, "Well, I looked around last week, and I'll probably need to spend most for the dress, but I found some jeans on sale. If I choose carefully, I'm sure I'll have enough money."

Inside the store, Natalie set aside several possible choices while her mother shopped in another department. After a few minutes, Natalie invited her mother to look at her choices.

Holding up a dress with lines around the middle, Natalie said, "Mom, look at this dress, isn't it beautiful?"

"That is a darling dress, Natalie. I like the color. Is it your favorite?"

"Well, yes, but I was wondering if the lines around the middle would make me look too short. What do you think, Mom?"

"Well," her mother said thoughtfully, "it might."

"My next favorite is this one," Natalie said, "but it has a roll-over neck, so I've decided no on that. Do you think that if I took some edging or lace and sewed it over the lines on this first one that maybe it would be okay?"

"That would probably soften the accent," her mother replied. "It sounds as if you've made up your mind?"

"I guess I have," Natalie said.

- Assuming that the jean selection follows a similar pattern, who made the selections? How might Natalie feel about her new clothes now?
- What does the dialogue reveal about Natalie's feelings?
- How do you think she feels toward her mother?
- What might Natalie say to her friends about her new clothes?

Unconditional Love— The Key to Effective Parenthood

A person's ability to love unconditionally can have powerful effects. Seeing another person in an eternal perspective, knowing that he is of infinite worth, helps us to look beyond his weaknesses. However, if we criticize his behavior, he may see the criticism as a personal attack. Likewise, when a family member makes a mistake, and we find fault or strike back, that person may feel justified in acting as he did. Our challenge is to reject the sin without rejecting the sinner, to reach out and treat him with dignity and respect when he seems to deserve it the least.

Perhaps the biggest challenge we face as parents is when our children choose to do things that are against Church standards. We may feel like forcing our children to do what we know is right, but does Heavenly Father force us to obey his commandments? One of our hymns reminds us that Heavenly Father will "call, persuade, direct aright, And bless with wisdom, love, and light, In nameless ways be good and kind, But never force the human mind" ("Know This, That Every Soul Is Free," *Hymns*, no. 90).

- Why won't Heavenly Father force us?
- Why do you think Satan was cast out of the pre-mortal council for wanting to use force?

Elder Jack H. Goaslind, Jr. related the following story about a mother whose daughter chose to go against Church standards:

"A good friend shared this story about how she learned the deeper meaning of love. Their family has always been active in the Church, trying their best to live the commandments. They were shocked and disappointed, however, when their daughter became engaged to a nonmember. The next day the mother was telling a good friend about her feelings. She knew her daughter's fiance was a fine young man, but she felt angry, hurt, betrayed, and numb and did not want to give her daughter a wedding or even see her. She said that the Lord must have guided her to talk to her friend because she received this reply:

" 'What kind of a mother are you that you only love her when she does what you want her to do? That is selfish, self-centered, qualified love. It's easy to love our children when they are good; but when they make mistakes, they need our love even more. We should love and care for them no matter what they do. It doesn't mean we condone or approve of the errors, but we help, not condemn; love, not hate; forgive, not judge. We build them up rather than tear them down; we lead them, not desert them. We love when they are the most unlovable, and if you can't or won't do that, you are a poor mother.' "

"With tears streaming down her face, the mother asked her friend how she could ever thank her. The friend answered, 'Do it for someone else when the need arises. Someone did it for me, and I will be eternally grateful.' " (In Conference Report, Apr. 1981, p. 79; or *Ensign,* May 1981, p. 60.)

The following twelve principles illustrate how integrity, agency, and unconditional love can help in making righteous family living both possible and enjoyable.

Achieving Oneness in Marriage

If each spouse is forever seeking the interests, comforts, and happiness of the other, the love . . . will grow" (Spencer W. Kimball, *Marriage and Divorce* [Salt Lake City: Deseret Book, Co., 1976], p. 23).

Unity in marriage is an important foundation for rearing children successfully. If a husband and wife do not support each other, they greatly weaken their influence with their children. However, if they are humble and strive to achieve greater unity, they can teach their children valuable lessons, both formally and informally.

President Spencer W. Kimball stated: "It is certain that almost any good man and any good woman can have happiness and a successful marriage if both are willing to pay the price" (*Marriage and Divorce*, p. 16). That is a bold statement in a time when so many marriages seem so troubled.

If one spouse is striving honestly to live a gospel-centered life, which includes unconditional love and proper respect for agency, the marriage may not fail. However, if both honor their gospel commitments, the marriage can certainly become a celestial marriage.

In examining your role in promoting oneness in your marriage, consider the following questions:

• Do I acknowledge myself and my companion as persons of worth and value (see Ephesians 5:28–29)?

- Am I willing to see my partner as my best friend?
- Am I willing to put the interest of my marriage and partner first?
- Do I see how my selfish acts hurt my spouse?
- Do I seek spiritual guidance in resolving disagreements?

Obedience to the commandments helps us achieve oneness in marriage. When husbands and wives repent of their wrongdoings, strive to overcome their shortcomings, and seek righteousness, they can become one.

President Ezra Taft Benson gave husbands the following counsel:

"Once you determine that a high priority in your life is to see that your wife and your children are happy, then you will do all in your power to do so. I am not just speaking of satisfying material desires, but of filling other vital needs such as appreciation, compliments, comforting, encouraging, listening, and giving love and affection." (In Conference Report, Apr. 1981, p. 47; or *Ensign*, May 1981, p.34.)

The following example shows how one unhappy marriage was improved because of a simple change in attitude. Each of us should pray for help in recognizing and overcoming our own imperfections and not be overly critical of our spouse.

Linda's Change of Heart

Linda was suffering in an unloving marriage. When asked to name one good quality her husband possessed, she resisted. It seemed ridiculous to her that any good thing remained in her husband. She was pressed to think of something.

Finally, she thought of one positive trait and then another. She began to soften her heart toward her husband. She knew he was not perfect, but she no longer condemned him. Rather, she turned her heart to him, and her suffering decreased. She saw that by her own hardness of heart she had unknowingly helped promote much of their contention.

"A marriage may not always be even and incident-less, but it can be one of great peace. A couple may have poverty, illness, disappointment, failures, and even death in the family, but even these will not rob them of their peace. The marriage can be successful so long as selfishness does not enter in." (Spencer W. Kimball, *Marriage and Divorce*, pp. 19–22.)

Resolving Conflicts in Marriage

Sometimes in our desire to have an ideal marriage, we set unrealistic goals and expectations for our spouses. When they do not meet our demands, we may forget their agency and harbor resentments, becoming blind to our part in marital problems. We think that only our spouses are at fault, and we justify our feelings because of what they have done to us. Elder Carlos E. Asay reminded us to avoid contention:

"*Do not contend or debate over points of doctrine.* The Master warned that 'the spirit of contention is not of me, but is of the devil.' (3 Nephi 11:29.) We are inconsistent if we resort to Satanic tactics in attempting to achieve righteous ends. Such inconsistency results only in frustration, loss of the Spirit, and ultimate defeat." (Carlos E. Asay, in Conference Report, Oct. 1981, p. 93; or *Ensign*, Nov. 1981, p. 68.)

In resolving conflicts in marriage, we must concentrate on our own weaknesses. Elder Neal A. Maxwell, in discussing how to fellowship inactive members, noted a principle important to each of us, particularly to spouses:

"If the choice is between reforming other Church members or ourselves, is there really any question about where we should begin? The key is to have our eyes wide open to our own faults and partially closed to the faults of others—not the other way around! The imperfections of others never release us from the need to work on our own shortcomings." (In Conference

Report, Apr. 1982, p. 57; or *Ensign*, May 1982, p. 39.)

Notice how the couple in the following account followed this principle to resolve conflict.

Ben and Della

It was one of those days. No matter how fast she ran during the day, Della was not able to keep up with the demands of her family. Her neighbor, with even more children than she, seemed so cheerful that Della began to doubt her own ability as a woman, a wife, and a mother.

Ben felt hungrier than usual on his way home. An extra eighty miles to deliver farm equipment had been necessary, but now he was tired. Being home sounded better all the time. Peace. Food. Rest.

Della heard Ben's car in the driveway and glanced at the clock. Oh no! Almost 7:00 P.M.? Now what? She had wanted to have dinner ready, but. . . . She heard the door open as she hurriedly placed the last biscuit on the baking sheet.

Ben strode through the door, leaned around the corner, and smiled at Della. She looked tense, and he noticed the empty table. He paused and took a deep breath.

- If Ben's concern is for his wife, how might he respond?
- If Ben's concern is only for himself, what might happen?

Ben exhaled, smiled at Della, and said, "Looks as if I got here just in time to help." Her tension disappeared. Relieved, she kissed him and said, "It's good to have you home, Ben.

You've had a long day, and I wanted to have dinner ready for you!" She gestured toward the empty table.

"We'll finish it together," he said, placing his arm around her. They then began to share the different challenges each had faced. While Ben set the table, Della put the biscuits in the oven and told him how rushed she had felt—even over-whelmed—all day. Ben forgot about how hungry he was and thought about ways to make her days easier.

Is it realistic to be so interested in your spouse's welfare that hunger seems unimportant? At baptism, and each time we partake of the sacrament, we covenant with God "to bear one another's burdens, that they may be light" (Mosiah 18:8). Whose burdens could be more important for us to bear than those of our spouse? We would do well in our marriages to follow Alma's counsel when he commanded Church members "that there should be no contention one with another, but that they should look forward with one eye, . . . having their hearts *knit* together in unity and in love one towards another" (Mosiah 18:21; italics added).

Family conflict—marked by hostility, resentment, anger, defensiveness, or criticism—is simply not of God and should be repented of. However, when people have conflicts, the counsel to repent may seem unrealistic. That is partly because we cannot feel anger and humility, resentment and compassion, defensiveness and a willingness to

learn at the same time. If you are resentful toward someone, you cannot, at the same time, feel charitable toward him. If you are defensive, you cannot, at the same time, be willing to learn from someone.

Ben and Della were interested in and appreciated each other in spite of their trying circumstances. They avoided frustration and negative feelings by turning their hearts to each other.

To help avoid conflict and contention, ask yourself the following questions:

- Have you searched your own heart for your role in the problem?
- What is the real issue in the conflict?
- What are you willing to do to help solve the problem?
- Will obedience to some gospel law suggest solutions to the problem?
- Do you need to forgive your spouse or repent of anything yourself?

There is no magic formula that will instantly free you from current marital conflict. The only solution is living the gospel. Your own humility and obedience must be the starting point for seeing possible solutions. (See also the "Lesson Ideas" section of this manual and "Contention.")

Teaching by Example

Elder H. Burke Peterson spoke about a father's duty to his family and of the need to be prepared and "listening." "Remember, fathers, you are always teaching—for good or for ill. Your family is learning your ways and beliefs." ("The Father's Duty to Foster the Welfare of His Family," *Ensign*, Nov. 1977, p. 88.)

General principles for helping us improve our families were outlined at the beginning of this section. But when parents wish to teach their children specific values, they do so most powerfully by example. Through love and willingness to listen, to understand, and to share their deepest beliefs, parents teach by example. The following example illustrates how what we think we are teaching may not be what is really learned.

What David Learned

The lesson in family home evening that night was on love. The family discussed ways they could show love for one another. Seven-year-old David said he could show love for his younger sisters by not being mean to them—even if they got into his things. "I won't even push or shove or hit them," he said proudly. Father agreed that that was a good idea, and David left family home evening that night with a new resolve to be kinder to his sisters.

The next night David was trying to fix the pedal on his bicycle when his mother called him to come to dinner. He answered, "I'm coming," but continued to work on the pedal because he was just about finished. His

mother called again. David answered, "All right," but still didn't leave.

As his father sat down at the table, David's mother said, "I've called David twice, but he still hasn't come. I wish he'd mind better." David's father, who was hungry and growing impatient, got up from the table and went outside. David was still working on the bicycle. "What's going on out here, David?" his father yelled. He grabbed David away from the bicycle and shoved him toward the house.

"But Dad, I only . . ."

"No excuses, David! I'm getting sick and tired of your constant disobedience! Now get in the house!" And he gave David another push in that direction.

David was upset as he went into the house. He thought, "Dad doesn't want me to push and shove the girls when they make me mad, but he shoves and pushes me. He says I should be nice to my sisters and show love for them, but he doesn't act like he loves me."

- If we tell our children to be loving and kind in family home evening and yet treat them with harshness and impatience at other times, what will they learn?

- If David's father feels his harshness is justified, of what value are his words on love?

- If David's father does not repent of his harshness, what might David learn?

- Even though David's father might be imperfect at times, how can he still be a proper example to his son? (Admit his

faults and show his son that he can repent.)

Often parents fail to see that they are teaching more than they intend. Example has more meaning to a child than we may think. Elder Vaughn J. Featherstone told of one father who did understand the importance of his day-to-day relationship with his son.

"Some years ago when Aldin Porter was president of the Boise North Stake, he dropped by the home of Glen Clayton, who was the Scoutmaster in his ward. Glen and his son were working together repairing a bicycle. President Porter stood and talked to them for a few minutes and then left. Several hours later he returned and the father and son were still working on the bike together. President Porter said, 'Glen, with the wages you make per hour you could have bought a new bike, considering the time you have spent repairing this old one.'

"Glen stood up and said, 'I'm not repairing a bike, I'm training a boy!' " (In Conference Report, Oct. 1976, pp. 153–54; or *Ensign*, Nov. 1976, p. 103.)

- Can you identify some times when your children learned from you just by the way you related to them?

- When did your children learn something important from you, even though you weren't trying to teach anything in particular?

- What does such an event teach you about love and teaching by example?

"I am convinced," said President Ezra Taft Benson, "that before a child can be influenced for good by his or her parents, there must be a demonstration of respect and love" (In Conference Report, Apr. 1981, p. 46; or *Ensign*, May 1981, p. 34).

Listening As an Example. An important way of passing our values to children is to listen to them. It is by listening to them that they learn to listen to us. President Ezra Taft Benson has offered counsel on how this might work:

"Encourage your children to come to you for counsel with their problems and questions by listening to them every day. Discuss with them such important matters as dating, sex, and other matters affecting their growth and development, and do it early enough so they will not obtain information from questionable sources." ("The Honored Place of Woman," *Ensign*, Nov. 1981, p. 107.)

• What may result when we do not listen and share with our children?

• What are the consequences of listening and sharing?

Elder Robert L. Backman of the First Quorum of the Seventy related the following example of the influence of good communication between a parent and child:

"I know a father who has a great relationship with his son. The lines of communication are wide open between them, creating a bond of trust and confidence that is beautiful to behold.

Working in the garden one summer day, he could hear his son in serious conversation with a friend on the other side of a hedge. The friend was asking some of those questions we all worried about as we grew up. Instead of answering the questions, the son asked: 'Why don't you ask your dad about that?' His friend replied: 'You mean you can talk to your dad about such things?'

"As I interview young men who have broken God's moral law, I ask myself how many of them could have been spared that soul-shattering experience if they had had open communication and consistent moral teaching from their fathers." ("What the Lord Requires of Fathers," *Ensign*, Sept. 1981, p. 8.)

In evaluating your communication with your family, consider the following questions:

• Do I really listen to each family member?

• Do I spend quality time alone with each family member?

• Do I express and show my belief in each family member? How?

What if your children do not respond to your example? Many parents insist that their children be perfect, even though the parents are not. Children may not respond to example in ways parents would wish, but that does not mean the children are wayward.

Teaching our children correct principles and providing the proper example does not guarantee they will live the principles or follow our example. Their

agency gives them the choice. However, we should never give up on them.

President Kimball gave the following counsel: "I have sometimes seen children of good families rebel, resist, stray, sin, and even actually fight God. In this they bring sorrow to their parents, who have done their best . . . to teach and live as examples. But I have repeatedly seen many of these same children, after years of wandering, mellow, realize what they have been missing, repent, and make great contribution to the spiritual life of their community. The reason I believe this can take place is that, despite all the adverse winds to which these people have been subjected, they have been influenced still more, and much more than they realized, by the current of life in the homes in which they were reared. . . .

"There is no guarantee, of course, that righteous parents will succeed always in holding their children, and certainly may lose them if they do not do all in their power. The children have their free agency. . . .

"What we do know is that righteous parents who strive to develop wholesome influences for their children will be held blameless at the last day, and that they will succeed in saving most of their children, if not all." (Spencer W. Kimball, in Conference Report, Oct. 1974, p. 160; or *Ensign*, Nov. 1974, pp. 111–12.)

Your children learn values more from what you do than from what you say. Consider the following questions as you teach your children values:

- Am I living in a way I wish my children to live?

- Do I share with my children the spiritual meaning of my daily experiences?

- When my children complain or ask questions, do I teach them or become impatient?

- If my children make wrong choices, do I work to teach them better or abandon them?

- If my children are miserable because of their wrong choices, do I offer discipline in love or do I reject them? Do I feel hostility for them or do I mourn as the father of the prodigal son mourned?

- When I teach values, am I willing to walk by faith and never give up?

Reasoning with Children

Observe what happens when a father reasons with children—even when they aren't his own:

John's Concern

Two days before John was to return to his military assignment, a construction crew began digging a large hole in the empty lot north of his home. By the end of the day, a fifteen-foot hole lay ready for cement forms to be placed. Within minutes after the crew left, neighborhood children swarmed on the "diggings." Teenagers were running, and smaller children were climbing, as well as some preschool boys playing with a toy wheelbarrow. Among those little ones was John's four-year-old son, Jason. They were trying to dump a little gravel from the wheelbarrow into the large hole, but the earth beneath their feet was crumbling. Seeing this, John raced out on his balcony and yelled, "Get off that lot, you kids! What do you think you are doing?" The children all scattered, and John went down to bring the little ones away from the hole and into his backyard.

Within minutes after he returned to his house, John saw all the children swarming over the lot and dirt pile again. His little boy's friends were there. "A lot of good my yelling did," thought John. "Maybe I could reason with them so they see the danger in playing there." John walked outside and beckoned to the older children on the dirt pile. Some of the older ones hesitated, but John encouraged them with a wave of his hand. "Listen," he said "I was kind of nutty to yell at all of you a minute ago. I guess in one way it is none of my business where you kids play. But my concern is that the little ones see you over here and they come over. If you fall, maybe you will break an arm or get bruised, but I'm worried about what might happen to the little ones if they fall. What happens if a lot of that dirt caves in on them? If you play on the hills, they play on the hills. Do you see any way we can work together to protect them?"

- What is the difference between John's first approach and his second?

Reasoning	Commands and Demands
1. Are you teaching a principle?	1. Are you issuing orders?
2. Are you reasoning sensibly and calmly?	2. Are you blaming and accusing?
3. Are you exploring consequences	3. Are you making decisions single-handedly?
4. Are you identifying wise alternatives?	4. Are you allowing only one possibility?
5. Are you sharing necessary information?	5. Are you demanding blind obedience?
6. Are you listening?	6. Are you doing all the talking?

- What was he teaching?
- What do you predict will be the teenagers response?

In the actual situation, the teenagers began policing the lot, kept the little children away, and even avoided the construction site themselves.

Do you reason with your children? or do you command them? Read the comparisons to help you evaluate whether your children understand why they should be obedient or if they are merely learning that you use power over them.

It is important to remember that reasoning involves persuasion, long-suffering, and love unfeigned (see D&C 121: 41–46).

Building Confidence

Have you ever heard parents make such comments as these to their children:

"Boy, are you dumb!"

"Can't you do anything right?"

"Why are you such a pack-rat?"

"Stop being such a loud-mouth!"

If you flinched when you read the above comments, you probably sensed how negative, harsh, and uncompassionate they are. What do such comments communicate? Concern? Patience? Gentleness? Love? Or do they show disrespect, insensitivity, or dislike?

We are told that we should not negatively label our children. But when we use such language, we do more than give a hostile label. We show we do not really care about them. How can we avoid using such labels? We must repent of unloving feelings and show compassion and patience. It may be that our task is not as much to build confidence in our children as it is to quit stealing it from them.

Jeremy Is Misunderstood

While the family was moving into a new home, eighteen-month-old Jeremy wrote in ink all over one of the new kitchen chairs. Upon seeing this, his father scolded him and angrily took him to his room.

A few hours later, Jeremy's father found him in the middle of another mess. This time he had dumped a box of powdered soap all over the chair and the floor! Father grabbed Jeremy, ran all the way back to the boy's bedroom, spanked him, and left him there.

Looking at the kitchen, his father suddenly realized that Jeremy hadn't been making another mess. He had simply been trying to clean the ink off the chair.

Feeling remorseful, his father recalled how Jeremy had looked at him, his eyes filled with both fear and hope for understanding. Realizing what he had done, the father went to Jeremy's room and humbly asked for forgiveness.

When children lack confidence, it may be a response to how they have been treated. Jeremy's father had restored his son's confidence by understanding and asking for forgiveness.

- What might have happened if he had not apologized to his son?
- How could Jeremy's father have avoided misunderstanding his son?

We can also strengthen a child's confidence by encouraging him to serve others. Teenagers especially benefit from such service. When we are concerned about others, we can forget ourselves. Even little children can serve unselfishly. Therefore, we need to offer our children the chance to serve.

Sherry

Four-year-old Sherry constantly interrupted her parents, especially when her two-year-old brother was sick and had to be carried by her mother. Finally her mother shared her feelings with her four-year-old:

Teaching Responsibility

"Sherry, I am really tired today, and I need your help. Jack has a cold, and I've got to get dinner ready. I've noticed how well you can read picture books. Would you help me by reading Jack some books?"

- How did Sherry's mother help her increase her confidence?
- What probably happened?

What about children who lack confidence and feel left out, clumsy, ugly, or unwanted? Encouragement and love are still the foundations you must use to help them. It is important to listen to their concerns when they want to talk, however small the concerns may seem. They know you care when you can ache with them or share their embarrassments.

In addition, you can encourage them to help others and to develop their talents at home, church, and school. By not belittling their fears, you can help them to overcome them. In fact, any activity suggested in this section to build families can be a confidence-builder.

In order to teach our children responsibility, we must allow them to make certain decisions and choices for themselves. However, parents first have the responsibility to teach the principles and laws to their children. Then they must see that their children clearly understand the positive and negative consequences of their choices.

Sometimes, as in the following example, it requires giving a child time to make a wise choice.

Richard's Violin Lessons

Seven-year-old Richard's parents thought it would be a good idea for him to learn to play the violin. An excellent teacher lived nearby, and it seemed a good opportunity for him to learn. When his parents asked Richard if he wanted to learn to play the violin, they told him he could think about it and decide for himself. They explained that learning to play would be fun, but not easy. It would take a lot of hard work and practice. After thinking about it for a couple of days, Richard decided he wanted to try.

At first he was excited with his lessons and practice time. He was thrilled to learn new things, and he enjoyed playing each new piece.

After a couple of months, however, the newness of learning to play the violin wore off. Richard's daily practice sessions became a chore. The weather turned warm and he wanted to spend his afternoons riding his new bicycle. His mother reminded him that he could do both things if he used his time wisely. But he wanted only to ride his bike. Practicing was no longer

fun. "I don't want to play the violin anymore," he announced. "I want to quit right now."

- If you were Richard's mother, would you let him quit?
- What might the consequence be if Richard's mother gave in at that moment?

Richard's mother explained that it would not be possible for him to quit right then. "You will need to go to your lesson this afternoon because your teacher is expecting you," she explained. "Tonight when Dad comes home we'll tell him what you're thinking of doing, and then we'll talk about it."

Richard's mother talked to his father alone as soon as he came home, explaining what Richard wanted to do. Together they decided that it would be unwise to let Richard quit the violin just because he was excited about his new bike. They knew that if they let Richard quit right then that he might develop an attitude of quitting in the middle of any project or task.

When they sat down with Richard that evening, they told him they understood his feelings. They also told him that it wasn't a good idea to make a hasty decision.

"But I decided to play the violin, so I can decide to quit," he countered.

"We know it was your decision," his father said. "And it will be your decision to quit if you want to. Your mother and I will let you make that decision if you attend your lessons and practice daily for another month without complaining. If at the end of the month, you still want to quit, then you may do so."

Richard's mother then helped him plan his afternoons so that he could both ride his bike and practice his violin. Richard remembered that he needed to practice and attend his lessons with no complaint to be able to decide at the end of the month.

By the end of the month Richard was seeing the results of daily practice and did not want to stop learning to play the violin. He had discovered that by planning his time he could do the things he wanted to do in the afternoon—and that included violin practice. He decided to continue playing.

- How was Richard learning to be more responsible?
- What do you think Richard learned about decision making and responsibility?

As parents, we will find that our children are more likely to respond favorably if we guide them with love rather than force. Consider how three-year-old Michael reacted to his father's loving guidance in the following example:

Michael's Prayer

"Three-year-old Michael was getting ready for bed when he announced to his father, 'I don't want to say my prayers tonight.' His father did not scold him or shame him or try to force him to say his prayer. Neither did he let Michael get into bed without praying. [Although he was young, Michael needed to learn to be responsible in saying his prayers.] He gently lifted him to his lap and said, 'Michael, I would like to tell you why I say my prayers.' He then told of the blessings for which he wanted to thank our Heavenly Father and of the good feeling he had when he asked Heavenly Father to watch over him. Soon Michael was naming his own blessings. After a while he jumped down from his father's lap, saying, 'Now I want to say my prayer.' " (*Love Makes Our House a Home*, Family home evening manual, 1974–75, p. 215.)

Although Michael was young, his parents knew he had to learn that there are certain things we do, not just because our parents want us to, but because we want to. His father taught him responsibility and integrity in a gentle way. While Michael learned that there are things we should not avoid doing, just because we don't want to do them at the moment, he also learned that it was still his choice to say his prayers or not.

Part of the teaching of responsibility to children includes teaching them to accept the results of their choices. For example, Heavenly Father lets us experience the consequences of our choices. As parents, we should apply the same principles to our children.

Darlene Forgets

Father called to say that he was bringing a guest home for dinner. Mother had an appointment she could not change, so she prepared most of the dinner early. She prepared a roast and left a note asking her teenage daughter, Darlene, to place it in the oven as soon as she came home. Darlene found the note and saw the roast, but when the phone rang, she forgot all about it and went to her friend's house.

When her parents returned, the uncooked roast was still sitting on the table.

- If you were Darlene's parents, what would you do to help her learn that she must take responsibility for her actions?
- What should the consequences of her irresponsibility be?
- How can Darlene's parents both forgive her and discipline her?

Guidelines for Teaching Responsibility

1. Accept responsibility yourself. A child will learn more from your example than from what you simply tell them.
2. Help children understand why responsibility is important by pointing out consequences and considering the future.
3. Set rules and discuss responsibility.
4. Reason together with your child, discussing the alternatives and the responsibilities of each alternative.
5. When a child avoids responsibility, discuss with him why and help him either plan how to complete his responsibility or set new responsibilities he can do.
6. When a child breaks a rule, help him accept responsibility by letting him suffer the consequences.
7. When we as parents make mistakes, acknowledge them, and accept the consequences, we teach our children that it is possible to grow from our mistakes and become responsible.

Setting Limits

The limits and boundaries that parents set can help teach children the best ways to live as well as demonstrate love and concern.

As children grow and develop, they explore many ways of behaving. Children try different behaviors to develop their personalities and to learn what is acceptable. Not everything a child tries is right or acceptable. It is important that children not be allowed to develop without proper direction from their parents. The purpose of setting limits is to show children the paths to happiness. It is part of what it means to "train up a child" (see Proverbs 22:6).

Letting Amy Play

Amy was a vivacious nine-year-old who loved to play with her friends, especially on Saturdays when school was out. Amy's parents told her she needed to do several jobs at home on Saturday before she could play. Her older sister even made an attractive chart so that everyone knew what jobs they were assigned.

Every Saturday, however, Amy bounded out of the house anxious to be with her friends. She left her jobs at home undone. As her mother went about the task of doing Amy's jobs she thought, "She enjoys being with her friends so much I hate to make her do her work before she goes out. It makes me happy to see her having so much fun. I really don't mind doing her work for her."

- What is Amy's mother teaching her?

- What would you do to help Amy learn to do her work?
- When would you talk with Amy?
- What would be the first thing you'd say to her?
- How would you help Amy make her own decision to fulfill her responsibilities?

By consistently being allowed to play without having to do her work, Amy is learning that the rule her parents have established has little meaning for her. It will be easy for her to develop the same attitude toward other rules her parents establish.

The rules and limits you set should not be taken lightly by you or your children. When you enforce those rules, you help your children learn important lessons, such as doing necessary tasks and distinguishing right from wrong. If you set and administer rules fairly and considerately, they can become guidelines that will help your children attain self-discipline. Undoubtedly, Amy's mother mistook letting Amy do as she wanted as a sign of love for Amy. In order to really show love and concern, Amy's mother should have been consistent in seeing that Amy followed the rules before she went to play.

Barbara's Practice

Sixteen-year-old Barbara is involved in many school activities. She and her mother have an understanding that unless Barbara has some activity specifically planned in advance or some special occasion arises and she calls her mother, she is to come home right after school. Recently, Barbara worried her mother by staying after school for a practice without telling her mother where she was or what she was doing.

- Were Barbara's mother's expectations reasonable?
- Why might Barbara's mother be worried?
- What should Barbara's mother do?

Guidelines in Setting Limits

1. Involving children in setting limits helps them understand rules and consequences from the parent's perspective.

2. Real love and concern for children is not shown by allowing them to do whatever they want. Rather, it is having them obey rules and limits and face consequences when those rules and limits are broken.

3. Being consistently allowed to cross limits without facing consequences fails to teach children the purposes of rules.

4. Firmness, fairness, and love go together when teaching dependability and setting limits. Indulgence, injustice, and indifference to limits teach irresponsibility.

Helping Children Learn

Children learn from the world they live in. It does not have to be a world rich in material goods, but if you are interested and willing to give of your time and talent, you will give your children a rich world in which to learn.

Mom Helps Doug

Doug was in his third year of school and was behind in reading. The doctors had said his vision was good and he had no learning disabilities. He did resist reading, however, and instead of studying spent every afternoon hiking in the hills behind his home. When his parents sent him to his room to read a chapter in his book before he could come out, he would build a castle out of blocks or draw pictures.

One day, Doug's mother sat on the bed with him and said, "Let's read this book together, one word at a time. You read a word; then I'll read a word." Doug was sullen at first, and resentfully whispered the words when it was his turn.

He soon became encouraged by his mother's enthusiasm. She congratulated him often, and his reading improved. He began to enjoy the daily, thirty-minute reading time with his mother. (For his mother it meant that her eleven-year-old daughter would take care of the baby, and her teenager would start preparing dinner. The reading time became a regular part of their family routine.)

Gradually, Doug's reading speed and comprehension improved. Doug and his mother would then alternate sentences, then paragraphs, then pages. By the end of the school year, Doug's reading skills were above average.

Doug's mother did not use a magic formula for helping him read and learn; she helped him learn a correct principle. She taught Doug that if he wanted to learn and improve he would have to work, consistently and with faith in his efforts. As a result, he did improve.

- What did Doug's mother do that encouraged him?
- What might have happened if Doug's mother had made him read without making the effort to help him?

Helping A Child Overcome Failure. Usually when a child has failed at something, he already knows it. It is not necessary to tell him again of his failure. Instead, we should help him find out what went wrong and encourage him to try again, as Peggy's mother did in the following story.

Peggy's Cake

Twelve-year-old Peggy cried as she took the burnt cake out of the oven. Her mother, hearing her cry, came into the kitchen, saw the cake, and said, "What happened?"

"I burned the cake," Peggy replied unhappily.

"I can see that. Let's find out what happened," her mother said as she put her arm around the distressed girl. "I know you didn't do it on purpose, and I can see you feel badly about it. Dry your eyes and let's read the recipe together."

Peggy and her mother read over the recipe and found that the temperature control on the oven had been set too high. "Now that we know what went wrong," her mother said, "let's wash the dishes and you can try again."

Peggy's mother turned a discouraging situation into a positive learning experience by encouraging Peggy to find out what was wrong and how to correct it. She acknowledged her daughter's feelings and did not condemn her. Peggy was encouraged to try again, and her confidence remained intact. Sometimes the way we respond to our children affects the way they learn and accomplish a task. (Adapted from *Relief Society Courses of Study, 1984,* "Mother Education," lesson one.)

Give Children Opportunities to Help and Grow. Sometimes we ask little of our children because we underestimate their true capacities. As Shawn in the following story illustrates, children often need only a chance to help. They learn and are able to learn much more than we may expect.

Shawn Helps

Diane was struggling to change her baby's diaper. "Oh dear," she said, "I left the clean diapers downstairs." Eighteen-month-old

Shawn disappeared and returned a moment later clutching a wad of clean diapers. Although he hadn't learned to speak yet, he understood what his mother needed.

She was surprised. Diane had assumed that he knew less than he did. In the next weeks she began to make more requests of her toddler. She was amazed at his ability to find things, to look for lost items, and in general, to respond eagerly to her requests. When asked, he would open the door and let the cat in. He would stand by the baby while Diane answered the front door. He stayed away from the hot oven when told. As Shawn grew and developed, Diane found herself asking him to do more and more tasks. She was pleasant and appreciative, and he was so willing and eager that he seemed to thrive as his mother's helper.

When you offer your children opportunities to help, you give them the chance to discover their strengths and their limits.

Randy

Dad attempted to respond encouragingly to Randy's report card. "Well, you got poor marks in English, but look how good your math was!"

Unfortunately, Randy will not live in a math-only world. He will live in a world where he will need to read, write, and communicate. And apparently his English skills are limited.

It may be true that Randy prefers math; he may even have a gift for it. And there may be a variety of reasons for his poor grades in English. But even though his father should encourage Randy to continue to excel in math, he should also encourage him to improve in English. Allowing math achievements to justify a lack of effort in English would be irresponsible. Randy and his parents need to first find out exactly where he needs help, and then they each should do their best to help him improve his English skills.

• What is Randy's responsibility?
• What is his dad's responsibility?
• How could Randy's dad help him learn?

Sharing Sorrows

How might parents communicate compassion in situations like the following?

Ida's Field Trip

Fifteen-year-old Ida had worked hard in her history class to qualify for the field trip. Only the top twenty-five percent of the class could go, and she had earned a seat on the bus only two days before the deadline. The night before the trip Ida contracted strep throat. Her father wanted to say something to comfort her, but wondered what he could say.

Daniel and Soccer

Twelve-year-old Daniel had been left out again. After school the boys quickly organized soccer teams that had no position for him. He waited on the sidelines for someone to invite him in, but no one did. Daniel's mother saw him shuffling home alone with his hands thrust deep in his pockets. How could she help him?

Judy and Fluffy

"Mother!" Judy screamed, "Fluffy's been hit by a car, and I think she's dead!" Sister Elton wondered what the loss of such a beloved pet would mean to her six-year-old daughter, and how could she comfort her and help her understand?

Children's sorrows such as these are real. By sharing them with your children you can enrich their understanding and their relationship with you. Another example of how a parent might share his child's sorrow follows.

Eric's Decision

Without having to ask, John could tell his son was troubled. Eric blurted it out. "They only kept me on the team so I could provide practice for the guys who play. The coach said I would probably never be in a game—unless we play a girl's school!"

Eric had practiced for months and had come home late but excited the night he had survived the last cut and had made the team. Now the season was more than half over, and Eric had not played in one game. He knew the rest of the season would be the same. He wanted to quit the team.

Eric's dad could feel his son's discouragement, and he sat quietly on the bed while Eric kept talking. Finally his dad said, "You've worked hard at this. I've watched you, and I think you deserve the best, son. I don't know whether the coach is right or wrong on this, but have you thought about what you believe would be right for you to do?"

Eric didn't think his father's question made any sense. "What can I do!" he muttered. "You could quit," his father said. In an instant Eric knew that quitting was the last thing he would do.

Eric began to understand his father's question. "What I believe is right? It was the right question," Eric said to himself. Whether the coach was right or wrong, wise or foolish, Eric could best meet the situation by being true to what he believed. Did he believe he should quit?

He thought out what he could do. He would be true to what he knew was right. He felt he had to be charitable to his coach, work hard on the team and in school, and learn as much as he could from his experience. He said to his father, "Dad, I don't like what's happening, but I'm not going to give up."

In sharing children's sorrows, you are seeing their sorrows as your own. You become one with them. You also help them to see that no matter what the sorrow, they should not lose hope.

Dealing with Problems Privately

Spending regular, private time with each child and with your spouse can effectively prevent some problems and help you deal with those that do arise. By regularly communicating on a one-to-one basis, you share not only your thoughts and feelings, but your burdens as well. Then, when an occasion arises that you need to correct a child or discuss a misunderstanding, it will be natural to do so on a one-to-one basis.

Think about your child's or spouse's need to speak with you privately as you read the following stories:

Dad and Darren

Darren was hurrying to finish cleaning up the kitchen. When his work was complete, he would be free to play soccer with his friend, Chuck, who was waiting for him at the kitchen table. Darren's parents were preparing for an evening out. His father came downstairs, saw the unfinished work, and said, "Aren't you through yet? At the rate you're going, you'll be here all night! Now, hop to it or Chuck will just have to go on without you."

Darren was embarrassed to be scolded in front of Chuck. He finished the kitchen and went to play soccer. However, after he returned home, he continued to resent his father. Even after midnight, Darren lay awake in bed, troubled by his resentful feelings. He got up to go to the kitchen. Maybe a midnight snack would help him forget. Darren was surprised to find his father sitting in the dark at the kitchen table.

Darren's father asked him to sit down and said, "I'm sorry about what I said to you tonight. I know you were trying to get your work done, and I shouldn't have said what I did. I know it embarrassed you in front of Chuck. Will you forgive me?"

Darren's resentful feelings for his father melted. He even felt a little foolish for holding them so long. "That's okay, Dad. Did you have a good time tonight?"

Father and son enjoyed eating and talking together. Then they went to bed feeling better about themselves and each other.

Elder F. Enzio Busche related the following story in a general conference address:

"One day when circumstances made it necessary for me to be at home at an unusual time, I witnessed from another room how our eleven-year-old son, just returning from school, was directing ugly words towards his younger sister. They were words that offended me—words that I had never thought our son would use. My first natural reaction in my anger was to get up and go after him. Fortunately, I had to walk across the room and open a door before I could reach him, and I remember in those few seconds I fervently prayed to my Heavenly Father to help me to handle the situation. Peace came over me. I was no longer angry.

"Our son, being shocked to see me home, was filled with fear when I approached him. To my surprise I heard myself saying, 'Welcome home, son!' and I extended my hand as a greeting. And then in a formal style I in-

vited him to sit close to me in the living room for a personal talk. I heard myself expressing my love for him. I talked with him about the battle that every one of us has to fight each day within ourselves.

"As I expressed my confidence in him, he broke into tears, confessing his unworthiness and condemning himself beyond measure. Now it was my role to put his transgression in the proper perspective and to comfort him. A wonderful spirit came over us, and we ended up crying together, hugging each other in love and finally in joy. What could have been a disastrous confrontation between father and son became, through the help from the powers above, one of the most beautiful experiences of our relationship that we both have never forgotten." (In Conference Report, Apr. 1982, pp. 98–99; or Ensign, May, 1982, p. 70.)

- What might the outcome have been if Elder Busche had not approached his son in love?

- How did going into the living room by themselves effect what happened between father and son?

Sometimes, even when you genuinely want to approach your child or spouse in love, the moment is not private. However, your concern for the feelings of your child or spouse will suggest to you the necessity of "private time." That way, other family members will not hear personal discussions or have the chance to tease a brother or sister afterward.

Reclaiming a Wayward Child

What can you do when a child raised in light and truth turns his back on the gospel? Too often, friends, leaders, and sometimes parents, lose faith. They assume that they have failed or that there is nothing that can be done to bring the children back. Such attitudes deny hope in the future. The Lord has taught us otherwise; he would have us have faith in ourselves and in our children.

When children break the laws of God and stray from the path he set, there is both parental and godly sorrow. To earthly parents, Elder Gordon B. Hinckley offered the following comfort:

"I recognize that there are parents who, notwithstanding an outpouring of love and a diligent and faithful effort to teach them, see their children grow in a contrary manner and weep while their wayward sons and daughters willfully pursue courses of tragic consequence. For such I have great sympathy, and to them I am wont to quote the words of Ezekiel: 'The son shall not bear the iniquity of the father, neither shall the father bear the iniquity of the son' (Ezekiel 18:20).

"But such is the exception rather than the rule. Nor does the exception justify others of us from making every effort in showing forth love, example, and correct precept in the rearing of those for whom God has given us sacred responsibility." (In Conference Report, Oct. 1978, p. 27; or Ensign, Nov. 1978, p. 19.)

If you are a parent whose child has abandoned gospel living, your faith in his capacity to come back is the foundation of whatever help you have to offer him. By your faith in him and in the gospel, you stand as a light to him. But as in any matter, faith without works is dead. Consider the following questions:

- Are you willing to act in love and firmness toward your child without demanding, in advance, a guarantee of success? In other words, are you willing to walk by faith?

- What do you believe love would require of you? What would you need to do in addition to having faith?

Jay and the Runaway

When Jay's fourth son, Sam, ran away from home at age seventeen, Jay had every reason to be discouraged. But Jay tried to know what his love for his son would require of him. What should he do about Sam's being away from home?

After praying and questioning some of Sam's friends, he found out which friend Sam was staying with and decided to visit his boy. The mother of Sam's friend nervously ushered Sam to the front door. Jay asked, "How are you doing?" Sam responded with a muffled "ok."

Jay then told his son he was interested in him and loved him. He said he hoped Sam would stay in school, but offered to help him get a job if he were determined to work. Jay explained again that there would always be a bed at home for Sam. How-

ever, if he chose to work, he would need to help pay for his keep. If he went to school, his parents would help with living expenses. Then Jay gave his son a hug and said, "Let me know what you decide or if you want to talk some more."

- What do you predict for Jay and Sam's future relationship?

- What if Sam doesn't move home? Will Jay's actions have been in vain?

- What do you see about faith, hope, and charity in this example?

- What should Jay do in the future about Sam?

Guidelines in Seeking "Lost Sheep"

1. Seek the guidance of the Holy Spirit in all you do.

2. Never give up. (Faith is the starting point.)

3. Teach your child correct principles in a loving way.

4. Review alternatives and their consequences with your child.

5. Help your child carry out responsible decisions.

6. Be firm in allowing your child to experience the consequences of his choices. (However, if consequences could be very destructive to either the child or others, then parents are correctly prompted to intervene.)

7. Acknowledge your imperfections.

Teaching about Procreation and Chastity

God expects parents in the Church to teach their children about procreation and chastity and to prepare them for dating and marriage. This responsibility should not be left to schools, friends, playmates, or strangers. Heavenly Father wishes his children to understand how to use this great and holy power wisely and reverently. If parents will seek the guidance of the Spirit in humble prayer, he will help them teach their children about this sacred power.

Elder Mark E. Peterson explained:

"Sex education belongs in the home, where parents can teach chastity in a spiritual environment as they reveal the facts of life to their children. There, in all plainness, the youngsters can be taught that procreation is part of the creative work of God and that, therefore, the act of replenishing the earth must be kept on the high plane of personal purity that God provides, free from all form of perversion.

"Unskilled parents can learn to teach their children properly. In fact, God commands it, and who are we to disobey?" (In Conference Report, Apr. 1969, p. 64; or Improvement Era, June 1969, p. 78).

Responding to Your Children's Questions. When a very young child asks a question, a simple matter-of-fact answer will usually satisfy him. For instance, consider the following:

" 'Mommy, where do babies come from?' Alan asked.

" 'Alan, where do you think

babies come from?' his mother replied.

" 'I think,' Alan said, 'they come from hospitals.'

" 'I can understand how you might think that,' his mother explained, 'but let me tell you how Heavenly Father planned for his spirit children to come to earth. There is a special warm place inside Mommy called a womb, where babies grow until they are ready to be born. Then Mommy goes to the hospital and the doctor helps bring the baby from the womb to the outside.'

"Answers to questions should be geared to the age and level of understanding of the child. If an older child would like more detailed information about childbirth, the mother might say, 'Babies pass to the outside through a channel called the vagina. This channel is not the same as [the one you use when you go to the bathroom].'

"At a young age the child has no desire to have additional details. If a child holds out his small cup of inquiry, we should not try to pour an ocean of explanation into it. Generally, he will be content with an accurate but simple answer.

"Teenagers who might ask more detailed questions should also receive frank and accurate answers. In response to questions about physical intimacies, emphasis should be placed on the fact that when husbands and wives share intimate moments, they are expressing their love for each other. Their actions are sanctioned because they have taken marriage vows, but such intimacies are not sanctioned by the Lord outside of marriage." (*Relief Society Courses of Study, 1979–80,* p. 110.)

How we react as our young children display curiosity about their bodies also helps them form attitudes. "A child quite naturally touches his ears, nose, genitals, and other parts as a learning experience. When different feelings occur a child may touch again. Harsh words and punishments are unwise. It's more helpful to say, 'It is better not to do this,' and then give the youngster something else to do." (*Relief Society Courses of Study* [1972–73], p. 199.)

If children do not ask questions, parents should plan some means of approaching their preteen sons and daughters. This approach should emphasize the eternal plan of a loving Father in Heaven, a plan that enables us to have eternal families.

Teaching Your Children Before Puberty. As children approach puberty, the time when a person physically becomes capable of being a parent, they should be prepared for the bodily changes that will occur.

Parents should tell their children before their bodies change that these changes are normal. Children need to understand that their bodies are simply preparing to fulfill the roles Heavenly Father intended them to have. Parents should also explain that each person develops at his own rate of speed, some faster than others, some a little slower.

Girls should be taught about menstruation—the body's discharged flow of blood and tissue from the uterus when an ovum has been produced but not fertilized. After puberty this period occurs approximately every twenty-eight days; however, irregularity in duration and timing can occur, especially in the first few months.

A boy should be taught about the power of creation within his body and that the Lord intended that this power should be used exclusively in marriage. He should be cautioned against sexual self-stimulation (masturbation). The Church has printed an excellent pamphlet, *To Young Men Only* (PBAP0210). This pamphlet is a reprint of an address given by Elder Boyd K. Packer in the priesthood session of the October 1976 general conference and can help fathers counsel their sons regarding their growth and physical maturation.

Parents should teach youth that although it is normal to feel attracted to the opposite sex, they must keep these feelings under restraint. "Youth need to understand how to interpret these [normal feelings according to their divine purpose]. Young people can counteract worldly attitudes with this attitude: 'This power of procreation is a spark of divinity within me. It is not part of my life now, but will be later. There is a proper time (marriage) for this spark of divinity to find expression with a proper person (my wife or husband). Self-mastery now will help me be capable of a celestial love and a celestial marriage. This is the future I want, and I must strive for it.' " (*Relief Society Courses of Study, 1979–80,* p. 111.)

Parent-Child Discussion. Parents need to be patient with teenagers and let them know that they are trusted. They should discuss questions about morality in an open and relaxed manner. Parents can be understanding and loving and hold fast to high principles. They shouldn't become angry or embarrassed as they answer their teenagers' questions, although some questions may seem to show irreverence for Church principles.

Parents can build rapport with each child as they have private conversations with the child. A parent could begin such a conversation as follows: " 'I understand much of what you are feeling. I probably don't fully understand how you feel, because I am not you. But I too have feelings like what you're feeling. Every person has felt these physical desires, so perhaps if we talk and share . . . feelings we can understand each other and I can be of help.' " (*Relief Society Courses of Study, 1979–80, p., 115.*) Such an introduction to a conversation can create an atmosphere of honesty, trust, and openness.

The words of Elder Boyd K. Packer to the youth of the Church can be helpful as parents and children talk together:

"This creative power carries with it strong desires and urges. You have felt them already in the changing of your attitudes and your interests.

"As you move into your teens, almost of a sudden a boy or a girl becomes something new and intensely interesting. You will notice the changing of form and feature in your own body and in others. You will experience the early whispering of physical desire.

"It was necessary that this power of creation have at least two dimensions: one, it must be strong; and two, it must be more or less constant.

"This power must be strong, for most men by nature seek adventure. Except for the compelling persuasion of these feelings, men would be reluctant to accept the responsibility of sustaining a home and a family. This power must be constant, too, for it becomes a binding tie in family life." ("Why Stay Morally Clean," *New Era*, July 1972, p. 5; also available as a pamphlet, PTMI0079.)

"A young teenage girl felt grateful as her mother explained to her the beauty of physical expression of love between husband and wife: 'As my mother tried to tell me about the urges and desires I would begin to experience, at first I was embarrassed. But she was so sincere that I wanted to listen. She said, "Your father and I share strong feelings of attraction for each other. These feelings are beautiful. These feelings make us respect and care for each other. We convey these feelings in words, in things we do for each other, and in physical expressions of our love. . . . Through the strong feelings of love which men and women have for each other, families are established and children are brought into the world. It is part of the Lord's great plan that we can establish an eternal family. It is so important to reserve the physical expression of these feelings for marriage so you can have the great blessings of this eternal plan."

" 'That one conversation with my mother undid all the wrong ideas I had formulated from listening to the girls at school. I knew then that the feelings I had felt for boys were normal but had to be controlled.' " (*Relief Society Courses of Study, 1979–80, pp. 115–16.*)

In addition to parent-child talks, parents can help children in other ways to accept and fulfill appropriate male and female roles. For instance, parents should establish and discuss proper dating guidelines with teenagers so they will have decided issues before they actually start dating. The following counsel from President Kimball will be helpful.

"In order to avoid difficulty and possible temptation, I suggest again the following standard. Any dating or pairing off in social contacts should be postponed until at least the age of 16 or older, and even then there should still be much judgment used in selections and in the seriousness. Young people should still limit their close contacts for several years, since the boy will be going on his mission when he is 19 years old." (Spencer W. Kimball, "President Kimball Speaks Out on Morality," *New Era*, Nov. 1980, p. 42.)

Encourage teenagers to participate in group activities and not to date steady until they are ready to consider marriage. Early dating is best done in groups, where teenagers can establish many friendships. Parents can explain that dating is for getting to know each other and to enjoy being together. Dates are not occasions for displays of affection, which should be saved for marriage.

Parents can further help youth control these new emotions by helping them develop feelings of self-worth. Young people who know that they are children of God and who understand their divine purpose will seek activities that are consistent with the eternal plan.

The Eternal Purpose of Sex. It is important to teach children that Heavenly Father did not intend sex to be something evil and corrupt. Rather sex has two basic purposes: first, to enable us to have children to fulfill God's command to "be fruitful, and multiply" (Genesis 1:28), and second, to express that special kind of love shared between a husband and a wife. When a husband and a wife use sex properly in their marriage, the Lord will bless them. However, when people abuse this divine gift, they please only Satan and his followers. President Spencer W. Kimball has clearly stated: "We strongly warn all our people from childhood to old age to beware of the chains of bondage, suffering, and remorse which come from improper use of the body.

"The human body is the sacred home of the spirit child of God, and unwarranted tampering with or defilement of this sacred tabernacle can bring only remorse and regret. We urge: stay clean, uncontaminated, undefiled." (In

Conference Report, Apr. 1974, p. 8; or *Ensign*, May 1974, p. 7.)

We should teach our children that self-gratification inside or outside of marriage will not fulfill the eternal purpose of sex. Sex is to establish eternal families and to unify a husband and wife. When viewed in this way, sex is an uplifting influence.

If a young man really admires, respects, and cares for a young lady, he would never do anything that is debasing or selfish, or that would bring sorrow and guilt. Rather, he would defend her virtue at all costs. A young woman would respond with the same respect and concern for a young man she cares for.

The Lord Has Given Us Clear Rules of Conduct. "Our Heavenly Father has commanded that sexual intercourse take place only between a lawfully married husband and wife. (Exodus 20:14, 17; D&C 49:16–17; 132:41–45.) Most children can understand the basic law of chastity if parents explain it clearly at the children's level of understanding and expand upon it as they grow older.

The Lord has made it clear that immorality involves more than extramarital sexual intercourse. Some other things that the Lord has clearly told us to refrain from include necking and petting, masturbation, pornography, and homosexuality.

Necking and Petting: President Spencer W. Kimball strongly declared that "among the most common sexual sins our young people commit are necking and petting. Not only do these improper relations often lead to

fornication, pregnancy, and abortions—all ugly sins—but in and of themselves they are pernicious evils, and it is often diffficult for youth to distinguish where one ends and another begins. They awaken lust and stir evil thoughts and sex desires. They are but parts of the whole family of related sins and indiscretions. Paul wrote as if to modern young people who deceive themselves that their necking and petting are but expressions of love: 'Wherefore God also gave them up to uncleanness through the lusts of their own hearts, to dishonour their own bodies between themselves.' (Romans 1:24.) How could the evils of petting be more completely described? . . .

"Our young people should know that their partners in sin will not love or respect them if they have freedom in fondling their bodies. Such a practice destroys respect, not only for the other person but for self. It destroys the ultimate respect for virtue. . . .

"Too many have lost themselves completely in sin through this doorway of necking and petting. The devil knows how to destroy our young girls and boys. He may not be able to tempt a person to murder or to commit adultery immediately, but he knows that if he can get a boy and a girl to sit in the car late enough after the dance, or to park long enough in the dark at the end of the lane, the best boy and the best girl will finally succumb and fall. He knows that all have a limit to their resistance." (*The Miracle of Forgive-*

ness [Salt Lake City: Bookcraft, Inc., 1969], pp. 65–66.)

Masturbation: "As boys and girls reach physical maturity, curiosity in one's body may result in self-stimulation (masturbation)" (*Relief Society Courses of Study* [1972–73], p. 203).

The world rationalizes that masturbation is natural and healthy. However, President Spencer W. Kimball states the Lord's view as follows: "Prophets anciently and today condemn masturbation. It induces feelings of guilt and shame. It is detrimental to spirituality. It indicates slavery to the flesh, not that mastery of it and the growth toward godhood which is the object of our mortal life. . . . No young man should be called on a mission who is not free from this practice." (*The Miracle of Forgiveness*, p. 77.)

Pornography: "There are magazines today publishing pictures and articles which . . . beckon to the baser instincts of men and women and young people. There are newspapers around the world which, seeking greater circulation, boldly flaunt sex. Some of our newspapers continue to publish illustrated advertisements which are basely provocative, inviting their readers to pornographic motion pictures. It is in such advertisements and motion pictures where seeds are sown for rape, unfaithfulness, and the most repulsive of deviant sexual transgressions." (Spencer W. Kimball, in Conference Report, Apr. 1978, p. 67; or *Ensign*, May 1978, p. 45.)

Homosexuality: Although many in the world today claim that homosexuality—sexual desires for or sexual relations with those of the same sex—is merely an act of nature, the Lord has repeatedly said otherwise through his prophets. President Spencer W. Kimball declared that "homosexuality is an ugly sin, repugnant to those who find no temptation in it, as well as to many past offenders who are seeking a way out of its clutches. . . . All such deviations from normal, proper heterosexual relationships are not merely unnatural but wrong in the sight of God." (*Miracle of Forgiveness*, pp. 77–78.)

Part of this sin's seriousness is in its destruction of marriages and homes. President Kimball explained that homosexuality "is hostile to God's purpose in that it negates his first and great commandment to 'multiply and replenish the earth.' If the abominable practice became universal it would depopulate the earth in a single generation. It would nullify God's great program for his spirit children in that it would leave countless unembodied spirits in the heavenly world without the chance for the opportunities of mortality and would deny to all the participants in the practice the eternal life God makes available to us all." (*Miracle of Forgiveness*, p. 81.)

Teaching the Lord's Rules of Conduct. We have the responsibility to teach our children the eternal purposes of their creative powers and of the sexual desires they will experience. We should use the teaching moments when children are most receptive to

instruction and learn to create such moments if they do not arise naturally.

Following are some of the Lord's principles that we should teach our children and some ways of helping them live those principles.

1. **Avoid and dismiss thoughts that might tempt you to do wrong.** We should teach our children that they must keep the commmandments and then the Lord won't allow them to be tempted beyond their ability to resist if they are humble and prayerful (see Alma 13:28). Some practical ways of resisting temptation that we can teach our children are:

a. **Prayer.** The Savior taught that we can avoid temptation by praying always (see 3 Nephi 18:15, 18). He taught that during temptation, we should pray for help or deliverance (see Matthew 6:13; see also Joseph Smith Translation, Matthew 6:14). Earnest prayer removes temptation and fills the mind with determination to act righteously. If we and our children follow the Savior's counsel to "pray always, lest ye be tempted by the devil" (3 Nephi 18:15), Satan's influence in our lives will be greatly reduced.

b. **Hymns.** In a conference talk directed to young people, Elder Boyd K. Packer suggested this to control our thoughts:

"Choose from among the sacred music of the Church a favorite hymn, one with words that are uplifting and music that is reverent, one that makes you feel something akin to inspiration. . . . Go over it in your mind carefully. Memorize it. Even though you have had no musical training, you can think through a hymn.

"Now, use this hymn as the place for your thoughts to go. Make it your emergency channel. Whenever you find these shady actors have slipped from the sidelines of your thinking onto the stage of your mind, put on this record, as it were.

"As the music begins and as the words form in your thoughts, the unworthy ones will slip shamefully away. It will change the whole mood on the stage of your mind. Because it is uplifting and clean, the baser thoughts will disappear. For while virtue, by choice, *will not* associate with filth, evil *cannot* tolerate the presence of light.

"In due time you will find yourself, on occasion, humming the music inwardly. As you retrace your thoughts, you discover some influence from the world about you encouraged an unworthy thought to move on stage in your mind, and the music almost automatically began." (In

Conference Report, Oct. 1973, pp. 24–25; or *Ensign*, Jan. 1974, p. 28.)

c. **Fasting.** Our children should understand that our Father in Heaven knows that we will be sorely tempted, and therefore he has provided us a way to increase our resistance—fasting. We increase our spirituality and our resistance to temptation as we fast and pray. When we have a testimony of the power of fasting, we should bear it to our children so that they will understand the importance of using fasting to escape Satan's snares.

d. **Sabbath worship.** The Lord promises us that we will keep ourselves unspotted from the world as we keep his day holy (see D&C 59:9).

2. **Make decisions right now about proper conduct.** If we help our children decide now how they will act in tempting situations, they will be more likely to act righteously when a real situation arises.

"Other young people may tempt your children to be unchaste. You can fortify your children against such threats by rehearsing with them ways they might respond in such circumstances. For example, when someone says, 'If you loved me, you would do what I want' they could say in return, 'If you loved me, you wouldn't ask me to do such a thing.' " (*He*

that Receiveth My Servants Receiveth Me, [Melchizedek Priesthood personal study guide, 1979–1980], p. 109.)

Elder Hartman Rector, Jr., gave an allegory about deciding beforehand to keep a safe distance from temptation:

"In my experience, I have found that it is very, very dangerous to fly just high enough to miss the treetops. I spent twenty-six years flying the [U.S.] navy's airplanes. It was very exciting to see how close I could fly to the trees. This is called 'flat hatting' in the navy, and it is extremely dangerous. When you are flying just high enough to miss the trees and your engine coughs once, you are in the trees.

"Now let's pretend that the navy had a commandment—'Thou shalt not fly thy airplane in the trees.' As a matter of fact, they did have such a commandment. In order to really be free of the commandment, it becomes necessary for me to add a commandment of my own to the navy's commandment, such as 'Thou shalt not fly thy airplane closer than 5,000 feet to the trees.' When you do this, you make the navy's commandment of not flying in the trees easy to live, and the safety factor is tremendously increased." (In Conference Report, Oct. 1972, p. 172; or *Ensign*, Jan. 1973, p. 131.)

Suppose, for example, a young girl decides that she

never wants to attend an R-rated movie. Later, however, when a boy comes to pick her up to go to a movie, he tells her that they are double-dating and the other couple has decided to go to an R-rated movie. If she has already made a decision about R-rated movies, it won't be as difficult to tell him that she doesn't go to R-rated movies and would like to go to a different one. It may not always be a convenient decision, and it may seem easier to go along with the group, but she will be blessed if she can live up to her decision.

3. **Avoid or leave tempting situations.** Elder Rector commented on this principle as follows: "The scripture records that Joseph stoutly resisted the advances of Potiphar's wife, but one day as he went into the house 'to do his business,' it so happened that 'there was none of the men of the house there within.' (Genesis 39:11.)

"Now, this is always a dangerous situation and should be avoided if at all possible. Potiphar's wife became particularly insistent, even to taking hold of his coat and attempting to draw him to her. But Joseph did the very best thing he could do under the circumstances. The scripture records, '. . . he left his garment in her hand and fled, and got him out.' (Genesis 39:12.) Or, in today's language—he ran.

"Maybe that doesn't sound like a very sophisticated thing to do, but sometimes running is the only thing to do. This was such a time." (In *Conference Report*, Oct. 1972, p. 172; or *Ensign*, Jan. 1973, p. 131.)

Our children might also find themselves in situations where the only thing to do is literally run—and fast!

How can we teach our teenagers to recognize when they should leave a group, a dance or a movie, or turn off the television? Some guidelines follow:

a. If you can't invite the Spirit of the Lord to attend a dance, a movie, or whatever you are doing, leave.

b. If you feel your pulse racing and your mind fantasizing immoral acts, leave immediately. It's better to miss half a movie than to implant images in your mind that might take years to root out.

c. If you would feel uncomfortable if your bishop, parents, or brother or sister were there, you probably shouldn't be there.

4. **Establish family rules.** After prayerfully counseling together, you can ask your children to help develop family rules that will be useful in avoiding compromising situations. For example Elder Rector suggested the following possible rules:

"1. Never go into a house alone with one of the opposite sex.

"2. Never, never enter a bedroom alone with one of the opposite sex.

"3. Do not pet or neck. . . .

"4. Never park on a lonely road with just the two of you alone.

"5. Do not read pornographic literature.

"6. Do not attend R- or X-rated movies, and avoid drive-ins.

"7. Do not spend time in drinking or gambling establishments." (In Conference Report, Oct. 1973, p. 173; or *Ensign*, Jan. 1973, p. 131.)

5. **Take part in worthwhile activities.** We should help our children develop their talents and participate in sports, music, drama, and hobbies. Encourage them to get involved in worthwhile school and Church functions and to choose friends with clean speech and actions. Provide them with uplifting reading material or direct them to it. Control your family's television viewing. Help your children choose modest clothing, encourage double dating or group dating during the teenage years. But above all, set an example of profound respect for the power and privilege of procreation.

A Final Thought. A teenage boy was so impressed with a discussion that he and his mother had on chastity that he saved and prized this quote she gave him: " 'Young Man . . . the girl whom you are going to marry is now alive. You may never have met her, but somewhere she is walking down a path which in the providence of God some day will cross yours. Wherever she may be, she keeps herself for you, and in her imagination you are even now a prince who some day she will gladly marry. Not for the wealth of the world would she be grossly untrue to you. How, then, are *you* living? You have no right to take to such a girl a life smirched with unchastity. If you do, there is a secret shame you will never outgrow, a pang that you will feel whenever your children clamber to your arms. To have a home free from all that, with memories high and beautiful, is worth anything that it may cost." (Harry Emerson Fosdick, quoted in Hugh B. Brown, *The Abundant Life* [Salt Lake City: Bookcraft, Inc., 1965], pp. 57–58.)

"How glorious and near to the angels is youth that is clean; this youth has a joy unspeakable here and eternal happiness hereafter. Sexual purity is youth's most precious possession; it is the foundation of all righteousness." (James R. Clark, comp., *Messages of the First Presidency of The Church of Jesus Christ of Latter-day Saints*, 6 vols. [Salt Lake City: Bookcraft, 1965–1975], 6:150.)

NOTE TO PARENTS

You may want to use some of the ideas, resources, and references in the "Lesson Ideas" section, "Chastity," in this manual.

Understanding the Personality Development of Children

Children are not just little adults. They go through typical characteristics of growth—intellectually, emotionally, and socially—on their way to becoming adults. When parents realize these things, there is less strain on both parents and children. Family home evenings can be more enjoyable and successful when a child's personality development is considered. Remembering that a child does not think like an adult, have the same attention span, or see the world the same way adults do, can help a parent plan a home evening everyone can enjoy.

Sometimes we may think that children are too young to understand a gospel principle or that we really don't have much influence with our older children. But Joseph Smith taught that "all the minds and spirits that God ever sent into the world are susceptible of enlargement" (*Teachings of the Prophet Joseph Smith*, sel. Joseph Fielding Smith [Salt Lake City: Deseret Book Company, 1938], p. 354).

The Spirit of Christ is striving to help each of Heavenly Father's spirit children. In addition, Satan cannot tempt little children until they reach the age of accountability. Therefore, parents have a powerful ally in God and a clear opportunity to help their children develop a sure and safe foundation for future gospel living.

Although Satan cannot tempt little children directly, their innocence and trust make them very open to suggestions and to the influences of others. They

look to their parents, older brothers and sisters, and other children and adults for examples and models of behavior to follow. For these reasons, childhood is a crucial time for laying the proper foundation.

Parents need to be constantly alert to the influences around their children and work hard to teach them the gospel. Parents often unknowingly lead children astray through uncaring, unthinking, and inconsistent behavior. Perhaps this is one reason why the Lord has said that the iniquity of the fathers will be visited upon the children (see Exodus 20:5) and why he holds parents responsible if they have not taught their children the things they must know (see D&C 68:25).

The following chart lists some common characteristics of children's behavior, arranged by broad age groupings, with reasons for that behavior and the implications that behavior may have on planning enjoyable and productive family home evenings. However, when considering any growth or behavior chart, remember that not every child will necessarily fit into described patterns. Individual children grow and develop differently and at different speeds. For instance, all children in one family will not walk or talk at the same age. Each child should be respected as an individual. The descriptions in this chart identify general behavior only, and you will note that the age groupings overlap.

CHARACTERISTICS	REASONS	IMPLICATIONS
Birth to 3 years of age		
1. A child likes affection, being held and cuddled. He especially likes motion—being carried, tossed, and sitting on a lap.	Infants and young children learn trust and love first through touch. They are absorbed in exploring the world through their senses and movements, and they are gradually getting more control over their muscles.	Give lots of affection, holding, cuddling, talking and listening. He is unable to understand rules, so correct his behavior with patience and love. He has a limited attention span. He will listen only to those things that interest him.
2. He loses interest quickly and will interrupt conversations, stories, or activities with cries, noises, and wiggling. He enjoys simple, repeated gestures and touches, playing with objects, putting them in his mouth and throwing them.	Children at this age are only aware of their own viewpoint, wants, and experiences. Doing things over and over helps them learn about things.	Provide short, vivid stories and games (peek-a-boo, patty-cake) that challenge his mental and sensory abilities. Provide repetition and practice short behaviors. Talk about Heavenly Father and Jesus and how to please them.
3. A child stops "naughty" behavior when you tell him to, but he soon goes back to it as though he doesn't care what you want.	Children have no understanding of rules and cannot understand how one situation has any relationship to another. They lack the ability to foresee consequences.	Do not try to teach concepts or rules; he cannot understand them. But do have rules and be consistent in applying them. Respond to him in positive ways to help him feel good about himself.
2 to 7 years of age		
1. A child will display affection at odd moments. He may run to you for a quick hug and then go on with his play. He likes affection but only in brief doses. He may sometimes push unsought affection aside when his attention is elsewhere. He rejects your help even though there are many things he cannot do for himself, like drawing and other tasks requiring good finger and hand coordination.	Parents meet most of a child's needs and satisfactions. As a child begins to conquer his world, he needs to know that this source of security is still there. He has an equally important need to do things, to be active, and to explore his world as his control over his body improves.	Give him simple things to do—holding pictures, leading songs. Increase these and add talks as he gets older. Let him feel he is an important part of family home evening. Give affection and praise. Practice "good" behaviors like folding arms and bowing heads, kneeling for prayers, drinking from a sacrament cup, and sitting still. Teach him about Jesus Christ and the gospel and how you feel about them.
2. A child may seem selfish, not sharing. He wants things others are using and does not play *with* children so much as *along side* them. Disagreements and frustrations are common. He interrupts others and cannot stay long with one activity if others are not doing it. He likes stories and imitates others.	A child still thinks the world is the way he sees it, not understanding that there can be more than one reason for anything. He cannot understand others' needs. He cannot keep a lot of ideas in his head for very long, so he turns to other things when his attention lags or he gets bored.	Read or tell scripture stories. Explain the "hard" parts. Choose stories that give "good" behavior to copy. Explain in concrete terms, not in abstract principles. Define gospel words like *repentance, faith*, and *forgiveness* with familiar examples. Use examples, simply told, from your own or other family members' lives.
3. A child may seem willful and disobedient and unable to justify "naughty" behavior. His reasons may be illogical: "Jimmy (an imaginary friend) made me." He is often slow to obey and must be reminded.	"Good" means "satisfying" to him; he still doesn't understand that rules apply to many situations. He doesn't reason the same way adults do. He learns by testing the limits imposed upon him.	Introduce rules but keep them simple. Be firm and consistent. Help your child to be sucessful so he can develop self-confidence. Show how obedience will help him grow.

CHARACTERISTICS	REASONS	IMPLICATIONS
7 to 12 years of age		
1. Boys may appear less open to affection than girls, particularly around others, but may accept it more willingly when hurt or frustrated. Both are active, like games, and prefer the company of their own sex.	Boys and girls are learning what they are all about. They play at the roles set for them much of the time. Although they look to each other for examples, parental love and approval are very important.	Be ready to listen. Give each child some personal time. Support your child in his problems. Provide real-life examples (stories and short examples) of good role models.
2. They like games and may spend much time discussing rules, fairness, and cheating. Some are aggressive while others lack self-confidence. In school, girls may be more successful, obedient, and more interested than boys. A child might be interested in clubs, cliques, or neighborhood gangs, seeking friends outside the home.	Games and clubs help the child learn about himself and how rules apply to his life. He is very aware of competition and concerned about his performance. Because girls are usually more adept at language and social skills at this age, they may do better than boys who may feel inferior or rejected.	Provide challenging games that teach sportsmanship, honesty, and cooperation. Help boys get ready for priesthood service. Teach the commandments and obligations as children of our Father in Heaven. Choose activities that build family unity.
3. He questions parents' decisions, wanting to know "why." When your explanations are fair or logical, he will accept them; if arbitrary or inconsistent, he will question them, but usually obey.	A child has discovered that things that happen are governed by or explained by rules. Knowing the rules and how they apply is extremely important because it helps him predict consequences.	If your child questions decisions, do not become angry. Explain and then allow him to respond. Be fair and impartial in applying rules, helping him understand how Heavenly Father's rules are for our good.
11 to adulthood		
1. A boy may become awkward and clumsy, while a girl may become silly and self-centered. Both may seem irresponsible.	Physical growth and changes are emotionally upsetting; the youth feels that things are happening faster than he is ready for them. He feels more socially than physically awkward.	Discuss gospel and life principles with your child. Avoid arguing over his different views; rather teach by sharing your own faith, experiences, uncertainty. Be supportive, encouraging, and accepting. Be consistent in applying rules and explain them in terms of principles.
2. Youth may enjoy sports, group activities, and discussions about "life," values, and principles (justice, equality, peace). But they may show great intolerance for others' opinions. They may want to escape the family but be afraid to do so.	Sports and play are no longer ways of exploring rules. They reassure youth about their abilities as they watch and copy others while establishing their own adult identities. Youth are especially concerned about relationships with each other. They may be insecure and uncertain about what society expects.	Encourage family support for your children's activities. Be friendly and open to their friends. Discuss marriage goals and how priesthood and service activities express the principles of love, brotherhood, and forgiveness. Find ways to bring their friends into family activities rather than competing for time and loyalty.
3. Youth often question values and come to distrust rules, especially rules without any strong ethical or moral basis. They may insist upon their "rights" to be independent. They may seem uncertain of what is meant by "right" and "wrong" for a time. They often reject authority as a reason to approve or disapprove of a behavior.	Youth have found by now that rules are not infallible. They are now able to handle abstract concepts and are busy building their own guiding philosophy of life. They now look behind the rules for the principles.	Teach the idea of baptism, priesthood, and marriage covenants. Help your children see scripture as a record of people trying to cope with problems. Give them opportunities to become involved in challenging discussions of ethical problems and gospel applications. These discussions are practice for making decisions on their own later.

FAMILY
Activities

Activities
and games for family
fun and learning,
plus activities to teach
emergency
preparedness

CONTENTS

FAMILY UNITY
Activities

OUR CULTURAL HERITAGE

What do you know about your family's cultural heritage? This activity is designed to help your family feel a sense of unity as you find out about the culture of your forefathers.

Activity

First see if you can answer these questions about your ancestors. You may find answers in family records, histories, and journals.

1. What country did they come from?
2. When did they live?
3. What was their life-style like?
4. What were their occupations?

Now find books, magazines, tapes, films, or pictures that relate to the countries your ancestors lived in and the things people did in those countries. The public library might be a good place to start. See if you can find information about some of the following in your ancestors' countries: music, arts, dance, literature, food, customs, the flag, and recreation.

You should not have to do too much research to find out how your ancestors may have lived and what they may have enjoyed doing. Discuss what you have learned, showing pictures and focusing on things that would especially interest your family.

Additional Activities

You may want to plan one of these activities for another night:

1. Have an evening featuring the music, art, literature, or dance of your ancestors. For example, find out who the composers of that time were and what musical instruments people played. Play tapes or records of their native music, and discuss how it makes you feel.

   Or, you could show photographs of paintings, carvings, and sculpture from the countries of your ances-

tors. Who are the artists and what do you like about their art?

Or, talk about the literature people read at the time your ancestors lived. Find a book, story, or poem to read from together. You might make a family project out of reading a whole book together.

If someone in your family is a dancer, have that person learn a native dance from the country of an ancestor and teach it to the family. Or, you can teach each other. Find pictures to show native dance costumes.

Watch for cultural activities in your area that feature arts from the countries of your ancestors. Attend as a family.

2. Celebrate Christmas by making presents that were popular during your grandparents' time (see Janet Brigham, "Christmas Presents from the Past," *New Era*, Dec. 1980, pp. 40–41).

3. Serve a heritage dinner, with several kinds of foods if you have ancestors from several different cultures. Let the children make and decorate place mats. Also, make a pretty centerpiece for the table, perhaps out of flowers native to your ancestors' countries.

4. Make flannel-board figures and use them to tell stories from family journals and histories.

5. Past Relief Society Cultural Refinement lessons, which have covered many countries, may help you learn about the countries of your ancestors. Check with your ward library for copies of past Relief Society manuals, tapes, and filmstrips.

6. Decorate your home with the colors of your ancestors' flag. If you have Italian ancestors, use green, red, and white. If your people are Scottish, try to find out what their clan's plaid looked like. Use these colors in a throw pillow, a patchwork quilt, Christmas decorations, or a family banner.

7. Do you have artists or craftsmen among your own ancestors? Family histories—written or oral—may tell of the talents and interests of your ancestors. Talk about carrying on the arts and crafts in your family and about starting your own traditions.

Notes

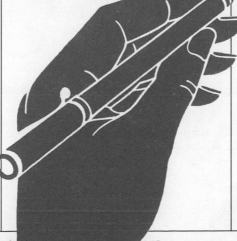

A GREAT WAY TO COMMUNICATE

This activity will show your family how to use notes to express their love for each other in a creative way.

Activity

A note can communicate love and appreciation over and over as the person who receives it reads it and rereads it. As a family, discuss these suggestions for writing your own personal notes:

1. Make them simple and sincere.

2. Express how you feel inside.
3. Use creativity to make your message personal.

Here are some examples of creative notes:

Daisies won't tell, but I will. You're the greatest, and I love you.

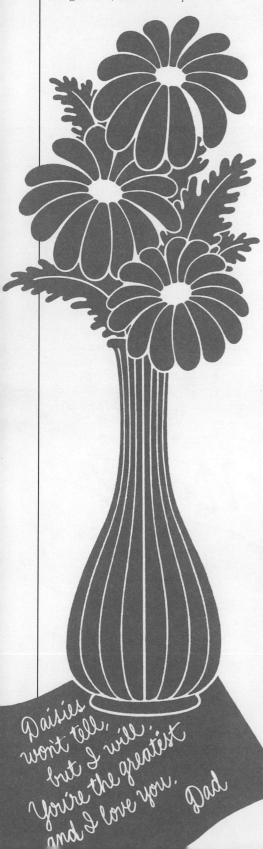

Daisies won't tell, but I will, You're the greatest, and I love you. Dad

Thank you for planting the seeds of what really matters in my life. You have helped me grow so much. (To Young Women leader or school teacher)

I acted like a nut. Please forgive me! (Peanut butter is good, too.)

Pack two lunches in two brown paper bags. On the outside of one bag write, "What do you say we 'bag' our differences and just enjoy each other today? Where shall we go? The park? The beach? You name it."

Mother, write a note to your deacon son. Let him know how special he is and how much you appreciate his service to you.

Teenagers and young adults, tuck notes in the pockets of your friends to let them know that you care about them and have faith in them. Think of clever ways to deliver your notes without getting caught.

Mother, tuck a love note in your husband's briefcase, scriptures, sandwich, or newspaper.

Dad, set a note for your wife inside the refrigerator, washer, checkbook, under the pillow, or in a dozen different places.

Small children appreciate a note that says, "I love you because_____."

SERVING OTHERS TOGETHER

People in need are all around you—in your own extended family, in your neighborhood and in your community. And some of the most rewarding activities your family can take part in together are those designed to help these people. The possibilities are endless, limited only by your imagination, your sensitivity to others' needs, and your willingness to give. Even very young children can feel the joy of serving. Your whole family can feel closer to each other as you work together for a good cause and share the satisfaction that comes in helping others.

Here are some suggestions to keep in mind as you consider the kind of service you will plan:

1. Carefully, even prayerfully, think about the needs of those close to you. Do not overlook those you

know best. If you want to visit an elderly person, for example, remember those in your own family.

2. Remember that an unneeded or unwanted service may not be a service at all. Also, keep in mind that what you would appreciate may not be what another would appreciate, or even be able to use. For example, a gift of a sack of wheat might be merely confusing to a refugee family unfamiliar with Western foods and cooking methods.

3. Consider serving anonymously. This can help you and your children feel the pure joy of giving without concern for recognition or reward. Also, anonymous service is sometimes easier for others to accept. Often, though, your personal delivery of a gift will make it even more meaningful to the person who receives it.

4. Help the whole family feel that the service activity is *their* project, not one you are imposing on them. Let each person contribute ideas and help make final plans for the activity. Children, who often have great spontaneity and natural generosity, can make a real contribution to your planning.

Activity

Choose one of these:

1. *Choose an elderly person* or couple who needs some kind of help. As a family, decide what you could do to help the person you have chosen— for example, raking leaves,

shoveling snow, caring for a lawn or garden, cleaning or repairing a house, or reading aloud to one who cannot see well. You might also prepare and present a talent show, invite an elderly person to family home evening, or buy something the person needs. And remember that the elderly will appreciate your friendship, as well as your help.

2. *Share dinner with a new neighbor* or one who is alone. You could also take dinner to a shut-in. A neighborhood potluck supper could help those who live around you feel a spirit of friendship and acceptance.

3. *Share a gift or even money* with someone who needs help. Each member of the family could contribute a certain amount toward a gift of money or an item that the person could not afford. Also, consider sharing fruits and vegetables from your garden or other goods your family may have. Homemade gifts of food—a loaf of bread or canned fruit—may also be appreciated. And remember that every family has two precious resources— time and energy—that they can use to help others. A day's yardwork might be the most welcome gift you could give.

4. *Be a "Substitute for Santa"* at Christmas for someone who may not have the means to enjoy a special meal or buy needed gifts. Look first to your extended family, then to the neighborhood and community. The bishop or a local newspaper or welfare agency can help you make a selection.

Have a member of your family, preferably mother or father, sensitively interview the family or person you chose to find out what would be appropriate Christmas gifts. Be careful not to make the family feel ashamed. If they would feel uncomfortable receiving the gifts, choose another family.

Assign family members to make or buy some of the items you have decided to give. Children can help make Christmas stockings or wreaths and everyone can help put together food baskets. Your family may even want to sacrifice a few of their own gifts. It may be fun to get

a Christmas tree and decorate it with the recipient family. Present the gifts, either anonymously or as a family.

5. *Have a family Deseret Industries drive.* Gather unneeded clothing, toys, and other items. Then take these things to the Deseret Industries store nearest you.

6. *Prepare a musical program* to take to a foster home, hospital, or old folks' home. You could invite another family to join you. Your program could include vocal or instrumental solos, duets, trios, or quartets; and be sure to include some familiar sing-along tunes that your audience could join you in singing.

7. *Clean up an outdoor area* near you —a park, roadside, or campground. Pick up litter in any public area.

8. *Make simple puppets* to take to a children's ward of a local hospital. Put on a puppet show of a favorite children's story. Then let the children keep the puppets.

9. *Volunteer to spend some time working* on a Church welfare project together.

BUZZ SESSIONS

Do you need help getting all of the members of your family to take more active part in group discussions in family home evening lessons or family councils? Try this idea: Divide the family up into small groups for short "buzz sessions." Have each group discuss the topic among themselves and then present its ideas to the family.

This is a good way to get quick reactions to new ideas or questions. This activity is designed to increase family communication, cooperation, and involvement through buzz sessions.

Preparation

Study these suggestions to make sure you know how to hold a successful buzz session.

1. Bring the entire family together and then divide them into groups of from two to four people, depending on the size of your family.

2. Assign a topic for the groups to discuss. You could have all the groups consider the same idea, or have each group consider a different aspect of the same problem.

3. Have each group appoint someone to write down the group's ideas and make sure that all have a chance to express their views.

4. Tell the groups they will have three or so minutes to discuss their ideas and come to some conclusions.

5. At the end of the time, call for reports and questions.

6. Have the family listen to each group's ideas and discuss them briefly.

7. After all buzz groups have responded, have the family discuss all the ideas presented. Let the person in charge of the discussion sum up the ideas.

Activity

Explain how a buzz session works. Then choose a topic you would like to discuss as a family. You might, for example, use a buzz session to find ideas for a family vacation or to make a plan for getting family chores done or for saving money. You could show a film, read a story, or watch an uplifting television program together; then ask each group to discuss their reactions to it. Buzz sessions can be a helpful way to make sure that every family member is part of family decision making.

BRAINSTORMING

Creative thinking—seeing facts in a different light and finding solutions beyond the obvious—is one of our most valuable tools for solving difficult problems. And all of us have this tool, but not everyone uses it to its full potential. Too often, fearing failure or rejection by others, we consider only obvious or familiar solutions. Brainstorming is a problem-solving technique that can tap the capacity for creative thinking. To brainstorm an idea—

1. Choose an idea or problem that has no obvious right answer or solution.

2. Ask the family to freely suggest as many ideas or solutions as they can think of.

3. Accept all ideas and write them down. Do not make or allow any comments or criticisms.

4. After two or three minutes, evaluate all the ideas and decide on the most promising solution.

Activity

Present the purposes of brainstorming, as explained above, to your family. Then initiate them into the brainstorming process by writing just one word, such as *white* or *faith* on a chalkboard or paper. Have everyone call out anything that comes to mind when he thinks of this word. Accept all ideas, even the least practical, and write them down. Do not allow anyone to comment or criticize another's idea at this stage. Do this for two or three minutes. You can allow much longer if participation is good. See if you can fill the whole chalkboard or paper with ideas. Build an atmosphere of acceptance and creativity.

Then present a real problem or situation that your family needs to resolve. Have family members suggest ideas for solving the problem or reaching an

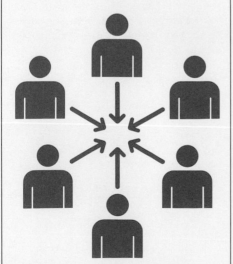

objective. Use the same process as you used with the single word. Once all ideas are in, have the family evaluate each one and decide on the most promising solution or course of action. Do this with love and concern for all. Amazingly enough, this little technique has been credited with producing spectacular results. It can help you in family council meetings, in family home evenings—any time you have a problem to solve.

ROLE PLAYING

In role playing, the participant acts out the part of someone in a real-life situation. This kind of activity can give those involved a better understanding of the feelings and behavior of others in situations they have not actually experienced themselves. It can also help them better understand how they should act in various real-life situations.

Roles are not memorized. They may be planned or practiced, but are more often impromptu. Role playing is a good teaching device, especially when you want to make a point about people, their actions, and their beliefs. And it can be effective in helping those involved see how gospel principles would apply to everyday life.

Have a member of your family study these guidelines for role playing and present them to the rest of the family.

1. Choose a simple problem to center your role play around. The role play should require only a few roles—two to four roles for most problems. Have the whole family discuss the problem and the roles needed to portray the problem or situation adequately.

2. Encourage family members to portray the right ways to handle situations. They will learn that it is easier to show several things not to do than to show one that should be done. But role playing is most useful when it shows correct ways to do things.

3. Select family members for roles. You can do this in advance or after the family has defined the problem. Brief family members on the general nature of their roles. Stress that they will only be pretending.

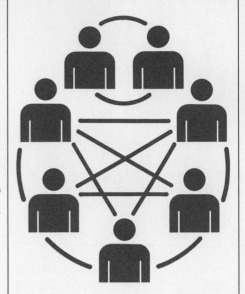

4. Role-play the situation and have the rest of the family be the audience. Encourage the role players to act naturally, but do not interfere with them as the role play progresses. When the situation or problem has been fully explored, or when participation seems to lag, stop the role play.

5. Discuss the role play. Either have the whole family discuss the presentation, or discuss it first in buzz sessions. Have the family identify strengths and weaknesses in the choices and behavior of the role players. Ask them to reach a conclusion about how to solve the problem. It is not necessary that everyone agree on one point of view.

Activity

Have an assigned member of the family outline the mechanics of role playing. Choose a situation or a problem that concerns your family or start with one of the situations outlined below. Role-play the situation you choose, following the suggested guidelines.

Situation 1: Judy Blacker missed taking driver's education in high school when her father received a job transfer to another state. She has just turned sixteen and wants to get her driver's license. Her father has promised to help her learn to drive.

Mr. Blacker wants to keep his promise to help Judy learn to drive and get her license, but the family car is new. He is a little nervous about her using it to learn and has put off teaching her.

Today is Judy's first lesson with father. They go out to the garage and get in the car.

Now role-play what happens next.

Situation 2: Bill Reynolds is sixteen. He has been taking a course in salesmanship in high school and is going for his first job interview for part-time work.

Mr. Godfrey owns a small hardware store in Bill's town. He needs a part-time worker, but is not sure he wants a high school student. Bill comes into the store for his scheduled appointment. Mr. Godfrey is waiting for him.

Role-play this interview.

Situation 3: Jerry, a ten-year-old, and Joshua, a nine-year-old, are playing softball in Jerry's backyard. Jerry hits the ball extra hard and it flies over the fence and hits Mrs. Darger's small bathroom window. The boys hear a sharp noise as the window cracks. Jerry's heart sinks. He has been in trouble with Mrs. Darger before. Then he remembers that Mrs. Darger is at her daughter's house for two days helping with a new granddaughter. And she lives alone, so no one else is there.

The boys look at each other. They have to decide what to do.

Role-play what they say and do.

You might also role-play one of these situations:

An instructor with students in a practice teaching session

Two missionaries tracting

A nonmember and a Church member who have just listened to the President of the Church talk about tithing in general conference

Proper etiquette on a first date when the boy picks up the girl

The proper way to pass food at a dinner table

Noah and his sons building the ark with two unbelieving and critical people looking on

You may get other ideas for good problems or situations to role-play from television programs, books, stories or personal experiences, Church speakers, and scripture stories.

DEMONSTRATIONS

One of the best ways to teach a skill or show a process is by a demonstration. Demonstration is a "show-and-tell" technique. You may use charts, pictures, drawings, or films to show the skill or process. Most members of the family have some skill they could share, and sharing these skills with each other is a good way to build confidence.

Preparation

These suggestions will help you give an interesting and motivating demonstration.

1. Choose a skill or process that is simple enough to show in a few minutes' time.

2. Decide how you will teach the skill or process. For example, if you want to demonstrate how to make a cake, you could bring the ingredients and actually make the cake. Or, if you wanted to show how to calculate tithing, you could use a chalkboard, a poster, or real coins.

3. Divide the process or skill into its most important steps or parts. Build the demonstration around these basic steps or parts.

4. Let the members of the family use the materials you brought to practice the skill or process you are demonstrating.

5. Use chalkboard outlines or other visuals to clarify concepts when needed.

6. Explain any terms you use that might be new and unfamiliar to the family.

7. Give handouts if needed to help the family remember what you have demonstrated.

Activity

Set a time to share skills, information, and talents through family demonstrations. You will be surprised how much family members have to share and how much they will enjoy learning new ideas. Let even the young children take part. Here are some skills your family might want to demonstrate:

How to make bread
How to cook in a wok
How to make crepes
How to set a table
How to plan a well-balanced meal
How to arrange flowers
How to decorate cakes
How to make a baby quilt
How to change a tire
How to survive in the water
How to bat a ball
How to sharpen a saw
How to change a washer in a faucet
How to respond to various emergencies
How to find locations on a map
How to preserve insects for a collection
How to treat shock
How to give mouth-to-mouth resuscitation

REUNIONS BY MAIL

Holding a family reunion can be difficult when family members live many miles from each other. With this activity, you will not need to worry about this problem of gathering the family physically. This reunion will be held by *mail*.

Activity

As with all reunions, planning is essential. Choose several family members to determine what kind of activities will work best for your family reunion by mail. (Note that the

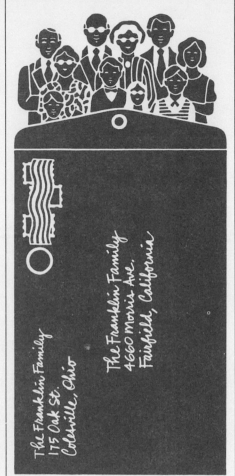

activities suggested here could also be used at a conventional reunion.)

Set up a system that lets everyone know to whom they will send their material. For activities that require passing items on to someone else, the best system may be to send them to the next youngest family member. But some activities require that you send your material to the person in charge of that activity.

The following are ideas that you could use or adapt. Don't be afraid to try them and even to develop some of your own activities. You can try them with the grown members of your own family, or with the members of your extended family—grandparents, aunts, and uncles.

1. Make up a genealogy quiz and have each family complete it and then send it back to the one who made it up. That person will score and return it.

2. Have each family send questions about family history to a knowledgeable family member. He can answer the questions and send a copy of all the answers to each family.

3. Have each family send in favorite recipes to the activity leader, who will compile them for everyone.

4. Have each family report their past year's most unforgettable experience.

5. Have each family commit to give another family a gift of service each year. (Choose by drawing straws the first year and rotate after that.)

6. Collect a baby picture and a current picture of some members of each family. Send the pictures to one family at a time. Have them try to correctly match the baby pictures and the current pictures. They could send their answer sheets back to the activity leader and pass the pictures on to the next family.

7. Send a cassette tape in rotation to the families. Have them record their feelings on subjects such as "What I Remember Best about Grandfather."

8. Have a family scavenger hunt. Make a list of questions about family members. For example, find someone in the family who is a farmer, someone in the family who is a bishop, someone who was born on a specific date, someone who was married in the Manti Temple. Send the list to each family and have them complete and return it.

LARGE GROUP FUN

These activities, which are easy to prepare, are great for large family and neighborhood gatherings. A simple activity like one of these can make the difference between a dull get-together and a very successful activity. Each activity can be adapted for all age-groups and areas.

Activity

Use any of these activities in a family or neighborhood get-together. Or use your creativity to find ideas from other people or to make up your own.

1. *Treasure hunt.* This activity is designed for preschool- and early elementary-age children. It is especially good for a park or other outdoor area, but children will also enjoy an indoor version on a rainy day.

Make a list of items that the children could find fairly easily. If your hunt will be on the beach, include such items as sea shells, driftwood, and so forth. If your hunt will be in the mountains, use evergreen branches, rocks, and so forth. Make a copy of the list for each child. If some of the children cannot read, draw or glue on a picture of each item so even the young ones can find the items by themselves.

Have the children find all of the items on their list, as they can, and put the treasures in their bags. Have them bring the items back to be checked off when they are finished.

Award prizes—to the first person finished, to the person who found the most treasures, to each person, or for each treasure found. Simple prizes will turn this activity into a real favorite of the little ones.

2. *"Can You Find Out?"* This is a good activity to get everyone talking and learning new things about each other.

Each person will need a copy of the worksheet "Can You Find Out?" and a pencil.

Instruct everyone to get the signature of someone in the room or area who answers the question asked in each box on the worksheet. You can set a time limit or see who finishes first. You may change the questions or make up your own if you wish.

CAN YOU FIND OUT?

Directions: Find people in the room who fit the questions below. Get one person's signature in each box.

Who has the same first initial as you?	Who has a birthday in the same month as yours?
Who is a grandparent?	Who was born out of the state of _____?
Who has a toothbrush the same color as yours?	Who has been to Hawaii?
Who went to the University of _____? (a college in your area)	Who has been out of _____ in the last month? (your city)
Who is wearing a gold wedding ring?	Who is wearing the same color dress or suit as you are?
Who is wearing glasses?	Who plays the piano?
Who is not married?	Who has on blue shoes?
Who wears the same size shoe as you do?	Whose family has the same number of children as yours?
Who went to Brigham Young University?	Whose eyes are are the same color as yours?
Who has served a mission in another country?	Who has a beige carpet?

LEARNING *Activities*

MAKING WORK FUN

If the word *dishes* triggers your family's disappearing act, or if you hear "just a minute, mom" from a distance, this activity is for you. Helping your family enjoy working will take creativity. Try some of the ideas given below.

Activity

1. *Make a vest* with two pockets for each child. Appliqué a turtle on one pocket and a rabbit on the other. Write jobs to be done on three-by-five-inch cards and put them in the turtle pocket. (If the child is too young to read, use a picture for the job description.) You may wish to start out with tasks as simple as brushing teeth or washing hands. The child can put the cards for the jobs he completes in the rabbit pocket.

2. *Make an apron* for each major household job with a job description written on each one. The person responsible for the job wears the apron until the job is finished. You may even include a hat for the cook. Use your favorite apron pattern and embroider, iron, stencil, or write the jobs on the aprons.

   Sew a ring onto this apron to hang a dust cloth from. Make this apron of vinyl or plastic.

3. *Make a chart* to show whose turn it is to set the table or wash the dishes. Slip the spoon of the assigned family member out of the container and into the paper strip on the day that it is his turn to set the table.

   On the day that someone is to wash the dishes, put his plate into the dishpan.

4. *Make a "Looking Good" chart* and hang it in your bathroom. List on it the things each person is to do as he gets ready. This is especially good for little children, who may need to be reminded of what they should do each morning.

5. *Make a work list* for family duties. Have family members brainstorm for a minute, thinking of all the jobs that need to be done around your house (prepare meals, go shopping, iron the clothes, set the table, cook food, do dishes, tend the baby, take out the garbage, pick up the clutter, mow the lawn, wash windows, or sweep the sidewalks).

   Next, arrange these jobs according to how often they need to be done— daily, twice weekly, weekly, monthly, semiannually, or annually.

   Now decide together who is capable of performing these duties and who enjoys doing them. Write those names beside the duties.

P O C K E T

To assign unwanted jobs, write them all on slips of paper. Place these slips inside balloons; blow up the balloons and tie them. Attach the balloons to a board or heavy cardboard with tape. Pass out darts and let the family throw them at the balloons. Each family member gets the job inside the balloon he pops. Decide together how long each person will keep doing the job. Record this on the work list.

Brainstorm for a few minutes on the subject of the unwanted jobs. Think together of ways to make the burden light. For example, what are five fun ways to carry out the garbage? (Whistle while you're doing it, carry it out on a skateboard, walk backwards, grumble and mumble, carry it in a wagon, pay somebody to do it for you.) Come up with all the creative solutions you can, and use them.

Instead of a list, you may want to use a job jar to draw your jobs from. A job wheel works well with older children.

6. *Reward yourself* when you have completed all your work. Hold a victory party. Have a weiner roast, an ice cream party, or a water fight. You may want to divide the family into two teams and see which one can get their work done fastest. The losing team could then cook dinner for the winners, take them to a movie, or do anything else they can think of.

7. *Make dinner time more fun.* Try some of these ideas:

• Have a formal dinner party in the middle of the week. Brush up on table manners.

• Have all the boys, including dad, become waiters for an evening. Dress them like waiters and make sure they use good manners all evening.

• Let your family go shopping with you through the advertisement section of your newspaper. Let them help decide on good buys. Write the items you choose on a sheet of paper and plan your next week's menu around them.

• Use shopping time as a one-to-one time with your children. Tasks such as peeling potatoes, folding napkins, or cleaning out drawers also provide moments for listening and sharing.

• As a family, set some basic guidelines for table manners, eating schedules, snack times, and clean-up.

8. *Play games* to make work pleasant:

• Have your children pretend to be puppets, robots, or soldiers. Wind them up and let them do their work.

• When the house is wall-to-wall clutter, hold a family "panic-pick-up-time." Set your timer and see how many things can be picked up and put away in ten minutes.

• Scrub to music, especially fast, rousing music.

• Wash the dishes for ten minutes; then dry them for ten minutes.

• Play "Beat the Clock." Time a job to see how much time it normally takes to complete it. Then set your timer and race against the clock. Try to cut down the time without giving up quality. You can even have a family contest to see who can set the family time record.

LEARNING FUN FOR INFANTS AND TODDLERS

Infants and toddlers learn mostly through their senses, so they need to have a stimulating environment. These activities are especially designed to give infants and toddlers many opportunities to use their senses.

Activity

Have the family share ideas about how to help very young members of their family have fun learning. Talk about how little ones learn best and choose a fun activity to do with them. They usually learn best in an informal,

everyday setting. You may want to use some ideas from those listed below.

For Infants

1. *Stimulate feeling*

• Hug your baby, rock him, kiss him, hold him firmly.

• After a bath, rub him firmly with the towel.

• Have your baby hold objects with different textures in both hands.

You might try objects like the following:

Different textures of cloth	Keys
	Paper (wax paper,
Yarn pom-pom	newspaper,
Metal objects	tinfoil, etc.)
Plastic objects	Ice cubes, snow
Sponge	Water
Dough	Grass
Sandpaper	Flowers
Pot scrubber	Flour, sugar,
Beans, macaroni, rice	cornmeal

• Let your baby crawl or walk on a variety of surfaces—carpet, linoleum, wood, grass, and sand, for example.

2. *Stimulate seeing.*

• Use colored sheets and blankets.

• Hang a bright mobile on the baby's bed. A newborn keeps his head to the side and will not see toys hung over the middle of the bed, so attach a bright object to the side of the crib nine to twelve inches from his nose. Try to change the mobile in some way every week.

• Take the baby from room to room with you.

• When your baby is lying on his back, dangle a brightly colored toy or rattle about ten to twelve inches above his eyes. When the baby focuses on it, move the object in an arc or half-circle.

• Hold him or sit him in an upright position occasionally so he can see how things look from that angle.

• During the day, shift the crib to another part of the room. Put it by a window, if possible.

3. *Stimulate hearing.*

• Talk to your baby. Tell him what you are doing for him, what you are cooking for dinner; what your feelings are about life, people, and politics.

• Sing to him or say a nursery rhyme.

• When your baby makes a sound, imitate it. Show him your delight in his "speech" by smiling, hugging, or praising.

• Let the baby hear noises around your house. You don't have to keep the house quiet.

• Let him hear the radio, television, or stereo for a short time.

• Let him play with noise-making toys like rattles and musical animals.

4. *Stimulate smelling and tasting.*

• Let your baby smell many things, such as soaps, lotions, perfumes, spices, and food.

• When your doctor says your baby is old enough, gradually introduce a variety of foods to him.

For Toddlers

1. *Stimulate large- and small-muscle development.*

• Ramps and chutes can be made from large cartons or several shoe boxes. Cut off the ends of shoe boxes and tape the boxes together into a long chute. Place it on a slant, and the children will enjoy sliding various objects down it. The boxes may also be used to make the cars of a train. Connect them with string or rope, decorate them, and

paint or glue on some wheels and watch how much fun this train can be for the children.

• Children love to punch holes with a hole puncher. Colored paper and hole punchers will keep children busy for quite a while. Save the dots in an envelope or bag for art projects or confetti for a party. Have the children punch holes from wax paper and put the dots in a jar filled with water. Screw on the lid, shake it, and watch the children's very own snowstorm.

• Make or buy some beanbags and have the children toss them to each other or throw or drop them into a box or bucket.

2. *Develop language and cognitive skills.*

• Write out a list of about five items (rock, leaf, grass, dirt, etc.). You carry the list and let the child carry a small paper bag. Go for a walk and see if you can find the items. Encourage the child to find each item by asking, "Can you find a rock?" Look for one thing at a time. When all the items are found, sit down together and talk about the items. Smell, touch, and look at them. Talk about color, shape, texture, and weight.

• Fold a piece of paper or cardboard in half. Draw a picture of a bowl of water with an object on top of the water on one side, and a bowl of water with an object on the bottom of the bowl on the other side of the paper.

Provide a small bowl of water and various objects from around the house which will float or sink. Sitting down with the child, place an object in the water and talk about whether it is on top of the water or at the bottom. Does it float or sink? If the child does not grasp the concept, do not pressure him. Let him place things in the water and talk about "on top" or "on the bottom."

• On a piece of poster board or cardboard, trace around four or five small objects you have in the house such as a cookie cutter, clothespin, battery, or scotch tape dispenser. Use a wide, dark colored magic marker. Put the items in a box where they can be kept perma-

nently. The child can take objects out of the box and match them with the outline on the cardboard, feel the objects, and talk about them.

• Cover a piece of heavy cardboard with felt or flannel. Cut out various shapes and colors from felt, flannel, nonwoven interfacing, wool, or other fabrics. Make up stories together, holding the flannel board on your lap and using the shapes you have cut out to illustrate the stories. Magazine pictures backed with flannel will also work well. Children can also name shapes, colors, or objects while you work together. They love putting things on the board and taking them off. A felt person cut into parts to be put together will help teach body parts.

• A child can glue squares of cloth on paper and make colorful scenes. To teach children to notice similarities and differences, cut two squares of each scrap of material and mix them up in a box. The children can match them or sort them by color, texture, or design.

• Use a tape recorder to record familiar sounds (washer, vacuum, or car) so the child can identify these as a game. Record short stories and then play them back when the child wants you and you are busy. He can hold a book and listen. Talk and sing together on the tape and then play back the recording and let the child listen to his own voice.

• Miscellaneous items: Let children make a collage out of beans and macaroni and scraps of material. Make it on newspaper, paper grocery bags, or paper plates. Use flour paste as glue.

Take a walk in the house and feel a variety of items (wallpaper, bedspreads, rugs, curtains, wood).

When setting the table, talk about the shapes on the table—round plates, squares, or rectangles. What shape is the table?

Sort the knives, forks, and spoons and let the child put them away.

Let him help dry and put things away. Make it a game.

Go on a shape hunt in your house. Look for circles, squares, rectangles, and triangles.

Count! Count the chairs in the kitchen, the books, buttons, steps, windows, beans, or plates.

Make up guessing games. "I live on a farm. I'm little and black, I like milk and say meow, meow. What am I?"

3. *Develop memory and listening abilities.*

• Take a button and tap it on the table two times, then say, "Now you do it." Have the child repeat a rhythm you clap. Or say several words and have him say them back to you.

• Children love to put puzzles of themselves together. Have a photo of a child's face enlarged to eight-by-ten inches. Mount the photo on heavy cardboard with rubber cement. Cut it into three or four pieces. Store it in a box.

4. *Develop creative expression.*

• Different kinds of dough or clay are favorites of many children. Here are some easy recipes:

Play Dough

2 cups flour	3/4 cup water
1 cup salt	colored with
1 tablespoon oil	food coloring

Mix the dry ingredients. Add the water and oil gradually. Add more water if the dough is too dry, or add more flour if it is too sticky. The oil preserves the dough and keeps it soft so it can be used many times. Store it in a plastic bag in the refrigerator.

Provide rolling pins and cookie cutters to use with the play dough.

Craft Clay

Combine:

1 cup corn starch	2 cups baking
1 1/4 cup salt	soda (1 pound box)
	1 tablespoon oil

Cook until thickened to doughlike consistency. Turn mixture out on pastry board and knead. Cover with a damp cloth or keep in a plastic bag. Good for plaques and other models. It can be painted when dry.

Modeling Clay

2 cups salt	1 cup corn starch
2/3 cups water	1/2 cup cold water

Stir salt and 2/3 cups water over heat four to five minutes. Remove from heat. Add corn starch and cold water. Stir until smooth. Cook again until thick. Store in plastic bag. This clay will not crumble when dry.

Baked Clay

4 cups flour	1 cup salt
3/4 cup water	

Press out dough and have child make his handprint on it. Bake at 325° for 1 hour. Will be light brown in color.

• Almost every child loves to finger paint. Here are some basic recipes. This is one activity that can be repeated several times throughout the year, and the children never grow tired of it. It may be wise to provide old shirts for paint smocks.

Flour and Salt Finger Paint—Cooked

2 cups flour	3 cups cold water
2 teaspoons salt	2 cups hot water
food coloring	

Add salt to flour, then pour in cold water gradually and beat mixture with egg beater until it is smooth. Add hot water and boil until it becomes glossy. Beat until smooth; then mix in coloring.

Soap Finger Paint

soap flakes	food coloring or powder paint

Beat soap flakes in small amount of water until it reaches the consistency of whipped cream. Add color and mix well. Use on smooth table top (it washes off easily), construction paper, or balloons, as well as on paper.

Plastic Starch Finger Paint

liquid plastic starch (available in grocery stores)
water soluble powder paint in salt shakers

Pour a small amount of liquid starch on dry paper. Shake powder paint on paper and spread with hands.

You might even want to try finger painting with instant pudding. Everyone loves this one! Shaving cream is also fun to finger paint with.

• Let the children try using water colors.

If you use tempera paints (powder paints mixed with water), add some

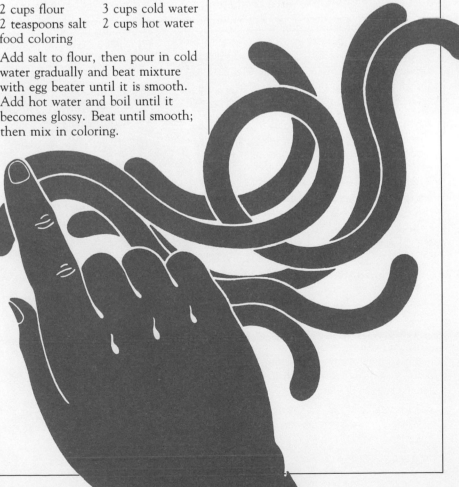

dishwater soap to the paint so it will wash out of clothes.

• Let the children try painting on rocks.

If paints aren't available or practical, give the child a can of water and a brush and let him paint the house!

• Draw on paper with chalk. Put butcher paper on the wall and have the child draw a mural on it. Try wetting paper with a sponge and then drawing on it with chalk. Chalkboards are a good addition to a toy supply.

• Cut out pictures from magazines and show the child how to paste them on paper, boxes, paper cups, or plates. Talk about the pictures. Tissue scraps, material scraps, colored paper shapes can also be cut and pasted.

Make pinwheels, hanging mobiles, paper-bag or paper-plate puppets (attach popsicle stick to paper plate and make a face on it). Make a chain out of construction paper. Hook one link inside another, and talk about colors.

• Put some powdered paint in an old salt shaker. Take the child for a walk in the snow and let him shake paint on the snow to color it. Make a picture on the snow.

5. *Miscellaneous activities:*

• Have the child lie down on a piece of butcher paper. Trace around the outline of his body. Talk about what you are doing. "Now I'm drawing around your fingers." Color the picture together. Talk about body parts and where they belong. Hang it up.

• Take a head-to-toe picture of the child. Have it enlarged so that it measures ten to twelve inches high. Mount the picture on 1/8-inch hardboard (or heavy cardboard). Use white glue or rubber cement to mount the photo. Hang the picture on the wall or set it on a stand. (A short piece of one-inch diameter half round moulding with a slot makes a good stand.)

• Cans are easily made into a variety of toys. Poke holes in cans, and run a string through the holes. Toddlers will enjoy pulling this toy behind them. Cans, as well as cartons, also make interesting blocks to stack and build with. Let children play with them in the kitchen area, putting them on the shelves with food for the family, or using them to play store. (If cans have sharp metal edges, cover with tape or avoid using them.)

• Buy a little bottle of soap bubbles or pour some dish soap, diluted with a little water, into a paper cup. A piece of bent wire or a plastic ring will do as a blower.

• Even a two-year-old can help load silverware into a dishwasher or sit on a stool and help mother wash some dishes. Before mealtime, when a little one is underfoot and impatient for meals, try this: Give him an apron, a stool, some sudsy water and the cooking utensils you've finished using. For additional fun, add a few drops of food coloring to the water.

• Going shopping? Take along labels from empty fruit and vegetable cans or cereal and cracker box fronts, and let your child help shop for the groceries by matching labels.

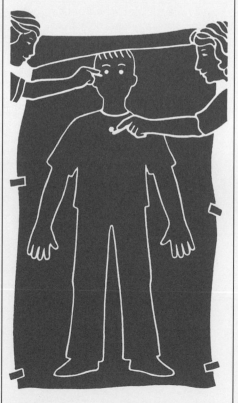

• Let the child choose which vegetable, fruit, or dessert the family will have for supper. Let him select the pan to cook it in.

LEARNING FUN FOR PRESCHOOLERS

These activities are especially designed to help preschoolers have fun as they develop skills in observing and classifying and in solving problems.

Activity

Have the family share ideas for having fun with preschoolers and helping them learn. Talk about how preschoolers learn and interact. Remember, learning should generally take place informally, as part of everyday activities. Parents should take advantage of the many teaching moments that occur daily in every home and family.

The following suggestions will help you know better how to play with preschoolers.

1. Allow time for the child to discover for himself.

2. Let him change the rules if he wants to.

3. Stop the game or activity when he loses interest.

4. Use this play guide to avoid problems: (1) infants to three years—parallel play (children playing side by side but not necessarily together), (2) 4 and 5 years—cooperative play, (3) 6 and up—competitive play.

5. Help the child feel good about himself and feel that he can do things himself.

Choose a fun activity to do with your preschoolers or get some ideas from those listed below.

1. *"What's Missing?"* You will need a tray and various objects like jar tops, a spoon, a spool of thread, and crayon.

Place the tray with the objects on it on the table or floor. Start the game by asking the child to look closely and try to remember everything that is on the tray. Allow the child time to look at each object; he may want to touch and ask questions about each object.

Then ask him to close his eyes. While his eyes are closed, take one thing off the tray and hide it. Then ask the child to open his eyes and try to tell which object is missing. You can make the game harder by adding more objects.

2. *"What Do You See?"* You will need one large envelope and cut-out pictures of familiar objects such as trucks, cars, or animals. Place the cut-out pictures in the large envelope. Pull one picture out slowly to show only part of the picture. Start the game by asking, "What do you see in the picture?" (Four wheels, two legs, etc.) "What do you think it might be?" If the child, after several guesses, seems to lose interest, show the picture and name the object. A variation of this game would be to write the letters of the alphabet or numbers on pieces of paper and play the same game.

3. *Magnets.* One fun game is "fishing." You will need a magnet (some potholders have a small magnet stitched inside that can be easily ripped out, or you can get a small one at the dime store for less than a quarter), an empty egg carton, and a piece of string. Also collect about a dozen assorted objects—paper clips, bobby pins, safety pins (closed), buttons, bottle caps, and beads. Be sure to include some objects that a magnet will not attract.

Put the objects in a deep box (a half-gallon milk carton works well).

Tie a string to the magnet long enough to reach the bottom of the box.

Let the child use the magnet to "fish" in the box and put his catch in the egg carton—paper clips in one section, safety pins in another, and so on.

The objects that a magnet will not attract are left in the bottom of the "pond." When the child has finished, ask him to tell what is the difference between the things in the egg carton and those left in the box.

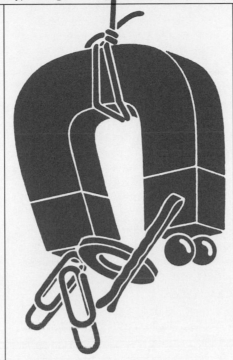

4. *Beanbag toss.* Get three beanbags of various colors and shapes if possible (yellow, red, blue, round, square, and triangular). If you make them, they should be about five inches in diameter. You will also need a box or basket.

Have each player take three turns trying to throw the beanbags into the basket. If the child can do it without missing, suggest that he move farther back.

You can use this game to help the child understand such space relationships as in front of and behind, in the middle, to the right, to the left, and over and under.

You can also play catch with a beanbag. Stand a foot away from the child and move farther back as the child's catching ability improves. Alternate beanbags with each game and say the color and shape. For instance, "Let's play catch with the square, red beanbag today."

5. *Riddles.* Gather some everyday objects from around the house, such as a spoon, scissors, crayon, or thread.

First place three items in front of the child. Say something like, "I am going to make up a riddle about one of these things. Look at

the things and listen to see if you can guess which one I am talking about." Then give clues, one at a time, until the child guesses correctly: "You see me on a table. You cannot eat me. But you use me to eat your soup. What am I?" "Yes, I am a spoon."

See if the child can make up the riddles for the other two items. Remind the child not to say the name of the object. Give help, if necessary, by whispering suggestions to the child.

Expand this activity by describing something in the room that both of you can see. Have the child tell you its name from what you tell about it. Then let the child describe something for other family members to guess.

6. *"What Would You Do?"* Begin by saying something like this to the child: "Sometimes things happen to us and we have to think what is the best thing to do about what happened. I will tell you some make-believe things that might happen to you, and you tell me what you would do."

Present some situations like these for the child to solve.

• The baby is crying and your mother is busy.

• You spilled your juice.

• You just broke your mother's vase.

• You are lost in the grocery store.

• You have spilled paint on the floor.

Make encouraging comments about the solutions the children present, and discuss with them some other ways they might solve these problems. Explore the possible results of each solution with the child.

7. *"It Starts Like This."* Say to the child something like, "Tell me a word that starts like *milk.*" At first, give such hints as these:

"It shines at night." (Moon.) "It makes fire." (Match.) "You see yourself in it." (Mirror.) "It's a little animal that likes cheese." (Mouse.)

Later on you can stop giving hints. The child will soon get the idea that many words start with the same sound and will enjoy thinking up words that "start like" the word you provide.

8. *"Things That Start with the Same Sound."* Give the child scissors and old magazines and let him cut out some pictures of things that start with the same sound—a car, a coat, a cake, for example—and paste them on a brown paper bag. To get the child started, you could cut out the first picture, then have the child find pictures of things that begin with the same sound. You can also print the first letter of the words on the bag.

9. *Look-alike letters.* Print these capital letters on a piece of paper.

AATA   FFOF   NMNN
RSRR   HDHH   DBBB
WWDW   GGGP   CCGC
MMMB   LLKL   JJLJ

Ask the child to pick out the letters that are just alike in each group of four letters. Start with the combinations where the two letters in the group look very different. Later, use combinations where the two letters look more alike.

Play this game another way by asking the child to pick out the letter that is different. You can play this game with small letters too.

Don't be upset if you have to do this many times for the same letter. It may be as hard for the child to memorize the name of a particular letter as it would be for you to memorize someone's seven-digit telephone number.

10. *"What Is the Missing Word?"* Say to the child: "I'll say something and leave out the last word. You tell me what word you think I left out." A typical sentence might be: "I guess I'd better open the _____ ." If the child responds with any word that makes good sense—*door, window, gate, package, envelope,* or *bottle,* give some encouragement, such as "good thinking" or "good choice." Ask for suggestions of other words that would make sense there. Try to use sentences in which many different words would make sense at the end.

Be sure to make this game enjoyable and fun by not making it too hard or pushing too fast.

TRAVEL GAMES

Travel with children is not always fun and games. Particularly on long automobile trips, you can travel to a constant chorus of: "Are we there yet?" "I need a drink of water." "When can we stop?" "I want an ice cream cone." "How much longer?" "I have to go to the bathroom!"

But with a little preparation, parents can make travel both educational and entertaining. This activity is intended to help families do just that.

Preparation

To help children get the most from traveling, include them in the preparations for the trip. Get a road map for each school-age child, and check the library for books about the places you will see. Read the books together and take some of them along. Then as you travel, talk about the things you will be seeing and their significance.

Activity

Try some of the following games on your next family trip. You can also adapt some of them for use in family home evening. Encourage family members to make up their own games. The games suggested are intended for automobile trips, but can be adapted for plane, train, or bus trips.

1. *Junior navigator.* Get a road map for each child. At home have a basic lesson in map reading and have the kids mark the routes you will be traveling. On the road, show how highway signs relate to the map. Make a game of estimating how long it will take to

reach a certain town. Let kids take turns giving directions. Older children can also help keep track of mileage, miles per gallon, and trip expenses.

2. *Talk show.* Have children take turns pretending to be a talk show host. They can use a tape recorder and have other passengers discuss what impressed them most about attractions or pretend to be historical characters related to the sites. The tape makes a nice trip souvenir.

3. *Trip journal.* The type will vary with the skills of the children. Little ones can draw pictures of their impressions; grade-school children can write and illustrate; older ones may want to gather materials for scrapbook collections—brochures, postcards, leaves, or flowers.

4. *"Roots."* Take along a collection of family stories for long stretches of highway. Stories that relate to the area are nice. But family stories need not be old to be interesting. Parents can tell about their childhood, courtship, wedding day, or other events.

5. *License games.* Various games can be played by spotting license plates.

Alphabet: Look for the letters of the alphabet—in order—on plates. The first one to spot the next letter gets one point.

Doubles and triples: Look for double or triple digits on license plates, such as 22 or 333. Score two points per double, three per triple.

Bingo: With twenty-five squares marked off and numbered with two-digit numbers like a bingo card, the leader calls out the first two digits of the license plates for players to mark on their cards.

States: See how many different states you can spot on license plates.

6. *Word games.* Write down scrambled names of places along your route and see who can unscramble them first. Or see who can make the most words from the name of a city or river.

Older children often like to make their own crossword puzzles. The puzzles can be designed around the trip's itinerary, duplicated, and taken along on the trip.

7. *"I'm Going to the Alamo."* The first player says, "I'm going to the Alamo and I'm taking my camera." The second player says, "I'm going to the Alamo and I'm taking my camera and sweater." The third might take his camera, sweater, and sneakers. The object is to add to the list, while repeating in order all the previous articles. Players drop out when they make a mistake.

8. *Scavenger hunt.* Each player has a list of common items that might be seen along the highway. The first to spot an object and call it out can cross it off his list. For team play, divide into two teams and take opposite sides of the road.

9. *"Al from Alaska."* The first player says something like "My name is Al; I come from Alaska; and I like airplanes." The next player may say, "My name is Ben; I come from Baltimore; and I like badminton." Continue in this way through all the letters of the alphabet.

10. *Counting cars.* Take any common object, such as red cars, vans, black and white cows, or red barns and see who spots the greatest number in a given time.

11. *Blank maps.* Before leaving home, make a photocopy for each child of the map of the country. Have

them color the states or areas they'll be touring.

12. *Travel quizzes.* Before leaving home, prepare quizzes on such things as state capitals or the geography along your route. Have children complete the quizzes and score points for each correct answer.

13. *"Mile for Mile."* Ask children to say "here" when they think they have gone one mile, five miles, or any arbitrary distance. One person watches the odometer and announces who came closest after all the results are in. A variation would be to choose a point down the road and give a piece of candy to the person who guesses most accurately how far away it is.

14. *"Follow the Leader."* This game requires at least four people. Any person in the group starts an action, such as clapping his hands, raising one arm up and down, or repeatedly touching his nose. All must follow this person, but at any time any other person in the group may start another action. The object of the game is for everyone to watch and follow the new action when it starts, while the person who is "it" must touch the person who starts the new action. The person who gets caught then becomes "it."

The more people involved in this activity, the more exciting it becomes.

15. *"Categories."* The players in this game decide on a category, such as makes of cars, flowers, colors,

vegetables, or fruits. The younger the children, the simpler the category. The first player names an item in the chosen category, then the next player does, and so on around the circle until someone cannot think of an item that no one has said yet. He is then out. The last player in is the winner.

16. *"Inkie-Pinkie."* This game will be fun for adults. It requires creativity and ingenuity. Any one of the players thinks of two words that rhyme. He then thinks of a simple sentence that describes these two rhyming words, and says it to the other players. The other players then try to guess what the two rhyming words are. To help the players discover the two rhyming words, the following clue is given:

If the two rhyming words are one-syllable words, the player giving the descriptive sentence says, "It is an ink, pink." For two-syllable words, the player giving the descriptive sentence says, "It is an inkie-pinkie." For three-syllable words, the player giving the descriptive sentence says, "It is an inkety-pinkety." For four-syllable words, the player says, "It is an inkety-pink, pinkety-pink."

There can also be other variations.

The following are examples of how the game might be played:

• Ink-pink—a tidy vegetable
Answers—neat beet, clean bean

• Inkie-pinkie—a friendly corpse
Answer—chummy mummy

• Inkety-pink, pinkety-pink—a very happy patient
Answers—effervescent convalescent, exhuberant recuperant

17. *Scrapbook bag.* Plan with each child to take along some sort of a bag to collect souvenirs, brochures, and cards for scrapbooks and journals. These can be designed and made by hand especially for the trip, or be simple inexpensive ones.

18. *Songs for the road.* There are many fun songs to sing while traveling. You can use family favorites or this is a good opportunity to teach new ones.

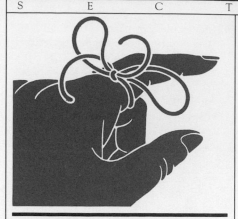

MEMORY MAGIC

All of us have good memories. We see, hear, and speak thousands of words in our own language with good understanding. But many of our memories are untrained. Improved memory can help us prepare for a mission, give talks, and teach lessons. It can help us gain self-confidence, meet and remember people, and be well informed and well organized. This activity is designed to help us gain mastery of our memory power.

Preparation

In advance, assign a family member to teach one of these memory-power techniques.

1. *Visualization.* Picture in your mind the things you want to remember in a systematic way. Pretend you are going shopping. You need to buy the following things:

A large ball-point pen	A can of red paint
An apple pie	A new hat
A bottle of glue	A mouse trap
A box of matches	A jar of mustard
	A pair of sunglasses
	A hammer

Now that you have read these items, see how many of them you can recall without looking at them. Take forty seconds to write down as many as you can. How many did you remember? Now reorganize the list in this way:

Visualize an empty table. Then picture yourself standing *a large ball-point pen* on end. Then balance the *apple pie* on it. You then pour the *glue* on the pie, letting it drip on the table. Around the table edge stand the *matches* and start them burning. Then picture a friend standing beside the table pouring

red paint from the *new hat.* Just as you are ready to clean up the mess, you hear a loud snap and glance around. You see a *mouse trap* closing on your new *sunglasses.* It has broken one lens and the other is smeared with *mustard.* Someone is beating on the lens with a *hammer.*

Now take another forty seconds and see how many you can recall. You will do better than before.

2. *Association.* By associating, or linking in your mind, an unfamiliar thing with one that is familiar or easy to remember, you can remember the unfamiliar thing better. Rhymes, codes, initial letters, and familiar songs are all good memory aids.

Almost everyone knows the rhyme, "Thirty days hath September." Many of us still use it to help us remember the number of days in a given month. Rhymes like this one can effectively improve memory.

Codes can also be very effective memory aids. For example, to recall the names of the spaces on the treble music clef, just remember that FACE spells face. To call the names of the lines on the treble clef, remember "Every Good Boy Does Fine" which stands for EGBDF. Make up your own codes for things you have to remember.

Using initials can also be helpful. For example, to remember the capitals of the six New England states—Boston, Concord, Hartford, Augusta, Montepelier, and Providence—think of the cities' initials—BCHAMP. Then think to yourself, "Boston is largest, so B is the champ."

You can also use initials to help you remember outlines for Church and public speeches. If you had to give a talk on salesmanship, for example, and the points you will include are fairness, intelligence, gratitude, honor, and truth. These spell *fight* when the initials are put together.

Set the words of a list you need to memorize to the music of a song you know. For example, the books of the New Testament can be sung to the tune of "Praise to the Man" (*Hymns*, no. 147).

Activity

Have the assigned family member introduce the memory aids he has studied. Then try one or more of these exercises.

1. Try to remember mom's shopping list using visualization.
2. Have an older child invent a code for remembering the Articles of Faith.
3. Memorize the books of the Book of Mormon by putting them to music.
4. Use the principle of association to remember family birthdays or other special events.

STRIP PUZZLES

Test your problem-solving abilities with this puzzle. Using trial-and-error and repetition is the only way to solve these problems. The activity is designed for school-age and older children, but preschoolers can try the first parts of it.

Preparation

Cut out eight strips of paper the size indicated below. Family members can take turns using this set, or they can make or duplicate sets. Cardboard will work well.

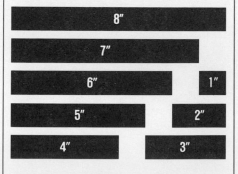

Activity

Show the family the eight strips that make up the strip puzzle. Explain that they must make the following shapes using the strips. There is only one rule they must follow: All eight strips must be used for each of the puzzles. None can be left out and no more can be added. They cannot be overlapped.

Decide who is going to try first, and have him begin. Make sure everyone has a turn doing at least one.

1. Make two equal rows.

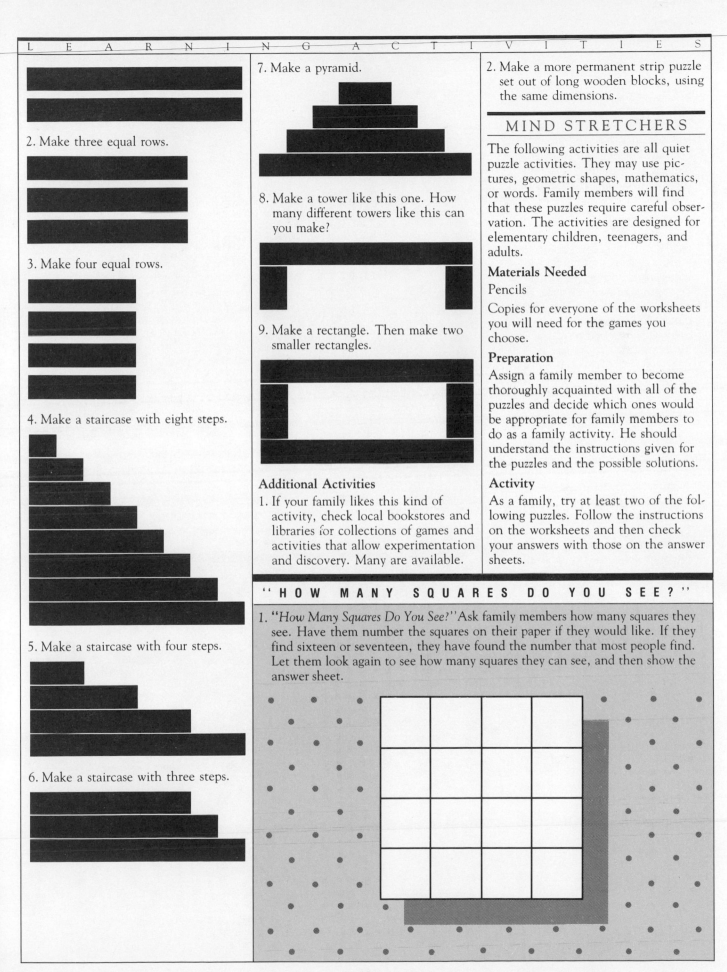

2. Make three equal rows.

3. Make four equal rows.

4. Make a staircase with eight steps.

5. Make a staircase with four steps.

6. Make a staircase with three steps.

7. Make a pyramid.

8. Make a tower like this one. How many different towers like this can you make?

9. Make a rectangle. Then make two smaller rectangles.

Additional Activities

1. If your family likes this kind of activity, check local bookstores and libraries for collections of games and activities that allow experimentation and discovery. Many are available.

2. Make a more permanent strip puzzle set out of long wooden blocks, using the same dimensions.

MIND STRETCHERS

The following activities are all quiet puzzle activities. They may use pictures, geometric shapes, mathematics, or words. Family members will find that these puzzles require careful observation. The activities are designed for elementary children, teenagers, and adults.

Materials Needed

Pencils

Copies for everyone of the worksheets you will need for the games you choose.

Preparation

Assign a family member to become thoroughly acquainted with all of the puzzles and decide which ones would be appropriate for family members to do as a family activity. He should understand the instructions given for the puzzles and the possible solutions.

Activity

As a family, try at least two of the following puzzles. Follow the instructions on the worksheets and then check your answers with those on the answer sheets.

"HOW MANY SQUARES DO YOU SEE?"

1. *"How Many Squares Do You See?"* Ask family members how many squares they see. Have them number the squares on their paper if they would like. If they find sixteen or seventeen, they have found the number that most people find. Let them look again to see how many squares they can see, and then show the answer sheet.

2. *"What Is This Thing Called Love?"* In the heart, there are thirty-four hidden words that describe what love is. See how many you can find. Words run in all directions, left to right, right to left, top to bottom, bottom to top, and diagonally. Circle them as you find them. Then look at the answer sheet to see how many you missed.

Answers: accepting, bond, communicating, loyalty, happiness, exciting, joyful, caring, trusting, fulfilling, receiving, giving, forgiving, understanding, tender, lovely, belonging, respect, natural, sharing, ageless, open, warm, nice, patient, faith, alive, always, hope, true, real, forever, right, wed.

"WHAT IS THIS THING CALLED LOVE?"

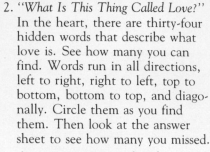

```
              S L G K P Y X                    K O F L F G
              S L G B C N E P O W N        S R V T T O P S C G
            Q H J M V W P I L G Q D R      L M D Q C R S T Y X P L
          S F A I T H T Y X D O J E I M  B F J N V E W O K G G C D H
        N S V L E M W P S C N A T U R A L H S T L V P G B A E M A I U
        D H B Q N P K J K M A Q O A R A S C U E X S H A R I N G N O
        Q L F H D H L E L N B C T B W A E D V R W H E Y P B O M E Q A
        R P J K E P O H I O A D C S A D R T E L C A R I N G Z U L Z R
        S X N U R K V M H G F E N Z R B R W X B A P N A Q S V T E B Y
        T W R P S S E L K J I D Q E C E F Q H K M P B A L W A Y S X S
        Y T B H I J L O G A D R C M L G D C Z L H I G D B R V S S Y T
        C V G J O Y F U L U E J I K F J N Y G R N H I F U M W A J
        J H E I D F L F I I T T Y E C D J U X I E I G V P Z T W X
          A J V K W E S V W S R Q H K U E F T O S G K R I G H T
          A F S I Z B I E X C I T I N G T A F B S J S W T N L S
            R G V J N N F G H B G D H N C I G W K F V K J F G
            E F G N I V I G R O F E I J H N J E L U O L R
              J S I A M C D E F I N T G N I G N O L E B
              F C M B R X N T U X P K L L R M D T K
                E L E O R A M G A E S G L Y S N P
                M N O P P M F N Y C F T I Q C O M
                J G B O B Z I Z C U E F R P B
                  U C Q J Y T L A Y O L U A
                  N X A E S W E D V U D
                    B O L U C R W C F
                    J P R K O B X
                      K Q T D A Y H
                      H E G Z L
                        C F P
                          X
```

3. *"The Tricky T."* Make patterns for these shapes by tracing them onto lightweight paper. Then use the patterns to make cardboard cutouts. Number them, and keep all the numbered sides facing you.

See if you can make the four pieces fit together to make a capital T.

"THE TRICKY T"

This *T* is exactly the same size as the puzzle pieces when they're put together properly.

282

4. *"Lots of Triangles."* There are thirty-five triangles in this pentagon. Can you find them all?

5. *"Division."* There are seven tennis balls inside this square. Can you divide up the square so that each tennis ball is left in its own compartment without any others—by using only three straight lines?

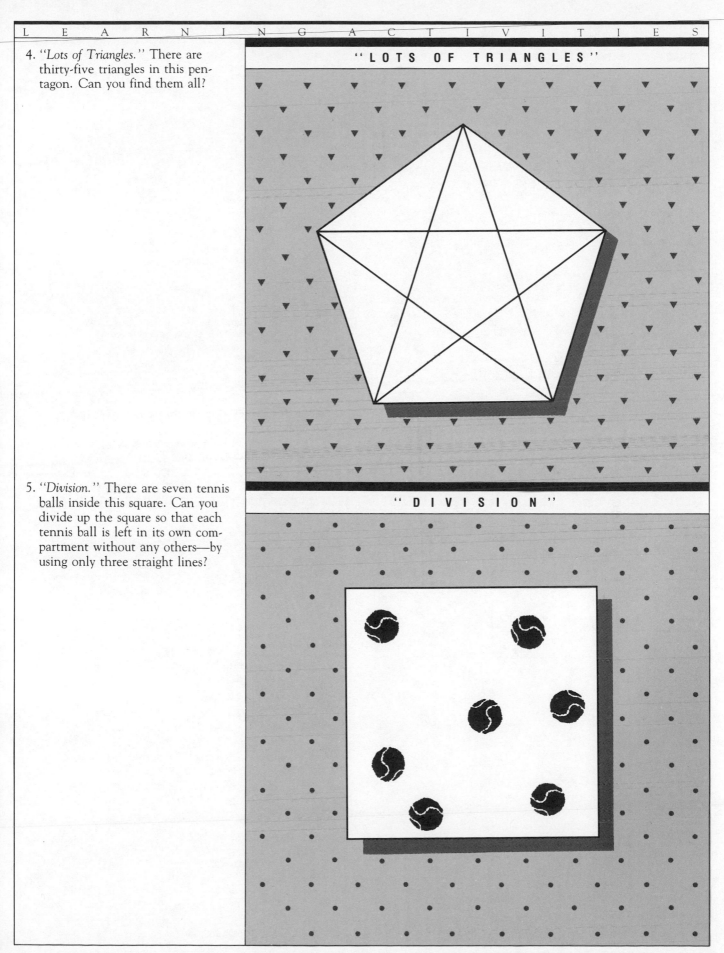

"L O T S   O F   T R I A N G L E S"

"D I V I S I O N"

"S N A T C H   A   M A T C H"

6. *"Snatch a Match."* Arrange twelve used matches to make four equal squares as shown. By moving only three matches, try to make three equal squares.

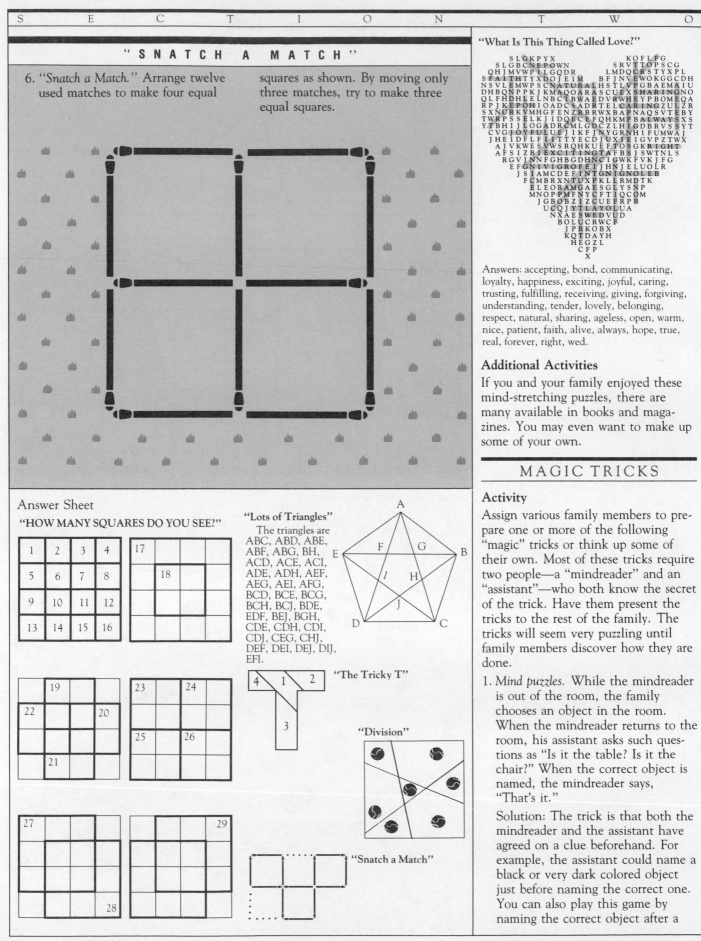

"What Is This Thing Called Love?"

```
      S L G K P Y X                    K O F L F G
    S L G B C N E P O W N          S R V T T O P S C G
  Q H J M V W P I L G Q D R      L M D G C R S T Y X P L
S F A I T H T Y X D O J E I M    B F J N V E W O K G G C D H
N S V L E M W P S C N A T U R A L H S T L V P G B A E M A I U
D H B Q N P P K J K M A Q O A R A S C U E X S H A R I N G N O
Q L F H D H L E L N B C T B W A E D V R W H E Y P B O M E Q A
R P J K E P O H I O A D C S A D R T E L C A R I N G Z U L Z R
S X N U R K V M H G F E N Z R B R W X B A P N A Q S V T E B Y
T W R P S S E L K J I D Q E C E F Q H K M P B A L W A Y S X S
Y T B H I J L O G A D R C M L G D C Z L H I G D B R V S S Y T
  C V G J O Y F U L U E J I K F J N Y G R N H I F U M W A J
  J H E I D F L F L I T T Y E C D J U X I E I G V P Z T W X
    A J V K W E S V W S R Q H K U E F T O S G K R I G H T
    A F S I Z B I E X C I T I N G T A F B S J S W T N L S
      R G V J N N F G H B G D H N C I G W K F V K J F G
      E F G N I V I G R O F E I J H N J E L U O L R
        J S I A M C D E F J N T G N I G N O L E B
        F C M B R X N T U X P K L L R M D T K
          E L E O R A M G A E S G L Y S N P
          M N O P P M F N Y C F T I Q C O M
            J G B O B Z J Z C U E I R P B
            U C Q J M T L A Y O L U A
              N X A E S W E D V U D
                B O L U C R W C F
                J P R K O B X
                K Q T D A Y H
                  H E G Z L
                  C F P
                    X
```

Answers: accepting, bond, communicating, loyalty, happiness, exciting, joyful, caring, trusting, fulfilling, receiving, giving, forgiving, understanding, tender, lovely, belonging, respect, natural, sharing, ageless, open, warm, nice, patient, faith, alive, always, hope, true, real, forever, right, wed.

Additional Activities

If you and your family enjoyed these mind-stretching puzzles, there are many available in books and magazines. You may even want to make up some of your own.

MAGIC TRICKS

Activity

Assign various family members to prepare one or more of the following "magic" tricks or think up some of their own. Most of these tricks require two people—a "mindreader" and an "assistant"—who both know the secret of the trick. Have them present the tricks to the rest of the family. The tricks will seem very puzzling until family members discover how they are done.

1. *Mind puzzles.* While the mindreader is out of the room, the family chooses an object in the room. When the mindreader returns to the room, his assistant asks such questions as "Is it the table? Is it the chair?" When the correct object is named, the mindreader says, "That's it."

   Solution: The trick is that both the mindreader and the assistant have agreed on a clue beforehand. For example, the assistant could name a black or very dark colored object just before naming the correct one. You can also play this game by naming the correct object after a

Answer Sheet

"HOW MANY SQUARES DO YOU SEE?"

1	2	3	4
5	6	7	8
9	10	11	12
13	14	15	16

17		
	18	

	19	
22		20
	21	

23		24
	25	26

27		
	28	

		29

"Lots of Triangles"

The triangles are ABC, ABD, ABE, ABF, ABG, BH, ACD, ACE, ACI, ADE, ADH, AEF, AEG, AEI, AFG, BCD, BCE, BCG, BCH, BCJ, BDE, EDF, BEJ, BGH, CDE, CDH, CDI, CDJ, CEG, CHJ, DEF, DEI, DEJ, DIJ, EFI.

"The Tricky T"

4	1	2
	3	

"Division"

"Snatch a Match"

284

red article the first time, a white one the second time, and a blue one the third time.

2. *Read the number.* The family chooses a number while the mindreader is out of the room. When he returns, the assistant calls off numbers, and the mindreader identifies the right one.

Solution: The first digit of the first number called out by the assistant tells when the selected number will appear. For example, if 45 were the number, the assistant might call "39, 75, 45, 62." The mindreader would reply "forty-five is the number." The first digit of 39 is 3. This told the mindreader that the right number would be the third one called.

3. *Reading the map.* This requires a globe or a map. While the mindreader is out of the room, have the family choose a city. When he returns, the assistant names one city after another. When he says the correct one, the mindreader identifies it.

Solution: The assistant names the correct city two cities after a city with two words in its name, such as Baton Rouge or New York. You can also use this trick with countries.

4. *Reading sentences.* Have each member of the family write a short sentence on a slip of paper, fold the paper, and place it in a container. (Make sure that everyone uses the same kind of paper.) The assistant pretends to write on his, but actually does not. Mix up the slips in the container. The mindreader then draws a slip, places it against his head, and says any short sentence. The assistant says that the slip was his. The mindreader nods, unfolds the paper, and reads it silently. When he does this, he memorizes the sentence that is actually written on the paper. He throws away that slip of paper and repeats the performance, this time repeating the sentence he has just memorized. When this one is claimed by a player, he repeats the performance again, and so forth.

5. *Temple reading.* The mindreader leaves the room while the group chooses a number from one to ten. When he returns, he puts his hands on the temples of each player, one at a time, stopping at each as if he is meditating. When he does this with his assistant, the assistant secretly tells him the chosen number by tightening his jaws and relaxing them, which makes the muscles in his temples move, the correct number of times. The assistant must be careful not to move his mouth and cheeks so no one will find out the trick.

6. *Pick a color.* The magician shows five new crayons to the family. He then gives them to a member of the family and turns his back to the group. The family member mixes the colors while the magician's back is turned and puts the crayons in the magician's hand, behind his back. The magician then turns back around to face the group as members of the family call for a certain color. After much concentration, the magician brings each color forth correctly.

Solution: The audience doesn't realize it, but the magician has five identical crayons secretly tucked under the back of his belt. He has memorized their order ahead of time. As someone calls for a color, he puts one of the original crayons in his back pocket and takes out the right crayon from his belt.

7. *Invisible writing.* Invisible writing is a method of secret writing with ink that is invisible until something is done to "develop" it. Below are several formulas for invisible ink:

• Dip a sheet of paper in water: then flatten it against a windowpane or large wall mirror. Place a dry sheet over it. Print your secret message on the dry sheet, using a ball-point pen or a pencil with a medium hard lead and a point that is not sharp. Press hard as you write. When you finish the message, remove the dry sheet and throw it away. The printing will be clearly visible on the wet sheet. When the sheet dries, the letters will vanish without a trace. Plunge the sheet into water. The writing immediately becomes visible again.

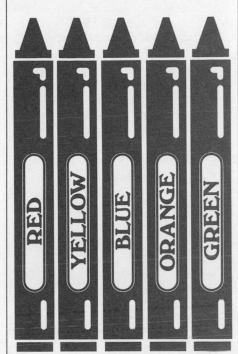

• One of the best inks of this type is ordinary milk. Apply it with a brush on a thick, hard-surfaced paper or thin cardboard, such as a file card. To bring out the writing, rub any kind of dark powdery substance over the dry page. A good way is to scrape the point of a lead pencil, letting the powder fall on a sheet of paper. Tap your fingertips on the graphite powder, then rub them over the invisible writing.

• Take one tablet of a laxative and mash it up thoroughly in about half an ounce of rubbing alcohol. Be sure the entire tablet is dissolved. Use a brush to print the message. The writing will be invisible when the ink dries. To develop it, moisten a piece of cotton or cleansing tissue with household ammonia (or any other strong alkaline, such as washing soda dissolved in a small amount of water) and dab it on the page. The writing will appear.

RIDDLES

Guessing riddles is fun, and you can do it anywhere. Use this activity to stimulate your mind and your funny bone.

Activity

You could have one activity night where all you do is tell riddles or you could intersperse riddles throughout several activity nights. Riddles can also be fun when you are traveling.

Many riddle books are available at bookstores and libraries. Get some for your family and let family members take turns telling riddles. You could even create some riddles of your own, if you have that special talent. Listed below are some Bible riddles that you can try on your family.

1. Who was the most successful doctor in the Bible? (Job, because he had the most patients [patience].)

2. Who was the most popular actor in the Bible? (Samson. He brought the house down.)

3. When is high finance first mentioned in the Bible? (When Pharaoh's daughter took a little profit [prophet] from the bulrushes.)

4. At what time of day was Adam created? (A little before Eve.)

5. What evidence does the Bible give to show that Adam and Eve were rather noisy? (They raised Cain.)

6. What did the cat say when the ark landed? (Is that Ararat?)

7. What simple affliction caused the death of Samson? (He died of fallen arches.)

8. Who was the best financier in the Bible? (Noah. He floated his stock [animals] while the whole world was in liquidation.)

9. What man in the Bible had no parents? (Joshua, the son of Nun.)

10. Why should we be encouraged by the story of Jonah and the whale? (Because Jonah was down in the mouth, but came out all right.)

11. Who was the straightest man in the Bible? (Joseph, because Pharaoh made a ruler out of him.)

12. What was it that Adam and Eve never had and yet they gave to their children? (Earthly parents.)

13. When was the longest day in the Bible? (When there was no Eve in it.)

14. Did Eve ever have a date with Adam? (No, it was an apple.)

15. How long did Cain hate his brother? (As long as he was Abel.)

16. Who in the Bible was the cham-

pion runner of all time? (Adam. He was the first in the human race.)

17. When was tennis first mentioned in the Bible? (When Joseph served in Pharaoh's court.)

18. What was the first theatrical venture in the Bible? (When Eve appeared for Adam's benefit.)

19. When was the first meat mentioned in the Bible? (When Noah took Ham into the ark.)

20. When was medicine first mentioned in the Bible? (When the Lord gave Moses two tablets.)

21. How do we know that Noah was preceded from the ark by at least three other people? (Because the Bible says that Noah came forth [fourth].)

22. Why was the giant Goliath very much astonished when David hit him with a stone? (Because such a thing had never before entered his head.)

23. Why didn't Noah catch more fish than he did during the voyage of the ark? (Because he had only two worms.)

24. Where was Noah when the light went out? (In the d'ark).

25. Who was the strongest man in the Bible? (Jonah, because the whale couldn't hold him even after he got him down.)

26. What proof have we that there was sewing in the time of David? (He was hemmed in on all sides.)

27. In what place did a rooster in the Bible crow where all the people in the world could hear him? (In the ark.)

28. What reason is there to think that Moses wore a wig? (Because he was sometimes seen with Aaron [hair on], and sometimes without.)

29. Which are the two smallest things mentioned in the Bible? (The widow's mite and the wicked flee [flea].)

30. Who was older, David or Goliath? (David must have been because he rocked Goliath to sleep.)

TANGRAMS

A tangram is a puzzle. It can be enjoyed by the entire family. It does not require a great amount of skill. But it does require patience; time; and, above all, imagination. There are at least 1,600 possible designs that can be constructed with one seven-piece set.

Activity

Divide a thick piece of cardboard or a panel of wood (1/4 inch [1/2 cm] thick and 6 inches [15 cm] square would be ideal) into sixteen smaller equal squares with a pencil and ruler. See figure 1.

With pencil and ruler, draw the pattern that you desire, as shown in figure 2. Then cut the block where you have marked it.

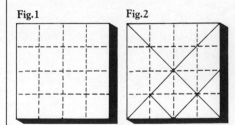

Fig. 1   Fig. 2

You can make a variety of different figures—birds, dogs, men, cats, and so forth—with the seven tans that make up this square. The only rules are that you must use all seven pieces, and none of the pieces may be overlapped.

Variation

Give each member of the family his own square or rectangle piece of paper and a pair of scissors. Each then cuts his paper apart with two straight cuts (see illustration). When each has cut apart his own paper, he mixes his pieces and passes them to the player on his right. Each player has five minutes to arrange the pieces so that they form the original square or rectangle. The player who first completes his puzzle scores ten points. Once a player has scored, shuffle the pieces again and pass them on to the next player to the right. Play continues as before. The game ends when each player has had the opportunity to work all puzzles but his own.

MAKING AND KEEPING AIDS FOR FAMILY HOME EVENINGS

Every effort has been made to make this manual as interesting for your family as possible. Pictures and games necessary for the success of the home evening are provided. You may want to make your own cutouts using patterns from the manual or by cutting materials from old family home evening manuals. By using the ideas below, you will increase the effectiveness of the activity and the ease in presenting the material.

1. *Removing cutouts from old manuals.* To remove the cutouts from old manuals, use a razor blade or a sharp knife. Place a thin pile of newspapers or a piece of cardboard under the page you want to remove, and make a clean, straight cut. This will protect the other pages in the manual and prevent jagged edges that may result from using scissors.

2. *Mounting cutouts.* Cutouts are usually more useful if you mount them before using them in the home evening activity. To mount a cutout, cover the back of it with paste or glue and then attaching it to heavier paper. Mount a picture

to be used in a game or jigsaw puzzle on heavy paper or cardboard. Cutouts for flannel board may be mounted on lighter-weight paper.

3. *Flannel boards.* The flannel board is an inexpensive and easy-to-make device. It consists of a piece of flannel or felt fastened to a stiff surface. A large sheet of rigid corrugated cardboard makes a good backing for the flannel board. Plywood or masonite can also be used. Cut a piece of flannel a little larger than the cardboard backing. (Felt can be used, but it is more expensive.) Stretch the flannel over the face of the backing material; wrap it around the edges; and tape it securely to the back with wide masking tape or packing tape.

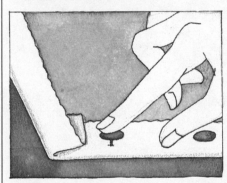

• Use a wide tape to fasten flannel on cardboard or masonite.

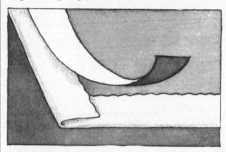

• On plywood or celotex, use tacks or heavy-duty staples.

To use the flannel-board figures, glue pieces of flannel to the figure

in several places, or use masking tape formed in a ring with the sticky side out so that it will stick to both the figure and the flannel board.

4. *Other ways of displaying cutouts.* You need not use a flannel board to display cutout figures. The following suggestions can be effective:

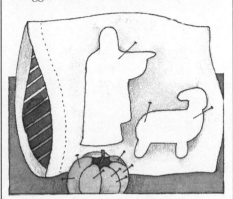

• Use a pillow and straight pins. Stick the pin through the cutout and into the pillow in the position you want it.

• Have the family sit around a table and lay the figures flat on it.

• Place the cutouts on the floor where all can see them.

• If you wish to move the cutouts as the story progresses, use spools or small blocks of wood or plastic. Make a ring with masking or transparent tape (with the sticky side out), and attach it to the back of the cutout and to the blocks or spools.

• Cut grooves about an inch deep in the top of some of the blocks or spools. Mounted cutouts can then be inserted into the grooves and will stand upright on your table or floor to give a three-dimensional effect.

5. *Chalkboard.* The chalkboard is a familiar and convenient means of presenting visual materials. Lightweight, commercially made chalkboards are available at furniture and variety stores at moderate cost. But building your own chalkboard can be a fun family activity.

One of the best materials available for making a chalkboard is tempered masonite. This is a smooth, durable, and inexpensive material. You may make your chalkboard any size, but three feet by four feet is adequate for most purposes.

When the masonite is cut to size and the edges are smoothed with sandpaper, it is ready for painting. It should be coated with a paintlike material called "chalkboard slating," which should be available at most paint stores and can be applied easily with a clean, soft brush. Chalkboard slating is also available in spray cans. Whether you brush or spray, be sure to follow the directions on the label of the container. Let the slating dry thoroughly. Also, let it age for several days before using.

Never write with chalk on a new or freshly cleaned board without first "sizing" it or coating it with chalk dust. Do this by patting or rubbing a loaded chalkboard eraser over the surface. If you fail to do this, it will be difficult to erase marks from the chalkboard. After use, a chalkboard can be cleaned with a dry cloth or chalkboard brush. Never use wet or oily rags. Once in a while, you may use a slightly damp cloth to clean chalk dust from the chalkboard. But the board must then be resized. Use soft, good-quality chalk. Colored chalks, which create added interest for young children, may also be used.

6. *Chalkboard substitute.* A piece of heavy, white poster board can make an excellent substitute chalkboard. Cover the whole poster board with a piece of clear, medium-weight plastic. Tape the plastic over the front of the poster board, using tape around the edge and over the back to secure it permanently. You may write or draw pictures on the plastic surface

with wax or grease pencils, marking pencils, or soap crayons. The wax markings can be wiped off easily with tissues or a soft rag. If they do not come off easily with a soft rag, use a sponge and a mild liquid detergent or soap.

7. *Bulletin board.* A bulletin board can be very useful in family home evenings or for general family use. It can be made very inexpensively out of celotex or similar fibrous building material. These materials are generally available with a white-painted surface on one side, which is satisfactory for a bulletin surface. To hide the pin holes, cover the board with a coarsely woven cloth, such as burlap. Use your imagination to decorate the board, perhaps with an interesting border.

8. *Posting board.* This simple teaching aid consists of a series of horizontal slots or pockets on a folded board that will hold wordstrips or pictures. Fold butcher paper or heavy kraft wrapping paper like pleats; then tape it to the front surface of the board.

9. *Puppets.* Simple puppets can help you dramatize stories and important lesson ideas. Children love to be involved in these types of dramatic presentations, and they enjoy the use of all kinds of puppets. A variety of puppets made from paper sacks, socks, and other common items are shown below.

CREATING FANCY FOODS

Have the family spend this family home evening in the kitchen together creating unusual ways of making and arranging ordinary foods.

Activity

This activity can be used many times during the year. Be as inventive as you can in what you do. You may want to divide the family into teams and see who can create the most unusual dish.

Be imaginative about the arrangement and color combinations of your displays. Make this a *visual* as well as an *eating* experience for the whole family.

1. *Creative cakes.* A bunny cake can be made with two round cakes put together as illustrated. Frost and decorate it with eyes, nose, and a mouth.

A heart cake can be made with one square cake and one round one put together as illustrated. Frost and decorate it with designs of your own imagination.

Any holiday can be remembered by special decorations on a cake. Be imaginative; use unusual things. For instance, this Christmas cake,

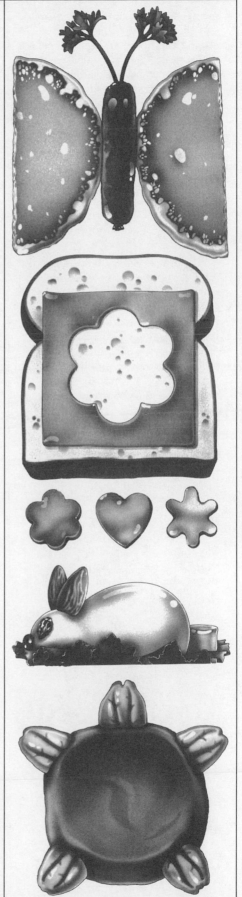

made of two large square cakes, sectioned as shown, can be frosted a dark green and then decorated with small cranberries and spaghetti dyed with food coloring.

You can make castle cakes, carousel cakes, almost anything you can think of. Sometimes you may want to build with crackers or cookies also. One young teenager created a "monster cake" by putting a single round layer of cake on a large piece of cardboard that was covered in aluminum foil and decorating the cake with carefully sliced vegetables to make the facial features. The eyes were egg slices; the nose a small carrot; the mouth a half slice of tomato; the ears, green pepper strips; the hair, noodles.

2. *Butterfly breakfast.* Try this one for breakfast some morning—or as a snack for family home evening. Serve one sausage, one pancake, cut in half, and two small pieces of parsley as shown.

3. *Sandwich cutouts.* For attractive open-faced sandwiches, use a cookie cutter to cut out shapes from cheese slices. You can use both parts of the cheese for two different sandwiches. Some meat under the cheese pieces will give color contrast as well as good taste.

4. *Bunny salad.* Take half of a sliced pear and put it on some lettuce with a small dab of cottage cheese for the tail. Marshmallows also make good tails. Use cinnamon candies for the nose and raisins for the eyes. You can use blanched almonds for the ears or pink paper cut in shapes like ears.

5. *Brownie turtles.* Put dabs of brownie dough on a cookie tin and place five pecan nuts in each cookie in the proper places to represent a turtle's feet and head. Bake the special cookies and ask everyone to eat them very slowly.

6. *Silly salads.* Many families have molds that set gelatin desserts and salads into various shapes that can be decorated in many very interesting ways. But to do something really creative and add sparkle to your salads and desserts, have each

member of your family select some odd-shaped object that you have around the house and set the gelatin in that. They may pick vases, toys, or nicknacks of various shapes and sizes, the sillier the better.

This looks as good as it tastes.

7. *Food flowers.* To make radish rosebuds, mark five or six lines from one end of the radish to the other with a paring knife tip. Start at the end away from the stem. Peel thin slices of the radish away between the lines to form the petals.

You can make larger flowers to fill a salad plate by using fruits and vegetables for petals, with celery sticks for stems and mint for leaves. Watermelon and cantaloupe balls, cherry tomatoes, or tomato slices, apple and orange slices, and even cauliflower pieces would look good enough to eat with an olive or cherry at the center of the bloom.

Slices of green pepper could be the outline for a bloom with creamed cheese filling in the center, again finished off with an olive or cherry in the center and a celery stick stem.

Make orange peel roses by cutting a slice of orange peeling about three inches long and one inch wide. Roll the peeling into a ball and secure it with half a toothpick. This makes a good garnish.

8. *Delicious dolls.* Raggedy Ann has a peach head, grated cheese hair, clove or raisin eyes, a sliced cherry mouth, a lettuce dress, and carrot or celery stick arms and legs. Her feet are made out of cheese.

Make a snowman out of three scoops of potato or macaroni salad. Decorate him with olives, raisins, carrots, parsley and red pepper or pimento.

9. *Colorful candles.* To make candles, pour gelatin into an empty juice can, using one color or different colors for each can, as you wish. When the gelatin is set, unmold it, cut it in half crosswise and put it on a serving dish with a lettuce leaf under the base. Drizzle with mayonnaise or whipped cream dressing. Cut a wick from a piece of cheese.

10. *Sandwich cutouts.* Make ABC sandwiches by cutting a prepared sandwich into strips and forming alphabet letters to spell out names and words.

Make lady's fingers by cutting the shape of fingers in an ordinary slice of buttered bread. Use jelly to paint on the fingernails. Rings can be made with peanut butter, cheese, or olive slices.

To make cheese sailboat sandwiches, cut cheese slices for the base of the boat; three inches is a good size. Use a toothpick, or straw for the ship's center pole. Cut a slice of bread diagonally into quarters and place one quarter on the pole for the sail.

FUN WITH GAMES

Have fun making up your own games. See how creative you can be. You may have as much fun making them as playing them.

Activity

This activity can be used many times during the year. There are many kinds of games your family may want to create. Three kinds are illustrated below, just to give you ideas of how to make up some in your own family. All of these games are "homemade." See what you can do.

Thought Games

1. *"What Animal Am I?"* Have each member of the family think of an animal he would like the family to guess. Choose one person to start. Have him act out what that animal does until someone guesses what animal he is pretending to be. The person who first guesses correctly gets a chance to act. Be sure everyone gets a turn to be the animal at least once.

2. *"Guess Who."* Have one member of the family think of some favorite or unusual scripture character. One at a time the rest of the family can ask him questions about this person, taking turns around the family circle. The first one who thinks he knows the correct name raises his hand and asks to answer the questions about the character himself. If his answers are right (the one who chose the personality will know), he continues until someone else guesses and takes over the answering. If someone's guess is wrong, he will answer the next few questions incorrectly (as judged again by the person who chose the name) and will be out of the game to sit by and watch while the others play until everyone in the family knows the correct personality. If two people

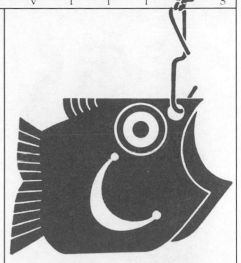

guess on the same turn, the first gets to answer at least one question before the second one takes over as the answerer.

Board games

Invent a game of travel, taking the players from some famous scripture site to another. Decide on where you want the game to start and end. (See the game illustrated below.) You may want to take Abraham from Ur to Haran and down into Palestine, or

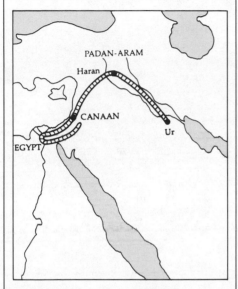

you may want to have him go from Palestine to Egypt and return.

On a big poster board or large piece of paper, draw a rough map of Egypt and Palestine, putting in all the major cities, lakes, and rivers. Draw in squares between these landmarks as shown in the illustration. Have the family choose some things to use as their "men"—buttons, thimbles, pebbles, beans. Work out some way to determine the number of spaces each will move each turn—using a spinner, dice, or drawing numbered cards.

You may want to add more excitement to the game by coloring every seventh square red. If a player lands on one of these red squares, he must go back three spaces.

Activity Games

1. *"Ringer."* Get three soft-drink bottles and line them up with a piece of paper under each designating the number of points possible.

Have each member of the family toss fruit jar rings to see what score they can achieve by getting ringers.

Each should get three tosses a turn. To balance skill and ability for various ages, allow small children to stand closer to the bottles. Keep score for as many turns as you want each to have, but be sure you decide the number of turns *before* the game starts.

2. *"Ball tag."* Play tag with a ball by letting everyone run around and dodge the ball that the person who is "it" is trying to touch players with. The player who is touched becomes "it" and tries to touch someone else with the ball.

3. *"Baseball with marbles."* Set up four blocks of wood and three glasses as shown in the illustration, with the glasses on their sides. Mark the blocks "first base," "second base," "third base," and "home run," consecutively. Each represents a hit.

Divide into teams as fits your family size and ages. The object of this homemade game is to pitch or shoot the marbles and hit one of the blocks. If you miss and the marble goes into a glass you are out. If you miss a block and the marble does not go into a glass that is a strike. The other rules of baseball can be applied, or you can make up your own rules. Keep careful score as to how many runs you make, who are on the bases, how many outs the team has, and the number of innings. You may want to make the game much more difficult if your family is good at marbles. You can put more glasses around where they will complicate the pitching and make accuracy more important. (See illustration.)

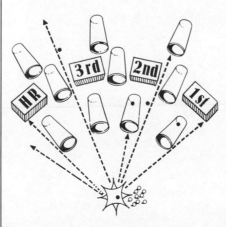

4. *"Fishing."* Make a fishing pole out of a stick and a long string. On the end of the string attach a paper clip, hairpin, or anything else with which you can make a hook. Make about ten fish by drawing them on either side of a folded piece of paper as shown in the illustration. The hole through which you must hook them to get a "catch" should be cut on both sides of the folded paper.

Put the ten fish on the floor all spread out and see how many fish each one can catch in turn within a one minute time limit. The fishermen must get the fish from the floor into his hand to count it as a catch.

You may wish to vary the game by seeing how long it takes each one to catch all ten fish. Make up your own rules—and your own game. It's fun!

5. *"What Do You Hear?"* Have all the family members close their eyes for one whole minute, listen, and note all the sounds they hear. After a minute, have them open their eyes and take turns naming the sounds they heard.

6. *"Mother Goose Charades."* Divide the family into two teams, with an adult or teenager heading each team. One team acts out a Mother Goose rhyme in pantomime. The other team guesses what the nursery rhyme is. Then they switch roles.

7. *"Whirlwind."* All stand or sit in a circle. One person says, "I'm thinking of something." He then

gives three clues, such as, "It can swim. It doesn't live in the water. It has webbed feet." When someone thinks he knows the answer, he whirls around in his place and says, "Whirlwind." Then he tells what he thinks it is. The one who guesses correctly gives the next three clues.

8. *"Buzz."* The players sit in a circle. They begin counting with one, each player taking a turn calling the next number. When seven is reached, the person says, "Buzz," instead of the number. This is true of any number with seven in it (such as seventeen) or any multiple of seven (such as twenty-one). When reaching seventy, the players say, "Buzz," for all the numbers; but when seventy-seven is reached, the player must say, "Buzz, buzz." Each player who fails to say "Buzz" or "Buzz buzz" when he should is out of the game. The last one out wins.

9. *"How's Your Memory?"* The players are seated in a circle. The first player starts by saying, "One old ostrich." The next player repeats this phrase and adds another phrase, saying, "One old ostrich and two tree toads twisting tendrils." Each time the phrases are repeated in order and the player adds one of his own. This goes on around the circle until there are at least ten phrases. When a person makes a mistake, he is eliminated. There should be a prize for anyone who can finish without a mistake.

Use phrases such as the following.

1. One ostrich
2. Two tree toads twisting tendrils
3. Three tiny titmice tapping trees
4. Four fat friars fanning flames
5. Five fluffy finches flying fast
6. Six of Susie's sisters sewing shirts
7. Seven seashells in Sarah's shawl
8. Eight elves eating Easter eggs
9. Nine nimble noblemen nibbling nuts
10. Ten throbbing thrushes twittering tunes in time

10. *"Ghost."* The players sit in a circle. The first player says the first letter of a word he is thinking of. It must be a word with more than two letters. The next player thinks of a word beginning with that letter and adds the second letter. The third player adds another letter. The game continues in this way until someone makes a complete word. Each player tries not to complete a word. Suppose the first three players had named the letters *n-e-x* and the fourth player can think of nothing but the word *next* and adds the *t*; he then becomes a "half-ghost." The next player starts another word. If a half-ghost ends another word he becomes a "ghost" and may no longer participate in forming words. Anyone who speaks to a ghost becomes a ghost also. The ghost remains in the game by trying to draw others into conversation with him.

A player must always have in mind a word of more than two letters. If one player doubts that another has in mind a legitimate word, he may challenge that player. The player challenged must then state the word. If he cannot, he becomes a half-ghost or a ghost. If he does state a word, the person who challenged him becomes a half-ghost or a ghost.

11. *"The Old Hen and the Chickens."* One person is chosen to be Old Hen. That person leaves the room. The family decides who will be Little Chick. Then they all sit with bowed heads. Old Hen comes back into the room and says, "cluck, cluck." Little Chick answers, "Peep, peep." After they all raise their heads, Old Hen tries to guess who her chick is. Then Little Chick becomes Old Hen and leaves the room. If in three tries Old Hen does not guess who Little Chick is, she should be told.

12. *"Animal Farm."* The family sits on chairs in a circle. They choose one member to be the farmer. The farmer kneels blindfolded in front of another family member and says the name of an animal. That person disguises his voice and makes the sound that animal makes. The farmer tries to guess who the person making the animal sound is. If he guesses correctly, the person who made the sound becomes the new farmer.

13. *"Buckle-Buckle Beanstalk."* Family members are shown an object—a block or small toy—which they are to look for later. Then all except one person leave the room. The one left places the object in sight somewhere in the room. When the others return, the first person to spot the object cries, "Buckle-Buckle Beanstalk." He then takes a turn placing the object while the others leave the room.

14. *"The Boy and the Bell."* The family members are seated on chairs in a circle. One person, who is the "bell boy," sits in the middle of the circle with a small bell under his chair. He is either blindfolded or closes his eyes tightly so he cannot see. Another member of the family creeps up, grasps the bell, holds the clapper to keep it from ringing, and takes it to his seat.

He puts both hands behind him, still holding the bell. All the rest of the family put their hands behind them, also. The one who has the bell rings it softly. The bell boy takes off his blindfold and tries to guess who has the bell. It may be necessary for the bell to be rung several times.

15. *"Fruit Basket."* One member of the family is chosen to be the caller. The rest of the family members sit in a circle on chairs. The caller gives each member, including himself, the name of a different fruit. When he calls out the names of two fruits, such as apples and pears, the two who were given the names of those fruits must change seats. The caller tries to slip into one of the seats, leaving someone else without a seat. The one without a seat is the new caller. At any time the caller may say, "The fruit basket tipped over." Then all must change seats, and the caller tries to get any empty seat, leaving another person as caller.

16. *"Dress-Up Race."* For each child, prepare a sack containing items of clothing such as a scarf, a ribbon, shoes, a belt, or a wig. Each child starts from a certain point with his sack. Upon reaching a given point, each opens his sack, puts on the items of clothing, and returns to the starting point. The first one to return wins. Older children could be given more items of clothing to put on. This game will be most successful with at least six players. It is a good game to play when you invite another family to join with you for a home evening.

17. *"Feather Volleyball."* Tie a string or rope between two chairs for a net. One team stands on each side of the net. One team starts the game by tossing a feather (a downy one that will float) into the air and trying to blow it over the net and onto the ground on the other team's side. The opposing team tries to keep the feather from falling on their side, and tries to blow it back over the net. When the feather falls on one side of the net, the team on the other side wins a point. Play continues until one team wins the game by gaining eleven points.

18. *"Bottle Build-Up."* Give each member of your family ten or fifteen toothpicks or matches. All should have the same number. Place a narrow-necked bottle on a table. The object is to stack the toothpicks or matches on top of the bottle across the opening. Each player in turn places one toothpick across the opening of the bottle. This continues until one of the players upsets the pile. The person who upsets the pile must take all the toothpicks that fall. The winner is the player who gets rid of all his toothpicks. If your family consists of only older children and adults, increase the number of toothpicks each has to make the game more difficult.

19. *"Jinx-Up—Jinx-Down."* Divide the family into two teams. Have the teams sit on opposite sides of a sturdy table. Choose someone to be captain of each team. No one but the captain gives orders. Give one team a coin about an inch in diameter. On the signal to start, this team starts passing the coin among themselves from player to player under the table. At the call "Jinx-up" from the captain of the opposing team, all members of the team with the coin must raise their hands above the table, keeping their fists clenched. At the command "Jinx-down" by the captain of the opposing team, all must slap their hands flat on the table.

The opposing side then consults together to guess who has the coin. The captain orders the hands raised, one at a time. When he orders the hand up that is hiding the coin, his team wins as many points as there are hands left on the table.

The coin is then given to the other side. The team that first scores twenty-one wins.

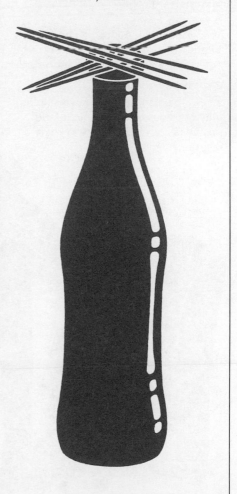

CULTURAL *Activities*

SINGING PRAISES: LEARNING OUR HYMNS AND CHILDREN'S SONGS

Sunday is a good day for the family to spend some time learning our hymns and children's songs. Singing together brings joy, and knowing the words to a song makes singing more fun. Encourage all family members to sing. Remind them that if only the birds with the prettiest songs were allowed to sing, the forest would be a mighty quiet place.

Materials Needed

A copy of *Hymns*
Sing with Me or *Activity Songs and Verses*
Squares of paper or 3-by-5 inch cards

Activity

These five games all involve singing. Playing them often can help family members learn the words to their favorite hymns.

Game 1

A number of words are used in more than one of our hymns. Here is a list of some of these words: *come, home, mountains, high, how, fire, Zion, let, there, sing, now, hills, guide, O, Oh, we'll, hark, light, thank.*

The family leader calls out a word, and each family member has a chance to sing part or all of a hymn using the word in the lyrics. When no one can think of any other hymn using this word, go on to the next word. Everyone stays in the game to the end, even if he misses a word. There is no particular winner in this game. It is a participation game. After the last word is given, the whole family can sing a hymn suggested by that word.

Game 2

Each person takes turns clapping or tapping out the rhythm of a Church hymn or children's song. The first person to guess the song may sing along with the clapping.

Game 3

Have family members sit in a circle around the room or on the floor. Choose a hymn or song from *Hymns* or *Sing with Me* that family members want to learn better. The leader will read the words to the song. Play the melody if you have a piano or other instrument available. The family then sings the first verse two or three times.

The leader then gives each person a turn to sing one word alone. The leader sings the first word, then points to another member to sing the second word, another to sing the third word, and so forth until someone misses. Starting where they left off, the leader points to the next members to sing a word at a time until the song is completed. The leader should try to keep the rhythm going as each sings his word in turn. At another time, each of the verses might be learned in the same manner.

Game 4

From *Hymns* or *Sing with Me*, pick as many songs as there are family members playing the game. Then pick one extra hymn or song. Divide each song into four fairly even sections or phrases and write each section on a separate card. Include the page number of the hymn in the lower left-hand corner of the card. In the upper right-hand corner, the cards should be numbered 1, 2, 3, or 4 according to the position of the phrases in the song. Also, make several free sing cards, according to the number of players as follows:

two players: 2 free sing cards
three players: 3 free sing cards
four players: 1 free sing card
five players: 2 free sing cards

No more than five players can play this game effectively. If there are more in the family, divide into two groups. One could be for younger children, using easy songs.

Mix up all the cards and give each player an equal number. There will be one extra card. Turn the extra card face up on the table as a discard or an exchange card if desired.

The first player sings a phrase from one of his cards. He then can pick up the discard or draw one card from another player. He puts one card down as a discard. If he draws from a player, that player picks up the discard on the table. Players rotate turns around the table. The second player has the same choices. He sings one phrase from his hand and either picks up the discard or draws one card from another player. If he picks from another player, that person picks up the discard to keep his original number of cards.

The point of the game is to find out who holds phrases from the different hymns and try to choose those that complete a hymn for you. The free sing cards can be used in place of any phrase to complete a hymn as long as the player can sing the missing words. The first person to collect all four cards for one hymn or to complete a hymn by using the free sing cards is the winner.

A player should pick a different phrase to sing each time he has a turn or at least until he has sung them all. Then he can repeat as he chooses.

Game 5

Divide the family into teams, or individuals if the family is small. Each team or person will choose a well-known Church hymn or song and act it out as a charade. The other members try to guess the title of the song. When the correct title is guessed, the family sings the hymn together.

Additional Activities

1. Make up your own musical games.
2. Listen to the Tabernacle Choir sing hymns on records and tapes.
3. Purchase *Songs and Hymns for Latter-day Saints* from a Church distribution center (records: PCSI0149; cassettes: PCSI015A; booklet with words: PCSI0160). This is a recording of thirty hymns and thirty children's songs. On one side of the record or tape the words are sung. On the other side there is a piano

accompaniment alone and you can sing along.

4. Advanced singers might hum the alto, tenor, or bass parts to a hymn and see if the other family members can guess what the song is.

APPRECIATING MUSIC

There are many kinds of good music, and each has its place. Even very small children enjoy listening to music that expresses different feelings.

Materials Needed

Collect some music by well-known classical composers. Many libraries have records and tapes you can check out with a library card. And many radio stations play music written by these composers. If you live in a western culture, you may want to select one of the following compositions:

Peter and the Wolf (Prokofiev)
Nutcracker Suite (Tchaikovsky)
Scheherazade (Rimski-Korsakov)
Sorcerer's Apprentice (Dukas)
Sixth Symphony (Beethoven)
The Messiah (Handel)
Fireworks Music (Handel)
Grand Canyon Suite (Grofe)
Mother Goose Suite (Ravel)
Carnival of the Animals (Saint-Saens)
Peer Gynt Suites (Grieg)
Pines of Rome (Respighi)

Ask the librarian or salesman at the record store to help you find descriptive music, music that tells a story or creates a mood.

Preparation

Select a piece of music to listen to as a family. Have a family member summarize the information on the jacket of the record. If you are using the radio, the announcer may give a brief summary before playing each selection.

Family members might want to sit on pillows on the floor or just on comfortable chairs. Very young children might be encouraged to move quietly to the music. Shorter selections will hold their attention best.

Activity

When the music begins, ask each person to close his eyes and imagine what the music might be expressing.

Tell the others that we are almost always surrounded by sounds, but we learn to "tune them out." Tonight we want to "tune them in."

After listening to the music for a few minutes, ask the following questions:

1. How does this music make you feel?
2. What colors do you think of when you listen to this music?
3. Can you imagine what might be happening?
4. Is it fast or slow? Loud or soft?
5. Can you hear a melody? Is it played more than two times?
6. Can you tell when the melody changes a little bit?
7. Can you hear the sounds that are made by the different instruments?
8. Do you feel like quietly moving your hand to the beat of the music? Do it if you like.

Do not expect immediate answers. Tell family members to think about their answers while the rest of the music plays. Let them sit back and relax. Avoid loud talking, which could be distracting.

Ask the same questions when the music is finished. Respect each person's answer. Each family member is unique and will have a unique response to the same music.

Additional Activities

1. Repeat the activity described above on another night. One of the pleasures of listening to music more than once is that the melodies become familiar to us. We enjoy recognizing a melody and anticipating what comes next.

2. Choose a kind of music other than classical—perhaps jazz or folk music. Bring some examples to enjoy together.

3. Have a "Name That Tune" night. Guess the names of songs played by the family member in charge.

4. Pick one composer and bring several recorded examples to listen to. Or you could bring several records featuring the same instrument—the piano, guitar, or violin, for example. Or bring several examples of music from one country or one historical period.

5. Attend a concert as a family.

6. Take a walk in the country and pay attention to the sounds of birds, babbling brooks, the wind, and even silence. Talk about the sounds. Go home and listen to the third movement of Beethoven's Sixth Symphony.

7. Take a walk on a busy street in town. Listen to the horns honking, cars screeching, and jackhammers working. Go home and listen to George Gershwin's *An American in Paris*.

ARRANGING FLOWERS

Knowing a few basic principles of flower arranging can help you add beauty and life to your home. This activity will help your family learn these principles.

Materials Needed

Flowers from your own garden, or cut flowers from a florist

A container, usually one of simple design

Tools or materials to hold the flowers in place such as one or more of the following:

1. A metal pinpoint "frog," available at variety stores

2. A block of "oasis," available from florists

3. Some pebbles or sand

4. Some crunched up pfitzer juniper or other branches to be stuffed in the vase

Florist's clay to hold frog in place (if you are using a metal frog)

Scissors or snippers (some prefer a sharp knife to cut flowers on a slant)

Preparation

To help flowers last longer—

Use clean containers to slow bacterial growth.

Use a sharp knife or scissors to make a clean cut on the flower stem.

Cut most flowers the evening before using them and place them in a bucket of warm water (too hot or too cold may shock the flowers).

Fill the bucket of water up to within a few inches of the heads of the flowers and put them in a cool place overnight.

Roses are best picked in midafternoon, when the sap is up in the stem.

Dahlias and poppies are often burned at the end of the stem, or recut under water.

Activity

Remove all dirt and old leaves from the flowers. Remove leaves that will be under water. Place a frog firmly in the bottom of the container with clay. You may use other items to hold the flowers in place, such as oasis, sand, or chicken wire.

Have a design in mind when you start arranging. Geometric shapes are most commonly used. Try a triangle, a half circle, an S shape, or a rectangle (see illustration). Start by placing the longer stems with smaller flower heads in the background.

Usually place the larger flowers closer to the lip or edge of the container. Cut the larger flower stems shorter. Cut each flower stem a different length. The arrangement is more effective when the stems are at all different levels.

Keep in mind that simplicity is the key to a beautiful floral design. You don't need a lot of flowers. Actually, each one will show better when the arrangement is not overcrowded.

Look for gracefully bent branches and let them form the outer design. Follow these lines with other flowers and filler branches, but don't cover the original graceful line. Experiment with color harmonies to see which colors blend well.

Keep the following things in mind as you choose flowers for a vase: scale of flowers to container (smaller flowers in smaller vase, large flowers in larger vase); balance of flowers (see that the arrangement is not too heavy on one side); harmony with the other furniture or surroundings. When putting flowers on a dining table, keep the flower arrangement rather low, usually below eye level, so that it won't interfere with conversation.

Use the following illustrations as guides for flower arranging:

Isosceles Triangle

Circle

Crescent

Vertical Rectangle

Additional Activities

1. Make Christmastime arrangements with pine branches and red carnations or holly and other evergreens.

2. Make dried or artificial flower arrangements using the principles of design discussed above. Have a family outing to gather the dried materials—weeds, pods, and leaves.

3. Try making arrangements in different types of containers from your kitchen—on a bread board, in a frying pan, in a kettle. Look for toys that might hold flowers for a child's room.

4. In the summer, have your own flower show. Each family member can make a design to brighten the home.

5. Visit the local flower shows in your area.

6. Consider planting in your garden different varieties of flowers that could be used as arrangements in the home or as corsages.

ARTS AND CRAFTS

A simple art or craft activity can be a truly satisfying experience for your family. Develop your family's creativity and self-confidence by trying one of the crafts described below.

Materials Needed
The materials listed for the craft you choose.

Activity
The following are simple arts and crafts that one person, or the whole family, can try:

1. *Spiderweb print.* A spiderweb is a thing of intricate beauty. Find a freestanding web in the weeds or bushes. This may be easiest in the early morning, when dew is on it. Then, later in the day, when the web is dry, go back to prepare it for printing. Do not break the web away from its support. Prepare it while it is still in place.

   To prepare the web, spray it on both sides with white enamel paint. Be careful not to hold the can too close, or you might tear the web. Be sure the spiderweb is completely covered with paint; but don't use too much, or it will sag. Hold a piece of black construction paper under the web. Center the web on the paper and break the main fibers that hold the web in place, allowing the web to fall onto the paper.

   This print will be nice enough to frame or mount on cardboard.

2. *Wooden buttons.* Family members can have fun making their own buttons for articles of clothing they sew.

   You will need a piece of dowel 1 inch (3 centimeters) in diameter. Place the dowel between pieces of cardboard to shield it, and put it in a bench clamp or vice. Father can drill two or three holes into the end of the dowel. Center them so you can use them for the holes in the buttons. If you don't have a drill with a bit, make holes by twisting an awl or leather punch into the wood.

   Use a hand jigsaw to saw off rounds of the dowel to the thickness you desire for a button. If you have a triangular file, you can file a design in the top of each button. Make four or five similar buttons so you can use them for a set.

   Use a fine sandpaper to smooth off the rough parts. You can stain, paint, or wax the buttons to the desired finish.

3. *Weathered wood or driftwood sculptures.* Interesting wood pieces can be found in deserts and along beaches. The wood is often twisted and gnarled by the weather. Find an artistic piece of wood. It can be any size, but a size that is easy to work with is about 12 by 4 inches (30 by 10 centimeters).

   Fill a bucket with water and add one cup of household bleach. Use this solution and a wire brush or stiff brush to clean the wood. Sand it with varying weights of sandpaper to get it smooth. Then stain, varnish, paint, or wax it.

   Make a square stand to place the sculpture on by cutting a 4-by-4-foot (1-by-1-meter) post 4 inches (10 cm) high. Drill a hole in the center of the square and one in the center of the wood sculpture. Glue a piece of dowel 4 to 8 inches (10 to 20 cm) long into the hole in the sculpture and then glue that to the hole in the stand.

4. *Sand candles.* Some people who live on the oceanfront like to make sand candles in the sand along the beach. Not everyone has a beach handy, but you can usually get a bucket of sand.

   Fill a bucket with clean, damp (not wet) sand. Hollow out any shape you like with your hands. Whatever you hollow out will be the shape of the completed candle. You might want to push a round cereal bowl or a jello mold into the sand to make your shape.

   You can use commercial candle wax purchased at a crafts shop or you can use 1 ounce (25 grams) of paraffin wax mixed with 1 ounce (25 grams) of stearin. A colored wax crayon will provide the color or you can purchase candle dye.

   Heat the wax carefully to 120° F (49° C). Cut a piece of string or wick and prepare it by placing it in the melted wax with a spoon or tweezers. Straighten it by pulling it out tight and setting it aside to harden.

Carefully pour the wax into the sand mold. The sand should be damp, but not too wet or it won't stick to the wax. As the wax begins to cool, the sand will drop, forming a hollow in the wax. Keep refilling the hollow with hot wax. If you want a thick crust, you need to use hotter wax. The hotter the wax the thicker the crust. But be careful: hot wax can cause severe burns.

Let the candle set for two or three hours in a cool place. Use a candle needle or a piece of thick wire to make a hole for the wick. Cut the wire as long as the candle is deep. Leave it in the mold overnight until the wax hardens.

Dig the candle out of the sand the next day. Carefully brush any loose sand from the candle. Remove the wire and insert the prepared wick. You may have to melt a little more wax and pour it around the wick to help the wick stand in place.

You can decorate the outside sand crust by gluing on sea shells, or you can carve a design in the sand with a sharp instrument.

5. *Fine pen drawing.* This is especially good for young children to do alone. No preparations are necessary.

Observation is the key to drawing. Pick a flower or a leaf. Look at it and memorize how it looks. Now put it away and make a line drawing with a fine-line pen.

After you have completed your first drawing, hold the flower or leaf in one hand while you draw it with the other hand. Look at it very carefully as you draw each part. See how much easier it is to draw when you can look at the object at the same time.

Try drawing your favorite toy by memory. Now get the toy and observe it carefully as you draw.

6. *Drawing with scissors.* You can create some interesting designs by cutting or tearing paper. You will need some different colors of construction paper or tissue paper.

See what different shapes you can cut or tear from the tissue or construction paper. Paste them on a full sheet of construction paper in any design that pleases you. You can even overlap some of the pieces you paste on.

7. *Fingerprint art.* Get an ink pad and some notepaper. Make your own designs by placing your thumb or finger on the ink pad and printing it on the paper.

Use felt-tipped pens of different colors to complete the design. You can add petals around the thumbprint to make flowers. A few strokes with the pen can turn thumbprints into people. Print three thumbprints, one on top of another. Draw two big ears at the top to turn it into a bunny. There is no end to what you can make.

8. *Pressed flowers.* Gather flowers just before they reach full growth and

when there is no dew on them. Place them between the pages of a magazine that you carry along as you pick the flowers. When you get home, put several books on top of the magazine for weight and leave the flowers to press for four or five days. Use the pressed flowers in—

- Glass pictures. Place several different kinds of pressed flowers and grasses between two squares of glass. Tape the two pieces together around the edges with black electrical tape. Display the picture on a plate stand or attach a fine wire under the tape so that the picture can be hung in a window.

- Framed pictures. Buy a small oval or square frame at a variety store. Place the flowers on a paper or cloth mat inside the frame.

- Place mats. Place pressed flowers on a rectangular piece of cloth. Cut a piece of clear contact paper one inch smaller on each edge than the cloth. Stick the contact paper to the cloth over the pressed flowers. Fringe the extra cloth outside the contact paper border.

- Notepaper covers. You will need notepaper, wax paper, and tissues. Separate the tissue so that you only have one ply in thickness. This is so the pressed flowers will show through. Cut the tissue and wax paper the same size as the notepaper.

Mix one part household glue with one part water. Cover the wax paper with diluted glue. Place the pressed flowers in a design on one half of the wax paper. Place the single-ply tissue over the flowers and glue the two sheets together.

Fold the wax paper in half and place it over the folded note paper. This forms a cover to place over the notepaper.

Additional Activities

1. Set up a family arts and crafts exhibit. You will need to choose a place for the exhibit—a table outdoors, a dining room table, an empty bookcase, or a place on the floor. Have each person display his craft with a tag or card telling about it.

2. Invite your extended family to visit your arts and crafts exhibit.

3. Ask neighbors to set up their own exhibit the same evening. Take a walk around the neighborhood to see their exhibits.

4. Suggest to the ward activity chairman that he arrange a ward arts and crafts exhibit. Encourage ward families to display what they have made.

5. Display some of the crafts in your home permanently.

6. Put tags on the things already in your home that family members have made, such as drapes by mother or fireplace by father. Have a surprise recognition night.

CHRISTMAS CRAFTS

Homemade Christmas decorations can become a special family tradition that will draw your family together, as well as beautify your home.

Materials Needed

Materials needed are listed below under each activity.

Activity

Choose one of the crafts listed below and let each member of the family take a part in gathering the materials needed for making the item.

1. *Fresh wreaths.* Popular around the world, wreaths can be hung on a wall or door or placed flat on a table with a large candle in the center. Be creative with decoration. Gather these materials:

   Metal coat hanger carefully bent into a circle
   Florist's tape (optional)
   Branches from evergreens such as juniper, spruce, fir, yew; branches from broadleaf trees such as magnolia, laurel, holly, Oregon grape
   Spool of wire (may be covered with green cloth), 24-28 gauge
   Garden pruners
   Pinecones, seed pods, other ornaments
   Ribbon bows

   To make the wreath, cut the branches into 6- to 15-inch (15- to 51-cm) lengths. If you have some green florist's tape, wrap the wire frame so that the branches will not slide on the wire.

Pick up a cluster of branches as thick as you want your wreath to be. Lay them all going the same way on the wire frame. Using a continuous piece of wire, begin wrapping the branches to the frame. Pick up another group of branches and place them in the same direction overlapping the ends of the last bunch. Wire to the frame. Keep going in the same direction until the frame is covered. When you have finished, clip any branches that extend too far out so that the wreath will be an even width. Any thin spots can be corrected by wiring more branches on top of those already in place.

Decorate the fresh wreath any way you wish. Use your own creativity. Here are some suggestions: wire on pinecones, make poinsettia flowers from milkweed pods sprayed gold and sprinkled with glitter, use other natural pods and nuts. Combine shiny ornaments with natural materials. Tie a ribbon bow at the bottom, side, or top. Let ribbon streamers hang down.

You could entwine a string of popcorn around the entire wreath. A cluster of popcorn balls can form a center of interest at the bottom or they can be wrapped in plastic and tied to the bottom of ribbon streamers. This wreath makes a nice gift for families with children.

To wire a pine cone, use a 24- to 28-gauge wire for medium size cones. Larger cones will require a heavier wire, about 20 gauge. Cut the wire into lengths of about 6 inches (15 cm) plus the diameter of the cone. A large cone will require a longer wire. Catch the wire in the crevice behind one of the last rows of scales. Bring it completely around the cone under the scales and twist the two ends of the wire together. Make sure the wire is firmly in place.

Use the remainder of the wire to attach the cone in place.

2. *Straw wreaths.* If you live on a farm, you should have no trouble finding straw. If there is a field or roadside nearby, you can cut some of the wild grasses before winter. You may also be able to buy a commercial straw wreath to decorate yourself.

   Gather these materials:

   Wire coat hanger carefully bent into a circle
   Brown florist's tape (optional)
   Tissue paper or newspaper (necessary only if you don't have enough straw)
   Straw or wild grasses (soak in water fifteen to twenty minutes before using)
   Jute twine or nylon fishing line
   Pinecones and other ornaments
   Ribbon bow

   Cover the wire coat hanger with florist's tape. If you have plenty of straw, tie it by handfuls directly onto the wire. If you don't have much straw, prepare the wire by placing damp crumpled paper around it and attaching the paper with twine or masking tape. Cut the straw or grass into bunches and tie it in place with a continuous piece of twine or fishing line. Overlap each handful over the last bunch of straw. Continue to do this until the frame is completely covered with straw or grasses. Set it aside to dry.

   Decorate with a bow at the bottom, wild grasses, plaid ribbons entwined around the complete wreath, artificial red apples, berries of holly or other bushes and trees, or anything you can think of. This wreath can be saved for years if stored in a plastic covering.

3. *Cornhusk wreaths.* This kind of wreath can be saved from one year

to the next. If you grow your own corn, save the inside husks. (The outside husks may be a little too coarse.) You can also buy bags of cornhusks at most craft stores. If you live in the tropics, try using banana leaves or broad leaves from bamboo.

Gather these materials:

Wire coat hanger bent into a
  circle
Brown florist's tape (optional)
Your own cornhusks or three bags
  from craft store
Jute twine or fishing line
Scissors
Large darning needle
Cones, pods, or other ornaments
Ribbon bow

Cover the wire circle with brown florist's tape. Soak the cornhusks in a pan of water for fifteen to twenty minutes before using. Cut fifteen pieces of twine into 6- to 8-inch (15- to 20-cm) lengths.

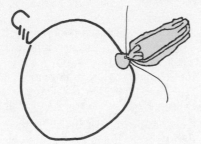

Place four cornhusks together with the small ends facing the same direction. Put 1 inch (2.5 cm) of the small end of the husks under the wire frame. Fold this 1 inch (2.5 cm) back against the rest of the husks. Pinch the two parts of the husks together and tie them close to the wire frame with a square knot.

Continue to tie on the remaining groups of four husks until the wire frame is filled. Put the groups close to each other; they will shrink when they dry. While the husks are still wet, take a darning needle and, beginning about 1 inch (2.5 cm) from the twine knot, shred the husk to the end. Make these shreds about every 1/4 inch (.5 cm). This gives the shaggy look to the wreath.

Now take a continuous piece of twine and bind the wreath

together so it will keep its shape. (Do this by taking about a 1-inch (2.5-cm) group of shredded husks until you have gone around the complete frame.) Tie off in a square knot. Shake the wreath to make it fluffy and set it aside to dry for about one day. You can hang it on a clothesline to dry.

When it is completely dry, fluff it again, and separate the shreds with your fingers. Decorate with any ornaments you may have. Add a bow for the final touch.

4. *Candle centerpiece.* This is an easy craft for small children.

Gather these materials:

Plaster of paris
A small round plastic container
  approximately six inches (15
  cm) in diameter and three
  inches (8 cm) high
Small candle
Gold spray paint
Pinecones, pods, twisted twigs,
  and other small natural objects

Mix a small batch of plaster of paris. Pour it into the round plastic container to the height you would like your candleholder to be. When the plaster of paris gets a little firm, place the candle in the center of the bowl. Decorate with small pinecones, pods, or twigs which are stuck into the plaster all around the candle.

When the plaster is hard, remove it from the container. Spray the cones, twigs, and plaster with gold spray paint. Let the paint dry. This will make a festive centerpiece. If you wish, place a few evergreens underneath and around it.

5. *Nativity scene.* Making your own nativity scene can be a fun family project. The finished scene can be an important addition to your family Christmas tradition.

Have all family members help make the figures and manger. There are many ways to make the figures, and many craft stores and holiday craft magazines will tell how.

You can make the figures of Mary, Joseph, baby Jesus, shepherds, wise men, sheep, and other animals from rolled or molded dough clay, from straw, from cornhusks, from carved wood, or from cardboard or construction paper with acorns or nuts glued on as heads. You can make the manger out of wood, cardboard, clay, or twigs tied together with twine. The smallest child can be part of this activity by gathering some dry grass to be used as straw for the baby.

Salt Dough
2 cups (500 ml or .5 liter) flour
2 cups (500 ml or .5 liter) salt
About 1 cup (250 ml) water

Mix flour, salt, and water to make

a stiff mixture. Knead mixture for about ten minutes to dissolve salt.

Cornstarch Clay Dough (Porcelain type)

2 cups (500 ml or .5 liter) cornstarch

2 cups (500 ml or .5 liter) baking soda

1 1/4 cups (310 ml) cold water

In a saucepan, combine cornstarch and baking soda. Gradually add water until the mixture is smooth. Heat, stirring constantly, until the mixture reaches a moist mashed-potato consistency.

Turn onto a plate, cover with a damp towel. Knead dough when cool enough to handle.

Mold the clay into figures. Or roll out the dough about 1/4 inch (.5 cm) thick on a floured board and cut out the figures by placing a pattern on the rolled dough and tracing it with the pointed end of a knife.

Bake the figures on a flat cookie sheet at 225° F (107° C) for two or three hours. Turn them over occasionally to keep them from curling.

Paint on faces and clothing with poster paints that have been mixed with a little white glue.

Make cardboard stands and glue them on back of the figures.

6. *Christmas tree cookie ornaments.* Use either the salt dough or the cornstarch clay dough described above. Roll out the dough and cut it with cookie cutters into stars, bells, circles, or other shapes. Make a hole in the top of each ornament so you can tie yarn through for hanging it on the tree. Bake the ornaments and paint them in the same way as the nativity figures.

7. *Christmas tree ornaments.* You may decorate your tree with pinecones, seed pods, dried flowers, or a combination of these things along with your sparkling ornaments. Homemade decorations will make your tree one of a kind.

You can do many things with pinecones. Leave them their natural color and wire them onto the branches of the tree or up the center of the tree trunk. Spray them

different colors or spray them with clear plastic and sprinkle them with glitter. Try combining them with two milkweed pods to form the wings of a bird and add plume grass for a tail.

Make milkweed pods into contrived flowers that look like poinsettia and spray them red, gold, or other colors. Tie small straw flowers of various colors together with thin ribbons and place them in small bunches on the tree. Clusters of berries, such as holly or pyracantha, look lovely tied onto the branches of a Christmas tree.

Wire different nuts on the tree in clusters. Drilling a hole in the nut and wiring it takes quite a bit of equipment. An easier way is to cover the nut with a layer of plastic wrap and tie the plastic with thin florist's wire. Twist the wires of five or six nuts together like a cluster of grapes.

8. *Yule log.* Many families already have a tradition of bringing in the Yule log. It is fun to decorate one for the house, even if you don't have a fireplace.

Gather these materials:

A wood log or piece of twisted driftwood

Evergreen boughs

Pinecones

Wire or strong twine

Ribbon

Find a log. It can be just one that you burn in the fireplace, or it can be an interesting twisted piece of driftwood.

Cut the evergreen branches a little less than one-half the length of the log. Tie the stems to the center of the log with twine or wire, so that the tips of half the branches point toward one end of the log, and the tips of the other half point toward the other end of the log.

Wire about five or six pinecones in a cluster near the center of the log and tie a big red ribbon around the very center.

If you have a fireplace, you can make this log part of your Christmas Eve tradition. Throw the log on an already burning fire. The pinecones will burn with blue and green flames. Tell the Christmas story around the fire.

9. *Rose potpourri.* This activity begins in the summer when roses are in full bloom. Collect and dry the rose petals to make potpourri or sachet bags for Christmas giving. Any age child can help collect the materials.

Gather these materials:

Rose petals or other fragrant flowers that grow in your climate (plumeria, gardenia, camellia, lavender, geranium)

Flat pan, such as a cookie sheet

Salt

Fixatives, such as dried lavender or oak moss (sold in herb and spice shops and many drugstores)

Cinnamon sticks, whole cloves, vanilla beans, or dried grated lemon peel

2 to 3 drops of perfume

Pick the petals from roses just after their prime and before they start to turn brown. Some roses are more fragrant than others. Pink roses are especially fragrant. Lay them flat on a cookie sheet one layer deep. Sprinkle a little salt over them. They will dry in a few days. Shake the salt from the petals, and to every quart of petals add one tablespoon of the fixative.

Place the petals in a glass container. Add other herbs and spices you may have and two or three drops of your favorite perfume. Close the container tightly and shake it well. Shake every other day for ten days.

Put this potpourri in colorful glass containers and decorate them with ribbon. Or put it in sachet bags for dresser drawers or closets. To make sachet bags, sew squares of nylon, organdy, or other light-weight materials into little bags. Leave one side open so you can fill them with the rose petal mixture. Blindstitch the open end together. Decorate with lace, ribbon, or embroidery. An easy-to-make pouch bag can be made from a small square of cloth such as organdy, silk, or fine cotton. Gather the square at the four corners with the rose petals enclosed and tie with a ribbon.

10. *Greeting cards and wrapping paper.* It is fun to work as a family making wrapping paper and greeting cards. There are many methods. Here are a few:

Wax rubbings: Remove the paper covering from several large wax crayons. Place a piece of paper over the wrong side of a broad leaf, such as holly, or over a pine branch. Begin rubbing the broad side of the crayon on the paper. Work from the stem of the leaf outward, holding onto the stem as you work.

Potato block prints: Draw a design on a piece of paper the size of a potato cut in half crosswise. It can be a holly leaf, a bell, a Christmas tree ornament, or any other simple Christmas design. Trace the design onto the potato half with a sharp pencil.

Remove excess moisture from the potato with a paper towel. Cut around the design with a knife so that the design stands up and the background is cut away.

Using poster paint or water-soluble

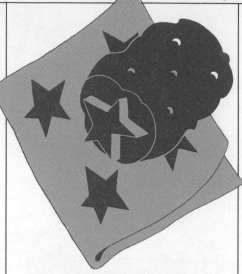

ink, paint the design on the potato with a brush. Print it on a card or folded piece of paper. You can use this potato design on greeting cards or wrapping paper.

Additional Activities

1. Take some of the crafts you have made to other families. (See "Serving Others Together.")

2. Combine giving crafts with a caroling activity. Take crafts to your friends and sing Christmas carols to them.

FUN WITH
STORIES AND POEMS

Have fun together being creative with stories and poems. No great talent is needed, although some may be discovered. Just have fun together using your imagination freely.

Activity

1. *Continued stories.* Relax with your children lying on the floor around a warm fire, on a big bed with a child on each arm, or anywhere that you all feel close and comfortable. Tell them that each is going to participate in telling a story you are going to create together. The first person will start the story and then stop at some critical moment. The next person will have to continue the story in his own words using his own imagination. Then he stops and lets the third person take over until all have had several turns and a story has unfolded. Set up some sequence or order in which you will participate. Encourage the children

to be completely uninhibited in what they want the story to be like. You may want to make up several stories in one home evening, letting different members of your family start and finish each story.

Example

First person: Once there was a beautiful little girl who loved the color purple. Her favorite game was to sneak out to the airport near her home and paint airplanes this favorite color, bright purple. Oh, it was messy! She often got into trouble because she would spill paint all over the runway where the airplanes came in. One dark night she crept out to paint the biggest airplane in the whole world, to paint it purple. When she got there she was surprised because . . .

Second person: When she got there she was surprised because somebody had already been there and painted that huge airplane yellow like a great big canary. She was so mad that she sat down and cried and cried. Suddenly the airplane opened up its big mouth and said . . .

The third person goes on by having the airplane say some ridiculous thing.

One variation to this kind of storytelling is to give each person a word that he must weave into his narrative in a natural way. Pick interesting words or funny ones.
Examples: volcano, stupified, rhinoceros, magnificent, ugly, etc.

Another variation is to prepare a rather long piece of string that the person telling his segment of the story winds into a ball or onto a stick. He must talk as long as it takes him to wind up the string. Yarn, thread, or even rope could be used instead of string.

Little children like to make up stories about themselves, using their own names. Consider one like the following:

One morning, _____ (your child's name) got up and found a cute little bluebird singing on the windowsill.

"Good morning, Mr. Bluebird," said _____ .

"Good morning, to you,
_____ ," said the bluebird.

Have the child go on telling what happened. Encourage him to use his own name frequently throughout the story you tell together.

2. *Personal poems.* Children love to make up their own poems. They will not always rhyme or fit a particular meter, but they are very refreshing and revealing. The following poem was written by a little girl eight years old who loves dogs. When she was six, she told her mother, "When I grow up, I'm not going to have babies; I'm going to have puppies."

What If Dogs
Took Over the World?

What if dogs took over the world?
What a sight to see,
People tied to a tree.
What would happen to me?
There would be a dog police.
Animals in the zoo would be
    released.
Dogs would walk us as we walk
    them.
They'd wear dresses with a hem.
They'd drive cars.
And have bazaars.
They'd roll and run,
And have such fun!
I hope dogs don't take over the
    world!

Let your family write some poetry about their pets, their hobbies, their concerns, their troubles, their interests—whatever they may be. Some of the poetry may turn out to be beautiful. Never correct your child's efforts. Let him feel his expression is good enough to be unconditionally accepted.

Older children may want to create funny limericks. Following is an example of the form they take:

There once was a girl named Janet
Who came from another planet.
Her hair was green
With a beautiful sheen,
And skin so white you could tan it.

They may want to make them up about their own names or those of other family members.

Another activity is to have each family member write new words to his favorite song. For example:

Sing to: "Jingle Bells"

Elephants, elephants, elephants are
    fat.
They each have a big long trunk
Where their nose is at;
Elephants, elephants, elephants are
    fat.
It appears their great big ears
Should cover where they sat.

You may want to use a favorite hymn and write some new words that are very meaningful to the music. *Caution:* Because of later association, it would not be wise to write humorous words to a sacred hymn, but some serious, thoughtful expression would be appropriate.

Sing to: "We Thank Thee, O God, for a Prophet"

We thank thee, O God, for our
    family
To guide us through our younger
    days
We thank thee for wise and good
    parents
To teach us of thy righteous ways.
We thank thee for brothers and
    sisters
Who fight, tease, but help some-
    times, too.
We hope to grow more close and
    loving,
And living the gospel's the clue.

Try some of your own favorites. Make up serious words for the hymns or funny ones for other songs. It does not matter as long as you do something original.

3. *Family poems.* Let your family compose a poem as a group. This is called a "mosaic" poem. Have each one express in a short sentence how he feels about some selected subject. Write down each expression as it is given. Sometimes it is best to have each keep his sentences secret until you all read them aloud. Sometimes you may want to give each line out loud right at first, expecting the first ones to influence what others may say, and thus build a more harmonious poem. Try both ways.

After each family member has contributed, you may want to rearrange the sentences to make more sense or create more unity in the poem. Any subject you are all interested in would be a good topic to start with.

4. *Expressive language.* Little children like to express themselves. They may not be able to create poetry or stories but they will enjoy completing phrases like the following:

As soft as _____
As slippery as _____
As green as _____
As scary as _____
As tall as _____
As happy as _____
As big as _____

Let them say whatever comes into their minds. Some of their responses can be very revealing and surprisingly wise. Make up many more than the seven examples given. It will be fun for you too.

5. *Haiku poetry.* This form of Japanese expression and appreciation for nature can be a really creative experience for the adults in your family. Find some beautiful picture from nature and have each one write three sentences about it, each on a separate line. Then cut down the first sentence to just five syllables, selecting the most expressive words. Cut the second one down to seven syllables; and the third, to five again. This is your haiku poem. See how simple, yet moving, your expressions can be.

Example

Viewing a beautiful picture of a mountain stream, one amateur wrote the following in the two steps of creating this kind of poetry:

Three Sentences

I love the verdant mountain streams with their fresh, icy water.
To sleep lightly by a stream like this and listen in half slumber to the cascades would be heaven to me.
I hope I can sit by some cool, bubbly bank forever.

The Poem

Verdant mountain streams.
Sleep lightly, listen. Heaven!
Cool bank, forever.

Now you try some.

CREATING PICTURES AND THINGS

Use your imagination to create some pictures, puzzles, and other things. Have fun together as a family being inventive and original.

Activity

1. *Drawing for fun.* Have each family member draw his favorite thing around the house—for example, a Chinese vase, a doll, the tree in the front yard, the cat, the big swing in the back, or the old pioneer cradle. The children may wish to draw a picture of the happiest moment they can remember or the most impressive—for example, blessing the new baby, Christmas morning around the tree, the flood in the basement last summer, or a family picnic. You could also have the family illustrate favorite scriptures—for example, Noah and the ark, David and Goliath, or Christ visiting the Nephites.

2. *Crazy creations.* At the bottom of a piece of paper, write the following sentence: "This is a _____ ." Fill in the blank with some silly word that you make up yourself—*ziggybob, twirple, babookit,* or *gabbygook,* for example. Have everyone then draw whatever they think that silly word looks like.

3. *"What's This?"* Draw a crazy line on a piece of blank paper, one for each member of the family, and ask the children to use their imagination to create a picture from it.

4. *"Color Bright."* Draw a lot of intersecting lines on a piece of paper for each family member. Have everyone color in all the geometric shapes thus formed, using a different color in each. Little children love to do this.

5. *Collage.* Have your children cut out odd-shaped pictures and colored shapes from a magazine and paste them onto a piece of wood or cardboard. You can use newspaper, Christmas cards, or even pieces of colored paper or tissue to add variety and give different textures to the creation.

6. *Mosaics.* Almost any material can be used for a mosaic: tiles, broken glass, nutshells, macaroni, wood pieces, or stones. Have your family each find several small things in your yard, on the beach, in the park, or in the school yard and arrange them on a piece of wood, gluing them down in some design. You may want to spray the whole piece with gold paint after the glue dries.

The next time you go on a vacation, take a box to keep little mementos of the trip. Then when you get home, make a mosaic of them to keep for years of memory.

7. *Family mural.* Pick a wall or floor in your home where you can spread out a large piece of butcher paper and attach it securely. Then have each person draw or paint on this great big picture. Each one can add the shapes or colors he feels will make it more artistic. Be sure all get a chance to contribute. You may want to take a long time to finish this and have fun with it for several days. Some families have even painted on their walls permanently, giving each one in the family a chance to make his effort a part of that room forever.

You can use any medium you have available: oil paint, crayons, chalk, water colors, poster paint. Make a collage, a mosaic, or anything together. The main thing is to have fun and do something the entire family will enjoy and feel free to participate in.

8. *Puzzles and blocks.* Little children may enjoy cutting out their own puzzles. They could draw, color, or cut out a picture from a magazine and then cut it up in pieces to make it into a jigsaw puzzle.

You can cut blocks out of scraps of wood and paint them bright colors. If you do not want to work with paint, soak the blocks in food coloring.

You could even go to a lumberyard and pick up scraps and board ends to make a set of blocks. Take them home and sand them during your home evening after cutting them into the shapes you want.

9. *Silly sculpture.* Try making some sculpture by gluing pieces of junk together. This can really be fun. Just about anything small can be used. You may want to divide into teams and see who can come up with the most interesting piece.

   If you want to use more conventional materials, have the children make things out of clay or carve something from a bar of soap. If it happens to be a snowy day, you may want to create a snow sculpture, something a little more original than a snowman. Try a sleeping giant or a dragon.

10. *"This Is Me."* Get a large piece of poster paper, butcher paper, old wall paper, or wrapping paper. The children will enjoy coloring themselves life-size. Have each child lie down on the paper you have selected and some older child or parent can trace his outline onto it. Then the child who has been traced fills in the details, adding the facial features, hair, and clothes, until he has made a life-size picture of himself. Children love to do this, and the entire family will enjoy the results.

ENJOYING DANCE AND DRAMA

Have a creative time together dancing or dramatizing. Let yourselves go. This kind of physical expression is satisfying and can be a lot of fun.

Activity

Choose one of these activities:

1. *Dance your feelings.* Play a record, a tape, the radio, or create your own music. Let the children dance the way the music makes them feel. Have them one by one take a turn to dance for the family so that each gets a turn to have everyone's complete attention. It is important that you allow them to be graceful, silly, or even clumsy as long as they are expressing something. If you are understanding, they will enjoy being inventive.

   The children will want to dance only two or three minutes each turn. Vary the fun by grouping them now and then in different ways between solo acts. This is a simple activity, but one the children find extremely satisfying.

   You may want to use some variations to their free expression by giving each a certain activity that he is to dance. For example:

   Be a skater.
   Be a flower coming up in the spring.
   Be a lion in the forest.
   Be a skier coming down the mountainside.
   Be a princess at a ball.
   Be a swimmer.
   Be a horse on the prairie.
   Be a tree swaying in the breeze.

   Another variation to this activity is to have each one dance and then have the family try to guess what he is depicting.

   One family has a dance night at least once a month. The children look forward to it with real enthusiasm and plan what they are going to do, especially their dances in pairs and groups.

2. *Statues.* This game is fun to play with children in a yard or field outside. Have everyone form a circle around someone. The person in the middle is the statue maker. He has each one come to him in turn to be swung around two or three times and then released. The position in which the one being swung comes to rest must be kept until all have been swung. All this time the statue maker has in mind what he wants them to be. The one who is most like what he has in mind wins and gets to go to the center and be the next statue maker.

3. *Charades.* Have each person one by one take a pose and have the family guess what each is trying to be. This activity can be made exciting if you let the children dress up and make their own costumes. They are very inventive and love to express themselves. You may even encourage them to pantomime stories from the Bible, Book of Mormon, or Church history that they particularly like.

   Words could be added to make a play if they so desire. Some props and scenery that they choose or create can make the evening even more fun.

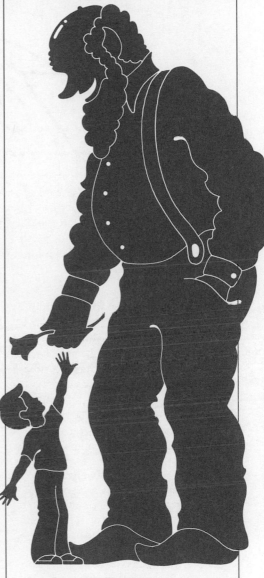

4. *Fairy tale fun.* Your children may enjoy acting out scenes from their favorite fairy tales. Let them be Snow White, Cinderella, Billy Goat Gruff, Prince Charming, or a great big giant. They may do the whole story or just one part of it. Let them dress up and have fun pretending.

5. *Hand puppets.* Your children may have fun making a stage using a small table or desk. They can make props and curtains and everything they need to furnish their stage. Let them make up a play with hand puppets or dolls and present it for the family. Children will have some marvelous ideas if you encourage them to be imaginative.

NATURE
Activities

HIKING WITH SMALL CHILDREN

One of the best ways to appreciate the outdoors is by hiking with your family off the beaten path. This activity will give you ideas to help make hiking fun for your whole family.

Activity

If you want to make hiking a family activity, here are some hints to make it fun for the younger ones:

1. Start hiking with children on small treks that do not get them so tired that they cannot enjoy themselves.

2. Forget your adult rules about how fast you want to go. Instead, think about how your children would enjoy spending their time. Walk for fifteen to twenty minutes, then look around for fifteen to twenty minutes. Throw rocks in a creek, float sticks in the stream, flip a bug on its back and see how it turns itself over. Look at and smell weeds, flowers, moss, rotten logs, and interesting rocks. Watch a hawk in the sky, a squirrel in a tree, a bird in a thicket, a rodent on the ground, a bug on a log, or other people on the trail.

3. Promise a party at the next bend of the trail. For the party, have a surprise piece of candy, bring a small toy to play with, have a story ready, make a stick whistle, or imitate a bird call.

4. Sing songs on the trail. Make up a song, rhyme, poem, or story with your children as the characters. Count the number of animals you see or see who can be first to spot a certain colored flower.

5. Avoid major changes in elevation; young babies and children up to two years of age have trouble adjusting to major changes in altitude. They may fuss, have an earache, or show

symptoms of stress in breathing.

6. Using a child back-carrier is much better than carrying a child on your shoulders. The weight of even a small child on the neck and shoulders can cause dizziness or even a temporary paralysis of certain neck muscles of an adult.

7. Have young children three or four years of age carry a small knapsack containing a sweater, a special toy, a doll, or some of their favorite food. Increase the load as they get older. Have children pack their own knapsacks.

8. Allow some freedom and independence in hiking, but set limits for how far children can move away from you.

ACTIVITIES IN THE RAIN

How many of your plans for family outings have been upset by rain? There are many activities that you can do in the rain or after a rain, some of them so fun that you might want to actually plan an outing for a rainy day. These rainy day activities can help your family appreciate rain rather than dread it.

Activity

Choose from the following activities for your rainy day outing:

1. Collect rain in containers and use it to wash your hair, put in mom's iron, water the houseplants, or put in your car battery.

2. Paint some paper with powdered tempera paints and water. Then set the paper in the rain to allow the water to run and make designs.

3. Have each person mark a line on a container showing where they think the water line will be when the rain stops. The person closest to the actual line is the winner.

4. Tell stories in which rain plays an important part—Noah and the ark, the early Saints in St. George paying their tithing so that rain would come, Elijah prophesying the end of three years without rain.

5. Have a water fight.

6. Talk about the kinds of animals that like the rain.

7. Go for a walk in the rain and notice the changes in nature. Observe what happens to the birds, bugs, worms, trees, flowers, and people. Notice the sounds and smells that this change brings.

8. Choose a long word that is related to the rain (*umbrella*, for example) and have each player write it in the center of a piece of paper. Then

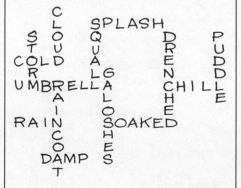

allow them two minutes to build up as many other words as they can from the basic word. All the new words must in some way be related to the first word. The player with the most words wins.

9. Discuss questions about rain, such as the following:
What causes rain?
What causes thunder?
What causes lightning?
What does the rainbow mean?
What are the rainfall records in our area?

10. Sing songs with words about rain.

GARDENING IN CONTAINERS

Many people who live in apartment buildings or houses with little or no yard space may think they cannot follow the prophet's counsel to plant a garden. But you can grow quite a bit of food in pots and hanging planters inside your home or on a balcony. This activity will help you get started gardening in containers. Even if your family has plenty of outdoor garden space, you might want to try growing some of your vegetables indoors.

Activity

You can plant in almost any kind of container. Try using plastic jugs, garbage cans, milk cartons, cans, plastic bags, baskets, a wagon bed, kitchen canisters, or clay pots. The bottom of the container should have several small drain holes and be lined with 2 to 3 inches of small gravel before you put in the topsoil. Hang containers from windows, put them on windowsills or in window wells; line your sidewalk or driveway with them, or hang them from your ceiling.

The following chart shows you how much dirt you will need in a container to grow some common vegetables. This will give you an idea of what size container you need to use. It also tells you when to plant and harvest the vegetables and how big they will get. These are not the only vegetables that grow well in containers. You can try almost any kind that is common to your area.

Additional Activities

Make an indoor herb garden on a window sill.

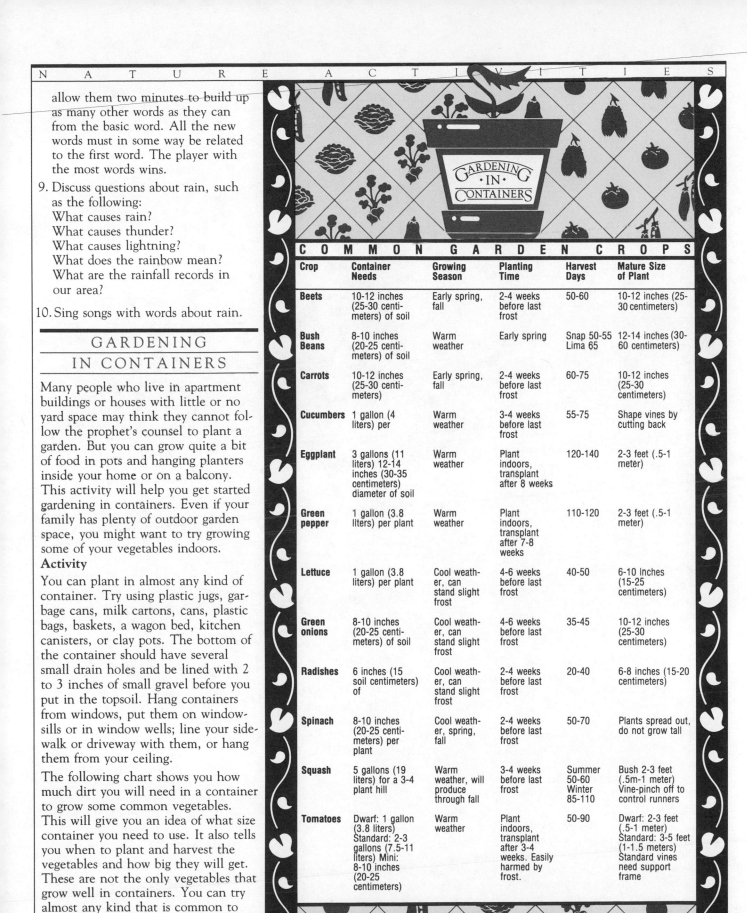

COMMON GARDEN CROPS

Crop	Container Needs	Growing Season	Planting Time	Harvest Days	Mature Size of Plant
Beets	10-12 inches (25-30 centimeters) of soil	Early spring, fall	2-4 weeks before last frost	50-60	10-12 inches (25-30 centimeters)
Bush Beans	8-10 inches (20-25 centimeters) of soil	Warm weather	Early spring	Snap 50-55 Lima 65	12-14 inches (30-60 centimeters)
Carrots	10-12 inches (25-30 centimeters)	Early spring, fall	2-4 weeks before last frost	60-75	10-12 inches (25-30 centimeters)
Cucumbers	1 gallon (4 liters) per	Warm weather	3-4 weeks before last frost	55-75	Shape vines by cutting back
Eggplant	3 gallons (11 liters) 12-14 inches (30-35 centimeters) diameter of soil	Warm weather	Plant indoors, transplant after 8 weeks	120-140	2-3 feet (.5-1 meter)
Green pepper	1 gallon (3.8 liters) per plant	Warm weather	Plant indoors, transplant after 7-8 weeks	110-120	2-3 feet (.5-1 meter)
Lettuce	1 gallon (3.8 liters) per plant	Cool weather, can stand slight frost	4-6 weeks before last frost	40-50	6-10 inches (15-25 centimeters)
Green onions	8-10 inches (20-25 centimeters) of soil	Cool weather, can stand slight frost	4-6 weeks before last frost	35-45	10-12 inches (25-30 centimeters)
Radishes	6 inches (15 centimeters) of soil	Cool weather, can stand slight frost	2-4 weeks before last frost	20-40	6-8 inches (15-20 centimeters)
Spinach	8-10 inches (20-25 centimeters) per plant	Cool weather, spring, fall	2-4 weeks before last frost	50-70	Plants spread out, do not grow tall
Squash	5 gallons (19 liters) for a 3-4 plant hill	Warm weather, will produce through fall	3-4 weeks before last frost	Summer 50-60 Winter 85-110	Bush 2-3 feet (.5m-1 meter) Vine-pinch off to control runners
Tomatoes	Dwarf: 1 gallon (3.8 liters) Standard: 2-3 gallons (7.5-11 liters) Mini: 8-10 inches (20-25 centimeters)	Warm weather	Plant indoors, transplant after 3-4 weeks. Easily harmed by frost.	50-90	Dwarf: 2-3 feet (.5-1 meter) Standard: 3-5 feet (1-1.5 meters) Standard vines need support frame

BIRD WATCHING CLOSE TO HOME

Bird watching, even through the kitchen window, can teach your family much about the world of nature. This activity will help your family set up situations in which they can watch birds close to home.

Activity

Invite birds to your home by choosing and doing one or more of the following simple activities:

1. *Birdbath.* Build a wooden frame with a bottom 2-feet square (60 cm square) and sides 4 inches tall (10 cm). Cover the bottom with plywood. Mix together one part cement, two parts sand, and three parts pea gravel; moisten with water so the mixture flows slowly. Pour into the frame and, before it hardens, slope the sides until the center is depressed about 2 inches (5 cm). Molding the cement mixture around a wire frame will reinforce the basin. Allow the mixture to harden, and mount the bird bath on a pedestal or above ground level so cats can't prey on the bathing birds. Then watch the birds enjoy the water.

2. *Windowsill observatory.* Fasten a wooden board to an outside windowsill or ledge. Nail two or three dowels to the board to act as perches for birds. Place some small pans on the sill to hold food and water. Make a "blind" by putting a small hole in a piece of cardboard and by placing the cardboard against the inside of the window. You can then watch birds from inside the house without distracting or frightening them. Place honey on a donut or a bread crust, sprinkle it with nuts, and see how many birds are attracted.

3. *String feeding.* String bits of food—such as bread, nuts, or popcorn—on a thin string or thread. Space the food several inches apart and tack both ends of the string to a tree trunk or limb. Watch the birds' different methods of feeding. This is especially effective in wintertime.

4. *Nest building.* Place colored yarn, string, or straw in an easy-to-find

place for birds. Watch to see which birds pick which material to build their nests.

5. *Hummingbird feeder.* Attach a small or medium-sized tube or vial to a tree twig or a stem of a flower. Decorate the vial with bright ribbon and place a mixture of one part sugar to two parts water in the container. Watch the birds hover and sip the nectar. It may also attract moths, butterflies, and other insects.

If you are interested in learning to recognize different kinds of birds and understand their habits, check local libraries and bookstores for the numerous guides to bird watching. The following ideas will give you some information with which to start learning about the birds you watch:

What time of year is best for observing specific activities? Summer is the best time to watch nesting, hatching, feeding the young, and hunting for insects. Fall is best for watching migration, flocking, and molting. Winter is best for watching the hardy birds struggle to survive and to watch feather changes. Spring is best for watching migration, courting and mating, nest building, and spring molting.

What time of day is best for watching? You have the best chance to hear the songs in early morning or late evening.

How do you keep track of what you see? Write down what you see in a notebook. You might include the following information about each bird you see:

Name of bird
Where you saw it
When you saw it
What the bird was doing
Characteristics: color, size, wing shape, beak, feet

What do bird sounds mean? You may hear a mating call, a morning or evening greeting, a cry of danger, a call to communicate with other birds during migration, or a means of self-expression. Each kind of bird has its own special calls, and getting to know the calls can help you recognize the different kinds of birds.

Additional Activities

1. Build a birdhouse.

2. Record bird songs on a sensitive tape recorder. Play the song back and see if you can attract a bird with the same song.

3. Learn which kinds have migratory paths in your area. Watch the semiannual migration of various birds.

4. Make a bird calendar. Let your family record the first time one of you sees a robin, the first bird's nest you see, or the first baby bird you hear. Think of unique things to observe and record.

ROCK HOUNDING

Rocks can be fascinating to young and old. A simple collecting trip requires little more than the desire to get outdoors and to notice the geological wonders of the earth. Collecting rocks, or just looking at interesting ones, can be a fun family activity.

Materials Needed

1. Cold chisel for breaking off a sample

2. Magnifying glass for examining what you collect

3. Knapsack or heavy canvas bag for carrying samples home

4. Pocket knife for cleaning

5. Newspapers to wrap fragile specimens

6. Old gloves to protect your hands

7. Mineralogist's hammer (blunt on one end, pointed on the other) for breaking off samples

Activity

Prepare for your rock hounding trip by first chosing an area that has interesting rocks. You may need to check with local experts at a rock shop, university, or gem club for advice on where to collect. The best areas are where rock is exposed—a quarry, mine dump, excavation gravel pit, stream, beach, road cut, dry wash, or plowed field. The best time for finding good material is often in the spring or after a storm, when fresh rock is exposed.

Be careful to obey the laws of your country. In the United States, rock-hounding is usually legal on public lands, but not in national parks, national monuments, and other restricted areas. It is also against the federal law to collect vertebrate fossils and Indian artifacts in the United States. Collecting on private lands requires the permission of the owner. Obeying the laws of your country, using courtesy, and taking good safety precautions can help to make your trip more enjoyable.

Once you have chosen a place to hunt, plan your trip. You may want to take a whole day with the family to collect rocks, eat lunch, and enjoy the outdoors.

Use moderation in gathering your rock samples. Take only the most interesting ones. It's a good idea to devise a labeling system so you can keep track of your collection in the field and at home. A simple system is to label each rock as you find it with a number on a small piece of adhesive tape. Record the number in a notebook with a description of the rock, the place you found it, the collector, and the date.

There are many things to notice in the rocks you collect, including hardness, crystal form, color, cleavage, fracture, possible magnetism, and luster. You might find it interesting to test the hardness of the stones you find. Knowing the hardness of rocks can help you identify them.

The Mohs scale, developed by Friedrich Mohs, is the hardness scale used by mineralogists. On this scale, 1 is the softest and 10 the hardest.

The minerals named in the scale are the ones that are typical for that hardness.

1. Talc
2. Gypsum
3. Calcite
4. Fluorite
5. Apatite
6. Orthoclase feldspar
7. Quartz
8. Topaz
9. Corundum
10. Diamond

Other rocks and minerals will have their own typical hardness. You can find their hardness by finding what will scratch them and what they will scratch. These common items have the following hardnesses:

Penny (3.0)
Knife blade (5.5)
Glass (6.0)
Steel file (7.0)

So if glass will scratch your rock and a knife blade will not, your rock must have a hardness between 5.5 and 6.0.

You can do a rough test in the field by scratching your specimen with your fingernail. If it can be scratched, then its hardness is approximately 2.5.

Rocks have many other distinct characteristics, too. A good handbook can help you distinguish these characteristics in the rocks you find and perhaps identify your samples.

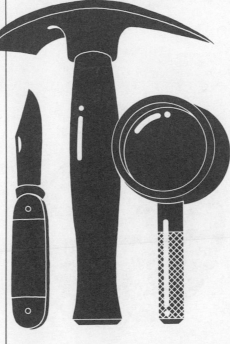

Additional Activities

1. Join or visit a gem and mineral club.

2. Check your library for books or magazines on rock collecting.

3. Visit a natural history museum to see mineral collections and learn how rocks are formed.

4. Attend a rock show sponsored by a local gem club.

5. Check government sources for pamphlets or other information on rock collecting.

6. Visit rock shops in your local area or as you travel. Most rockhounds will be glad to share collecting tips.

7. Build display shelves or cases to house your collection.

8. Take a class in lapidary (rock polishing) or jewelry making.

9. Take a geology class through a college or university. These classes often include field trips to local areas of interest.

10. Make gifts, a fireplace, a rock wall, a wishing well, a birdbath, or other garden ornaments out of unique rocks.

MAKING SNOW SCULPTURES

Wintertime in some areas can be long and tedious. Making snow sculptures can involve your whole family, and even your neighbors, in creative outdoor fun.

Activity

First, sketch on paper the sculpture you want to make out of snow. Figure out the approximate dimensions of the parts of the sculpture. For best results, use snow that is wet or packed in compact drifts and shape it into dense balls, squares, or related forms. Use a knife, spatula, shovel, hoe, wood scraper, or other tool to carve the packed snow. This will keep your hands from getting too cold. Add snow as required to give proper form.

Add color to your snow sculpture by dissolving food coloring or clothing dye in water and painting it on the sculpture or mixing it with the snow. Spray water, using a clothes spray or garden spray. Brushing on water with a paint brush can add a nice glaze to your object. Try an igloo, snowman statue, dog, cat, spaceship, or nativity scene for starters.

Additional Activities

1. Have a family contest and award prizes for form, style, creativity, or color. Invite your neighbors to join the competition.

2. Use sand in areas without snow.

3. Take pictures of your sculpture.

COLLECTING AND PRESERVING SHELLS

The sea holds a fascination for people of all ages. Fishing, building sand-castles, surfing, snorkeling, people watching, playing beach games, and swimming are just a few of the activities you can enjoy at the beach. Shell collecting can also be a good family activity.

Preparation

You need very little equipment for collecting shells: a cloth bag, bucket, or similar container will do. If you are going to explore exposed rocks, you may need a pair of sandals or canvas shoes. Be alert to the tides, exposure to the sun, and breakers that could knock a person off his feet. Don't allow members of the family to explore isolated beaches alone.

Before you go collecting, check local regulations on collecting shells. Also watch for dangerous forms of sea life, such as jellyfish, Portuguese men-of-war, or sharks. Visiting curio stores and sea life museums can give you an idea of the types of shells to collect and the hobbies associated with collecting.

Activity

Shells are simply the hard coverings of animals. So you must remove the remains of the animals from the shell to prevent odor from decay. You can use a small penknife or fishhook to remove the meat from the shell. Placing shells in a box of ants also cleans them well.

Clean hard shells with a mild solution of hydrochloric acid, and rinse and polish them with a soft cloth. Many shells are fragile, so be careful when you work with them. To file rough edges or make holes in the shells so you can use them for jewelry, use jewelry files, fine emery boards,

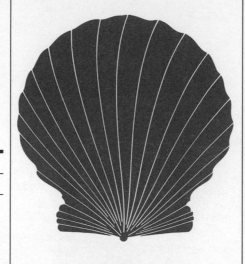

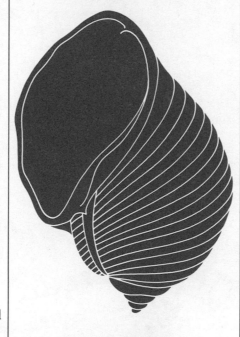

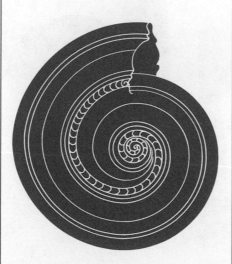

and small electric drills for minimal breakage.

Try making rings, cameos, necklaces, bracelets, or buttons out of especially pretty shells. You can decorate a picture frame with shells or make a hanging mobile. Use broken pieces of shells to make a mosaic or use a large shell as a paperweight. Decorate an aquarium or a sandcastle or make a unique dinner set using shells as plates, cups, saucers, and napkin rings.

If you become very interested in collecting shells, check out books from the library and learn the names of the shells you have found and what kinds of animals lived in them. You might try to collect samples of the five classes of mollusks.

1. Collect, dry, and preserve sand dollars, sea urchins, crabs, starfish, and coral.

2. Try to find shells near local fresh-water lakes.

3. Collect driftwood and display it with your shells.

PHYSICAL *Activities*

CARPET SQUARE CHALLENGE

It has been said that playing and moving are the full-time jobs of little children, just as daily work is the full-time job of adults. And, indeed, play is one of the first ways children learn to use their bodies. Families can help little ones by spending time helping them to both identify body parts and to learn how the body and its parts can move. It is essential for a healthy, growing child to feel good about his body. This activity gives young children problem-solving experiences as they try to place different parts of their body on a carpet square, newspaper, reed mat, or other kind of mat. Teenagers and adults can also join in to get a workout, as well as to have fun.

Preparation

Get a carpet sample, reed mat, hand towel, or something similar for each family member. Choose a space inside or outside where each person can move on and around his carpet sample without bumping into anyone. Prepare in advance a lengthy list of movement challenges (see sample list) to verbally give to participants. Start with simple problems and gradually increase the difficulty.

Activity

Have each family member find his own space and position himself with his carpet square on the floor or grass. Have the family member leading the activity call out body parts to be placed on the carpet sample. By calling out opposites such as front—back, bottom—stomach, right hip—left hip, the leader can intensify the physical activity. By calling out body parts quickly one after another, this activity can turn into a vigorous game. The leader can also call out two body parts to be put on the carpet square at the same time. Giving each family member a chance to be the leader helps them learn body parts and allows them to observe the many different ways family members may be solving problems.

Try to challenge the problem-solving abilities of family members. The following are sample instructions:

Simple	Complex	More Complex
Nose	Right hip	Right ear and left knee
Top of head	Left foot	Left shoulder and right foot
Chin	Left hip	Top of head and right hand
Back of head	Right foot	Left elbow and right knee

Feet	Left ear
Hands	Right knee
Knees	Right ear
Bottom	Left knee
Stomach	Right shoulder
Back	Left ankle
Chest	Left shoulder
Shoulders	Right ankle
Elbows	Right hand
Ankles	Left elbow
Wrists	Left hand
Forehead	Right elbow
Toes	
Fingers	

Caution: Keep it simple, lively, and fun for small children. Remember, learning right and left takes time. Be patient in helping them learn.

Additional Activities

1. Try these challenges on top of the carpet sample.
   - Place *one* body part on and *one* part off the carpet. Find *five* different ways to solve this problem using different body parts and different positions each time.
   - Place *two* body parts on and *two* off the carpet. Find *five* different ways to solve this problem.
   - Place *three* body parts on and *one* off the carpet. Find *five* different ways to solve this problem.
   - Place *four* body parts on and *two* off the carpet. Find *three* different ways to solve this problem.
   - Place *five* body parts on and *one* off the carpet. Find *three* different ways to solve this problem.
   - Place *six* body parts on and *two* off the carpet. Find two different ways to solve this problem.

2. Try these challenges over the carpet. Move your body through the air from one side of the carpet to the other in these ways:
   - Hop in *three* different ways.
   - Jump in *three* different ways.
   - Step in *four* different ways.
   - Leap in *three* different ways.
   - Change your body support from your feet to your hands and back to your feet in *two* different ways.

3. Play the game "Simon Says" by calling out body parts to be placed on the carpet sample.

4. Create a new game your family can play using carpet samples.

5. Lie on the floor and spell your name, one letter at a time, by forming the letters with your body.

6. Make different numbers with your body while lying on the floor.

7. With two or three family members on a team, see which team can make numbers on the floor the most quickly, for example, 25 for two participants, 147 for three participants.

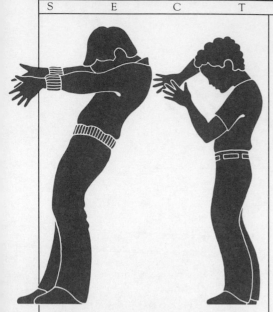

NUMBER AND ALPHABET GRID CHALLENGE

This activity offers not only an enjoyable family activity, but also hours of self-directed and small-group problem-solving play for children. It involves using different body parts and basic motor skills. It will help children recognize numbers and do simple arithmetic problems and also recognize letters and spelling words, including family names.

Preparation

Mark a number or alphabet grid on some hard surface (driveway, floor, or sidewalk). Use paint or chalk, masking tape, white shoe polish, or other substances depending on how long you want the grid to last.

Number Grid
— 6 feet (183 cm) —

4	0	2	1	3	9
7	5	3	6	4	2
9	6	0	7	5	3
2	4	2	6	1	7
1	8	5	0	8	3
6	2	4	9	7	1

12-inch (30.5-cm) squares

Activity

Pose different problems and challenges to family members to solve. Use the following or make up your own:

1. *Number grid.*
   - Step on each number in order from *one* to *nine.*
   - Hop on each number in order from *one* to *nine.*
   - Jump on each number in order from *nine* to *one.*
   - Jump backwards on ten different *even* numbers.
   - Hop on each number in order from *one* to *nine, twisting* your body *one-quarter turn* in the air each time.
   - Jump on ten different *odd* numbers, *twisting* your body *one-half turn* in the air each time.
   - Jump on five different *even* numbers, *twisting* your body *one full turn* in the air each time.
   - Solve simple addition, subtraction, and multiplication problems by stepping, hopping, or jumping on the numbers that equal the answer. For example, $3 + 2 + 2 + 1 = 8.$

2. *Letter grid.*
   - Step on the letters of your *first name* in order.
   - Hop on the letters of your *last name* in order.
   - Jump on the letters of the alphabet that are *vowels.*
   - Jump on the letters of ten *consonants.*
   - Spell simple words by placing a different body part on each letter of the word being spelled.

Letter or Alphabet Grid
— 7 feet (214 cm) —

Y	T	P	L	F	G	W
S	D	A	X	K	U	C
O	N	E	B	R	J	V
Z	U	M	T	P	I	M
H	W	I	L	Q	E	H
K	O	R	C	A	B	D
J	S	G	S	P	N	F

12-inch (30.5-cm) squares

- Correctly spell the name of your father and mother by hopping on the letters in correct order.
- Hop or jump on the letters of simple words while doing one-quarter, one-half, or full twists in the air between each letter.

Additional Activities

1. Using both grids, hop on the numbers and letters in your home address, both street numbers and name; your grandmother's address; your dad's work address.
   - Jump on the numbers and letters in today's date, month, and year.
   - Put a different body part on each number of the emergency telephone number for your community.

2. Assign family members to create unusual challenges and solutions using both the number and letter grid.

3. Encourage family members to create different games using the number or letter grid.

MARKED YARD GAMES

Simple yard games can help children learn to take turns, play by simple rules, and win and lose. Because they involve hopping, jumping, catching, throwing, bouncing, hitting, and striking, the games described also develop motor skills and coordination. These games require little equipment and space, and you can mark the game area on indoor or outdoor surfaces.

Activity

As a family, select two or three yard games to be marked on your sidewalk, driveway, or floor. Although nine sample designs are given here, you may want to choose some activities to mark that are best suited to your family or culture. You will need chalk, paint, or floor marking tape.

Mark the two or three activities you have selected using the dimensions given here. Show and talk about different ways each game can be played. Encourage young children to make up some games of their own. For instance, they might jump or hop the hopscotches without throwing a marker.

1. *Tetherball.* You can make your own tetherball pole from an 8-foot (2.5-meter) to 10-foot (3-meter) piece of 1 1/2- or 2-inch (3.8- or 5-cm) pipe, two 10- to 12-inch (25-or 30-cm) pieces of rebar (concrete

reinforced steel rod) welded to the bottom of the pole, an eyebolt attached at the top of the pole, an old rubber tire, and a small amount of concrete mix.

Usually two players play at a time. The goal is to hit the ball hanging from the rope so that the rope will completely wrap around the pole. Each player must stay in the marked hitting area of the court. Variations may be played where the ball is caught and then hit.

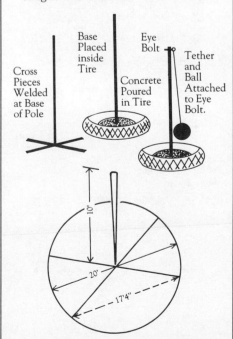

Cross Pieces Welded at Base of Pole

Base Placed inside Tire

Eye Bolt

Concrete Poured in Tire

Tether and Ball Attached to Eye Bolt.

2. *Hopscotch.* The player tosses a stone or some flat object into the first square, hops into that square and picks it up or kicks it out, and then hops back out. The stone must not land on any lines, and the player must not touch any lines with his hand or foot. The goal is to do the same thing in each square from 1 to 10. If the player throws his stone outside of the square he is aiming for or touches a line with his hand or foot, he must begin again or let someone else take a turn.

3. *Snail hopscotch.* The player does not throw an object, but merely hops in the squares from 1 to 30 on one foot and then hops from 30 to 1 on the other foot without touching any lines.

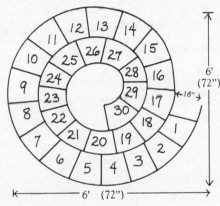

4. *Toss-and-reach hopscotch.* The player always tosses the object into the center square, then hops to each square in order. From each square, he must reach in to pick up the object without losing his balance or stepping on any lines.

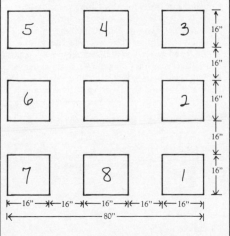

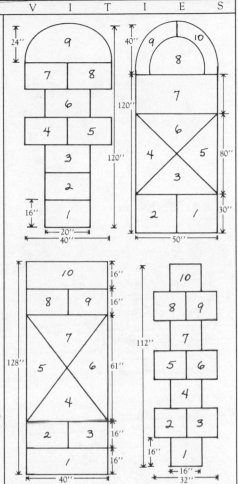

5. *Agility hopscotch.* This game is more difficult. The player must hop back and forth across the center line without touching any lines or losing his balance. He must hop on his left foot in squares marked *L* and on his right foot in squares marked *R*. He may rest with both feet down where the *L* and *R* are marked opposite each other.

313

that promote health and physical fitness. Other benefits include increased personal discipline and positive self-image, weight control, release of unwanted stress, and family fun and communication.

Activity

Get from your ward physical activities specialist a copy of the *Physical Fitness Awards Program* (brochure; PBAC0271) for each family member. Or make copies of the physical fitness activities chart and the physical fitness progress chart printed here for each family member. (Note: The physical fitness awards program is available through the Church distribution center in your area.)

Activity

Encourage each family member to participate in the physical fitness award program with the goal of earning a

6. *Four-square.* Four players usually play at a time. The player in square A usually bounces the ball to the player in another square. This player must control the ball and bounce it to a player in a different square. A player misses and goes to square D if he steps on a line, bounces the ball on a line, or cannot control the ball. The goal is to move up to square A. More than four players may play by having another person waiting outside each square. When the person in the square bounces the ball to another square, he must then jump out of his square and the waiting person then jumps in before the ball is bounced back to that square again.

Additional Activities

1. Have a family hopscotch tournament. Draw a ladder and put each family member's name on a rung. Players may challenge any person above their name on the ladder. Involve mom and dad, as well as the children.

2. Plan a neighborhood or extended family hopscotch, four square, and tetherball activity night with refreshments.

3. Identify and mark a new yard game to add to your family's ready-to-go games.

PHYSICAL FITNESS AWARD PROGRAM

Physical fitness is important in the lives of all of us. But we sometimes neglect our physical health, only to realize how precious it is once it is gone. This activity is designed to encourage families and individuals of all ages to take part *regularly* in activities

Physical Fitness Progress Chart

Check off the numbered boxes in sequence as you earn points. Each box represents one point.

GOLD	381	382	383	384	385	386	387	388	389	390	391	392	393	394	395	396	397	398	399	400
	361	362	363	364	365	366	367	368	369	370	371	372	373	374	375	376	377	378	379	380
	341	342	343	344	345	346	347	348	349	350	351	352	353	354	355	356	357	358	359	360
	321	322	323	324	325	326	327	328	329	330	331	332	333	334	335	336	337	338	339	340
	301	302	303	304	305	306	307	308	309	310	311	312	313	314	315	316	317	318	319	320
SILVER	281	282	283	284	285	286	287	288	289	290	291	292	293	294	295	296	297	298	299	300
	261	262	263	264	265	266	267	268	269	270	271	272	273	274	275	276	277	278	279	280
	241	242	243	244	245	246	247	248	249	250	251	252	253	254	255	256	257	258	259	260
	221	222	223	224	225	226	227	228	229	230	231	232	233	234	235	236	237	238	239	240
	201	202	203	204	205	206	207	208	209	210	211	212	213	214	215	216	217	218	219	220
	181	182	183	184	185	186	187	188	189	190	191	192	193	194	195	196	197	198	199	200
	161	162	163	164	165	166	167	168	169	170	171	172	173	174	175	176	177	178	179	180
	141	142	143	144	145	146	147	148	149	150	151	152	153	154	155	156	157	158	159	160
	121	122	123	124	125	126	127	128	129	130	131	132	133	134	135	136	137	138	139	140
	101	102	103	104	105	106	107	108	109	110	111	112	113	114	115	116	117	118	119	120
	81	82	83	84	85	86	87	88	89	90	91	92	93	94	95	96	97	98	99	100
	61	62	63	64	65	66	67	68	69	70	71	72	73	74	75	76	77	78	79	80
BRONZE	41	42	43	44	45	46	47	48	49	50	51	52	53	54	55	56	57	58	59	60
	21	22	23	24	25	26	27	28	29	30	31	32	33	34	35	36	37	38	39	40
	1	2	3	4	5	6	7	8	9	10	11	12	13	14	15	16	17	18	19	20

Physical Fitness Activities Chart

To accumulate points toward your individual or family award, participate in any of the physical activities listed below, earning points as shown. Points may be earned in any or all activities. You receive one point for accomplishing the minimum standard listed in any of the eight areas. The awards are designed to provide minimum standards in various age groups. We encourage you to participate in your selected activities at least three times per week for at least fifteen minutes or more. (Activity should promote deep breathing, but not be so intense that a person cannot carry on a conversation.) Keep a record of your points earned by recording them on the progress chart.

Age Group	Running	Walking	Cycling	Swimming	Stationary Run 75 steps/min. or rope jump	Basketball Soccer or Team Sports	Racquet Ball Handball Tennis	Participation in other events*
Under 30	1.5 miles 14 min.	2 miles 27 min.	4 miles 14 min.	400 yds. 8 min.	15 min.	30 min.	30 min.	1 event
30 to 39	1.5 miles 15 min.	2 miles 28 min.	4 miles 15 min.	400 yds. 8.5 min.	15 min.	25 min.	25 min.	1 event
40 to 49	1.5 miles 16 min.	2 miles 28 min.	4 miles 16 min.	400 yds. 9 min.	15 min.	25 min.	25 min.	1 event
50 and over	1.5 miles 17 min.	2 miles 29 min.	4 miles 18 min.	400 yds. 9 min.	12 min.	20 min.	20 min.	1 event
Fitness Points	1	1	1	1	1	1	1	1

*Ward physical activity specialists may approve a broad spectrum of activities in this category. Activities should be large-muscle type and last at least fifteen minutes.

bronze, silver, or gold award certificate during a twelve-month period. You may also want to work together as a family for a family award certificate.

Post the progress charts for each person in a place where everyone will be continually reminded of their commitment to physical health through regular physical activity.

Additional Activities

1. If you can arrange to, watch one or more of the excellent films available on physical fitness. *What Makes Millie Run?* is excellent for women. *Run Dick, Run Jane* is good for all ages. *Coronary Counterattack* shows how vigorous aerobic activities help prevent heart disease. Check your stake or regional film library for these films.

   If these films are not available to you, contact sport clubs, libraries, or schools that may have similar films you could use.

2. Add a 5,000- or 10,000-meter road race to the activities of your family reunion. Or enter a local or neighborhood road race as a family.

RHYTHMICAL EXERCISE PROGRAM

This activity offers an inviting and invigorating exercise program for those who may be less able to take part in active sports or games. Although it can be fun for all ages, it is designed especially for older members of the family. The exercises can be done in and around a chair in any home setting.

Preparation

Assign a family member to put the exercises in this activity to music of his choice. Have that person bring a cassette tape player or record player and become familiar with the exercise routine so he can teach it to others.

Activity

Before beginning this activity, make sure everyone understands that they should stop or slow down if they become too tired. You may also want to talk about the need for regular physical activity in your family's daily routine.

Have the assigned person introduce the music and exercises to the family.

Have everyone follow him as he leads them in the exercise program. Going through the routine several times is helpful in learning the different exercises.

Schedule and participate regularly (four to six days a week) in these exercises or some other large-muscle exercise program.

1. Arm Raises

2. Side to Side Trunk Bending

3. Hip Flexion-Forward Trunk Bending

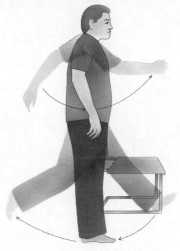

4. Arm and Leg Swinging

5. Foot Flexion and Extension

6. Foot and Leg Rotation

7. Head Rotation

10. Wing Stretcher and Arm Rotation

13. Knee Lifts and Trunk Flexion

8. Toe Raiser and ½ Knee Bends

11. Arm Push and Pull

9. Hip Flexion While Sitting

12. Toe Raiser and Alternating Arm Lifts

14. Hopping and Arm Swinging

Additional Activities

1. Invite or assign family members to make up a new exercise routine using a chair to some of grandma's or grandpa's favorite music. Teach it to the family and use it in your fitness program.

2. Older members of the family might join with nearby neighbors for daily participation in a rhythmical exercise program.

3. In addition to a rhythmical exercise program, begin a program of regular walking. Walking is the best exercise for many older people. You can walk and talk with a friend, a grandchild, or other family members.

Begin with easy walking while shaking your hands loosely and breathing naturally. This helps prepare the body for more vigorous activity. After walking easily for five to eight minutes, increase to a brisk walk. Step heel first in order to minimize strain on the joints. Gradually increase your time until you are able to walk comfortably for thirty minutes.

4. Consider working toward a bronze, silver, or gold physical fitness award.

FAMILY PHYSICAL ACTIVITY CENTER

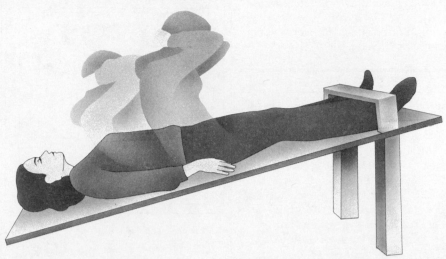

A family physical activity center can help children and youth develop physically and also help the whole family achieve and maintain physical fitness. It can also provide inexpensive recreation close to home.

Activity

In a family council or home evening, discuss what you might do to develop a family physical activity center. First, find a small area, outdoors or indoors, which you might use. Visit a park, school playground, health spa, or athletic club for ideas. Consider equipment that will help family members work on balance, flexibility, strength, coordination, and endurance. Include items for the ages of your family members. Try to find inexpensive ways to build your center. You probably won't need everything listed below. A few versatile items may be all you can afford and all you have room for. And remember: you can build it over several years' time, getting one piece of equipment at a time.

1. Make an *overhead ladder* from two 2-by-4-inch (5-by-10-cm) boards, 8 feet (about 2.5 meters) long, and several lengths of 1-inch or 1 1/8-inch (2.5- or 3-cm) dowels. Hang it from basement ceiling joists or install it on posts outside.

2. Make a *balance board* from a small log 12 to 16 inches (about 30 to 40 cm) long, and a cleated board 10 inches (25 cm) wide and about 24 to 26 inches (61 to 66 cm) long.

3. Hang a *climbing rope* (even if it is short) from ceiling joists in the basement. It can also serve as a swing where children use their arm and shoulder strength to hang on instead of sitting on a seat. It can also be mounted outside from a tree limb.

4. Make a *chinning bar* out of three lengths of 1 1/2-inch (about 4-cm) galvanized pipe and a bag or two of concrete mix.

5. Make a *shinny pole* or fireman's pole out of a 10- to 12-foot (about 3- to 4-meter) piece of 2-inch (5-cm) galvanized pipe and a bag of concrete mix.

6. Make a *tire vault* by burying one-third to one-half of a large truck tire in the ground.

7. Make *tire trees* from 12- to 14-foot (about 3- to 4-meter) logs about 10 inches (25 cm) in diameter with three sets of four used passenger car or truck tires mounted up the log so that they overlap a little. Putting two tire trees close together allows children to jump from one tree to the other. Installation in the ground should be *firm.*

8. Make a *log walk* (balance beam) from a pole 6 to 8 inches (about 15 to 20 cm) in diameter and about 12 to 14 feet (about 3 to 4 meters) long. Mount it on two hewn-out small pieces of log.

9. Make a *log jam* using varying heights of logs 10 to 12 inches (about 25 to 30 cm) in diameter. Mount them vertically in an irregular arrangement, side by side.

10. Make a *trapeze bar* out of four eye-bolts, two short pieces of chain, and about a 30-inch (about 76-cm) piece of 1 1/4-inch (about 3-cm) dowel. It can be mounted from basement floor joists, outside on an A-frame, or from a tree.

11. Make *beanbag targets* from plywood to look like clowns, animals, or trees. Bags can be tossed through holes shaped like mouths, eyes, or fruit.

12. Mount a *dart board* on a cloth-covered piece of celotex 4 feet by 4 feet (about 1.25 meters by 1.25 meters). Then there is less chance that darts will hit walls and floors.

13. Make a *jumping board* out of a 10-by-42-inch (about 25-cm-by-1-meter) piece of hardwood. Mount a 2-by-4-inch (5-by-10-cm) board securely under both ends.

14. *Tumbling mattresses or mats*

15. *Sit-up or abdominal slant board*

16. *Basketball backboard and hoop*

17. *Tire swing*

18. *Volleyball and badminton standards and net*

19. *Stationary bicycle*

20. *Jogging trampoline*

21. *Weights*

22. *Ballet bar and mirror*

23. *Gym scooters*

24. *Tetherball pole*

25. *Skip ropes*

26. Any other *device for exercising muscles* in which the resistance can be progressively increased

After you have decided which items you want to make or buy, work toward having them installed. Encourage regular use of the equipment.

FAMILY SUPERSTARS

This activity offers wholesome fun for the entire family, practice in many basic sports skills, and vigorous to mild physical activity. In it the family, in pairs or small teams, take part in a wide variety of challenging events. A "Family Superstars" event requires several weeks of planning and would be a good activity for times when the extended family or guests will be present.

Preparation

Choose or invent eight to twelve different events that you can hold in your yard, at a park, on the church lawn, or at a school near you. Assign different family members to prepare for one or two events, including getting or making the needed equipment and materials. Choose a date several weeks in advance and invite other family members or a neighborhood family to join you. Your family can also use one or all of the events without staging a formal superstars day.

Make a small banner advertising your superstars day and display it a week or two in advance. Be sure to establish simple and easy-to-understand rules for each event. Don't be afraid to make up your own rules. You may choose not to keep score or have winners and losers if it is more appropriate for your family. If your family has small children, you might want to give teenagers and adults a handicap when they compete against the children. This might include throwing or kicking with the arm or leg they do not usually use, running backward, or giving the child a head start.

A week or more in advance, have a family member prepare a special award certificate for each person who will take part. A simple hand-lettered certificate (see example) will do.

Invent or create your own events, or you may find it helpful to try some of the following:

1. *Milk carton field goal kick.* You will need three half-gallon (2-liter) milk cartons filled with crumpled

1. Milk carton field goal kick

3. Jump and reach ballon.

newspaper and wrapped with masking tape, and a makeshift goalpost approximately 5 feet (1.5 meters) high and 8 feet (2.4 meters) wide. Each person tries six times to kick a milk carton over the crossbar and through the upright. Keep score by counting the number of times each person makes it.

2. *Flying saucer throw for accuracy.* You will need a target made from a hula-hoop, inner tube, tire, or other circle. Each person tries six times to throw a frisbee, ice cream bucket lid, or stiff paper plate through the target. Keep score by giving each person one point for hitting the circle and two points for going through the target.

3. *Jump-and-reach balloon.* You will need twenty to thirty small balloons, masking tape, five or six pins, and a wall. Tape the balloons to the wall with masking tape at approximately the heights shown in the drawing. Measure how high each person can reach while he is standing flat on the ground. Then give him a pin and allow him three tries to jump and pop a balloon as high as possible above his head. The person who pops a balloon the highest above his standing reach wins.

4. *Hula-hoop agility race.* You will need ten hula-hoops, inner tubes, tires, or circles of some sort 2 1/2 to 3 feet (about 75 to 90 cm) in diameter. Lay them on the ground in two parallel lines, spaced out so that each line is 30 feet (about 9 meters) long. Have each person run up one row of circles and down the other, making sure that both feet land in each of the circles. The person who can run down and back the fastest wins. Give each person three chances to run and take his best time.

5. *Standing long jump.* Mark an area for the long jump on the grass, sidewalk, or floor. A sewing tape measure taped or pinned down will do. Give each person three tries to jump as far as he can.

6. *Rope skips in one minute.* You will need two or three ropes 7, 8, or 9 feet (about 2, 2.5, or 3 meters) long. Little children can use a

7-foot (2-meter) rope; adults require a 9-foot (3-meter) rope. Have each person count how many times he can successfully skip the rope in one minute.

7. *Throwing for accuracy.* You will need five soft balls—newspaper balls, foam balls, or yarn balls— and several cans. Let each person try ten times to throw a ball into a can some distance away. Give two points for each can hit and one point for each can knocked over.

8. *Soccer dribble.* You will need eight chairs, boxes, or cones for markers and two playground or soccer balls. Set up the chairs or boxes as shown in the drawing. Have each person try to kick and guide the ball with his feet, up and back as shown by the dotted line. The person who can do it successfully wins.

9. *Basket shooting.* You will need a basket, box, or garbage can and a basketball, rubber ball, foam ball, yarn ball, or large paper ball. Draw a circle 10 feet (about 3 meters) in diameter around the basket for adults, 6 feet (about 2 meters) for children. Have everyone stand outside the circle and make fifteen tries to get the ball into the basket. The person who throws it in the most times wins.

10. *Wrestling sticks.* You will need two smooth wood sticks, each 5 inches (about 13 cm) long. Two people face each other, grip the stick between them, and try to wrestle the stick out of the hand of their opponent. The opponents can use one hand or two hands and cannot move their feet. The person who wins two out of three times is the winner.

11. *Shuttle agility race.* You will need four boxes, baskets, or small garbage cans and ten old stuffed socks, newspaper balls, or blocks of wood. Arrange the boxes as shown in the drawing. Put five balls in each of the far boxes. Have two players begin by the full boxes and move the balls to the empty boxes as fast as they can, one ball at a time. Items must be placed in the container, not tossed in. The person who transfers all five balls the fastest wins.

12. *Pioneer pillow push.* You will need two soft pillows. Mark a 10- to 12-foot (about 3- to 4-meter) circle on the grass or the floor. Contestants stand inside the ring and try to push one another out using the soft pillow. Both feet must be out of ring to count as a fall. Play for the best two out of three falls.

Activity

With all family member assignments completed and the eight to twelve events ready to go, divide the family into pairs or teams. The teams need not match exactly in age, height, and weight, but do not put all the young children on one team. Pairs or teams take part in an event while others cheer them on. If there are more than six pairs or teams, have two different events going on at the same time.

At the conclusion, give a "Family Superstar" award certificate to each participant. Encourage family members to display their certificates on the family bulletin board or in their rooms.

Additional Activities

1. Buy or make a simple little surprise (candy, cookie, or small toy) to give participants at the end of each event.

2. Change your superstar day to a challenge day. Omit competition between pairs or teams and merely challenge all family members: Can you do this?

3. Take pictures of your superstar activity and make a collage of superstars for your family photo album.

4. Plan and conduct a "Neighborhood Superstars" activity. Be sure to invite some nonmember friends or neighbors.

5. As a family, volunteer to stage a superstars day for the extended family at a reunion.

6. Give a prize to the family member who invents the best new event for your family superstars.

7. Adapt the superstars activity to an indoor activity. You will need to adapt the events listed and invent new ones.

8. Soccer dribble.

4. Hula-hoop agility race.

11. Shuttle agility race.

LET'S GO FLY A KITE

The following activity teaches family members how to build and fly a kite and is good for all ages. It takes two to three hours and requires breezy weather.

Materials Needed

A brown paper bag or brown wrapping paper

Reed stems, twigs, bamboo barbecue skewers, or any other lightweight wood about 1/16 inch (about .16 cm) in diameter

Thread

A nail to punch holes

Strips of paper or cloth 1/2 inch (about 1.25 cm) wide and 6 feet (about 2 meters) long

Scissors

Activity

To build a Bermuda kite, follow these steps:

1. Trace the pattern on the cut-apart paper bag or on the brown wrapping paper. Then cut out the pattern.

2. Use the nail to punch holes in the pattern as shown in the drawing.

Since kites are so inexpensive at the store, you may want to buy one instead of making one. The following are some activities you can do with your kites. Your neighbors might enjoy getting involved with these activities.

1. *Reeling-in race.* The kite string should be 100 yards (about 90 meters) long. The contestants launch their kites and, at a signal, begin to reel them in. The first to reel in his kite wins.

2. *Altitude race.* The object of the altitude race is to make your kite reach higher than the other kites in a certain time period. Each person starts at a starting line and has five minutes to get his kite in the air and return to the starting line.

3. *Messenger race.* Thread a cardboard circle on each kite line. While the kites are in the air, contestants try to maneuver the cardboard disc up the kite line to the kite.

4. *Kite fighting.* In a clear, open area such as a field with few trees and no electrical lines, two contestants launch their kites and take a position 40 to 60 feet (about 12 to 18 meters) from each other. The object is to cut the opponent's line before he cuts yours. This is done by entangling the lines and making a vigorous sawing motion. The kites should be flown lower than normal height. When one line is cut, the game is over. Prepare the kite line by applying glue and then sand to the 100 feet (about 9 meters) of kite line nearest the kite.

Additional Activities

Have each family member design and decorate a kite. If you want to judge them, do it according to construction, design, appearance, materials used, and flying ability.

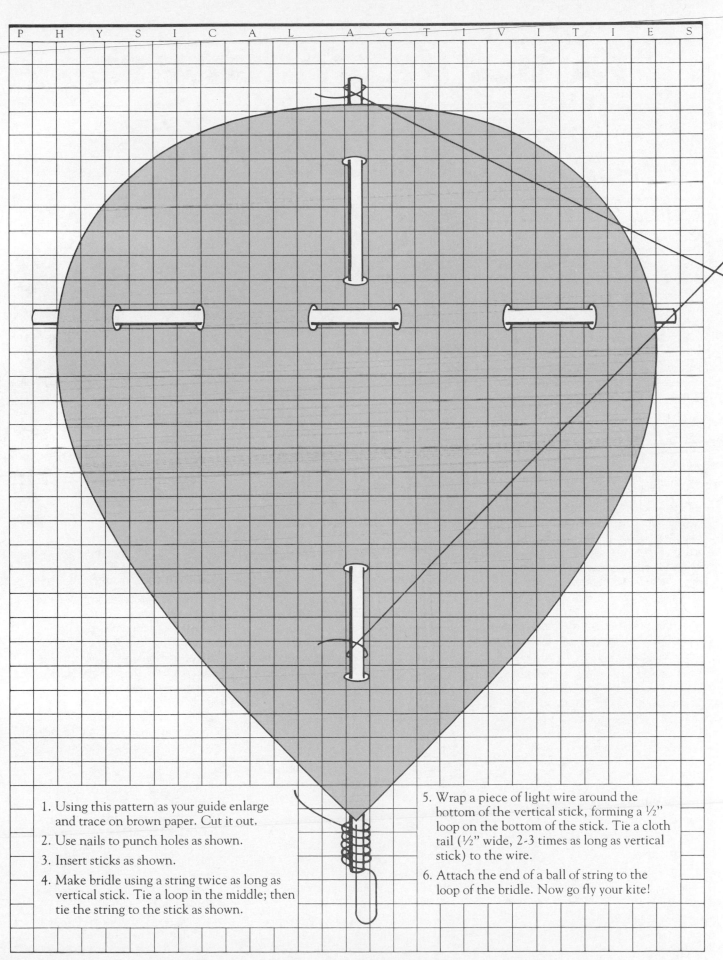

1. Using this pattern as your guide enlarge and trace on brown paper. Cut it out.

2. Use nails to punch holes as shown.

3. Insert sticks as shown.

4. Make bridle using a string twice as long as vertical stick. Tie a loop in the middle; then tie the string to the stick as shown.

5. Wrap a piece of light wire around the bottom of the vertical stick, forming a ½" loop on the bottom of the stick. Tie a cloth tail (½" wide, 2-3 times as long as vertical stick) to the wire.

6. Attach the end of a ball of string to the loop of the bridle. Now go fly your kite!

FAMILY PREPAREDNESS
Activities

EMERGENCY SUPPLIES

Do you have the supplies your family would need in case of emergency? Are those supplies in good working order and in a place where you could find them quickly? Or are they scattered all around your home? When emergency supplies are in a central place, your family will be better able to handle emergency situations. This activity will help your family gather and organize the emergency supplies that can make your family more secure.

Activity

Recall together some emergencies that have happened in your home or area: a blackout in the city, someone's falling and bumping his head, someone's cutting his finger on a knife, or a fire in the kitchen. When these things happened, where did you find the supplies you needed? Did you have to search for candles or antiseptic or bandages? Perhaps you could not find or did not have what you needed. Talk about how important it is to have emergency and safety supplies stored near the place where the emergency is most likely to happen and where everyone could find them quickly.

First decide where in your home you can put a central store of supplies. Then assign several family members to find the safety and emergency items that are scattered throughout your house. You likely have many of the items you need already. Look over the following suggested list of items. You may want to buy those on the list you do not have, as well as others you feel you might need.

1. A flashlight in good working condition.

2. Extra batteries for radio and flashlight. Do not keep batteries in the flashlight or radio. Keep them in an airtight container.

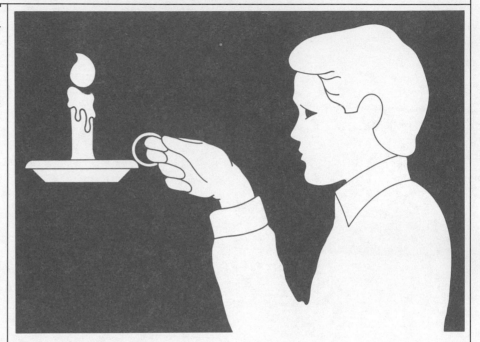

3. Portable battery powered radio. Use for receiving emergency instructions.

4. Candles (bowl type). Keep in case of power failure. Bowl will help prevent fire in case candle is overturned. (You can make these inexpensively out of parafin wax.)

5. Wooden matches. Use for lighting candles and relighting pilots on gas appliances. Be sure matches are kept in a metal container out of the reach of small children.

6. Fire extinguisher (ABC or dry chemical type for all classes of fires). Be sure you know how to handle and use it. Check it regularly.

7. Fuses (if your home has a fuse box). Numbers on the end of the fuse indicate size. When replacing blown fuses, be sure the number on the end of the new fuse is the same as the number on the old fuse.

8. First-aid instruction book.

9. First-aid supplies. The following list suggests minimum items to be included in your first-aid kit.

Aromatic spirits of ammonia—one unbroken tube

Aspirin—100-count bottle

Calamine lotion (for insect bites, hives from allergic reactions, or exposure to stinging nettle or poison ivy)—one tube

Thermometer—one oral and one rectal for small children or babies

Scissors and tweezers—one of each

Safety pins—one package of assorted sizes

Adhesive tape—one roll

One large box of assorted adhesive bandages

Matches (for sterilizing)—one box of wooden matches

Absorbent cotton—one box

Rubbing alcohol—one unbreakable bottle

Antibiotic ointment (Neosporin or Bacitracin)—one tube

Bicarbonate of soda (used for shock and upset stomach)—one box

Diarrhea remedy (Kaopectate or Pepto Bismol)—one bottle

Elastic bandages (for sprains and aches)—one 3-inch (about 7.5-cm) and one 6-inch (about 15-cm)

Gauze—one roll

Hot water bottle

Hydrogen peroxide—one unbreakable bottle

Ipecac syrup (induces vomiting)—one bottle

Finger splints (popsicle sticks)—ten splints

Roller bandages—two 1-inch (2.5-cm) and two 2-inch (5-cm)

Three-by-three-inch (7.6-cm) sterile pads—one box

Triangle bandages—four or more

Hand soap—one bar

Water purification pills and/or bottle of 2% tincture of iodine

Eye drops and medicine dropper

Razor blades

Needles

Measuring cups

Knife

Consecrated oil

Soothing throat lozenges—one package

Place all these items in a waterproof container (metal, heavy plastic, or wooden). Also store blankets, sheets, and at least four thin board splints 30 inches (about 76 cm) long.

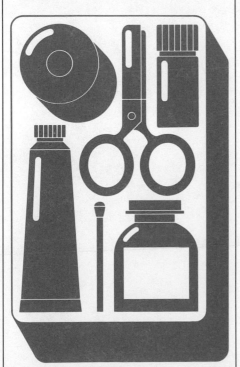

You may wish to add items to the kit as you need them. For example, if you have small children, you may wish to add liquid aspirin. If someone in the family needs special medication, add this to your kit.

Label your supplies, and date all medicines. Check supplies periodically, replacing them as they are used and throwing away old or contaminated supplies. Do not throw old medicines into trash cans around the house, where small children could find and eat them. Instead, flush them down the toilet or dispose of them in some other safe way. Perishable items should be rotated regularly to reduce spoilage.

After you have gathered your safety supplies and decided what you need to buy, divide up assignments. Assign some family members to buy items you need, and others to label the items. Buy things as you can afford them. It may take a while to get all the supplies you would like to have.

After you have gathered and stored your supplies, you may want to have a series of family home evenings where you discuss how to use them.

Additional Activities

1. Hold a family home evening and invite neighbors and extended family members. Learn together what to do in emergency situations.

2. Take a first-aid course from a school or organization in your community.

3. Assign a family member to periodically inspect your supplies to make sure they are kept current.

4. Take your first-aid kit along on a trip or campout.

5. Put together a kit of emergency supplies to keep in your car. You could include the following:

   Standard first-aid kit

   Reflector and flares in case your car stalls on the road or is involved in an accident

   Flashlight and batteries

   Blanket to be used for shock, cold weather, fire, or other emergencies

   Tow chain

   Fire extinguisher

   Flat block to be used as a car jack support

6. Sing this song together to the tune of "Yankee Doodle."

Be Prepared

Verse 1:

Our prophet's told us to prepare
For famine and disaster.
If we obey, our family will
Live happy ever after.

Chorus:

"Be prepared," our prophet said.
Store your wheat and honey.
Plant a garden; learn first aid;
And don't forget some money!

Verse 2:

When Father Noah built an ark,
The people laughed and shouted.
But when the rain began to pour,
Those people never doubted.

Chorus: Repeat

Verse 3:

We have been warned in latter days
There will be floods and earthquakes.
So put your house in order and
Prepare before the dam breaks!

Chorus: Repeat

Verse 4:

Please do not procrastinate.
Excuses have no muscle.
You'll never find a better time
Than NOW! So better hustle.

Chorus: Repeat

EMERGENCY TELEPHONE NUMBERS

In case of emergency, can you immediately find telephone numbers that could bring help to you and your family? In a crisis, just a few minutes of time can make a lot of difference. In this activity, your family will post all emergency numbers and learn how to use them.

Activity

With help from all family members, look up in the telephone directory the following numbers:

Fire department
Police, sheriff, or constable
Department of Public Safety
Ambulance rescue

(In some areas, the numbers listed above can be reached by dialing a special number for emergencies. Check and see if there is such a number in your area.)

Doctor—home and office
Hospital
Poison control center
Highway assistance
Home teachers
Visiting teachers
Bishop
Relative or close friend

List these numbers on a piece of paper to post by each telephone in your home. At the bottom of the list, write the words *who, what,* and *where.*

Make sure all family members know how to report an emergency. Explain that, when the person they are calling answers, they should always first say, "This is an emergency." Then they should tell—

Who (give their name). *What* (tell what is the matter—whether anyone is trapped or injured). *Where* (give address and directions).

Then they should answer questions about what first aid has been given and listen for instructions about what to do until help arrives. If for some reason they cannot stay by the telephone until the call goes through, they can give the necessary information to the operator. If the number they call is busy, they should dial "0" to get faster action.

Make sure that each family member knows which numbers to call for which kind of emergency and can relate all important information. It is also a good idea to have small children memorize their names, ages, addresses, and parents' names.

If your family does not have a telephone, find out the location of the nearest telephone or source of help. Because you may need to use a pay telephone in an emergency, it is a good idea to carry change with you. Since you probably will not have emergency numbers with you at a pay telephone, dial "0" for the operator. As soon as the operator answers, tell her, "This is an emergency." Give her the number of the telephone from which you are calling. Then tell her who, what, and where and wait for confirmation.

After you have posted your emergency numbers and taught the proper report-

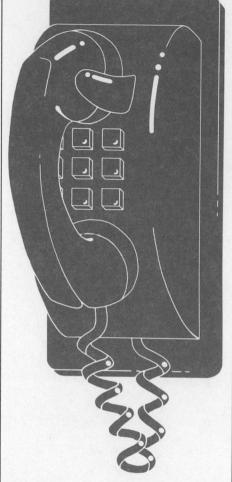

ing procedure, have everyone practice making an emergency telephone call. Leave one or two members of the family home to role-play the operator, fireman, doctor, or other person you might call. Have other family members go to another phone and call their home telephone number.

Sample emergency phone number card:

Emergency Telephone Numbers

Rescue Squad
 (paramedics or EMT) _____

Fire Department _____

Police _____

Doctor _____

Hospital Emergency Room _____

Life Support Unit _____

Poison Control Center _____

Other numbers _____

Who? _____

What? _____

Where? _____

MOUTH-TO-MOUTH RESUSCITATION

Smoke inhalation, heart attack, drowning, choking—all of these can stop a person's breathing. Mouth-to-mouth resuscitation may well be a gift of life to one of your own family members. You never know when an emergency will arise that requires you to use it. All family members should know how to perform this life-saving technique.

Preparation

Have a family member become familiar enough with the following instructions that he can teach them to the rest of the family:

When you encounter someone who is not breathing, start mouth-to-mouth breathing right away. Do not wait to call for a doctor or aid. Don't try to move the person or give secondary first aid before giving mouth-to-mouth resuscitation.

The following chart explains the procedures in giving mouth-to-mouth resuscitation.

If a victim appears to be unconscious:

Tap victim on the shoulder and shout, "Are you okay?"

If there is no response:

Tilt the victim's head, chin pointing up. Place one hand under the victim's neck and gently lift. At the same time, push with the other hand on the victim's forehead. This will move the tongue away from the back of the throat to open the airway.

Immediately look, listen, and feel for air. While maintaining the backward head tilt position, place your cheek and ear close to the victim's mouth and nose. Look for the chest to rise and fall while you listen and feel for the return of air. Check for about five seconds.

If the victim is not breathing:

Check for and clear any foreign matter from the victim's mouth. Give four quick breaths. Maintain the backward head tilt, pinch the victim's nose with the hand that is on the victim's forehead to prevent leakage of air; open your mouth wide; take a deep breath; seal your mouth around the victim's mouth, and blow into the victim's mouth with four quick but full breaths just as fast as you can. When blowing, take only enough time between breaths to lift your head slightly for better inhalation. For an infant, give gentle puffs and blow into both the mouth and nose, and do not tilt the head back as far as for an adult.

If the chest does not rise when you blow, it may help to reposition the head and try again.

Again, look, listen, and feel for air exchange.

If there is still no breathing:

Change rate to one breath every five seconds for an adult.

For an infant, blow into mouth and nose at the same time. Give one gentle puff every three seconds.

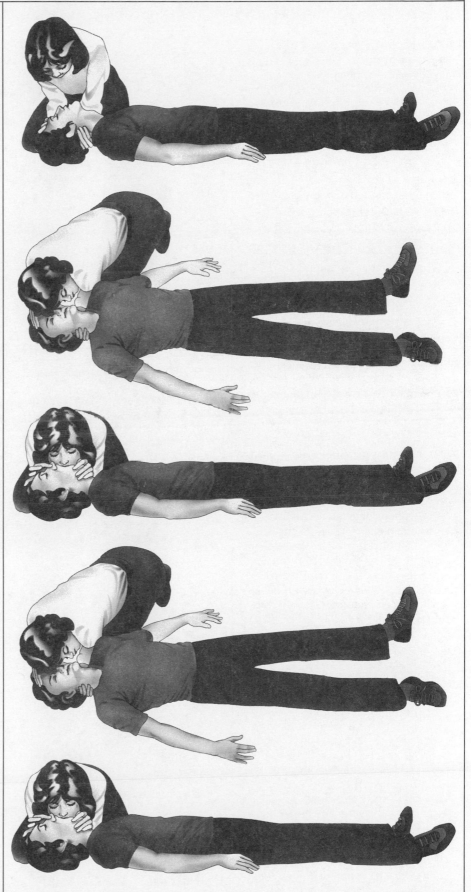

Mouth-to-nose method. The mouth-to-nose method, instead of the mouth-to-mouth method, can be used in the same sequence described above. Maintain the backward headtilt position with one hand on the victim's forehead. Remove the other hand from under the neck and close the victim's mouth. Blow into the victim's nose. Open the victim's mouth to look, listen, and feel for breath.

For more information about these and other lifesaving techniques, contact your Red Cross chapter for training.

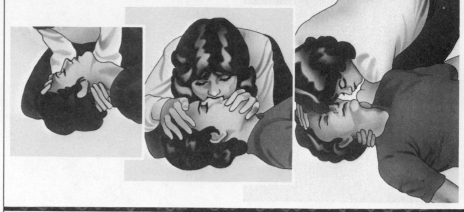

TREATING CHOKING

A series of simple techniques could save the life of someone who is choking on food or other objects. This activity will teach your family how to use these techniques.

Preparation

Have a family member become familiar enough with the following material to present it to the rest of the family:

If the victim can cough, speak, or breathe, do not interfere.

When someone is seriously choking, he will become pale and turn a bluish color. He may perspire and collapse. The signs of choking are often confused with those of a heart attack. But you can tell when someone is choking because he will be unable to speak. Time is a critical factor when someone is choking. Breathing must be restored within four minutes, or else brain damage may result. The person will die within eight minutes. So there is no time to call for a doctor or rescue vehicle.

Here are several life-saving techniques—

1. *The abdominal thrust, or Heimlich maneuver,* is the preferred method. With the victim standing or sitting, stand behind the victim and wrap your arms around the waist (see fig. 1). Place the thumb side of your fist against the victim's abdomen, slightly above the navel and below the tip of the breastbone. Grasp your fist with your other hand and press it into the victim's abdomen with four quick upward thrusts.

2. If the abdominal thrust method does not work or is impractical, use *the back blows method.* With the victim

Fig. 1

Fig. 2

standing or sitting, stand at his side and slightly behind him (see fig. 2). Place one hand high on the chest for support and position the victim's head at chest level or lower so that gravity can assist the procedure. Give sharp blows with the heel of your hand over the victim's spine between the shoulder blades. Do not just pat him on the back; use a series of quick, sharp blows. Give the blows as rapidly as possible. If the victim is in the lying-down position, roll him toward you and deliver the back blows (see fig. 3). Figure 4 demonstrates back blows to an infant.

If the victim is lying down, roll the victim on his back and straddle his hips or one thigh. Place one of your hands on top of the other, with the heel of the bottom hand in the middle of the victim's abdomen, slightly above the navel and below the rib cage. Move forward so that your shoulders are directly over the victim's abdomen and press upward toward the diaphragm with four quick thrusts (see fig. 5). Do not press to either side.

For infants and small children (fig. 6), place the victim face up on your forearm, with his head down. This maneuver may be performed more easily by resting your forearm on your slightly elevated thigh. Place two or three fingertips on the middle of the victim's abdomen, slightly above the navel and below the rib cage, and press into the victim's abdomen with four quick upward thrusts.

If you are choking and there is no one around to help you, perform the abdomen thrust on yourself.

3. If neither of these procedures works, you must repeat the sequence: four quick upward thrusts and four quick back blows.

Press your own fist into your upper abdomen with a quick upward thrust, as described for the victim standing. Or you can lean forward and press your abdomen quickly over any firm object, such as the back of a chair, the edge of a sink, or a porch railing.

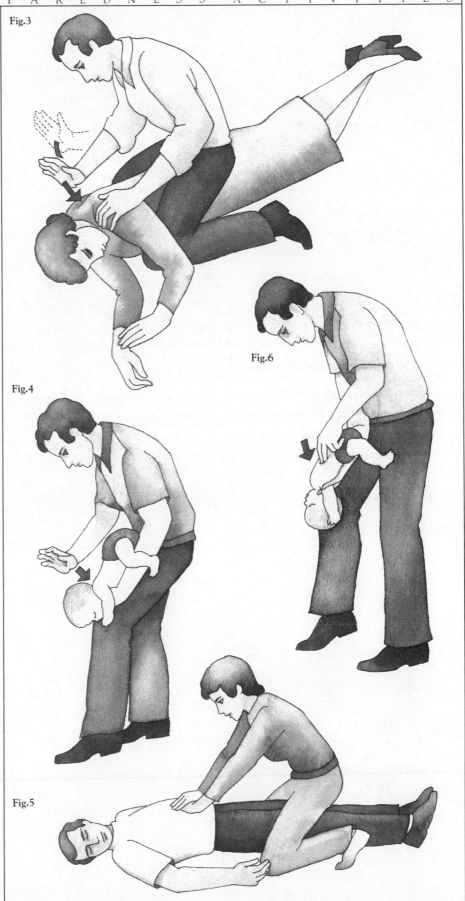

Fig.3

Fig.6

Fig.4

Fig.5

4. *The chest thrust technique* is an alternate technique that can be used for women in advanced pregnancy or people who are so overweight that your arms cannot encircle the victim's abdomen.

If the victim is standing or sitting (see fig. 7), stand behind him, place your arms under his armpits, and encircle his chest. Place the thumb side of your fist on the breastbone, but not on either the lower tip of the breastbone or the lower edge of the ribs. Grab your fist with your other hand and make four quick inward thrusts.

If the victim is lying down, place him on his back and kneel at the side of his body (see fig. 8). Locate the tip of the breastbone, at the upper abdomen. Measure two to three finger widths—1 to 1 1/2 inches (about 2.5 to 4 cm) up from this point. Place the heel of your other hand toward the victim's head, on the lower half of the breastbone, next to the two fingers used to locate the tip of the breastbone. Put your other hand on top

Fig.7

of the first and lean forward to bring your shoulders over the victim's breastbone. Make four quick downward thrusts with your arms, which will compress the chest cavity.

If you use any of the above procedures properly, the food or other blocking object should pop from the patient's mouth.

Have the assigned family member explain the above procedures to the family. Have everyone get a partner and practice; the children could practice on dolls. Spending a few minutes now may prepare you to save a life.

TREATING SHOCK

At least one of your family members may well experience shock during his or her lifetime. Shock is extremely dangerous, and, unless it is recognized and treated, it can kill. This activity will help your family learn to recognize and treat shock.

Activity

Before you begin, write down on slips of paper a few situations that could cause shock and could actually happen in your family (see list below for ideas). Put the papers in a jar.

Shock may be caused by any of the following:

- Loss of blood through internal or external bleeding
- Loss of plasma (the liquid part of the blood) through burns
- Loss of body fluids from vomiting, dysentery, or dehydration
- Allergic reactions
- Infections
- Heart trouble, heart attack, or stroke
- Poisoning by chemicals, gases, alcohol, or drugs
- Snake and animal bites
- Respiratory problems
- Lack of oxygen
- Chest wounds
- Broken ribs
- Obstructions in the throat that cause the victim to choke
- Injuries to the respiratory system
- Damage to the spine that paralyzes muscles
- Water-related accidents

Fig.8

- Injuries of all types, both severe and minor
- Occasionally, fear, bad news, or the sight of blood.

Explain to your family that tonight you are going to discuss something that could happen to any one of you sitting in this room—shock. Shock is the severe condition that depresses body functions and can keep the heart, lungs, and other organs from working normally. Many different things can cause it, and almost all medical emergencies involve some form of shock. Unless it is treated, shock can kill a person, even if his injuries are not serious.

1. *Causes of shock.* Discuss the causes of shock as outlined above. Stress that if any of these things happen, you should always treat for shock as a precautionary measure.

2. *Recognizing shock.* Discuss the following signs:

- One common form of minor shock is fainting or faintness.
- The skin may be pale or bluish and cold to the touch. If the victim has dark skin, look at the color of the inside of the mouth or of the skin under the eyelids or nails.
- The skin may be moist and clammy.
- The pupils of the eyes may be dilated. The eyes may be dull and lackluster, a sign of poor circulation.
- The victim is weak.
- Breathing may be shallow, panting, labored, or irregular.

- The pulse is usually fast (over 100 beats a minute).
- There may be nausea, vomiting, anxiety, and thirst. The victim may collapse.

As shock grows worse, look for these signs:

- The victim may become apathetic and not respond. This is because he is not getting enough oxygen.
- The eyes may become sunken. The victim may have a vacant expression.
- The victim's skin may become spotty because of very low blood pressure and congested or collapsed blood vessels.

Unless the victim is treated, he will eventually pass out. His body temperature will fall, and he may even die.

3. *Treating shock.* Tell family members that you treat for shock as soon as you have dealt with stopped breathing and severe bleeding.

A first aider cannot give complete medical care for shock; only a medical facility can do this. However, a first aider can give care that will help prevent shock.

- For minor shock, such as faintness, have the victim sit down and put his head between his knees. As blood flows to the brain, the body's normal functions will usually resume.

- Have the victim lie down. Do your best to comfort, quiet, and soothe the victim. Keep him comfortable, and keep the body temperature normal. If it is hot, provide shade; if it is cold, put blankets or other protective coverings both under and over the victim.

- Choose the best position for the victim according to the nature of the injury. The following illustrations will help you make a decision.

A trained medical person can help prevent shock by giving intravenous fluids to replace body fluids lost through an injury or illness. If you cannot get medical help within one hour and the victim is likely to die, giving fluid by mouth may help prevent shock.

Do *not* give the victim fluid to drink if he or she is unconscious or semiconscious, vomits or may vomit, or appears so severely injured that surgery or a general anesthetic may be needed.

Make a salt and soda solution. Mix 1 level teaspoonful of salt (about 5 ml) and 1/2 level teaspoonful (about 2.5 ml) of baking soda in a quart (or liter) of water that is neither hot nor cold. If you mix this solution in an ordinary drinking glass or cup (250 ml or 8 ounces), use about 2 pinches of salt and 1 pinch of soda.

Never give alcoholic beverages. If you do not have salt and soda, give

Standard position for giving care for shock: feet up, injury elevated. Warning: Do not elevate the injury if you think a bone may be broken. Do not elevate *any* unsplinted fracture.

The victim should be flat on the back if you think a bone may be broken and it is not splinted, if elevation is painful, or if you are unsure about which position is correct.

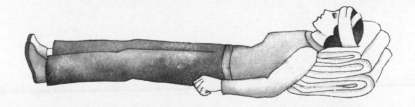

If the victim has a head wound or is having trouble breathing, elevate the *head and shoulders.* Do not elevate the feet and the head at the same time.

A victim who is bleeding from the mouth, vomiting, or may vomit should lie on one side, so fluid will drain from the mouth.

plain water in the amounts listed below:

Adults who are conscious and not vomiting: Give half a cup (about 120 milliliters) or glass of salt and soda solution over a period of fifteen minutes. Have the victim sip it slowly. Give the same amount during the next fifteen minutes, and the next, if the person is still conscious and not vomiting.

Infants and children who are conscious and not vomiting: Give the same salt and soda solution in smaller amounts. To a child, give about 1/4 cup or glass over each fifteen-minute period. To an infant, give about 1/8 of a normal glass over each fifteen minutes. You may need to use a nursing bottle.

If someone has not already left for help, take all necessary precautions and be fairly sure the victim is stable. Then go for help yourself. Return as fast as you can.

After you feel your family understands what shock is and how to treat it, take turns drawing from the jar the situations that could cause shock.

For example:

- Janie is allergic to many foods. She ate one.
- Grandpa has heart trouble.
- Grandma is a diabetic. She has to be very careful of what she eats and what she does.
- Bobby loves to swim and spends a lot of time at the pool. As energetic as he is, he could very easily have a water accident.

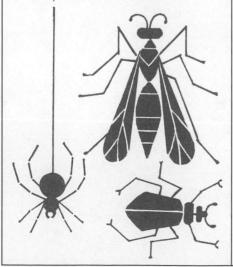

- We all camp out a lot. We have been bitten many times by insects.
- Aunt Joan went into shock when she heard about Uncle Bill's accident.

Have the person who draws the slip read the situation to the rest of the family and then pretend to be the victim. Have the rest of the family take the necessary steps to treat him. Continue until all the slips have been drawn.

TREATING BLEEDING

How often has a child come running through your door holding up a finger and announcing tearfully, "Mommy, my finger is bleeding. Can you make it better?" Most of us could handle that emergency. But what if you came upon a really serious accident where someone was bleeding—perhaps a car accident or a more serious household accident? This activity will teach your family how to handle bleeding.

Materials Needed
Cotton
Handkerchief
Cloth
Strips of cloth

Preparation
Have a family member learn these steps to control bleeding. Have him present them to the rest of the family.

1. The best way to control bleeding is to hold a thick pad of clean cloth over the wound with your hand and apply direct pressure. A folded handkerchief will do, but it is best to use a sterile cloth if possible. If you cannot get a pad right away, use your hand until you can get a pad. Put your hand, palm flat, directly over the wound. Press firmly and evenly as necessary to stop the bleeding. Pressing will make the flow of blood slow down and clot.

2. Keep the original covering on the wound. Changing the covering will disturb the blood clot that has formed. If the pad becomes saturated, add other layers of material to the top as needed and keep pressing. Keep these pads in place until the blood has clotted and bleeding subsides.

3. Unless you think a bone may be broken, raise the victim's bleeding limb above the level of his heart as you continue to apply pressure. Gravity helps to reduce blood flow in the injured area, which slows down the loss of blood through the wound.

4. After the bleeding is under control, apply a pressure bandage to the wound. Steady the victim's limb. Keep the original covering on the wounded area and place the center of a strip of material or gauze over the middle of the covering. Wrap this strip around the middle of the covering, around the limb, and back to the starting point. Repeat until the strip is used up. Tie it in a knot directly over the center of the covering. Keep the bandage tight enough to prevent bleeding, but loose enough to allow blood to circulate.

5. If direct pressure does not stop the bleeding, you may need to use the pressure point technique. With this technique, you press the main artery above the wound in order to stop bleeding. You can identify the artery by feeling a strong pulse beat. Fig. 9 shows the locations of major pressure points.

Lay the victim on his back. Press with the flat of your hand directly over the pressure point. If the bleeding does not stop, use the flat of your fingers to apply more direct force. Place the fingers of one hand over the artery and use the other hand over those fingers to add greater pressure.

To apply pressure on the pressure point in the wrist, for example, hold the victim's arm in the air. Place your fingers on the inside of the wrist and your thumb on the outside. Press your fingers firmly toward your thumb.

The pressure-point technique stops circulation within the limb. Use it *in addition* to the other methods already in progress. As a rule, do not use the pressure-point technique alone to stop bleeding. If bleeding should start up again, however, be ready to reapply pressure at the pressure point.

6. Using a tourniquet can be very dangerous. It can cause the victim to lose a limb. But, if you cannot stop serious bleeding any other way, you may need to use a tourniquet as a last resort to save a person's life.

Wrap a band of cloth about two inches wide twice around the limb between the wound and the heart. Do *not* use wire or cord. On the arm, place the tourniquet no less than a hand's width below the armpit. On the leg, place it no less than a hand's width below the groin. In either case, place it as close to the wound as practical, but there must be unbroken skin between the tourniquet and the wound. Tie the ends of the tourniquet into a half knot; place a stick across the knot; then tie the

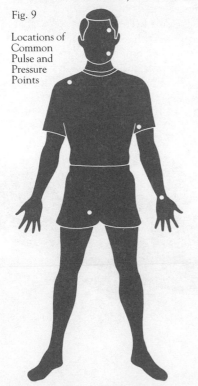

Fig. 9

Locations of Common Pulse and Pressure Points

ends above the stick in a tight knot. Twist the stick to apply just enough pressure to stop the bleeding. Use a second bandage to tie the end of the stick in place so it will not untwist.

Do not loosen the tourniquet. This will only allow more bleeding, which may be fatal. A tourniquet can safely remain in place for 30 to 45 minutes. *Get medical help immediately.* Make sure the tourniquet is visible and that everyone concerned knows that it is there.

7. Always treat a bleeding victim for shock (see "Treating Shock").

8. For nosebleed take these steps:
 - Tilt the head forward.
 - Pinch the nose just below the bone in the bridge of the nose and hold for five minutes.
 - If the bleeding does not stop, blow the nose to clear the nasal passage on the bleeding side.
 - Pinch the nose again in the same spot.
 - Do not blow the nose to clear the clotted blood once the flow of blood has stopped.
 - Do not remove the blood clots from the nose for several hours.
 - Ice held on the bridge of the nose can also help stop the bleeding.

9. A fall or an automobile accident may cause dangerous bleeding inside the body. Watch to see if the victim coughs up blood or if there are traces of blood in the bowels. Do not give the person anything to drink; move him as little as possible; and go for help immediately.

10. For bleeding from the ear, get a doctor quickly.

11. Stay calm. Seeing lots of blood can be very alarming. But realizing that you know what to do to stop it can help you be calm.

Activity

Have the assigned family member present the material he has prepared. Using the cotton and strips of material, have family members practice on each other the steps in treating bleeding in different situations. The small children could use dolls or stuffed

animals. Use the situations below or make up some of your own. Divide into teams if you wish.

Remind the family that the instructions to be calm and apply pressure to the wound apply to *all* bleeding problems, large or small.

1. Barbara cut her finger on a kitchen knife. What should we do?

2. We are hiking and John falls off a ledge and injures his left leg. He is in pain and is bleeding. Now what?

3. We are driving down the road and hear the screeching of tires. In the road is a small boy who has just been hit by an automobile. He is injured and is bleeding from the mouth. What should we do?

4. Greg was playing with a stick, and he fell and punctured his arm. It is bleeding. What should we do?

5. The boys have been mowing the lawn. Jenny comes running in and announces that the lawn mower has just cut Mike's toe. It is bleeding and he is in a panic. What now?

Make sure that family members understand the basic steps in treating bleeding. You may need to review these skills periodically.

Additional Activities

1. Talk over some safety rules that might prevent accidents which cause bleeding. For example, teach

your children how to use knives properly. Show the proper way to carry scissors. Discuss how to use hand tools and power tools.

2. Support your local and ward blood drives.

PROTECTING YOUR HOME AGAINST FIRE

Every year thousands of people lose their homes or their lives by fire. But many fatal fires could be prevented by basic knowledge and practical precautions. Every family should have a fire safety program to teach family members how to prevent fires and how to react in case one occurs. This activity teaches your family basic steps to prevent and deal with fires.

Activity

Study the checklist "Fire Safety All around Your House." Discuss it with your family. Then with the checklist, a black pencil, and a red pencil, walk together through each room in your home. As you do, discuss whether your family takes all the safety precautions listed. With a black pencil check off the precautions you are already taking. If you need to improve in an area, make an X with a red pencil. If you have red Xs, your home is not as safe from fire as it could be. Assign family members to correct each problem. As they do, erase the red marks.

Fire Safety All around Your House

1. Kitchen

—Never fight a grease fire with water. Have a lid available for every pan in which a grease fire could start.

—Keep towels available for drying hands before using any electrical appliance.

—Turn pot handles inward on stove.

—Wear close-fitting sleeves when you cook.

—Keep stove and exhaust fan clean and grease-free.

—Don't hang clothes, dishtowels, or decorative objects, that could catch fire over the stove.

—Keep a fire extinguisher handy. Know how to use it.

2. Laundry and Furnace Room

—Keep the lint trap around the dryer free of lint after every load of drying.

—Replace furnace filters regularly. Clean dust and lint from around the furnace motor and burners.

—Service fan motor and check fan belt regularly.

3. Bedrooms

—Be sure windows open easily.

—Always sleep with bedroom doors closed if you don't have a fire detector.

—Plan two escapes from each bedroom.

4. Storage

—Never leave greasy or oily rags lying about.

—Store gasoline and other flammable substances in tightly closed metal containers.

—Keep the basement, attic, and other storage areas clean. Do not store old clothes, cardboard boxes, magazines, newspapers, or other items that catch fire easily.

5. Electrical Outlets

—Don't overload circuits. Avoid plugging more than two appliances into one outlet.

—If a fuse blows or circuit breaker trips, find the cause.

—Don't use extension cords under rugs, over hooks, or through door openings. They can become worn and cause short circuits.

6. Care of Children

—Never leave a young child unattended.

—Do not let children play around stoves, open fires, or electric heaters.

—Keep matches and combustible fluids out of reach.

—Instruct babysitters on what to do in case of fire.

7. General Fire Safety Practices

Keep a garden hose with a nozzle attached to a water outlet at all times in case of fire. Be sure the hose is long enough to reach all areas of the home.

Make sure each family member has a whistle for warning others. Have the family keep their whistles by their beds.

Turn off or unplug appliances when you finish using them.

Protect children by buying them flame-retardant sleepwear and costumes for special holidays. If clothing catches on fire, remember to stop, drop, and roll—don't run, lie flat on the floor or ground, and roll over several times then back, leading with the legs. Keep the arms drawn in and the hands over the face. Practice this skill with each family member.

Additional Activity

1. Memorize these four rules of fire safety:
   - Eliminate fire hazards around the house.
   - Teach every family member safe fire habits in daily life.
   - Install a smoke detector system, if possible.
   - Be sure that everyone knows exactly what to do in case of fire.

2. Discuss the possibility of installing a smoke detector system in your home. You will need one smoke detector for each level of your home. You will also need one for each sleeping area if the bedrooms are not grouped together.

3. Develop a home emergency escape plan. With your family, find the best possible escape route from different parts of your home, giving special attention to the bedrooms. Every room needs two escape routes, one normal and one emergency exit. Consider using doors, halls, and windows.

   If you choose a window for an emergency exit, make sure that it is possible to reach the ground safely. You may need an escape ladder or rope. If a bedroom window does not open, keep a hammer under the bed to break out the glass if necessary. In emergencies when no one can help you in getting down from a high window, rip up bed sheets and tie them together to form a rope.

   Make a master home emergency escape plan. Draw a map of each floor, showing emergency and normal exits, as well as the location of windows, doors, stairs, and halls.

   Decide on a place outside to meet after you leave the home. Mark it on your master plan map. Make sure your family knows this is where you will all meet.

Post copies of the master plan in several areas of your home. You may also want to post individual plans in every room.

4. Fire drills reduce the chance that someone will be hurt in a fire. Hold family fire drills regularly—at least three times a year. Use your home emergency escape plan as the plan for your fire drill. Make sure that everyone understands the exit procedure. You can hold a drill in several ways.

   To start the drill, have everyone go to their bedrooms, close the doors, and wait for a prearranged signal. When the signal is given, have them use the emergency escape from their bedrooms and meet in the assigned place outside the home. Or have someone give the prearranged signal when no one is expecting it and see how fast family members can meet outside in the assigned place. As part of each drill, have someone practice going to a phone *outside* the home so that family members will remember that they must call the fire department.

   Review these rules each time you have a drill:

   - Post emergency telephone numbers at all telephones. See "Emergency Telephone Numbers" for instructions on how to make emergency calls.
   - Do not return to a burning building once you are outside.
   - Do not try to put out the fire, unless you see that it is confined to a very small area.
   - When you hear the alarm, get out of the house immediately. Don't stop to dress, get valuables, or call the fire department. Go to a neighbor's house to call.
   - Do not rush into a hallway. Touch the closed door with the palm of your hand. If it is hot, use your emergency exit. If it is not hot, open the door with caution. If there is fire and smoke, close the door immediately. It takes ten to fifteen minutes for fire to burn down a door.
   - If you become trapped, don't panic. There is a good chance of survival. Cover the vents with cloths, and stuff cloths in the cracks in the door. If there is a telephone in the room, call the fire department and tell them exactly where you are. Then signal from the window with a light or bed sheets. Don't jump from a high window unless someone is holding a net to catch you.
   - If your room is filled with smoke, get down on the floor and crawl. Cover your face with a cool, wet cloth if possible.
   - Always close windows and doors behind you as you leave. This will slow down the spread of the fire.

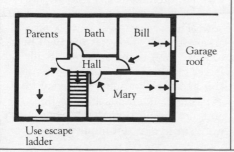

Use escape ladder

COPING WITH
A BLACKOUT

This activity will help your family be prepared to deal with power failures that result in loss of light and heat.

Materials Needed

Matches and candles
Battery-powered radio
Flashlight and batteries
Fuses (if you have a fuse box that requires fuse replacements)
Food storage items: food requiring no refrigeration or cooking such as crackers, canned meats, fruits, dried meats, fish, juices, water, and powdered milk

Activity

Decide on an evening when your family can practice coping with a blackout. Parents might want to plan the evening together and then surprise the rest of the family.

Before dinner, announce that in a few minutes you will be turning out the lights. Tell everyone that for a specified amount of time they will not be allowed to turn on the lights again because tonight your family will be learning what to do during a blackout. Have all family members follow these steps:

1. Don't panic and don't walk around in the dark. You can get hurt if you wander about in the dark, especially if you are outside or in a strange place.

2. Check the inside of your home to see if the problem originates there. Check the fuse box or circuit

breaker box. Find the replacement fuses and make sure all family members know how to replace them. If your home is run from breaker switches, check them for malfunctioning circuits.

3. If you find the problem does not originate from these sources, look out the window to see if other lights are off in the neighborhood. If they are not working, turn on your battery-powered radio for information. Use your telephone only for serious emergency needs to avoid jamming the lines.

4. Get the flashlight, candles, batteries, and matches.

5. Discuss how best to prepare your evening meal. Since you have no electricity, you must prepare food that requires no cooking. Also, you must prepare your meal from food storage or from food on hand. The water you will be drinking must also be supplied from your food storage. (Use purification tablets if necessary.) Use your creativity.

6. After your meal, plan some activities that will keep family members from feeling frightened or anxious. Following are a few suggestions you may wish to use:

- Create shadow pictures.
- Tell stories.

- Whistle or hum songs, and play "Name That Tune."
- Play games.
- Create an add-on story. One person starts with the background, the next person adds the characters, the next states what they do, the next creates a problem, the next complicates that problem, and finally the last person solves the problem and concludes the story.

Here are some things to keep in mind during a blackout:

1. If someone in the home depends upon electrical medical equipment, such as an iron lung, contact the police or fire department immediately, or take the patient to the hospital at once.

2. Even in a power shortage some appliances remain in service. While gas furnaces cannot heat homes when there is no electricity, gas water heaters still make hot water. A gas oven will not work, but a gas range-top will.

3. Telephone lines are separate from electrical lines.

4. Most burglar alarm systems have battery backups.

5. It is suggested that you unplug appliances when there is an outage. When power is restored, plug them in slowly, one by one, to prevent an overload.

6. If the power outage is from a source other than your own home, turn off the main circuit breaker.

MAKING YOUR
HOME A TOUGH
TARGET FOR THIEVES

In about 20 percent of burglaries, the burglar was able to enter the home without forcing entry. Either he has a key or has found an open door or window. This activity will teach your family security measures that will help to make your home a more difficult target for thieves by making it as difficult and time-consuming to steal from as possible. A burglar likes to be in and out of your home with what he wants in five or ten minutes.

Activity

Choose some or all of the following security measures and do them as a family:

1. Lock up your valuables. Money, silver, and jewelry are obviously valuables. But your most prized possessions may be items that cannot be replaced, such as family heirlooms.

2. Choose hard-to-reach or hard-to-find hiding places. Bedrooms are the worst hiding places. They are generally searched first. Also, dirty clothes hampers and backsides of dresser drawers are unsafe hiding places.

3. Don't keep large amounts of cash at home.

4. Etch identification numbers onto your valuables—your drivers license number, your phone number, or other identifying number. Give a record of these numbers to the police department. Most police departments will furnish you with an engraving tool free of charge.

   Call your local police department to determine if they have a crime prevention program that offers the service of engraving identification numbers. If they do, make the necessary arrangments to have this done. If they do not, you may want to organize a neighborhood or family project to purchase the tool and share it to mark your valuables.

   On items that cannot be engraved, such as silverware or paintings, write identification numbers on white tape and place the tape on the items. Then take a picture of these items. Keep an itemized record of all property and pictures in your safety deposit box or other safe place.

5. Make and record a room-by-room inventory of your possessions. Identify each item and record its serial number, if it has one. After recording this information, place the document in a safe, fireproof place (perhaps your refrigerator freezing compartment).

6. Install a peep-hole viewer with a wide-angle (180°) lens. This is an inexpensive way to view those who

are on the outside without opening the door. Don't rely on a chain guard, which can be easily broken. Always talk to strangers through a closed door.

7. Beware of people you are not expecting. A stranger at the door may claim to be a repairman, police officer, or someone in need of your help. If a stranger comes to your door—

   • Offer to call for anyone in need or in trouble. Make sure the stranger waits *outside* while you make the call.

   • Verify that he is who he claims to be before opening the door by calling the company he claims to be representing. Always look up the number yourself and check his name and description. Never call the number the stranger may give you. There may be a fellow conspirator on the other end of the telephone. Remember that official-looking identification can be easily forged.

   You may want to have family members role-play a situation with a stranger at the door.

8. If you are a babysitter or child left alone at home, always answer the phone. A burglar may call and think the house is unoccupied if there is no answer. Never admit

that parents are gone. Tell a phone caller that your parents are busy right now, and they will call back when they are finished. Ask the caller for his name and number.

   Never open the door to a stranger. Say that your parents are busy and cannot come to the door. If the person persists, call the police.

9. Make sure that your windows and doors can be safely locked. If you need more security, see the illustrations "Pin Double-Hung Sash Windows" and "Pin Doors with Outside Hinges."

Pin Double-Hung Sash Windows

Drill a hole through the lower sash window, and halfway through the upper.

Insert a pin, dowel, or nail into the hole to prevent the window from being opened from the outside.

Drill additional holes in the upper sash to allow the window to be secured while left partially open for ventilation.

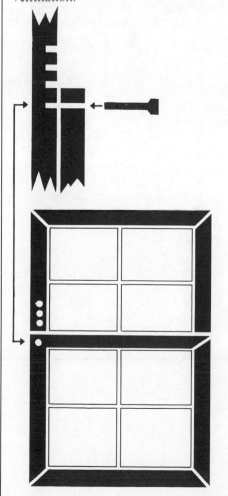

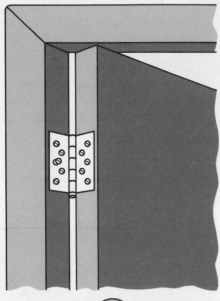

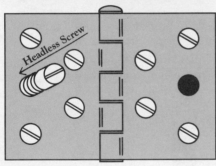

Pin Doors with Outside Hinges

To prevent doors from being lifted off the hinges if the hinges are located on the outside of the door, simply remove the two center screws from the hinges. Insert a headless screw into one of the holes, allowing it to protrude approximately 1/4 inch. When the door is closed the screw will engage the other hinge, and even if the hinge pin is removed, the door cannot be removed.

10. Establish a family security system. Assign family members to lock the doors, shut and lock all windows, and check the stove and electrical appliances, making sure they are properly turned off and disconnected. Turn on the burglar alarm if you have one. Don't forget to assign someone to shut and lock the garage door and all access doors. Make any other assignments necessary for your safety.

11. Decide where you are going to keep your house keys. It is a good idea not to leave them under the mat or on a cup hook. Also,

thieves will often look for keys left on door ledges.

12. Invite a police officer in your area to a family activity evening and discuss the security of your home.

13. Find out about the possibility of installing a burglar alarm system in your home.

14. Get a film from your local library on crime prevention. See the film and discuss the information.

EARTHQUAKE PREPARATION

What are earthquakes? The earth's crust is constantly subjected to stresses from deep inside the earth. First the crust bends, and when the stress exceeds certain limits, the crust breaks. This breaking process causes the vibrations we call earthquakes.

We have been warned by the Lord to expect earthquakes in our day. "And there shall be earthquakes also in divers places, and many desolations" (D&C 45:33). There is no plan that can eliminate all earthquake danger. But you can greatly reduce damage and injury by following several basic guidelines.

Activity

As a family, discuss the following guidelines for protecting yourself in an earthquake. You may want to role-play some of the steps.

1. Try to stay cool and calm. Think through what you should do. Try to reassure others.

2. If you are indoors, stay there. Protect yourself in one of the following ways and wait out the earthquake:

   • Take cover under a heavy desk, bed, or table. This will protect you from falling debris.

   • Move into a strong doorway, or sit or stand against an inside wall. If you are large enough, brace yourself in a doorway. A door frame or the structural frame of a building are the building's strongest points.

   • Stay away from glass, as the earthquake may shatter it.

   • Move away from bookcases, ceiling fixtures, or china cupboards.

• Try to keep your children with you.

3. If you are in a tall building, get under a desk. Do not dash for exits, since stairways may be broken and jammed with other people. Power for elevators may fail.

4. If you are in a crowded store, do not rush for a doorway since hundreds may have the same idea. If you must leave the building, choose your exit as carefully as possible.

5. If you are outdoors, get away from buildings, tall objects, and electric wires. Falling debris can injure or kill you.

6. If you are in a moving car, stop in an open area if possible. Don't stop on a high overpass or bridge, or where buildings can topple down on you. Stay inside the car until the shocks stop, even if the car shakes a great deal. A car is a fairly safe place to be.

7. Be prepared for additional earthquake shocks, called "aftershocks." Although most of these are smaller than the main shock, some may be large enough to cause more damage.

When the earthquake stops—

1. Check your water line, gas line, and electrical lines. If there is a gas line into your home or building, turn off burners and pilot lights. Do not light candles, matches, or lighters until you determine there is no leak. Gas leaks can cause explosions. Report damage to the appropriate utility companies and follow their instructions. If there is a leak, stay out of the house.

Do not flush toilets until you know that sewer lines are unbroken.

Electric lines can cause fire. Shut off all electrical power if there is damage to your house wiring. Do not operate electrical switches or appliances if you suspect a gas leak. They can create sparks which can ignite gas from broken lines.

2. Check your household for injured members.

3. Check your neighborhood for injured people who need help.

4. Immediately clean up spilled medicines, drugs, and other potentially harmful materials.

5. Turn on your radio (battery-operated or car). Listen for damage reports and instructions.

6. Don't tie up the telephone unless there is a real emergency to report. The lines will be urgently needed.

7. Don't go outside to see the damage. The area will be cluttered enough and you may hamper rescue. Keep the streets clear for passage of emergency vehicles.

8. Do not touch downed power lines or objects touched by the downed wires.

9. Stay away from damaged buildings. Aftershocks can collapse them.

10. Stay away from beaches and waterfront areas. Not all quakes cause tidal waves, but many do. If you are near the ocean or tidal inlet following an earthquake, be alert for tidal waves. Move inland.

11. If water is off, you can get emergency water from water heaters, toilet tanks, melted ice cubes, and canned vegetables.

12. Do not eat or drink anything from open containers near shattered glass. Strain liquids through a clean handkerchief or cloth if you think broken glass may be in them.

13. Respond to requests for help from police, fire fighters, civil defense and relief organizations. But do not go into damaged areas unless your help has been requested. Cooperate fully with public safety officials.

MAKING A SURVIVAL KIT

Outdoor activities are no fun when someone gets lost. Adequate preparation will usually keep this from happening, but some simple equipment can prepare a family member to survive if he does get lost. This activity will teach family members to make a lightweight survival kit that they can easily carry with them.

Activity

First make sure that family members understand a few simple rules:

1. Wear a shrill whistle around your neck when you are hiking or fishing in an isolated area.

2. Tell someone where you are going and when you are coming back. Don't leave the camping area by yourself.

3. Orient yourself to the area and do not explore longer or farther away than your family feels is safe.

4. Remember when you are lost to—

• Keep calm, find a sheltered place, and stay put. Get out into the open if planes are overhead.

• Build a fire if possible, conserve your heat and energy.

• Mark your location. Move out from it to seek familiar landmarks and return to it.

• Shout, use a whistle, and concentrate on being found—not on finding someone.

• Prepare for the night, gather wood, build a shelter before dark.

Then have all family members help construct a survival kit. Make sure they know how to use each item. The following items can be put in a 2 1/2-by-4 1/2-by-16 1/2-inch (6-by-11-by-16-cm) leather pouch and will weigh less than one pound (.5 kilograms).

SURVIVAL KIT

Item	Uses
Pocket knife with cutting blade, can opener, leather punch	Carving, cutting, spearhead
Metal canister 1 1/2-by-3 1/2-by-4 1/2 inches (4-by-9-by-11-cm). Many of the following items can be put in this canister.	Cooking pan, reflector, cup
Surgical tubing, 40 inches (100 cm)	Drinking tube, tourniquet, flipper
100 halazone tablets	Water purification
Six small cotton balls	Swabs, pad, dressing
1/32-inch (5-mm) twine, 96 inches (30 meters)	Fishing line, snare, sewing
Aluminum foil, 12-by-18 inches (30-by-45 cm)	Cooking, heat reflector
Wire survival saw 15 inches (36 cm)	Sawing
Three razor blades	Cutting, snares
Twelve safety pins, 1 inch (1.5 cm)	Repairs, clothespins, securing shelter to rope
Six No. 12 fish hooks and 12 feet (3.5 meters) of line	Fishing, snares
Three balls of steel wool	Tinder for fire in wet weather
Waterproof matches, candle, metal match	Fire
Metal whistle	Signal, reflector
Small sharpening stone	Striking matches, sharpening
Pencil and paper	Leaving notes or directions
Twelve heat tablets	Cooking
Electrician's tape, 120 inches (3.6 meters) (wrapped around canister)	Repairs, fastening shelter to rope
Six small band-aids	First aid
Card showing ground-air signals	Giving directions, sending distress signals, signaling location
Six bouillon cubes, dried soups	Food, morale, body heat
Two plastic sheets 9-by-12-feet (2.6-by-3.6 meters)	Shelter, ground cloth, water collection
1/8-inch (2-cm) nylon cord, 12 feet (3.5 meters)	Shelter rope, snares
Sewing kits: two needles, three buttons, 6 feet of thread (1.8 meters)	Patches, first aid
Small compass with mirror on back	Directions, signaling

Additional Activities

Try each component in your backyard or on a simulated exercise to prepare yourself and your family for possible use.

WATER SAFETY SKILLS

Most drownings happen because people fail to practice safety rules for water activities. This activity is designed to help each family member learn water safety and water survival skills. You will need to have access to water (ocean, lake, river, lagoon, or swimming pool) along with instruction and careful supervision.

Activity

If you live in an area where water safety classes are taught, plan to take a class as a family. If you do not, have a family member learn the following basic safety techniques and present them to the rest of the family. Have all family members practice the techniques until they feel comfortable with them.

1. Survival Floating

• Resting position. Let the body float in the water with the knees tucked up against the chest.

• Exhaling position. Exhale.

• Preparing to exhale position. Make swimming motions with arms until head is above water.

• Inhaling position. Inhale.

• Resting position. Allow body to return to resting position.

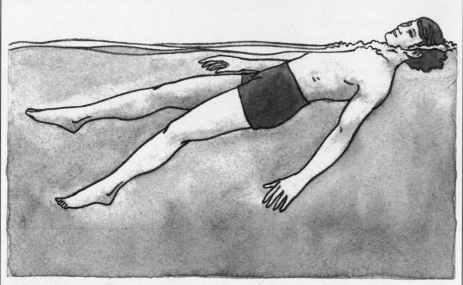

2. Back floating or sculling. Lie back, kick feet slightly and move arms from side to side. Very little motion is required to remain afloat.

3. Emergency flotation device. Practice removing clothing such as pants or shirts in the water and filling them with air to make a flotation device. Tie off the pant legs or shirt sleeves and raise them above the head scooping air into them.

4. Treading Water

Besides helping family members learn these safety techniques, teach them the following essential water safety rules:

1. Learn to swim.

2. Never swim alone. (You may want to use the Scout buddy system.)

3. Swim at a safe place, preferably with lifeguards present.

4. Don't swim when overheated or overtired.

5. Before diving, make certain the water is deep enough and that there are no hidden objects.

6. Don't swim further away from shore than you are able; distances in water are misleading.

7. When distance swimming, always be accompanied by someone in a boat who remains close by.

8. Learn and practice the skills of survival floating, treading water, and back floating.

9. Learn and practice the skills of removing shoes and clothing in the water. (In very cold water the clothes should not be removed.)

10. Learn and practice the skills of emergency rescue in the water.

11. Learn and practice the skills of mouth-to-mouth artificial respiration (see pp. 322-26) and CPR (cardiopulmonary resuscitation).

Caution: Require each family member to pass a minimum swimming and water survival skill test before being allowed to play in deep water. Always take a rope or some floating item to throw to a person who may get into trouble.

Additional Activities

1. After drown-proofing all family members, plan a family outing or camp at a nearby beach, lake, or resort.

2. Pursue other family interests such as river running, kayaking, surfing, or snorkeling. Encourage all family members to wear flotation devices during such activities. Many LDS families have a standing rule that some flotation device must be worn whenever anyone is in the water. This significantly reduces the chances for a mishap while boating or swimming.

INDEX